CAMBRIDGE TEXTBOOKS IN LINGUISTICS

General Editors: B. COMRIE, R. HUDDLESTON, R. LASS, D. LIGHTFOOT, J. LYONS, P.H. MATTHEWS, R. POSNER, S. ROMAINE, N.V. SMITH, N. VINCENT

PSYCHOLINGUISTICS

In this series:

PSYCHOLINGUISTICS

MICHAEL GARMAN

DEPARTMENT OF LINGUISTIC SCIENCE
UNIVERSITY OF READING

CAMBRIDGE
UNIVERSITY PRESS

Published by the Press Syndicate of the University of Cambridge
The Pitt Building, Trumpington Street, Cambridge CB2 1RP
40 West 20th Street, New York, NY 10011-4211, USA
10 Stamford Road, Oakleigh, Melbourne 3166, Australia

© Cambridge University Press 1990

First published 1990
Reprinted 1991, 1994, 1996

Printed in Great Britain at
the University Press, Cambridge

British Library cataloguing in publication data
Garman, Michael
Psycholinguistics – (Cambridge textbooks in linguistics)
1. Psycholinguistics
I. Title
401'.9

Library of Congress cataloging in publication data
Garman, Michael.
Psycholinguistics / Michael Garman.
        p.   cm. – (Cambridge textbooks in linguistics)
Includes bibliographical references.
ISBN 0 521 25675 5 (hardback) – ISBN 0 521 27641 1 (paperback).
1. Psycholinguistics.   I. Title.   II. Series
[DNLM: 1. Psycholinguistics.   BF 455 G233p]
P37.G33   1990
401'.9 – dc20   89–18645   CIP

ISBN 0 521 25675 5   hardback
ISBN 0 521 27641 1   paperback

ETA

CONTENTS

Contents

ILLUSTRATIONS

ILLUSTRATIONS

TABLES

PREFACE

This book provides an introduction to the field of language study known as *psycholinguistics*. Language can be studied in a number of ways – as a corpus of data in *descriptive linguistics*, as an abstract system of knowledge in *theoretical linguistics*, as a social phenomenon in *sociolinguistics*, and so on. Psycholinguistics is, as its name implies, basically concerned with language as a psychological phenomenon; and, most characteristically, with language in the individual. Hence it addresses such questions as 'How does a listener recognise words in the stream of speech, or in patterns on the page, and arrive at an understanding of utterances?' and 'How does a speaker go about putting ideas into forms that can be expressed as patterns of articulatory, or manual, movements?'

Two important aspects of these concerns are well captured in the term *microgenesis* of language (Campbell 1979). First, *micro-* in this connection refers to the rapid, moment-by-moment nature of everyday language processes, by virtue of which we understand and produce utterances on a time scale that is marked off in seconds and milliseconds. This contrasts with what we may refer to as the *macrogenesis* of language, in either of its main forms, (i) the individual's learning of a first or subsequent language (the ontogenesis of language), on a time scale of days, weeks, months and years or (ii) in the species' development of linguistic abilities (the *phylogenesis* of language), on a time scale appropriate to human evolution. The other part of the term, *-genesis*, draws attention to the creative nature of language use that is involved, not just in producing utterances (where something is self-evidently 'put together'), but also in understanding (where what is produced is abstract, internal to the language user, and altogether more difficult to study objectively).

The time-scale of microgenesis itself may be further highlighted by reference to a distinction between *microchronic* and *macrochronic* dimensions of speech (Catford 1977). In these terms, the very rapid microchronic *processing* events may be thought of as taking place within a hierarchy of phases, from neurolinguistic programming to execution of vocal tract muscle movements, with each phase being of the order of tens of milliseconds in duration. The result is a macrochronic *product*, a succession of speech sounds which range from constituents having durations of tens of milliseconds up to indefinitely long stretches of utterance. Such concepts as these, in written as well as spoken language forms, and in comprehension as well as production, help to define the field that the psycholinguist is involved in.

It may be as well to say something here about who psycholinguists are, and what brings them to psycholinguistics. Terms such as 'linguist' and 'psychologist' are too broad to show either the inter-disciplinary similarities or the intra-disciplinary differences of approach, which appear to depend more on the immediate goal of study than on the demarcations between academic disciplines. Thus, linguists, philosophers of language and psychologists working in cognitive-semantic aspects of language performance constitute an interdisciplinary research community, and one that is rather distinct from, for example, that which concerns itself with the production and perception of speech. Concerning the latter, 'speech scientists' as they may best be called, we may observe that they too represent a number of disciplines, including acoustic physics as well as phonetics and psychology.

We should perhaps mention, in passing, that among this research community, there is a tradition that occupies a particularly important place in the development of psycholinguistics: within the academic discipline of linguistics, it is phoneticians who have most conspicuously and consistently focussed on the processes of actual human performance, as well as their products, in language. This focus is evident even in the idealised classical phonetic description of speech sounds, in terms of the movements of articulators that are required to produce them. In a sense, the goal of a more general psycholinguistics may be regarded as extending this approach to the rest of language performance. In this regard, it is unfortunate that linguistic science has (with some honourable exceptions) not devoted comparable efforts towards the study of the visible forms of language.

So psycholinguistic research may be thought of as constituting, appropriately enough, a mosaic of specialisms, focussed on different aspects of a highly complex phenomenon. As a result, it can be very difficult for the beginning student to develop a sense of where all the research activities and findings belong, in the larger field of psycholinguistics. This difficulty can be compounded by some real differences of approach between disciplines. In this connection, I should declare my own background as that of the interested linguist, teaching courses over the years to various undergraduate and postgraduate groups in the Department of Linguistic Science at the University of Reading.

One experience arising from this situation is that I have had to address those elements of psycholinguistics that are least well represented in my students' (and my own) experience – not an easy task, and one which writing this book has given me the further opportunity to labour at. Another has been the need to caution students from other disciplines against equating 'linguistics' with any single school of thought, and not to regard the view from linguistics (of any school) as having automatic authority within psycholinguistics. What balance I have been able to strike in my interpretation of psychological issues remains to be seen, but I should admit to a long-standing sympathy with the view expressed by N.S. Sutherland (an experimental psychologist), in the context of a discussion of Chomsky's (1965) account of linguistic competence, that

> the task of psycholinguistics is not to confirm Chomsky's account of linguistic competence by undertaking experiments ... The task of psycholinguistics is to my mind very much more difficult and interesting. It is, by doing experiments, to find out what are the mechanisms that underlie linguistic competence. (Sutherland 1966, pp. 161–2)

Inevitably, developments have taken place in the years since this view was expressed in just these words. For one thing, our notion of 'doing experiments' has come under scrutiny; and it might be added that an important role for linguists in such a general enterprise is to provide suitable descriptions of observable language behaviour, in naturalistic as well as in experimental situations, in order that resulting theories about underlying mechanisms may be suitably founded.

Psycholinguistic approaches to language are, as we have noted, quite varied, from those that are concerned with the more concrete operations of the physiological systems involved in producing and perceiving language *signals* to the more abstract cognitive systems, including memory, which are involved in the construction and interpretation of *messages*. This book tries to cover something of this range, for both spoken and written forms of language. But it inevitably leaves a good deal out of account, particularly on those areas which are represented elsewhere in this series of textbooks by other specialists, such as Elliot (1981) for child language acquisition, Klein (1986) for second language acquisition, Brown and Yule (1983) on discourse analysis, and so on. By and large, however, what is left for our consideration is arguably central to our field.

The organisation of the topics in this book results from an attempt to identify *elements* (Part I) and *issues* (Part II) of psycholinguistics, focussing on the most general language abilities of *normal, adult* and *monolingual* individuals. The final chapter pushes the discussion into the field of adult language pathology, but only very briefly, and in order to evaluate a further potential source of evidence.

In concluding this Preface, I should like to acknowledge my debt to the research communities for the intellectual excitement that has come from the tenacity and ingenuity through which valuable sightings (sometimes perplexing and conflicting) have eventually been made of so many apparently intractable and inaccessible aspects of language processing in humans. I should also point out to the reader that I have not tried to produce a survey of all, or even most, of the recently published studies on psycholinguistics, since I did not know how to make such a diet digestible. Instead, I have tried to identify a fairly balanced range of issues and approaches, most of them with research roots going back about a decade, and have tried to discuss their implications. This book will do well if it helps students to go to the primary sources of current research with a reasonable sense of perspective; if it also serves to help them to identify areas where further research is needed, then it will do better still; it will do best if it stimulates some students sufficiently that they eventually become contributors to the research field themselves.

ACKNOWLEDGEMENTS

Many people have helped me with this book in many ways, at various stages of its preparation. I should like to thank them all. The first group of people I am indebted to are those students who have attended my psycholinguistics courses over the years at the University of Reading: they may recognise more or less of the material that is covered here, depending on the number of years intervening. I have also received much helpful advice from colleagues who gave unstintingly of their time at moments that were more to my convenience than theirs: in alphabetical order, they are: Professor R.E. Asher, Colin Biggs, Andy Butcher, Margaret Davidson, Susan Edwards, Janet Fletcher, Paul Fletcher, Patrick Griffiths, Mark Hanson, Professor Bill Hardcastle, Arthur Hughes, Professor Ray Kent, Professor P.H. Matthews, Professor Lesley Milroy, Professor F.R. Palmer, Professor Philip Smith, and Lin Wang. Outside this order, and most particularly, I thank John Trim, my series editor, who has provided a constant flow of judicious advice and patient encouragement, throughout a very long period. The book doubtless has many faults still, and those I must acknowledge as my own.

Penny Carter of CUP also deserves a special mention, for her seemingly endless patience and encouragement. Hazel Bell, Barbara Barnes and Jill Tozer of the Department of Linguistic Science generously and efficiently took on much of the typing and retyping of the book, at various stages of its development. Last, in the chronological sequence, comes Jenny Potts, for her blend of expert sub-editing skills and great patience in the face of daunting problems.

A textbook in an interdisciplinary field such as this must rely a good deal on previously published ideas. As far as the text is concerned, I have tried to make due acknowledgements, while attempting to preserve the flow of the text in the interests of the reader who wants the ideas, rather than a bibliographical survey. I should like to learn of, and apologise for, any omissions in this regard. For the figures and tables, I am grateful to the following sources for permission to use previously published material: Academic Press: figures 2.4,

2.7, 2.8, 2.10, 2.18, 3.8, 4.11, 4.12, 5.7, 6.10, 7.6, 7.7, 7.8, 7.9, 7.10 and 7.11, tables 3.8, 7.3, 7.4, 7.5 and 7.7; Acoustical Society of America: figure 4.6; American Psychological Association: figures 4.4 and 4.5; American Speech–Language–Hearing Association: figure 1.4; Bell Telephone Labs: figures 1.1 and 2.3; Binet Archives, Paris: figure 2.18; Blackwell: figures 2.1 and 2.7; Bounty Books: figure 2.9; Cambridge University Press: table 7.2; Churchill Livingstone: figures 4.10, 6.2 and 8.3; Cole and Whurr: table 8.10; College-Hill: figure 2.2; Croom Helm: table 8.9; Edinburgh University Press: figures 2.17 and 4.3; Elek: figure 5.9; Elsevier: table 6.5; Grune and Stratton: figures 8.1, 8.4, 8.5, 8.6, 8.8 and 8.9, tables 8.3, 8.5, 8.6 and 8.7; Harper and Row: figures 2.4, 2.6 and 2.12; HMSO: figure 1.7; Holt, Rinehart and Winston: figure 7.2; Lawrence Erlbaum Associates: figure 5.2, tables 3.9, 5.2 and 5.3; Longman: figures 3.1 and 8.10; Macmillan: figure 2.14; McGraw-Hill: figure 2.13; MIT Press: figure 6.9; Mouton: figures 6.6 and 6.7; North-Holland: figure 5.5, table 8.8; Open University: figure 3.6; Prentice-Hall: figure 4.8; Routledge and Kegan Paul: figures 5.11 and 5.12; *Scientific American*: figure 2.11; Springer: figures 1.3 and 2.15; Taylor and Francis: figures 2.3, 2.4, 2.6, 2.9, 2.12 and 2.13; Williams and Wilkins: figures 2.16, 4.4, 4.5, 4.6 and 4.7, table 4.1; Wiley: tables 6.2 and 6.4.

ABBREVIATIONS

A	*adverbial*
AdvP	*adverb phrase*
AER	*average evoked response*
AI	*artificial intelligence*
APG	*abstract performative grammar*
Art	*article*
ASL	*American Sign Language*
ATN	*augmented transition network*
Aux	*auxiliary*
BSL	*British Sign Language*
C	*complement*
CAT	*computerised axial tomography*
CN	*cranial nerve*
cons	*consonantal*
CVA	*cerebral vascular accident*
decl	*declarative*
dem	*demonstrative*
det	*determiner*
EEG	*electroencephalography*
ELI	*English language interpreter*
EMG	*electromyographic*
ERP	*event-related potential*
ESB	*electrical stimulation of the brain*
FCU	*functionally complete unit*
FP	*fluent phase*
GPC	*grapho-phonic correspondence*
GPSG	*Generalised Phrase Structure Grammar*
GPT	*grapho-phonic transposition*
HP	*hesitant phase*
LG	*linguist's grammar*

MG	*mental grammar*
MV	*main verb*
N(P)	*noun (phrase)*
Nprop	*proper noun*
O	*object*
obstr	*obstruent*
PP	*parsing procedures*
Pr	*preposition*
Pron	*pronoun*
rCBF	*regional cerebral bloodflow*
REA	*right-ear advantage*
RN	*radionucleide*
RT	*reaction time*
RTA	*road-traffic accident*
RTN	*recursive transition network*
S	*subject*
SIS	*sensory information storage*
STM	*short-term memory*
TM	*transcortical motor (aphasia)*
TG	*transformational grammar*
TS	*transcortical sensory (aphasia)*
V	*verb*
VOT	*voice-onset time*
VSSP	*visuo-spatial scratch-pad*
WAB	*Western Aphasia Battery*

Note on transcription: the transcription used for phonetic representation is that of Gimson (1970).

PART ONE

Elements of psycholinguistics

1
Characteristics of the language signal

1.1 Introduction

1.1.1 *Preview*

The first part of this book (chs. 1 to 3) surveys the elements of psycholinguistics. For this purpose it is convenient to think of most types of observable language behaviour as comprising three levels: (a) the *language signal*, which we shall take to cover all the forms of language expression which are generated and perceived by language users, including writing as well as speech; (b) the *neurophysiological activity* involved both in the first and the next level; (c) the *language system*. While the first two levels relate to physical entities, the third is abstract, and may be implemented even when we are not using palpable language signals at all, as in silent verbal reasoning, contemplation of our language, and general language knowledge.

These three levels define the first three chapters. In this first chapter we shall review the properties of the language signal. Since these derive, at least in part, from the operations of our neurophysiological systems, they can help to determine the limits of functioning of those systems. In the second chapter we shall consider aspects of the neurophysiological systems themselves: since they are involved, in some way, in constituting whatever mechanisms subserve language behaviour, a knowledge of them must be a necessary, if not a sufficient, basis for theories of language processing, which we shall deal with in the second part of the book. Finally, in the third chapter we shall address the issue of the language system: not directly, since this is too controversial a task, but indirectly, by reviewing the sorts of evidence that are to hand for an empirical approach.

We start by reviewing the more important characteristics of the speech signal (section 1.2), both as it is generated by the human articulatory apparatus (1.2.1) and carried through the air (1.2.2) for processing by the auditory system (1.2.3). Then, because a very large part of our everyday contact with language is based on signs which we perceive and produce as writing, we review some properties of writing systems (section 1.3), looking at some of the major types of writing system (1.3.1.–1.3.3) before considering the English system in some detail (1.3.4). Finally, we consider briefly the adaptation of a writing system to tackle the difficult task of representing the characteristics of the speech signal, in however limited a fashion (section 1.4). This helps to remind us that the representation of speech in such a written medium as this book is necessarily indirect and tends to be selective of certain characteristics over others.

1.1.2 *Language processing*

First, to set the scene for our discussion, let us consider two very simple diagrams of language processing, as set out in figures 1.1 and 1.2. The first is of a quite familiar sort, reproduced here from Denes and Pinson (1963), who refer to it as 'the speech chain'. It shows schematically two heads, one talking to the other. The talking head is listening to (monitoring) its own speech output via a feedback link which is important for maintaining good control of articulatory targets. But the main channel of information flow is from the talking head to the listening head. In this flow three stages, or levels, are distinguished: the *linguistic*, concerned with the formulation of the message; the *physiological*, concerned with the expression/reception of the signal carrying the message; and the *acoustic*, which is distinguished by being the only level which is outside of, and common to, both individuals – the air gap which has to be bridged for the speech chain to be completed between the heads. It is the acoustic level which is placed at the centre of this picture, the central link in the chain. Now consider the second diagram (fig. 1.2). It has just one (schematic) head, which is busy acting as a central language processor, both receiving and sending signals, through two channels, the articulatory–auditory (speech), and the manual–visual (writing). We might refer to

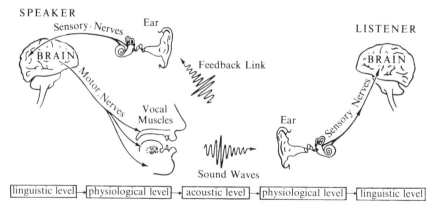

Figure 1.1 The 'speech chain'. (From Denes and Pinson 1963: fig. 1.1, p. 4.)

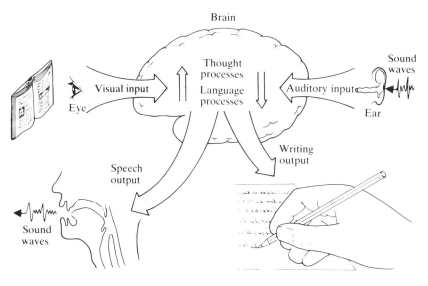

Figure 1.2 The 'language switchboard'

this picture as 'the language switchboard'. At the centre of these input–output events is the brain, capable of reconciling the considerable physical and physiological differences between these events, so that it can recognise and generate the 'same' message in different forms. We tend to take this ability so much for granted that we may not fully appreciate what a task this is that the brain manages so well. Consider, for example, what is going on when someone says something like the following:

(1) I've got the *j, e, l, l, y* (/'dʒeɪ 'iː 'el 'el 'waɪ/) in the fridge

(perhaps in the presence of a child who is about to be given a surprise treat). Notice, first, that such an utterance would not be possible except in a language community that has a way of speaking the written forms of words. Your auditory system perceives these speech signals, and delivers the results of this processing to your brain; at this point, the events are interpreted, not as a sequence of words (thus, for instance /'waɪ/ is not interpreted as the word *why*), but as spoken versions of letters. The appropriate letter-sequence is somehow assembled in such a way that it can be used to address the dictionary of stored written forms of words that you carry in your head, and you find the item *jelly*.

This is just one, albeit quite complex, example of input–output relations in language processing. There are numerous other 'special' examples, including

5

Table 1.1 *Some input–output relations in language use*

Input	Output

Visual–linguistic
    reading the word *jelly* on a box in the
    fridge
	Manual–non-linguistic
	    picking the box out

Visual–non-linguistic
    seeing a jelly in the fridge
	Articulatory
	    'can I have some of this jelly?'

Auditory–linguistic
    hearing a request to say what you would
    like for tea
	Articulatory
	    'can I have some jelly?'

Auditory–linguistic
    hearing a request to find the jelly in the
    fridge
	Manual–non-linguistic
	    picking out the right item

Intentional
    wishing to label the box containing jelly
	Manual–linguistic
	    writing on the lid

the ability to recognise words from letter shapes traced in the palm of the hand; and a host of others that we carry out as part of our everyday activities, such as those set out in table 1.1. Both diagrams in figures 1.1 and 1.2 are attempting to sketch the same thing, which is an impressionistic picture of the framework within which these and other sorts of language processing are carried on. One could easily add a written language dimension to the first diagram, for example, to bring it more into line with the second. But even if we did this, their emphases would be rather different, with the first putting the physical signal (whether acoustic or graphic) at the centre, while the second puts the brain at the centre, and asks us to consider how all the input–output events in language use might be mediated. It is this second picture that this book attempts to deal with.

In so doing, we encounter a problem. If we attend first to the auditory/articulatory systems, say, and then shift our attention to the brain, we are not thereby making the transition from the 'physiological' to the 'linguistic' level, as figure 1.1 implies. The brain is a physiological entity but language is not, so looking for language in the brain is a problematic matter. It is possible, however, to approach this problem from a number of complementary angles:

1. to examine the physiological foundations of language in the brain, as well as in the auditory/articulatory systems, and the visual/manual systems (ch. 2);
2. to consider the basic elements of the language system, as one

source of evidence concerning what sorts of constructs the human language faculty manipulates, together with aspects of human language performance, as revealed in experimental and naturalistic situations (ch. 3);

3. to construct processing models (the second part of the book, chs 4–7);

4. to examine how language processing breaks down in relation to specific brain injury (ch. 8);

5. to approach the issue from the standpoint of formal theories of language.

In this latter way, we can ask how formal properties of language must constrain our theories of the *mind*, and we may then consider the relationship of this construct to what we know of the brain. This approach is the most ambitious one, at least in respect of the role it envisages for linguistic theory in this enterprise, and is beyond the scope of this book. (Aspects of it can be found in Fodor 1983, Bever, Carroll and Miller 1984, and in Chomsky 1986.)

1.1.3 *Language signals*

Returning to the main point of this chapter, we should consider how it is that we normally make contact with the signals of language. Apart from the written forms of English, for example, there are other forms such as sign language, semaphore, morse code, braille and so on. Some of these systems are direct encodings of particular forms of a language, as in the case of semaphore, morse code and braille. Among sign languages direct encodings are found in so-called 'finger-spelling', and in aspects of the Paget-Gorman sign system, which is based on English and has signs that signal particular morphemes (e.g. word endings) as well as others that more abstractly represent the vocabulary of English words. In contrast to this, British Sign Language (BSL) and American Sign Language (ASL) are independent of English or any other language (see Woll and Kyle 1983 for detailed discussions of sign language characteristics). In this book we shall be concerned with just the spoken and written forms of language, since speech as a form of language is universal and the written forms are also basic in all the language communities that have them.

Another point which may not be immediately obvious, perhaps, is that within both of these forms of language, spoken and written, distinctions may exist from the point of view of the producer vs the receiver; speaker vs listener, and writer vs reader. For the speaker 'speech' involves the control of the movements of the articulatory organs (Hardcastle 1976), while for the listener it involves searching the acoustic signal for auditorily significant properties (Repp 1982). For the writer 'written language' involves the sweep of the pen across the page, or the finger-pressings of keyboard operation (Viviani and Terzulo 1983), while for the reader it involves the control of eye movements over two-dimensional arrays consisting of contrasts of dark and light (Rayner 1979). There is much more to language processing than this would imply, of course; more generally, starting with an idea and then finding the formal means of its expression is a very different sort of activity, involving distinct parts of the body, from what is required in perceiving speech sounds or letter sequences, and processing them in ways that yield understanding of the intended message (Miller 1981). Psycholinguistically, then, we have to be prepared to find certain fundamental differences in the way we process language in ordinary use (processing for production vs processing for comprehension, as well as in processing for speech vs written forms of language), and a basic question that arises is how far we may be able to see these distinct processing systems converging on, or deriving from, some unitary set of 'language abilities'.

But the most striking characteristic of the language signal is its perceptual *invariance*, by which we mean that in both speech and writing it constitutes a stable and salient form which stands out against its physical environment. In speech, for example, the signal is embodied in patterns of air turbulence, which may be thought of as constituting a three-dimensional dynamic entity (see further below), and is produced by human vocal tracts that vary a good deal in size and shape. Some of these variations are linked to genetic factors such as race and sex (Catford 1977 has a brief review of some studies), and we should also mention age in this connection; others are more idiosyncratic. Such differences, both structural (size, shape) and functional (e.g. individual rate of articulation), give rise to tremendous physical variation in the actual sounds produced from these vocal tracts; but against this, what we typically perceive is a standard, normative language signal, and only secondarily may we notice such contingent properties as husky voice quality, slow delivery, nasality and so on (Laver 1980). In the case of writing we are dealing with, most typically, two-dimensional contrasts of light and dark, which are essentially static; but here again, invariance of perception is a notable characteristic. The 'same' letter, or word, may be easily perceived against a range of physical differences that may derive from the sort of writing implement used, the type of letter form aimed at (a printed vs a handwritten form), individual styles of handwriting, imperfections of execution (leaving a smudge or broken line) and so on. In our perception of such forms, gaps are closed, and irregularities are overlooked: indeed, such constancy, or invariance, of visual perception was a prime motivation behind the development of the concepts of *figure* vs *ground* in the school of Gestalt psychology (Woodworth 1931).

1.2 The speech signal

We shall discuss the nature of the speech signal in the context of how it is generated (articulatory factors), how it is transmitted (physical properties) and how it is perceived (perceptual factors). These three issues will be addressed, in turn, in sections 1.2.1–1.2.3 below.

1.2.1 *Articulatory factors*

Students of linguistics are familiar with the concept that the output of a generative model of language (more precisely, that part of the model that constitutes the *phonological component*) is a set of instructions to some (appropriately idealised) model of the speech organs (Postal 1968). Taking the generative models that have been proposed by linguists together with the traditionally strong emphasis on articulatory mechanisms in phonetics, we have the outline of a field of enquiry where the relationships between linguistic descriptions and psycholinguistic structures and processes can be fruitfully explored. At first sight it would seem that the field of speech production is much better fitted to this sort of enquiry than that of speech perception, if only because the observable data in production – the recorded movements of the articulatory organs – constitute the *endpoint*, rather than the *input*, to the process. (There are thus no problems analogous to those in speech perception, where the input cues of the acoustic signal are in themselves hypothetical.) Surely, we can argue, there can be no doubt as to the status of the units of articulatory dynamics: they are observable movements and relations between movements. As such, they provide us with a concrete basis on which to build our theories.

To a very large extent, this is the case. However, recent research in speech production theory (MacNeilage 1983) reveals that there are still a large number of unknowns, many of them surprisingly (to the newcomer, at least) at a basic level of description, e.g. the neural control of muscles. Lack of sufficiently detailed information at this level naturally provides insufficient constraints for theorising about higher level processes. It turns out, then, that speech is such a complex species of coordinated motor patterns that it defies many of the techniques and theories that have permitted significant advances to be made in our understanding of simpler patterns (e.g. locomotion, limb and head movements: see Bizzi 1983).

9

The object level of description

We are not concerned immediately here with the description of the organs of speech, or how they are controlled; these topics will be addressed in the next chapter. Our purpose at this stage is to consider the signal as it arises from the movements of the articulators.

A good place to start from is the sort of record that is produced from cine-fluorographic film (Kent 1983), as illustrated in figure 1.3. In this technique, very small radio-opaque metallic pieces are attached to crucial articulators in such a way as not to impede their natural performance, and a radiographic film is then taken (usually from one side of the head) on which dynamics of speech show up as traces of the interactive movements of the metallic pieces on the articulatory organs. These can then be plotted as separate traces, all co-ordinated with reference to a single time scale.

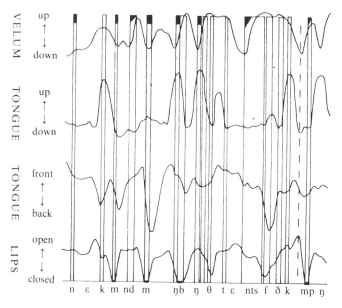

Movements of the velum, tongue, and lips recorded by lateral cinefluo-rography during the sentence 'Next Monday morning bring three tents for the camping trip.' Movements of velum and tongue were recorded as displacements of radiopaque markers attached to these articulators. The segments blacked in at the top are nasal consonants. A partial phonetic transcription at the bottom of the illustration identifies major articulatory events. The dashed vertical line marks one example of nearly simultaneous movements of two articulators, in this case, velum and lips.

Figure 1.3 Lateral cine-fluorographic record of velum, tongue and lip movements in continuous speech. (From Kent 1983: fig. 4.7, p. 69.)

Most outstandingly, perhaps, in this articulatory display, several *channels* (each representing a particular articulatory organ) are in simultaneous activity. This immediately leads to very great difficulties of *segmentation*, since the articulatory cycles of one channel are more or less independent of those of another. Thus, what is a segment boundary for one channel may not be one for another. And we have no way of deciding, in advance, which channels, if any, are more 'important' for our purpose than others. All we can do, it seems, is to look for points of coincidence between channels; the more channels that agree on any particular 'segment', the better established that segment will be. But for the most part, we find it more difficult to segment the articulatory record than to ascertain sound segments in the acoustic record. This is simply a fact of articulatory phonetics, springing from the many-to-one relationship that we have observed to exist between the speech organs and the complex acoustic signal. The segmentation provided in figure 1.3 is only partly derivable from the information contained in the recorded traces; for the most part it has been imposed on them, derived independently from a simultaneous audio-recording. Nevertheless, there is much to learn from representations like these. Consider first the lips trace, at the bottom of the chart in figure 1.3. There are four points where the lips close: for *Monday*, *morning*, *bring* and *camping*. There is also a further point where they approximate: for the labiodental fricative in *for*. Apart from these points, however, it is emphatically *not* the case that the lips simply remain passively in the 'open' position. Instead, the upper areas of the trace show continuous movement. This is fundamentally for two reasons: first, because the lips are, fairly passively, reflecting other movements, e.g. of the lower jaw, which carries the lower lip up and down with it; and second, because the lips may be involved in *secondary articulations*, as shown in this example at the point in *three*. Here the lips approximate to the same degree as in *for*, reflecting the secondary lip-protrusion on the /r/ segment. Thus, the upper part of the trace both carries general information about other aspects of speech dynamics and indicates specific types of (non-primary) articulation. Notice, finally, that the lips trace indicates that considerable velocities can be achieved by these articulators, in the relatively vertical traces shown leading into, and out of, full closures – particularly, from the open vowel in *camping*.

There is something more like an identifiable base-line in the case of the tongue trace, although here too passive movement effects are found as a result of jaw movements (e.g. the jaw partially closes for the initial consonant in *morning*). Notice, however, that this is over-ridden in the case of *Monday*, where the following vowel requires a lower tongue position. Finally, consider the velum trace (up indicating an oral articulation, down allowing for degrees of opening into the nasal cavity). Here, it may be surprising to note that the points of relatively complete closure are fairly few and far between, occurring in the sequences of oral closures that immediately follow nasal consonants in *Monday, morningbring, tentsfor* and *camping*, and also in *three*, and *forthe*. For the rest, about 60 per cent of the time, the velum is lowered by some appreciable amount (around one third). But probably the most significant pattern to spot in the velum trace is that, in nasal-plus-oral consonant sequences like those just identified, the velum is actually moving towards closure during the oral closure for the nasal consonant, and in some cases prior to that. In other words, the consonant, as defined by tongue/lip closure, ends less nasally, as defined by velic closure, than it began. This can be observed in the case of *Monday, morning, bring, tents, camping*. And, in the case of *camping*, the velic closure starts to occur even before the vowel is terminated by oral closure. Against these instances, compare the velic trace for *next, Monday* and *morning*, where the velum is consistently lowered through the oral closure for the nasal consonant. We therefore have to reckon with *variability* in speech production, as in perception. One sort of variability is the product of *articulatory context*: thus, the tongue may be readied for the next vowel even while maintaining position for a preceding consonant; or it may move with greater or less precision depending upon some external factor, such as *speech rate*. Another sort of variability is found as the product of *articulatory timing*: essentially the same gesture (e.g. velic closure) may be traced to coincide with one or other aspect of articulatory movement in other channels. In the case of *camping* above, the coordination is such that, simultaneously, the tongue is maintaining positions for /a/, the lips are moving to close for /m/, and the velum is rising to close for /p/. Both these types of variability result in what is referred to as *coarticulation*.

What this means is that, at any given point in time, the articulators may be observed to be carrying out aspects of both preceding and following speech targets, in an overlapping fashion. If we take a cross-sectional slice through the articulatory continuum, therefore (like the vertical lines in figure 1.3), we find a complex signal, in which anticipatory movements for upcoming targets are interleaved with the execution of current targets. This means, in turn, that coarticulation is related to the concept of articulatory variance, since it follows that the articulatory movements associated with any one target will vary from one context to another.

Another instrumental approach, which is particularly revealing of coarticulatory aspects of tongue-contact patterns in speech production, is found in electropalatography (Hardcastle 1984; Hardcastle, Morgan-Barry and Clark 1987). The sorts of phenomena that can be recorded by this technique are

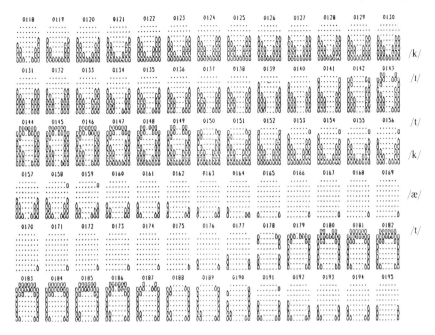

Computer printout of lingual–palatal contacts during production of the word *kitkat* by a normal speaker. Sample interval is 10 msec., and frames are numbered from left to right. In each palate diagram the electrode positions are arranged schematically, the top representing the anterior part of the oral region and the bottom, the posterior part. For descriptive purposes in the text, the palate is divided into zones based on traditional phonetic labels: the top three rows are referred to as the 'alveolar' zone, rows 4 and 5 as the 'palatal' zone, and rows 6, 7 and 8 as the 'velar' zone.

Figure 1.4 Computer printout of electropalatographic record of lingual–palatal contacts during production of the word *kitkat*. (From Hardcastle, Morgan-Barry and Clark 1987: fig. 1, p. 174.)

illustrated in figure 1.4. The layout consists of six rows of thirteen 'frames', each frame representing a picture of tongue–palate contact, sampled at intervals of 10ms (starting from the top left and running to bottom right). Each frame represents schematically an artificial palate worn by the speaker and having eight rows of contact points, each row except the first (at the front of the palate, at the top of the frames in the figure) having eight contact points (sixty-two contact points in all). Where the tongue makes contact with any of these points, an electrical circuit is closed for the duration of the contact, and the contact is recorded; the frames in the figure show dots (.) for points that are not currently contacted by the tongue, and empty circles (○) for those that are.

The top three rows represent the alveolar position, the middle two the palatal and the lower three the velar. In these terms, we can see the initiation of the word *kitkat* with a lingual contact bilaterally in the palatal to velar areas, closing to a full velar contact, maintaining bilateral palatal contact (row 1). This bilateral palatal contact is characteristic of the following /ɪ/ vowel, as can be seen in the next row; toward the end of row 2 we observe the beginnings of alveolar closure (for the /t/) being overlaid on the bilateral palatal pattern, and this is effected at the start of row 3. Also in this row, however, we can see the overlap between alveolar and velar closures (for the medial –/tk/– sequence). Row 4 shows the minimal contact pattern characteristic of the open vowel following, and this continues also into the fifth row. Towards the end of the fifth row, we have the beginnings of the final /t/ segment, showing first as a narrow bilateral palatal–velar contact (distinct from the thicker contact observed in the corresponding phase of the first /t/ closing from the high front vowel /ɪ/), and subsequently as full alveolar closure, extending into the final row. It may be appreciated that, while the rows are organised here in terms of the six main articulatory segments, they show considerable overlaps and contextual specialisations, reflective of the coarticulatory processes of connected speech.

Linguistic segmentation and articulatory variance

Given this complex phenomenon of articulatory variance, we should consider its implications for relationships between observed speech production and linguistic descriptions. One, fairly standard, viewpoint has been to adhere to the notion of linguistic–phonetic input (comprising elements of the systematic phonetic level, in the terms of Chomsky 1964 – see also Postal 1968). Several models derive from this viewpoint, one of which (Perkell 1980) we shall be considering in some detail in chapter 4. All such approaches need to account in some way for the mismatch between discrete input segments and coarticulated output.

A well-established alternative view (MacNeilage 1970) is that the input to speech production processing is essentially non-linguistic. Instead of encoding abstract linguistic segments into articulatory movements, speech production is viewed as starting from target articulatory goals (such as 'velic closure', 'labial opening', etc.) which are essentially invariant in their sensory-motor implications. By definition, however, such targets are teleological in nature: that is, they lie 'out there' as end-states to be worked towards, so that articulatory variance tends to enter the picture as the inevitable consequence of degrees of success in achieving the targets. The inevitability arises because of the probabilistic nature of human behaviour and the fact that successive targets may make conflicting demands on the articulators (e.g. 'velic opening' immediately followed by 'velic closure'). Such targets may actually be *perceptually* based:

they may be represented by, for example, ideal formant patterns for vowels, whose attainment is monitored by auditory processes providing feedback into, and adjustment of, the specification of ideal points of approximation, for ideal relative segment durations, within the speaker's mental representation of articulatory space. Other feedback channels may operate via peripheral sensory receptors, e.g. in the lips and gums, from contact by the tongue; in the tongue, from contact with the palate, and vice versa; and also possibly from generalised intra-oral sensation resulting from supralaryngeal air pressure, etc.; and via central pathways, in the central nervous system itself. The concept of articulatory space is, at the ideal level, to be understood as the speaker's mental representation of the vocal tract, a cognitive structure built up ontogenetically through experience of use. From this view also, a number of specific proposals are derived.

A third view also has come to be represented (Fowler *et al.* 1980). This may be referred to as the 'synergistic' approach – where by 'synergy' is meant the concept of discrete and even anatomically unrelated muscle groups coming into play as collective systems, for particular functions (such as speech). The implications of such functional collaboration extend to neural pathways and brain centres also. According to this approach, coarticulation phenomena arise, not from 'smeared' boundaries of linguistic segments nor as a falling away from ideal targets, but from the very inception of the neural control of muscle systems, wherein interactive processes are of the essence. These are the 'dynamic patterns' of coordinated structures (Kelso, Tuller and Harris 1983).

We shall note certain parallels in these viewpoints with some of the approaches to perception of the acoustic signal, in section 1.2.3 below. As in the case of perception too, current disputes arise largely out of ignorance of certain critical stages in processing; and the ignorance derives largely from the richness and complexity of the problem. The suspicion is widely shared among speech researchers that the relatively few physiological parameters that can be observed and measured (such as those in figs. 1.3 and 1.4) are influenced by overlapping control strategies at a number of levels in the hierarchy of articulatory organisms. The way forward is, as Cooper (1983) suggests, to balance research that starts from directly or indirectly observed events near the output end of the hierarchy with research that works from specific concepts of the nature of input, or from general concepts of the nature of neural control systems, at the top end of the hierarchy.

Prosodic factors

As well as the blurring of segment boundaries by coarticulation phenomena, we also have to consider the existence of *prosodic* characteristics in the articulated signal. These are suprasegmental phenomena which are perceived in terms of relative *pitch*, *loudness*, *rhythm* and *tempo* (or rate of articulation), and are embodied in the signal as fundamental frequency, amplitude and durational characteristics (which we shall examine in more detail in the next section).

Prosodic phenomena are typically observed extending over domains that may be described in terms of units such as the syllable, the word and the phrase. Some of these signal properties appear to derive from *words* having characteristic *stress* (pitch and loudness) and rhythmic patterns which appear to be both independent of, and interactive with, segmental qualities. Thus, the noun *estimate* and the corresponding verb (a different word, in one sense of this term) have distinct patterns, involving different degrees of stress on the third syllable, which in turn is bound up in different qualities in the third vowel segment ([ə] vs [eɪ]).

Other prosodic properties in the signal may derive from higher levels of organisation, such as *syntactic units*; others still may have to be seen as belonging to independently specifiable phonological patterns of *intonation*, which may be laid over utterances to yield particular meanings in context. In addition, some of the long-range frequency, amplitude and durational characteristics in the signal derive from factors that are either *non-linguistic* (deriving from a speaker's having a cold or speaking while running, etc.) or *paralinguistic* (as when speech shows emotional effects which may be attributed to the speaker's attitude to what is being said).

There are many controversial issues in interpreting these data, some of which we shall encounter later (see the discussion in Cutler and Isard 1980). For now, we have simply to recognise that the signal carries information that may be interpreted well beyond the bounds of individual articulatory segments.

1.2.2 *Physical properties*

We are concerned here with what Fry (1979) refers to as 'the physics of speech'. His review should be consulted for further details. We shall simply highlight certain points here which will make for easier understanding of material to come in the next chapter.

The first point to notice is that air is the crucial medium for the transmission of speech; it is the link in the speech chain (as we have seen in fig. 1.1) between speaker and listener, present in the speaker's lungs and oral tract, in the air between speaker and listener and in the listener's ear canal. When the speaker's articulatory organs move – the lungs, the glottis, the tongue, the velum, the lips, etc. – air moves. More precisely, air particles are set into

motion in the locality of the articulatory gestures. They then disturb neighbouring air particles, which in turn transmit the motion to others, while other
articulatory gestures modify and control the nature of the particle movement
that results. Eventually, the acoustic signal that is so generated acts directly on
the tympanic membrane of the listener's ear. At this stage, the airborne phase
of the signal ends.

Fry points out that there are two sorts of particle motion that can be described as waves. One is that of a wave across the surface of water, where the
particles (of water) move up and down, at right angles to the direction of the
wave (it is the wave that moves transversely, not the particles of water) – this is
the *transverse* wave. The other is the *longitudinal* wave, in which particles of
the transmitting medium move to and fro in the same line of movement as the
wave itself. This is the case with wave propagation in air. The air particles may
be likened to people in a chain carrying buckets of water to a fire, each individual moving backwards and forwards within a restricted space, alternatively
receiving and delivering the next bucket. As particles of air crowd together,
local air pressure increases, and as they pull apart, it decreases: these represent
the peaks and troughs of the air pressure wave.

Amplitude, frequency and intensity

There are three dimensions to such waves which we must recognise: they have *amplitude, frequency* and *intensity.*

Amplitude is the displacement of particles from their position of rest, either
in one direction or the other. Elasticity is the property that tends to hold particles of any medium in one position, hence resisting displacement and leading
to a pendulum-like reaction against displacement in one direction, resulting in
an overshoot-displacement in the other direction. Gradually, with no further
external force being applied, the particle will come to rest in its original position.

Frequency is the number of times that the pattern of displacement either
side of the position of rest occurs in a unit of time. It is conventional to refer to
cycles of displacement (one cycle being described by the motion of a particle as
it goes through each pattern of displacement and overshoot) per second:
originally abbreviated as cps (cycles per second), this unit is now more generally referred to as Hertz (after the German physicist, Heinrich Hertz), and
abbreviated as Hz (kiloHertz, kHz, 1,000 cycles per second, are also convenient large units for speech).

Intensity is the hidden member of these three dimensions of the sound signal, since it relates to the energy in the sound, and this may be expressed in
terms of greater amplitude (displacement of particles at a given frequency) or

17

frequency (more rapid oscillation of particles at a given amplitude). The intensity of a sound must be increased by n squared for an increase of n in the frequency of a sound of given amplitude; and by n squared also for an increase of n in the amplitude of a sound of given frequency. Intensity is measured in decibels (dB), units on a logarithmic comparison scale ranging from 0dB, on the threshold of audibility, to 130dB, equivalent to the sound of a jet aircraft at 120 feet. Conversation at normal levels and distances is rated as 60dB. The ear is used to handling speech arriving as whispers (30dB) to the loudest shouting that speakers can manage (75dB) (Fry 1979).

Simple versus complex waves

Any departure from a perfectly regular, symmetrical wave form (a *sinusoidal* form, or a *sine wave*) results in what is referred to as a complex wave form. Simple wave forms arise from such instruments as a tuning fork, where the to-and-fro motion of the prongs is evenly distributed either side of the position of rest. Most of the sounds we find in everyday experience, and speech sounds are among these, are produced from instruments that are more complex in their vibrating properties than tuning-fork prongs; they move more easily in one direction than another, for instance, or they are constrained (damped) by some other instrument contacting them. These situations give rise to complex wave forms, which can be analysed out in terms of constituent simple wave forms in particular time (or phase) relationship to each other. The constituency is expressed in Fourier's Theorem, and the process by which complex wave forms are recognised by calculating their constituent simple wave forms is referred to as Fourier analysis.

Sound quality and harmonics

For complex wave forms, the constituent sinusoidal wave forms – or components – consist of (a) the lowest-frequency component, called the fundamental frequency, and (b) other components that are at whole-number multiples of this frequency (i.e. twice that frequency, three times that frequency, four times that frequency, and so on). These latter are called the harmonics of the fundamental (second harmonic, third harmonic, fourth harmonic, etc.). Depending on the characteristics of the sound-producing system, some of these harmonic frequencies may be of greater amplitude than others, and it is this harmonic structure of a sound that gives it its characteristic quality. The shape of the vocal tract at any given moment is related to the harmonic–amplitude structure of the sound that results.

18

Periodic versus aperiodic sounds

Certain sounds do not have this orderly relationship between fundamental and harmonic frequencies, however, and these are referred to as aperiodic sounds. Sounds generated by taking frequencies at random and adding them together are of this type. Fry (1979) notes that these sounds are 'those which the ear and brain class as *noises*; the sound of escaping steam and the sound of something being fried in the pan are good examples of natural noises' (1979: 83). In speech, sounds that have a supraglottal source, e.g. the turbulence of air escaping through an oral constriction, as for [s], are aperiodic; by contrast, sounds that arise through pulse waves deriving from the opening and closing of the glottis in the larynx are periodic (and hence have harmonics on which differential amplitude characteristics can establish a structure).

1.2.3 *Perceptual factors*

The acoustic signal properties

A good way to start considering the nature of the acoustic signal is to look at a spectrogram. Figure 1.5 shows a spectrogram of a phrase, *rapid writing*, with the broad phonetic identification of segments indicated. One of the features you will notice is that the relative timing of these segments as represented in the acoustic signal is quite varied: some are of relatively long duration, while others are very brief. Another feature is that the segments do not have sharp boundaries, by and large: the centres of the segments are more clearly identifiable than are their boundaries. Indeed, the phonetic identification provided in this example has been carried out in this way; the positioning of the phonetic symbols is in line with their spectrographic centres, and the boundaries have been left unmarked. These two features, then, belong to the *time* dimension of the signal. The next feature to notice is that different parts of the signal, as identified along the time line, have distinct energy patterns spread vertically. The vertical axis represents the *frequency* dimension of the display, and it is possible to see at once that it would be too simple to say that some sounds are of higher or lower frequency than others. Rather, each identified sound has a *pattern* of frequencies – a frequency profile – and these profiles are distinct from each other. But, because speech is basically a continuous phenomenon, these frequency profiles do not show *sharp* discontinuities from those on either side of them. They merge and flow, one into the other, along the duration dimension. This is why the boundaries are harder to locate than the centres. There is also a third dimension, of *intensity*, which is indicated by relative darkness in figure 1.5 but can be seen more clearly in figure 1.6. The

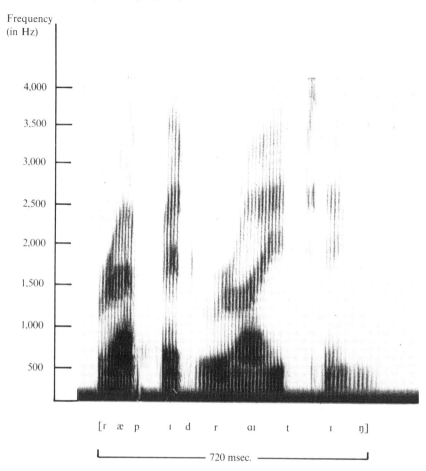

Figure 1.5 Spectrographic representation of the phrase *rapid writing*

peaks of intensity appear on the spectrogram as dark bands of energy, known as *formants*. These reflect the changing resonance characteristics of the vocal tract as it assumes different configurations. These three dimensions, of time, frequency and intensity (amplitude may be thought of as the overall intensity of a section of the signal, across all frequencies), represent a good deal of the acoustic aspect of the speech signal. But we must bear in mind that the acoustic form of the signal derives from the aerodynamic effects, which in turn result from the consequences of articulatory movements on surrounding air particles – and there is certainly some loss of information through these transduction stages. First, there are quite palpable articulatory distinctions which appear to get lost in aerodynamic encoding, and hence cannot be identified in the acoustic signal: e.g. the distinction between alveolar [n] in *ten* and dental

20

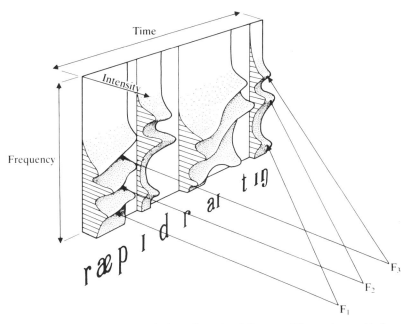

Figure 1.6 Schematic three-dimensional diagram of the spectrographic form of *figure 1.5*

[ŋ] on *tenth* (Fudge 1967); or the velar closure coarticulated with alveolar closure in the case we noted above in figure 1.4; or the momentary drop in air pressure in the forward part of the oral tract which results from a sudden enlarging of that cavity, obliterating a continued increase in pressure below the larynx; and so on.

Secondly, the normal possibilities for contamination of the aerodynamic/acoustic relationship are endless, as will be appreciated by anyone who has made a spectrogram of speech recorded in a less-than-soundproof environment. Typically, what comes in at the ear is not just what is being said by the person you are listening to at the moment, but a host of other sounds, speech as well as non-speech. Consequently, a major issue in the understanding of speech perception in normal, noisy environments is the ability to 'lock on' to a subset of the acoustic information arriving at the ear, and to define it as a distinct channel, which may be kept open, or abandoned in favour of another, in spite of the fluctuating real-time values both within and around it. In this connection, we should bear in mind that phase relations, which can prove important in discriminating speech from non-speech sound, are not found in the spectrographic record.

Processing the acoustic signal

Let us take it, then, that the three-dimensional construct of the acoustic signal provides the basis for speech perception. Our first task must be to understand the relationship that might exist between this signal and our perception of it. But how we conceive of this task will depend on what we take 'our perception of it' to mean.

A standard view (see the review in Borden and Harris 1980) is that the auditory system might be thought of as converting the continuously varying input at an early stage into a succession of discrete segmental percepts ('phonemes', as they are usually called in the speech perception literature). In this case, the system might achieve this task on the basis of detecting *cues* to such percepts (with the implication that the stretches of signal between these cues are not strictly relevant, and may not be sampled). Such a response system would carry 'phonemes' to the brain, where they might be assembled as known word sequences. Current work on the cues that might actually be used in speech perception (e.g. Blumstein and Stevens 1981) suggests that they may be 'spectral templates' of stable composition but very short duration.

Alternatively, we might ask whether the auditory system works like a sound spectrograph (e.g. Whitfield 1967). If so, then it takes in continuously varying data on frequency and intensity along the time dimension, and delivers an analysis through the operation of filters, or specialised resonating devices. Such a response system might carry a continuous and faithful display of 'spectrograms' to the brain, where they might be interpreted as (sequences of) known, discrete, word shapes. The possibility that a mediating stage of phoneme identification may not be directly involved in speech perception (e.g. Studdert-Kennedy 1981) is compatible with this view (regardless of how literally we may wish to take the spectrogram analogy).

We shall discuss the implications of these approaches in chapter 4. It is sufficient for our purpose here to note that, by either account, the auditory system must (a) register the changing intensity and frequency characteristics of the wave-like motion of air particles arriving at the air/ear interface, and (b) represent these characteristics within those parts of the system in which air is no longer the transmitting medium. We should also understand that the ear and its associated neural system is dealing with energy levels that are extremely low (from 10^{-16} watts to 10^{-4} watts); that acuity of the system is greatest for these low energy levels between about 1kHz and 8kHz frequencies; and that phase differences among sine-wave components of complex wave forms are not nearly as important as frequency analysis to the way we hear these sounds, so that the ear appears to operate more as a frequency-spectrum analyser than as a phase-spectrum analyser (Denes and Pinson 1963: 29).

Prosodic information

We have already noted the information that prosodic characteristics may carry regarding the words, grammar and meaning of utterances (see our discussion in section 1.2.1 above). In addition, speech perception may rely on such factors as pitch continuity and continuity of internal spectral composition of segments (each of which may be characteristic of a particular speaker) in order to identify and track a continuing speech signal, in a situation where there is more than one voice or a certain level of other potentially masking background noise (see Laver 1980 on the description of voice quality). It is also likely that the speech rate in the local environment of segments is monitored and used in the determination of certain segments as being contrastively 'short' or 'long'; this may involve retrospective (or 'backward') perceptual calibration of segment duration, on the basis of later-incoming auditory information on durational characteristics of the signal (see the discussion in Nooteboom, Brokx and de Rooij 1978 and Summerfield 1979).

1.3 Writing systems

We shall now consider some properties of writing systems. These are based on essentially two-dimensional space, but the ways in which they exploit these resources are not all the same. There are examples of minor differences of detail, as between the Cyrillic and Roman forms of the alphabet, but there are also some fundamental differences in terms both of the sorts of units that are represented on the page, and the relations these bear to the speech signal, and to the properties of linguistic systems (Klima 1972: Lotz 1972; Taylor 1981).

Orthographic forms of language are perhaps most typically produced by the manual system and offered to the visual system as patterns of different shades of grey (e.g. typewriting or print on the page); but we should not forget that this may not always be the case (e.g. illuminated letters against a dark background or letters distinguished from background by colour, etc.). We should also bear in mind that, as in the case of speech signals, there is considerable variation to be found. This may exist in letter shapes as between upper and lower case print; one type of print vs another (e.g. italic or roman); between print and handwriting; between one person's handwriting and another's; right down to variations in one person's attempts at the same letters. There is, then, a considerable challenge, in terms of pattern recognition, to the visual system (and in terms of pattern production, to the manual system); the 'same' pattern must be perceived in a variety of objectively distinct sizes and shapes, a constancy of response maintained despite a host of physically varying circumstances (see ch. 4 for further discussion).

It is not necessary or possible to provide an exhaustive review of different writing systems in what follows (aspects of this study may be found in Edgerton 1952; Gelb 1963; Pei 1965; Haas 1976a; and Sampson 1985). Instead, we shall concentrate on some of the major differences of organisation, and then discuss the system that English uses in this context. We may also note that it is not appropriate for us to go into the physical properties of light, and the ways in which the photoreceptors of the eye are activated by the wavelengths involved in processing written language symbols. There is no real parallel here to the role of air as the transmitting medium of speech. Light does not serve as the expressing medium of written language (hand and finger movements do not manipulate light in the act of writing). Thus writing can be accomplished in the dark, whereas no speech is possible in a vacuum (apart from the indirect skill of lip-reading); and switching out the light does not erase the symbols from the page. Accordingly, we shall not organise our discussion in terms of production, transmission and perception here, as we did in discussing the auditory signal (section 1.2), since these aspects do not relate in a straightforward way to the conventional differences that we are concerned with. These are represented in

1. ideographic systems
2. syllable-based systems (syllabaries)
3. alphabetic systems

which we shall consider in sections 1.3.2–1.3.4 below. The processing implications of such distinctions will be reserved for discussion in chapters 4 and 5. However, we shall briefly review some general issues regarding production and perception in 1.3.5.

The status of writing systems

From a linguistic point of view, it is usual, and appropriate, to stress the derivative status of written forms of language, in spite of the degree of independence that some written language forms may attain (Lyons 1968). The argument is based on numbers (relatively few of the world's languages are possessed of a native script), on history (writing emerged comparatively late on in the evolution of languages) and on logic (a spoken language is not affected by the rise, or the loss of, a written representation for it). There are many difficult points of detail with this last argument, since certain distinct features of style, involving all levels of language, may rest upon the existence of a written representation for a language, but these hardly affect the main issue. From a psycholinguistic point of view, however, the visual modality of language processing gives rise to questions that go to the heart of our understanding of how language is instantiated in the individual. Certainly, reading and writing develop later in the individual's language development than do speaking and listening abilities; but how they develop, and what subsequently happens to the individual's total language capacities, are fundamental issues.

One logical possibility is the situation where a new means of expression/perception is developed for one and the same language ability; another is where a totally new language ability is developed in relation to the written means of expression and perception. It may be suspected that most people's experience lies somewhere between these extremes of compound and coordinate relationship, but exactly where is dependent on a number of factors, including the way in which the writing system is taught and acquired, the degree of literacy achieved and the formal properties of the system. We are mainly concerned with the latter here.

1.3.1 *Possible writing systems*

General linguistic accounts of written language (conveniently reviewed in Henderson 1982) frequently start by establishing the boundaries of possible scripts and continue by elaborating three main types within these. The continuum of graphic representation is bounded at one extreme by a variety of *pictographic* possibilities. These may be relatively unstereotyped, as in the case of a representational picture, telling a story; or symbolically constrained, as in the case of internationally agreed road signs, where a red border signifies a warning or prohibition. Even in these latter, conventionalised pictographs, however, the relationship to linguistic forms of the message tends to be approximate and variable. For intance, the sign in figure 1.7 might be ver-

Figure 1.7 A standard warning sign from the British Highway Code. (From *The highway code*. London: HMSO.)

balised as 'Warning: stone chippings are liable to be thrown up from vehicles' wheels along this surface', but this particular linguistic version is only as good as all the other possible paraphrases. In short, the sign is directly representing a message, rather than a particular linguistic form of a message, and hence falls outside the accepted scope of 'written language'. At the other extreme, we shall wish to exclude machine-based recordings of the acoustic signal (spectrograms, mingograms, and the like), since they selectively present formal features of language for the purpose of refining the analysis of these features, rather than for the more ordinary purposes of communication (Marshall 1976).

In between these extremes, the sort of picture set out in figure 1.8 is frequently recognised. This sort of taxonomy is usually accompanied by reference to the diachronic interpretation of these types, whereby meaning-based systems tend to become sound-symbolic over time; and all known alphabetic systems are said to derive from some relatively recent (conventionally, Phoenician) development representing the high-water mark of orthographic development. Thus, it is argued, for example, that no further refinement of alphabetic writing systems into feature-based notations is possible, since this would actually worsen their practicability and efficiency; the ratio of graphic information (marks on the page) to perceived speech distinctions would become unacceptably high.

Problematically, this sort of typology can create the misleading impression that actual writing systems are purely of one type or another. Possibly the most striking example of a mixed system is Japanese, where logographic and syllabary symbols coexist in the written forms of utterances; a more mundane example is to be found in English, which has a number of non-alphabetic elements, as we shall see. But even in the less obviously mixed types, we shall note that Chinese logographs contain sound-representative components; and that among the alphabetic elements of English, words may be distinguished by their visual spelling patterns, within certain limits of sound-representativeness. Thus, for example, being able to read and understand forms such as *boy* and *buoy* is a matter of relating letter structure to word meaning as well as to word sounds.

First, however, let us sketch out more neutrally the different sorts of representation of language that may exist – and coexist – with an orthographic system. As figure 1.9 shows, there are three relevant orders of unit, which may be illustrated in the threefold ambiguity of the word *word*: we may mean a word in the sense of its sound shape (phonological word), or in the sense of its grammatical properties (grammatical word), or in the sense of its lexical iden-

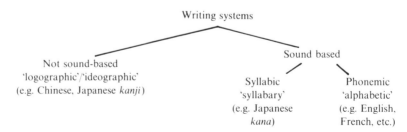

Figure 1.8 A generalised typology of writing systems

Components of language structure

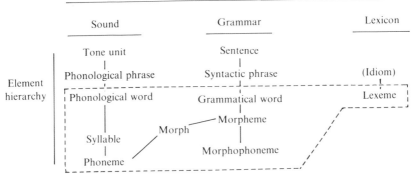

(Elements within the dotted lines are available for orthographic mapping)

Figure 1.9 Possible points of contact between language elements and units of writing systems

tity (the word as a lexeme). As an example, consider the word *foolish*. Phonologically, it consists of two syllables, organising five phonemes, /fu:-lɪʃ/, with stress on the first syllable. Grammatically, it consists of two morphemes, {fool} and -{ish}, the first being a noun, the second an adjectivalising suffix, and the whole form being an adjective. Lexically, it is a member of the set *fool, foolish, foolishly, foolishness, folly* (which, in this sense of the term, are all forms of the same 'word').

It is no accident that we have chosen to illustrate these three orders of language structure from the level of the word. In the phonological hierarchy, word forms constitute phonological phrases, which build into tone units; in the grammatical hierarchy, words are constituents of syntactic phrases and thence of sentences; and lexically, there are no other units to select (apart from idioms such as *hit it off*). Presumably, no orthographic system builds on phonological or syntactic phrases, or larger units still, for the same reason that these do not constitute the basic units of form–meaning correspondence in language structure: this would entail having different symbols to represent each of *the boy, a boy, the girl, a girl* and so on. So, given that orthographic representations map from units of word size (or less), we can see at once that any particular system might represent *either* aspects of the *form* of words (whether phonological, morphological or lexemic) *or* the semantic aspect. And if the orthographic system maps from units of less than word size then these will either be the semantically empty phonological units of the syllable and the phoneme, or, in the grammatical hierarchy, morphemes which again can be captured either as form-based or semantic entities. For our discussion here, the item morph in figure 1.9 may be considered to be a grammatically relevant phonological entity, as in the alternative forms of the stem in *knife*, *knive-s*.

Given this framework, we shall now briefly characterise some of the salient features of Chinese orthography, followed by Japanese as an example of a 'mixed' script, then illustrate from a typical syllabary, as used for Kannada, a Dravidian language of southern India, and finally turn to a consideration of English.

1.3.2　*Chinese* (*Mandarin*)

The spoken languages (often referred to as 'dialects') that are Chinese include Mandarin, Cantonese, Hokkien and other mutually unintelligible languages. They can all be written in the same traditional script; the examples given here are illustrated with phonological forms from Mandarin. There are basically three sorts of character to consider.

Simple characters
These include:

(2)　　　　人　　　　木　　　　　　其
　　　　　rén　　　　mù　　　　　qí /tɕʰi/
　　　　　person　　tree　　　　his, her, its, etc.

The first two of these illustrate the simplest sort of meaning-based symbol, even preserving something of their representational (pictographic) basis: we might use the term *ideographic* for them. The third is representationally much more abstract, as well as being more complex in terms of its component strokes; for this we might use the term *logographic*, since there is no hint of an attempt here to portray the idea of the word, only to provide a distinct symbol for the word itself. Of all these characters we may say that there is no connection between their stroke structure and the sound structure of the words they represent: nothing marks the tone or the phonemic sequence in any way; we shall say that there is nothing *phono*-graphic about them.

However, some simple forms may represent more than one word, such as that for *gōng* /kʊŋ/, 'public' (also 'male of species'), and the character for *gàn* /kàn/, 'trunk' (also 'work'). The fact that the same character may be used for two (or more) words that happen to share the same phonological form is important: it means that, in such cases, the character is taking on a phonographic function. It may be regarded as logographic in respect of one of the words it stands for (usually one is seen as basic to it), but when we say that it 'stands for' this word, we cannot rigorously exclude its potential for representing the sound as well as the meaning; and it is the sound aspect that is exploited in the extension of the same character to certain homophonous items in the language.

Compound characters

These are of two major types, of which the first may be illustrated very simply by:

(3)   木   + 木   = 林   *or* 森
          mù   mù   lín   sēn
          tree   tree   woods   forest

There is graphological compositionality here, quite clearly; but it is not linked to any phonological relationship. The written form of *lín* thus forms a type of compound ideogram, as also does that of *sēn*. Note that a compound character is distinct from a character sequence, which we shall discuss below: it may be graphologically complex in a fully compositional fashion, but it represents a single word. This is true of the forms for both *lín* and *sēn*, notwithstanding the incidental difference between them, namely that *lín* 'woods' is a fully free word capable of standing on its own, while *sēn* 'forest' is restricted to appearing in the sequence *sēn lín*.

Compound characters may also involve reduced forms of simple characters:

(4)   人   + 木   = 休
          rén   mù   xiōu /ɕiǝu/
          person   tree   rest

Here 亻 in the compound is the reduced form of 人 *rén*: it functions in this compound as the *radical*, a type of element of which we shall have more to say in a moment.

There may appear to be a subtle distinction of type here, beyond the use of a reduced symbol, however. The 木 *mù* + 木 *mù* = 林 *lín* relationship seems literal and straightforward, while 人 *rén* + 木 *mù* = 休 *xiōu* involves a rather metaphorical relationship, such as 'a person against/under a tree is in a state of rest'. In each case, however, the symbol-to-sound relationship is abstract: *xiōu, lín, sēn*, etc. are all represented by non-phonographic symbols.

A second type of compound has clear phonographic aspects:

(5)(a)   木   + 卜   = 朴
          mù   bo   pò
          tree   (*final particle*   species oak tree
                   with no
                   inherent tone)

(5)(b) 木 + 反 = 板
      mù   fǎn   bǎn
      tree   to turn over   board; printing block
               or back; to
               rebel

(5)(c) 竹 + 其 = 箕
      zhú
      zhú /tʂú/   qí   jī /cī/
      bamboo   his, etc.   winnowing basket

In the first two cases, the leftmost element of the compound, 木, is called the radical (cf. also 亻 in 休 in (4)), and is not represented in the pronunciation of the word at all. It is often – even typically – representative of the meaning of the compound, as can be seen clearly in the case of 朴 *pò* in (5a). Graphically, the radical element of a compound is often smaller, or abbreviated, compared to its full form, and in many cases has the graphological status of a diacritic. Depending on the design characteristics of the whole symbol, the radical may appear in any position, not just on the left – see, for example, the third character 箕 in (5c). For any particular compound character, the position of the radical element is conventionally fixed: i.e. ⺮ in 箕 cannot appear in any other position. The remaining element of these compounds is a full graphic symbol and serves the function of marking the phonological form of the word. The degree to which it achieves this may be less than absolute, as in (5a): really, what 朴 tells the reader is something close to 'a tree, pronounced like *bo*', and similarly 板 in (5b) says in effect 'related to tree and sounding like *fǎn*'. The phonographic function of 其 in 箕 in (5c) is not fully accurate, but it is in

(6)   木 + 其 = 棋
          mù   qí   qí
          tree his, etc. Chinese chess

where the compound says 'related to wood, and pronounced like *qi*'.

    Finally, these compounds may be subject to the same homophonic extensions that we have already noted in simple characters. Thus:

(7)   木 + 公 = 松   *but also* 松
          mù gōng sōng   sōng
          tree public pine tree   loose

Character sequences

    In introducing the concept of this latter type of compound character (consisting of the 'radical' plus what is often called the 'phonetic'), we have rather literally interpreted the sort of information that these characters convey. In practice, only a learner of the Chinese script would interpret 松 in (7) as 'sort of tree, and pronounced like *gōng*'. For a fluent reader, the character as a whole would map onto the lexical item {sōng: 'pine tree'}; and indeed onto its homophone {sōng: 'loose'}. What this means is that the force of the radical component is frequently lost, and the result of this may be seen in the existence of certain sequences such as:

(8)　　　木　　　板
　　　　　mù　　　bǎn
　　　　　tree　　　board = wooden plank or board

Here, no new character is formed, but rather a (syntactic) sequence of characters. But notice that the first character, the full form of *mù*, is required to distinguish *wooden* from other sorts of *board*.

In all, there are now 214 radicals, which serve as the organising principle of Chinese dictionaries. There are 1,585 compound characters listed in the largest Chinese dictionary as being built on the radical 木 *mù*. Most, but not all, of them have something to do with wood; but the full symbol 木 *mù* also functions in many other characters as a 'phonetic' component.

Finally, we should stress the point that it is too much of a simplification to say that the Chinese script is not phonographic. We have tried to show that it does indeed have phonographic aspects, and that the control of it by native writers and readers requires skilful interplay of both sound and meaning dimensions in the script. Historically, this can be seen in the way new characters have been devised for the language: Ong Tee Wah (1980) relates the story of how the second-century lexicographer Xu Shen provided a character for the word *xī* /ʃī/, 'west', by using the form 西 which also appears in 栖 *qī* /ʃī/, 'nesting bird', with the gloss that the bird went to its nest at the time of the setting of the sun in the west (possibly the forms involved were phonologically more similar in his day). The same sort of interplay can be found today, for instance in the devising of suitable characters for newspaper reports to use in referring to visiting foreign dignitaries (S. E. Martin 1972 notes the possibilities that exist for intentional sound–meaning interplay in this connection).

There are many details that have been left out of this account (see French 1976, Sampson 1985), but it should suffice to make the point that the Chinese writing system does embody certain phonographic principles. We have to observe also that the phonographic aspects tend to be related to whole word-forms, rather than to phonological segments, and that individual component strokes of the written characters do not themselves represent aspects of the phonological pattern; that is to say, the phonographic representation is fundamentally non-compositional. Or, putting it another way, it is sound *similarity* rather than *components* of sound structure, that the characters capture.

1.3.3 *Syllabaries*

Among those writing systems that are fundamentally phonographic, we shall expect to find the ability to represent components of sound structure. One very important type is that of *syllabaries*, which are based on the syllable unit of the spoken language; and in this connection a question immediately arises as to how far they are radically distinct from those, *alphabetic*, systems that are based on individual consonant and vowel segments.

We shall look first at the writing system of Japanese, which uses a syllabary alongside a Chinese type of system. Having briefly noted the main characteristics of the Japanese syllabary, we shall then consider a rather different type, as found in Kannada, a Dravidian language spoken and written in Karnataka state in south India. This is an example of a highly compositional syllabary, within which the consonant and vowel segments can easily be discerned; as such, it will take us towards our consideration of the alphabetic system used in English (section 1.3.4).

Japanese

The Japanese writing system is a hybrid of (a) *kanji* characters, deriving from Chinese ideo-/logographs, and (b) *kana*, syllabary elements that belong to either of the subtypes *hiragana* (cursive kana) or *katakana* (square kana) (Morton and Sasanuma 1984). The overall characteristics of this mixed system, particularly the interplay of meaning-symbolic and sound-symbolic elements, are well described in Martin (1972). The kanji characters are used for major lexical items (nouns, verbs, adjectives), while, of the kana elements, hiragana is used for grammatical morphemes (particles, auxiliary verbs, etc.), and katakana is used for representing loan words and foreign names. Each of these syllabary systems has seventy-one characters, using basic forms and diacritics (see Morton and Sasanuma 1984). Both systems appear to have arisen from simplifications of kanji characters, and hence share some general similarities; but there are nonetheless some striking differences of form between corresponding symbols in the two systems.

Each system is typical of syllabaries generally in having two fundamental types of sound syllable directly represented in terms of characters: the vowel-type (V), without preceding or following consonant; and the open-syllable type (CV), consisting of a consonant followed by a vowel. In Japanese kana, as traditionally organised, there are five vowel characters, corresponding to the alphabetic symbols *a, i, u, e* and *o*. In addition, there are separate symbols for each of the CV combinations arising from the following consonants with these vowels: *k, s, t, n, h, m, r, g, z, d, b, p*. Some other symbols represent CV sequences with a restricted range of vowels: *ya, yu, yo, wa, wo*. There is also a symbol for the nasal consonant without included vowel. The total inventory is seventy-one symbols.

In such a system, it is clearly crucial to understand the nature of the relationship, in character composition, between those shapes that represent the individual V sounds and those that represent the CV patterns. In both forms of kana, this relationship is fundamentally obscure: while it is possible to spot similarities of form here and there among V and CV characters that represent the same vowel sound, this phonographic correspondence goes largely unrepresented. It is also important to observe how consistently individual consonant sounds are represented in CV symbols; and here the kana system again provides very little overt correspondence. The result is that kana symbols by and large are highly syllabic, possessing very little internal structure which would permit their decomposition into constituent consonant and vowel shapes. See figure 1.10, where the top row consists of the *k*-series of CV symbols in hiragana; it will be quite apparent that it is impossible to detect a consistent *k*-feature across these forms. By contrast, note that the corresponding *g*-series (row 4 in fig. 1.10) is systematically related to the *k*-series by using the same basic symbol, with the addition of a voicing diacritic (two short strokes in the upper right corner). This feature is found on certain other voiced consonant series also. But it should be noted that this type of compositionality

Japanese (Hiragana)	か	き	く	け	こ
Kannada	ಕ	ಕಿ	ಕು	ಕೆ	ಕೊ
English	ka	ki	ku	ke	ko
Japanese (Hiragana)	が	ぎ	ぐ	げ	ご
Kannada	ಗ	ಗಿ	ಗು	ಗೆ	ಗೊ
English	ga	gi	gu	ge	go

Figure 1.10 An illustrative selection of Japanese (Hiragana) and Kannada symbols with English equivalents

operates from syllable level to *features*, rather than to the *segments* of alphabetic notation.

Kannada

By contrast, the Kannada language is possessed of a syllabary that has distinctly alphabetic implications. It may be thought of, as a first approximation, as having fifty basic symbols, made up of twelve vowel types (V), thirty-four CV types, and four other positionally restricted elements that need not detain us here. The count of thirty-four CV types, however, is based only on the included vowel *a*: i.e., there are thirty-four C + *a* symbols. In addition, these may be supplied with other vowel diacritics, generating separate symbols for each of the CV patterns recognised in the system – a total of more than 400 symbols in all. Perhaps because of the size of this system, it is systematically compositional in nature, with relatively consistent shapes for both consonantal and vocalic identities. And these identities are essentially segmental (alphabetic) in size. See figure 1.10, rows 2 and 5: these clearly show that there are distinct consonant symbols for the *k*- and *g*-series, and that there is consistency of both consonant and vowel representation in the CV symbols illustrated (not all the vowel possibilities that Kannada recognises are shown). A further aspect of this system that underlines its alphabetic potential is that it is possible to represent consonants alone (i.e. without an included vowel diacritic) by providing the basic consonant symbol with a 'vowel-deletion' diacritic: this is used, for example, in pedagogic contexts, in formulae such as 'k^o (the symbol with the vowel deletion diacritic) + $a = k^a$ (the symbol with the *a* diacritic)'. The other contexts in which such consonant-alone symbols might be used is in consonant clusters: thus the word /yatna/ 'effort', might be represented as $y^a t^o n^a$. In practice, this solution is much less used nowadays, in favour of a range of consonantal diacritics below the base symbol; in these terms, /yatna/ would be represented as $y^a t_n{}^a$. This solution reflects the fundamentally syllabic nature of the symbols, as does the practice of ignoring word boundaries in continuous text, in favour of syllabic structure: thus /ond(u)/ 'one' + /iṭṭige/ 'brick', which in speech usually shows elision of the parenthesised vowel, is representable as $ond^i \d{t}_i{}^i g^e$. (The symbol 'ṭ' represents a retroflex consonant.)

The Kannada writing system, then, is fundamentally syllabic, but has, as we have seen, a number of alphabetic aspects. The existence of more than one organising principle within a single writing system should not surprise us: after all, the speech signal contains syllables as well as smaller and larger units, and it is the function of a phonographic script to provide useful clues to the sound structure of the language forms that it represents. But, beyond this, we have also seen that phonographic clues may even sit alongside logographic ones. At this point, we may turn to the case of the English writing system.

1.3.4 *English*

Examining the nature of our own writing system (see also Haas 1969; Albrow 1972) is in some ways a harder task than looking at other systems, since we have to step back and examine our assumptions (e.g. that ours is basically an alphabetic system, that it is therefore phonographic, and at the level of the phoneme, and so on).

We may start by considering the inventory of alphabetic elements that English makes use of, and for this purpose it is convenient to use the keys of an ordinary typewriter, as set out in figure 1.11.

Non-alphabetic elements

Perhaps what is immediately striking about this array is the fact that there are so many non-alphabetic elements, such as £, &, %, etc. (Edgerton 1941). Furthermore, this list could easily be extended: . in *9.186* ('nine *point* one eight six'); × in *5 ×4* ('five *times* four'; in computer applications, * has this function); *X* in *Xmas* ('*Christ*mas', also '*Ex*mas') and in common abbreviations such as *Xian* ('*Christ*ian') and *KingsX*, *QueensX* (abbreviating the major railway stations on the London–Aberdeen route), + similarly in *Kings +* and *Charing +* (the usual form for 'Kings *Cross*', 'Charing *Cross*' on London buses), and so on. Further extensions still can be effected by compiling basically alphabetic elements into such conventional units as *ms*, *dB*, *Hz*,

$$1 \quad 2 \quad 3 \quad 4 \quad 5 \quad 6 \quad 7 \quad 8 \quad 9 \quad 0 \quad \tfrac{3}{4} \quad =$$

$$* \quad " \quad / \quad \$ \quad £ \quad \_ \quad \& \quad ' \quad (\quad) \quad \tfrac{1}{4} \quad +$$

$$q \quad w \quad e \quad r \quad t \quad y \quad u \quad i \quad o \quad p \quad - \quad [$$

$$Q \quad W \quad E \quad R \quad T \quad Y \quad U \quad I \quad O \quad P \quad ? \quad !$$

$$a \quad s \quad d \quad f \quad g \quad h \quad j \quad k \quad l \quad ; \quad] \quad \tfrac{2}{3}$$

$$A \quad S \quad D \quad F \quad G \quad H \quad J \quad K \quad L \quad : \quad @ \quad \tfrac{1}{3}$$

$$z \quad x \quad c \quad v \quad b \quad n \quad m \quad , \quad . \quad \tfrac{1}{2}$$

$$Z \quad X \quad C \quad V \quad B \quad N \quad M \quad , \quad . \quad \%$$

Figure 1.11 The character inventory of a standard English typewriter

lb, *oz*, *etc*, and so on. Many of these retain some connection with alphabetic principles, as do *ms*, *dB*, and *Hz* in this list; but *lb* does not, and hardly *oz*. Similarly *ft*, *in* are partially alphabetic, but ', " are not, either in this function or in the case where they represent minutes and seconds. The use of / is a particularly interesting case: it is usually taken to represent *per* in contexts like *lb/in²* ('pounds *per* square inch'), but in *syllabary/alphabet* it seems to represent *or* which is specialised as 'non-disjunctive or' (= *and/or*), and is coming increasingly to be verbalised as 'stroke'.

Leaving detailed consideration of these and other non-phonographic forms aside, let us simply recognise that English orthography apparently has considerable resources which are strictly non-alphabetic. The proportion of their use is presumably highly variable, depending on the style and nature of the text, but it seems likely that we have to recognise a situation wherein fluent English readers make effortless transitions between radically distinct forms of character as their eyes scan a representative sample of print, and disambiguate such ambiguous symbols as +, ", . and /.

Punctuation markers

These represent an interesting class of elements, which are phonographic without being alphabetic: that is, they represent aspects of sound structure which typically have to do with supresegmental (often prosodic) aspects, such as pause, shift of pitch (particularly for material contained within parentheses – or even set off by hyphens – as in this example which you are reading now), and intonational patterns. As such, they typically mark (as do their phonological counterparts) features of structure at the level of the clause and the sentence.

Alphabetic elements

It is well known that there are twenty-six of these, but we really have to consider them as fifty-two: i.e. comprising both upper and lower case. In standard lower-case text, use of upper-case letters for sentence-initial position has a similar function to that of the full stop punctuation mark. But English readers can also scan whole texts in upper case, so we must include them in our survey of basic alphabetic elements.

Upper and lower case

The first point to notice is the variable degree of correspondence that exists between upper- and lower-case forms of the same letters (table 1.2). As far as most print founts are concerned, the eight items listed here as having 'direct' relationship between upper- and lower-case forms are clearly distinct

Table 1.2 *Three categories of upper- to lower-case relationships in English letters*

Direct (8 items)		Intermediate (7 items)		Abstract (11 items)	
W	w	Q	q	E	e
U	u	Y	y	R	r
O	o	I	i	T	t
S	s	P	p	A	a
Z	z	F	f	D	d
X	x	J	j	G	g
C	c	K	k	H	h
V	v			L	l
				B	b
				N	n
				M	m

in relying on size alone to mark the case difference. (For some print founts (e.g. italic), and for many styles of handwriting, some of these items would show an indirect relationship, e.g. *W–w*, *X–x* and *V–v*.) There is room for disagreement about the borderline between the 'intermediate' and 'abstract' categories, but it is not our concern to pursue such details here: one reason for this being that we do not yet know which features of similarity and difference readers use as cues in recognising letters (see further in the next chapter).

Phoneme–grapheme correspondence

The second major point to notice about this system of alphabetic elements is that it is not straightforwardly suitable for representing the phonemes of English: there are no ready symbols for /ʃ/, /θ/, /ð/, etc. among the consonants, and the five 'vowel' symbols, *a, e, i, o, u*, are quite inadequate for representing the contrasts of the phonological vowel system. These considerations take us to the heart of the nature of English orthography, and accordingly need to be looked at quite carefully.

The phonemic principle

The way the English spell their language has been an intellectual football for hundreds of years. Approaching the system as it is today (e.g. Venezky 1970), one notices three principal ways in which the phonemic principle of 'one symbol for each distinctive sound-segment' is apparently violated.

The first is found in the use of sequences of (usually two) letters to represent a phoneme: *sh* for /ʃ/, *ng* for /ŋ/, *ee* for /iː/, and so on. In these cases, we have to recognise a set of digraphs, or complex symbols, in which the constituent elements are not compositionally phonographic (though, as in the cases of *sh*, *ng*, etc., they are clearly chosen on a 'near neighbour' principle). Essentially, then, these violations are more apparent than real, and we should extend our list of basic alphabetic symbols to include *sh, ng, ee, th,* and a host of other digraphs. However, this does not eliminate all problems: *th,* for instance, is used for both /θ/ and /ð/; and *ti* in *nation, ration,* maps on to /ʃ/. Furthermore, in *cushion, fashion,* we may wish to recognise a trigraph *shi* which is related to both *sh* and *ti*. We should, however, consider these problems to derive not from the existence of polygraphic letter sequences as such, but from a distinct characteristic of English orthography, which affects single letter symbols as well; this is the phenomenon of many-to-many mappings between sounds and letters. Figure 1.12 illustrates the situation. It is perhaps not surprising that, traditionally, English spelling has been seen as essentially unsystematic: cf. G. B. Shaw's deliberately perverse spelling of *fish* as *ghoti* (*gh* as in *rough, o* as in *women, ti* as in *nation*). We should mention here also the well-known problem of 'silent letters', as in *sword, scissors, psychology, mnemonic* and the like. Note that in other cases, such as *e* in *sale,* the so-called 'silent *e*' is usually described as having the function of determining the phonological correspondence of the preceding vowel symbol: a sort of discontinuous digraph, perhaps, *a–e*. But this is complicated further in words like *face,* where *e* also is said to function in 'softening' *c*: a convergence here of *a–e* and *ce*. We may conclude, then, that there is a considerable body of evidence that tends towards the view that English spelling is compositionally phonographic only *postlexically*; in other words, the grapheme–phoneme mappings become apparent *after* the word in question has been identified, and are not an adequate basis on which to achieve its identification.

Spelling patterns in English

Contrary to possible first impressions, however, English spelling is not simply perverse. Three types of example will suffice to make the point.

First, consider again Shaw's outrageous *ghoti*. This example partly makes its point by selecting from the exceptional use of *o* in *women,* but also by ignoring positional factors. Thus, *gh* = /f/ is a feature of word-final position only, as in *cough, rough;* and so also in *coughing, roughly* where the forms are built up by suffixation onto a word. Similarly, *ti* = /ʃ/ is only found word-medially. So we learn from Shaw's example not that English spelling is simply perverse but that it is complex, and involves positionally restricted grapheme–phoneme mappings.

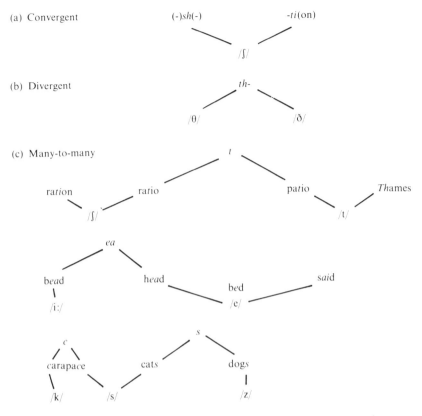

Figure 1.12 Examples of convergent, divergent and many-to-many letter-to-sound relationships in English

Secondly, consider *cats* vs *dogs*: the use of *-s* captures the predictable phonetic relationship between -[s] ~ -[z] in this environment. And in *lint, link*, the use of *-n-* for the homorganic nasal consonant shows the same principle at work. There is a limit to the adherence to this principle, however, as shown in *foxes* (where the syllabic form of the affix is distinctly represented with a vowel symbol – but notice that *s* is preserved) and in *limp* (apparently marking the quantal divide between labial and lingual articulations). From these examples it seems apparent that English spelling actually implements the phonemic principle, up to some (imprecise) limit of phonetic difference.

Thirdly, it has more recently been suggested, within the framework of generative phonology, that much of the systematicity of English spelling has been missed by failing to look for it in the right place, i.e. at an abstract level where lexical relationships are to be stated. Thus, in

op*aque* – op*ac*ity
pro*f*ane – pro*f*anity
electri*c* – electri*c*ity

the stability of orthographic -*a*- and -*c*/-*c*- help to mark word identities in a language where these are obscured by phonological changes to the base forms. Again, the orthography only departs from this principle, in these examples, where a limit on its operation is encountered: in the case of -*qu*-/-*c*-, **opaquity*, with -*qu*- = /s/, would look odd against *electricity*; and **opace*, with -*c*- = /k/, would look odd against *pace*.

These three examples, taken together, suggest that English spelling may indeed be seen as violating a very simple spelling-to-sound correspondence, but that it actually embodies a set of relationships that are considerably more sophisticated, and which carry a number of advantages. The fact that these advantages – e.g. the capturing of positional effects, environmental constraints, and abstract representations – are open only to those who already know the language well is undeniable but, clearly, not a criticism of the orthography as such.

Residual problems, and conclusions

Contrary to these justifiably emphatic second impressions, however, it is still the case that there are many inconsistencies in the way that English words are spelled. Many of these derive from ancient scribal practice (e.g. writing *o* for *u* in letter environments where *u* would have been easily confused, hence *woman*), from regional differences of both pronunciation and spelling tradition, from attempts at reform that were more or less thorough, or misguided, and so on. There is no 'reason' for *head* to exist alongside *bead*, in the language as it is today; the cause is essentially external, located in the historical accretions that culminated in the present-day script.

What, then, is the nature of the English alphabetic system of orthography? It tends to be phonographic, but is compositionally so only in comparatively few cases (it is no accident that *cat*, *sat*, *mat* are routinely used for beginning readers). Differences in spelling between homophones such as *two* vs *to* vs *too*, *for* vs *four*, *bee* vs *be*, *oar* vs *or*, etc. mark distinctions of grammatical-word identity, in a way which over-rides, yet does not conflict with, their identical status as phonological words. The essence of such differences is that they are visual rather than phonological. As a result, the semantic distinction between, say, *flare* and *flair* is marked, as far as production is concerned, in terms of strokes of the pen, or sequences of typewriter key pressings, and, in perception, in partially distinct visual arrays. The similarity between this state of affairs and what was noted for Chinese will be apparent; and it is somewhat reinforced by the consideration that, in terms of pen-strokes, roughly the same number of elements, on average, go to make up a written word in each of these languages.

Words – real, possible and impossible

It will have become apparent, but is worth stating explicitly, that the basic unit of English orthography is the word. Alphabetic characters exist to spell words (rather than, say, syllables), and orthographic word-forms reveal themselves to be highly resistant to variability (as witness *elevate– elevation–elevator*). Higher-level units than the word, such as the syntactic phrase or sentence, are spelled in a way which is a strict function of the spelling of their constituent words (with no contextual modifications such as are found, for instance, in Kannada). Furthermore, English orthography consistently marks the word status of alphabetic sequences by use of spaces (which thus function as a type of word-level character in the system) and, more-or-less consistently, the hyphen. If the way that words are spelled represents the heart of the system, it will be appropriate for us to concentrate attention on what constraints exist on the form of letter strings between two word spaces.

Constraints on letter sequences

We have stated already that the English alphabet is not phonologically compositional in a strict or thorough-going manner. However, precisely because it is an alphabet, and because individual letters have nominal sound correspondences, the resulting system (a) allows for *literal* compositionality – i.e. we can take individual letters and put them into any sequence, and (b) recognises that these strings have some nominal pronounceability. It is easy to spot **gjmwbk* as an impossible literal string and *gippit* as possible but not having word status. But it is less easy to disentangle these observations from the fact that the nominal pronounceability of **gjmwbk* (as something like [gə'ʤimwəbk], let us say) violates phonological sequencing constraints in English, while *gippit* (either as /'gɪpɪt/ or /'ʤɪpɪ't/) does not. So the question arises: are there any purely literal sequencing constraints? Consider first the case of *qu-* in *quash, queen, quiz*, etc. where the occurrence of *u* is completely determined by the preceding *q*. At first sight this looks as if it must represent a literal sequence constraint, since of course there is no phonological constraint that /w/ should follow /k/. But the issue is complicated by the fact that *u* in these sequences does represent the phonological element /w/. The grapheme– phoneme correspondence here is something like 'If /k/ is followed by /w/, it is represented by *q*, and /w/ by *u*'. So again, the literal and phonological factors are difficult to disentangle. The search for purely literal constraints is more profitably conducted at points where literal sequences have contextual variants which do not change their nominal pronunciation value, e.g. the letter clusters *tt*, *ck* in *butt*, *butter*, *back*, *backing*, compared to **ttub*, **ckub*, etc. However, even here it is possible to provide a sound-based observation for the letter-cluster forms: they occur only after phonologically short vowels, hence **cacke* (for *cake*), etc.

Grapheme–phoneme correspondences

One of the points to emerge from this discussion is the issue of grapheme–phoneme correspondences. We have seen that as far as real words of the language are concerned, their pronunciation is, by and large, *not* a function of segment-by-segment mappings between letters and sounds. Instead, the letter *sequence* maps on to a *word*, and the word then guides the interpretation of the component letters: thus -*gh* in *cough*, *rough* is /f/, -*ou*- in *cough* is /ɒ/, and so on. It is in this sense that the phonographic compositionality of English spelling can be said to be *postlexical* as opposed to *prelexical*.

On the other hand, we have also recognised the existence of nominal pronunciation values of individual letters, and the fact that these elements are fully compositional. This is clearly crucial to the pronunciation of *non-words* (both possible and impossible types). It is also crucial to the pronunciation of those words which we come across in print for the first time. These are actually of two types, which we may refer to as the *blick* type, and the *misled* type. The *blick* type consists of words having dictionary status, but existing in the personal lexicons of relatively few people (e.g. architects use *blick* to refer to a glimpse of a building between surrounding buildings). The *misled* type is a convenient label for the situation where we are misled (/mis'led/)) into pronouncing a commonly used word in the wrong way (/'maɪzəld/) when we encounter it for the first time written down. In each case, a first scanning of the graphic form relies on (a) our knowledge of the nominal pronunciation values, or grapheme-to-phoneme correspondences, of individual letters, and (b) our knowledge of the phonotactic constraints of the language (since we naturally assume that the item in question is a word which we are simply ignorant of). As it happens, the grapheme-to-phoneme correspondences of *blick* are uniquely constrained, but this is not a defining characteristic of this type. We may actually come up with an incorrect pronunciation for other words of this type, which may persist until some authoritative source (someone who knows, or a dictionary) puts us right. The *misled* type may likewise be either straightforward or complex in terms of grapheme-to-phoneme correspondences. What distinguishes it from the *blick* type is the fact that, at some point, con-

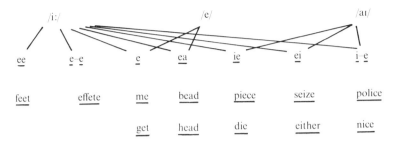

Figure 1.13 Overlapping patterns of regular spelling-to-sound correspondence in English

tact will be made between the graphic form and the existing phonological form (resulting in an 'aha' experience). This may happen quite early on in the scanning of the word for the first time. Where, as in the case of *misled* itself, the grapheme-to-phoneme correspondences are complex, it may be long delayed, and even lead to the 'back formation' of stems such as **misle*.

Regular versus irregular words

Related to the issue of grapheme–phoneme correspondences is the distinction, among real words of the language, between regular and irregular patterns of correspondence. At first sight, it might seem feasible and appropriate to define a set of 'regular' correspondences, letter by letter, or phoneme by phoneme, and to treat all other correspondences as 'irregular'. This, indeed, is quite routinely done, in controlled investigations of reading abilities, as we shall see in chapter 5. But the simplicity of such a distinction flies in the face of the evidence. Instead, we need to recognise a number of 'regular' patterns, which may overlap, as in figure 1.13. Against these, 'true' irregularities such as *quay*, *Beauchamp*, *people*, *foetus*, *eye*, *buy* may be recognised. The important point is that 'regular' should not be taken to mean 'unique' or even 'highly constrained', in the context of phoneme–grapheme correspondences.

When we come to consider non-words, we find ourselves dealing once more with the phenomenon of 'nominal pronunciation values' of individual letters. There seems to be a distinction between contextualised grapheme–phoneme correspondences of the sort that are found in words (as just illustrated above) and the decontextualised variety which apparently play an important role in interpreting novel letter sequences. Thus, while *ea* may be /iː/ or /e/ in words, in non-words such as *geap* it seems to map most naturally onto /iː/. One could, of course, use this criterion to define the real words *bean*, *leap*, *heath* etc. as 'regular' and *death*, *head*, *lead* (the metal), *breath* etc. as 'irregular'. But, in view of the relative numbers involved, it would seem preferable to reserve the concept 'irregular' for words such as *ate, said, bury* and the like, and to distinguish *head* vs *bead* in terms of whether or not they conform to 'nominal' pronunciation values.

1.3.5 *General remarks*

We should pause at this point to sum up the last three sections, 1.3.2–1.3.4. The main point is that we should beware of assuming that language scripts fall into neat watertight categories. Chinese characters are fundamentally meaning-representative, but they often have phonographic characteristics also; the development of Japanese kana out of Chinese characters reminds us that, once a word is represented on a page by a written symbol, that symbol is open to interpretation as embodying the phonological form of the word as well as its meaning; we have seen also that, among syllabaries, some (e.g. Kannada) embody the phonemic principle quite straightforwardly; and that, in an alphabetic system like that of English, phonographic values and compositionality are not the whole story.

Native readers and writers tend therefore to be presented with a range of characteristics to exploit in the written forms of language. The psycholinguistic implication is that we should not simply envisage English or Japanese readers as switching from one, meaning-based, system to another, sound-based, system, and back again, as their eyes scan a text. Rather, we should probably envisage parallel use of meaning-based and sound-based strategies most of the time, for most writing systems. And not just these strategies alone. The basic task in reading is to relate the marks on the page to what we know of our language: in this task, a whole range of strategies can be deployed, including those based on grammatical knowledge and real-world knowledge, in addition to strictly sound- and meaning-based cues in the script. Scripts vary in the balance and variety of cues that they provide, and this variation has to be considered in the light of the differences of linguistic structure between languages. Korean perhaps affords the most striking example of a language whose script (Hangul) cues a number of different levels of linguistic structure (Taylor 1980): articulatory features (since some of the symbols relate to articulatory postures); phonemes (since the basic elements are phoneme-sized); syllables (since the elements are packaged into syllabic clusters); and morphemic/lexical (since there is a strong relation between syllable structure and morphemes and lexical items in the language). All these cues, then, are offered to Korean readers; but their strategies may not after all be so different from those who read other scripts, since (a) there may be no need for, say, the articulatory features to be processed at all in normal reading, and (b) there is no reason to suppose that Korean readers do not use, for example, real-world knowledge, even though it is not directly represented in their script.

We must conclude that, while it is possible that different types of organising principles in writing systems may affect the nature of the perceptual and production processes that are called into play, it may be very difficult, in practice, to determine what the precise relationship might be between script properties and processing strategies. Certainly, it would appear that such gross distinctions as 'logographic' vs 'syllabary' vs 'alphabetic' provide at best a very haphazard basis for determining the nature of individuals' reading and writing performance.

1.4 Conclusions

1.4.1 *Spoken versus written language signals*

The speech signal is highly complex. It is representable as a dynamic three-dimensional acoustic entity, which, although it has, in some obvious sense, segments within it that correspond to our intuitions regarding speech sounds, is essentially continuous. It is marked by its linear compression, or the interleaving of preceding speech sounds with later ones. This arises as a natural consequence of the parallel and independent operation of the articulators in the vocal tract, which may be thought of as constituting a multichannel transmitting system. The resulting signal is ideally structured for reception by the auditory system, which is able to resolve the frequency and intensity information contained in the signal in a parallel, multi-channel and continuous fashion; it would be incapable of processing the same information in the form of discrete linear events per unit of time. In this respect, and in respect of the frequency and intensity range of their operation, the ear and the mouth work within their mutually compatible ranges (see ch. 2 for further details), and constrain the form of the signal to a high degree.

By contrast, the situation with the written language signal appears to be much less constrained. Many shapes may be generated by the hand–arm system, and many patterns recognised through the visual system: the mutual compatibility of these systems and their characteristic signal properties, are much less at issue than is the case with speech. There is nothing corresponding to the immediacy of the mouth/air/ear transmission chain in written language (though, to be sure, the role of the hand–arm system in signalling to the visual system is much more comparably direct in the case of signing systems such as are found in American or British Sign Languages). Less constrained too is the fashion in which the written language signal may represent the language in question: it may be essentially meaning-based or essentially sound-based, and yet, as we have argued, remain free to mix a range of meaning and sound cues.

It is the product of language awareness within given speech communities; and, in all its various forms, it has been devised as a sufficient and convenient way of representing the language knowledge that has been established first in such communities through the spoken medium.

1.4.2 *Writing the spoken language*

Standard writing systems, even those that are phonographic, do not attempt to represent the properties of the speech signal as such. Instead, they provide clues as to the nature of the linguistic elements being used, and native speakers can use their knowledge of their language to make the connection between written and spoken forms. Thus, for example, when we see a full stop or a comma in written English, we can interpret this in terms of some higher organisation of meaning and grammatical relationship between the elements involved (which may be single words, or longer sequences, representing the parts or wholes of utterances), and can also supply one of the appropriate intonation patterns for the sort of linkage that is conventionally signalled by these devices.

Instrumental representations of the speech signal are also not comprehensive; instead, they focus on certain aspects (some articulatory movements rather than others, or some acoustic properties rather than others), and leave the integration of these with other aspects to the human researcher.

For the scientific study of language, it has been desirable to have a written representation of spoken language, but undesirable to make use of standard writing systems with their reliance on inexplicit native-speaker knowledge. Various systems of phonetic notation have been developed in order to fill this need, and it is convenient to consider them under the headings of *segmental* and *suprasegmental* transcriptions. The fullest sort of phonetic transcription, of course, marks both segmental and supresegmental information, but this is quite rarely used, in practice, outside the field of phonetic analysis. More commonly, and particularly for discussions of grammatical and lexical structure and function, an orthographic transcription is used, supplemented by segmental and suprasegmental phonetic information only where the analyst thinks it necessary.

There are, in general, two problems with traditional segmental phonetic transcriptions for the sort of purpose that we have in this book. The first is that they are too reliant on auditory–impressionistic judgements on the part of the transcriber, and hence may provide a not sufficiently reliable basis on which to build a discussion of, say, speech perception. For this reason, in section 1.2 above we made reference to three types of machine representation of speech.

The second problem is that such transcriptions are loaded with phonetic detail that may be irrelevant for the purpose of representing language units such as words and sentences. Here we have to be careful, however, since it is tempting to 'clean up' a transcription of conversational speech to such a degree that many potentially informative features might be lost. Such features might include hesitations, false starts, filled (e.g. *um* and *er*) and unfilled pauses, repetitions, and so on. In English orthography, a great many of these features can be represented, in terms of their position in the speech stream, and in terms of their nature or identity, in a fairly straightforward fashion. It is also possible to include in such a transcription certain details of intonation (pitch and stress) and certain other details (such as creaky voice, slow onset, etc.). Such details are selected, however, from the full range of speech characteristics that are actually in the signal, so we must bear in mind that the transcription embodies certain decisions about what will be displayed to us for our consideration. We must also recognise that a transcription of this sort does not in any sense give us ready-made language units, such as affix vs word vs phrase vs clause vs sentence, except in so far as (and possibly misleadingly) it provides us with spaces between institutionalised words.

We shall be making use of just such a transcription in chapter 3, where our discussion will focus partly on how we arrive at viable units of analysis out of this sort of representation. For now, it suffices to note that, for all intents and purposes, there is, apparently, no possibility of representing the spoken language on the page in faithful, detailed and comprehensive fashion: it is as well to be aware of this at the outset of a book that will at many points attempt to deal with the spoken language in terms of written symbols.

2
The biological foundations of language

2.1 Introduction

2.1.1 *Preview*

The language signal is generated, and perceived, by the operation of some highly specialised biological systems: auditory and visual pathways from sensory organs to the brain, and motor pathways from the brain to the vocal tract and the hand–arm system. Within the brain itself are ultimately founded not just the representations of the language signal, in its various forms, but also those mediating functions that constitute our general language and cognitive abilities. Before we launch into a consideration of a large and technical research field, we should pause to ask ourselves what we may expect to learn of the nature of language processing from a consideration of what is currently known about these biological systems.

In general, the situation may be likened to one or other of the following: in the best case, monitoring the observable performance of some device such as a television set while systematically inspecting and manipulating its circuitry; in the worst case, speculating on the functions of a building by considering its architectural properties. We cannot expect, in even the best case, that biological investigation will explicate concepts such as 'hearing speech', or 'knowing a language', any more than we would expect to get closer to the images on a TV screen by looking in the back of the box. Our expectations must rather be in the direction of gathering evidence that will eventually constrain our understanding of the principles of language processing.

There is a fairly direct relation between what we know of these biological systems and what we know of the auditory and visual signals conveying language and the articulatory and manual generation of such signals. However, there is a much less clear relation between biological concepts and the abstract phenomenon we know as language. This arises partly as a result of uncertainties in the biology of central processing, as well as differences of view among linguists concerning the formal properties of language; and partly because of the difficult problem of relating abstract systems such as language, which belong to the domain of the mind, to specific brain structures and functions (Eccles 1977). Even so, it is necessary for students of psycholinguistics to have some awareness of (a) the general organisation of language-relevant components in the central as well as the peripheral nervous systems, and (b) the characteristic manner of communication within and between these systems. Even such an elementary introduction to these issues as is attempted here may provide a framework within which constraints on theorising might fruitfully be sought. Calvin and Ojemann (1980), Draper (1980), Espir and Rose (1983), Perkins and Kent (1986), Schneiderman (1984), Selnes and Whitaker (1977), Thompson (1967) and Walsh (1978) may be consulted for further details. Helpful illustrations are to be found in standard anatomical references, such as *Gray's Anatomy* (Pick and Howden 1901), or *Cunningham's Manual* (Romanes 1979).

2.1.2 *Functional relationships*

First, though, we shall introduce the main properties of the human nervous system, to provide the proper setting for our focus on language processing.

Peripheral versus central nervous systems

The human nervous system is conventionally divided into the *peripheral* and the *central* nervous systems. The central nervous system comprises all the neural tissue contained within the skull (the brain) and the spinal vertebrae (the spinal cord) (Perkins and Kent 1986). The peripheral nervous system consists of all the neural tissue outside these bony structures, and connects the central nervous system with the muscles and sensory organs of the body. The brain occupies the superordinate position in this hierarchy, and thus connections which are involved in the brain's control of muscles are said to be *descending* (or *efferent*), while those involved in carrying sensory information to the brain are *ascending* (or *afferent*). For complex motor and sensory activity, however, both afferent and efferent activity is found, since (a) the brain needs to 'feel' the effect of its motor-control output, and (b) sensory perception may require motor-control adjustments to the sensory apparatus for optimal performance.

Descending and ascending connections between the brain and the body may be of three types; the most general one is *contralateral*, whereby, for example, an area of the left side of the brain controls movement in, or registers sensation from, a portion of the right side of the body (and vice versa); in the facial region, however, *bilateral* connections are found, whereby left and right sides of the brain jointly control muscles on both sides of the face; and *ipsilateral* connections are those (usually subsidiary types) where the same side of the brain and the body are involved (Thompson 1967). Fundamental to these types is the phenomenon of *decussation* of connections, which literally means a division into a cross-over pattern (after the X-shape of the Roman numeral *decem*). From each side of the brain, connections are established in groupings of neural tissue, which may decuss at a certain point, with some members of the group crossing the anatomical midline. If most of the connecting tissue crosses the midline at decussation, we speak of contralateral control (with minor ipsilateral input): but if the connecting tissue innervates the ipsilateral side as well as decussing to the contralateral side, bilateral connections are found.

The distinction between peripheral and central nervous systems does not, it should be noted, lie exactly between what we have described as signal processing (ch. 1) and what we shall describe as aspects of the language system (in ch. 3). This is because signal processing involves brain centres, in the central nervous system, as well as peripheral sensory-motor structures.

Cortical versus subcortical structures

For psycholinguistic purposes, there is a basic distinction to be drawn between the cerebral *cortex*, which is the outer surface of the *cerebrum* (divided into left and right *hemispheres*), and various *subcortical* elements. This distinction ought to be set in the context of the traditional anatomical divisions, however, which are illustrated in figure 2.1, and comprise: (1) the *telencephalon*, comprising the two cerebral hemispheres, and internal structures such as the *basal ganglia*; these surround (2) the *diencephalon*, more deeply located, and including the *thalamus* and associated structures, and the *optic tracts*; these are located on top of, and around (3) the *mesencephalon* or *midbrain*. This forms the upper part of a complex known as the *brainstem*, behind which is found (4) the *cerebellum*, and which comprises also (in descending order) (5) the *metencephalon* or *pons* and (6) the *myelencephalon* or *medulla*. The lower extension of the brainstem is (7) the *spinal cord*.

The cortex is a thin layer of specialised cells called *neurons* (presenting a greyish appearance, hence 'grey matter') arranged in approximately six strata over the outer surface of the brain. This surface is highly convoluted, into depressions (*sulci*; larger ones are referred to as *fissures*) and ridges (*gyri*) permitting a greater surface area over the cerebral hemispheres. Neurons are composed of cell *bodies* and projecting *fibres*. The cell bodies have the ability to integrate a range of inputs which affect their electrical charge, which in turn may lead to the generation of small electrical impulses, or *action potentials*, on an all-or-nothing principle. They receive input from other neurons via afferent fibres called *dendrites*; and transmit electrical impulses to other parts of the

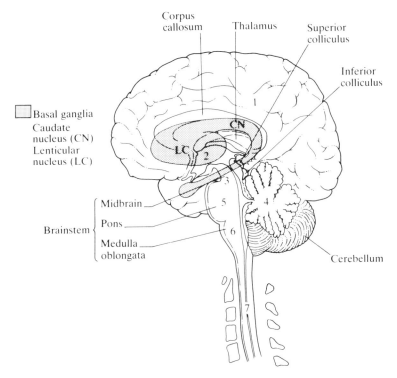

Figure 2.1 Principal structures of the brain. (Based on Harré and Lamb 1983: Figs. 5, 6, 15, pp. 63, 67.)

nervous system via efferent fibres called *axons*. The transmission of electrical activity from the axon of one cell to the dendrite of another takes place across biochemically bridged gaps called *synapses*.

Certain motor and sensory neurons have long axons passing through the brain between the cortex and relays in the brainstem and spinal cord; these are known as *projection* fibres. Other neural connections link cells in different parts of the cortex: these are the *commissural* fibres (Sperry 1964), linking the two cerebral hemispheres, and the *association* fibres, linking structures in the same hemisphere. Some axons are coated with an insulating substance called *myelin* (having a whitish appearance, hence 'white matter' to refer to the subcortical mass of brain tissue). Thus, one sense of the term 'subcortical' refers to the connections to and from cells of the cortex, and their interconnections with each other below the level of the cortex within the cerebrum. Another sense of 'subcortical', however, refers to specific structures, containing masses of cell nuclei, at the centre of the brain, buried deep within the cerebral hemispheres, and copiously linked with each other, and with the cells of the cortex.

These structures include the structures of the brainstem, and also the inter-brain, including the *basal ganglia*, the *limbic system* and the *thalamus* (fig. 2.1). Finally, we should mention here the *cerebellum*, a motor coordinating centre with its own two-hemisphere structure, situated above and behind the brain-stem, just below the posterior areas of the cerebrum.

2.2   The auditory system

The human auditory system is a sensory-neural complex which has quite general capacities for processing a range of sounds but which also shows some specialisation for the sorts of sounds that are ordinarily used in speech. It has a total frequency range of between 15Hz to 16kHz (Romer 1971a), but is most sensitive in the 1kHz to 4kHz range; stimuli outside this inner range have to be of greatly increased intensity in order to be audible. The linguistically significant parts of most articulated speech sounds are located within about 600Hz to 4kHz, so the mouth and the ear work within com-patible limits of comfortable operation.

The auditory system may be thought of in terms of the following organisa-tion:

> the first stage: the outer- and middle-ear system (collection and transmission of the airborne signal) (section 2.2.1);
>
> the second stage: the inner-ear system (mechanical analysis of the signal in the cochlea) (section 2.2.2);
>
> the third stage: the mechanical–neural interface (also in the coch-lea) (section 2.2.3);
>
> the fourth and fifth stages: the relays of the sensory system, in the brainstem and subcortical nuclei, and finally up to the auditory cortex (section 2.2.4).

2.2.1   *The outer- and middle-ear systems*

The external ear canal (sound-wave reception)

Situated in the *outer ear* (with the ear *pinna* as a collecting device), the *ear canal* has certain acoustic properties as a result of its size and shape (fig. 2.2). Much larger ear canals, as in the elephant, favour lower frequencies, while smaller ones, as in cats, help to extend the upper range to around 70kHz. In humans, the 2–6kHz frequency range resonates within the canal (Stillman 1980), and this has the effect of increasing the intensity of sounds within this range. Perkins and Kent (1986) suggest an increase of two to four times for $2\frac{1}{2}$–4kHz sounds. The canal ends in the *tympanic membrane*, which vibrates in sympathy with these amplified sounds (Stillman 1980). Møller (1983) reviews recent work on tympanic membrane dynamics.

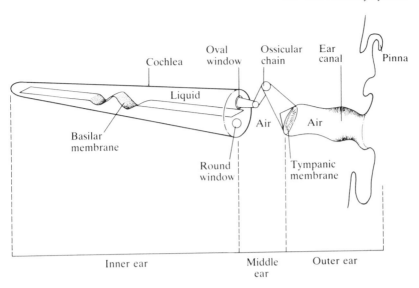

Figure 2.2 Schematic diagram of the outer-, middle- and inner-ear systems.
(The basilar membrane is shown displaced in a wave-shape typical of response
to a middle-frequency sinusoidal tone.) (Based on Schneiderman 1984: fig. 69,
p. 140.)

The ossicular chain (from air waves to mechanical oscillations)

As the tympanic membrane vibrates, the *ossicular chain*, located
in the *middle ear*, transfers the frequency, amplitude and temporal characteristics of these movements to the *cochlea* (in the *inner ear*). That is to say, there is
a direct correspondence between events arriving at the ossicular chain and
those leaving it. What, then, is its purpose?

First, it boosts the incoming signal, preparatory to passing it on to the cochlea. This is necessary because the end of the ossicular chain interfaces with the
cochlear liquid, and this is rather resistant to the passage of sound waves. So
the ossicular chain transduces the sound waves to mechanical oscillations.
These are then boosted to some extent by leverage within the ossicular chain
and, more importantly, by the fact that the output area (the *oval window* into
the cochlea) is smaller than the input (tympanic membrane) area. In other
words, large-amplitude, low-energy compressions and decompressions of the
air (the airborne sound) are converted to low-amplitude, high-energy oscillations, or mechanical vibrations, suitable for activating the cochlear mechanisms (see below).

Secondly, the ossicular chain has in-built damping abilities which reduce
the potentially harmful effect of very intense sounds.

Thirdly, the ossicular chain has a reflex ability to attenuate low-frequency sounds while preserving (even slightly enhancing) sounds in the higher 1–2kHz range by muscle contraction (Stillman 1980). This is very important for speech, because important acoustic distinctions are carried in the higher-frequency ranges for many sounds. We shall see (below) that certain neuro-mechanical properties of the auditory system respond in a very gross way to low frequencies, and, because of this, low-frequency sounds have the potential to mask higher-frequency sounds. The ossicular chain thus provides for a first defence against this tendency. Perkins and Kent (1986) estimate that the combined effects of the ossicular chain multiply the mechanical force fourteen times.

2.2.2   *The inner-ear system*

The inner ear is made up of the *cochlea*, which is basically a tube, filled with a liquid, in which is supported a long, flexible structure called the *basilar membrane* (fig. 2.3). The cochlear tube is anatomically a helical structure, like a snail shell. The ossicular chain delivers oscillations to the cochlea via the *oval window*, at the base of the cochlea, to the cochlear liquid, and thence to the basilar membrane. This is narrower, and stiffer, at the oval-window end of the cochlea, and gradually widens, and becomes more flexible, along its length. As a result, it is displaced to its maximum extent at different points, depending on the frequency of the input oscillations: highest-frequency input causes a wave-form displacement of the membrane where it is narrowest (nearest the oval window), and successively lower frequencies result in wave forms which, while propagating from the oval-window end, travel further down the basilar membrane before reaching maximal displacement (fig. 2.3(a)).

Overall, it takes about 5msec. for a travelling wave to reach the farther end of the basilar membrane, and it slows down as it travels (Perkins and Kent 1986). The wave displays a rather abrupt cut-off beyond the point of maximal displacement; by contrast, the build-up to that point is more gentle, particularly for lower-frequency sounds. This means that different frequency sounds have distinct 'wave envelopes' as well as distinct points of maximal displacement (fig. 2.3(b)). It is because lower-frequency sounds yield waves that involve larger areas of the basilar membrane than high-frequency sounds that they tend to have a masking effect. Differences in amplitude of sounds are represented by degrees of displacement of the basilar membrane. It may be appreciated that larger degrees of displacement also involve larger areas of the membrane, so that it is not possible to say, neatly, that frequency is represented purely as distance along the basilar membrane, and amplitude purely as distance of the maximally displaced portion of the membrane from its posi-

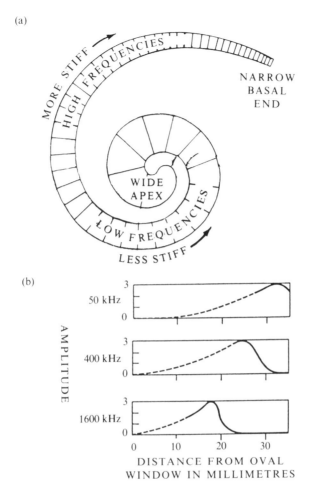

(a)

MORE STIFF

HIGH FREQUENCIES

NARROW
BASAL
END

WIDE
APEX

LOW FREQUENCIES

LESS STIFF

(b)

AMPLITUDE

50 kHz

400 kHz

1600 kHz

DISTANCE FROM OVAL
WINDOW IN MILLIMETRES

Figure 2.3 Schematic representation of basilar membrane characteristics:
(a) the layout of the higher- to lower-frequency response areas; (b) envelopes
of displacement for sinusoidal tones of three frequency levels. (From Denes
and Pinson 1963: fig. 5, 7, p. 73; Perkins and Kent 1986: fig. 10.1, p. 272.)

tion of rest. The effect of increased amplitude on area of displacement is particularly strong on the higher-frequency side of the wave (the gentler slope of
the wave envelope). There is, therefore, an interaction between these two
dimensions of sound reception in the mechanical responses of the cochlea.
Current understanding of the way the cochlea works builds on the Nobel-
prize winning research of von Békésy (see von Békésy 1957).

We may summarise the foregoing by saying that up to this point, the cochlea provides another mechanical analogue of the input signal. But also within

the cochlea is another component which has the important task of carrying out the first transduction of the signal from mechanical to electrical response (Stillman 1980): this component is the *organ of Corti*.

2.2.3   *The organ of Corti and the auditory nerve*

The organ of Corti lies along the basilar membrane and effects the link between the movements of that membrane and the nerve impulses which travel along the fibres of the *auditory nerve* (fig. 2.4). (Anatomically, we would strictly have to speak here of the *cochlear nerve*, since the anatomical structure known as the auditory nerve consists of two components; one, the cochlear nerve, involved with hearing; the other, the *vestibular nerve*, part of the system concerned with balance. But we may conveniently refer to the former as the auditory nerve here.)

The organ of Corti consists of a series of *hair-cells* which are attached along the surface of the basilar membrane in such a way that they flex when it is displaced. Each flexing of the hair-cells causes chemical changes which generate small electrical impulses (action potentials) in them that are transmitted along the associated fibres of the auditory nerve. The organ of Corti is responsive to flexing movements in one direction only: that is, on each displacement of the basilar membrane, it responds to the degree and location of movement, and then is passive as the elasticity of the membrane reverses the displacement.

These displacements of the basilar membrane therefore generate patterns of neural impulses which travel along the auditory nerve. The task involved may be appreciated in the light of the number of fibres in the auditory nerve (less than 30,000; by comparison, the optic nerve has about a million), in relation to what they convey, encoding the frequency and amplitude characteristics of the input sound in such an efficient and sensitive fashion that more than 300,000 single tones can be discriminated (Thompson 1967). It is not easy to be clear about how this state of affairs is achieved, as we shall see.

Early attempts to understand this encoding process appealed to (a) the 'frequency' theory (Rutherford 1886), and (b) the 'place' theory (Helmholtz 1863). In our discussion, we shall refer to the first of these as the 'time' theory, to help avoid a confusion between the frequency characteristics of the signal, which are uncontroversial and constitute the datum to be accounted for, and the encoding principles which have been advanced to account for the way in which they might be analysed in the auditory system.

The time theory, then, sees the frequency characteristics of an input sound as being encoded in terms of the timing of the discharge of neural impulses from the organ of Corti along the auditory nerve. Thus, if we assume a rigid

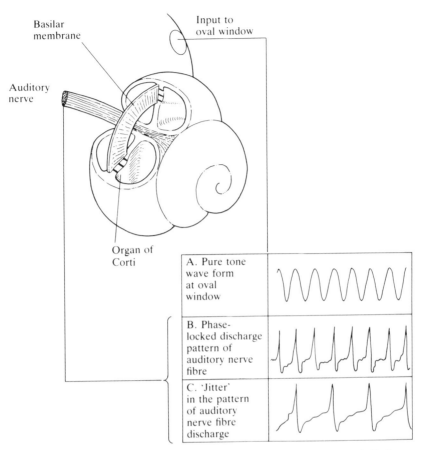

Basilar
membrane

Input to
oval window

Auditory
nerve

Organ of
Corti

A. Pure tone
wave form
at oval
window

B. Phase-
locked discharge
pattern of
auditory nerve
fibre

C. 'Jitter'
in the pattern
of auditory
nerve fibre
discharge

Figure 2.4 Mechanico-neural transduction through the cochlea. A, B, C
show the relations between input and output for a 0.3kHz tone of low
intensity. (Based on discussion in Thompson 1967: 264–8; Møller 1983: fig.
3.2, p. 195; Perkins and Kent 1986: fig. 9–10, p. 259.)

relationship between (a) airwave oscillations, (b) basilar membrane displacements, and (c) the generation of action potentials in the organ of Corti, we can
think of a 200kHz sound resulting in neural impulses passing a particular
point in the auditory nerve 200 times per second.

The place theory, by contrast, sees the frequency of that sound as encoded
in terms of (a) the displacement of particular regions of the basilar membrane,
(b) the flexion of particular associated hair-cells of the organ of Corti, and (c)
the travelling of impulses along certain of the fibres within the auditory nerve,
thus preserving the *receptotopic*, or spatially organised, arrangement of the
basilar membrane frequency response.

Now, the time-encoding theory has to take account of a basic property of the system, which is that the refractory period of fibres in the auditory nerve is 1msec. (i.e. it takes an individual fibre 1msec. to recover after one impulse before it can pass another; see Thompson 1967). This effectively keeps the impulses travelling along a fibre some minimal distance apart. This in turn imposes an absolute upper limit on transmission frequencies along a particular fibre of 1,000 impulses per second, corresponding to (again, assuming a rigid relationship) an input sound frequency of 1kHz. But the basilar membrane, in its narrower regions, and the organ of Corti, can transmit much higher frequencies than this, of course. So how does the time theory cope with this observation?

An ingenious answer seemed to lie in what was referred to as the 'volley' strategy (Wever 1949). According to this, for input sounds up to around 800Hz (comfortably within the auditory nerve's refractory capacity), the time-encoding principle is employed; but as input sound frequency increases beyond this point, half of the hair-cells/nerve fibres serving a grossly defined frequency region halve their workload to every even-numbered phase of the oscillation cycle, while the other half take over the transmission of the intervening phases. This volley-firing strategy is viable up to around 1600–1800Hz, whereupon again the limit on the refractory capacity of the nerve fibres is being approached, and a further division in responsibility for transmission takes place. This allows the auditory nerve, considered as a whole, to transmit frequencies up to around 4kHz, but only at a cost.

The cost is measured in terms of the number of nerve fibres available for transmission, which reduces as frequency increases; and the significance of this may be appreciated when we consider that amplitude is (at least partly) encoded in terms of the number of activated hair-cells/auditory nerve fibres. Hence, for the higher-frequency sounds fewer and fewer fibres are available to discriminate higher vs lower amplitudes in this way.

A further problem with the time-encoding theory is that the assumption of a rigid locking of neural impulse generation to phases of the oscillation cycle ('phase-locking') appears to be rather too strong (although many authorities state it as a fact). Observation reveals that, even at low frequencies, there is rather a *probabilistic* relation between basilar-membrane displacement and the occurrence of action potentials. So, the basis of the time theory is actually much more complex than we have allowed for in our discussion, given that the intervals between impulses travelling along the auditory nerve are at best an indirect and complex representation of the frequency of the input sound (see fig. 2.4, and Møller 1983).

But the place theory of frequency encoding also has its problems. Accord-

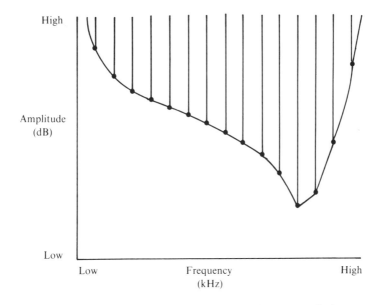

Figure 2.5 Schematic 'tuning curve' of a typical auditory nerve cell. (Lower ends of vertical lines indicate the lowest-amplitude stimuli to which the cell responds at tested frequencies.) (Based on discussion in Thompson 1967: 270–1.)

ing to this theory, adjacent auditory nerve fibres transmit impulses generated on adjacent hair-cells in the organ of Corti, which relate in turn to adjacent regions of the basilar membrane. In this receptotopic arrangement, frequency is encoded as the activation of certain cells and not others. Certain auditory nerve cells exhibit a selective response profile, or 'tuning curve' for particular frequencies, especially those at lower-amplitude levels: see figure 2.5, which shows a fairly typical tuning-curve pattern, with a sharp high-frequency cut-off, and shallower low-frequency slope. Such a response profile acts as a template for frequency analysis of the signal generated in the cochlea. While this interaction of amplitude and frequency in triggering the cell's response is not a problem for the theory, it suggests that the frequency response may be more complex, and variable, than a pure place theory would expect.

More seriously, though, we can see, by referring back to figure 2.3(b), that different wave envelopes along the basilar membrane may overlap to a greater or lesser extent. So, for a given sound at a middle range of amplitude (around 40dB), between 15 and 20 per cent of the basilar membrane and the organ of Corti may be involved. This in turn involves around 10,000 auditory nerve fibres in the transmission of the signal from the cochlea to the higher auditory-processing centres. If the frequency of the sound alters by some small amount,

59

up or down, we may think of a few hundred fibres being lost, or added, at the end points of the activated range, while the central range of activation is maintained. Likewise, small changes in amplitude for a given frequency will show a small proportionate change in the overall pattern of activation. If more than 90 per cent of the action potentials are maintained for slight but perceptible changes of the input sounds, it is a problem to know how the encoding of the input is achieved (Pickles 1982 has further discussion).

For our purposes, it is sufficient to appreciate that frequency and amplitude encoding in the auditory nerve overlap in subtle and complex ways, precisely in the 'speech range' of 1–4kHz. So, to summarise, we may say that:

> the organ of Corti converts the oscillating fluid pressure signal to the form of electrical impulses, for transmission along the auditory nerve and thence to higher auditory-processing centres;
>
> frequency is encoded partly in tonotopic organisation of responses and partly in temporal rate of firing, in ways that are not fully understood;
>
> amplitude is encoded partly in terms of the number and type of auditory nerve cell activation, and partly in terms of the rate of discharge of individual fibres;
>
> within the auditory nerve, there are cells that have 'best frequency' response characteristics, but as amplitude increases a progressive broadening of the response band is observed, especially towards the low frequency end;
>
> frequency and amplitude characteristics of the input signal are observed to interact even at the level of the basilar membrane responses, and it may be that our understanding of how the auditory system encodes these characteristics will improve only with a more precise knowledge of basilar membrane mechanics.

2.2.4 *The relays of the sensory system*
The cochlear nuclei: the first relay

The auditory nerve conveys neural impulses from the cochlea to the brainstem (fig. 2.6). It enters the medulla high up, near the border with the pons, and connects with groups of nerve cells called the *cochlear nuclei*. These are found each side of the medulla; the left ear connects with the left-side cochlear nuclei, and the right ear with those on the right side. The cochlear nuclei cells effect further refinements in the signal: they effectively extract critical features from the arriving impulse arrays of the auditory nerve. Some respond to the onset of a tone; others discharge continuously while the tone is presented; still others fire to rapid frequency or intensity changes; and so on. A

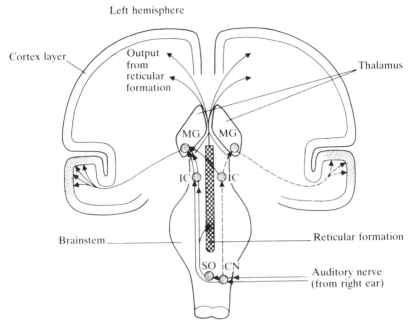

Figure 2.6 Diagram of inputs from right ear, through the higher levels of the auditory system, to the auditory cortex in the left hemisphere; minor input to the right hemisphere is shown by dotted lines. Major cell nuclei in the auditory system are shown as follows: CN, cochlea nucleus; SO, superior olive; IC, inferior colliculus; MG, medial geniculate. (Based on Thompson 1967: fig. 10.28, p. 629; Perkins and Kent 1986: fig. 13.3, p. 350.)

further function is to prevent any spontaneous firing activity (i.e. without stimulus) in the auditory nerve from reaching higher centres and thus reducing the discriminating ability of the system (Thompson 1967).

The superior olivary nuclei: the second relay

Elsewhere in the medulla, in the *superior olive*, extremely important processing of temporal interactions takes place, which requires, crucially, a *bilateral* blending of inputs, from left and right ears. If a sound occurs to the right of your head, there is a small but measurable difference in the time the resulting sound waves will arrive at each of your ears. The right ear will be reached first, then the left. Inter-aural time differences as small as 20µsec. can be processed in the medulla (Stillman 1980). Some medullary neurons respond only to truly simultaneous input to each ear; others only for sounds that arrive at the right ear some critical time intervals before the left, or vice versa. Still other medullary computations involve the 'head shadow' effect, which relates to the drop in intensity at the ear that is further away from the sound source.

This latter is found particularly for high-frequency sounds, and depends in part on the fact that in the medulla, as indeed at every level from the auditory nerve upwards, individual cells are tuned to particular best frequencies, with increasing precision and sharpness of high-frequency cut-off; it also partly results from the fact that the head as a structure tends to filter out lower-frequency components. The medullary coding of sounds in relation to their spatial location, by either method, allows for higher brain processes such as those involved in *attention* to make a selection on the basis of information coming in via other channels.

Fibres from the medullary areas pass through the brainstem bilaterally, with connections being made to the *reticular formation* and the *cerebellum*. The reticular formation is a net-like complex of grey and white matter (nuclei and interconnecting fibres) in the brainstem, and is responsible for integrating as well as relaying sensory inputs, and for readying the cortex as a whole for the arrival of these inputs (French 1957). The cerebellum, while primarily associated with motor inputs and outputs, has a number of sensory inputs including the auditory one, and, like the reticular formation, has rich connections with the cerebral cortex.

The inferior colliculus: the third relay

Further complex intermixing of binaural input takes place in the nuclei of the inferior colliculus, in the midbrain. Neurons of these nuclei include many that are specialised for contralateral (rather than ipsilateral) stimulation (Pickles 1982). Many of the cells exhibit very sharply defined tuning curves, suggestive of further refinement in the processing of the signal characteristics, and cell responses to frequency at this level may be affected by either amplitude or by *frequency modulation* (the phenomenon whereby, in complex wave forms such as are found in speech, certain frequencies of oscillation recur in sufficiently stable cycles to have their own frequency – cycles of cycles, as it were). Pickles (1982) suggests that the inferior colliculus has some of the complex-frequency analysing capacities of the cochlear nucleus, and some of the sound-localising abilities of the superior olive. The inferior colliculus also has a motor output, which appears to be involved in orienting responses (via the superior colliculus, at the top of the midbrain).

Thalamic and cortical auditory systems: the fourth and fifth relays

The major output of the inferior colliculus (apart from that to the superior colliculus) is to an area of the thalamus, represented bilaterally, known as the *medial geniculate body*. While this may be seen as the fourth relay, it has two-way connections with the cells of the auditory cortex, and hence is rather more than simply a relay station (Stillman 1980). Indeed, one of the problems in defining precise cell functions at these highest levels of the auditory system is that their responsiveness depends increasingly on such brain processes as attention, emotion, memory, etc. (in which an important role is played by the reticular formation). In addition, the existence of two-way connections between the cortex and thalamus raises the issue of descending (centrifugal) control in the auditory system, whereby higher centres can 'reach down' to regulate the lower-level processes: about 2 per cent of the auditory nerve fibres carry descending information down to the cochlea and the muscles of the ossicular chain.

Fairly precise locations in the cortex have been demonstrated (e.g. by removing areas of auditory cortex in animals after a period of auditory stimulus training, and observing whether the effects of training are impaired); but interpreting these findings is hard, since the nature of the *training method* used to establish the particular discrimination skill in the animal also has an effect, as well as the actual *portion of cortex* that is removed. It is also not yet possible, from such work with animals, to shed light on the processing of *speech* sounds; but it is possible to show that certain areas of the auditory cortex seem to be involved in *temporal pattern* discriminations. This is important, for the ability to discriminate between a tone sequence ABA vs another tone sequence BAB must involve some form of brief memory (Thompson 1967). This consideration takes us a tiny but welcome step towards the processing of complex temporal sound patterns of speech.

The organisation of the auditory cortex is complex. As for the perception of other sensory modalities, it appears that it is arranged into a 'map' or *projection field*, of the relevant parts of the body (in this case, of the basilar membrane), and that more than one projection field is involved (the cat has six), although one is primary. A special property of the projection field in the auditory cortex may be that, while for *frequency* we can consider the basilar membrane to be laid out on the cortex (as it were, east–west), the dimension of *intensity* is represented at right angles to this (or north–south).

A feature of the organisation of cells in the primary auditory cortex is their columnar arrangement. In certain other areas of the cortex (e.g. the visual cortex) this arrangement is thought to allow for groups of cells of similar response characteristics to be grouped vertically, with sharp differences between them and their columnar neighbours. This in turn may permit rather sharp, discrete, categories of perception. As far as frequency is concerned, however, the columnar organisation of the primary auditory cortex appears to show smooth transitions; but, almost at right-angles to this, the columns mark discrete, step-wise, discriminations of binaural dominance (Pickles 1982).

Furthermore, while the relationship between best-frequency and distance along the basilar membrane itself tends to be logarithmic (proportionately greater space along the membrane being devoted to low frequencies), the projection-field relationship in the auditory cortex is much more linear. This allows as much space in the auditory cortex for a given high-frequency band as for a comparable lower one. And, while cells with lower best-frequencies in the auditory cortex have the typical shallow slope for lower frequencies in their tuning curve, those devoted to higher best-frequencies exhibit a sharp cut-off on either side of the relevant tone (Thompson 1967).

At this point we shall leave the processing of the incoming speech signal, and turn to consider how the other major input modality, vision, processes the signals of written language. We shall return to the relation of auditory and other types of language processing in the final section of this chapter.

2.3   The visual system

As your eyes scan these lines of print, perceptual processes are initiated that are, at least in their early stages, quite independent of the auditory system which we have been considering thus far. Yet language input via each of these systems, auditory and visual, appears to converge ultimately on the same product of comprehension. This conclusion seems clear from the consideration that, *prima facie*, your understanding of these sentences is not affected by whether you read them yourself (silently), or have them read out to you by someone else. If we accept this, we are implicitly defining a fundamental issue: at what point or points do the auditory and visual pathways merge? Simple answers are not ready to hand, and we shall start to consider the issue here with a survey of the neurophysiological properties of the visual system, and continue the discussion, in terms of models of behaviour, in chapter 4.

We shall start our review of the visual system with the eye, whose main function is the collection and focussing of light (section 2.3.1). We shall then look more closely at the retina, which is responsible for the first three stages of signal processing (section 2.3.2), and the optic nerve (section 2.3.3), which projects to the midbrain nuclei which are responsible for the fourth stage of signal processing (section 2.3.4). Finally, we shall consider the visual cortex, in which the fifth and sixth stages of processing take place (section 2.3.5).

2.3.1   *The eye*

We may think of the formal features of orthographic representations as passing into the visual system in the form of patterns of greater and lesser illumination, from a two-dimensional surface. The refraction of these patterns, first through the *cornea* and then through the *lens*, is a preliminary

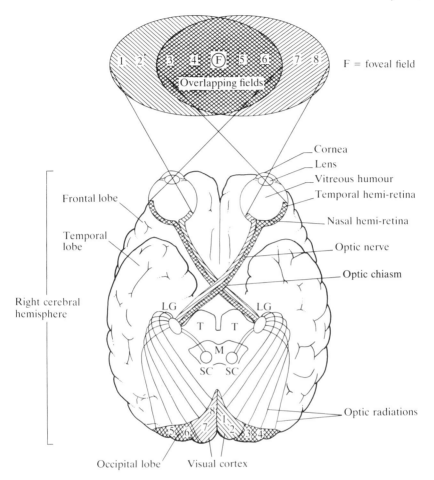

F = foveal field

Figure 2.7 Elements of the visual system. The brain is viewed from the underside, showing the structure of the eye, the optic nerve and the radiations to the visual cortex. Other elements are shown as follows: T, thalamus; LG, lateral geniculate; M, midbrain; SC, superior colliculi. (Based on Harré and Lamb 1983: fig. 23, p. 70; Lindsay and Norman 1977: fig. 2.10, p. 74.)

sort of signal processing, so that an inverted image falls on the *retina* at the rear of the eye (Romer 1971b; see fig 2.7).

These patterns represent the *visual field*: i.e. that part of the external world which is currently imaged on the retinae of both eyes. Two sets of muscles are involved in maintaining and changing the contents of the visual field; one for focussing the lens and the other for swivelling the eyes bodily, from side to side down. When the eyes are held steady, to maintain a given visual ~~re said to be in~~ *fixation*; normal fixations during the reading pro- the order of 250msec. Moving from one fixation to another is ~~moved~~ by movements that are called *saccades*. These movements are 'ballis- tic'; that is, they are executed without an on-line guidance system (like lobbing an object into a particular spot, where everything depends on the accuracy of your preliminary aiming and impelling of the object). They are also very rapid – of the order of 10–20msec., though up to around 50msec. for return sweeps from the end of a line. There seems to be an upper physiological limit of around five saccades per second, so the figure of 250msec. for a fixation is right at that limit. Perception only occurs during fixations, but is nevertheless available, on this basis, during more than 90 per cent of total reading time (at least in principle). Ideally, the procedure for scanning for reading starts with an initial fixation just a few letters in from the start of the first line, covering eight or nine characters; then shifts through 1–4° of visual angle to the right, for the next fixation, which is centred some ten to twelve letter spaces further along the line; and so on (McConkie and Rayner 1975; Bouma 1978; Rayner 1979). In practice, regression movements also occur, particularly if the text is complex, or if the reader is a novice.

The retina of each eye has the form of a hemispherical cup, mounted on a slightly off-centre stalk (the *optic nerve*), which fits snugly into the rear of the eyeball. It is conventionally divided into the *nasal hemiretina* (the area extend- ing from the centre point towards the midline of the head) and the *temporal hemiretina* (the part towards the outer side, or 'temple' of the head). Because the image falling on the retina is passed through the lens, elements in the left visual field impinge on the temporal hemiretina of the right eye and the nasal hemiretina of the left eye; and, conversely, elements in the right visual field are picked up by the left temporal and right nasal retinae. Because of the orien- tation of the eyes in man, most of our visual field is processed by both eyes (*binocularly*); but there is little or no crossing, or separating, of the responsibi- lities of the hemiretinae, so that the left and right visual half-fields are norm- ally continuous, without overlap (fig. 2.7). The central area of each retina is particularly sensitive; it has a slight depression, the *fovea*, which has the effect of increasing the retinal surface area in this region, and which is made still more sensitive by virtue of the fact that it has a thinner layer of covering cell- tissue, without blood vessels, and by its composition of photoreceptors (see section 2.3.2). The *foveal field*, at the centre of the visual field (fig. 2.7), is thus particularly well represented on the retinae, and it is those parts of written language that fall within this field that are most available for detailed analysis in the course of reading.

2.3.2 *The retina: the first three stages of signal processing*

From what we have said thus far, it might be thought that the retinae are simply photosensitive membranes which serve the limited function of gathering relevant sense data for higher centres to process. It would, however, be nearer the truth to say that the retinae are actually parts of brain-matter, outfolded from the main mass of the brain (Romer 1971b) in such a way as to be in a position to gather light signals; but their internal cell-structure is sufficiently complex to initiate the processing of these signals too. It may also be that this 'outfolding' concept accounts for the strange orientation of the retinal photoreceptor cells in the eyes – they are so arranged that they point *down* through the retinal tissue, facing away from the incoming light, and towards the outer walls of the eyes. This aspect has been ignored, however, for the sake of convenience, in the discussion and illustration that follows.

The photoreceptors: photo-electrical transduction

Each eye has about 130 million photoreceptors. These are of four types, *rods* and three different types of *cones*. Generally speaking, any area of the retina will be found to have a mixture of these types, but towards the fovea there is an increasingly dense population of cones. Cones require strong illumination, whereas rods are effective in faint light; cones as a group are better for detailed analysis of form (they tend to have one-to-one connections to higher cells), and for colour, while rods give a blurred picture (with many-to-one connections to higher cells) in lighter and darker shades of grey (Hubel 1963; Barrington 1971; Romer 1971b).

These photoreceptors perform the essential first stage in the processing of the stimulus: the sensory transduction into a code of electrochemical impulses. They exhibit a number of horizontal connections, so that different parts of the retinal mosaic (as the banks of receptors are often called) can act together.

Bipolar cells and ganglion cells: the second and third stages

But their chief projections are to the next level of cells (*bipolar cells*) in the retina, where further hierarchical groupings are achieved, and thence to the third and final stage of retinal processing, in the *ganglion cells*. By virtue of their complex connections, these ganglion cells receive input from a number of photoreceptors, and a single photoreceptor may serve more than one ganglion cell (Hubel 1963). In lower animals, ganglion cells are more simply connected to their receptors, and are known to be specialised for certain key visual features, such as *contrast* (i.e. the edge between areas of differential illumination), *movement, direction* (of movement), *orientation* (of edge), etc. (see, e.g. Maturana *et al.* 1960, on the frog retina). In mammals, both

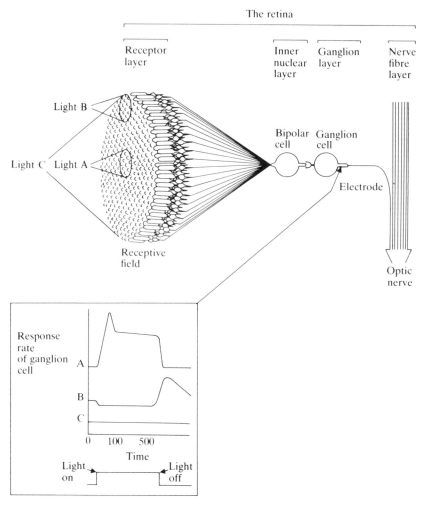

Figure 2.8 Schematic view of a portion of the retina, showing receptive field of a ganglion cell and the corresponding response rate of the cell to three distinct patterns of light stimulation, A, B, C. (Based on Lindsay and Norman: figs. 6.18, 6.19, 6.20, pp. 215–17.)

excitatory and inhibitory connections exist between neighbouring receptors and the ganglion cell served by them. Figure 2.8 (A, B) shows a typical sort of 'on-centre, off-surround' arrangement of a portion of the retina serving a ganglion cell (its receptive field) in the retina of a cat (based on Lindsay and Norman 1977). In situation A, light falling on the central portion of the receptive field causes an increase in the response rate of the ganglion cell (curve A), while, in B, light falling on the surrounding area of the receptive field causes a decrease in ganglion-cell activity, with a brief burst as the light is switched off (curve B). Such a pattern of increased and inhibited cell activity leads to an edge effect in perception. If light falls diffusely over the area C, there may be no increase in the activity of the ganglion cell. In man, it is not certain that such a high degree of specialisation exists at this level as in the case of the lower animals, but it is certain nonetheless that considerable abstraction of stimulus properties does take place. A highly simplified version of this abstraction would posit a limited set of 'trigger' *features*, being processed *in parallel* by specialised cells, with *invariance* of detection as between one feature and another. In practice, invariance is approached rather than achieved, so that, e.g. a cell that fires in response to a particular *edge contrast* (in terms of absolute illumination-levels) may do so only if the edge is in a particular *orientation*, or *location* (in the visual field), or is above some threshold *illumination* value, or shows some combinations of these. Similarly, a simplified view would assume an 'all-or-none' firing response. But this assumption may also require modification, as the response from a particular ganglion cell may be *gated*, or provided with limits of occurrence, in relation to the presence or absence of particular stimulus features. And, within the gated response, differential impulse frequency of discharge may serve as a measure of goodness-of-fit of the stimulus to the characteristics of the detector cell: i.e. a *tuning curve* may exist, as in the case of the auditory system. Any given ganglion cell may thus transmit information simultaneously about, for example, illumination, edge, orientation, etc., thus contributing simultaneously to a number of different higher-level processing systems. It would seem that these stimulus properties are ultimately disentangled by virtue of their parallel transmission by a variety of neurons having different but overlapping sensitivities, along a hierarchical chain. Already, before the signal leaves the retina, something of this hierarchical processing has taken place (Blakemore 1975).

We have already noted that, for lower animals such as frogs, retinal processing goes as far as to distinguish certain environmentally salient feature complexes in a cell-specific way. Most strikingly, certain ganglion cells, highly specialised for convex-edged objects that are moved into and around the visual field, are 'bug-perceivers' (Maturana *et al.* 1960). It would appear that this can only be a partial account of visual perception of objects – otherwise, there would need to be as many uniquely specialised object-detector cells as there are visible objects in the animal's environment (Weisstein 1973). Further, it is not clear that such specialisation exists at this level in man. But it raises the intriguing issue of the link between the optimal modes of operation for ganglion cells (or possibly higher levels of cells) in man and the optimal formal features of man's various writing systems.

2.3.3 *The optic nerve*

Ganglion cells from all parts of the retina send about a million fibres (Thompson 1967) together from each eye in the form of the optic nerve. This should really be thought of as a brain-internal connecting pathway, rather than as a connection from peripheral to central nervous systems. The fibres are organised in a way that roughly preserves the spatial distribution of the cells over the retina – that is to say, in a *retinotopic* manner. However, cells near the fovea have narrower *receptive fields* than those of the periphery, so the retinotopic bundle of nerve fibres represents the central area of the visual field preferentially over the periphery.

The optic nerve projects to the *lateral geniculate nuclei* (to the rear of the thalamus, very close to the medial geniculate nucleus of the auditory system), and to the *superior colliculi* (also involved in the auditory system) in the midbrain (fig. 2.7). (Other projections of the optic nerve need not concern us here, as they relate to different phenomena such as the linking of biological rhythms to periods of light and dark, and the mediation of the pupillary response to levels of illumination.)

The projection to the lateral geniculate nuclei is part of the subsystem that eventually projects to the striate cortex area that is concerned with form vision, and which is generally referred to as the *geniculostriate* system.

The projection to the superior colliculi is part of the system which controls eye position and movement (fixation and saccade); because the superior colliculi are in the roof (*tectal* area) of the brainstem, this is generally referred to as the *retinotectal* system (Chamberlain 1983).

The optic chiasm

In the geniculostriate system, the optic nerve fibres innervate the lateral geniculate nuclei in retinotopic fashion; but *en route* from the eyes, a remarkable division of channels has taken place, at the *optic chiasm* (an equivalent term to decussation, from the Greek letter *chi* χ). By virtue of this, the left lateral geniculate nucleus receives input from the right visual field (via the left temporal and right nasal hemiretinae), while the right lateral geniculate nucleus receives that from the left visual field (fig. 2.7). The decussation of fibres in the optic chiasm is roughly 50/50. As a result, each side of the visual system receives an almost identical version of something like the complete half visual-field; *almost* identical, because of the very slight difference in vantage points of the two eyes, and *something like* a half-field because of the slight peripheral area which is not binocular. This 'double exposure' phenomenon, effected at the optic chiasm, lays the basis of stereoscopic vision, which is achieved at higher levels of processing (Romer 1971b).

2.3.4   **The midbrain nuclei**

The lateral geniculate nuclei

Fibres of the optic nerve innervate the lateral geniculate nuclei in retinotopic fashion, integrating the inputs from both eyes. The cells of these nuclei, like the ganglion cells of the retinae, are thus driven by overlapping portions of the retinal receptive fields, and are in general served by ganglion cells in a nearly one-to-one fashion. They also function similarly to ganglion cells in that they are basically of two types: those that respond to bright centres/dark surrounds ('on-centre' cells) and those that respond to dark centres/bright surrounds ('off-centre' cells) (Hubel 1963). It may appear, then, that this fourth processing stage represented in the lateral geniculate nuclei is a relatively minor one; but it should be recalled that the input to these nuclei is of the 'double exposure' type, and it may be therefore that bringing these two views of the visual field into registration is a prime function that is achieved at this level. Certainly it is true of cells higher up the system, in the visual cortex, that they respond more strongly when being stimulated binocularly.

The superior colliculi

These are involved in controlling the more automatic aspects of saccadic eye movements in reading (as well as other activities), in directing visual gaze towards, for example, a sound source, and in maintenance of gaze during changes in body posture, etc. It is not very clear how the highly rapid and precise saccades are achieved, since the cells in these nuclei are rather gross in their receptive-field characteristics. Possibly the answer lies in complex structuring of large numbers of cells, having overlapping fields (Blakemore 1975). One of the intriguing results of work in eye movements in reading (Rayner, McConkie and Erhlich 1978; Levy-Shoen and O'Regan 1979) is the observation that a good deal of text processing goes on *prior* to the form perception of characters (in terms of features or whatever). How far eye-movement control is determined on the basis of visual input at the earliest level (grey-level intensities of the visual array), or by high-level processing (including word recognition, and syntactico-semantic knowledge resulting from this) is a matter of dispute (Brady 1981; Underwood 1985).

2.3.5   **Cortical processing**

The lateral geniculate nuclei project, via the *optic radiations*, to the *visual cortex* in the occipital lobe. It is here that the most extraordinary specialisations are found, among cells that are grouped functionally into banks of columns about $\frac{1}{2}$mm in diameter on average, arrayed perpendicularly to the upper and lower surfaces of the cortex like the bristles of a brush (Hubel

1963). Thus, all the thousands of cells in a particular column may respond to a particular *orientation* of an edge; each of these is presumed to be connected to a large number of lateral geniculate cells, which are in turn connected, via the ganglion cells, to receptors whose fields have their centres occupying a straight line at a particular angle across the retina of each eye. In this fashion, there are unimaginable numbers of cells, dedicated to particular inputs, some responding to slits, or to bars, or to edges, in certain orientations arranged in retinotopic fashion throughout the columnar banks of the visual cortex. These, the simple cells of the visual cortex, represent the fifth level of processing in the system. But interspersed among them, in the same columns, are the complex cells of the sixth stage, which used to be thought to derive their inputs only from the simple cells, allowing for the unified tracking of edges in preferred orientation, from one part of the retinal field to another. According to this view, a strictly hierarchical relationship was thought to exist between the six stages of processing, whereby features abstracted at a lower stage were handed up for integration and further analysis at successively higher stages. It would appear, however, that the hierarchy is not so neat or rigid as this, since, for example, at least some complex visual cortex cells (sixth stage) receive input directly from the lateral geniculate nuclei (fourth stage), and perhaps even earlier than the simple cells, along fast-transmitting fibres (Blakemore 1975). This, together with our earlier observations regarding the multi-channel nature of cells in the visual system, seems to cast doubt on the simple trigger-feature view ('one feature, one neuron'), at least as a comprehensive account. Instead, we may have to posit neuronal specialisation for whole assemblies of features, where these assemblies do not relate uniquely to any single object. This, in turn, suggests that the perception of visual input must ultimately depend on some integration of these multi-channel devices. Just possibly, though, there may be relatively stable 'assemblies of assemblies', or explicit object detectors, at least for certain frequently occurring and important visual stimuli, the synthesis of which may take place as a direct result of early training or experience. This is largely speculative, but it is a question that ought to be asked: how far such detectors may exist for forms of written language in literate adults, and whether they correspond to individual letters, or to smaller or larger units.

Further processing

Beyond the primary retinotopic projection in the visual cortex, further anatomical detail becomes exceedingly complex, but there appear to be a large number of localised visual projection fields between the occipital lobe and the underside of the temporal lobe. Conceivably it is in these regions that integration and synthesis of visual input from the primary visual cortex takes place. However that may be, it is appropriate to conclude this section with the reminder that visual perception is not just the result of extraction processes, but crucially involves active integration, under pressure from *expectations* of *how things should be*. Imposing an active organisation on sensory data thus makes contact with general knowledge as well as specific expectations, and is known to be both fallible and at least partly under voluntary control (witness visual illusions, impossible figures and our ability to transform certain ambiguous stimuli; see Sharpe 1983). And again we return to the point that the role of training and learning may be quite considerable in the sort of visual skill that fluent reading requires, in facilitating synthetic processes of perception that might otherwise be inefficient, prone to error and difficult to transfer from one version of the 'same' stimulus array to another.

For most children, fully stable fixation patterns are observed to be attained by around ten years, considerably after the age at which they are reported to be able to 'read' (Foss and Hakes 1978). The discrepancy here probably relates to developments in central processing, allowing for efficient utilisation of material under fixation. Stein and Fowler (1982) recognise an ocular-motor basis for certain reading difficulties in young children. Since reading small characters at a normal reading distance requires such precision of eye control (down to a quarter of one degree of visual angle), with appropriate convergence of the eyes, they suggest that normally a 'leading (or reference) eye' strategy develops, whereby the signals being perceived from one eye are given priority in determining which foveal image constitutes the relevant input. They further suggest that inducing a 'leading eye' strategy in children who apparently do not use it spontaneously, is helpful in treating early types of reading difficulty. If so, it represents a further illustration of how lower levels (motor control) and higher levels (visual interpretation) are functionally related in the skills required for reading.

2.4 The organisation of language in the brain

Having reached the brain, as it were, by way of the auditory and visual systems, we shall now consider how their outputs to the cortex relate to other areas of language processing in the brain. We shall deal first with the cortex, in its structural and functional aspects (section 2.4.1); then the subcortical pathways and nuclei (section 2.4.2). Finally, we shall consider the roles in language processing of the dominant and non-dominant cerebral hemispheres (section 2.4.3).

2.4.1 *The cortex*

We shall consider the structural aspects of the cortex first, and then turn to the hypothesised functions.

Structural aspects

Structurally, the cortex presents: (a) a convoluted surface which can be mapped (the *topographical* approach); and (b) a cross-sectional structure which can be described in terms of its tissue composition (the *histological* approach). The latter leads naturally into a consideration of the various cell types and structures (or *cyto-architectonics*).

The topographical features constitute the most obvious starting point, since, as we have noted, the cortex is not smooth but folded into *gyri* standing between small *sulci* or large *fissures* (fig. 2.9). The major fissures are: the *longitudinal* (dividing the two hemispheres); the *central*, or *Rolandic* (demarcating the *frontal* and *parietal lobes*); and the *Sylvian* (separating the *temporal* lobe from the frontal and the parietal lobes). We should also note the *superior temporal* fissure dividing the upper surface of the temporal lobe from the lower. The temporal and parietal lobes share a boundary with the *occipital* lobe which is the posterior portion of the cortex. This is actually not very clearly distinguished in terms of surface features.

Histologically, the cortex is not uniform over the cerebral hemispheres. Overall, it comprises an envelope of roughly six layers of cells, of varying types, depth and organisation, about one-eighth of an inch thick (Perkins and Kent 1986). In detail, it has been mapped into distinct, conventionally numbered, areas (called Brodmann's areas; see Brodmann 1909). In many cases, histological evidence shows gradual, rather than abrupt, changes in cell composition between surface divisions such as lobes, although the occipital lobe does show a sharp histological boundary (Thompson 1967).

Functional aspects

Concerning the fundamental division of the two cerebral hemispheres, we have noted a parallelism of function that may be complementary (in the case of the contralateral connections between body and brain) or mutual (in the case of bilateral connections). But there is also striking asymmetry of function between the hemispheres: one hemisphere tends to be dominant for a range of functions, including handedness and certain aspects of language. Dominance is normally a left-hemisphere characteristic (thus, right-handedness is ensured by left-hemisphere dominance, by virtue of the characteristic contralateral control of the body by the brain). Although there are exceptions, we shall assume the left hemisphere to be the dominant one in

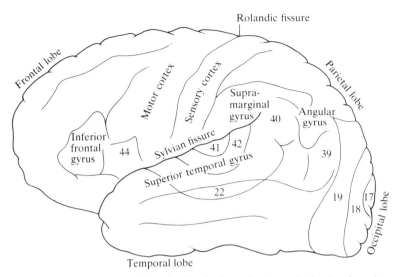

Figure 2.9 The left cerebral hemisphere, showing major landmarks and areas relevant to language functions. Brodmann's areas are indicated by numbers. (Based on Pick and Howden 1901: fig. 346, p. 648; Perkins and Kent 1986: fig. 15.3, p. 422.)

our discussion here (see Walsh 1978 for further discussion and references).

Within each hemisphere, the occipital lobe is concerned primarily with vision; the parietal lobe with body-surface senses and spatial orientation; the temporal lobe with hearing and time relations. In front of the central fissure is a strip of *motor cortex*, responsible for the control of movement over the whole body; just behind this fissure is the corresponding *sensory cortex*. In each of these areas, the body is represented in inverted fashion, with the cells controlling the upper areas of the body (including the muscles and sense receptors of the articulatory organs) located towards the junction with the Sylvian fissure. Large areas of the remaining cortex are apparently neither directly sensory nor motor in function, and have been called 'silent' or 'association' areas (Thompson 1967). However, the area just anterior to the motor cortex is often referred to as the *premotor cortex*, and is thought to be associated with the preplanning of motor goals, e.g. complex schemata or 'mental images' of what the articulatory organs have to achieve (fig. 2.9).

For language, the phenomenon of left-cerebral dominance is illustrated by the fact that the area demarcated by the inferior frontal gyrus and the precentral gyrus (fig. 2.9) in the left hemisphere (Brodmann's areas 44 and 45) is of special importance for speech output; this is what is referred to as *Broca's area* (after Paul Broca, a nineteenth-century neurologist who hypothesised that damage observed in this area was associated with certain spoken language output disorders; see ch. 8). Mohr (1976) points out that the histological evidence for this region is actually very weak, so that the Brodmann numbers are used (as indeed is the label 'Broca's area') more for convenience than to make any stronger claim. The area is thought to be involved in movement of the articulators, and appears to control specifically speech aspects of the oral tract (rather than chewing, swallowing, coughing, etc.).

The area of the angular gyrus (fig. 2.9) in the left hemisphere (Brodmann's areas 42 and 22) provides further evidence for specialisation of the left hemisphere for language functions. This is what is called *Wernicke's area* (after another nineteenth-century neurologist, Carl Wernicke, who hypothesised that damage in this part of the brain was responsible for certain other observed difficulties in processing spoken language, leading to strikingly fluent but meaningless speech; see ch. 8 for this also). Wernicke's area is situated on the *planum temporale*, the posterior portion of the superior surface of the temporal lobe. This area, which is anatomically quite well defined, is observed to be larger in the dominant hemisphere than the corresponding region in the non-dominant hemisphere, in neonates as well as in adults (Witelson 1977), a feature that suggests some evolutionary adaptation for language functions. Wernicke's area is therefore situated close to the primary auditory area, to the visual cortex and to the parietal lobe, and appears to be centrally involved in the meaning aspect of the production and comprehension of written and spoken forms of language.

Just anterior to Wernicke's area, on the upper surface of the superior temporal gyrus (fig. 2.9), is found the primary auditory cortex (Brodmann's areas 41 and 42). This area in the left hemisphere may have some specialised speech–auditory functions that are not found in the corresponding area of the right hemisphere (see section 2.4.3 below, and ch. 4, section 4.2.4). In the occipital lobe, the most posterior region (Brodmann's area 17) forms the primary visual cortex, with connections from there to adjacent anterior regions (Brodmann's 18 and 19), from where long association fibres make connections to other regions of the cortex (Romanes 1979). There is a body of evidence for right half-field (i.e. left hemisphere) superiority with verbal material (Walsh 1978).

Between the angular gyrus and the supramarginal gyrus (Brodmann's areas 39 and 40, and part of 22), lies an area that may be involved in relating visual and auditory input to stored meaning representations, where primary inputs from systems concerned with auditory, visual and body-spatial processing interconnect. Each sensory representation – how a word sounds, how it appears on the page, how it feels to articulate and to write, as well as what its referent looks like, sounds like, feels like, and so on – is complexly interconnected with each other. See Perkins and Kent (1986) for many useful diagrams and insights.

2.4.2 *The subcortical systems*

The picture we have presented thus far is fairly circumscribed, in two ways. First, it does not do justice to the less direct involvement of large areas of cortex in *both* hemispheres in language processing (see section 2.4.3 below on the role of the non-dominant hemisphere). Secondly, it fails to take account of subcortical structures and functions: as we noted earlier, these are of two types, involving cortical–cortical connections, and connections involving subcortical masses of cell nuclei.

Subcortical pathways

Among the former type, we should mention the *corpus callosum*, the principal grouping of commissural (transversely connecting) fibres between the two hemispheres, keeping each copiously informed of what the other is doing, and enabling them to function as a single brain. (We shall refer to this again in section 2.4.3 below.)

There is also the *arcuate fasciculus*, a bundle of association fibres connecting from Wernicke's area to Broca's area (fig. 2.9). The importance of the arcuate fasciculus from a language-processing point of view is that Wernicke's and Broca's areas are located rather distantly from each other, by virtue of the fact that they are close to their respective primary cortical areas (auditory–visual input, and speech output, respectively), and yet have a close input–output relationship. This is exemplified most vividly, perhaps, in so-called 'speech-shadowing' and simultaneous translation, in which auditory input is rapidly converted into speech output; but it may also be present in more ordinary uses of language, if we think of Wernicke's area as being involved in the processing of meaning in language production. The link in these different language functions (from meaning formulation to speech output) is made possible, on this view, via the arcuate fasciculus.

There are numerous other subcortical pathways of general relevance to language, e.g. projecting from the occipital lobe (visual cortex) to the temporal and parietal regions, but we shall not detail them here (see Walsh 1978; Perkins and Kent 1986).

Subcortical nuclei

Among the subcortical nuclei we should take note of the *thalamus*, the *basal ganglia* and the *limbic system* (refer back to fig. 2.1).

The thalamus

At the top of the brainstem, the midbrain eventually diverges into two branches, left and right, which marks the beginning of the division of the hemispheres of the brain (Perkins and Kent 1986). Each of these branches supports nuclei known as the thalamus and the basal ganglia, and around these nuclei is found the white matter of the cortex, in each hemisphere. The thalamus is a collection of sensory nuclei, and one of its functions is essentially as a sensory relay station (all sensory information, save olfactory, connects to designated nuclei within it, e.g. auditory input to the medial geniculate bodies, visual input to the lateral geniculate bodies, etc.). It has two-way connections with most of the cerebral cortex, and it also has the function of integrating, as well as relaying, sensory information from and to all parts of the brain. Language functions are lateralised in the thalamus, as in the cortex. Penfield and Roberts (1959) suggested that one role of the thalamus was to integrate frontal and parietal language areas. This is still an open issue, however, since this view would naturally predict more fundamental effects of *aphasia* (loss of language abilities; see ch. 8) resulting from damage to the thalamus than are normally observed: 'One explanation is that aphasia is not related to the destruction of a specific thalamic nucleus but appears to depend on the destruction of a "pattern" of nuclei' (Wallesch and Wyke 1985: 188). (Crosson *et al.* (1986), however, report a recent case of thalamic aphasia.)

Speech production, rather than comprehension, seems to be implicated in the functions of the thalamus; and the work of Ojemann and his colleagues has thrown light on the role of the left thalamic region in short-term verbal memory:

> the thalamic role in language may be related to an interaction with mechanisms involved in the maintenance of focal attention to specific and perhaps specifically verbal aspects of the external environment, mechanisms that are also important in at least short-term memory function. (Ojemann 1976: 128)

The basal ganglia

These comprise the *caudate* (tail-shaped) *nucleus* and *lenticular* (lens-shaped) *nucleus* (itself made up of the *putamen* and *globus pallidus*) (fig. 2.1). For speech they appear to function primarily as part of the motor output system: Perkins and Kent suggest that they may be important for generating motor programmes for voluntary speech activity that are then sent to the motor cortex for implementation (1986: 448). Automatic aspects of speech control may, by contrast, be stored as motor patterns in the subcortical structures.

The limbic system

This is a complex, spatially diffuse, and not very well defined system (including the *cingulate gyrus, hippocampus* and *amygdala*) situated around the basal ganglia. It is not shown in figure 2.1 because it would unduly complicate the picture: see Thompson (1967) and Walsh (1978). It is generally characterised as involved in emotional states, motivation, learning and memory. Anterior parts of the thalamus have anatomical and functional connections with parts of the limbic system. The hippocampus may be particularly involved in short-term memory (or that form of it which does not involve conscious attention to what is being experienced).

Finally, we should note that both the reticular formation (centrally located in the brainstem – refer back to fig. 2.6) and the cerebellum have important integrative and coordinative roles to play in speech production, as in perception. Wallesch and Wyke conclude by recognising three possible parallel pathways involving subcortical nuclei:

1. a cortical – sub-cortical (basal ganglia, thalamus) – cortical loop;
2. cortical – thalamic – cortical two-way connections;
3. ascending reticular formation – thalamic – cortical connections (1985: 194).

2.4.3 *Language in left and right hemispheres*

We have already referred to the phenomenon of cerebral dominance, whereby one side of the brain – usually the left – is more specialised in the control of certain functions. Right-handedness is usually linked to a whole range of left-hemispheric dominances, but the pattern may be more complex in particular individuals. For language we should ask what aspects of language function are lateralised in this way.

Methods of investigation

The first method to be mentioned is the *Wada test* (Wada 1949), a fairly direct, if gross, way of determining lateralisation of particular functions, developed for use prior to surgical intervention (e.g. in cases where brain damage, or malfunction, has to be attended to). It involves injecting a temporarily paralysing drug (sodium amytal) into the carotid artery in the neck on one side or the other. Injection into the left carotid artery will affect the left hemisphere of a conscious patient for a few minutes, and subsequent effects on that individual's abilities in speaking and perceiving speech confirm a pattern of left-cerebral dominance for language in that individual. This, however, is only a first step.

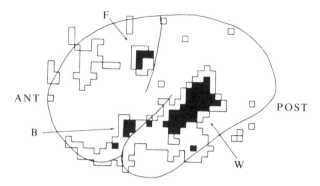

Figure 2.10 Regional cerebral blood-flow (rCBF) pattern during passive listening to speech. Dark areas indicate increased blood flow, mainly in Wernicke's area (W). (From Pickles 1982: fig. 9, 16, p. 282, adapted from Lassen, Ingvar and Skinhøj 1978.)

The functional topography of the brain is fairly well understood in general terms, but there are in this field, as in many others, considerable differences between individuals. As a result, surgeons who contemplate excision of part of the cortex for medical reasons (e.g. in the control of epilepsy) have to be particularly careful when working in areas known to be language-related. Direct mapping has been achieved, in a few cases, by electrical stimulation of the brain (ESB) (Penfield 1959) using a silver electrode on the exposed brain of a locally anaesthetised, but fully conscious, patient. Evidence from this type of procedure – expanded, under suitable controls, for the purpose of academic research in some cases – has provided some rather direct indication of a specialised speech-production centre in the left hemisphere.

Other methods involve less direct instrumental analyses, as in *electroencephalographic* (EEG) or *regional cerebral blood-flow* (rCBF) investigations. In these, simultaneous readings are taken from various points on the scalp, while the subject performs certain language-related tasks: EEG traces represent areas of changed electrical activity in the brain (average evoked responses, AER, and event-related potentials, ERP, over time), while rCBF displays those areas receiving increased blood flow during the performance of these tasks (see Gruber and Segalowitz 1977 for a review). Figure 2.10 shows a pattern resulting from a typical rCBF study.

Still other methods rely more on observable linguistic performance, as in a *dichotic* listening task (Broadbent 1954), or a *dichoptic* visual-perception task, each of which involves the subject in attending to competing stimuli presented simultaneously at each ear or eye. We shall refer briefly to dichoptic tasks during our discussion of so-called 'split-brain' individuals, below. Concerning dichotic listening tasks, in which auditory stimuli are used and the subject has to report what is perceived, the usual pattern of results obtained is one of faster, and more accurate, reports for the stimulus received via the right ear – often described as showing 'right-ear advantage (REA)' for speech over non-speech sounds (Kimura 1961, 1964, 1967). The observation of right-ear advantage is consistent with the pattern of left-cerebral dominance and the fact that the major auditory pathways cross over in the brainstem, by virtue of which the right ear delivers most of its sensory data to the auditory cortex in the left hemisphere. We shall now briefly consider what is involved in the distinction between 'speech' vs 'non-speech' sounds.

Right-ear advantage for speech sounds

First, not all speech sounds appear to show the effect at all reliably: steady-state vowels show no consistent REA; consonants such as /l/ and /r/, with strong vocalic structure, show it only weakly (Cutting 1973; Day and Vigorito 1973); and stop consonants show it best, particularly when they are fully contrastive (i.e. have nothing in common but their stop-ness) (Borden and Harris 1980). This pattern of findings appears to involve both acoustic (i.e. type of sound) and linguistic (i.e. function of sound) factors. Gruber and Segalowitz's (1977) review cites the work of Spellacy and Blumstein (1970), Haggard and Parkinson (1971) and Van Lancker and Fromkin (1973) in support of the view that psychological factors may also play a part: the same sounds, embedded in speech vs non-speech contexts, may show stronger vs weaker REA.

Secondly, we shall note some arguments in chapter 4 to the effect that sounds outside speech may be perceived in a similar way to speech sounds, including REA, if they have certain acoustic properties – specifically, highly dynamic, fast-changing spectral patterns (e.g. speech played backwards, and plucked (vs bowed) sounds produced from stringed instruments).

Accordingly, it is not entirely clear whether the dominant hemisphere effect in this type of observation arises from a specialised 'speech processor', or from a specialised 'dynamic sound-structure' processor. The difference between the two views is important for the interpretation of the 'language' abilities in the two hemispheres. Confirmatory evidence on REA in speech (though not refined enough to bear on the issue of 'speech' vs 'complex sound' specialisation) comes from EEG and rCBF studies, which tend to show increased activity in the area of the auditory cortex in the dominant hemisphere during speech perception (fig. 2.10).

Broca's area and the production of speech sounds

Another major function of language is speech output, and, as we have seen, it has been suggested that Broca's area, in the dominant hemisphere, is crucially involved in this. However, as we shall go on to see in the next section, the picture of hemispheric involvement in the innervation of muscles for speech as opposed to non-speech purposes is not particularly clear. Generally, it seems that both left and right hemispheres contribute to certain sensory (feedback) and motor (initiation and control) aspects of speech, but dominance is again a left-hemispheric characteristic. Given the routings of the upper motor neurons, and of the cranial and thoracic nerves, this dominance does *not* result in a lateral asymmetry of speech-muscle innervation, however. The dominance is *associated with* the cortical control of these muscles, rather than being strictly part of such control. So 'Broca's area' (fig. 2.9) is to be thought of really as an association between two control functions that are closely related and proximal to each other; one is the speech-control centre, which organises and sequences the input to the second area, which contains the large cells of the motor cortex which innervates the muscles used for speech.

Language functions in 'split-brain' individuals

So-called 'split-brain' individuals belong to a fairly small population of patients who have undergone radical surgery for the treatment of intractable epileptic conditions. The surgery involves cerebral commissurotomy, or the severing of the corpus callosum, the main commissure between the two hemispheres. After the operation, the patient has two effectively independent hemispheres, largely duplicating each other's function, but preserving their specialisations, including those we have noted for language.

Some striking features arise from this in what are, in other respects, apparently normally functioning individuals. Refer back to figure 2.7, and imagine that, above the brainstem, the corpus callosum has been severed. This has the effect that the contents of the left visual half-field (numbers 1–4), represented in the occipital lobe of the right hemisphere, *cannot be communicated to the left hemisphere* (or vice versa). The significance of this is that, unless the viewing subject can effect this communication by external means such as scanning eye-movements, only the right hemisphere 'knows' what is in the left field. Scanning eye-movements can be eliminated by presenting visual stimuli at short exposure durations (less than 200msec.). Because speech output is controlled from the left hemisphere, the subject is unable to say (by the left hemisphere) what is being seen (by the right hemisphere in the left visual field). The same situation arises with tactile input: information from the left hand (e.g. picking up an object) will be communicated only to the right hemisphere, as long as other information is cut out (e.g. the subject is blindfolded, or the object is handled under a screen). In these cases, the subject will be unable to say what the object is.

Under these conditions, two sorts of visual-field presentations can be effected. One is the dichoptic task referred to earlier, in which inputs can be made simultaneously via both visual fields, each going only to the contra-lateral visual cortex, by virtue of the hemiretinae connections discussed in section 2.3.3 above. An example of this is the word *heart*, with the letters *he-* appearing only in the left visual field, and the letters *-art* only in the right: subsequent verbal report was that the word *art* had been seen, but left-hand identification invariably picked out the card with the word *he* written on it (Gazzaniga 1967). The other type of presentation involves using just one half of the visual field (a visual half-field asymmetric presentation), such as show-ing a picture of a spoon in the left visual field: here, the subject was able to guide search with the left hand (out of sight) among a set of objects, and cor-rectly retrieve a spoon; but, having done this (via right-hemisphere control), he was subsequently unable to say what the object (still out of sight) in his left hand was (Gazzaniga 1967). Figure 2.11 summarises the main outcomes from visual and tactile input to split-brain subjects.

Language in the minor (non-dominant) hemisphere

Thus far it would appear that we have ascribed no language func-tions to the minor (non-dominant) hemisphere. This would be a misleading impression to convey, since no modern authorities believe that the minor hemisphere is 'silent' for language: but stating what language functions it fills is a less easy matter. In this respect, we have to consider how vague the state-ments are, really, for all but the most *speech*-based functions (auditory percep-tion, articulatory production) even of the dominant hemisphere. For example (as we shall see in ch. 8), there may be some links between the sequencing of speech sounds and certain aspects of syntactic organisation, inasmuch as they are frequently observed to be impaired together (in Broca's-type aphasia). The actual categories of language function involved, and their precise relationship with each other in the normally functioning brain, are a matter of some con-troversy. Part of the problem here lies in the difficulty in interpreting the find-ings from split-brain patients and other non-normal situations (including dichotic listening tasks); it is not clear how far it is possible to interpret data drawn from non-normal language use to shed light on what the normal situ-ation is like. If the minor hemisphere *can* be shown to perform certain

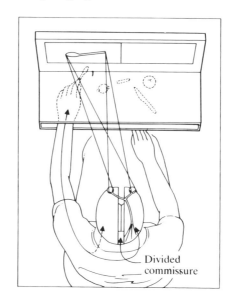

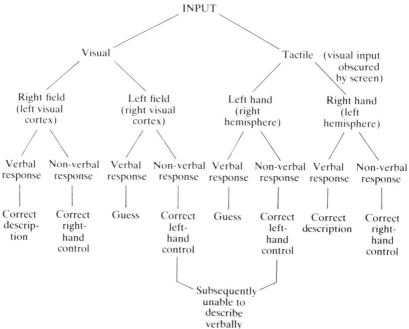

Figure 2.11 Summary of outcomes from visual and tactile inputs to 'split-brain' subjects. (Inset above shows typical testing situation.) (Based on diagram, p. 28, and discussion in Gazzaniga 1967.)

language functions, in certain demanding situations, this does not mean that it may *ordinarily* perform them.

Accordingly, it may be appropriate to confine our discussion here to the following observations that have been made on the possible involvements of the minor hemisphere in language:

The minor hemisphere can:

> perceive non-linguistic environmental sounds (Knox and Kimura 1970);
>
> comprehend visually presented words, especially concrete nouns (Gazzaniga 1967);
>
> match objects to auditory or visual naming or description (Gazzaniga 1967);
>
> spell auditorily presented words (Gazzaniga 1967);
>
> process kanji (logographic) word symbols better than the kana (phonographic), in Japanese (Yamadori 1975);
>
> develop considerable vocabulary skills (Fromkin *et al.* 1974);
>
> process intonation patterns (Ross and Mesulam 1979);
>
> mediate emotional responses (including recognition of emotional tones of voice) (Haggard and Parkinson 1971; Kent 1984);
>
> make inferences, understand jokes and process discourse organisation (Locke, Caplan and Kellar 1973; Gardner *et al.* 1983);
>
> perform general, holistic, cognitive skills (Gazzaniga 1967);
>
> generate good block design (spatial) (Gazzaniga 1967).

It is markedly less able to:

> control speech production (but see Gazzaniga 1983);
>
> discriminate speech sounds (but see Ades 1974);
>
> perceive temporal rhythms (Robinson and Solomon 1974);
>
> process syntactic constructions (Gazzaniga and Hillyard 1971).

It is not yet clear whether the analytic, linear, and sequential specialisations of the dominant hemisphere that favour certain crucial language (speech) functions are (a) the result of genetic programming (cf. the enlarged planum temporale in the left hemisphere), or (b) the result of a suppression, or inhibition, of those functions in the non-dominant side that the dominant side preferentially performs. See Moskovitch (1977) and Zaidel (1978) for discussion.

2.5 The articulatory and manual systems

The articulatory and manual systems may be conveniently discussed together, since they can each be conceived as having the following four levels:

the motor and premotor areas of the cerebral cortex (section 2.5.1);

the upper motor neurons (descending fibres of cells in the cerebral cortex), and the subcortical nuclei and the cerebellum (section 2.5.2);

the lower motor neurons (fibres of the peripheral nervous system) innervating the muscles of the articulatory and manual systems (section 2.5.3);

the muscles and organs of the articulatory and manual systems (section 2.5.4).

Additionally, we shall consider:

the aerodynamic phase, for speech, and the dynamics of written language output (section 2.5.5).

2.5.1 *The motor and premotor cortex*

As with the auditory and visual input systems, there is topical organisation of cells in the cortex that are involved in motor output. However, instead of a single crucial organ (such as the basilar membrane or the retina) being laid out, as it were, along strips of cortex, we find the various separate organs, indeed the whole body, laid out, over the motor cortex (running anteriorly to the Rolandic fissure; see fig. 2.9). The organisation is such that the representation of the body is inverted, with the lower limbs controlled by cells located at the top of the motor cortex (in fact the feet and toes are represented in the medial surface, between the hemispheres), followed by the hips and trunk, then the shoulders, elbows, wrist, fingers and thumb (relevant for manual output), and neck, brow, eyes and face, and then the lips, jaw, tongue and other muscles associated with vocalisation (as well as their other functions). (See fig. 2.12.)

Contralateral control is a feature of this system, whereby the left arm, for example, is controlled from the relevant portion of cortex in the right hemisphere, and vice versa. Ipsilateral connections are found also, mainly quite weakly, though they are more equivalent to contralateral connections in respect of the upper part of the face and head: for the speech musculature (located in the lower part of the head) and written language output contralaterality is a significant phenomenon. In this connection, we should bear in mind that, while handwriting is a single-handed activity, typing is typically two-handed: control aspects are to that extent distinct in the two activities, in so far as the motor areas of the cortex are concerned, but the evidence is that both hemispheres are involved in writing as well as in typing. There is also columnar arrangement of cells within the motor cortex, with cells having sim-

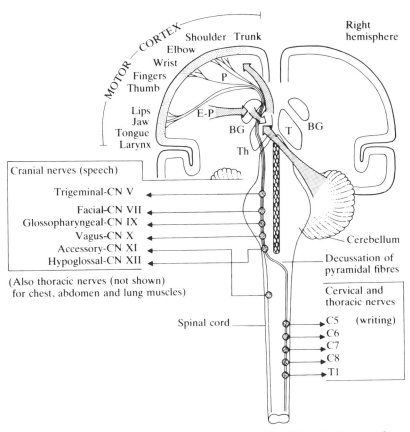

Figure 2.12 Motor control of speech and writing. Schematic diagram of inputs from left motor cortex via the pyramidal system (cortico-bulbar and cortico-spinal tracts) and the extra-pyramidal system. Broad arrows indicate functional relationships between the basal ganglia, thalamus, cerebellum and cerebral cortex. P, pyramidal fibres; E-P, extra-pyramidal input to basal ganglia; BG, basal ganglia; T, thalamus. (Based on Thompson 1967: fig. 13.2, p. 397; Perkins and Kent 1986: fig. 2.12, p. 460.)

ilar function in terms of motor control being stacked vertically, and with rather sharp transitions in cell function between the columns.

While the motor cortex is clearly of major importance, it operates in association with the premotor cortex which exerts a controlling influence, and the parietal lobe also contributes massively to the upper motor-neuron system that projects to the lower control centres. Parietal lobe involvement is perhaps particularly important for the organisation of written language output: within it are mediated the spatial aspects of forms (relative shape and position of letters) and movement (of the hand over the surface of the page, or pressing down keys in the spatial configuration of a keyboard); the visual properties of the letter sequence (as processed in the neighbouring occipital areas); and the control of specific motor commands to muscles of the arm and hand. Indeed, any precise and rapid movements such as those exhibited in speech or writing (including typewriting) require integrated involvement of not just motor but sensory areas as well, so that afferent feedback signals from the articulatory or manual organs may provide information on the extent to which efferent motor signals are having the desired effect.

Thus, the nervous system functions holistically, at this highest level, through subcortical connections over a wide area of each hemisphere; and the two hemispheres communicate through such channels as the corpus callosum, so that the input from the cortex for motor-control functions is bilaterally distributed, even though certain crucial aspects are lateralised. See Brown (1980) for a discussion of brain structure in relation to language production.

2.5.2 *The upper motor-neuron system*

The motor cells of the cortex with their descending efferent fibres projecting to certain subcortical nuclei, the cerebellum, the reticular formation and relays in the brainstem and spinal cord together make up the *upper motor neuron* system (fig. 2.12).

Pyramidal versus extra-pyramidal systems

Additionally, there is an important distinction to be made between the system served by the large pyramidal-shaped (Betz) cells of the motor cortex – the so-called *pyramidal system* – and those of the biologically older *extra-pyramidal system*. The pyramidal system has upper motor neurons that establish direct connections with relays in the brainstem and the spinal cord, and appears to be involved with voluntary movements. The extra-pyramidal system is served by cells over the whole cortex, and by the thalamus and basal ganglia; it is involved in inhibitory functions as well as excitation of movement, and in a range of reflexive movement patterns, including the adjustment and maintenance of posture.

The cerebellar system

A further distinction is to be made between these two systems and the *cerebellar system*, which appears to be implicated in the coordination of movement. It may be that both the cerebellum and the basal ganglia are movement-pattern generators (the basal ganglia for slower movement, the cerebellum for fast, highly coordinated patterns), and that they send these patterns to the cortex, via the thalamus, for implementation and regulation (Kornhuber

1974). In this view, the pyramidal subsystem regulates the patterns generated within, and transmitted through, the extra-pyramidal and cerebellar subsystems. The connections between these systems are sufficiently rich for them to be considered as functionally unified.

Cortico-bulbar and cortico-spinal neurons

Complex behaviours such as speech and writing require not only consciously willed movements but also semi-automatic and completely automatic control of sequences of movement: we speak and write fluently, and a skilled typist does not have to 'think' the connections between the three keypressings that make up the typed word *the*. Something of this range is also represented (in the pyramidal and extra-pyramidal systems) as upper motor neurons from the motor cortex, and other cortical areas, group together to pass down through the base of the brain. The neurons that most concern us here are those of the trunk projection (for control of the muscles of breathing), and of the shoulder, arm and hand (for writing), and of the head and neck region (for the vocal tract).

Some of these (pyramidal) fibres connect to relays in the brainstem; because of the bulb-like shape of this structure, they are often referred to as the *cortico-bulbar* fibres. Others pass down into the spinal cord: the so-called *cortico-spinal* fibres. Generally those that govern the vocal tract, including the larynx, are cortico-bulbar, while the remainder, controlling the respiratory functions of the thorax, and the hand–arm system, are cortico-spinal. Still other neurons, of the extra-pyramidal system, project to the basal ganglia, the thalamus and the cerebellum, and these nuclei also contain cells that have fibres that connect to the brainstem.

The cerebral cortex is thus able to influence the basal ganglia–thalamus complex, which in turn influences the cortex, the brainstem and spinal cord relays. There is also feedback to the higher centres at every level, with the cerebellum being closely involved with this, via its interconnections with the basal ganglia and thalamus complex. As consciously willed movements become increasingly automatic, they become part of the repertoire of the basal ganglia and the cerebellum. Other willed movements can then be overlaid on these, to build up extremely rapid and sensitively controlled articulatory sequences that would otherwise overcommit the resources of the motor cortex. There are both voluntary and postural inputs to the basal ganglia; postural information (e.g. where the tongue is at any moment) is crucial to appropriate modification of position, and it is one of the functions of the cerebellum to regulate postural reflexes and muscle tone (the ongoing level of contraction of the muscle fibres). We may think of the basal ganglia, thalamus and cerebellum as a complex, serving to organise and monitor semi-automatic and postural patterned movements.

As the upper motor neurons pass down into the brainstem, some project to the *reticular formation*, which appears to exert facilitating and inhibiting effects on certain types of neurons.

Most (around 80 per cent) of the pyramidal fibres decussate in the brainstem, just before passing down from the medulla into the spinal cord. The motor nuclei from which the cranial nerves that we are interested in proceed are located in the *pons* and the *medulla*.

The cortico-spinal fibres descend to the base of the brainstem and decussate just before entering the spinal cord, resulting in contralateral control of the main muscles of the body by the hemispheres.

To summarise, we may say that the output of the upper motor-neuron system is delivered to the brainstem and spinal cord relays via the pyramidal, the extra-pyramidal and the cerebellar systems. Fibres of the upper motor-neuron system are richly interconnected, derive from many areas of the cortex (not just the motor cortex) and show the regulating influence of many subcortical structures, in complex fashion. The brainstem and spinal cord relays they connect to contain the *lower motor neurons*, of the peripheral nervous system.

2.5.3 *The lower motor-neuron system*

Lower motor neurons are cells in the brainstem and spinal cord relays that connect to the muscles of the body. They receive the complex output from the upper motor-neuron system, and translate it into muscular activity, based on a summing of the total of efferent excitatory and inhibitory influences. Their output is a pattern of neural impulses which trigger contractions of the muscle fibres, which may either be attached to the bones of joints in the skeleton (as in the mandible or jaw bone, or the muscles of the hand and arm), or form some soft organ such as the tongue, velum or lips. The more fibres involved in the innervation of a muscle, and the more rapid the firing rate of the impulses along the fibres, the more powerful are the contractions. (See fig. 2.13.)

The motor unit

Each lower motor neuron, together with the muscle fibres that are innervated by it, constitutes a *motor unit*, of which there are some 200,000 represented in the spinal cord, responsible for all the contractions of the muscles of the body outside the head (Eccles 1977). When peripheral nerves are examined, they are found to contain two populations of motor-nerve fibres: large, or *alpha*, types (the axons of alpha cell bodies in the spinal cord);

Descending fibres (upper motor neurons)

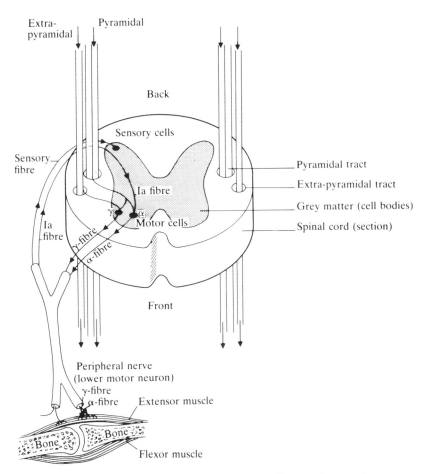

Figure 2.13 The lower motor neuron system. Horizontal section through spinal cord, showing connections between upper and lower motor neurons, and innervation of muscles via motor and sensory fibres of the peripheral nervous system. (Based on Eccles 1977: fig. 4–7, p. 117; Perkins and Kent 1986: fig. 12.3, p. 324.)

and smaller, or *gamma*, types (the axons of smaller, gamma cell bodies in the spinal cord).

At the muscle end, the alpha fibres are attached to the main muscle fibres which, when excited, cause the mass of the muscle to contract. The gamma fibres are attached to specialised muscle fibres called *spindles*. When these contract, they do not result in the whole muscle contracting, but they give rise to feedback neural activity along sensory fibres (the so-called *Ia* fibres) that are also attached to the spindle, and connect to the alpha neuron in the spinal cord. It appears that pyramidal impulses cause both alpha and gamma neurons in the spinal cord to fire. This results in (a) contraction of the muscle, via the main alpha nerve fibres and the main fibres of the muscle, and (b) contraction of the spindle, via the gamma nerve fibres. If the muscle contraction proceeds at a greater rate than spindle contraction, the spindle becomes slack, and the feedback via the Ia fibres moderates the degree of excitation in the alpha neuron. If the muscle contraction is less great, then the spindle is stretched, relative to the main mass of the muscle, and feedback along the Ia fibres increases the degree of alpha innervation. This not only lays the basis for a type of servomechanism in the motor unit, but also allows that the gamma input can bias the system towards greater or lesser levels of activity, and then monitor performance at a given level.

If we think of a finger joint as an example, one point that arises from this account is that all movement around the joint is achieved by muscle contractions (no neural activity directly leads to muscle elongations). The joint is supplied with two main groups of muscles: the *extensor*, on the outer side of the joint, which when contracting will tend to straighten or extend the finger; and the *flexor*, attached to the inner surfaces of the joint, which will tend to bend or flex the finger. Generally, where muscle groups oppose each other around a joint, as here, the prime mover is referred to as the *agonist*, the counteracting muscle being the *antagonist*. The innervation and servomechanism we have just illustrated is found in both agonist and antagonist muscles, thus allowing for graded and balanced movement of bones around joints in the body. A further refinement is that the Ia feedback loop from the agonist muscle connects not only to the alpha neuron innervating that muscle, but also, via an intermediate, inhibitory neuron, to the alpha neuron of the antagonist motor unit; so regulation can be carried on simultaneously on both sides of the joint (Eccles 1977).

The lower motor neurons involved in speech

These include the *cranial nerves*, which are numbered conventionally in anatomical discussions, based on the position of their nuclei, from top to bottom in the brainstem, from cranial nerve (CN) I to CN XII. Of these, we need to consider the following (refer back to fig. 2.12).

CN V (the trigeminal nerve) from the pons to the mandibular and tongue muscles, and involved in jaw and tongue movements generally, e.g. in chewing. It presumably has a function in at least the grosser jaw movements of speech, though its precise role is not clear. It also has a number of sensory fibres, carrying information about the jaw and tongue back to the brainstem.

CN VII (the facial nerve) from the medulla, which passes through the skull by the ear (accompanying the auditory nerve, CN XIII, as it does so); it has a small branch to the ossicular chain in the middle ear, providing a damping effect against very loud noises (see 2.2.1). It innervates the ring-like muscle that controls the lips, and muscles of facial expression. Its sensory fibres serve the soft palate and tongue tip.

CN IX (the glossopharyngeal nerve) has motor components that serve the tongue and the pharynx.

CN X (the vagus nerve) (running alongside CN IX) is, as its name implies, rather a vagabond; it has branches that go from the medulla to the *pharynx* and *larynx*, and also to the *palatoglossus* muscle of the tongue and soft palate. It also supplies chest and abdominal areas (though not importantly for speech functions).

CN XI (the accessory nerve) anatomically, this is hardly a cranial nerve at all; it originates in the upper spinal cord, just below the brainstem (in the *cervical cord*), but emerges alongside CN X into the cranial area, to serve muscles of the soft palate and the pharynx.

CN XII (the hypoglossal nerve) runs from the medulla to the main muscles of the tongue.

It should be emphasised that our discussion and illustration of these nerves here is concerned with only a fraction of the full range of their sensory and motor functions.

In addition to the cranial nerves just mentioned, certain of the *cervical* and *thoracic nerves*, from the upper and middle regions of the spinal cord, control the muscles of the ribcage and the abdomen. These operate to regulate breathing, and we can conveniently think of them as a complex group, serving the need of providing for the airstream on which speech modulation is overlaid.

The lower motor neurons involved in manual output

These include the *cervical nerves*, which emerge from the spinal cord vertebrae just below the level of the brainstem; numbered conventionally from C1 to C8. We are mainly interested here in C5, C6 and C8 (C7 is involved in movements of the arm above the horizontal); also in the first of the *thoracic nerves*, T1, emerging from between the next pair of vertebrae down. These nerves pass down through the arm, as shown in a dermatome (skin) map of their motor and sensory distributions (refer back to fig. 2.12). The *radial* (or outer) divisions of C5 and C8 are responsible for finger extension; the *medial* (or midline) divisions of C6 and T1 provide for thumb flexion and opposition, and for flexion of the first and middle fingers; and the *ulnar* (or inner) divisions of C8 and T1 control adduction of fingers and thumb (Goldberg 1979).

2.5.4 *The muscles and organs of speech and writing*
Speech

From what has been described so far it is quite clear that the articulatory system, as it is represented in physical form, is not nearly as integral or localised as the auditory system. It is spread out physically from the front of the cranium to the base of the thorax, and covers a wide range of bone and muscle types. For this reason, it is frequently observed that there are no 'organs of speech' as such; there are, rather, organs that have evolved for different purposes (i.e. breathing, coughing, swallowing, etc.) that have been phylogenetically recruited to the ends of speech. There is certainly something to be said for this view; but it does rather less than justice to the specialised nature of the system for speech production. Part of this specialisation is found at various neural levels, e.g. at the motor cortex and in the basal-ganglia–thalamus–cerebellar complex; but this level of specialisation of *control* would not have come about without a concomitant specialisation of the physical *structures* to be controlled. One way to appreciate this is to consider the human vocal tract from a comparative standpoint.

The vocal tract: general properties

The most obvious comparisons to be made are with other primates. To some extent, these observations can be supplemented by diachronic comparisons with earlier hominid fossil remains. There is also some correspondence between these observations and those that can be made in the case of the suckling human infant.

Some striking differences emerge in these comparisons, concerning the supralaryngeal area, in the middle of the vocal tract (see fig. 2.14). In the chimpanzee the *epiglottis* is high, and can make contact with the soft palate, yielding highly differentiated respiratory/digestive tracts. In adult humans the supralaryngeal cavity is much longer; the larynx and epiglottis are lower down and respiratory/digestive passages are harder to maintain separate (food can 'go down the wrong way'). However (setting aside the nasal cavity), this arrangement gives what is called a 'two-tube' shape to the vocal tract, which has advanced acoustic properties over the 'single-tube' system of the chimpanzee. One of the tubes is the oral part of the vocal tract; the other, set at 90° to this, is the very much extended pharyngeal part. Furthermore, the tongue also is orientated through 90°, permitting three-dimensional movement, and extending into both of these 'tubes'.

Acoustic modelling of the chimpanzee tract indicates a fairly restricted range of resonance patterns, which limit the range of vowels that can be produced. Effectively, the vowels of such a system are restricted to the central

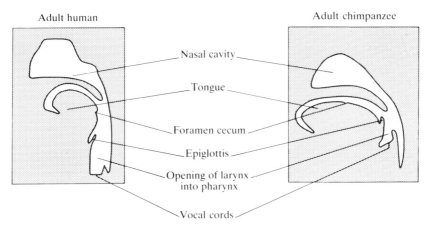

Figure 2.14 Diagram of casts taken of air passages in the supralaryngeal tracts of adult human and chimpanzee. (Trachea and oesophagus are not shown.) Shaded areas indicate anatomical structure around the passages. (Based on Lieberman 1975: fig. 9.4, p. 108.)

region of the conventional vowel trapezoid (defined roughly by the points half-open, half-closed, half-front, half-back). Thus, for example, such a tract could generate the more lax, central vowels [ɪ, ə, etc.] but not the more tense vowels on the periphery of the human vowel trapezoid [i, e, etc.].

Now, we must bear in mind that the English sound system employs a range of vowel distinctions that is much more complex than is commonly found in languages of the world. It is English that is unusual in this respect, and there is no reason to believe that the results of computer modelling of acoustic properties of vocal tracts demonstrate beyond doubt that the chimpanzee does not speak a human language because its vocal tract is the wrong shape for a particularly wide range of vowels. It is conceivable that restricted tongue movements are much more inconveniencing in this regard, for instance. The evidence is very hard to interpret, as it stands. Presumably, on a phylogenetic dimension, there have been complex interactions between gross structural realignments (e.g. upright posture of early hominids), vocal tract changes, social organisation and neural control (Borden and Harris 1980).

Vocal-tract structure and function

Ohala (1983) provides a clear and revealing schematic overview of vocal-tract structure and function (fig. 2.15). According to this view, the vocal tract is a complex device that has three *pistons*, four *valves* and three *chambers*. The pistons are: the *chest wall*, in the pulmonic cavity, used for *egressive*

95

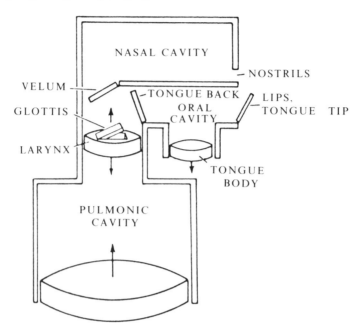

Figure 2.15 Diagram of the vocal tract as a device for producing local 'direct current' pressure changes. (From Ohala 1983: fig. 9.1, p. 191.)

pulmonic airstream generation; the *larynx*, used for both egressive and *in-gressive* airstreams; and the *tongue*, used for ingressive airstream generation (airstream direction is indicated by the arrows in the diagram). The valves are: the *glottis*, in the larynx; the *velum*, at the junction of the oral and nasal cavities; the *tongue back*; and the *lips* and *tongue tip*. The chambers are: the *pulmonic cavity* (not a resonating chamber, since it is below the glottis); and the two resonating chambers of the *oral* and *nasal cavities*. Noise sources in this system derive either from the glottis (periodic sounds, as in voice, or aperiodic sounds, as in glottal whisper), or from supraglottal constrictions in the oral cavity (producing aperiodic sounds only).

Ohala characterises the function of this complex device as the production of local *direct current* (dc), or one-way, air-pressure changes (*compression*, in egressive airstreams, or *rarefaction*, in ingressive airstreams), which result in generalised *alternating current* (ac) wave forms (through the elastic recoil effects of air particles). This dc-to-ac transduction is carried out with con-comitant modulation of the signal, certain frequencies being amplified over others, by means of the continuous adjustment of the shape and size of the resonating chambers.

Using this schematic overview as a guide, we shall now briefly examine the more important components in a little more detail.

The lungs

These are two large spongy masses, enclosed in an airtight sack (the *pleura*) inside the ribcage. As the thoracic muscles expand and raise the ribcage, and the diaphragm (the floor of the lung cavity) is tensed and lowered, the lungs expand within the pleura and air is drawn into them. As the thoracic and diaphragmatic muscles relax, the ribcage falls and the lungs are compressed over the abdomen, expelling the air. This process, cyclically repeated, results in normal (or *tidal*) breathing. The lungs never expel all their air; as much as 30 per cent remains behind, even with maximal expiration. Tidal breathing, and breathing for speech, can therefore best be considered against the remaining usable (or *vital*) capacity (constituting about 5 litres in a full-grown man).

Tidal breathing operates in the midrange, volumetrically, usually not expelling to less than 40 per cent, nor inhaling to greater than 60 per cent, of vital capacity. Breaths occur at the rate of about twelve to twenty per minute, with inspiratory and expiratory phases being of roughly equal duration (50–50 per cent) of the breath cycle. For speech, a number of changes occur. While the number of breaths per minute stays roughly the same, the breathing profile is markedly different. Inspiration is accomplished swiftly (only 13 per cent of the breath cycle), up to a typically higher percentage of vital capacity. The expiratory phase is then prolonged (to 87 per cent of the breath cycle, to sustain an efficient period of speech). This prolongation is achieved by the muscles of the larynx in controlling expiration; and by the muscles of the ribcage only gradually returning to their position of rest; i.e. they are acting against (a) the *elastic recoil* of the lungs and ribcage; (b) the constriction of the airflow through the larynx; (c) to some extent also the *torque* of twisted cartilages in the ribcage; and (d) the *gravitational pull* on the raised ribcage and lungs. (The gamma fibres of the thoracic nerves are crucial to this sustained, posture-adjusted movement.) As the vital capacity returns to its normal lower level (around 40 per cent), one of two things may happen: either sufficient speech has been articulated for a new breath to be taken; or the speaker wishes to go a little bit further. In this latter case, contraction of the ribcage muscles results in further air being expelled, down towards (but, of course, rarely reaching) the absolute lower limit of vital capacity. (See figure 2.16.) Thus, the control of breathing for speech, and the switching from muscles of the ribcage to those of the abdomen/diaphragm, may be intimately bound up with the planning ahead of what the speaker wishes to say, and how he or she wishes to express it.

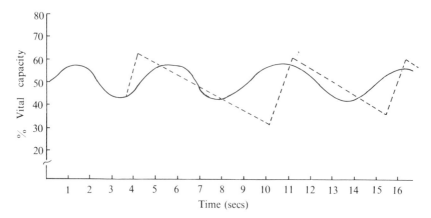

Figure 2.16 Breathing for speech (dotted line, superimposed on basic sinusoidal pattern of 'tidal' breathing). See text for discussion. (Based on Borden and Harris 1980: figs. 4.30, 4.31, p. 73.)

The larynx and pharynx

This is a cartilage complex, which forms a box-like extension of the *trachea* (windpipe) leading up from the converged bronchial tubes of the lungs. It is provided with movable plates at the sides (the *arytenoid* cartilages) and front (the *thyroid* cartilage) which can be tilted, slid and swivelled into various positions by (the arytenoid and cricothyroid) muscles. The arytenoid cartilage muscles are responsible for the adduction of two internally attached muscles which form the *vocal cords*, and which have their own range of movements. They can thus assume a wide range of postures, accurately controlled, in various states of tension. As they do so, the space between them (the *glottis*) is either closed off completely or set at two stages of opening. At fullest opening, for voiceless speech sounds, the glottal area in cross-section is only half that of the trachea below, and this produces the so-called Bernoulli effect, which speeds up the airflow (since speed of airflow, considered as the velocity of air particles, is inversely proportional to the cross-sectional area of the tract). At partial opening, the glottis is actually relatively closed, for the production of voiced sounds. The larynx can also be raised or lowered, to shorten or lengthen the lower (pharyngeal) tube of the supralaryngeal vocal tract. The pharynx can additionally be altered by movement of the root of the tongue and the muscles in the wall of the pharynx itself. All these modifications affect the acoustic properties of the lower tube.

The oral and nasal cavities

These two cavities can be utilised either simultaneously or independently by lowering or raising the velum, and by opening or closing the mouth at a number of points. The position of the velum is controlled by muscles which run round the rear of the oral cavity and the nasopharynx, innervated by the accessory nerve (CN XI).

The remaining (majority of) muscles of the tongue are innervated by the hypoglossal nerve (CN XII) and control all other movements of this organ. The velum and tongue can be thought of as valves for the stopping and guiding of the airflow in the supralaryngeal tract. The remaining valve that we should mention here is formed by the lips, activated by the ring-like orbicular oris muscle, innervated by the facial nerve (CN VII).

This concludes our survey of the main neurophysiological properties of the human articulatory system. What we have described is, at both neurological and physiological levels, a complex of many discrete components, whose functioning as an integrated system for speech production is dependent on the highest neuromotor (and neurosensory) skills that are to be found in any sort of human behaviour. We shall consider models of this system in a later chapter. But we must not forget that the story of speech production, as far as we have taken it here, needs to be taken a stage further, since the movement of articulators is only the beginning of the aerodynamic phase, the creation of the airborne signal (section 2.5.5). But first we must consider the case of the manual production system.

Writing

We shall not go into great detail here (see Stelmach 1978), since the operation of the fingers, hand and arm are accessible to casual observation in a way in which the vocal tract is not. But we shall make a few remarks on the nature of the system in the light of what we have noted for the articulatory system.

First, however, we must note a fundamental distinction. On the one hand, there is the situation where the movements of the hand–arm system are directly representative of the categories and distinctions recognised in the language being expressed (as in the case of sign languages such as British Sign Language or American Sign Language). See Bellugi (1980) for a discussion of such categories and expressive devices in American Sign Language, and for the view that, in such a situation, Broca's area may be involved in the sequencing of hand movements much as it is in the sequencing of the articulatory gestures of spoken language. On the other hand, we have the situation where the function of the arm–hand movements is to fashion symbols (characters) that have a conventional relationship with elements of the spoken language. Our remarks below relate to this latter situation. There is a further type of situation, in which manual gestures (key-pressings, arm movements, etc.) generate symbols (Morse code, semaphore, etc.) that represent a simple code on the characters of the written language – this too we shall leave out of our account below.

Our concern, then, is with handwriting and typing, since these are the ordinary types of language performance that most educated adults make contact with. As such, the physiological factors we shall consider are those that form the basis of the skilled arm, hand and finger movements that result in written language-forms, from the gross gestures of the graffiti artist wielding an aerosol can over a wall, to the small and careful emendations of a text editor.

Given this delimitation of the sorts of hand–arm functions we are considering, we may note the following characteristics:

> the hand–arm system is more integral and localised than the vocal tract;
>
> it is not specifically 'there for writing', hence is recruited to the expression of language, like the vocal tract;
>
> unlike the vocal tract, it is not obviously specialised for this function; the pen is made to fit the hand, rather than vice versa (though we may note that the usual 'qwerty' keyboard layout has its origins in the avoidance of key-clashing in early mechanical typewriters, rather than in manual convenience);
>
> in writing function, the hand and arm form a partly closed system, with fingers and thumb in reciprocal agonist–antagonist relationship (though with simultaneous and coordinated arm sweeps across the page); by contrast, in typing, they function more as an open system, with two hands, and fingers and thumbs acting in overlapping simultaneous and coordinated movements;
>
> the hand–arm system typically acts on a tool, rather than operating directly on the natural medium of impression; nor does the hand–arm system, or the tool it operates, directly manipulate light, which is the medium of reception through the optical system, so there is a fundamental discontinuity of transmission in the written medium;
>
> in writing, the spatial aspects of characters are those of shape, and are encoded in the manual movements that generate them; by contrast, in typing these shape aspects are already encoded, partly in terms of hand/finger identification and partly by the relative position of keys within a restricted space.

These considerations suggest not only that the hand–arm system has its own distinct biomechanics compared to those of the local tract, but also that it can function as one or another of two rather different biomechanical systems, in typewriting as opposed to handwriting: this latter observation is borne out by the common experience that learning to type properly is a matter of developing a new set of manual skills.

2.5.5 *The dynamics of speech and writing*

We bring our review to a close in this chapter with a consideration of the sorts of influences on the production systems that might arise from the nature of the substances to be acted upon: air, in the case of speech, and the various media of writing.

The aerodynamic phase

We shall start by considering the fundamental source of sound energy, in the larynx. Here, the vocal cords can be set to certain appropriate positions and degrees of tension so that, as air passes through them, they periodically open and close, at certain frequencies. Whatever laryngeal frequency is found at any point in the stream of speech, it is called the fundamental frequency (f_0). It may rise or fall, depending on the setting of the vocal cords and the subglottal air pressure. The more slowly the vocal cords open and close, the lower the pitch and vice versa. It is the subglottal air pressure overcoming the vocal-cord tension which forces the cords apart (the opening phase of the cycle). What causes them to close again is partly their elastic recoil (dependent again on their tension at any moment) and partly the Bernoulli effect, which is dependent on the speed of air passage through the glottis. The Bernoulli effect is found if you blow through the ragged remains of a burst rubber balloon; as you blow down the stem the limp rubber remnants will flap audibly as they are alternately pushed apart and sucked together by the air issuing through them. It is the bursts or pulses of air, 'chopped' off the airstream as it rushes through the glottis, that make the noise of speech (rather than the banging together of the vocal cords). Sound waves are thus set pulsating through the supralaryngeal vocal tract.

First in one 'tube' (the pharynx), then in another, divisible, 'tube' (the oro-nasal cavities), a series of complex modifications can now operate on this fundamental signal. As the tubes assume different shapes cross-sectionally, or effectively alter their lengths, different resonance patterns are superimposed on the signal, emphasising particular frequencies and damping others. This process gives rise to bands of energy, or *formants*, at various frequencies, which are thus characteristic of certain vocal-tract configurations.

In addition, the airflow can be interrupted and constricted at a number of places. When a fluid such as air, or water, is allowed to flow freely through a channel, it behaves as an integral mass. In these conditions it flows smoothly (exhibits 'laminar' flow). When the channel is constricted, however, there comes a point when the mass starts to break up (exhibits 'turbulent' flow). The degree of constriction required to produce this effect is inversely related to the velocity of the fluid: i.e. a lesser degree of constriction will produce the effect if the velocity is greater, and vice versa. This constant relationship is represented in the Reynolds number, which varies according to the shape of any given channel and the nature of the fluid flowing through it. The human vocal tract represents one type of channel, and air is one of the fluids that passes through it. The Reynolds number for airflow through a static vocal tract at rest is around 1700. Since this number may correspond to nothing in your previous experience, you may well find it uninterpretable. But what is important for us is that, if this relationship is plotted along two axes, one representing changes in channel area (since we are talking about constrictions of the vocal tract, we are dealing with areas of around 5mm^2 to 40mm^2), and the other the velocity of the volume of air (in cm^3 per second), a stable picture emerges. The turbulence that is produced in each case yields a source of noise, which is secondary to and quite distinct from, that of the f_0. Whereas the f_0 is a pulsar noise – it has cycles, or is said to be 'periodic' – the turbulence noises are all much less regular; they are erratic, or *aperiodic*. These aperiodic noises are typical of fricative consonants, [f], [θ], [s], [ʃ], [ʂ], [ɹ], [ç], [x], [χ]. Because these consonants are articulated with rather different degrees of constriction, they demand rather different volume velocities to bring about their characteristic 'tearing' or turbulent sond. The relationship between their volume velocity and the degree of constriction in the oral tract in producing them is constant, however, and is expressed by the Reynolds number of 1700, to a high degree of accuracy. That is, they all lie along the same slope, which also characterises the way air flows through the unconstricted vocal tract (fig. 2.17).

The point of this discussion is to emphasise the importance of the aerodynamic phase in considering the production of speech. After taking account of all the activity of the central and peripheral nervous systems, all the muscles (around sixty of them) and the individual articulatory organs (some half-dozen of these), we may consider that the air passing through the constantly altering vocal tract represents the ultimate organ of speech. If the articulators had to move some other fluid than air in speech, they would have rather different tasks to perform, and would show rather different characteristics of movement. Air is the medium, therefore, which helps to govern the movement of articulators which yield the sound signal, receive its modifications and finally transmit it beyond the lips of the speaker, in the form of complex sound

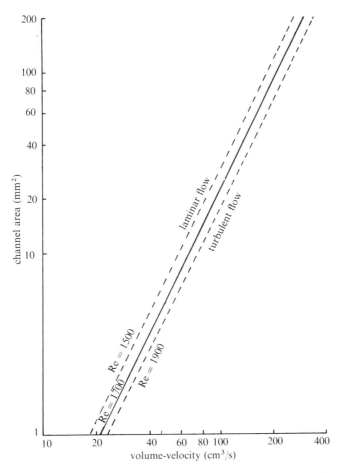

Figure 2.17 The relationship between cross-sectional areas of articulatory channel and volume–velocity for a critical Reynolds number of 1700. (From Catford 1977: fig. 8, p. 43.)

waves. And these sound waves have the sort of properties that the auditory system is designed to process.

The dynamics of writing

For handwriting, a number of features appear to derive from the physical characteristics of hand, pen and paper. We may start (see Viviani and Terzuolo 1983) by noting 500msec. as a typical execution time for the letter a, with a distance from start to finish being of the order of 15mm in this example. Average velocity along the figural line of the letter tends to increase or decrease in proportion with the size of the letter (the 'Isochrony Principle'; 1983: 110), a global property of handwriting that tends to be relatively stable, though it can be varied at will. However, velocity along the line of the letter shape is not constant, but varies (between 0 and 200 + mm per sec.) in inverse proportion to the degree of curvature at any point along the line, such that segments of similar radius of curvature tend to be executed in similar times (the 'Isogony Principle'; 1983: 107). (See fig. 2.18.) This is a local property that may reflect the inertia of the hand–pen mass. Relatively large mass-changes (heavier or lighter writing implements) can be swiftly accommodated by the system, but increasing the frictional properties of the system (e.g. smooth vs rough surface, ballpoint vs pencil) has the effect of reducing the size of writing, though the phenomenon of 'Motor Equivalence' (1983: 110) is observed, in that form characteristics are preserved, across variations in size.

In typewriting (see also Viviani and Terzuolo 1983), we are dealing with movements of the order of seven to eight strikes (key-pressings) per second, with interstrike intervals of around 120 to 140msec., and reaction times (from letter choice to completion of strike) of around 300msec. The speed of strike sequences systematically varies according to the degree of independence of muscle systems involved: thus, it is greatest in the case of alternating hands (around 110msec. intervals), rather less in alternating fingers of the same hand (around 130msec.), and least in successive strikes with the same finger (around 160msec.). There are other determinants of speed of striking, including word structure, which we shall more appropriately address in chapter 4. But we may note that established word-rhythm patterns are to some extent individualistic, and, once established in an experienced typist, tend to be invariant across changes in mechanical loading of the keys (e.g. the sort of difference found between a heavy old manual typewriter and a modern electronic type). But these patterns do depend on touch/pressure exteroceptive feedback: 'imaginary' typing, with no keyboard, fails to maintain the stability of developed typing patterns.

2.6 Conclusions

2.6.1 *Comparative considerations*

We have already drawn some comparisons between the written and spoken language signals (ch. 1). Among the relevant comparisons to consider here, we shall concentrate on the biological aspects of how the two sorts of language signal are perceived, centrally processed and generated.

Perceptually, two very different sorts of biological system are involved. The auditory and visual systems are chiefly alike only in that both are located in the head, involving short pathways to the central processing areas in the brain.

Figure 2.18 Binet's nineteenth-century recording of the dynamics of handwriting, using a modified version of Edison pen which burned the paper with a spark every 5msec. Velocity can be estimated by the inverse of the distance between successive points. (From Viviani and Terzuolo 1983: fig. 1, p. 107, courtesy of the Binet Archives, Paris.)

Beyond this, the differences are more striking. The auditory system has a number of preliminary signal-processing stages, mediated via accessory structures (Davis 1961) prior to the point at which mechanical-to-neural transduction takes place. By contrast, the visual system allows for neural encoding to a considerable level of complexity before the processing of the signal leaves the eye. The significance of this observation may be sought in the fact that the auditory system is closely linked with the vocal-tract system, by virtue of the signal properties of the speech channel, whereas the hand–eye channel is fundamentally discontinuous. Biologically, this distinction may be reflected in the possibility of an articulatory–motor involvement in speech perception (without there being a corresponding manual involvement in reading). If this is so, there may be a case for the physical, and biological, priority of the spoken over the written language. The auditory system, like the vocal tract, appears to be rather specialised for processing the sort of signal which is found in speech. It is also a widely held view that speech perception (as well as production) is a particularly impressive category of biological performance. By contrast, the visual system, equipped to face the challenge of perceiving the physical world, with its moving, three-dimensional objects and events, may appear to have no biological capacity constraints in the processing of the typical two-dimensional, rather stable shapes of written language symbols. They are typically presented to the visual system as figures that are both well formed and relatively uncontaminated by background features; e.g. they are usually presented on a clean page or other surface. (Handwriting samples may violate the first of these conditions, and may cause distinct problems as a result.) What may be particularly difficult for the visual system, as far as written language signals are concerned, is the sustained processing of rather dense linear arrays, as typified within alphabetic systems by the small letter-shape differentiation cues found, e.g., between *d* vs *b* vs *p* vs *q*. It seems likely that, as far as biological issues are concerned, these are problems that are associated particularly with initial or immature reading strategies that are based on individual letters rather than larger-sized units.

Concerning central brain processing, the impression we are left with is of a biological system that incorporates both speech and written language aspects, but with major speech-processing areas located more centrally and more locally to each other, while the major written language areas are situated more distantly. Notwithstanding this distinction, however, it appears that the integration of written-language processing and speech has aspects that are accommodated within the central language area. Functionally, we may say that the incorporation is achieved to some degree neutrally (reflecting the fact that the meaning of a spoken utterance may be identical with that of some written expression), and to some degree distinctly (acknowledging the frank differences between reading and hearing, or between writing and speaking). Thus, to illustrate from the case of acquisition, we may think of certain aspects of written language awareness as being peculiar to that modality (including learning how to manipulate writing implements, and the development of effective letter-scansion strategies); but other aspects are somehow integrated with existing language knowledge which is based on the speech mode. A striking demonstration of the distinct-yet-integrated nature of written language abilities *vis-à-vis* speech abilities is found in cases of disruption to language processing as a result of brain damage: it appears that both written and spoken language abilities may co-inhabit the central language area in such a way that they are regularly impaired together in instances of focal damage to brain tissue, yet differentially in terms of severity and quality (see some further discussion in ch. 8, section 3.2).

Concerning output, we have seen that, although the hand–arm and articulatory systems are quite distantly located from each other, their neurophysiological control characteristics are quite similar, down to the lower levels of muscle innervation. But the vocal tract appears to be rather specialised for producing the speech signal, which itself appears to be a rather special category of performance, in terms of both speed and complexity of operations; by contrast, we may wonder how far writing represents a challenge to the control of the hand–arm system, as compared to the control that is demanded in, say, spinning, weaving, knitting, modelling clay, or a host of other manual activities. In this connection, we should probably regard the phenomenon of skilled typing abilities (a late development in the means of written language production) as a rather specialised skill which is somewhat aside from the biological capacity for written language production; just as, for example, the dexterity shown in the manipulation of keyboard musical instruments by those who have trained in this skill is rather distinct from the biological basis for music.

2.6.2 *Parallel versus serial processing*

It remains to make a final point concerning the relevance of biological issues to language processing. We suggested earlier that we should not expect knowledge concerning these issues to provide direct answers to many of our questions about, for example, how we perceive speech sounds vs other sounds in our environment, or how we access words in our mental dictionary, or construct or comprehend utterances. But it may provide clues to the nature of the processes that may be involved in these operations, and such clues may eventually provide some constraints on models and theories of language processing.

To illustrate, we may take the issue of *parallel* vs *serial* processing. At many points in our discussion we have encountered parallel processing, for instance in the transmission of neural impulses along parallel fibres of the auditory and optic nerves, and in the upper motor neurons. In this type of processing different parts of the input signal, or the motor-control pattern, are carried independently by different elements in the transmission system. We have also at a number of points leaned rather to a serial view of processing, by suggesting that processing of some aspects of the signal may be completed in one part of the biological system before the results of this processing stage are handed on to another part of the system. Thus, for example, we have noted the boosting of the speech-relevant frequencies in the outer and middle ear before the auditory signal is transferred to the cochlea; and the generating of motor sequences in the subcortical nuclei before their transmission via the upper motor-neuron system.

There is actually an issue here which our attempts to describe the functioning of biological structures have not addressed. Which processes are truly carried out serially, with all aspects of an earlier stage being completed before the following stage is initiated, and which are handled by independent and parallel means? We shall not attempt to do more than raise this issue here, and to note that (a) apparently clear differences in serial vs parallel processing may be observed in some areas, but that (b) much processing may be carried on in a mixed fashion. Understanding how frequency and amplitude characteristics are encoded in the neural-firing patterns of the auditory system may be a case in point. The place theory works in terms of which elements in the system are activated in parallel, while the time theory looks instead to the information carried in the phasing of responses in relation to each other, where each phase, or package of activation, may represent a distinct stage in the analysis of the signal. The difficulty encountered by each of these theories may indicate that the biological processes involved have to be thought of as fundamentally mixed serial–parallel types.

3
Sources of evidence for the language system

3.1 Introduction

3.1.1 *Preview*

In this chapter, we consider the third of our designated elements of psycholinguistics: the nature of the language system. Information about the properties of this abstract system constitutes a further constraint – along with those arising out of our considerations in the previous two chapters – on the possible forms that language processing might take.

Our approach will review the available sources of evidence, and will concentrate initially on some general features of naturalistic language data, in contrast to experimentally elicited data. We shall introduce a sample of adult conversational speech (section 3.1.3); then we shall consider two specific types of property in this data, hesitation phenomena (non-fluencies) (section 3.2) and grammatical characteristics, including lexical, phrasal and clausal elements and patterns (section 3.3). It should be noted that, regrettably, we shall not have anything to say on hesitation phenomena in the production of written language, nor on the distinctive grammatical features of written language: these topics are too large to be adequately treated here. See Griffiths (1986) for a temporal measure of constituent structure organisation in copying of written language; and Perera (1984) for developmental aspects.

Finally, we shall examine the evidence that has been gleaned from various studies of spontaneously occurring errors, in speech production (slips of the tongue), auditory comprehension (slips of the ear), writing (slips of the pen) and reading (slips of the eye).

3.1.2 *Sources of evidence*

Gathering evidence on an abstract and complex entity such as the language system is not an easy undertaking. Certain clues as to the nature of the system to be investigated have come from linguistic sources: most influential among these has been the Chomskyan approach, which, since the early 1960s, has helped to define what may be called the modern period of psycholinguistics. In the early part of this period, experimental investigations were carried out quite intensively on specific aspects of language behaviour that were suggested by current theories of the language system. Within this framework, it was thought possible that psycholinguistic research might permit *performance* data to be interpreted in such a way as to shed light on the operations of the *competence* system which linguistic theory attempted to model (Chomsky 1965).

The sorts of specific questions that were addressed by these early experiments tended to focus on *comprehension processing*, and *syntax* (following the emphasis of Chomsky's work), particularly: (a) the nature of linguistic units and their phrase-structure configurations (form classes and phrases, as discussed, e.g. in Radford 1981: ch. 2); and (b) the role of transformational operations, as they were then conceived (there were some radical developments in how these were formulated during the period, e.g. Chomsky 1957; Katz and Postal 1964; Chomsky 1965). The use of experimental methods was effective in the rapid building up of a body of research evidence bearing on specific issues within the Chomskyan paradigm. For (a), linguistic units, the sorts of methods used included: getting subjects to perceive extraneous sounds in relation to auditorily presented sentences (the so-called 'click location' task, Fodor and Bever 1965); asking subjects to attend to a sentence and then presenting a single word from it, as a 'probe' for the recall of the next word to it in the original sentence (the 'probe latency' method; see Ammon 1968); asking subjects to press a button (stopping a timer) when they detected the presence of a predetermined phoneme in a sentence (the 'phoneme monitoring' technique; see Foss and Lynch 1969); and asking subjects to judge the degree of relatedness between words within sentences (Levelt 1970). For (b), transformational processes, subjects were asked, for example, to match sentences presented in sets (Miller 1962); to judge whether sentences were true or false, in relation to general knowledge, or some array or pictured event (Wason 1959); to recall presented sentences (Mehler 1963); to recognise a sentence from a passage, or against a noisy background (Sachs 1967); to judge the grammaticality of real and 'semi' sentences (Marks 1967); to provide paraphrases of sentences (Stolz 1967); and to handle various aspects of ambiguous sentences (Garrett 1970). Such experimental investigations formed the stuff of psycholinguistics in that period, and are much discussed in the earlier textbooks (e.g. Slobin 1971; Glucksberg and Danks 1975; Clark and Clark 1977; Foss and Hakes 1978); a penetrating review is provided in Levelt (1978).

An early finding was that different experimental tasks tended to yield results that supported conflicting conclusions about the organisation of underlying competence. For instance, on the matching task, the hypothesised relationship within the language system between affirmative and negative forms of sentences (construed as mediated by the operation of a transformational rule) appeared to be closer than that between active and passive forms: but on the true–false task, this finding was exactly reversed. In some cases (as in this example), the discrepancy could be accounted for in terms of a *task effect*: to perform well in a matching task, subjects have to pay attention to the *forms* of sentence stimuli, rather than their *meanings*, and, in terms of form, the negative version is only slightly different from the affirmative, while the passive is markedly different from the active. It was also pointed out that considerations of functional context play a role in the way subjects perform with linguistic structures such as sentences: thus, for instance, 'contexts of plausible denial' (Wason 1961, an early example of recognised context effects) facilitated the use of negative structures.

Competence and performance

It was generally concluded (e.g. Fodor and Garrett 1966), on the basis of such early findings, that the relationship between competence and performance was essentially indirect. A number of considerations tended towards this view, some of them relating to the concept of competence, others more closely to that of performance. For instance Hymes (1972) and Campbell and Wales (1970) independently pointed out that linguistic competence as described in Chomsky (1965) fails to make an important distinction between specifically grammatical competence (knowledge of the rules of sentence structure) and the more general competence involving knowledge of how to implement the rules, in situationally appropriate fashion: here was one possible source of the indirect fit between experimental data (reflecting contextual or task effects) and rules proposed in models of (grammatical) competence.

This was enough to suggest to some researchers that psycholinguistic enquiry might profitably disengage from particular versions of current linguistic theory, in order to pursue its own objectives (e.g. Sutherland 1966): essentially, these were taken to be bound up in the search for the 'mental grammar' (MG) (Fillenbaum 1971). From this standpoint, the existence of task and context effects suggested that the concept of performance was also in need of subdivision, to take account of the observation that different categories of performance might yield their own versions of how the MG was constituted. Suppose the MG, as a cognitive entity, is to be thought of not as a fixed, unitary system, but rather as a complex of elements, which might reorganise, in the face of particular task demands, in order to optimise performance in specific situations; then a natural further consideration was that, if the experimental tasks required subjects to perform in ways that were markedly different from everyday functions of language outside the psycholinguistics laboratory, their results might have little bearing on more ordinary sorts of language behaviour.

Regarding the performance–competence distinction, however, a more radical consideration was this: if the MG may reorganise to meet specific performance requirements, then the linguist's model of it (the linguist's grammar, or LG) may reflect the nature of such reorganisation. And, if the type of performance involved is fairly unusual – having linguistic intuitions, and subjecting them to hypothesis testing, in the search for significant generalisations – then the result may embody certain properties that are not present in the very different tasks called for by experimental investigations, and which in any case are 'irrelevant for most ongoing speech behaviour' (Bever 1970). For essentially this reason, Watt (1970) proposed calling the LG an 'abstract performative grammar' (APG), rather than 'competence', thus calling into question the very nature of the competence–performance distinction. See Fillenbaum (1971) for a review; and Hockett (1970) for some similar considerations, from the linguistic viewpoint.

At this point it is worth emphasising that it is not our purpose to say that subjective, intuition-based enquiry in linguistics leads to unrealistic results. The subjective method of observation is perfectly viable, as long as it is subjected to suitable constraints (e.g. hypothesis testing, and intersubjective agreement). It is not even radically different from the objective method (Woodworth 1931), and it is interesting to observe, within psycholinguistic methodology, a reintroduction of *subjective* methods, using *introspection* into ongoing language processing. Introspection was much used, and discussed, by psycholinguistic researchers in the last century (see Woodworth 1931; Blumenthal 1970), but fell out of favour subsequently, perhaps partly as a result of the emphasis on *objective* methods that characterised the *behaviourist* approach (see the introduction to Bloomfield's 1933 book, *Language*, for an indication of the impact of this tradition on language research, at least in the USA). Within linguistics, the systematic exploitation of intuitional data has proved highly successful, not just within the Chomskyan paradigm (see Bresnan 1978; Gazdar 1981), yielding some very sophisticated models of the LG; and current work involving subjective methods in psycholinguistics (Faerch and Kasper 1987) may have an important contribution to make to the study of certain language processes. The point is, rather, that, as far as the psycholinguist is concerned, the LG should be interpreted as one (particularly well-documented) sighting among many glimpses of the elusive MG. For a more recent statement of Chomsky's position, see Chomsky (1986), where the technical concepts 'E (externalised)-language' and 'I (internalised)-language' are used for essentially the performance–competence distinction. Chomsky's focus is, in these terms, on I-language, though he recognises that it is an 'inexact working hypothesis' that 'informant judgments give us "direct evidence" as to the structure of the I-language' (1986: 36).

3.1.3 *Naturalistic data*

We have looked at these issues in the recent history of psycholinguistics in order to provide a context for appreciating some current trends. Among these has been a general perception of a need to widen the basis of evidence, in two general ways: to broaden the range of investigation beyond the syntax of individual sentences to discourse structure and pragmatics; and to collect data from a range of different sources, in order to note the direction in which converging lines of evidence might lie, and to permit the documentation of task effects where necessary.

In particular, the *naturalistic* (as opposed to *experimental*) approach to gathering data for psycholinguistic research has tended to become increasingly central. 'Naturalistic' is a very general term, covering a range of situations that represent the natural, everyday, contextually embedded and communicatively informative uses of language. Surreptitious recording of spontaneous language behaviour is an example. Such data has traditionally been highly regarded as a potentially valuable source of evidence, but its use has been circumscribed by (a) the unstructured nature of the data – if the researcher is interested, for example, in certain types of temporal specification, it may be difficult to direct the elicitation towards this area, and very low incidences of the relevant data may be found; (b) problems in the analysing (and even the basic transcription) of large and frequently intractable bodies of data, full of hesitations, false starts and incompletions; and (c) difficulties in specifying descriptive baselines for effective comparisons between different samples.

In this book, we shall review a range of studies making use of experimental as well as naturalistic, and subjective as well as objective methods. However, it is still the case that the resources of naturalistic data have more potential than has been exploited hitherto, and in this connection there may be a particular contribution to be made by the use of descriptive linguistic techniques. In sections 3.2 and 3.3, we shall try to show some ways in which this contribution may be implemented.

For this purpose, we shall illustrate with reference to a sample that approximates to some suitable representation of conversational English, as set out in figure 3.1. This is taken from Crystal and Davy (1975), and represents a type of surreptitious recording of 'conversational' speech. This is actually a vague term, potentially varying along several dimensions, from formal to informal,

A well |what's the · |what's the 'failure with the ↑FÒOTBALL| I
   mean |this · |this I don't 'really ↑SÈE| I mean it · |cos the
   ↑MÒNEY| · |how 'much does it 'cost to get ìN| |down the ↑RÒAD|
   |NÒW|

B   I |think it ↑probably – it| 5
   |probably 'is the ↑MÒNEY| for |what you ↑GÈT| you |KNÓW| – erm
   I was |reading in the ↑paper this ↑MÒRNING| a a |CHÀP| he's a
   DI|RÈCTOR| of a |big ↑CÒMPANY| in |BÌRMINGHAM| – who was th
   the |world's ↑number 'one ↑FÒOTBALL 'fan| he |used to ↑SPÈND|
   a|bout a 'thousand a ↑YÈAR| |watching FÒOTBALL| you |KNÓW| 10
   (C: |CÒO|) – he's he's |watched 'football in ↑every n · on
   ↑every 'league · 'ground in ÉNGLAND| |all 'ninety TWÓ|
   (A *laughs*) – and he's |been to A↑M̄ERICA| to |watch ↑West
   BRŌMWICH 'playing in A'merica| he's · he's |been to the la
   · to |ÒH| · the |LÀST| f f |two or 'three 'world CÙP| · |world   15
   CÙP| · mat |THÍNGS| you KNÓW| · |TÓURNAMENTS| – – and he |goes
   to ↑all the 'matches AWÁY| you |KNÓW| |European ↑CÙP 'matches
   and 'everything| that |ÈNGLISH teams are PLÁYING in| he's all
   'over the ↑WÒRLD 'watching it you SÉE| – |THÌS YÉAR| he's
   |watched ↑twenty 'two GÀMES| – |SÒ 'far| |this YÈAR| which is   20
   a|bout · FÌFTY per 'cent| of his |NǑRMAL| (C: |good LÒRD|) · and
   |even ↑HÈ's getting 'browned ↑ÓFF| and |HÈ was SÁYING| that
   erm – you can |go to a NǏGHTCLUB| in |BǏRMINGHAM| – – and
   |watch ↑Tony BÉNNET| · for a|bout ↑thirty ↑BÒB| – |something
   like THÍS| a |night with ↑Tony ↑BÉNNET| – |have a 'nice ↑MĒAL| 25
   · in · |very · ↑plushy SURRŌUNDINGS| very |WĀRM|
   |NÍCE| |PLÈASANT| – says it |CÒSTS him| a|bout the ↑SÀME
   a'mount of MÓNEY| to |go and ↑ sit in a ↑breezy 'windy STÁND| –
   (A & C *laugh*) on a · on a |WÒODEN BÉNCH| – to |WĀTCH| a |rather
   BÓRING 'game of ↑FÒOTBALL| with |no ↑PERSONÁLITY| and |all   30
   DEFÉNSIVE| and |ÈVERYTHING| he |says it's just ↑KÌLLING itself|
   you |KNÓW| (A: |YÈAH| C: |M̀|) – they're |not 'giving the
   'enter'tainment they ÚSED to 'give| the erm – CON|DÌTIONS have|
   if |ÀNYTHING| are |not are f DE|TĚRIORATED| and er (C: in |what
   WÀY|) they're |charging f ↑three 'times what they ↑ÙSED to| ·   35
   or |four 'times what they ↑ÙSED to|

C in what |way have con'ditions DETÈRIORATED 'Gerry|

B well the |GRÒUNDS| are |scruffier than they ÚSED to be| I mean
   they |never DÒ these 'grounds ÚP| |DÒ they| I mean they're
   pro|gressively ↑ getting ↑ WÒRSE| 40

C   you |KNÓW| I |thought they ↑'ÀLWAYS had these
   'wooden 'benches and STÁNDS and 'that|

Figure 3.1   Illustrative sample of conversational English. (From Crystal and
Davy 1975: extract 1, lines 1–42, pp. 19–20.)

from contextually embedded to free, from attentive to inattentive, interested
to uninterested, and so on. Our everyday world is an environment that is constantly changing in such terms, and our language behaviour is normally responsive to such factors. So the first task is to consider the notion of 'some
suitable representation of the spoken language'. In view of this, we should first
consider the circumstances in which our passage was recorded.

The participants and the situation

The participants: the surreptitious recorder, A, is an academic
linguist; B and C are two men, aged around forty years, old friends of A. B, an
accountant, is originally from Ireland but has lived in Berkshire for some
years. C is a primary schoolteacher, originally from Yorkshire, and resident in
Berkshire for many years. The situation: B and C had been invited to have a
drink one evening at A's home (we are told that this was a regular event). The
evening started with A asking B and C to read some words into a microphone
linked to a visible tape recorder, to assist A in some research 'on accents'. This
over, the microphone was pushed slightly back, the visible tape recorder was
switched off, and the conversation started. Unknown at the time to B and C, a
hidden tape recorder was still functioning, linked to the microphone on the
nearby table. In this way, high-quality, naturalistic recording was possible.
The passage extracted comes from about an hour into the conversation. B and
C are very relaxed (as also is A). B has been complaining about falling
standards in entertainment and sport. A tries to steer him round from talking
about the state of the cinema to football.

The first point to notice about the situation from which the sample is drawn
is that language behaviour itself is in the forefront of the evening's activities.
This is underlined all the more by the considerations that the participants all
share in a high standard of education, and are present 'for a chat', in relation
to which other activities such as recording their accents, having a few drinks,
etc. are fairly clearly subordinate: a participant under these circumstances
who did not engage in the conversation at some point during the evening
would be regarded as not having played his or her proper role. The fact that
A, the host, is an academic linguist must also be considered to have played a
part in shaping the sort of attitudes that B and C bring to their primary social
task on this evening.

The second point to notice is that, in the extract, A is attempting to guide
the conversation into a new direction, while, for the moment, C is content to
form part of the audience (he takes the floor subsequently). A thus intervenes
briefly at the start of this passage, then leaves B to develop his theme. Towards
the end, C comes in with a couple of specific contributions, to which B

115

responds in a way which suggests that he has come to the end of his 'piece'. We have here, then, an extract which displays its own 'discourse contour', from initiation of topic, through its development and ending in its closure.

So, when we claim that this is 'representative' of 'normal' language behaviour, we are actually putting forward a fairly specific type of such behaviour. This is inevitable, and is no drawback, as long as we bear in mind that generalisation from this type to other types of normal language production may fail to hold. So much for our first requirement, of representativeness.

Other requirements

A second requirement is that we should be dealing with some reasonably comprehensive example of what we are trying to understand. To some extent, this is achieved inasmuch as we are looking at a complete discourse unit, in the sense suggested above. This, however, is as yet an undecided matter, and inevitably our expository sample is too small to be seriously considered in this respect.

A third requirement involves the issue of the *level* of representation. The text generally ignores segmental phonetic characteristics, other than those rough indications which are embodied in the standard orthography, but a number (not all) of prosodic features are marked, including some stress, pitch-change and pause phenomena. How do we decide what sort of information to include, and what to leave out? This is as yet an unanswerable question; but we shall see, as our discussion progresses, that the level of representation displayed here (as well as its limited degree of comprehensiveness) allows us to raise most, if not all, of the issues in current research on language production. We shall therefore finesse this requirement and proceed; but in section 3.3 below we shall recognise the need for a transcription of the data at a further level of representation, the *grammatical* level.

3.1.4 *Naturally displayed evidence*

After these preliminary considerations, we turn to the nature of the 'naturally displayed evidence' (Garrett 1982) that such a sample of speech affords. What, in principle, is available for description? And how far can we progress from describable effects to presumed causes? We shall take up the first question here.

The taxonomy set out in figure 3.2 displays what we intuitively think of as 'normal' speech production in the centre of an array of more or less 'normal' concomitants; to the left are *filled pauses* (*er*, *um*, etc.) which are frequently taken to be associated with difficulties in formulation and/or word-finding difficulties, and *silent pauses* and *breath pauses*. Silent pauses are often recognised

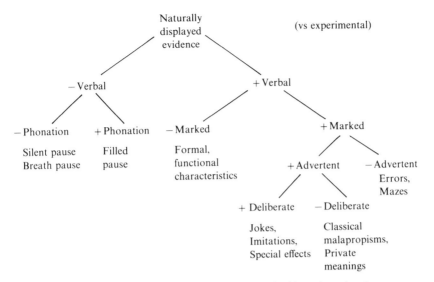

Figure 3.2 Taxonomy of naturally displayed evidence in spoken-language production. (Partially based on discussion in Garrett 1982: 21–4; Zwicky 1982: 116–23.)

as listener-orientated devices, inserted by the speaker in order to clarify the structuring of the message; others may be speaker-based, reflecting similar difficulties to those marked by filled pauses. Still others may be both speaker-based and 'listener-friendly', e.g. marking the beginning and end of a speaker's afterthought. They frequently occur with filled pauses, in a way that makes the distinction between filled vs silent pauses seem artificial: we may think of these as 'partially filled pauses'. Other sorts of partially filled pauses are found when verbal categories, such as *well, y'see, I mean, y'know*, and other forms are used, in certain contexts, as devices for maintaining production. The point is that they are, in these functions, not to be accorded full grammatical status (see the discussion in section 3.3 below), but are to be treated along with types of pause filler. Terminologising somewhat, we may refer to *er, um*, etc. as 'pause fillers' (the more usual term, 'filled pauses', is less satisfactory, implying that these sounds are coterminous with the pauses they fill) and to the more verbal forms, in these functions, as 'pause words/phrases'. Pauses may be partially filled, containing breaks as well as pause fillers and/or pause words.

Unmarked verbal behaviour can be analysed for its properties at various levels. This is essentially an exercise in corpus-based linguistic description, and as such is found chiefly in so-called 'text-linguistics' and 'discourse analysis' approaches (Freedle 1977; Brown and Yule 1983; Stubbs 1983). These are currently quite heterogeneous, with little agreed common ground except for the necessity to look at the grammatical properties of language structure and function beyond the domain of the sentence. Many such approaches tend to emphasise *either* the textual properties of the data, i.e. looking on the corpus purely as 'product' (text linguistics), *or* the psycholinguistic aspects, i.e. treating the data as potentially revealing of underlying processes (much of discourse analysis). It should be clear that, ideally, the 'process' view presupposes an adequate description of the 'product'. It is also necessary to avoid a rigid division of linguistic description into 'grammar' (sentence-based) vs 'discourse analysis' (beyond the sentence); phenomena such as *anaphora* operate within and between sentences (referring-links between words, as between an antecedent phrase *the boy* and a subsequent pronoun *he*). We shall illustrate the main features of a suitable sort of linguistic characterisation of our sample below.

We should note, before passing on, that unmarked verbal material will display a number of interesting articulatory characteristics, such as juncture phenomena and modification of articulations in specifiable grammatical environments. We shall refer more to this below and in chapter 4.

Marked, or unusual, verbal behaviour may conveniently be characterised as *advertent* or *inadvertent*, and the former as either *deliberate* or *non-deliberate* (these suggestions come from Zwicky 1982). The issue for ± advertent is whether the speaker, confronted with a transcript, or recording, would acknowledge or disclaim the intention to produce certain forms. Acknowledgement would extend to such advertent behaviour as *deliberate* distortions, ungrammaticalities, etc., e.g. for comic or imitative purposes; and also include *non-deliberate* uses of forms which the speaker believes, idiosyncratically, to be appropriate. Examples would include what Zwicky calls 'private meanings', e.g. where *raven*, of hair colour, is thought to mean something other than 'deeply black', and is used to denote some other colour (e.g. 'auburn') or property (e.g. 'lank'). Classical malapropisms also fall into this category, where idiosyncratic forms are used for certain meanings, as *exploded* for *explored*. One may also note the use of non-words, with the same intended meaning as certain real words, e.g. *acutate* for *actuate*. These last two subtypes each show form similarity between the word used and the normal word having the intended meaning, and so offer a form-based parallel to the case of private meanings.

Finally, inadvertent properties constitute the heterogeneous class of 'speech errors' – forms which the speaker attempts to correct either at the time of speaking or subsequently when they are brought to their attention. The essence of such errors in normal speech behaviour is that they do not represent the acknowledged system of the speaker. They comprise semantic misformulations ('slips of the mind'), word shifts and substitutions ('momentary malapropisms'), syntactic errors of various kinds (including 'talking oneself into a syntactic corner', see Garrett 1982), articulatory shifts and substitutions ('slips of the tongue'), and 'mazes' (including false starts, repetitions and reformulations; see Miller 1987). See section 3.4 below for further discussion.

3.2 Non-fluencies

In the transcription of our sample in figure 3.1, the following impressionistic pause markings are used (from Crystal 1969):

> . a 'brief pause', being 'perceivably shorter than (and usually half as long as) unit length';
> – a 'unit pause', being the length of 'the interval of an individual's rhythm cycle from one prominent syllable to the next';
> –– and ––– double and treble the length of unit pauses.

In addition, the pause fillers *erm*, *um*, etc. are used, frequently, though not always, in association with a pause preceding or following.

Apart from pauses, filled and unfilled (see Rochester 1973), there are a number of other phenomena that we may wish to take into consideration, under some general heading such as 'non-fluencies', or 'hesitation phenomena'. Paradoxically, some of them are characterised by a superficial fluency, at least in terms of the acoustic signal.

One type is repetitions, including those that appear to involve restarting the utterance from the beginning (e.g. *he's he's watched football . . . , it probably – it probably is the money . . .*) and those in which more local 'midstream' reformulations are attempted (e.g. *he's been to the la . to . oh . the last . . .*). Both subtypes may or may not be associated with breaks in the signal.

Another type is the use of what we have called pause words and phrases, frequently observed at the beginnings and ends of utterances (e.g. *well what's the . . . , and . . . for what you get you know*). These are often not associated with any break in the signal, but it seems useful to include them in a count of non-fluencies, since they represent abrupt troughs in the ratio of content to expression, in the production of speech.

A further type is constructional switches. These are frequently observed in constructional mazes, which end in some reformulation. These too may or may not be associated with breaks in the signal and are sometimes marked by word fillers (e.g. *conditions have if anything are not are f deteriorated, it was it in Madrid, I don't really see I mean it . . .*).

Table 3.1 *Categories of preceding context for forty-two non-fluencies immediately followed by a clausal utterance*

Preceding context	Illustration	Total
Clausal utterance	[... in Birmingham] . [who was ... football fan]	21
Other speaker	[C: coo] – [he's watched football ... in England]	8
Noun phrase	[the money] . [how much does it cost ... now]	4
Pause word/phrase	[you know] – erm [I was reading ... this morning]	3
Connective	[that] erm – [you can go ... in Birmingham]	3
Determiner	[the] . [what's the matter ... football]	3
		42

Now, there is clearly an issue concerning the use of impressionistically derived data on pause *duration* and pause *location* in the acoustic signal. We shall return to this issue below, but first we shall offer some observations on the distribution of all the non-fluencies, whether or not they involve a break in the acoustic signal (see also Blankenship and Kay 1964). For this purpose we shall make use of a longer stretch of the data than is provided in figure 3.1, covering 136 examples of non-fluencies. (See also Levelt 1983 for an analysis of non-fluencies and 'self-repairs' in Dutch speakers.)

3.2.1 *The contexts of non-fluencies*

One way to document the occurrence of non-fluencies in the data is to examine their preceding and following contexts. These may be quite diverse, and difficult to determine in a unique fashion. Table 3.1 shows the range of preceding contexts recognised for those forty-two non-fluencies that were immediately followed by a clausal utterance.

Tabulating all 136 non-fluencies in this way appears to require something like twenty-one preceding, and twelve following, context categories, or a total of 252 combinations. Actually, only sixty-three different combinations, a quarter of the possible total, are represented in the data, which suggests the operation of some constraints on the contexts in which such non-fluencies occur. Determining the nature of these constraints would help to shed some light on their possible processing origins.

The first step in interpreting these types of non-fluencies is to distinguish those signal breaks that demarcate constituents and utterances in ways that are helpful to the listener. Broadly, the test is whether such breaks would remain if the utterances in question were being produced under ideal conditions, for instance in rehearsed reading aloud. It is observed, too, that speakers may make use of signal breaks between utterances for breathing (see

Table 3.2 *'Same'* (*S*) *and 'reconstructed'* (*R*) *continuations from non-fluencies in three contexts*

	Preutterance	Preconstituent	Prelexical	Total
S continuations	7	16	29	52
R switches	15	3	7	25
	22	19	36	77

ch. 2, section 2.5.4), with the precise location and duration/volume characteristics of such breath pauses being affected also by planning activity for upcoming utterances (see below). Generally speaking, the pauses that satisfy the requirements of listener and speaker occur in between-utterance and between-speaker contexts, accounting for only about one-tenth of all the types of contexts recognised, but representing around one-third of all actual instances.

For the rest, we can recognise a category of 'same' element continuations from the point of non-fluency (S), where no apparent change of word or construction is involved. This type accounts for around half of the types and actual instances. There is a further category of 'reconstructed' continuations (R), in one-third of the context types and one-fifth of all instances. Standing outside this classification are just those instances where, usually after a pause, another speaker takes over. The pattern of S and R transitions from non-fluencies may be summarised in terms of whether the transition is to a word (lexical) or a phrase (constituent) within an utterance, or a whole utterance, as set out in table 3.2.

Most straightforward continuations are found to lead into a constituent phrase or lexical item; most reconstructed switches occur before a whole utterance. It is possible perhaps to discern different levels of functioning in operation here: a level of *planning*, associable with the sort of reconstructional switch that precedes a whole utterance; a level of *constituent assembly*, associable with the execution of constituent phrases; and a level of *lexical selection*, associable with the retrieval of particular lexical items. If the sort of distribution found in the analysis of this sample is at all reliable, it may constitute *prima facie* evidence that these are distinct psycholinguistic phases of the production process.

3.2.2 *The linear distribution of non-fluencies*

We should now ask what sort of *linear distribution* the 136 non-fluencies exhibit in the sample: do they occur evenly spaced out at fairly regular intervals, or do they tend to cluster at certain points, in ways that might be revealing of psycholinguistic processes?

A basic question here concerns the *domain* of distribution that we wish to analyse: two obvious candidates are the *text* as a whole, and the smaller unit of the *utterance* within the text. A second decision has to do with the *units* of linear distribution over a domain: e.g. for a particular domain we may choose units of time (e.g. seconds), or linguistic units such as utterance (within text), or word, syllable or morpheme (within utterance or text).

There are actually two sorts of structural description available for utterances: one phonological, the other grammatical. As a phonological entity, an utterance may be characterised in terms of: (a) its *tone-structure*, marked by prosodic features of pitch and stress, distributed within units which may be referred to as *preheads*, *heads*, *nuclei* and *tails* (see O'Connor and Arnold 1961); and (b) in terms of its *segmental* structure, including the minimal segments, phonemes, and building up to larger segments such as the elements of the *syllable* – *onset*, *peak*, *nucleus*, *coda* (see our discussion of speech errors in section 3.4 below), as well as the syllable itself, and *phonological words* (e.g. *I'll*, consisting of two grammatical elements, in one phonological sequence). As a grammatical entity, an utterance is usually described in terms of *sentence*, *clause*, *grammatical phrase*, *grammatical word* and *morpheme* (see section 3.3, below). The relation between these hierarchies is not one to one: tone units may contain sentence/clause boundaries within them, and vice versa; and phonological words, e.g. *John's*, may contain more than one grammatical word (*John*, *is*) or morpheme (*John* + possessive). However, it has been pointed out (Crystal 1980) that in the sort of data we are looking at, there is a better fit between tone units and clauses than between tone units and sentences or grammatical phrases (around 54 per cent of clauses are just one tone unit in length, more than twice as high as any other correlation). We shall therefore first consider a statement of non-fluency distribution over the clause domain, and then turn to the wider distribution of non-fluency over the domain of the text as a whole.

Within the clause: for this analysis, we have drawn on a body of seventy utterances from the text illustrated in figure 3.1 above, and which consist of just one tone-unit/clause structure each. Points of commonality were established between them in terms of their structural properties and the incidence of non-fluencies at each of these points was determined. The results are set out in figure 3.3. In order to illustrate the positions set out here, we shall need to refer to certain grammatical categories that are discussed further in section 3.3, below. The present discussion should, however, suffice for our immediate purposes.

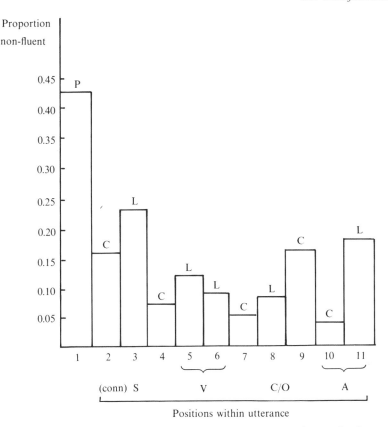

Figure 3.3 Proportion of instances associated with non-fluency, for eleven defined positions in utterances, in the conversational data. P, planning locus; C, constituent break; L, lexical choice

Eleven positions are recognised:

1. pre-utterance;
2. after a connective (*and, or, if, unless,* etc.) occurring in utterance-initial position (e.g. *and erm . it . . .*);
3. before a major lexical class word, an adjective or noun in the subject (S) noun phrase, frequently occurring after a determiner (as in *the erm – conditions . . .*);
4. before the verb phrase (V) (as in *they . build . . .*);
5. within the verb phrase, between auxiliary verb and following elements (as in *he's . he's been to . . .*);
6. some of the items in (4) and (5) stand directly in front of the main verb, and this position tallies with their combined incidence;

7. occurring between the verb phrase and the following phrasal constituent, either a complement (C) or object (O) (as in *they're
   charging f . three times . . .*);
8. before a major lexical-class word in complement or object constituents (as in *what's the . what's the failure with . . .*);
9. before an adverbial (A) constituent, if there is one (as in *and watch
   Tony Bennett . for about thirty bob . . .*);
10. between preposition and following noun phrase (one of the more
    commonly occurring phrasal types of A) (as in *about . fifty per
    cent . . .*);
11. before a major lexical-class word in an A phrase (as in *on every
    league . ground . . .*)

For each of these positions, the number of non-fluencies occurring was cal-
culated as a proportion of the number of instances of that structurally defined
position in the text. The result is the generalised 'non-fluency configuration'
for the clause patterns analysed. The most striking characteristic is that 0.43 of
clause-structured utterances in the sample are preceded by a pause – the bar in
position (1) in figure 3.4 is labelled 'P' to reflect the usual interpretation that
here is a major *planning* point for the upcoming utterance (Boomer 1970).
About 16 per cent of utterances having an initial connective show a pause
between the connective and the next *constituent* (subject noun phrase, in our
examples). This may also provide an opportunity for planning, but has been
labelled 'C' here to reflect the occurrence of the first major constituent boundary once vocalisation of the utterance is initiated. Around 24 per cent of non-
fluencies occur prelexically in the subject NP, often after a determiner, at a
point where either an adjective or a modifying or head noun are to be selected.
This state of affairs is labelled 'L' to reflect the likelihood that *lexical access* is
a major determinant of the non-fluency features observed at this point. From
this point on we can observe a gradual decline in the percentage incidence of
non-fluencies at C-points (4, 7, 10), except for a noticeable increase at position
(9), marking the boundary of a following adverbial element. Overall, apart
from this boundary, points of non-fluency are more strongly associated with
lexical selection – though here too there is a linear effect, with the percentage
incidence of non-fluencies at L-points (3, 5/6, 8) declining, until the adverbial
position (11), where again an increase is found to occur.

Within the text: if we now turn to the text domain we can plot a cumulative
graph of the non-fluencies over a suitable linear measure. We noted above that
it would be possible to choose either a temporal unit or some linguistic unit for
such a display. Since time is not recorded in the transcript we are considering,

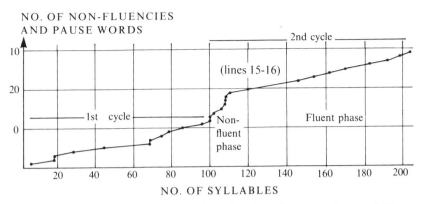

Figure 3.4 Cumulative plot of non-fluencies and pause words over syllables in the conversational data

it is convenient to use the syllable as a linear unit, yielding the result shown in figure 3.4. This curve actually includes not just the non-fluency types that we have described above, but also eight pause words and phrases, which also provide the speaker with opportunities to 'rest' and plan ahead. Notice how there appear to be points at which non-fluencies cluster, interspersed with relatively long, flat portions of the curve. Goldman-Eisler (1968) recognised 'non-fluent' and 'fluent' phases in spontaneous speech samples, and Butterworth (1980b) and Beattie (1983) have more recently argued for a macroplanning level on the basis of this sort of evidence. Their view is that speakers plan ahead, in terms of units that are several utterances long, and that the boundaries of these units (a) coincide with boundaries of semantic topic (as judged by observers), and (b) are characterised by non-fluencies. The alternating 'fluent' and 'non-fluent' phases, in this interpretation, represent what are called the speaker's 'encoding cycles'.

One problem with this view is that it may not account for all non-fluent phases in a sample – Goldman-Eisler herself recognised that other factors, such as topic difficulty, may contribute to non-fluency. Does the difficulty of the topic preclude advanced planning? Or does the non-fluency simply reflect the inherent intricacy of execution, in spite of preplanning? A more detailed analysis of the nature of the non-fluency may provide clues.

A second problem that has been raised is whether the 'encoding cycle' is a mere artefact; Jaffe, Breskin and Gerstman (1972) have claimed that a device which generates 'non-fluencies' and 'fluencies' in a random way will, for a given proportion of non-fluencies to fluencies approximating to that found in spontaneous speech, exhibit the sort of distribution that the hypothesis of the encoding cycle would expect; see also Power (1983).

We should mention here that, of the twenty-nine non-fluencies that straightforwardly precede a lexical selection, ten involve nouns all used for the first time in the sample; nine involve verbs, of which eight are used for the first time; and the remaining ten involve adjectives, eight for the first time. We shall return to these observations in our discussion below regarding some of the factors involved in lexical selection.

3.2.3 *Objective measures of non-fluency*

Our analysis thus far has been an exemplification of the major issues, based on an impressionistic record. While it would be inappropriate to dismiss such a transcription as simply too subjective to be of use, it is clearly desirable to supplement it with an objective measure of pauses. Two benefits immediately follow from an instrumental investigation: first, pauses too short to be perceived in certain contexts are made available to the analysis, and it may be that these carry information about the speaker's production processes; secondly, it is possible to carry out a finer analysis of the duration characteristics of both perceptible and imperceptible pauses – differences in duration also carry potential information about the nature of the speaker's behaviour.

Unfortunately, it seems an impossible task to review in a consolidated fashion the heterogeneous studies that have attempted to tackle various aspects of non-fluency measurement: there are too many different interpretations given to fundamental concepts such as 'pause', and too many differences in the sort of speech investigated (spontaneous, or oral reading; selected samples, or comprehensive). What we shall do, therefore, is to supplement our account of the impressionistic record above with a number of considerations and observations that seem permitted on the basis of the evidence to hand.

What sort of phenomena are measurable? These include *breaks*, i.e. portions of non-vocalisation in the acoustic record; *fillers*, i.e. stretches of non-verbal vocalisation; *juncture* phenomena, i.e. vowel- or consonant-segment lengthening at a juncture between linguistic units such as words, constituent phrases or clauses; *breaths*, as *inhalation/exhalation*; *pauses*, i.e. perceived breaks, either without filler (*silent pauses*) or with (*filled pause*), and with breath inhalation (*breath pause*) or without. Some pauses may actually correspond to no break in the acoustic record, being signalled instead by segment lengthening. The latter point is a particular benefit of objective measurement; it apparently serves as one basis for the often quoted 'linguistic' viewpoint that 'there are no gaps between words in the continuum of speech'. Such a view has been well motivated inasmuch as it has countered a naive tendency to think of words in speech as separated like words on the page (in Western alphabetic orthography); but, as we shall see, it contains only a partial truth.

Notice that phenomena such as lexical and constructional switching, and the use of pause words and phrase elements, may involve no break in the speechstream at all; while they are in principle measurable, they have not generally attracted the interest of the psychoacoustician.

What sort of variation is found between samples? First, there appears to be considerable *cross-linguistic* variation, although it is not clear what conditions it. Speakers of certain languages (e.g. French) pause less often but for longer durations, than speakers of English (Grosjean and Deschamps 1975). There is some evidence that pausing less often is compensated by greater length of pause; but it also seems that some languages do need more, or less, pause time overall. This may plausibly be related to phonological characteristics such as rhythm, i.e. the characteristic interstress interval, or to grammatical characteristics such as degree of permitted stem–affix complexity, or to both (and possibly other factors).

There is also some *inter-individual variation* – people appear to have more or less idiosyncratic pause-habits. However, this is not currently a well-documented observation. Much better studied – and more important for our purpose – is the factor of *task variation*: reading aloud yields (for well-practised readers) consistently more fluent performance than speech; rehearsed speech (as in retelling a story, or telling a story for which major topics and vocabulary have been provided) is more fluent than spontaneous speech; cognitively demanding spontaneous speech is likely to be least fluent of all. For English, Goldman-Eisler (1956) found variations between subjects of 4–54 per cent of total pause time in interview situations, 13–63 per cent in discussions, 16–62 per cent in picture descriptions and 35–67 per cent in impromptu speech.

Are patterns of pause distribution discernible? The answer appears to be yes, within the constraints of variability just mentioned. For the sort of conversational sample that we have been considering, we may refer to the findings of Butcher (1981), for spoken German (see also Grosjean and Collins 1979). Figure 3.5 shows the elements of a typical utterance, starting with (1), the *breath pause*. These pauses are elements of what we may refer to as the *phonation sequence*, but they also exhibit a correspondence with the *grammatical sequence*, inasmuch as they are $2\frac{1}{2}$ times more likely to occur between sentences than within them, in all conditions (reading, rehearsed speech and spontaneous speech); and are still more likely to occur between clauses rather than

127

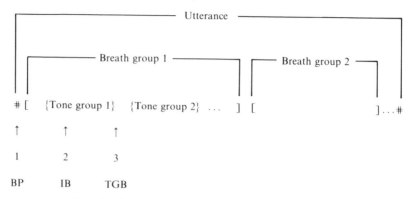

Figure 3.5 Patterns of pause distribution within the utterance. BP, breath pause; IB, interruption break; TGB, tone-group break; #, juncture. (Based on discussion in Butcher 1981: 60–2, 213–16.)

within them (though less markedly so in spontaneous speech than in reading or rehearsed speech).

They may be divided up into: (a) a *pre-inhalation interval*, which tends to be more frequently found, and to be longer, in spontaneous speech than in reading or rehearsed speech; (b) an *inhalation phase*, which is apparently physiologically determined, at around 400msec., regardless of grammatical location and of speech conditions; and (c) a *post-inhalation interval*, which tends to be three times longer in spontaneous speech than in reading. This initiates the *breath group*, which may be described as a sequence of *tone groups*. Tone groups represent 'the most readily perceivable, recurrent, maximal functional unit to which linguistic meanings can be attached' (Crystal 1969: 204). They are the domains over which perceived intonational patterns occur (e.g. a series of stressed and unstressed syllables terminating in one of a restricted set of nuclear tones, such as high rising, low falling, etc.). There may exceptionally be up to around six tone groups on a single expiration or breath groups; but usually the number is smaller – around two or three – and there is some degree of correspondence between these units and grammatical ones. In spontaneous speech, breath groups longer than three tone groups tend to correspond to sentences, and to be bounded by pauses that are relatively long, around 1,000–1,200msec. (i.e. containing significant pre- and post-inhalation phases). Shorter breath groups show a tendency for individual groups within them to coincide with clauses, or longer phrase-sequences within clauses (e.g. adverbials). Crystal (1980) found the coincidence for the sort of material found in our sample of English to be much greater than between any other units (see above). Butcher found it to be nearly four times as frequent as failure to coincide (although rehearsed speech and reading showed significantly higher frequencies, at between eight to ten times). In Butcher's data, individual tone groups averaged out at eight syllables in length, around 1.3sec., being slightly shorter than this in spontaneous speech, slightly longer in reading.

Once a tone group has been initiated, regardless of its position in the breath group, it is likely to be completed fluently. Particularly in spontaneous speech, however, it may contain what Butcher refers to as an *interruption break* (point (2) in fig. 3.5). This may be at any point within the tone group, but often occurs before lexical, or content, words, such as noun, verb, adjective, adverb, rather than before function words such as determiner, auxiliary verb, etc. Interruption pauses are usually brief, either around 170msec. (. in our transcription) or 600msec. (– in our transcription). It appears that ordinary listeners are more sensitive to shorter durations of break in this type of position than elsewhere: most of Butcher's subjects were able to identify interruption breaks down to 80msec.

At the end of a tone group, and particularly when this coincides with the end of a clause, there tends to be a tone-group *boundary break* ((3) in fig. 3.5). This is frequently signalled partly by increased length of the final consonant or vowel segments (cf. also Cooper 1980; Cooper and Paccia-Cooper 1980), of between 70–100 per cent of normal duration, regardless of the length of the boundary break. Perceptually, a boundary pause may be identified even where there is no break in the speech stream, but only final-segment lengthening. Shorter breaks tend not to be heard as breaks in this position: most of Butcher's subjects identified them only above 220msec. Paradoxically, then, physical breaks are less well perceived, though what one naively calls 'pauses' are perceived even in the absence of breaks. This may reflect the operation of higher levels, of grammatical and semantic processing.

From our data it would appear that, although tone groups are everywhere less likely to show interruption breaks than boundary breaks, most interruption breaks are likely to occur earlier rather than later in the tone group(s) corresponding to a clause, especially if the subject is a multi-word phrase.

Where a tone-group boundary break occurs at the end of a clause, and another clause or lengthy phrase follows within the same breath group, a break of linguistically sensitive duration tends to occur. Butcher found it to be longer between unrelated clauses, and successively shorter for related co-ordinate clauses, subordinate non-relative clauses, down to relative clauses. Where it is longest, it tends to be utilised for breathing, leading into a new breath group.

Within the framework of this temporal configuration, we may conclude with some general remarks on 'fluency' and 'rate'. Butcher found that perceived fluency was marked by (a) a greater proportion of breaks occurring at phonation/grammatical-sequence boundaries, (b) fewer and shorter breaks overall, and (c) a greater proportion of inhalation time to pre-/post-inhalation in the longer breaks, utilised as breath pauses. 'Longer' and 'shorter' here refer to 1,400msec. +, and around 500msec., respectively. Butcher found modal distributions of 3.9sec. breath groups to 0.6sec. pausing, which corresponds well with Lenneberg's (1967) estimate of 87 to 13 per cent, respectively. The breath rate (i.e. the incidence of breath pauses) tends to be distributed around the norm for tidal breathing, though it is rather shorter and more variable in spontaneous speech, and rather longer in reading.

Increase of tempo is generally agreed to involve a reduction of overall break time; Grosjean (1980) found no evidence of accelerated articulation rate, but Butcher did.

Earlier suggestions (Maclay and Osgood 1959) have been made about tendencies in the distribution of filled vs silent pauses; in Butcher's study they exhibited non-distinct distributions in intervals up to long breaks (around 1,500msec.), thereafter filled pauses occurring to the virtual exclusion of silent pauses. Beattie (1983) has evidence to support a 'floor-holding' role for the use of fillers in longer pauses.

Finally, we should note that this discussion of the temporal configuration of utterances has concentrated on phenomena that may be said to be *proximal*, i.e. located in and around utterance units. As such, it may be that the articulatory plan for individual utterances involves an 'ideal' pause-pattern, consisting of a minimum set of pauses, resistant to reduction and open to expansion, depending on tempo (Butcher 1981). Gee and Grosjean (1983) present evidence, from a study of oral reading of various sentence types, for a correlation between interword intervals and grammatical structure. And Beattie (1983) has argued for *distal* phenomena, by plotting total pause time cumulatively over total speech time (see fig. 3.6). This is a temporal version of the 'encoding cycle' pattern that we referred to earlier, and as such has similar implications for the interpretation of the speaker's production processes; it has been criticised as being artefactual, for the reasons already mentioned (see also Power 1983).

What are the functions of pauses? It is usual (see, e.g. Goldman-Eisler 1972) to recognise three functions: (a) physiological – to allow the speaker to inhale; (b) cognitive – to allow the speaker to plan ahead; and (c) communicative – to allow the speaker to signal certain demarcations in the speechstream to the listener. And Butcher's quantitative study shows three (or four) types of pause, in terms of modal distribution around certain duration values, as follows:

Type	Duration (mean length)	Crystal (1969) symbol
1	100–400msec.	.
2	400–800msec.	–
3	800–1,200msec	– –
(4	1,200msec +	– – –)

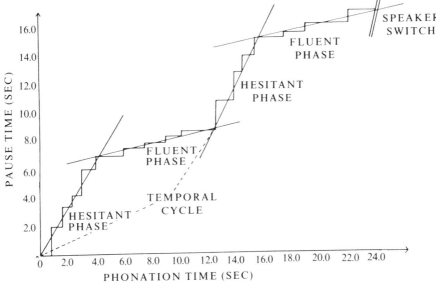

Figure 3.6 Temporal measure of 'encoding cycles'. (From Beattie 1983: fig. 3.1, p. 47.)

Further, we can recognise a number of linguistic positions of pauses, as follows:

(i)   between a function word and a content word;

(ii) between syntactic constituents (phrase, clause, sentence);

(iii) between prosodic constituents (tone group, breath group);

with a greater or lesser degree of correspondence between the latter two.

Let us now consider 'function (a)' – permitting the speaker to breathe. This is open to types (2)–(4) (type (1) is too short), and is typically found in positions (ii) and (iii). But note there is a fallacy in saying that, e.g. the *function* of a type (2) pause in position (ii) is to allow the speaker to inhale. The evidence is better interpreted by saying that the speaker (opportunistically) *utilises* positions like (ii) for inhalation, and that the resulting process *yields* a pause of at

131

least type (2). Thus, pause position is a *determinant*, and inhalation is a (physiological) *activity* (whose *function* is to provide a sufficient airstream for speech), which in turn (partially) determines pause length. 'Partially', because other activity, such as cognitive planning, may also be taking place simultaneously.

Similarly, with 'function (b)' – planning. Under the heading of cognitive planning we should include planning for content and for syntactic form, as well as word-finding activity. We shall say more about this in the next chapter. It *may* be that, on occasion at least, speakers pause *in order to* plan. But it is also likely that certain positions – presumably definable in terms of planning units – determine the points of further planning activity, which, if it is reasonably complex, may in turn determine the length of pauses in these positions. Note that, by this account, pauses involving planning may occur in a variety of syntactic/prosodic positions, since message units may be relatively independent of expression units. An example of this may be when a change of construction occurs part-way through a constituent, or after a phonological fragment. But it is hard to be clear about the demarcation of planning activity, as we shall see in chapter 7.

Butterworth (1980b) has attempted to shed light on the boundaries of planning, or 'idea', groups, by asking independent judges to divide samples of speech into 'ideas'. He found that those points in the samples where more than half the judges agreed on idea boundaries corresponded significantly with boundaries between encoding cycles, but also that the correspondence was not complete. One reason for this is that there may be a considerable degree of planning that is simultaneous with speech activity; it may not all be relegated to pause positions, expecially if (a) the planning is not specially complex, and (b) the speech activity in process is relatively simple or even stereotypic.

However, both idea and cycle boundaries 'almost invariably' correspond with clause boundaries (Butterworth 1975), 'and thus consist of a set of whole clauses. So we can say, at least, that at the semantic level, the speaker formulates a Plan which is supraclausal' (Butterworth 1980b: 165).

In Butcher's study, spontaneous speech showed many more longer, type (2) and (3), pauses than oral reading, with three-quarters of intersentence breaks being 800msec. +, and of intrasentence breaks being 400msec. +. The likelihood is that, whether or not these breaks were also utilised for breathing, they marked points of planning.

Thirdly, 'function (c)' – the communicative, demarcation function. According to this view, the speaker inserts certain breaks purely for the purpose of 'chunking' the speechstream in helpful ways for the listener. These are the breaks that are preserved in oral reading, and their location and duration characteristics are determined by syntactic/prosodic form (with a good degree of tie-up between these). All breath breaks will be communicative: the speaker is signalling a constituent boundary which is so major that it tolerates breathing activity. The constituents involved tend to be clauses and sentences, and the looser the structure, the longer the break between them. Within tone groups/clause constituents, Butcher found no relation between duration of break and linguistic structure, so pausing within these units appeared to have no communicative value. These breaks tend to be of type (1), shorter than required for inhalation, and occurring in positions (ii) and (iii). They tend not to be perceived at tone-group boundaries, so if they have a demarcation function at these locations, it is in the nature of preperceptual cuing. We should note here again that Gee and Grosjean (1983) have uncovered evidence from oral reading that very fine durational characteristics do map onto something like syntactic organisation.

3.3 Grammatical characterisation

How much of naturally occurring speech is grammatically well-formed? Garrett (1982) suggests that most of it is; Goldman-Eisler (1968) observes that most of the time speakers are engaged in other than fluent grammatically well-formed performance. It is actually possible to go some way to reconciling these apparently opposing viewpoints. First, it may be noted that much non-fluency may be fairly straightforwardly 'lifted out' from surrounding fluent speech, to leave grammatically well-formed utterances:

> well | [what's the- |] what's the 'failure with the ↑ FÒOTBALL |
> I | think [it 'probably -] it | probably 'is the ↑ MÒNEY | - - -

This allows for both views, for it should be noticed that one emphasises 'grammaticality', while the other emphasises 'non-fluency' – the two operative concepts here are not on the same continuum, and may therefore coexist, as these examples indicate. But there are fluently ungrammatical stretches (in bold print) also, as in:

> ... | what's the 'failure with **the** ↑ FÒOTBALL |
> ... - it – probably '**is the** ↑ MÒNEY for | what you ↑GÈT | you | KNÓW
> - erm I was / reading in the ↑ paper this ↑ MÒRNING, * **a a** CHAP |
> he's a DI|RECTOR | of a big ↑ CÒMPANY | in | BÌRMINGHAM | -

In the first of these examples, the use of *the* is surprising, as it would not have been had the speaker gone on to say something like *the* ↑ *FOOTBALL world*. The second case looks superficially similar, yet here *the* before MONEY is not simply better omitted (as in the first case); rather, something else has been omitted, perhaps along the lines of (... ' *is*) *a question of* (*the* ↑ MÓNEY) *you pay* (*for* | *what you* ↑ GÈT | *you* KNÓW). In the third example, there is actually some disfluency (*a a*) in the noun phrase we need to consider, but this is irrelevant to its essentially non-grammatical (or *paratactic*) relationship to the preceding and following material.

It is not always possible to be very precise about the nature of the ungrammaticality in such instances (e.g. in the particular repairs that are called for); but it is fairly clear that we are dealing here with examples of speech which, while they cause no surprise to, and are typically not noticed by, the listener, would naturally be 'grammaticalised' in other communicative contexts. These contexts are not confined to the conventions of the written language. Freed from the time pressures of ongoing speech production, people listening to their own recorded utterances tend to reproduce spoken 'verbatim' versions that are grammaticalised paraphrases of what they have originally produced. Indeed, as transcribers of speech are aware, it is a difficult skill to represent ungrammaticality faithfully in the transcriptional record.

A further consideration is linked to this last example: what one wishes to characterise as '(un)grammatical' is implicitly referred to some *domain* of grammatical distribution. Considered as an NP, *the football* is grammatical, although in a wider context (e.g. line 1 above) it is not. This in turn leads to the position where, apart from *fluent grammaticality*, we may observe *non-fluent grammaticality* (halting, repetitious, phrase-by-phrase production, with possibly paratactic linkage of smaller units into larger ones), *fluent non-grammaticality* (paratactic linkage, change of construction) and *non-fluent non-grammaticality*. There is scope here for rather different characterisations of different parts of one and the same corpus. What is required, and is not currently available, is a widely agreed set of criteria in terms of which the linguistic characteristics of different samples of 'everyday language' can be compared. In particular, the word 'grammatical' is usually appealed to (as here) without reference to the grammar it relates to. What might 'the grammar' of our sample look like? A first step towards establishing this involves the requirement for an adequate grammatical transcription of the data (a sort of grammatical analogue of a broad phonetic transcription at the level of sound structure).

3.3.1 *Minor versus major elements*

First, we shall make a distinction between *major elements*, that are describable in straightforward grammatical terms – e.g. as 'parts of speech' – such as determiners, nouns, prepositions, adjectives, verbs, and so on, and those, *minor elements*, that are not (Crystal, Fletcher and Garman 1976).

These latter have generally been rather neglected in most grammatical treatment. Some, including responses, greetings and vocatives, appear to function as whole utterances (they are said to have *holophrastic*, or *sentential*, status), e.g. *yes, hello, Gerry!* Others appear to depend on other utterances, which they may introduce, or conclude, or modify loosely in a variety of ways e.g. *well* ..., ... *y'know*, ... *sort of* ... We may say of these elements that the holophrastic types fail to show the expected internal grammatical structure of major utterances, and that the others, while they might superficially be subjected to a 'parts-of-speech' analysis, do not yield appropriate results (thus, *well* as an introducer element is not the adverb *well*; *y'know* as a concluder does not represent the grammatical structure of second person pronoun subject plus the main verb *know*, etc.). In a rather similar way, we may wish to identify other forms which appear superficially to have grammatical structure but which may be better treated as minor: stereotypical sequences, some of which may be holophrastic, are a case in point, e.g. *how do you do?*, which is not really a literally constructed question form but rather a stored routine, much like *hello*.

It will be apparent that minor elements constitute quite a mixed set of forms, and we should emphasise that the boundary between them and major elements may be difficult to draw in certain cases. The same forms may be found in both minor and major elements, and it is contextual *functions* that differentiate them. However, it seems important to recognise some such distinction, no matter how difficult it may be to carry it through in particular cases. We have already noted that, in minor functions, certain elements such as *well, y'know, I mean*, etc., may act as verbal pause fillers.

Levels of major function

For the remaining elements, we may recognise three levels of structure. The first, the *word* level, consists of the major syntactically defined classes of *lexical* items, including nouns, verbs, adjectives and adverbs; and also the traditionally distinguished set of *grammatical* words, including determiners, auxiliary verbs, connectives and pronouns and other proforms. At this level also we may specify the internal composition of words, in terms of stem and affix morphemes.

The next level, of *phrase structure*, recognises groupings of word-level elements into grammatical constituents such as noun phrase, verb phrase, adjective phrase, prepositional phrase, and so on. It is quite usual for the term 'verb phrase' to be used to cover both the verb and its postverbal complement or object, so that, for example, *watch Tony Bennet* is a verb phrase in this sense. But there is also a sense in which a sequence such as *have to keep on watching* is a phrasal group, with the main verb *watching* as its *head*, or central element. In the scheme of grammatical representation that we shall follow here, 'verb phrase' has this sense.

Finally, there is the level of *clause structure*, at which two aspects of grammatical organisation are defined: first, a set of grammatical relations holding between phrase constituents, in terms of which, for example, noun phrases may be characterised as subject (S), object (O), complement (C), or adverbial adjunct (A) in relation to the verb (strictly speaking, the verb phrase) (V); and a set of patterns of such relational elements, defining the clause structures of the language. This actually takes us further, into the domain of the *sentence*, which may most simply be treated as a larger unit of clausal organisation, in terms of which individual clauses (patterns of clause elements, such as SVO, SVA, etc.) may be established in relationship to each other (subordinate, or coordinate).

As an illustration, let us take the sentence

	you	*can*	*go*	*to*	*a*	*nightclub*	*and*	*watch*	*Tony Bennet*
Clause	S	V		A				V	O
Phrase	Pron	Aux	MV	Pr	Det	N		MV	Nprop

where just clause and phrase levels are marked, as being of principal interest. At clause level, we have a sentence unit, composed of two clause patterns, the first being SVA, in coordinate relationship (marked by the connective *and*) with the second clause pattern, VO (part of sentence structure here is marked by the ellipsis of the S element in the second clause).

At phrase level, we can specify the internal representation of the clause-pattern elements: thus, in the first clause, S is represented by a pronoun (Pron); V by the sequence auxiliary verb (Aux) and main verb (MV); and A by the sequence preposition (Pr) followed by determiner (Det) and noun (N). In the second clause, the subject is ellipted (as we have seen); the V consists just of a main verb (the auxiliary also being ellipted); and the O element is represented by a proper noun (Nprop).

Basically, what this scheme attempts to provide is a running sequence of word-class information (*you* is a pronoun, *can* is an auxiliary verb, *go* is a main verb, ..., etc.), on top of which is overlaid an indication of higher constituents (there is a constituency break between *you* and *can go*, etc.) and their relationship to each other (*you* is S to the V of *can go*, etc.). Our illustration is far from complete in the way it represents constituency groupings: thus, *to a nightclub* is a prepositional phrase, having the internal structure preposition +

noun phrase, and *watch Tony Bennet* represents a higher-order grouping of the clause-level constituents $V + O$, not marked in this illustration. It also provides only a very crude indication of the major grammatical relations at clause level.

In spite of these shortcomings, this type of representation may serve a very useful function, in allowing for an initial characterisation of textual data at the level of grammar – a sort of grammatical 'broad transcription', so that one can address a number of general questions regarding the grammatical properties of quite large bodies of data. A particular virtue of it is that it permits the transcriber to finesse certain decisions, which, in the context of the sort of data we are considering, are ones that we should postpone to the endpoint, rather than the beginning, of grammatical analysis: such decisions are typically involved in determining the subordinate vs coordinate status of clauses within the sentence, in defining the sentence itself, and in determining the relationship of A-elements to clause patterns (as we shall see below).

3.3.2 *Word level*

Our major interest at this level concerns the issue of lexical selection. In producing and understanding conversational speech, normal adults demonstrate the ability to access their stored information about words of the language – something we may think of as a mental dictionary – very rapidly. In our discussion above, we have suggested that certain pauses in the production of an utterance may be associated with lexical search (see fig. 3.3, above), particularly if the word in question (i.e. immediately following the pause) is a member of one of the larger word classes in the language, such as a noun, a verb, an adjective or an adverb. One possibility, therefore, is that items in larger word classes are less easily accessed, both by the speaker (word retrieval) and by the listener (word recognition). But we may also observe that certain words, e.g. *the, he, to, be, and,* etc. occur much more frequently than others, e.g. *company, surroundings, charging, warm, progressively.* A further possibility, related to this observation, is that frequently-used words are accessed more easily.

In this connection, we should note that traditional approaches to vocabulary have emphasised the distinction between the 'open-class', 'lexical', 'content' words of a language, vs the 'closed-class', 'grammatical', 'functor/function' words (see e.g. the discussion in Lyons 1968). Psycholinguistic discussions of lexical access have also paid attention to this distinction, as we shall see in chapter 5. At its clearest, the distinction is between: (a) words which belong to very large, indefinitely extendable sets, and which have independently specifiable meanings, in terms of objects, actions and relationships in the real world (rather, our perception of the real world); vs (b) words

137

which belong to restricted sets of items, and whose meanings therefore are to be specified in relation to the other members of the set; they may have referents in the perceived world, as in the case of pronouns, but their relationship to these referents may be constantly shifting, from one context to another.

How does our conversational data appear, from the point of view of these word-class considerations? To address this question, it is convenient to recognise the following ten word classes: (1) Minors, including stereotypical phrases such as *you see*; (2) Pronouns, both personal, such as *he*, and non-personal, *something*; (3) Determiners; (4) Adjectivals, including not just adjectives, but also numerals and nouns functioning as prenominal modifiers, as in *football* (*team*); (5) Nouns; (6) Preverbs, including auxiliaries, and catenatives such as *used to* (*go*); (7) Verbs; (8) Prepositions and verb particles such as (*playing*) *in*; (9) Adverbs, including intensifiers such as *all* (*ninety two*) and *even* (*he*); and (10) a class of 'Other' words, mainly comprising connectives, relative pronouns, the infinitive *to*, and *not*. These suffice for an exhaustive classification of the 250-word sequence making up participant B's contribution from lines 5 to 36 in figure 3.1 above (ignoring those words in repeated or abandoned attempts).

Some words turn up only once in this data: they are *types* that have only one *token* each. But others turn up much more frequently (have more tokens). Overall, there are 131 types (different words) among the 250 tokens (all words), a proportion of 0.52: but this overall proportion tells us very little, really, since the range of type–token proportions for individual words extends from 0.1 for words like *and* and *a* (they each occurred ten times in the data), up to 1.0 for words like *him*, *big*, *paper*, *think*, *over*, *away*, *who*, etc. (which each appeared just once). Notice that the fact that so many different word classes are represented among the latter group makes it difficult to talk about type–token proportions even for individual word-classes, let alone for the whole sample. So word-class distribution, in such small samples, and as measured by type–token proportion, may not be a reliable guide to the lexical characteristics of the data, and hence provide few clues for accessibility of individual lexical items.

Nevertheless, word-class information can be useful. Consider first the type–token proportion for the individual classes. It appears that Adjectives, Nouns, Verbs and Adverbs have generally high proportions, compared to those for Pronouns, Determiners, Preverbs, Prepositions and Others (with Minors somewhere in the middle). Furthermore, the incidence of types and tokens also reveals class differences in the data: Nouns and Adjectives are high for both types and tokens, while Adverbs, Minors and Preverbs are low on both.

Table 3.3 *Distributional measures for ten word classes in the sample of data*

Word classes	Type-token proportion	Incidence		Proportion		Types more than tokens
		Types	Tokens	Types	Tokens	
Nouns, Adj	high	high	high	high	high	yes
Verbs	high	mid	mid	mid	mid	yes
Pron, Det, Prep, Other	low	low	mid	low	mid	no
Adv, Min	mid	low	low	low	low	equal
Prevb	low	low	low	low	low	no

Verbs are in the midrange for both, and Pronouns, Determiners, Prepositions and Others show a pattern of low numbers of types but midrange values for tokens. It is also possible to look at word classes in terms of their proportions in the total sample, for both types and tokens: three classes – Adjectives, Nouns, Verbs – have more types than tokens, while others have fewer (Pronouns, Determiners, Preverbs, Prepositions, and Others), or equivalent proportions of each (Minors and Adverbs). Table 3.3 summarises these observations.

On this basis, we should think of a distributional continuum of word classes in our data, rather than a simple dichotomy between open vs closed, or lexical vs grammatical. But we have also seen that there may be considerable within-class differences in the way that words are distributed in a sample such as ours. In large part, such differences will reflect the topic of the conversation, and will be expected to change from one conversation to another: thus, for instance, it is likely that the topic, and style, of the conversation in our sample led participant B to make particularly rich use of adjectives. But to some extent, there may be differences that derive from the language system, and which would be expected to recur from one sample to another. In this connection, we should consider qualitative subgroupings of classes, e.g. the division of Nouns into those referring to common objects, place, time, activities, persons, abstract states, and so on. It may be that such subclassifications will prove relevant to the issue of access to the mental lexicon for particular words – possibly relating also to such factors as relative ease of imageability which have been argued to affect lexical access (Allport and Funnell 1981).

Our discussion thus far has been based entirely on the possibility of a satisfactory classification of words in running text. In practice, however, this exercise is not entirely straightforward. In many instances, the same word form may be assigned to one or another class depending on its context, e.g. *some* in *I've seen some good books* and *I've got some too* (Determiner vs non-personal Pronoun); *company* in *a company director* and a *big company* (Adjectival vs Noun); *big* used attributively in *a big company* and predicatively in *it was really big* (both classed as Adjectival above); and so on. Decisions about assigning words to *classes* thus regularly make appeal to syntactic context, and hence arguably take us beyond the realm of purely lexical considerations, in which, for instance, the word *be* is the same regardless of whether it is used as an auxiliary or as a main verb.

A further problem with classes of words is found with the complementary situation also, in which a class may contain disparate elements. For example, within the Preposition class there are words such as *(different) to/from*, *(similar) to*, and *(he goes) to (all the matches)* which, in their contexts, are typical of grammatical, closed-class elements, in that they are wholly determined, and hence do not represent any element of meaning in the utterance (Hurford and Heasley 1983); and there are also those, such as *beyond, over*, which tend to be much more like adverbs in having an independently specifiable meaning. Note also that certain prepositions, such as *on*, may be more grammatical in some contexts than others: Lyons (1968) draws a distinction between 'concrete' functions, where the literal meaning of the word is intended, as in *the pencil is on the shoebox* (as opposed to *inside* it, *underneath* it, *behind* it, etc.) vs 'abstract' functions, where the literal meaning may hardly be in evidence, as in *the fly landed on the ceiling*. Adverbs also provide a case in point, since some of them are quite restricted in their distribution and number, as in *(I don't) really (see)*, while others (not well represented in our conversational sample) show more of the characteristics of open-class words, e.g. *fractiously, furiously, aggrievedly*, and so on.

For all these reasons, if word class turns out to be a determinant of lexical accessibility, it will be likely to prove a highly indirect one – a conclusion which in no way runs from the apparent fact that words like *a* are very different from those like *match*. One respect in which they are different is in frequency of occurrence: is this likely to be a factor? It will be apparent that low frequency of occurrence, at least in a limited sample like ours, is no guide to class membership. If frequency of a word has anything to do with its accessibility, it may completely obscure the distinction between open and closed classes. Further, frequency in the language (as measured by word counts, usually of written texts, e.g. Kučera and Francis 1967, and Francis and Kučera 1982) may not be as relevant to the issue of lexical access as frequency in the context of a particular sample (cf. the case of *football* in our example). This in turn may suggest that frequency is merely a symptom of something much more fundamental to ease of word access, namely contextual plausibility. It is this factor, more than anything else, which may result in the sort of effect displayed in figure 3.3 above, where the incidence of lexical pausing declines successively through the utterance. Perhaps the best indication of the complex aspects of lexical structure in running text is to be found in *cloze passages*, in which certain words (in random cloze, every *n*th word) are deleted, and have to be supplied from context. This approach has been used explicitly to gauge points of lexical indeterminacy (highest number of alternatives in texts (Butterworth 1980b). It is particularly revealing (Garman and Hughes 1983) of how context (rather than whether a word belongs to an open or closed class) plays a determining role in the success with which either the original word, or some fully acceptable word, can be supplied, by normal adult speakers. A fruitful approach to the issue of word selection is to examine prelexical pause-characteristics (see fig. 3.3 above) to lexical determinacy, as measured by the cloze technique (Beattie 1980; Butterworth 1980b).

It is often found that, once a word has been used in a text, it has a tendency to turn up again and again. Apart from possible contextual reasons for this, we may also suspect a sort of self-maintaining 'lexical priming' effect – the system is that much more ready to make the same word available, having recently done so. Thus, the decision to refer back (that is, to make *anaphoric reference*) to a meeting of a staff–student committee as either *the meeting* or as *the committee* will to some extent be a self-sustaining one within a given discourse. Against this, there may operate some widely acknowledged but little-understood stylistic tendencies for speakers to vary their lexical selection, referring to one and the same thing as now *the meeting*, now *the committee*, and so on. But it is also to be observed that when, for instance, two meetings are to be referred to, e.g. a staff–student committee and a staff meeting, the speaker may early on refer to one as *the committee* and to the other as *the meeting*, and maintain these 'lexical anaphors' subsequently during the discourse. This is also a characteristic of newspaper reports. Generally, we may observe that, from the lexical encoding (and decoding) viewpoint, it is easier to use relatively few words many times (a type-to-token ration of few-to-many), but that many pressures variably operate against this state of affairs. At this point we shall leave the discussion of the word level, and turn to the next, phrase level.

3.3.3 *Phrase level*

Given the following two word sequences,

he did it there
the world's number one football fan kept on watching his team in
America,

it is clear that there are certain correspondences within the language system among the constituents of clauses, between those that are single lexical items, and those that are phrasal groupings, inasmuch as they may serve the same grammatical roles. In this sense, *he* corresponds to *the world's number one football fan*, and *there* to *in America*. The other correspondences, between *did it* and *kept on watching his team*, lead us into more difficult issues, since *it* does not correspond directly with *his team*, but rather with *keep on watching his team*. This leaves *did* answering to some grammatical feature of past tense, rather than a specific lexical item. By and large, though, we may say that individual words, and word groupings, may have corresponding grammatical roles to play in clause structure. We shall consider the sorts of phrasal structures that are found in our small sample of data, bearing in mind the following psycholinguistic question: apart from individual acts of lexical access, what sorts of structures does our speaker have to synthesise, and his listeners have to analyse?

Verb phrases

We shall start with verbs, and it will be helpful to set these out in terms of both the single lexical items and the phrasal groups that represent clausal V in the data sample, as in table 3.4. Surprisingly, perhaps, there are almost as many single verb exponents as phrase structures. Most of the former are accounted for by unmarked or third-person singular-marked forms of lexical verbs, and by the corresponding forms of the copula verb *be*. The low incidence of simple past-tense forms is determined by the topic of discourse, which naturally allows for an 'habitual present' narration of the football fan's activities and attitudes, and of the state of the grounds these days: past-tense forms tend to predominate when the speaker is relating what happened some time ago. For the phrase structures, more than half are of the *auxiliary + main verb* type; apart from *used to* constructions with a main verb, three-word phrase patterns are hardly used. There is, then, a limited range of structural types to deal with.

Noun phrases

Noun phrases in the data are distributed across the relational categories S, O, C and A as in table 3.5. There are as many single-word as

Table 3.4 *Exponents of clause-level V in the conversational data*

Single items	
Copula *be* (all forms)	8
Other verbs	
Unmarked	6
3rd person singular	5
Past tense	2
Participle -*ing*	3
	24
Phrase structures	
Auxiliary + main verb	18
used to ± main verb	5
Verb + particle	4
Two auxiliaries + main verb	1
Main verb + main verb	1
Auxiliary + negative + main verb	1
	30

phrase-structure types overall: but the single-word types are overwhelmingly not nouns but *pronouns*; and there is a skewed distribution of these elements, such that most of them (thirty-two out of forty) occur in *subject* position, all instances of this position being *preverbal*. Noun-phrase structures, therefore, are mainly found in postverbal positions, and there is a tendency for the longer structures to be reserved for the end-position in the utterance (particularly structures with phrasal or clausal postmodifications). Quirk *et al.* (1985) refer to this tendency as 'endweighting'. See Rochester and Martin (1977) on the referring function of noun phrases.

Putting these observations together (there are very few other types of phrase structure represented in the data), we may characterise a typical utterance as conforming to the pattern illustrated in

$$\underline{\text{he's}} \; \underline{\text{all over the world}} \; \underline{\text{watching it}} \; \underline{\text{you see}}$$
$$\text{S V A} \qquad\qquad \text{A} \qquad \text{(Minor)}$$

and

$$\underline{\text{they're}} \; \underline{\text{not giving}} \; \underline{\text{the entertainment they used to give}}$$
$$\text{S} \qquad \text{V} \qquad\quad \text{O}$$

Table 3.5 *Exponents of noun phrases in the conversational data*

	S	O/C	A After Preposition	A Other	Total (tokens)
Single items					
Personal pronoun	32	3	—	—	35
Non-personal pronoun	—	—	1	—	1
Proper noun	—	2	—	—	2
Single common noun	1	1	—	—	2
Total	33	6	1	—	40
Phrase structures					
Determiner + noun	4	1	5	2	12
Adjectival + noun	1	1	2	—	4
Determiner + adjectival + noun	—	2	—	—	2
Postmodifying phrase	—	2	2	—	4
Postmodifying clause	1	4	1	—	6
Coordinated plural	—	1	—	—	1
Other phrase	1	4	5	1	11
Total	7	15	15	3	40
All forms	40	21	16	3	80

in which the initial element is a pronoun subject, whose value is supplied by some antecedent expression earlier in the text, and the second element is the verb, which itself frequently shows full or partial *cliticisation* (i.e. where an element is made phonologically dependent, as *'s, 're*) upon the subject word. As a result, the first major lexical choice that has to be made in these utterances is located quite far on in the sequence of words, being either the main verb (as in *giving*), or (since the copula verb is usually treated as a type of grammatical rather than lexical verb), in some postverbal constituent (as in *all over the world*). To the extent that this is a favourite pattern for the sequencing of elements within an utterance, it may reflect the time pressures of producing and understanding utterances in conversation: the tendency appears to be to introduce major lexical selection, and structural diversity, within a partially established grammatical framework for the utterance.

Apart from, but linked to, these structural considerations, the resulting configuration may be described, in message-structure terms, as one in which *old* information is introduced first, and *new* information subsequently. We may also note, further to our reference to cliticisation above, that there are phonological consequences too: utterance-initial elements generally tend to be unstressed, or not so strongly stressed as the longer, more informative constituents that follow – in these examples, the tonic falls on *world* and on *used*, respectively.

Note that around half of the postverbal noun phrases occur after a preposition, i.e. within prepositional phrases: since these have adverbial function, there may be many more instances of this grammatical role than would be indicated by a list of all the lexical adverbs alone. We shall have more to say about adverbial functions in due course, when we consider clause structure.

We may conclude that our noun-phrase data affords evidence of the application of simple schemata, with the two-word patterns *Det + Noun* and *Adj + Noun* forming the most numerous group among the multi-word patterns. The more complex structures built out of these simpler schemata, or out of clausal sequences, are located towards the ends of utterances. Particularly at the beginnings of utterances, phrase-level exponence is mainly in the form of single words, most of them pronouns, and (it may be observed) having anaphoric function, referring to an antecedent element in an earlier utterance. The phrase-level organisation of utterances reflects the way they are 'shaped' to fit each other in the textual structure of discourse, with informationally light, pronominal, 'leading edges' that fit, or overlap, with the more informationally substantial portions of previously laid-down utterances. Pronouns have distributions that are in parallel with those of noun phrases, but their interpretation is quite different: the basic meaning of many noun phrases such as *a big company* or *football* or *Birimingham* can be thought of as contained somehow within the entries for their lexical forms in the mental lexicon. By contrast, the meaning of *he* cannot be so precisely pinned down: it is singular and masculine, but beyond that, its meaning is to be sought elsewhere than in the mental lexicon – in the built-up representation of the meaning of the earlier portions of the discourse. And the same can be true of those noun phrases that function as 'lexical anaphors', e.g. *all the matches* (= 'football matches'), and other phrases, e.g. *used to* (= 'used to charge (money)').

3.3.4 *Clause level*

We shall discuss this level in two parts, the first dealing with elements of clause patterns, the second with clause connectivity.

Elements and patterns

Looking at the distribution of relational elements in our sample, we find the following situation. There are fifty-four occurrences of V (either represented as a single verb or a verb phrase such as auxiliary verb plus main

Table 3.6 *Incidence of clause-level elements and patterns in the conversational data*

Element represented	External	Internal	Total
V	36	18	54
S	29	12	41
A (one)	14	8	22
(two)	4	—	4
(three)	2	—	2
(all)	20	8	28
O	13	4	17
(one case of O indirect + O direct)			
C	7	1	8
Patterns of elements in clause			
2 (SV)	1	6	7
(other)	2	4	6
3 (SVA)	5	3	8
(SVO)	5	—	5
(SVC)	4	—	4
(other)	3	—	3
4 + (+ A)	13	3	16
(− A)	1	—	1

verb). This provides a good approximation to the number of relational patterns, or *clauses*, that we must recognise, since there is (normally) only one V per clause. Of these fifty-four, eighteen occur in clauses that are clearly internal to another clause, e.g. in *how much does it cost [to get in down the road] now.* The remaining thirty-six clauses include those that are clearly independent, plus some that ought to be regarded as structurally dependent on others, while not being clearly internal, e.g. *which is about fifty per cent of his normal.* Setting things out in terms of 'internal' vs 'external' clauses in this way, we have the situation in table 3.6. From this we may observe:

1. V, S and A are the most commonly occurring elements, overall;
2. A, O and C are less common in internal clauses than in external ones;
3. most clause patterns are more than two elements in length, overall, but there is a clear preference for shorter patterns internally;
4. addition of A elements is a favourite means of extending clause patterns, especially the longer ones.

The evidence on A-elements here is particularly interesting. They have traditionally been viewed as unlike other elements of clause structure, in that: (a) they are optional (except for cases where main verbs such as *be, put,* etc, specify an adverbial); (b) they are mobile, being able to occur in a variety of positions within the clause; (c) it is possible to have more than one per clause. To this list, one might add that (d) they are extremely heterogeneous, both in terms of their structural exponence (as phrase structures they may be noun phrases, prepositional phrases or adverbial phrases, or various types of clause), and in terms of their functions apart from specifying time, place and manner (they may be used for a range of other functions, including instrumental, benefactive, comitative, purposive, etc.). The pause evidence we considered earlier (fig. 3.3 above) suggested a loose relationship between A-elements and the rest of the clause pattern; but the evidence we are now confronting speaks of A-elements as frequent, and hence presumably important, elements of clause patterns. There need be no conflict here, actually: we may say that A-elements are frequent in our data because they contain important modulations of message structure, rather than because they are integral parts of clause structure. As such, they may be regarded as providing rather direct insights into the way that message structure is organised, since, although they are part of clauses, they are not, apparently, subject to such stringent rules of grammatical distribution as are the other clause elements. Nevertheless, they are not completely free in their mobility; they are sufficiently part of clause-structure organisation that they observe the endweighting tendency, with most of them occurring in postverbal position in the data, and with all the complex A-elements (extended phrasal and clausal types) occurring in only this position. Apart from expressing message structure, one of the functions that A-elements may serve, in any position, is the linkage of clauses, our next topic.

Connectivity

If we now turn to the larger organisation of these clause patterns, we find a wide variety of types of interclause linkage, and considerable use of minor elements in introducer/concluder functions. In table 3.7, *connectives* include *and* (especially numerous) and others (e.g. *who, to, that,* etc); *pronominal* includes linkage achieved through coreferential pronouns (e.g. *he's all over the world...*) where no connective is present; *appositional* refers to examples such as *European cup matches...* and *very warm, nice...*; *elliptical* is found in *have a nice meal...* and *says it costs him* (with ellipsis of the subject element); and *topical* covers a number of more-or-less easily definable cases where the linkage seems to be achieved by maintaining the same topic across a clause

Table 3.7 *Incidence of various types of connectivity features in the conversational data*

Clause linkage		
	Connectives	15
	and	9
	other	6
	Topical	11
	Pronominal	7
	Elliptical	2
	Appositional	2
Minors		
	Introducers	8
	Concluders	6
	Other	2

boundary (other than in ways indicated above), as in *a a chap, something like this* ... In all, thirty-seven instances of such linkage occur, among the fifty-four clauses in the sample. In addition, sixteen minor elements occur, also contributing to the textual structure of the passage.

One feature that strikingly emerges from this sort of data is the lack of clear status for the *sentence*, defined as a sequence that may be either monoclausal (the simple sentence) or consisting of two or more clauses linked in some determinate grammatical relationship (subordinate or coordinate). This raises the possibility that the grammatical organisation of connected discourse may be radically different from what might be expected from the straightforward sequencing of units comparable to isolated sentences (see O'Connell 1977; Givón 1979; Ochs 1983). Crystal (1980) presents arguments, from the sort of data we are considering here, to the effect that, while words are organised in terms of phrasal and clausal constituency groupings, and these have a fair degree of correspondence with tone groups (see above) in production, there is, apparently, little or no evidence of a further domain of organisation, unless we take that as being the domain of the text, or discourse, itself.

To illustrate, consider the longish sequence, from participant B, in lines 5–36 of the data in figure 3.1 above. If we set part of it out here simply as a sequence of words (with non-fluency features omitted), we shall be able to appreciate that the issue of how to segment it into grammatical units in valid and reliable ways is one that is worthy of due consideration:

he's watched football on every league ground in England all ninety-two
and he's been to America to watch West Bromwich playing in America
he's been to the last two or three World Cup tournaments and he goes to
all the matches away you know and everything that English teams are
playing in he's all over the world watching it you see this year he's
watched twentytwo games so far this year which is about fifty percent of
his normal and even he's getting browned off and he was saying that you
can go to a nightclub in Birmingham. (lines 11–23)

It is possible to establish formal criteria for segmentation of this sort of data
into grammatical units, but we should not expect the resulting units to fit readily our notions of 'sentence'. One approach starts by making appeal to *verbs* as
the centres of clausal constructions, treating formal *connective devices* such as
and, *if* and relative pronouns as initiating new units, and recognising *unconnected phrases* and *minor* elements as constituting independent units (Garman
1989). This yields what are called 'text units'; they are, by design, fairly minimal units – involving the fewest assumptions about grammatical organisation. Using them as a basis, various sorts of 'higher-order' units may be
defined, as necessary. To illustrate the results of this approach on our
example, consider the following:

(1)   he's watched football
(2)   on every league ground in England
(3)   all ninety-two
(4)   and he's been to America
(5)   to watch West Bromwich
(6)   playing in America
(7)   he's been to the last two or three World Cup tournaments
(8)   and he goes to all the matches away
(9)   you know
(10) and everything
(11) that English teams are playing in
(12) he's all over the world
(13) watching it
(14) you see
(15) this year
(16) he's watched twenty-two games
(17) so far
(18) this year
(19) which is about fifty percent of his normal
(20) and even he's getting browned off
(21) and he was saying
(22) that you can go to a nightclub in Birmingham

We have here twenty-two text units, of which two are minor types (numbers 9 and 14), and six are phrasal (numbers 2, 3, 10, 15, 17 and 18): the remainder are clausal. A number of these text units would be candidates for higher-order groupings, of different types depending on the criteria used.

For instance, in (1) the object noun *football* satisfies a syntactic condition of the verb *watch*, and hence is included within the same text unit, but there is no requirement for a place specification such as is provided in (2). However, in the context of the passage, the form (1) *he's watched football* acts as previously established information (the conversation is based on this man's keenness to watch football), and the next text unit provides a communicatively effective extension of this, (2) *on every league ground in England*. So, if our purpose were to recognise communicative units containing topic/given-plus-comment/ new information, then we would wish to group these two text units.

By contrast, the phrase (3) *all ninety two* appears to be typical of the sort of conversational afterthought that is 'dropped' in place without any coherent linkage, either in terms of syntactic or communicative units.

In the case of (4) *and he's been to America*, followed by (5) *to watch West Bromwich* and (6) *playing in America*, we may observe that both the *-ing* form of *playing* and the *to* form of *to watch* serve to establish syntactic links between the text units involved.

We shall not go into further details here, but we should emphasise the importance of reliable and valid means of segmenting such data. For without such means we shall be unable to carry out even the simplest analytical procedures, such as: equating different samples for size; providing mean length of utterance measures for samples; calculating the ratio of clausal to non-clausal utterances; establishing the proportion of complex clauses; and so on.

We may conclude, at this point, that: (a) grammatical units are linked to each other in many and various ways, not all of which may be captured by statements regarding the syntactic distributions of the individual units; (b) overt marking of unit linkage (e.g. by connectives) is frequently ambivalent; (c) frequently the links between units are not marked by any formal connective at all, forcing the analyst who works in terms of specifiable grammatical types of linkage to impose decisions on the data (Crystal 1980 notes 'indeterminate ellipsis' as one of the features giving rise to this situation); and (iv) units that are linked together, in terms of topic and internal organisation, may not always be adjacent (what Crystal 1980 refers to as 'intercalation' of units in sequence). We do not yet know how far text units, or certain types of higher-order groupings, might correspond to, or shed light on, the actual processing units that speakers, and/or listeners, use in the course of natural conversation: but we may have taken an appropriate step towards appreciating the sorts of units that appear, at least superficially, to be involved.

At this point, we shall conclude our brief survey of the structural properties of our data, and turn to a consideration of another class of naturally displayed evidence, that of errors.

3.4 Errors

In this section we shall consider the evidence regarding naturally occurring errors that fall under the ' − Advertent' heading in figure 3.2. The taxonomy in figure 3.2 is actually not very satisfactory, inasmuch as it implies that such errors and mazes are far removed from the ' − Verbal' phenomena of pauses, whether filled or empty: mazes are actually frequently observed to occur along with pause phenomena, as may be seen in the data sample of figure 3.1. Errors have considerable potential to shed light on the nature of the language system, since they mark those points at which the system breaks down. The symptomatology of errors can thus, in principle, carry information on *where* in the system the breakdown has occurred, and *how*, in the sense of the possible mechanism involved.

Most speakers have had the experience of hearing themselves say something not quite as they intended it. Many of these naturally occurring speech errors are either articulatory in nature, as when speech sounds get transposed, e.g. in so-called 'spoonerisms' (named after Dr Spooner, Warden of New College, Oxford at the turn of the century, who was reputed to have made a good many of these errors; see Mackay 1970b; Potter 1980) such as *I think he's had a daw real* ('raw deal'). Others are more to do with grammar and meaning, as when whole words or constructions get mixed up, e.g. *you couldn't have hit that shot any better than Bernhard Langer* ('you couldn't have hit that shot any better if you'd been Bernhard Langer/Bernhard Langer couldn't have hit that shot any better than you').

Errors of both sorts seem to be quite normal, although they tend not to occur very frequently (Garrett 1980a estimates observing a few per week), so our brief illustrative data sample affords little evidence of them (see Garnham *et al.* 1982 for an analysis of 'slips of the tongue' in the larger body of texts contained in the London–Lund corpus of spontaneous English conversation). Much evidence concerning these errors has come through corpora dedicated to their collection, e.g. Fromkin (1973) (the UCLA corpus), and Garrett (1975) and Shattuck-Hufnagel (1975) (the MIT corpus).

It is tempting to restrict the concept of 'slips of the tongue' to just those errors that have an articulatory basis. However, the distinction between articulatory errors and those involving grammar and meaning is a difficult one to apply consistently to the data, and we shall use the term 'slips of the tongue' here to refer to all types of error manifested in speech production. In the same way, apart from slips of the tongue, we may also observe ourselves making slips of the pen: i.e. anything from letter-production errors that arise from momentary lapses in manual output, such as writing *-the* at the end of (intended) *with* (perhaps because of the frequency of *e* occurring after the sequence *th*), to grammatical and meaning-based errors, including leaving words out or writing the wrong words. (We should note here in passing that the term 'slips of the hand', which might seem an appropriate one for covering both writing and typing errors, has been used by Newkirk *et al.* 1980 in reference to their discussion of the errors made among users of American Sign Language.)

As far as input processing is concerned, we may also recognise slips of the ear, as when we start to hear a particular sequence, and then realise that we have misperceived it in some way; e.g. perceiving *the ambulance* at the start of *the yam balanced delicately on the top* . . . And slips of the eye also occur, sometimes persuading us that we have seen a word on a page that, on closer inspection, turns out not to be there (although the triggering elements may be discovered).

We shall briefly consider each of these types of evidence, paying most attention to those attested in speech production, since in this area the corpora are larger, especially in relation to grammatical and meaning-based types, than for the other categories.

3.4.1 *Slips of the tongue*

We shall illustrate our discussion here with data drawn from the MIT corpus. Our observations are based on the data and analyses presented in Shattuck-Hufnagel (1983) for articulatory errors, and in Garrett (1980a, 1982) for the grammatical and meaning-based types.

Articulatory errors

Shattuck-Hufnagel (1983) notes that nearly half the errors in the MIT corpus, which at the 1981 count stood at something over 6,000 items, have some articulatory involvement. The data have been collected by what we may call the pocket-book method, usually from errors observed in the speech of the researchers' colleagues or of the researchers themselves, and using orthographic notation supported where necessary by broad phonetic transcription. A strength of this method is that the recorder can check with the speaker (when this is another person) what the intended target was, on the spot; another is that the transcription is usually made within seconds of the error occurring. A weakness is that it relies on auditory-impressionistic judgements, which tend to filter out information about the less audible articulatory clashes, suggesting, falsely in such cases, that one sound is completely supplanted by another.

Of these errors, just over half are substitutions of one sound for another, which are classifiable in many cases as anticipatory or perseveratory, as in (examples from Garrett 1980a):

(23)   it's the /g/olly green giant (for 'jolly')
(24)   ... thir/θ/ and fourth ... (for 'third')
(25)   a clear p/l/iece (for 'piece').

We should also note that Stemberger (1985) cites errors such as

(26)   he could at /w/east – at least get them into line

where there is no apparent source for the substituting element.

Shifts may also be noted, as in

(27)   nasals, lides and /g/liquids,

although in this example the data may be interpreted as an exchange of /l/ and /gl/ onsets (as we shall see, below).

Nearly a fifth of the errors are exchange types, where two sounds are involved. Shattuck-Hufnagel (1983) looks at exchange errors as being of particular interest. One problem in this enterprise is that certain examples remain intractably ambiguous, as in *he's a cat fàt* (with the intonation pattern of the intended form, 'he's a fat càt', being unaffected). This might result from exchange of articulatory segments /k/ and /f/; or whole syllables; or morphemes; or words. Such examples are excluded from the discussion below. Certain other problem cases were also excluded from the analysis: intraword exchanges (e.g. ty/k/ipal for 'typical'), and exchanges involving function words (e.g. *s*hince *s*/i:/, for 'since she'), because they are said to show their own minor patterns and hence may represent rather different mechanisms of production; errors that were corrected at once (e.g. I *s*an't – can't see), because they might have turned out to be anticipatory errors (e.g. I *s*an't *s*ee) or exchanges (e.g. I *s*an't /k/ee); and errors that involved identical adjacent segments, because of their structural ambiguity (e.g. *t*ame *s*ape, or *t*ame *s*ape, for 'same tape'). After these exclusions, the corpus of exchange errors stood at just 210 items.

Considering first the *structural properties* of exchange errors, we find that an outstanding characteristic of the data is that the majority of examples – around two-thirds – can be described as involving *singleton* elements, i.e. occurring between single consonant or vowel positions, e.g.

(28) *b*ate of *d*irth (for 'date of birth'),
(29) cu*ck* ca*pe* (for 'cup cake'),
(30) *se*dden d*u*th (for 'sudden death'), etc.

This observation, and those following, need to be interpreted in the light of the proportion of singleton to sequences of segments in the phonotactics of the language, since the exchange statistics may simply reflect what is available in the language.

Among the remainder, those examples involving the exchange of whole syllables, e.g.

(31) *lin*ing it on the *lay* (for 'laying it on the line'),

only constitute 3 per cent of the total. Possibly their relative rarity is the result partly of their being open to interpretation as involving lexical, rather than sublexical, units. Between the singleton and whole-syllable types, there are in addition: exchanges involving a consonant cluster (16 per cent), e.g.

(32) *st*ee *fr*anding (for 'free standing');

those involving a vocalic complex, such as a diphthong, or vowel plus liquid (4 per cent), e.g.

(33) gr*ai*n gr*ee*p (for 'green grape')
(34) m*ur*k b*il*ning (for 'milk burning', in an accent with postvocalic /r/);

and consonant and vowel sequences which form part of a syllable (8 per cent), as in

(35) s*ole* ... h*ock* (for 'sock ... hole'),
(36) made my t*urls* c*oe* (for 'toes curl').

Only 2 per cent of examples in the corpus involve sequences that are heterosyllabic, i.e. straddling a syllable boundary.

Further observations include: that most exchange elements are consonants; that most are located in syllable-initial positions; most are found in stressed syllables; and, in all but two instances, a *syllable-position constraint* is adhered to, by which the elements involved in the exchange occupy corresponding positions in their respective syllables (as in (28)–(30) above). Thus the major pattern in the data may be represented by the schema:

(37)   Main stress   Main stress
     ... [...   [__ Vowel ...] ...]   ... [...   [__ Vowel ...] ...]
            Word Syllable   Word Syllable

There may be other (unstressed or stressed) syllables in the word sequence, and there may be words intervening between those involved in the exchange.

The favoured position for exchange is indicated by ___, located prevocalically in stressed syllables. Note that the factors of position and stress are conflated in the data, so that it is not possible to say that one or the other is the determinant of the exchange pattern.

The issue of phonotactic patterns is important. In the case of (28)–(30) we have straightforward single-segment exchanges, but the following

(38)   p*l*ay a *f*at fee (for 'pay a flat fee')
(39)   sp*r*it b*l*ain (for 'split brain')

are more problematic. In (38) we may interpret the error as an exchange type (as indicated), but it may also be an anticipatory movement error (involving *l* occurring in *p-ay* rather than in *f-at*). In (39) we are dealing at first sight with exchanging elements from rather different positions within words – the third element in a three-element cluster with the second element in a two-element cluster. But, within a syllabic framework of segmental phonotactics, the similarities may outweigh the differences here. A generalised structure of the English syllable is set out in figure 3.7. In these terms, example (39) involves an exchange of elements in position 3 (= final position within the *onset*). Within this framework, it is also possible to account naturally for the apparently mixed type of exchange (/sn/- cluster and singleton /ʃ/-) in (40),

(40)   *show* *sn*ovelling (for 'snow shovelling'),

as involving two syllable onsets. Using the concepts of *syllable, onset, rhyme, nucleus* and *coda*, it is possible to account for 96 per cent of the exchange-error data in terms of an exchange between structurally available and corresponding elements (which is the force of positional constraint referred to above). However, we should be cautious with such an approach, in case it leads us to impose such a rich descriptive framework on the data that *any* sequence is analysable as a viable exchange candidate. We may test this possibility by noting that, in terms of the syllable structure of figure 3.7, the sequence *onset + nucleus* is not a viable unit, and hence should not be easily available for exchange: it is observed that only 2 per cent of the data show this pattern. And we have already observed that heterosyllabic sequences occur at only the 2 per cent level. And it appears that errors which involve the splitting of sequences within onset, or nucleus or coda tend not to occur: in the light of which the case of (39) above possibly merits a further look. It may be simply an example of a rare type; or it may tell us that position 3 is a special case; or it may even be that the best interpretation of this example is that whole onsets, *spl-/br-*, are exchanged. By and large, it would appear that the descriptive framework provides a fruitful way of starting to refine the observations that may be

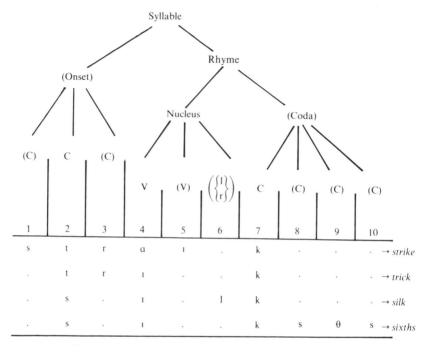

Figure 3.7 Generalised syllable structure for English words

appropriately made concerning the data. See Fudge (1969) and other 'non-linear' descriptions of phonological organisation, e.g. Goldsmith (1976), Kahn (1976), and Liberman and Prince (1977).

Concerning the possible *mechanism* of exchange errors, Shattuck-Hufnagel (1983) suggests that it is extremely unlikely that they arise through two unrelated segmental substitutions (which happen to cooccur). There is, it appears, no evidence to suggest that segmental substitutions occur frequently enough within the same utterance for this to count as a plausible explanation (see also Shattuck-Hufnagel and Klatt 1980). However, a real issue arises in respect of what we take the nature of the exchanging elements to be. Singleton exchange errors may actually involve two types of exchange, depending on whether we take the exchanging elements to be the *segments* themselves, or certain of their subsegmental *features*. Consider the example below, which may be described as the exchange either of the segments /p/ and /k/, or of the features [labial] and [velar] in the following way:

(41) intended form: cup cake
      output form: cu*ck* ca*pe*
      segment exchange: /p/ ↔ /k/

156

feature exchange: [cons]   [cons]
                   [obstr]   [obstr]
                   [oral]   [oral]
                   [labial] ↔   [velar]
                   [unvoiced]   [unvoiced]

Which of these descriptions is to be preferred? First, we should note that, in principle, any segment exchange can be described in terms of one or more features, since it is the purpose of features to provide cross-classifying analyses of segmental similarities and differences. Thus, for feature exchanges, to be convincing as distinct from whole-segment types, what should we be looking for? Consider the following:

(42)   intended form: tip of the tongue
            output form: tick of the tum
        segment exchange: none
            the sequence ... /p/ ...   /ŋ/ is produced as
            the sequence ... /k/ ...   /m/
        feature exchange: [cons]   [cons]
                             [obstr]   [obstr]
                             [oral]   [nasal]
                             [labial] ↔   [velar]
                             [unvoiced]   [voiced]

It will be apparent that only in example (42) can we unambiguously say that exchange of features, rather than segments, has taken place. If we restrict the feature-exchange type to just this sort of example, we may say of the other singleton types that, while features may capture the similarities and differences between exchange elements, the exchange itself is to be thought of as occurring between whole segments.

Grammatical errors

Using this term to cover errors involving everything except articulatory elements, e.g. morphemes, words, phrasal constituents and clause patterns, we may recognise the following general types (examples from Garrett 1980a).

Exchange errors

These involve transposed elements that are non-adjacent, before and after transposition. The elements involved may be phrasal (43) or words (44), but notice the second example in (43) is repeated as the first in (44), as an illustration of an undecidable type.

(43)   (a) I got into *this guy* with *a discussion*
        (b) forgot to add *the list* to *the roof*

(44) (a) forgot to add the *list* to the *roof*
       (b) once I *stop*, I can't *start*
       (c) as you *reap*, Roger, so shall you *sow*
       (d) everytime I put one of these buttons *off*, another one comes *on*

Nouns and noun phrases figure prominently in these examples, but verbs (44b, c) and prepositions/adverbs (44d) also are involved. What is striking is that elements of the same grammatical class are involved in each individual exchange – what one may suspect to be a defining characteristic of this type of error.

Most examples of this type show a minimal intervening element of just one word, many others have two intervening words, and some are like (44c) with four words, or more. Probably more important than number of intervening words, though, is the constituent structure. These exchanges tend to occur across boundaries such as NP–AdvP, or clause–clause, and not within constituents such as NP or AdvP. This also may be taken to be a defining characteristic of the type.

Stranding exchanges

Sometimes it happens that phrase or word exchanges involve movement of elements out of *stem#affix* constructions (# denotes a word boundary). In such cases a new stem is put into construction with the #affix. Example (45) shows a complex phrasal type,

(45) He *facilitat#*ed *what he was doing* to *remove the barricade*

and (46) a variety of word types,

(46) (a) you have to *square* it *face#*ly
       (b) I thought the *park* was *truck#*ed
       (c) I've got a load of *cook*en *chick#*ed

In the remarkable example (45), the exchange involves two sequences, each consisting of a verb and associated object (the first a clause), in which it is the verb that is put into, or taken out of, construction with the affix *#ed*. As far as word types are concerned, (46), the element that moves out of construction with the affix is in many cases a word that can act as an appropriate member of the new positional class it ends up in: thus, *square* can be a verb, as in (46a), and *park* can be a noun, (46b); but the example (46c) is a little unusual in this respect, with *cook* joining a pseudo-affix *-en* to create a non-word, *cooken*.

Before passing on to the next type, it is worth considering:

(47) it makes the *warm breath#*er to *air*.

This seems to involve both forward and backward movements as well as stranding (of words), as indicated. It may be possible to treat it as a complex *exchange* type as follows:

(47')　(a)　*Target:* the air warm≠er to breathe
　　　　(b)　*Exchange:* the *breathe* warm≠er to *air*
　　　　(c)　*Stranding exchange:* the *warm breath*≠er to air

Shifts

These appear as transpositions of elements which are adjacent before and after the transposition, and with no reference point such as is provided by affixes, as in stranding exchanges. Thus, they are of the general form (48)

(48)　X – A – B – Y　(X, Y may be null)

where the transposing elements are A, B. They are open to the following interpretations:

(48')　(a)　X – B – A – Y　　(exchange)
　　　　(b)　X – __ – B – A – Y　(right shift)
　　　　(c)　X – B – A – __ – Y　(left shift)

The examples in (49) show words transposing with phrases, and those in (50) words with words:

(49)　(a)　If you can't figure *what that out* is
　　　　(b)　Who *did you think else* would come?
　　　　(c)　You *have to do* learn that
　　　　(d)　Maybe that has *to do something* with it
(50)　(a)　Did you stay up *late very* last night?
　　　　(b)　Unless you got somethin' *to better* do?
　　　　(c)　They're *only the* ones that …
　　　　(d)　They'd tell me *to who* go see

It probably makes sense to see interpretation (48'c), left shift, operating in many of these cases. These may be related to blends (see below), where an element of a later subplan intrudes a little too early in the linearisation process. Why it should do so may in some cases be connected with the possible sequences illustrated in (49'):

(49')　(a)　… *figure what that* is
　　　　(b)　… who *did you think* would come?
　　　　(c)　… you *have to* learn that
　　　　(d)　… has *to do* with it

and (50'):

> (50′) (a) ... stay up *late* last night?
> (b) ... somethin' *to* do?
> (c) They're *only* ones that ...
> (d) ... me *to* go see

What may constitute another type of shift appears to involve stranding of an affix (which is element A in terms of the schema in (48′)) by a word (element B), as in (51):

> (51) (a) he point *out#ed* that ...
> (b) I'd forgot *about#en* that
> (c) the same as add *ten#ing*
> (d) easy *enough#ly*

A reverse pattern is apparently found in (52):

> (52) it dead#*s end*

And there may be something of the pattern of (51) in the otherwise articulatory-seeming (53):

> (53) does your *toas- *pass#t*?

Left-shifting may again be relevant in many cases, based on the cohesiveness of the sequences in (51′):

> (51′) (a) point *out* that ...
> (b) forgot *about* that
> (c) add *ten*
> (d) easy *enough*

The notion of 'competing plans' for the utterance may be appropriate in such cases.

Blends

Competing plans are most clearly in evidence here, as indicated in (54) for phrases:

> (54) (a) How much do you want? *As lot* ... as much as possible.
> (*As* much as possible/A *lot*)
> (b) How many *of there are you*?
> (*of* you *are* there/are *there* of *you*)

and in (55) for words:

> (55) (a) gone *mild* (mad/wild)
> (b) that's *torrible*! (terrible/horrible)
> (c) *enlicit* your support (enlist/elicit)

(d) he *misfumbled* the ball
   (*mis*handled/*fumbled*)

(e) have you ever *flivven* (*fl*own/dri*ven*)

In the word types of (55), we can observe a range of subtypes, from the fully fused, paradigmatically related elements in *mild, torrible* etc. through the more syntagmatically ordered compounds of *enlicit* and *misfumbled* (note the affix boundary marking off the two elements), to the concertina'd sequence of *flivven*, paralleled in my own speech by the example *hudition* (for 'human audition'). A stranding type of 'blend' may be apparent in (56):

(56)   sudden *quick*♯s – stops (sudden/quick stops)

All the word types shown here appear to involve competing results of lexical retrieval; thus each member contributing to the blend is linked to the other semantically. In (56), each member is fully retrieved (hence not truly blended at all), with the consequence that the second one displaces the planned head word from its slot.

Substitutions

A number of substitutions are semantically motivated, as in (57):

(57)   (a)   He rode his bike to school *tomorrow* (yesterday)
       (b)   You go *wash* (brush) your hair
       (c)   *Ask* (tell) me whether . . .

Notice that, in terms of semantic dimensions of descriptions, *oppositeness* of meaning and *incompatibility* of meaning are just as representative of general *relatedness* as are *sameness* and *includedness* of meaning. For obvious reasons, substitutions by *synonyms* (same meaning) and *hyponyms* (included meaning) would tend to go unrecorded (58):

(58)   (a)   Is anyone using this *seat* (chair), please?
       (b)   What a lovely *rose* (flower)!

though they may be glimpsed in blends. There is also a class of form-related substitutions, exemplified in (59):

(59)   (a)   because I've got an *appartment* (appointment) now
       (b)   No – I'm *amphibian* (ambidextrous)
       (c)   it doesn't *sympathise* (synthesise) it

These are interesting, inasmuch as they suggest that dimensions of form – including initial/final segments, syllable structure, stress pattern and grammatical class – are operative in lexical retrieval (Fay and Cutler 1977). The examples in (59) are, in terms of our taxonomy of error types, non-deliberate:

for this reason, Zwicky (1982) calls them 'Fay–Cutler malapropisms' in order to distinguish them from 'classical malapropisms'. In the same way, he distinguishes semantically related word substitutions (57) from the sort of instated 'private meanings' that form a (typically, very small) part of an individual's mental lexicon: cf. our illustration in section 3.1.4 above. Zwicky suggests that deliberate errors are not particularly revealing about psycholinguistic processes, although they may shed light on the circumstances of lexical acquisition, in childhood and beyond.

We may conclude this brief review with one observation and two further types.

The observation concerns what Garrett (1980b) has termed 'accommodation' of non-error elements to the changed situation in an utterance after some error has occurred. The accommodation may be grammatical, as in

(60)　most cities *are* true of that ('that *is* true of most cities') (Stemberger 1985)

or phonological, as in

(61)　it wait/s/ to pay (Garrett 1980a)

The two further types are cited by Stemberger (1985), as follows:

(62)　('bumper cars') I got a *paper* on my *test* ('an A on my paper')
(63)　we *always* never do that ('almost never').

In the first of these, *A* is 'bumped' out of the way by *paper* (with morphological accommodation of the preceding determiner), whose place is then occupied by a further, semantically related, element, *test*. In the second, both phonological similarity with the substituting word (*almost – always*), and a semantic relation between that word and another in the utterance (*always– never*) appear to condition the substitution error.

3.4.2　*Slips of the ear*

Browman (1980) presents an analysis of 222 misperceptions by listeners, of which 85 per cent involve a single word only, e.g. *Barcelona → carcinoma*; with others, ranging from feature-based types, e.g. *van → fan*, up through multiple sound-changes over word sequences, as in *popping really slow → prodigal son*, to examples involving whole-word deletions and insertions, as in *go to the car and get the tuna → get my car tuned up*. Garnes and Bond (1980) provide a taxonomy from a similar corpus of 890 items, which is presented in simplified form as table 3.8. From this, it will be apparent that certain problematic cases exist, e.g. in *raised → glazed* we may be dealing with a sound-based error involving the syllable onset, and in *some light → sunlight*

Table 3.8 *Structural properties of slips of the ear*

Type	Examples	Total
Sound-based	*cape → cake*; *nodes → nose*: *braise → braids*; etc.	237
Word-based	*raised → glazed*; *foreign → falling*, etc.	288
Multiple word	*mow his own lawn → blow his own horn*; *mystery dressing → Mr Dressing*; *swallowed → smiled at*; *herb and spice → urban spice*; etc.	226
Miscellaneous	*Iowa U → Iowa you*; *shed some light → shed sunlight*; etc.	139
		890

From Garnes and Bond 1980: table 1, pp. 234–5.

likewise we may wish to recognise a feature change (as Garnes and Bond note). Additionally, we may wonder how far misperceiving *U* ('University') in *Iowa U* as the homophonous *you* constitutes a slip of the ear at all, as opposed to a slip of the mind: Browman, indeed, makes a fundamental distinction between misperceptions involving an acoustic misanalysis vs those based on lexical selection (which may go wrong independently of, or in association with, some error at the acoustic level).

In spite of problems of interpretation in individual cases, Garnes and Bond find certain general properties in their data:

1. very few cases in which stress and intonation patterns are misperceived (as in *'ketchup → a 'chip*);
2. very few misperceptions of stressed vowels;
3. a high proportion of the misperceptions constituting real words of the language; and
4. very few cases where mis-segmentations (as in *herb and spice → urban spice*) involve phrasal boundaries (e.g. between a noun phrase and a following verb phrase).

Additionally, Browman, within an overall distinction between acoustic vs lexical types (see above), finds evidence for a number of restricted statements:

1. most acoustic misperceptions occur in word-initial position in unstressed syllables of polysyllabic words, and in both word-initial and word-final positions of stressed monosyllabic words;
2. most lexical-selection errors appear to involve a mismatch of word-initial elements in unstressed monosyllables (many of these being grammatical or closed-class words – see above, section 3.3.2);

3. for unstressed syllables in polysyllabic words, fewest lexical mismatches occur at the beginnings and ends of words; Browman points out that this characteristic agrees with what has been reported for word finding difficulties (the so-called Tip of the Tongue, or TOT, state; see Brown and McNeill 1966; Rubin 1975; and see further below), and for cueing word retrieval (Horowitz, White and Atwood 1968);

4. overall, there is a decreasing rate of acoustic misperceptions throughout the word, which may represent the effect of increasing lexical knowledge (what the word must be) on the processes of acoustic analysis.

These statements are considerably simplified versions of the discussion in Browman (1980), which should be consulted for further details. The complexity of the patterning of slips of the ear is further evident in the bias noted by Goldstein (1980), in terms of which perceptual confusions between one sound and another (e.g. between /θ/ and /f/) are more likely to occur in one direction (/θ/ → /f/) rather than the other. Goldstein notes that Shattuck-Hufnagel and Klatt (1980) report speech-error data to be basically without this sort of bias, and suggests that it is the result of speech perception being (unlike speech production) essentially a matter of hypothesis testing, with bias as one of the means of generating hypotheses about what has been heard.

3.4.3 *Slips of the pen*

Apart from the evidence (Potter 1980) that Dr Spooner made slips of the pen as well as oral spoonerisms, there exists a sizable body of data on the sorts of slips that people make in the ordinary course of producing written language. Hotopf (1983) provides a discussion and analysis based on the author's own writing (and typing) slips, the slips found in a draft of a thesis in psychology, slips observed in samples of writing by groups of psychology students, and forty scripts analysed by Wing and Baddeley (1980).

First, we should distinguish slips of the pen from 'spelling errors' – those established, advertent (see fig. 3.2 above) mis-spellings that are observed in particular individuals, especially children in the middle years of schooling who are still in the process of becoming fluent writers. We should also add here students at a later stage of development, who may establish mis-spellings for recently encountered technical terms (e.g. the fairly common spelling of *auxiliary* as *auxillary* among linguistics undergraduates).

By 'slips of the pen' we refer to inadvertent and non-established errors in writing, and our discussion will follow Hotopf (1983). Overall, it appears that pronunciation may be a factor in around 20 per cent of slips – those that can

(a)

(b)

Figure 3.8 Possible feature-based handwriting errors: (a) for the beginning of *paradigmatic*; (b) for *speed*. (In (a) the attempt was aborted at the point indicated by the arrow. (Example (b) from Hotopf 1983: 193.)

be attributed to confusions between phonological forms, e.g. *there/their*, with vanishingly few appearing to result from confusions along a visual dimension, e.g. *there/theme*.

Feature-based slips

The first type of slip we shall consider appears to involve what we shall refer to as letter *features*. (We shall use this term loosely, to refer to sub-letter parts that may have processing relevance.) The form in figure 3.8(a) was a handwriting attempt at the word *paradigmatic*, which was aborted at the point indicated by the arrow. The writer's interpretation of what went wrong suggests *feature omission* here (although it is also possible to see the influence of the letter pattern found in other lexical forms such as *parallel* and *para-linguistic*). By the feature-based account, the lower curvature of the letter *d* has been omitted, and the upward stroke of its ascender has been initiated (though its downward stroke is not completed prior to the abortion of the attempt). Conceivably, the similarity between the initial curvatures of the preceding letter *a* and the letter *d* may have played a role in precipitating the error.

Feature omission is not the only type of slip to be observed at this level: addition and substitution are also possible. In all cases, feature-based slips, if they result in legal output forms, may be difficult to tell apart from whole letter slips, as in figure 3.8(b) (for the target *speed*), where the open curvature of the letter *d* allows for the interpretation of it as *c* plus another letter. Pre-sumably, on-line visual feedback, from within the foveal field, plays a role in this. The addition of a final downward curvature transforms the final segment into the letter *h*, perhaps under graphotactic constraints on well-formedness. The result looks superficially like a substitution of the letter group *ch* for the single letter *d*. (This, and following, examples are from Hotopf 1983.)

Letter-based slips

The second type of slip to be described more truly involves whole letters. Forms like *inhibtions* (inhibitions), *vsual* (visual), *bothe* (both) and

165

colsed (closed) represent types of omission, addition and transposition which result in non-words. But words may also be formed as slips of these subtypes, as in *to* (too), *were* (where), *where* (were), *that* (than), *produced* (produce), etc. Some of the omissions and additions involve contractions across a word boundary, as in *his* (he is), and the interesting example *Freudiand &* (Freudian &). In the latter, the sequence *-and* is consistent with a contraction of *-an and*, and is particularly interesting not so much because the second word involved is retained (repeated) after the contraction (like writing *his is* for *he is*), but because the second word appears as the logograph *&*. This obviously has implications for the nature of the input to the writing process, and we shall return to it below. Some other examples appear to show the influence of forms from other parts of the visual field, as in *thant* (than) which was written on a line immediately below the word *predominantly*.

All these examples can be interpreted as involving single letters (except that transpositions by definition involve more), but we should also recognise within this type slips involving letter groups that do not systematically represent any unit of linguistic analysis – although, not surprisingly, most of them have *syllabic* consequences. Omissions are found in *repitions* (repetitions), *specifity* (specificity) and *scientic* (scientific), and in *has* (he has) and *wat* (was at), where contraction across a word boundary is involved.

Finally, in the whole-letter type, we should note examples like *ridgid* (rigid), *ques* (cues) and *8* (H), where similarity of sound may be a factor. We shall have more to say about these below.

Morpheme-based slips

Thirdly, there is the type of slip that involves subword grammatical elements, usually suffixes, that may be one or more letters in length. An omission is found in *has reach to*, where it is possible to argue for an effect of pronunciation (the *-ed* suffix has no separate articulatory identity in this context). Addition is found in the sequence *of using bothing approaches* (... both ...); and substitution in *slowing catching up* (slowly ...) and *difference intelligence tests* (different ...), where anticipation seems to be involved. In many cases, as here, the result is a related word (i.e. built on the same stem), and this is also seen in *psychoanalysis* (psychoanalyst). Contractions across a word boundary also occur, as in *forbiddencies* (forbidden tendencies).

Word-based slips

The fourth type involves whole words. Omissions occur, as in *went to* (the) *room*, *this* (is) *in experiment*, *that* (it) *is possible*. Addition is found in *saw the the movement*, and substitution in *even to give to the response*, with whole-word transpositions resulting in cases like *is it* (it is). Within this type, substitutions are either *semantically* related (frequently as antonyms or cohyponyms), as in *when we meet the students next term* (week), or else they are *sound*-related, as in *there* (their), *surge* (search), *scene* (seen), *good* (could), etc.

It should be emphasised once more that these types are purely descriptive and that it is not an easy matter to guess at the underlying processing errors that give rise to them. It is not even a straightforward matter to assign all slips to these categories; for instance, *societies* (society's), *reference* (referents) and *greater* (great a), all involve output that is homophonous with the target and hence might seem to be close to sound-related word substitutions; but they also bear similarities to suffixal slips.

3.4.4 *Slips of the eye*

Cowie (1985) reports a number of errors made while reading, normally and silently, during a three-month period. The total number of slips recorded was fifty-two, a small sample, suggesting a fairly low incidence of such errors: but twelve of these occurred in just the one hour that was devoted to collecting examples to the exclusion of all other activities, and this may be more representative of their actual frequency.

In spite of the relatively small sample, his data and analysis provide a glimpse into a complex range of phenomena that will ring true to most readers' recollections of their own, half-acknowledged, experiences. He suggests three types of *expectation* as playing a role in triggering the errors, and four types of *spatial structure* involved in the assembly of their constituents (see table 3.9).

Zero expectation most strongly implicates a low-level processing error, having to do with scanning of text, and is represented by errors that appeared to be triggered by no special significance of the elements involved. *External expectations* represent a mixed category, where significance of other elements, scanned elsewhere in the text, or in a neighbouring text, appears to intrude. *Internal expectations* most clearly represent the situation where significance is 'read into' the text being scanned, triggering errors that appear to impose themselves on the results of scanning.

Concerning *spatial structure*, this is classified as either *conservative* (conserving the word-elements of the errors) or *radical*, with the latter split into *conflated words, conflated strings* (each making use of disparate elements in the text, synthesising them into error forms) and *atmospheric* errors. These last are the most difficult to classify, involving associative significance derived from

Table 3.9 *Taxonomy of slips of the eye*

Spatial structure	Expectation		
	Zero	External	Internal
Conservative			
	extemporary → Stornoway	speech →speed	copies →Cowies
Conflated word			
	his pro*mised* . . . . . . *programme* → his programmised	Ba*thro*om *T*issu*e* → Toothpaste*	The co*ntr*act Gerald *Sey*mour → Sentry*
Conflated string			
	much more money Mar*ch* 31 → much, much more	st*ill more people* to camps or *chilly* . . . → more chilly people	Shadrach . . . Dom De- Luise *Jethro* . . . Richard B. Sh*ull* → *Jethro Tull*
Atmospheric			
	GLIDE PATH *STANERRA* → STAR TREK	Horse of the Year Show/Cannon → (see text)	

* In these instances, the text was inverted in the visual field.
Based on discussion in Cowie 1985.

disparate elements, driving some impression of the meaning of a word or phrase. In one case, that word or phrase did not actually occur (zero expectation): seeing the racing results with the horses' names GLIDE PATH and STANERRA, and feeling a sense of something to do with science fiction, perhaps 'Star Trek' (Cowie cites the associations of *glide*, *path* and the *sta-r* letter structure in *Stanerra*). In another case, the perceived sense derives from a form that has occurred, but has not been acknowledged until after the error has prompted a search for the basis of the slip (internal expectation): reading in the TV programme lists about the Horse of the Year Show (in one column) and feeling a sense of 'grim and determined' competition, presumably triggered by a subsequently discovered reference, in the next column, to the detective series 'Cannon', in which the phrase 'grimly determined' appears in the synopsis of the episode.

Cowie concludes that there is little or no evidence of 'acoustic effects' – that is, of the way words sound – in his data on slips of the eye. He suggests that these errors tell us a good deal about the way in which the eye goes about the task of reading, a task which may be fundamentally unnatural in its requirement of continued attention to fine detail, as opposed to the low spatial-frequency analysis that is sufficient to build the gross outlines of the solid, three-dimensional scenes of the world around us.

3.4.5   *Other errors*

Thus far, we have discussed errors under the headings of the main input and output modalities of language processing; but here, as in all aspects of language performance, there comes a point, or a level, at which we may wish to recognise some modality-neutral, or highly central, error types – perhaps approaching what we should wish to characterise as 'slips of the mind', and which are capable of being observed in more than one type of language performance. As we suggested earlier, this is not a distinction that we can straightforwardly apply, in the current state of knowledge, and it may be that some of the examples we have already discussed may turn out to have cross-modality implications. We shall offer here some further examples for consideration.

Environmental contaminants

The first example comes from Garrett (1980a), who notes that the semantic basis of lexical selection appears to be open to cross-modality influences. He cites two instances of what he calls 'environmental contaminants':

1. Target: Are you trying to send me a message, Dog?
    Situation: Speaker is addressing Dog; Dog is standing by front door looking woebegone. Immediately beside speaker at eye level on a shelf, is a novel with the cover blurb: 'A novel of intrigue and menace'. Speaker has idly read this while approaching the dog and preparing to speak.
    Output: Are you trying to send me a menace, Dog?
2. Target: People should take off their old bumper stickers.
    Situation: Speaker is looking at a car bumper with two year old sticker reading 'Dukakis should be governor'.
    Output: People should take off their old governor stickers.
    (1980a: 209–10)

In each case, the visual modality provides input which activates an item in the lexicon; this activated item subsequently appears incorporated into the otherwise unrelated oral utterance. A condition on this occurring may be a degree of (vaguely characterised) structural relatedness of the intruder and displaced items. In relation to the examples just cited, consider the modifier–head relation of *menacing message*, and *governor bumper stickers*, for example. A possible link between this situation and the blends we considered earlier may be apparent if we consider whether, under such environmental conditions, blends such as '. . . trying to send me a *menage*, Dog?', and '. . . remove their *gumper* stickers' might not occur (and go unrecognised, for lack of contextual information).

Tip of the tongue phenomena

Further examples of central-processing breakdown are found in the situation first documented and described by Brown and McNeill (1966) as the tip of the tongue (TOT) phenomenon. This is observed where a word is 'known', in terms of its meaning (or at least a substantial part of it), but whose form cannot be identified sufficiently for appropriate production in speech or writing.

TOT states can regularly be induced by presenting dictionary definitions of rare words, e.g. 'a navigational instrument used in measuring angular distances, especially the altitude of sun, moon, and stars at sea'. A TOT state may begin with an incorrect identification of a semantically related item, e.g. *astrolabe*. The next attempt may be to misidentify a word of similar sound to the target, e.g. *secant*. In some cases, the speaker may insist that this is indeed the target, at which point we may conclude that the TOT state is over (and that, for one reason or another, the lexicon has failed to operate appropriately on this occasion) – resulting in a malapropism (not of the classical type) (Fay and Cutler 1977). But the speaker may at once reject *secant*, and then the TOT state is protracted. More similar-sound items may be produced and rejected; typically, these will show a gradually increasing similarity with the target. In such a state, people are sometimes able to say which similar-sound items are closer to the target; they can often say that the target has certain global characteristics, such as having two syllables, with stress on the first; and they can usually identify sounds which they are confident occur in the target. In this ability, it has been noticed that sounds in word-initial position are best known, followed by those in final position and lastly those from the middle. And, of course, most importantly, people can distinguish the similar-sound items from the target – this is the defining characteristic of a TOT state. Such a state is dynamic, rather than static; progress towards the target may not be uniform and linear, but whatever fluctuations occur, there is a constantly changing situation. Finally, the TOT state ends in one of two ways: either the target is finally attained spontaneously, or it is *recognised* when provided. In either case, the target is recognised for what it is – in this case, *sextant*. See Rubin (1975) for discussion of what is known about the internal structure of words of a TOT state.

3.5   **Conclusions**

In this chapter we have reviewed some of the more obvious sorts of 'naturally displayed evidence' that normal speech-behaviour affords regarding the nature and limits of our language abilities. Interpreting this evidence, and modelling performance, is not an easy matter. In the second part of this book we shall attempt a review of the more important models that have been proposed. We shall conclude this chapter, and prepare for what comes later, first by observing that there is strong evidence for distinct *levels* of processing in language performance, and secondly, by recognising two very general *classes of model* which are distinguished in respect of the sorts of inter-level relationships that they envisage.

3.5.1   *Levels of processing*

We shall use just the evidence of speech errors, by way of illustration. Recall that in section 3.4.1 we circumscribed a set of 'articulatory' speech errors, and distinguished them from the grammatical and meaning-based types that we may assume to occur prior to the articulatory programming and execution stage. Now we should recognise that there is a whole class of errors that we have not so far illustrated, because in a sense they stand somewhere between these other two. They are particularly informative about operational priorities between different levels of processing.

The stored articulatory programme

We must envisage, from our discussion of articulatory errors, a level of segmental representation where successive articulatory segments are simultaneously present, in order to account for certain interactions between them. That is to say, lexical items are copied, from stock (the mental lexicon), in a pre-articulatory assembly which constitutes a sort of *buffer store*, just prior to the implementation of articulatory activities. It is in this buffer store that exchanges, shifts, perseverations and anticipations may take place. We have suggested that not just *segments* are represented in this store, but *syllable* structures as well, including constructs such as *onset, nucleus, peak* and *coda*.

How extensive might this programming domain be? The evidence (again, from Garrett 1980a) on perseverations, both of the intrusive and replacive kind, is illustrated in (64):

(64) (a) a c*l*ear p*l*iece (piece)
(b) ... take the GOP nomin*ow*ation away (nomination)
(c) ... wa*ll*op him in the cho*ll*ops (chops)
Replacive
(d) I don't understand the o*r*der at o*r* (all)
(e) I *d*reamt that he *d*roke both arms (broke)
(f) *e*xperiences become much more *e*xportant (important)
(g) a coat of *pr*imer, and then a *pr*oat of ... (coat)
(h) the *juice* is on the table. Is that en*uice*? (enough)

There is evidence here for intrusions extending over four syllables/two phrase-constituent boundaries, and for replacements extending over eight syllables/major constituent boundaries such as clause and sentence. However, it is possible that certain perseverative errors arise from interactions between memory for what has just *been* uttered and material about to be uttered. If we look to anticipatory errors, do we find such extensive domains? In so far as the illustrations in (65) are representative, they suggest not:

(65) (a) one b*ure* (beer) c*ure*s a bad dinner
(b) Yank*le* (Yankee) Dood*le* Dandy
(c) *g*olly (jolly) green giant
(d) curren*th* (current) mon*th*
(e) the *r*age (age) of _eason
(f) first, second, thir*th* (third) and ffour*th* years

and this may be a better indication of the normal operating limits of the articulatory buffer.

Evidence for a planning level

Exchanges and shifts involving articulatory elements suggest a similarly restricted domain. However, as we have seen, word and phrase construction exchanges occur over much wider domains, suggesting a distinct level of planning: in (66) *the mechanical mouse* is available for transposition before *an economy five and dime*, a domain of operation which may be appreciated from the linear extent of the target:

(66) I went to ↓ an economy five and dime for the mechanical mouse → I went to the mechanical mouse for an economy five and dime.

At the point marked by the arrow, the final noun phrase of the target must, in some sense, be already available for transposition – between seven and nine words 'upstream' in the planning process. If this is thought to be outside the limits of the articulatory buffer, then we have evidence of another level of operation here.

Articulatory accommodation

The strongest sort of evidence for more than one level of processing comes from certain accommodation phenomena, illustrated in (67):

(67) (a) a lot of po*n*/z/ and pa*t*/s/ to wash (pot/s/ and pan/z/)
      (b) it run_ out/*s*/ fast (run/z/ out)
      (c) eas[i·]_ enough*ly* (eas[i]ly enough)
      (d) a/n/_anguage *l*acquisition problem (a language acquisition . . .)
      (e) I deserve a/n/ *a*round of_plause for that (a round of applause)
      (f) m*usá*rpial (marsúpial)

In (67a, b) the transpositions occur in the articulatory buffer, prior to the realisation of the following fricative segments, which show modified voicing characteristics. In (67c) the second vowel of the target *easily* is modified in length and quality to reflect its prevocalic position subsequent to the transposition of *-ly*. These accommodations may be seen as occurring during the initiation of articulation, and hence to separate the levels of articulatory assembly (in the buffer) and implementation.

In (67d, e) we seem to have evidence of a compensatory process in the buffer itself: either the segmental form of *a(n)* is not specified until *after* the following lexical items have been assembled (and subjected to error), or it has been specified appropriately initially, and subsequently adjusted to take account of the following segmental transposition error.

Finally, errors like (67f) suggest that stress-syllable patterning may be specified independently of segmental characteristics. The vowels *u–a* in this exchange adjust their quality and length characteristics to their post-exchange environments. See Garrett (1980b) for a discussion of accommodation effects and their implications for distinct levels of processing.

3.5.2 *Relations between levels*

Given the presence of more than one level of operation, the issue arises as to how the levels relate to each other. We shall have more to say in detail about levels, and inter-relationships, in speech production in the next chapter: but we can introduce and illustrate some basic concepts here.

Serial versus parallel processing

We have referred to this distinction already, in concluding the previous chapter on neurophysiological processes. It is fundamental to more

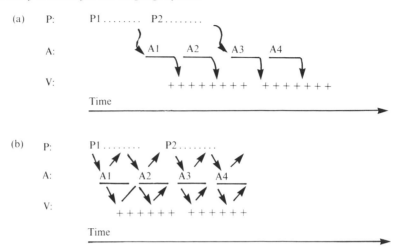

Figure 3.9 Schematic illustration of (a) serial and (b) parallel processing, for three levels of planning (P), assembly (A) and vocalisation (V) of utterances

abstract models of language processes also, as we shall see in subseqent chapters. We may illustrate with reference to the schematic layout in figure 3.9. Here, we have crudely identified just three levels for illustration of production processes for spoken utterances: P for a level of planning what to say, which may be thought of as partly involving message structure, delineation of topics, and so on, and partly the representation of these elements in terms of propositional or abstract syntactic structures: A for the assembly of the forms which are required for realising the plans, including lexical items and grammatical formatives; and V for vocal tract implementation of these assembled forms. Figure 3.9(a) illustrates a hypothesised serial-processing relationship between these levels: note that, for the purpose of this illustration, we are assuming just two main planning units, or domains, P1 and P2, each of which requires an assembly of two groups of lexical/grammatical forms, A1, A2, A3, A4, resulting in vocalisation that is largely continuous but may show breaks that reflect higher processing-unit boundaries. Figure 3.9(b) illustrates a similar set of processing units within a hypothetical parallel-processing system: the chief difference to note is that in this case assembly of the first group A1 can begin as soon as planning of the domain P1 has got underway; and likewise, vocalisation may start even before the assembly of group A1 has been completed. The output trace is similar, being essentially continuous, but showing occasional breaks which reflect higher-level processing boundaries. The most important difference, in terms of implications for the nature of processing, is that lower-level processes can influence higher ones within the parallel-processing model, whereas in the serial model, all higher-level processing is complete, for a given domain of processing, prior to any lower-level activity. By virtue of this, parallel models may be said to allow for interactive, on-line, bottom-up, influences during the time course of language processing.

It should be noted that it may be quite difficult to decide, in any given area of language processing, whether serial or parallel operations are effective in its implementation; and, again, that within a multi-level system it is conceivable that some levels may be serially ordered with respect to each other, while others may be parallel in operation. Finally, we should note that the distinction between serial vs parallel must itself be distinguished from the opposition of sequential vs simultaneous: there is sequential activity even in the parallel model, since one domain succeeds another, and elements within domains are likewise ordered in time (thus the term 'parallel' refers to independence of operation rather than to temporal relations); and simultaneity of operations is found within the serial model (where, for instance, all three levels may be simultaneously active, though within different domains of processing).

Relations between orders of description

Another sense of 'level' is that in which we speak, e.g. of the 'signal level' (ch. 1), the 'biological level' (ch. 2), the 'linguistic level' (ch. 3). To some extent, these refer to different orders of description, applied to the same phenomenon: language processing. What can we say of the relation between them? Figure 3.10 provides an illustration from the area of speech production. It focusses on linguistic and biological orders of description, since these may be seen as providing a framework within which it may be possible to establish a psychological (processing) order of description such as will concern us in the second part of this book.

The linguistic order of description is represented by the levels and categories recognised within generative phonology (Chomsky and Halle 1968); the biological order derives from some of the concepts we have introduced in chapter 2; and, between these, the psychological order is represented by a model we shall be examining in more detail in chapter 4, from Perkell (1980). Note that the psychological and linguistic orders tie in with each other at the point where sensory goal values are set up, in explicit parallel with the systematic phonetic representations of the linguistic model; and that the psychological order ties in with the biological order, first in its assumption regarding higher speech-control centres (which may be identified with the biological interaction of the cortex, thalamus and cerebellum), and secondly in respect of the motor commands that it recognises (corresponding to the innervation of the speech musculature). To some extent, the points of correspondence and divergence

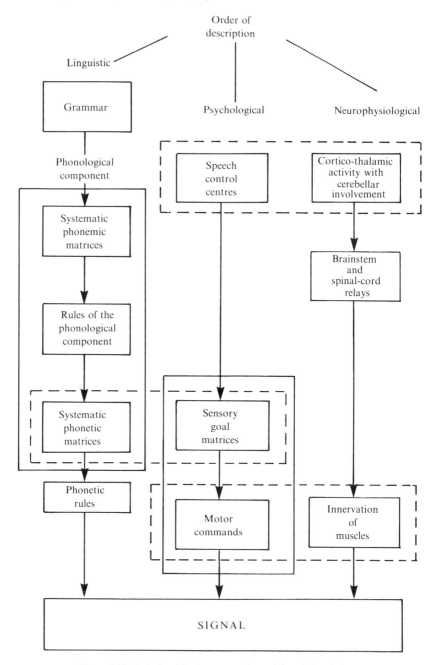

Figure 3.10 Relationships between orders of description in language processing, illustrated for speech production (see text). Dotted rectangles indicate areas of compatibility across orders of description

between these orders of description derive from the particular exemplars that we have chosen for our illustration. The main points to notice are, first, that each order of description is to be regarded as a hypothesis, subject to corroboration or falsification in its own terms; and secondly, that, in our present state of knowledge, we should not be surprised at the discrepancies between available orders of description, but make use of them in order to constrain our understanding of the nature of language processing.

PART TWO

Processes and models

4
Processing the language signal

4.1 Introduction

The main business of this chapter is to consider issues in the processing of the language signal: but, since it is also the first chapter in part II, it is also the place to set out the framework within which these issues will be set, and indeed those of the subsequent chapters.

4.1.1 *Preview*

We start, therefore, with a brief overview of the field of language processing, from the level of the signal up to message structure (4.1.2), before turning to signal processing, beginning with speech perception (4.2): this is the largest section, since it reflects a research field that has addressed such fundamental issues as the distinction between speech and non-speech signal processing in great detail. We then consider visual perception of written language (4.3). Sections 4.4 and 4.5 deal with production, in articulatory processes and in the organisation of handwriting and typewriting.

4.1.2 *The components of language processing*

What we can provide at this stage of the exposition is not so much a model, as a schematic route map. (See fig. 4.1.) The map basically indicates ways of getting from a *message* to be linguistically communicated to the *signal* that represents it, and vice versa. Two routes are provided: one, via the *lexicon*, carries the information flow for that part of utterance meaning and form which is represented in terms of constituent words; while the other, via *syntax*, does so for the constituent relations between words in utterances. Each of these routes is organised hierarchically, with respect to the message level, and to the lower level of *working memory*, to which they may contribute, and from which they may derive, information. Below this level are found the *production* and *perception* systems, which mediate between the upper hierarchies, of the *language system*, and the language signal.

In these terms, part II is organised with chapter 4 concerning itself with the production and perception systems between the language signal and the language system; chapter 5 deals with the lexicon; chapter 6 broadens the

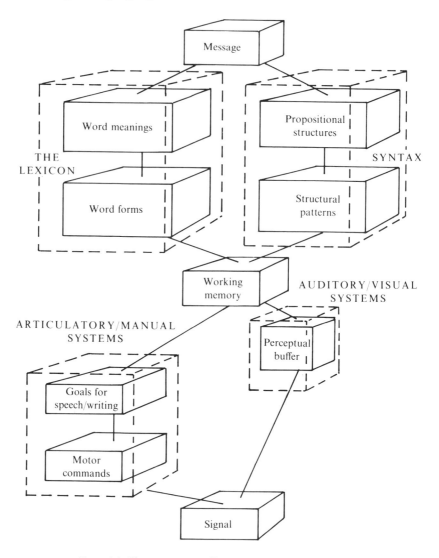

Figure 4.1 The components of language processing

scope to include syntax (as well as the lexicon), but concentrates on comprehension processing, while chapter 7 does the same for production. Finally, in chapter 8, we consider the evidence that derives from impaired language processing, involving a range of sources among these general components.

4.2   **Perceiving the speech signal**
4.2.1   *The time course of speech perception*

In part I, chapter 1, section 1.2.3, we considered the nature of the speech signal as a physical entity, and suggested that spectrographic representation (fig. 1.5) provides a reasonable basis on which to enquire into the ways in which the signal might be processed. We shall now consider some of the basic issues in the modelling of the ways in which this processing is effected, over time.

The processing window

The physical signal presents, in spectrographic form, some apparent segmentation: the vertical boundaries between consonant and vowel segments are fairly apparent. But we must beware of assuming that these straightforwardly define the *bases* of *auditory* processing: rather, they are apparent to us as the *results* of *visual* processing (our visual inspection of the spectrogram). Besides, given that speech processing is sequential over time, the fact that these apparent segments vary widely in their duration makes them unlikely candidates for initial stages of processing. Nooteboom (1979) speaks of 'a gliding time window, the contents of which are passed on to central processing mechanisms that extract auditory attributes like pitch, timbre, loudness and duration from the input signal' (p. 114). The aperture of this window is defined by the concept of an *acoustic buffer*, or store, distinct from what we may refer to as *auditory memory*, i.e., that part of the working-memory component of figure 4.1 which holds the results of processing the contents of the acoustic buffer. The more important characteristics of the acoustic buffer are:

it is faithful in the way it represents the physical properties of the signal (no analysis, or extraction and discarding of information has yet been carried out);

it is brief, with the contents fading rapidly;

it is determined, to a large degree, by the neurophysiological properties of the auditory system.

Nooteboom (1979) provides a review of studies relating to the time course of speech perception, including the rate of decay of the contents of the acoustic buffer. Plomp (1964) presented subjects with stimuli consisting of two sound-pulses, each of 200msec. duration, separated by a time interval of variable duration. The response of the auditory system to the first pulse decays over time (reflecting the recovery capacities of the neural fibres in the auditory

183

nerve and possibly also the more peripheral elements of the system): only after sufficient decay in the sensation level of the first pulse has occurred can the distinct onset of the second pulse be responded to. In other words, the first pulse will *mask*, for some brief period of time, the sensation of a distinct occurrence of the second pulse. Plomp found that the pattern for just-noticeable time intervals between the two pulses indicated a declining sensation level which, by extrapolation, reached zero somewhere between 200–300msec. Hence, post-stimulation auditory-system activity may persist for around 250msec. Nooteboom reviews some other studies (Slis and van Nierop 1970; Butcher 1973; Huggins 1975; Brokx 1979) and concludes that the estimate of 250msec. is about right for a sort of negative after-image of the original stimulus persisting in the auditory system. This allows for direct integration of one part of the incoming signal with another, within the 250msec. time-window. However, 'it cannot in itself explain the integration over time needed to explain word or morpheme recognition, firstly because its location is peripheral rather than central, secondly because it is too short-lived, and thirdly because its contents are acoustic, i.e. in terms of a time-frequency-intensity display, rather than auditory' (pp. 144–5). Possibly it is more suitable for the early identification of individual speech segments (phonemes), prior to the recognition of words and morphemes: this is an issue that we shall return to. Meanwhile, we shall follow Nooteboom's discussion of the time course of signal processing out of the acoustic buffer and into auditory memory.

Auditory memory

A shift from the strictly physical-acoustic to the more perceptual-auditory domain is accomplished in the transition from the acoustic buffer to auditory memory. Evidence for the nature of this auditory memory derives from work on the recall of verbal material. The findings are that, after each presentation of a number of novel sequences of seven digits or so (i.e. rather similar to telephone numbers), subjects are able to recall the beginnings and the ends of each sequence more accurately than the middles. The facilitation regarding the initial digits of the sequence is referred to as the *initial effect*, and may have something to do with memory strategies that are appropriate for the recall of individual items, or very small groups. This strategy collapses as more items are added, leading to the relatively poor recall of digits in the middle of the seven-digit series. The facilitation observed with the last few items is the *recency effect*, and may be thought of as resulting from an 'echo-chamber' function of auditory memory. The recency effect appears to be specific to auditory, rather than visually presented material: this property is known as the *modality effect*. A further effect is the *suffix effect*: this is found where an extra item, not to be recalled itself, is added to the list, and leads to the reduction of the recency (and hence the modality) effect (Crowder and Morton 1969; Crowder 1971). By varying the interval between the end of the list and the presentation of the suffix, it is possible to measure the decay of auditory memory for the (latter members of the) list. Rather than a consistent decay time emerging, however, it is found that estimated decay times vary considerably, depending on the acoustic characteristics of the items to be recalled. If these are potentially confusable with each other (i.e. harder to hold apart in auditory memory), then the effect of adding a suffix is quite small, for both consonants and vowels (Darwin and Baddeley 1974). This is consistent with a relatively brief decay in auditory memory for members of the list to be recalled: Nooteboom (1978) says 'When for a specific task a high quality of auditory information is needed, the survival time ... is very brief, say in the order of 150 or 200msec. If, on the other hand, low quality information is sufficient ... survival time of auditory information ... may be rather long, even in the order of seconds' (p. 146), and goes on to suggest that low-grade information is characteristic of intonation-pattern processing, while word recognition may be dependent on much more refined signal processing, and hence have to be accomplished much more rapidly.

Nooteboom (1979) also observes that, while the suffix effect reveals that auditory information is affected by subsequent auditory input, it 'does not tell us, however, how long auditory information may remain useful to the listener when it is immediately followed by other auditory information, belonging to the same stream of sound, as is normally the case in the perception of speech' (p. 133). But he is able to point to what he calls 'temporal reversals' in speech perception, where a later-occurring segment in the physical signal is effective in determining how an earlier segment is perceived. Such cases show that, in speech perception, auditory information persists *at least* as long as the time it takes for the offset of the first segment to be followed by the onset of the second. Studies by Remington (1977) suggested that, in the perception of CVC syllables, the initial consonant and vowel are perceived on the basis of the same acoustic information, and that the vowel segment becomes available in perception rather earlier than the initial consonant; Nooteboom and Doodeman (cited in Nooteboom 1979) found that listeners' perceptions of whether vowels of midrange duration were 'long' or 'short' were systematically influenced by the duration of a pause following the word or syllable containing the vowels in question.

Rather differently, because located at the level of word recognition, this sort of contextual perception is apparent in the findings of Warren and Sherman (1974) on 'phonemic restoration'. In this study, phoneme segments were excised from the acoustic signal representing a spoken utterance, and each was replaced by a burst of noise. The missing segment was uniquely specifiable, within the context of the word it occurred in. The possibility of acoustic cues to its identity remaining in the adjacent portions of the acoustic signal was eliminated by having the segment mispronounced prior to its excision. In spite of having no *acoustic* cues to the nature of the missing segment, listeners were satisfied that they had 'heard' it; they were unable to locate the burst of sound accurately within the word. Presumably what they 'heard' was the word, complete in all its segments, as stored in their mental lexicon (see the next chapter): but this was made available to them on the basis of subsequent (as well as preceding) acoustic signal processing.

Thus far, we have tried to set the scene within which speech perception takes place, and we shall now turn to consider specific aspects and issues. What does the processing window pick up from the acoustic signal? And what does it deliver to more central processes of speech perception? In chapter 1 (1.2.3), we have already introduced a distinction between two possible views of speech perception: it ultimately makes possible the identification of words (and hence of all utterances) in the language in question, but it may do so either *indirectly*, through an initial stage of speech-sound identification, or *directly*, by mapping the auditory perception of the acoustic signal onto the stored forms of words in the mental lexicon. The first of these possibilities accords with the traditional approach, and we shall consider it first. Notice that it involves two stages of processing, in a serial relationship: first, speech sounds are identified, and secondly they are assembled into sequences that are matched with the stored forms of words, for word recognition.

4.2.2 *Cues to phonemes*

Let us assume, for now, that phonemes are the immediate output of signal processing through the gliding time window, and that they are identified on the basis of subphonemic cues in the signal. Such a cues-to-phonemes approach may be illustrated as follows, in relation to figure 4.2, the spectrographic display of the phrase *rapid writing*. Here we have ten scanning steps, covering successive portions of the signal. They range in duration from 50 to 130msec. each, as a first approximation, and are defined in terms of a visual estimate of where the phonemic segment boundaries lie. Now, this is almost certainly an inadequate approach, given what we have noted already concerning the complexity of signal processing through the time window. But we may use it to illustrate the following points.

1. Speech processing cannot be carried out initially on a phoneme-by-

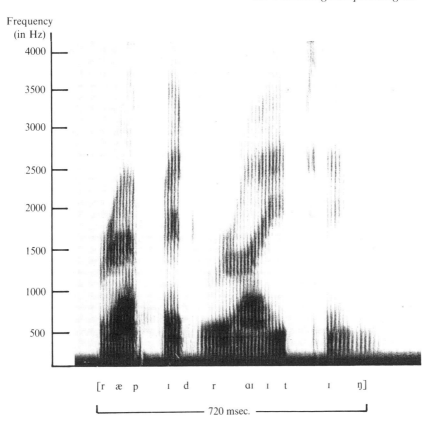

Step	Scan (msec.)	Phonemic identity
1	0–50	/r/
2	50–110	/a/
3	110–180	/p/
4	180–230	/ɪ/
5	230–280	/d/
6	280–360	/r/
7	360–490	/aɪ/
8	490–590	/t/
9	590–640	/ɪ/
10	640–720	/ŋ/

Figure 4.2 Spectrogram of the phrase *rapid writing*, and associated scanning steps for phoneme identification

187

phoneme basis, since the rate of their arrival at the ear, about fourteen phonemes per second in this example, would exceed the resolving capacity of the
auditory system. So there can be no question of simple 'phoneme-detectors' in
speech perception. The implication is that what are detected must be much
smaller than phonemes: acoustic cues, which can be processed within the time
constraints, and which provide sufficient information for subsequent identification of phonemes.

2. In fact – and this is only partially suggested in the scanning steps envisaged
above – phoneme-sized portions of the acoustic signal are not separated by
sharp boundaries, but rather interleaved with each other horizontally. Something of this is found in steps 3 and 8, where a voiceless stop is preceded and
followed by a voiceless vocalic segment. These voiceless vocalic sections
arguably belong to both the vowel concerned and the consonant, and are typical of the way in which speech-sound boundaries overlap. See also step 9, in
which nasality will be picked up on the final vowel, as a 'leading edge' cue to
the presence of the final nasal consonant.

3. Such an interleaved signal-structure as this implies points the way to the
resolution of the problem in (1), since a cross-section through any part of the
signal will typically yield information about more than one phoneme – preceding, current and following phonemes may be cued together.

4. Acoustic cues are presumably processed independently, in parallel, by
specialised cue-detectors which are sensitive to their occurrence in the signal.
In this connection, the presence of highly specialised cells in the auditory
system (ch. 2, section 2.2.4) is relevant to the earliest stages of speech processing.

5. The cues thus detected are transmitted through the auditory system to
some integrating component, which assembles and interprets the cues in the
form of language-specific distinctive sound-classes, phonemes, in a way that is
sensitive to their acoustic diversity in a range of different contexts.

6. Most importantly of all, perhaps, this approach makes it quite clear that
there is only an indirect relationship between properties of the acoustic signal
and the phonological representation which is ultimately derived from it. The
beginnings of speech perception are found in the response of the neurophysiological components of the auditory system to the physical properties of the
acoustic signal: the results of speech perception are found in our abilities to
identify the sounds and words of our language. The problem lies in knowing
what goes on in the middle region of these processes.

These points have led many researchers to conclude that speech perception is a highly specialised facet of human audition (e.g. Liberman *et al.* 1967). It is argued that, generally, the lack of a one-to-one relationship between properties of the input signal and the phonological percept, and everything which flows from this fundamental fact, demonstrate the need for a speech-processing capacity which is peculiar to speech and distinct from that required in the perception of non-speech sounds. Certainly, there is much evidence to suggest that speech perception is an extraordinary achievement. We shall briefly review some of its characteristics here, before going further into the issues that arise.

1. Speech perception is normally carried on in surroundings which are much less than ideal for 'good-quality' tape recording. Traffic in a busy street, doors slamming, telephones ringing, and more than one person talking, all around – these are some of the generally unnoticed accompaniments to successful speech communication. Just occasionally, the speaker will raise his or her voice intensity to overcome some particularly noisy intrusion; or the listener will lean forward, cup a hand behind an ear, or, very rarely, interrupt with 'Sorry, what was that?' But these are exceptional events. The normal situation is for speech perception to proceed apparently effortlessly.

2. Even without taking account of such seeming hazards as these, the signal that the speaker transmits is typically much less than 'ideal', if we compare it to the reasonably slow, careful style we think we might use if we really tried. When words are excised from tape recordings of speakers reading aloud, and presented for identification in isolation, many of them prove to be fairly unintelligible: a success rate of 50 per cent is typically found. In the case of naturally occurring spontaneous speech, the success rate can be still lower.

3. Speech is prosodically contoured, and an important feature of this contouring is the distinction between stressed and unstressed syllables. Many consonant and vowel sounds in unstressed syllables tend to be articulated further away from their ideal targets than their counterparts in stressed syllables; they tend to have shorter duration, too, and the articulatory gestures which underlie them are more schematic, yielding acoustic spectra that are less distinctive. Taking this last sentence as an example, there are rather more than twice as many unstressed as stressed syllables, so there is an important source of potential processing difficulty, if we believe that speech processing proceeds on a segment-by-segment, syllable-by-syllable basis.

The last two points here relate to the fundamental issue of perceptual *invariance* (perceiving the 'same' sound) in the face of acoustic *variance*, which we shall now consider in a little more detail.

Acoustic variance

A speech sound is said to be acoustically variant when it exhibits distinct acoustic forms in different environments. It appears that acoustic variance in speech is strikingly common. As a result, the problem of speech perception – at least the detection phase – becomes correspondingly complex. Acoustic variance may arise for a number of reasons, which we shall briefly consider here.

Probabilistic variance. Because human beings are not automatons, there is (inherent) variability between repetitions of the same activity; this is as true for articulatory gestures as for the rest of human behaviour patterns, and hence it is found also in the acoustic signal.

Different utterances of the same word or phrase by the same speaker under the same conditions give rise to variable forms. These variables are, individually, unpredictable; but, over repeated utterances, they will tend to cluster around common articulatory–acoustic centres. They can therefore be termed probabilistic variants.

Individual variance. Different speakers have individually distinct vocal tracts, which give rise to slightly different articulatory gestures and acoustic results. Some of these differences are linked to such controlling factors as sex and age. Sex differences are not simply a question of smaller/larger vocal tracts; the internal proportion between the oral and pharyngeal tracts is different. So a simple 'perceptual transformation' to compensate seems not to be adequate. Bear in mind also the radical differences between the infant's vocal tract and those of older humans (see fig. 2.14 and discussion). We should also bring under this heading the sort of differences that are linked to language varieties, both regional and social, since these partially determine individual differences in signal properties; and we should note that some sex and age differences may derive from sociocultural, rather than purely physical factors.

Dynamic variance. This covers a whole range of articulatory, aerodynamic and acoustic factors, accounting for perceptible *allophonic* variants (such as /a/ → [æ] in *man*, /k/ →[k] in *keel*, etc.) and for inaudible spectral characteristics of the speech signal. What is common to all such variants is that they are *contextually dependent*; they arise from coarticulations, from inertial forces in the aerodynamic phase, and from acoustic inter-relationships.

It is dynamic variance in particular that has motivated a whole range of studies aimed at determining the cues to speech sounds. These have been investigated most intensively, within the cues-to-phonemes approach, by the use of synthetic-speech stimuli which permit the selective and systematic manipulation of certain properties of the acoustic signal, while maintaining other properties at constant values.

4.2.3 *The evidence from synthetic-speech perception*

Illustrating from English, we may review here the sorts of acoustic cues that have been postulated as input to the speech-processing capacity. Some of them we have already mentioned in passing. There are fundamentally two types of cue, those that are *dynamically invariant* (i.e. unaffected by articulatory, aerodynamic and acoustic context) and those that are *dynamically variant*. In the case of certain sounds, both types may be operative. Among the variant group, we may distinguish between those cues that vary within the segment characterised by the percept (*segmental variants*) and those that vary in a neighbouring (preceding or following) segment (*contextual variants*). The situation is set out in table 4.1, based on the discussion in Borden and Harris (1980). It will be seen that variant cues become more involved in the lower part of the table with certain consonants.

As far as the vowels are concerned, high-intensity periodic sound cues are found in the relative positions of formants F_1 and F_2 (F_3 is also involved, but not distinctively and hence is not included here in the table). A low F_2 in a vowel segment correlates with back articulation; high values of F_1 and F_2 mark open and front vowels respectively. (To some extent, as will be seen from fig. 4.3, the terms 'high' and 'low' here are simplifications, since 'high F_2' has a higher absolute frequency value in conjunction with a low F_1 than with a high F_1, for example. However, the critical values of F_1 and F_2 are quite stable for particular steady-state perceived vowel qualities.) Monophthongal quality is the result of steady-state formant-positioning over time; diphthongal quality results from one position-pattern succeeding another, through gentle transitions. It is noted that the stressed component of the diphthong is of greater duration, and that the unstressed component may consist of transitions towards, but not quite reaching, the perceived endpoint vowel. The non-syllabic semivowels /j/, /w/ similarly have brief duration and consist in (sharper) transitions towards, rather than steady-state formants at, their perceived points. The liquids /r/ and /l/, like the vowels and semivowels, have a distinct formant structure, where F_3 appears to play a distinctive role; F_1 is low, F_2 in its midrange, and F_3 is either low (close to F_2), for /r/, or not, for /l/. The core of /l/ seems to demonstrate acoustic variance in respect of F_3, since it is high for /l/ following a close front vowel, which has a high F_2, but is mid after other vowels.

For the nasal consonants, the opening of the large resonating chamber in

Table 4.1 *Hypothesised speech cues in the acoustic signal, and their corresponding percepts in the phonological system of English*

Steady state formants F$_1$	F$_2$	Aperiodic noise	Closure characteristics	Transitions of formants F$_2$	F$_3$
Low	High				
High	High				
High	Low				
Low	Low				
Low	Mid				Low
Low	Mid				Mixed
F nasal	Locus low				
F nasal				Locus 1.8kHz	
F nasal				Mixed	
Short Locus low	Locus low		Extra duration		
Short Locus low		(High burst)	Extra duration	Locus 1.8kHz	
Short Locus low			Extra duration	Mixed	
Locus low	Locus low		May be voiced		
Locus low		(High burst)	May be voiced		
Locus low			May be voiced		
	Locus low	Wide band	Extra duration		
			Voiced		
		Wide band	Extra duration	Locus 1.8kHz	
			Voiced		
		High band	Extra duration		
			Voiced		
		Mid band	Extra duration		
			Voiced		
		Wide band			
		Mid band	Extra duration	Locus 1.8kHz	
			Voiced		

Based on Borden and Harris 1980: figs. 5.19, 5.20, pp. 184–6.

			Speech percepts

— Variant ───────────────────			
	┌─Contextual─┐		
Aperiodic noise	Preceding segment	Following segment	

			Speech percepts
			Close front ⎫ ⎧ Syllabic monophthongal
			Open front ⎪ ⎪ and diphthongal
			Open back ⎬ ⎨ vowels; non-syllabic
			Close back ⎭ ⎩ semivowels
			/r/
			/l/
			/m/
			/n/
			/ŋ/
(Mixed burst)	Devoiced	Devoiced onset	/p/ ⎫
	Devoiced	Devoiced onset	/t/ ⎬ (released)
(Locus F_2 burst)	Devoiced	Devoiced onset	/k/ ⎭
(Mixed burst)	Extra duration		/b/ ⎫
	Extra duration		/d/ ⎬ (released)
(Locus F_2 burst)	Extra duration		/g/ ⎭
	Devoiced		/f/
	Extra duration		/v/
	Devoiced		/θ/
	Extra duration		/ð/
	Devoiced		/s/
	Extra duration		/z/
	Devoiced		/ʃ/
	Extra duration		/ʒ/
			/h/
	Devoiced		/ʧ/
	Extra duration		/ʤ/

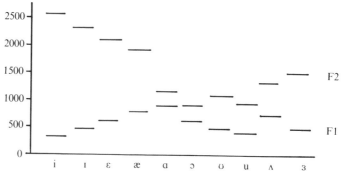

Figure 4.3 Formant positions for some steady-state English vowel sounds. (From Catford 1977: fig. 19, p. 59.)

the nasal cavity is shown by the presence of a low-frequency, very intense nasal formant, F_N, which obliterates low F_1. In the table 'low T' for F_2 indicates a transition *from* a low value (before a vowel), or a transition *to* a low value (after a vowel), or both (intervocalically). This is the invariant property of /m/. /n/ and /ŋ/ have variant F_2 transition cues. For the alveolar place of articulation, the F_2 transition is linked to a locus of around 1.8kHz. For the palato-velar consonants, it is linked to a locus of around 3kHz for front vowels, but to a lower frequency value for back vowels. The resulting acoustic discontinuity (found for /k/ and /g/ also) is partly the result of articulatory placement distinctions (postpalatal to postvelar, depending on the vowel environment), but also owes something to aerodynamic-acoustic effects of constrictions occurring in the back part of the oral cavity. F_2 transitions are steeper for front-oral release/closure, and shallower for the back-oral case; this results from the greater ballistic properties of the lips and tongue tip compared to the back part of the tongue (an altogether more massive articulator).

For stop consonants, place of articulation cues are as for nasals. Additionally, released stops have a characteristic burst (10msec. or so), which is variantly of low frequency (for more open vowels) and of higher frequency (for more close vowels) for /p/; invariantly of very high frequency for /t/; and variantly close to F_2 of the following vowel for /k/. These cues are parenthesised in the table, as properties only of those stops that are released. Additionally, again, a voicing contrast is cued in more than one way. Invariantly, F_1 transition is attenuated initially for voiceless stops, and duration of closure is shorter for voiced stops, and the two contextual cues, typified in the case of preceding and following vowels, show variant distinctions. Voice onset time (VOT), to the following vowel, is longer for all voiceless stops, but relatively less so for /p/ (around 25msec.) than for /t/ (around 35msec.) and /k/ (around

40msec.). A longer preceding vowel, with no devoiced offset, is also characteristic of voiced stops. This cue, together with the F_2 transition, is sufficient for
place and manner identification in the absence of the burst that is characteristic of release.

Among the fricatives, /s/, /z/, /ʃ/, /ʒ/ are cued invariantly by frequency and
duration of closure, presence of voicing; and variantly by duration of the preceding vowel. Additionally, /f/, /v/ vs /θ/, /ð/ are variantly cued by F_2 transition. /h/ has no cues relating to oral constriction, nor a voicing distinction.

Finally, the affricates show place of articulation and voicing cues that are
characteristic of stops; the relative duration of the aperiodic noise to the preceding closure and the following F_2 transition is critical to their perception.

This brief survey of possible acoustic cues is largely based on perceptual experiments involving synthetic stimuli. As a result, there are certain difficulties
in drawing direct conclusions regarding the perception of natural speech; for
example, it has been shown that synthetic F-structure differs systematically
(though slightly) from what is found in natural speech vowels, for optimum
perceptual clarity. Nevertheless, while the exact nature of the cues involved in
natural speech perception remains unclear, the experimental literature has
provided a good deal of preliminary information. It is already clear, for instance, that certain perceptual distinctions, such as voiceless vs voiced, have
no unitary acoustic cue: the fact that *tip/dip* and *sip/zip* can be contrastively
articulated and perceived in whispered speech indicates that the opposition in
such cases may crucially depend on the relative timing of other events than
laryngeal voicing.

4.2.4 *The speech mode: a critical review*

Apart from the phenomenon of variance, at least three other important arguments have been used in favour of a specialised speech mode (e.g.
Wood 1975): from categorical perception, from selective adaptation and from
right-ear advantage for speech. However, these arguments have not gone
unchallenged (e.g. Cutting 1978; Schouten 1980). We shall review the main
issues in a little more detail now.

Categorical perception

When people are asked if they can *perceive* something, two sorts
of behaviour are being sought. One is *discrimination* (perceiving the difference
between X and Y). Another is *identification* (perceiving that all Xs are instances of X). Discrimination has to do with same/different judgements
between items; identification concerns individual items, one by one, in relation
to some pre-existing category or 'label'.

Categorical perception shows itself when discrimination of equidistant (evenly different) stimuli is poor within a category label (e.g. 'those sounds are all /b/') but good between category labels ('that one was /b/, but this one is /p/'). Voice onset time (VOT) is an example of an acoustic dimension along which such categories can be revealed, and we shall consider it in more detail in a moment. First, figures 4.4 to 4.7 illustrate some other sorts of contrast that have been investigated using synthetic speech stimuli with equidistant graduations of one feature.

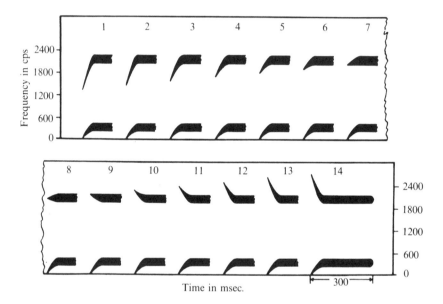

Figure 4.4 Fourteen synthetic speech stimuli formant patterns, covering the range /ba/–/da/–/ga/. (From Liberman *et al.* 1957: fig. 1, p. 359.)

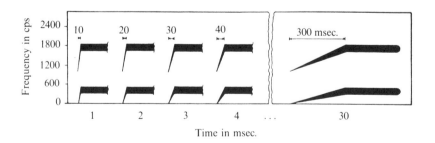

Figure 4.5 Thirty synthetic speech stimuli formant patterns, covering the range /be/–/we/–/ue/. (From Liberman *et al.* 1956: fig 2, p. 130.)

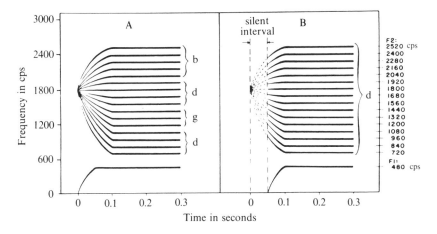

Figure 4.6 Synthetic speech formant patterns for the identification of /d/ before different vowel qualities. (From Delattre *et al.* 1955: fig. 4, p. 771.)

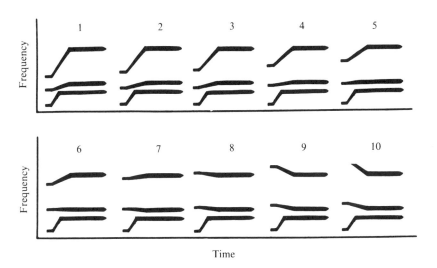

Figure 4.7 Ten synthetic speech stimuli formant patterns, covering the range /ra/–/1a/. (From Borden and Harris 1980: fig. 5.25, p. 192.)

Voice onset time

Now let us return to VOT. The timing of voice, in relation to release of an occlusion or constriction of the oral tract, is independently controllable. It can start *before* the release, to give 'prevoiced' consonants; though, if the consonant involves oral occlusion, there is an upper limit to this prevoicing period, represented by equal pressure of air above and below the larynx. But with oral constriction (for fricatives) the only limit is the time taken to exhaust the vital capacity of the lungs. This sort of timing difference is conventionally marked in *negative* values (e.g. '−40msec.' means 40msec. before oral release). Or voicing can start coincidentally with release (a VOT of 0). Finally, it may start after release (e.g. '+40msec.').

Along this dimension, synthetic speech stimuli can be constructed at regular intervals, in order to test people's perception of VOT differences. In a typical experiment of this sort, monolingual English speakers reported hearing /ga/ for all presented negative VOT values, for 0 VOT, and for all positive VOT values up to +40msec. At this point, and for all higher presented VOT values, they reported /ka/.

We therefore have two identification categories, *ga* and *ka*, with the boundary between them set at +40msec. VOT. What about discrimination abilities? These were tested as follows. An interstimulus interval was decided on (e.g. adjacent stimuli, in one trial; alternate stimuli, in another, and so on). Then two stimuli differing by this amount were presented; call them A and B. They were then followed by a third stimulus which was *either* A *or* B; call it X. Then the observer had to judge whether X was the same as A or B.

Using this 'ABX' method, the whole range of VOT values was investigated. It was discovered that, at the interstimulus interval that was sufficient to permit discrimination, and for larger intervals than this, people were much better at distinguishing between intercategory items (e.g. a high VOT-value *ga* and a low VOT-value *ka*) than equivalently VOT-spaced intra-category items (e.g. two *ga*'s, two *ka*'s). What does this tell us about speech perception?

The interpretation of categorical perception

A number of questions are raised by this sort of finding. Is categorical perception peculiar to the domain of speech? Can we relate it to known properties of the auditory system? Are only certain speech sounds perceived in this way? If so, can we say why? Is it acquired or present at birth? Is it found only in humans?

The safest generalisation seems to be that it is involved in the perception of sounds that involve rapid changes in their acoustic characteristics. So rather static speech sounds such as vowels with relatively stable formants are not categorically perceived. Nor are non-speech sounds such as pure tones, which are also static. But when vowels are of quite short duration and placed within a consonant–consonant frame, they tend to be more categorically perceived. In these circumstances, they are acoustically dynamic, with a formant structure rapidly assembling for the vowel and then disassembling equally rapidly.

However, in the main it is consonants that are involved in categorical perception. It was, indeed, first demonstrated for place of articulation on synthetic stimuli such as *pa – ta – ka, ba – da – ga*, where three categories – Labial, Alveolar, Velar – were reliably elicited and were then shown to affect discrimination in the required fashion. This experiment systematically varied the onset transition of formant F_2, keeping everything else constant. Further experimentation, involving manipulation of formant F_3 in VCV synthetic-speech stimuli, has shown categorical perception of *ara* vs *ala*. On another dimension, graded synthetic stimuli manipulating the duration of aperiodic noise of given frequencies in CV syllables have shown categorical perception of *tʃa* vs *ʃa*. In this case, *one* end of the continuum involves rapidly changing acoustic characteristics (the onset to the affricate). A similar sort of relative dynamicity is involved in the stimulus series *ba* vs *wa* vs *ua*, where the duration of formant F_2 transition is systematically varied, from short (*ba*) to long (*ua*). This also yielded categorical perception.

Not all consonants are categorically perceived, however. The difference between the fricatives *fa, θa, sa, ʃa*; or *va, ða, za, ʒa*, for example, is largely a matter of relative frequency of aperiodic noise. This is quite static, and is found to be continuously perceived. The hardest pairs to discriminate by frequency alone are *fa* vs *θa* and *va* vs *ða*. In these cases, there appears to be some formant F_2 transition cue, which might thus yield categorical perception, if frequency were held constant.

Categorical perception of at least some speech sounds therefore appears to represent a good foundation for the view that there must be some specialised decoding device for the perception of speech. However, this argument would be considerably weakened if evidence can be gathered suggesting that categorical perception is also found in the processing of some non-speech sounds. This appears to be the case. Categorical perception has been claimed to exist in non-speech perception such as 'noise-buzz' sequences (Miller *et al.* 1976), tone onset time (Pisoni 1977) and the 'pluck–bow' continuum (Cutting and Rosner 1974), where slow-rise, round-backed sine waves are characteristic of what are perceived as 'bowed-string' sounds, while fast-rise, saw-tooth sine waves are perceived as 'plucked-string' sounds. The difference between the two, acoustically, is in terms of 'hyperdynamic' (extremely fast-changing) properties at the fast-rise end of the continuum, and perception shows a discrimination-function peak at the boundary between 'plucked' and 'bowed' categories, but very low discrimination within these categories. Furthermore, and quite strikingly, human infants and one species of non-human animals (chinchillas) have been found to show human adult sorts of categorical perception of synthetic-speech sounds (Jusczyk 1981; Kuhl 1981), suggesting that the effect derives from a type of processing of acoustic events that is not specific to speech sounds.

At this point we should reconsider the phenomenon of categorical perception, in the light of what we noted earlier regarding auditory memory.

In the standard ABX elicitation procedure, the subject has to store stimulus A, then add to this the stored form of stimulus B, then add further the stored element X. Only when all three items are present simultaneously in auditory memory can the required comparisons be effected.

Now, let us assume a processing window in which fine acoustic detail fades very rapidly, leaving only gross linguistic information. In such a case acoustically distinct b_1 and b_2 will, in some very short time, be stored identically as two instances of [b]. If b_1 represents A in the ABX triad, b_2 B, and one of these – say b_1 – represents X, then effectively, by the time the triad is presented, it may have the representation [b] [b] b_1. On this basis the subject cannot say whether X is more like A or B. The phenomenon of within-category failure to discriminate will be discovered. If, however, A is b_8 (the last of the b-stimuli, acoustically) and B is d_1 (the first of the d-stimuli), the triad will, on the same assumption, be completed as [b] [d] [b_8]. On this basis, the phenomenon of intercategory discrimination will be found. So it has been suggested that categorical perception is possibly to some degree an artefact of the ABX format. It is real enough as a subsequent stage of processing (linguistic rather than auditory), but it is not necessarily characteristic of the first auditory stage of analysis. Consistent with this view, it has been found that finer discriminations within a linguistic category can be elicited by presenting two-element sequences for comparison, in series: 'Which pair is more alike? AA, AB' (with the order of sequences counterbalanced).

It has also been found, consistently with this view, that increasing the interstimulus interval between sounds such as steady-state vowels, which are not normally perceived categorically, can yield categorical effects: making the vowel sounds shorter and putting them into interconsonantal environments appears to give similar results.

So we may conclude this section by noting that the basis for categorical perception may lie in the rapid decay of information in the processing window. And this, in turn, may be quite consistent with the proposed acoustic basis for it in the hyperdynamic characteristics of the acoustic signal, regardless of the speech–non-speech distinction.

Selective adaptation

We have seen how the cues-to-phonemes approach naturally leads to the hypothesis of specialised acoustic-signal property-detectors, at the first stage of signal processing, and that these are, however hypothetical, assumed to function in a way that is similar to the sorts of neural detectors that have been isolated and empirically investigated in the auditory system (ch. 2). It is known that such detectors tend to operate in parallel with others, and that some are highly specialised for certain properties of the acoustic signal, e.g. frequency, or amplitude, but with a slight overlap of coverage between them. Each detector has a characteristic response-threshold pattern in the form of a tuning curve, whereby it responds best to stimuli falling within the centre of its range of coverage. It is also known that neural detectors can be fatigued by repeated stimulation. Within speech-perception research, an experimental paradigm has been developed (Eimas and Corbit 1973) which permits the investigation of boundary shifting between speech categories, as a result of repeated presentation of stimuli from one side of the boundary. In figure 4.8, two hypothetical cue detectors are illustrated for the VOT continuum, (following the discussion in Foss and Hakes 1978: 90–1): let us suppose that the VOT ranges to which the two detectors are sensitive overlap slightly, with one responsive to voiced stops (with short VOT values), and the other responsive to voiceless stops (having long VOT values), then stimuli falling within the overlap region will activate both detectors, and perception will depend on which detector is activated more strongly (situation A). If, however, the short VOT detector is fatigued by repeated stimulation with stimuli within its range, then stimuli subsequently falling within the overlap region will be less likely to activate that detector (to be perceived as voiced). The result will be an effective shift of the category boundary down towards the lower values on the VOT continuum.

This sort of approach has been seen as holding out considerable hope for the determination of speech property detectors (Ades 1976). But since a whole range of non-speech auditory stimuli show selective adaptation effects, it has provided a basis for arguments for the essential similarity between speech and non-speech processing, and hence against the existence of a specialised speech mode.

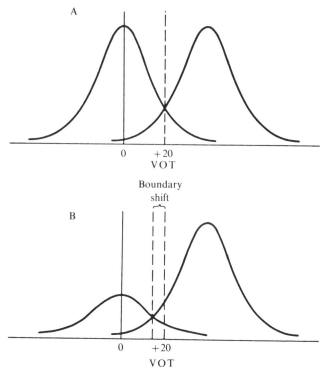

Figure 4.8 Hypothetical sensitivity functions for detectors sensitive to VOT values for /b/ and /p/: (A) before adaptation with a repeated stimulus; and (B) after adaptation. (From Foss and Hakes 1978: fig. 3.11, p. 91.)

Right-ear advantage for speech

This phenomenon derives from cerebral hemispheric specialisation in the form of the lateralisation of speech functions in the (normally dominant) left hemisphere (see ch. 2, section 2.4.3). The argument here has been from the existence of certain non-speech stimuli also showing left-hemisphere processing, to the conclusion that speech shows left-hemisphere processing only in so far as it happens to share those characteristics which the left hemisphere is specialised for.

Reactions

Against these criticisms of the speech mode, however, Repp (1982) points out that there are a number of problems with the arguments, and that there is some more recent evidence to support the notion of a speech mode.

First, concerning the supposed parallel between non-speech and speech-sound categorical perception, there are a number of methodological problems. As we have seen, it is possible that the basis for categorical perception actually lies in the use of labels in discrimination tasks, and from the time pressures of the processing window. In this connection, speech categories may be rather different from non-speech, in that they 'are not only more deeply ingrained than many other categories, but they also bear a special relation to the acoustic signal. As Studdert-Kennedy (1976) put it, speech sounds "name themselves"' (Repp 1982: 84).

Regarding the criticism from selective adaptation, Repp observes that this effect has been argued to result from quite early stages in auditory-signal processing (Roberts and Summerfield 1981), prior to the involvement of central mechanisms of speech (i.e. it arises in *acoustic* rather than in *phonetic* perception). The proposal to hypothesise phonetic-feature detectors to explain selective adaptation has come under particularly heavy fire from Studdert-Kennedy (1982), as an example of redundant conceptualising. As a result, the selective-adaptation paradigm is not currently in a fit state either to support or contest the view of speech as a specialised mode of perception.

Thirdly, the argument from hemispheric specialisation may turn out to be more complex than has been assumed: 'insofar as lateralisation presumably evolved to support some behaviour important to the species, it seems more likely that lateralisation of motor control preceded or caused lateralisation of speech processes, which in turn may be responsible for the superior analytic capabilities of the left hemisphere' (Repp 1982: 85).

Finally, Repp reviews some new evidence pointing to a special status for speech perception, from so-called 'trading relations' between speech-sound cues. Take, for example, the perception of voiced vs voiceless stop consonants in prevocalic position: for this, both VOT and F_1 transitions are contributory cues, and they may trade against each other in the following way: a low onset frequency for F_1 transition may be compensated for by an increased setting on the VOT parameter, yielding an equivalent phonetic percept (Lisker 1975). It is a challenge for non-speech auditory approaches to explain why such acoustically different cues as F_1 transition onset and VOT should conspire in perception in the way they do. However, it must not be thought that trading relations are only found in speech sounds: Darwin (1987) points out, rather, that speech is unique 'in the particular form of the trade-off. The same sounds heard either as speech or as a non-speech sound give different trade-offs between cues' (p. 72).

Best, Morrongiello and Robson (1981) got subjects to listen to stimuli in which the complex wave forms of normal speech had been replaced by sine waves of the same frequencies as the formants. When instructed to interpret the sounds as speech, they were able to do so, but subjects not so instructed perceived the sounds as non-speech whistles. In the 'speech' condition, the *say–stay* contrast (the presence vs absence of a stop closure between fricative and vowel) was more effectively perceived when the cues, silent closure duration and F_1 transition onset frequency, were operating together than when they were working against each other. By contrast, in the 'non-speech' condition, the results were unaffected by the nature of the working relation between the cues.

It seems that the possibility of the existence of a specialised speech mode goes to the heart of much of the motivation behind current speech-perception research. If one may hazard a guess, it is that crucial experimental data will prove elusive, and that competing interpretations of the available evidence will continue to be put forward.

4.2.5 *Alternative approaches*

Perhaps the best characterisation of our current understanding of speech perception is that we are working with two unknowns. On the one hand, it is not yet settled which properties of the naturalistic speech signal are truly functional, over what temporal domains, in speech perception. On the other, it is at best only a working assumption that the percepts cued by these properties are the linguistic elements (e.g. features, or phonemes) of phonological description. In this situation, it is possible for research to become unproductively circular; hypothetical and highly specialised detectors may be set up in order to account for the auditory system's apparent sensitivity to hypothetical acoustic cues having highly specialised properties such as variance. Discussions of whether particular detectors are 'phonetic' or 'acoustic', and of whether all detectors are one, or the other, rapidly become increasingly detailed and abstract. Faced with this potential quagmire, researchers are starting to probe in new directions.

The search for invariant cues

One way forward is to cling to the view that speech processing results in a phonological representation, but to renew the search for acoustic cues, with the emphasis this time on possible *invariant* properties of the signal (Stevens and Blumstein 1978; Blumstein and Stevens 1979, 1980, 1981). If these can be demonstrated to be available for all speech sounds, then a straightforward mapping between signal and percept will have been uncovered. The possibility that such cues are actually functional in speech perception would be an attractive one, therefore. This approach takes us into what we might call the *microstructure* of the acoustic signal. It is hypothesised that unique, invariant cues to phonetically distinctive features may be found in very short (tens of msec.) stretches of the signal. So two research questions arise: first, where in the signal is the search to be carried on?, and secondly, what is being looked for? Such evidence as is currently available is strongest on the perception of place of articulation. It appears that, within about 20msec of the consonant release, and thus prior to the F_2 transition curve, gross spectral configurations (i.e. on the frequency dimension) can be detected which are unique for labial vs alveolar vs velar place of articulation. In spectrographic data collected on over a thousand speakers, Blumstein and Stevens (1979) claim that such *spectral templates* can be observed about 85 per cent of the time. Subsequent perceptual tests have shown consonant identification on the basis of the initial 10–20msec. of consonant release, and synthetic spectral templates have been reported to lead to the expected perceptual shifts (Blumstein and Stevens 1980). Other contrasts, relating to manner and voicing, are currently being researched in similar fashion. If this proves to lead to reliable findings, this approach could usefully set limits on the initial phase of signal processing.

The search for holistic properties

The approach we have just outlined is in many ways a logical extension of mainstream studies of the last three decades; we might say that it views speech perception as, essentially, the processing of speech for linguistic (phonological) properties. A second recent approach, as expounded in Studdert-Kennedy (1981), is rather more radical than this. It rejects the assumption that the immediate end of speech processing is a phonological representation, claiming that this has actually distorted our view of the problem. We should not ask 'Why does the signal not contain straightforward cues to phonological elements?' but rather 'What exactly does the signal convey?' By adopting this essentially empirical attitude, it is claimed, we should avoid extraordinary artefacts such as the specialised speech-processing device.

Now, while this view claims that background assumptions may distort one's view of the acoustic signal and how it is processed, it turns out to have its own assumptions, which we should look at here.

Studdert-Kennedy's (1981) argument starts from two observations; first, speech perception is for language understanding; and secondly, the point at which the (essentially arbitrary) sound–meaning relations are established in language is the *lexicon*. Each word in the lexicon is represented as a complex of semantic, grammatical and phonological information. In its latter aspect, what this means is that it has a physical manifestation as a unit of neuromotor activity. Moreover, this neural pattern must also be considered to have a neurosensory pattern, linked to the neuromotor one, since the ordinary speaker is also a listener.

In this view, then, the input signal stimulates the neurosensory aspect of a neural composite pattern that represents a stored form in the lexicon. The information that it conveys is the dynamic pattern of articulatory activity that represents the spoken word. The immediate goal of speech perception is not the distinctive feature, or even the phoneme, but the stored lexical form that corresponds to the spoken word.

If we then ask, how is it that individual phonological segments such as consonants and vowels form part of our linguistic awareness?, the answer is that these emerge from the shared properties of the innumerable stored forms that make up our lexicon. Since the range of independent articulatory gestures and components is quite small in relation to the vastness of the lexicon, these elemental properties emerge as the recurrent components of successive neural patterns. But they are derivative, rather than functional in normal speech-processing. The functional property of the speech signal is its capacity to call up a stored neural complex, which may be quite abstract in its shared sensory-motor characteristics.

What properties are we looking for in the speech signal, according to this view? Not microstructure so much as *macrostructure*, not so much concrete spectral detail as abstract configuration. Evidence that supports this type of search comes from the following sorts of considerations. First, as we have seen, a contrast such as voiced–voiceless may be manifested in different ways in the acoustic signal. Some of these ways may be complementary, such that if one sort of cue is dominant (e.g. attenuated F_1 onset), the complementary cue is weak or absent (e.g. delayed voice onset): see our discussion of 'trading relations' above. Such a relationship suggests an abstract representation of the contrast at higher levels of processing. Secondly, it seems to be possible to strip the speech signal of particular amplitude and intensity characteristics and yet preserve perception, at least to a large degree (Remez *et al.* 1981). This suggests that it is the grosser dynamics of speech that are central to perception. This might also provide the basis for the perception of speech across a wide range of individual variation. Thirdly, it has also been shown that auditory perception can be dramatically influenced by visual input, where this is available. Looking at a face that actually says *ga* and hearing a voice, which appears to come from the face, but actually says *ba*, produces the percept *da* (McGurk and MacDonald 1976). The possibility of such cross-modal influences suggests that the critical properties of perception are essentially *abstract*, and thus modality-neutral, as well as *dynamic* and *holistic*.

Such different approaches as these may seem to be incompatible, but this is not necessarily the case. They may capture aspects of different and complementary processing strategies used in human speech-perception. In the current state of knowledge, it is far too early to accept one over another. It may turn out that the microstructural approach will improve our understanding of the stimulus-driven early stages of signal processing, while the macrostructural approach may tell us more about the higher processes involved, once preliminary information about the signal is available, and the task is to make that information compatible with what the listener knows (a) about the language and (b) about the current utterance.

In this connection, we should also mention Klatt's (1979) proposal that speech perception maps directly onto a stored phonetic network of all the possible words in the language having the form of sequences of spectral templates. The chief characteristic of these templates is that they cope with acoustic variance of speech sounds by containing their context-dependent onsets and offsets. They are thus more macro- than microstructural in nature, and recall the 'Wickelphones' of an earlier proposal (Wickelgren 1976; Pisoni 1981).

There is also much interest in the contribution of *prosody* to speech perception (Nooteboom, Brokx and de Rooij 1978), and one good reason for this is that it serves to link the earlier and later stages of speech perception. It is manifest in various ways in the acoustic signal, in modification of formant patterning, voice onset time, duration of aperiodic to periodic noise, changes in fundamental frequency, and so on. To that extent, it is part of the acoustic microstructure. But it also represents certain linguistic changes, such as the alternation of stressed and unstressed syllables, and the pitch contours of tone units. As such, it is a guide to abstract macrostructure. (Consider how often you have been unable to find the word that you wanted, but were nevertheless able to say that it had three syllables, and that the first was stressed.)

Our survey of speech perception has appropriately taken us close to higher levels of language structure, particularly the words in the lexicon. As we have seen, it is a characteristic of some recent thinking that the term *speech perception* properly applies to more than just the phonological level of language structure. In this sense, we shall be pursuing the study of speech perception later on, in chapter 5. But we shall first turn to consider other aspects of signal processing.

4.3 Perceiving the graphic signal

In spite of a wide range of typological differences, writing systems consistently represent language as patterns of light and dark in two-dimensional space. We have suggested (ch. 1, section 1.3.1) that we have no need to concern ourselves here with the physics of light, but this does not mean that we can ignore the issue of how the nature of the visual array might affect the way that written language is perceived. This question takes us into the field of visual perception (see Marr 1982), and we shall briefly review some of the more important aspects here, in preparation for our discussion of the basis of the perception of the graphic signal.

Henderson (1982) laments the 'general neglect of the elementary level of pattern analysis in [visual] word recognition' (p. 220). Pinker (1984a) has subsequently provided a clear review of the research that bears on this issue, and we shall draw on it in the following paragraphs.

Properties of the visual array

Consider the following orthographic version of the phrase whose spectrographic form we considered earlier:

rapid writing

In this printed form (we shall deal with handwritten representation a little later), it is quite apparent that there are segments with determinate boundaries, twelve letter characters, and one internal word space. It is not quite so clear how far the minimal segments may be regarded as clustering into letter groups – possibly *wr-* and *-ng* might be singled out in this regard. Nor is it clear whether perception of these letter segments is achieved by some sort of segment-matching process, or via an analysis of subsegment features such as 'vertical line', 'left curvature', 'closed loop', and so on, or by some other subsegmental properties of the array. We shall look at these issues in a little more detail below.

4.3.1 *Processing the visual array*

Two striking properties of writing systems, as compared with natural objects, is that they are typically composed of just two-dimensional elements (rather than three), and have a highly conventional structure. Letters of the alphabet do not (like tables) have objects lying on top of them, obscuring or extending their outlines; nor do they move about (like animals), or change their size and shape as you look at them (as balloons do while they are being inflated). They consist of a limited number of light–dark contrasting patterns, in terms of vertical, horizontal, slant, straight and curved edges, in various, but limited permutations. As such, writing systems constitute visual arrays that avoid many of the really problematic issues in our understanding of visual-shape perception. It is tempting to conclude from this that they are in some sense easy to process, a convenient feature for a system whose task is to represent the complexity of language for the reader or writer. But it is not clear what sort of early processing is involved, since it is a matter of debate as to what sorts of properties of the array the visual system makes use of.

The visual buffer

Our description of the visual system in chapter 2 (section 2.3) noted an upper time limit of around 250msec. for fixations achieved in visual scanning, during which time letters in the foveal field are available for uptake by perceptual processes. During these brief exposures, the retinal image contents of each fixation are processed in parallel, and retinotopically, initiating activation of successively higher levels within the visual system, up to the level of the primary visual fields in the striate cortex of the occipital lobe. It would appear that 250msec. fixation times are not required for this purpose, however, since 50msec. exposures will actually contain more information than can subsequently be recalled. Sperling (1960) showed that, with such brief exposures of an array of nine individual letters (not making up words), subjects were usually able to recall only about four or five of them. He could 'cue' a particular letter to appear reliably among the subset that were recalled, by placing a small bar marker next to it, and asking subjects to pay attention to the cued letter. Most importantly, he showed that the bar marker was effective in cuing a particular letter in the array, even when it appeared on the screen, in the appropriate position, but *after* the exposure of the letters had been completed. The image of the bar merged with that of the letter array, so that the subjects 'saw' the two together, just as if they had been physically copresent on the screen. By systematically increasing the interval by which the bar marker was delayed, Sperling was able to show that this *visual buffer* image effect permitted randomly designated letter recall in a way that smoothly declined, till at 500msec. delay it was no longer effective. The term 'visual buffer' is used here in explicit parallel with the 'acoustic buffer' (4.2.1 above); it is also called *sensory information storage* (SIS) (Lindsay and Norman 1977) and *iconic memory* (Dick 1974; Long 1980).

Sperling also noted that, if a letter was cued by a circle enclosing it (instead of a bar), it was not cued in perception, but *erased*: the array was recalled with an empty circle where the cued letter should have been. This demonstrates a masking of earlier information in the visual buffer by later information, and this is presumably important in 'wiping the slate' in the transition from one fixation to another. Instead of creating a palimpsest effect, like the overlaying of one transparency with another, making both difficult to read, the contents of a subsequent fixation obliterate those of the preceding one. Thus the visual buffer contains more information than subsequent stages of processing are able to extract; it represents its contents continuously (e.g. smoothing out eye-blinks), faithfully, exhaustively and pre-analytically, and decays completely within half a second. Fixation times of around 250msec. therefore do not reflect the time required for the uptake of information from the printed page into the visual buffer, but rather the time required for the contents of the visual buffer to be transposed to *working memory*.

Working memory

Information extracted from the visual buffer is passed to an analogue of the auditory memory store that we discussed in section 4.2.1 above. There, is, however, a puzzle in knowing how far this memory store for reading works on auditory or visual principles. We have seen, in chapter 1, section 1.3.4, that the English writing system (not alone among writing systems generally) has both sound-representative and word-representative aspects. The degree to which letter–sound correspondences such as we discussed in chapter 1 play a role in the reading process is an issue which is as old as reading research itself. The possibility or otherwise of contact between written language and speech processing-paths is central to many models and theories. Those that view reading as mediated via speech in some way are often referred to as 'indirect' theories of reading. We shall refer to them generally as *grapho-phonic transposition* (GPT) theories, since there are considerable differences of detail in how the 'graphic' and 'phonic' elements in the process are conceived of. One possibility is that the contact is effected in the way that information is stored after it has been extracted from the visual buffer.

Baddeley (1979) refers to this next phase of processing as *working memory*, and recognises within it both an *articulatory loop* for the rehearsal of verbal material, and a *visuo-spatial scratch-pad* (VSSP), for the maintenance of spatial and other aspects of visual material. It is the articulatory loop that concerns us here. The articulatory-loop theory holds that information from the visual buffer is converted into a phonological form, for further processing. Evidence consistent with this view comes from the deleterious effect on immediate recall ability of having phonologically confusable items (such as B and C, which do not look alike, but share the same vowel in their letter names), or long words, in the verbal materials to be recalled; and from the finding that phonological confusability and word-length effects in this task can be dispelled by getting subjects to articulate an irrelevant word over and over (presumably preventing the subvocalisation behaviour on which the transfer of information to the articulatory loop is based; see Conrad 1964; Baddeley and Hitch 1974; Baddeley, Thompson and Buchanan 1975). It is also suggested that the articulatory loop may play an important role in learning to read (Conrad 1972; Liberman *et al.* 1977). Concerning fluent reading, Baddeley notes that research 'has shown that [the articulatory loop] is not essential for comprehension (Baddeley 1979), but provides a supplementary source of information that may be important when a high level of accuracy is required' (1981: 19).

It is not clear how far the loop may be *articulatory*, as opposed to auditory, in nature, or possibly involve some abstract level of phonological representation that is neutral between these two. Subvocalisation behaviour in normal fluent reading, where it exists, may not bear on this question, since it may result from, rather than work towards, lexical access (i.e. may be *post-* rather than *prelexical*). The likelihood of subvocalisation being postlexical is underlined by the consideration that reading a word aloud involves latencies of around half a second up to the initiation of the vocal output, whereas comprehension of the same word can be demonstrated to have occurred in rather less than half of this time. Similarly, reading rates are generally at an order of magnitude faster than the 300 syllables per minute that would be the upper limit on the basis of (sub)vocalisation: 300 *words* per minute is quite a normal sort of reading rate, with words containing more than one syllable each on average.

So it seems likely that grapho-phonic mapping, in so far as it occurs prelexically in reading, takes place at a more abstract level. It may account for the subjective impression that readers have, of some 'inner voice', even when reading at high speeds, and for the sensation of the 'para-phonological' characteristics of the words on the page even while simultaneously vocalising some irrelevant material. Such grapho-phonic mapping is essential to our ability to read aloud non-words, and words that we have not encountered before. It may very well exist in parallel with the more direct, visual route, whereby the letter forms on the page are somehow mapped onto stored graphological forms of words in our mental lexicon. Below, we shall consider how far the print-to-lexicon mapping procedure, whether phonologically mediated or not, may involve an intermediate level of representation that is based on whole letters, or *graphemes*. First, however, we must look in a little more detail at the possible nature of the first stage of processing of the visual array.

4.3.2 *Pattern recognition in the graphic signal*

Just as we considered earlier the possible cues to speech perception, we shall now enquire into which properties of the graphic array might actually be utilised in reading. Pinker (1984a) provides a convenient review of recent approaches.

Template-matching versus structural descriptions

Visual pattern recognition has often been seen as essentially a process of matching the patterns of light stimulating the retina with stored templates of either whole objects (the simplest type of template theory) or features of objects (more sophisticated 'feature-detector' theories). It is usual for whole-object template theories to be dismissed (e.g. Neisser 1967), in the context of natural-object perception, as being hopelessly incapable of accounting for the sheer numbers of variations of shape/size in retinal image and of orientation in the visual field that natural (and man-made) objects exhibit. Thus, for example, an eagle seen from close up is very different in the area of retinal stimulation it gives rise to compared with the same eagle viewed from a distance; and as it flies overhead it presents continually changing outlines of wings and body shapes as it changes orientation in the visual field of an observer on the ground. There is also the figure vs ground problem, in which natural objects may be partially camouflaged by their surroundings.

However, some of these problems do not arise in the context of conventional letter shapes, which are few in number (compared to the natural objects of our environment), and restricted in dimensionality, orientation, size, and sequential distribution. Figure/ground characteristics are usually ideal, too. In any case, Pinker (1984a) points out that some arguments against simple templates may have been prematurely made, in view of current neural models of recognition and imagery (Trehub 1977), in which each template is stored in a single cell, rather than distributed over the cells of the entire retina. Each such cell receives inputs from many others in the retina, and is able to compute best matches from a variety of partial matches, such as 'P' for 'R'. Accordingly, it is not inconceivable that the visual array for written language consists of whole, character-sized patterns of light–dark edges that the visual system is readied to process.

Feature models of visual perception (based on the early work of Selfridge 1959) rely on part- or feature-templates, for recurring parts of shapes. So, in the upper-case English printed alphabet, the letter 'A' would trigger responses from feature detectors specialised for left and right slant lines, a horizontal line and a vertical angle (see e.g. Fisher, Monty and Glucksberg 1969; Briggs and Hocevar 1975). In such a case, the visual array might consist of feature-sized patterns of light–dark edges, with some economy of storage, at the cost of extra processing (assembling the feature-responses into larger complexes).

Structural descriptions (Winston 1975a; Oden 1979) are, in a sense, propositional templates, or recipes for shapes, specifying components and spatial relationships between them. However, they are rather abstract, and it is not

clear exactly what sort of components are envisaged at the earliest stages of
signal processing (Pinker 1984a).

Fourier analysis

A way of specifying components in the visual array is provided in
the work of Kabrisky (1966), Kinchla (1977) and others. A pattern of light–
dark edges can be thought of as a set of alternate increases and decreases in
light intensity, along a particular dimension. If these increases and decreases
are perfectly regular, say, along a horizontal plane, then one component of the
visual array in question is describable as a sine wave having peaks and troughs
of light intensity. If the pattern is not symmetrical, but is also not random, it
can be described as a complex wave, having component sine waves within it.
The parallel with our discussion of the speech signal above will be apparent.
High spatial-frequency information relates to sudden changes of light intensity (e.g. within small degrees of visual angle), associated with individual letters
in a word; low spatial frequency is also present in gross word shapes, however
– the sort of information that is contained in the array after extensive blurring
of the image (Henderson 1982). It is conceivable that both amplitude and
phase spectra of these high- and low-frequency complex wave forms constitute the essence of the visual signal (Pinker 1984a).

As we noted above for the speech signal, there is still the issue as to whether
the visual system works directly from spectral analyses of the input, to stored
representations (spectral templates) of whole-word shapes (both in terms of
gross and fine detail), or whether at some point an intermediate construct, the
letter (or 'grapheme', as it is frequently called), is established in perception
(McClelland 1976: see the discussion in Henderson 1982: chs 9, 10). There is
also a question concerning the *modality* of further processing, since there is
some evidence for a connection from visual input to phonological encoding.
We shall take up this latter issue first.

4.3.3 *Graphemes and allographs*

In contrast to our printed orthographic version above, consider a
handwritten form of the phrase, as in figure 4.9. It is much less clear how segment boundaries may be determined in this representation. Even the centres
of segments are severely distorted from their canonical forms, presenting a
more challenging problem in understanding how perception may be achieved.
While certain landmarks appear to stand, as (initial) *r-*, *-a-*, *w-*, other forms
are much less easy to identify. The form of the first *-i-* here might be interpreted as *r* in another context; that for *-d* might be *cl*; after the *w-*, the form for

-r- might be *v* elsewhere; or, together with the following downstroke (for *-i-*), it might be *n*; and so on. And, if the identification of *g* depends in part on a component of an upper closed loop, then the lack of such a feature in this case is surely a problem. In such cases, we may want to recognise an essentially dynamic form of variance, such as we noted in the case of the speech signal. Interestingly, perhaps, language users are apparently much less proficient at handling such variance in the graphic signal, however: it is much more usual to be unable to interpret someone's handwriting than it is to fail to understand their speech. Further parallels with speech may be sought in the personal, regional and educational influences on the way that individuals develop their 'hand' in writing.

Figure 4.9 Handwritten production of the phrase *rapid writing*

Such considerations as these tend to the view that interpretation of the visual signal is not satisfactorily accounted for in terms of a signal-driven process of letter identification, followed by assembly of these letter percepts into word sequences, and so on. Contextual integration would appear to play a vital role in the identification of component letters. However such variant forms might be processed, there seems to be some point in the parallel between *allographs* with allophones, and *graphemes* with phonemes, at least in the case of handwriting. Henderson (1982) is generally dismissive of the notion of allographs and graphemes in the case of other forms of the graphic signal, since printed characters tend not to show dynamic variance, and the concept of allography relates simply to such phenomena as the more or less arbitrary link existing between lower- and upper-case forms of letters. However, in writing systems other than English (for example, the Kannada syllabary discussed in ch. 1), we may note that allographic variation is much more important than in English, and may serve to demarcate word boundaries in examples of the script where spaces are not used for this purpose.

The issue of whether graphemes are perceived prior to lexical access, or as a result of it, parallels that of the role of the phoneme in speech perception, above. It is partly bound up in the nature of written-word representations in the lexicon, to which we shall now turn.

4.3.4 *Graphological forms in lexical entries*

The next issue to consider is how the written forms of words might be stored in the mental lexicon. At the neurophysiological level, they may be thought of as neurosensory schemas, but at the perceptual level are they organised as sequences of individual graphemes, or more holistically? Direct evidence is difficult to come by, but we may assume that evidence that supports the notion of the grapheme as a mediating element in lexical access will be consistent with the view that lexical entries are stored in terms of graphemes, and vice versa.

Words stored as visual patterns

According to this view, the graphological form of a lexical entry is stored as a holistic visual pattern, which may be either a word-shape 'envelope' reflecting the pattern of individual letter-shapes within it, or, more complexly, in terms of the concept of spatial frequency (see Groff 1975, and section 4.3.1 above). We can illustrate the difference between high vs low spatial frequency by considering a visual array such as a page of print. Under ideal conditions, the print stands out clear and sharp from the page. Even such closely spaced edges as those marking the sides of the vertical stroke in *d* are clearly perceived; these are high-frequency spatial components. Under less than ideal conditions (e.g. without reading-glasses), characters like *d* are 'blurred', their individual edges can no longer be picked out, and what are perceived are the grosser – more widely spaced – components of letter structure, i.e. the low-frequency spatial component. Now, somewhere within this frequency spectrum, it is argued, reside patterns (relations between components) that are characteristic of particular orthographic words. And it is these patterns that are stored in the graphological form of lexical entries.

It is instructive at this point to consider the parallels between this view and the holistic theory of speech perception that was briefly introduced in chapter 2 (section 2.5.1). In each case, stored word forms are held to be directly compatible with their perceptual counterparts and the percepts themselves are characterisable in terms of subsegmental, featural properties (the phoneme, and the letter, are irrelevant concepts). Now, whatever the merits of this view in speech perception theory, there is no compelling reason to adopt the same view in orthographic perception. As Henderson (1982) points out, although some studies (e.g. Havens and Foote 1963) have found that words with distinctive envelopes are more easily recognisable than other equally common words, their results 'are perfectly compatible with a model based on individual letter identification' (p. 232).

Further, it has been found that changing letters from *uPpEr* to *LowEr* case in a word, and effecting $_{o}{}_{t}h^{e}{}^{r}s^{o}r^{t}s$ of distortions, does not impair access in a way that would be consistent with visual-pattern theory. For example, if we have never encountered the specific visual pattern *uPpEr* before in our lives, it should behave like a non-word, up to the point of lexical access. But it is found instead that real words (like *upper, uPpEr*) are easier to access than non-words, regardless of case, fount and positional and other sorts of mutilations of the visual pattern (McClelland 1976). What these results strongly suggest is that access, for both real words and non-words, is mediated via letter percepts (in our terms, *graphemes*) that are themselves abstract enough to transcend such dimensions of form as case and fount. But, of course, such studies do not tell us what graphological forms of words in the lexicon are really like.

Words stored as graphemic structures

If words are stored in the mental lexicon with graphological forms that are organised as strings of graphemes, then these must presumably be structured in some way that captures their 'wordness'. Otherwise, it is difficult to explain why words should have a perceptual advantage over random sequences of such well-known entities as letters (see further 5.2.3). A parallel may be found here with phonological representations of words: those that are organised in terms of phonemes were initially conceived of as linear strings (Chomsky and Halle 1968), but subsequent emphasis has been placed on their non-linear properties (e.g. syllabic structuring: Fudge 1969; Goldsmith 1976; Kahn 1976; Liberman and Prince 1977).

We should note that, if lexical entries are taken to have graphological as well as phonological forms, then these must be inter-related within each lexical entry in such a way that a given word may be visually perceived, then pronounced, or judged as rhyming with another, auditorily perceived word; or auditorily perceived, then spelled, or judged to have regular or irregular spelling, and so on. This sort of grapho-phonic inter-relationship is not *pre*-lexical, since it forms, by hypothesis, part of the lexical entry itself. It thus represents a type of convergence between visual and auditory perception that cannot form a mechanism of lexical access: it allows for direct access to word-specific graphological form, *after* which phonological properties of the word in question also become available.

4.4 Articulatory processes

In part I, we reviewed some of the articulatory-source properties of the acoustic signal, the neurophysiological elements involved in its generation, and some potential sources of evidence, from slips of the tongue, regarding the nature of articulatory-control processes. There are three basic levels of processing for us to consider here. The first concerns the 'loading' of target articulatory patterns into the speech-production mechanism. This is basically a matter of accessing the stored articulatory patterns for individual words, in the lexicon, and making them available to a transient output store – in terms of figure 4.1, from *word forms* within the lexicon to *working memory*. But output reflects not just individual word patterns, but also, in the case of multi-word utterances, the constituent structure within which words are set – in figure 4.1, the input from *structural patterns* to working memory: so we have to consider the consequent adjusting and integrating of the sound sequence, resulting in various word-boundary effects, both segmental and suprasegmental (Cooper and Paccia-Cooper 1980), and prosodic organisation (Cutler and Isard 1980). It is not easy to locate the source of all such effects: some may result from the level of working memory, while others may be derived within the *articulatory system* of figure 4.1. We shall recognise, for the main framework of our discussion, a level where 'ideal' targets are established for each part of the sequence, in *goals for speech*; and a subsequent level, of *motor commands*, from which control of the articulatory organs is effected.

4.4.1 *The input to working memory*

Shattuck-Hufnagel (1983), on the basis of speech-error evidence, proposes a *scan-copy* device which deals with the lexical input to working memory, and Lapointe (1985), on the evidence of certain processing disorders, has suggested a *read-copy* mechanism, from a structural-pattern store.

The scan-copier model

Going back to the evidence from slips of the tongue, we need to make just two additional observations before proceeding. First, that most consonants (apart from /ʃ, ʒ, tʃ, dʒ/) are equally likely to function as *intruder* or as *target* elements, e.g. in *bate of dirth*, /b/ is intruder for target /d/ and /d/ is intruder for target /b/; secondly, the frequency with which certain segments occur in error patterns appears to match their frequency of occurrence in the language. Armed with these considerations, we can attempt to outline a model of how stored lexical representations come to form the input to a motor-command model.

Of course, the concept of simply lifting the stored lexical representation out of memory and articulating it is wildly inappropriate. The memory which underpins the lexicon is not like a warehouse, from where items of stock can be physically removed. We do not forget a word the moment we have uttered it, which is presumably what 'removal' would imply. Stored lexical representations should perhaps be thought of rather as catalogue entries, which describe

217

the properties of lexical items. Our model must therefore be able to *scan* these entries, and to *copy* them into the motor-command processing device. It is at this level that speech errors may plausibly be located. We may think of an entry as consisting of two parts; one relates to the skeletal framework of the word, and is essentially rhythmic and syllabic; the other specifies the segments that can be inserted into the framework. Notice that splitting these two types of entry information achieves considerable economy of representation. The hundreds of thousands of words that are in the mental lexicon are, in the main, phonologically distinct from each other (homophony exists, but is much less common than heterophony). But there are a relatively few skeletal (CV...CV) patterns that occur again and again; and, likewise, a limited set of segmental elements that fit into the positions defined in these patterns. Thus, if economy of representation is a goal of the model, then this would be one way of achieving it. The cost is to be found in the necessity of postulating a copying process, which inserts segmental representations into skeletal representations; in this combinatorial activity, speech errors may arise. (See fig. 4.10.)

On the basis of some of our earlier discussion, we may legitimately question whether economy of representation is so all-important, of course. For instance, the segments may be quite richly specified in terms of their coarticulatory patterning. But some sort of skeletal-frame vs segmental-filler distinction is probably required in any case, if a large number of intralexical relationships are to be captured (e.g. *sing – sang – sung*, which all show the same partially filled frame).

We may postulate also a monitor, which checks the copying process, in order to prevent multiple copying of the same element, and to 'edit' sequences of suspiciously similar segments (which might have arisen through copy error). In its editing function, the monitor may occasionally actually introduce error into certain unusual but correct sequences (e.g. *be behaving* →*be-having*). Other possible outcomes from this model would include:

> on-line corrections, as the monitor catches a copy error in time, e.g. *top – shop talk*;
>
> next-best target, as the monitor catches a copy error but fails to amend it at source, substituting instead the element that has been left out by the copier, e.g. *top shalk*;
>
> monitor failure after copy error, e.g. *top talk* (for 'shoptalk').

Of these, on-line corrections appear to be the simplest types of error, and it is confirmed that they constitute the most frequent single type in the MIT corpus.

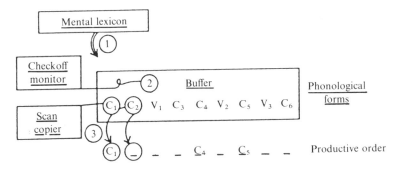

Figure 4.10 Schematic diagram of Shattuck-Hufnagel's scan-copier model,
1, a word form is entered into a buffer memory store; 2, the check-off monitor
erases segments from the buffer as they are dealt with; 3, the Scan Copier,
which copies them into the speech-production system. (From Buckingham
1985: fig. 5.5, p. 129, based on Shattuck-Hufnagel 1979.)

Finally, there is the question of suprasegmental structure, particularly
stress. In errors such as *photo'graph, photo'grapher* it is just possible that we
are dealing with a type of exchange, stressed ↔ unstressed, in the skeletal
framework; but it is perhaps more likely that one skeletal framework (for
photo'graphic) is somehow influencing the others. In general, we can say of the
framework that it exists to guide the scan copier, since there are constraints on
which elements can fill which positions (e.g. /ŋ/ is not a segmental candidate
except for syllable-final positions in English).

4.4.2 *The components of the production system*

Perkell (1980) has provided a convenient framework of a processing model which works from sensory goals to motor commands. It deliberately reflects a fairly traditional approach to the issue of how a *segmentally
structured* input, in the form of target articulations for individual segments
within a sequence, may be transposed into motor commands for the implementation of an *essentially continuous* speech signal. The framework accordingly hypothesises an input level consisting of segments specified in a binary
(+ or −) fashion for various *sensory goals*. Moreover, these segments and
sensory goals are assumed to correlate with the *phonemes* and *distinctive
features* of linguistic (phonological) descriptions (Chomsky and Halle 1968).
So we are dealing with an account that is basically concerned with the transposition of a linguistic-type input to a neurophysiologically-based output.
There is a parallel between this approach and that which we noted in the case

219

of speech perception, in the role of the phonemic level between the signal and the representation of it in the language system.

The sensory goals

These are of two types: those that are specified for individual segments, and those that extend to two or more segments (suprasegmental sensory goals). Notice that the particular linguistic/behavioural relationship in this model allows for insights from these two viewpoints to be combined at this level of representation: the segments/goals are quasi-linguistic (at the least), yet the sensory goals themselves reflect an essentially teleological or target-oriented type of processing, supported by feedback. This is the peculiar characteristic of the input matrix at the top of figure 4.11. From what has been said so far, it will be appreciated that there will be only an indirect relationship between these sensory goals at the input level and the output of motor commands to particular muscles. Thus, a prime function of this model is to account for the transduction processes that are required to relate these levels. The sensory goals themselves (e.g. 'maintenance of intra-oral air pressure', or 'constriction of oral passage in alveolar/tongue-tip articulation') typically refer to more than one articulator (e.g. jaw *and* tongue) or more than one muscle group within an articulator (e.g. 'flatten tongue body' *and* 'raise tip'). They therefore have to be broken down into discrete motor commands. But this is only a part of the transduction process, because they also have to be specified for temporal value. One of the fundamental issues in any model of speech production is the point of entry for the *temporal* dimension. At the input level in this model the segments are in *sequence*, but have no temporal values. And thus the same is true of the sensory goals that cross-classify them. So the next stage in the model is to implement the transduction along these lines. Before proceeding, however, we should note that sensory goals (like distinctive features) are not completely independent of each other. There are dependencies that are language-specific, such as, in English, that *nasal* consonants are (at this ideal level) all *voiced*; and dependencies that may derive from biomechanical interactions among articulators (e.g. lip rounding tends to raise the jaw). Thus the lack of variance at this level, while considerable, is relative rather than absolute.

Finally in this section, we should consider the *quantal* basis of the sensory goals. By quantal is meant the package-like structuring of distinctions along a given dimension. Thus, apical contact along the postdental ridge is essentially uniform in acoustic effect for different positions, from the base of the teeth to the alveolar point; but a small movement further back still, to just behind the alveolar point, will yield a perceptually large effect. This is a transition from

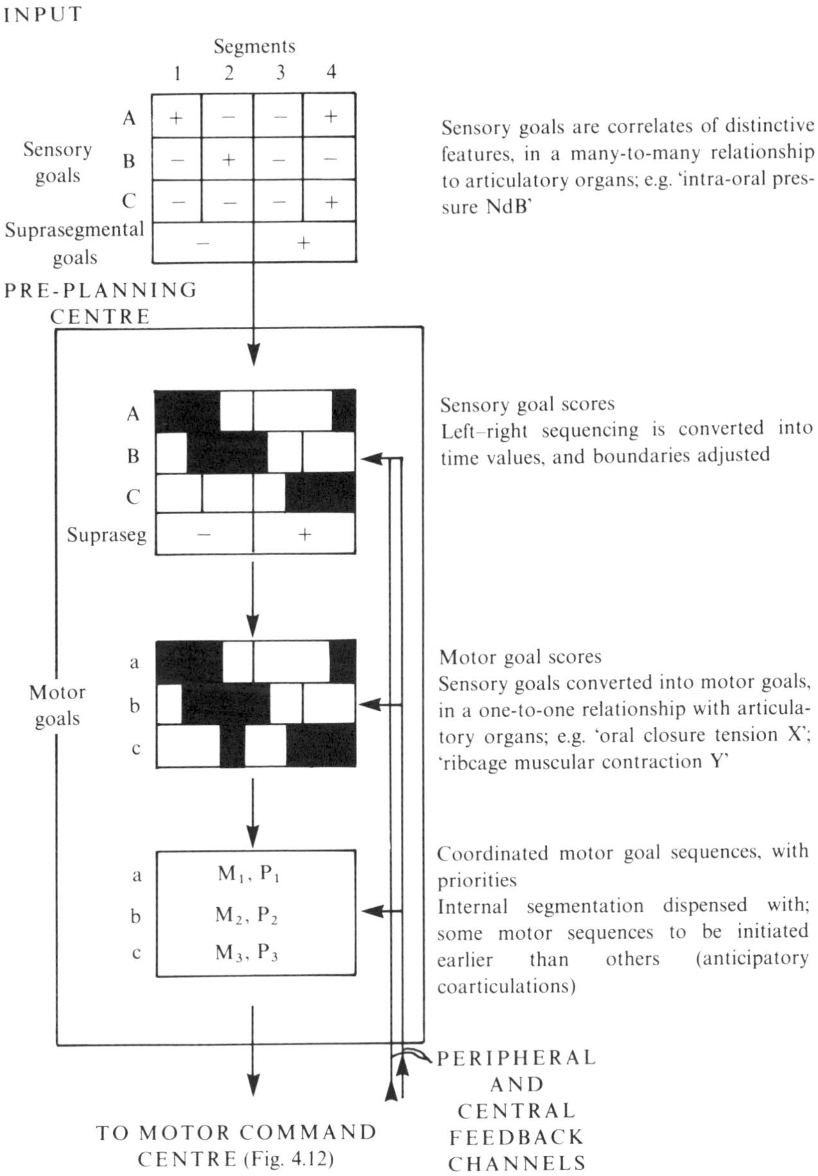

INPUT

Segments

	1	2	3	4
A	+	−	−	+
B	−	+	−	−
C	−	−	−	+

Sensory goals

Suprasegmental goals

	−	+

Sensory goals are correlates of distinctive features, in a many-to-many relationship to articulatory organs; e.g. 'intra-oral pressure NdB'

PRE-PLANNING CENTRE

A

B

C

Suupraseg

	−	+

Sensory goal scores
Left–right sequencing is converted into time values, and boundaries adjusted

Motor goals

a

b

c

Motor goal scores
Sensory goals converted into motor goals, in a one-to-one relationship with articulatory organs; e.g. 'oral closure tension X'; 'ribcage muscular contraction Y'

a M_1, P_1

b M_2, P_2

c M_3, P_3

Coordinated motor goal sequences, with priorities
Internal segmentation dispensed with; some motor sequences to be initiated earlier than others (anticipatory coarticulations)

TO MOTOR COMMAND CENTRE (Fig. 4.12)

PERIPHERAL AND CENTRAL FEEDBACK CHANNELS

Figure 4.11 The upper components of the sensory goal model of speech production. (Based on Perkell 1980: fig. 2, p. 363.)

one articulatory *quantum* to another. The inter-quanta boundaries are perceptually relevant, therefore, and in some respects provide an articulatory basis
for categorical perception. By and large, the targets that the sensory goals
represent coincide with articulatory quanta.

The preplanning centre
Sensory-goal real-time values

The first stage of articulatory processing, as suggested above, is to convert the
sequential input into actual temporal values. Perhaps it would be more accurate to say that they are relative time-values, since the result of this stage of
processing is to establish timing in such a way that it will survive, as a pattern,
in slow or fast rates of speech. The relative timing is certainly affected by such
suprasegmental factors as stress (both inherent word-stress and contrastive
stress), but depends also on the following: articulatory displacement (the distance that an articulator must move to achieve a sensory goal); the dynamic
response properties of the articulator; the capabilities of the motor-control
system; and the auditory perception of the output. The relative nature of the
timing that is established will ensure, for example, that vowels are longer
before voiced consonants than before their voiceless counterparts (possibly
because of the more forceful closure required for the higher intra-oral air pressure of voiceless stops).

The importance of this transduction, in terms of the overall model, is that it
is at this point that the segment boundaries are adjusted in a way which is
compatible with the coarticulatory nature of the output. By the same token, of
course, if the sensory goals are understood to be fundamentally non-segmental at the input level, then this first stage of processing is rendered unnecessary.

Motor-goal values

By virtue of the preceding stage, then, all subsequent stages of processing have
relative time-values specified for them. In addition this next stage breaks up
the many-to-many relationships of sensory goals to motor commands, so that
the *motor goals* fit many-to-one or one-to-one with the eventual articulatory
output. In this level of processing, information is used which derives from the
suprasegmental as well as the segmental sensory goals; thus, for example,
muscular effort under conditions of a stressed segment will be specified as of a
higher degree than for a corresponding unstressed segment. Even quite simple
articulatory gestures need reorganising in terms of muscle operation: for instance, the levator palatini muscle that raises the velum has to be specified for
a higher degree of contraction to maintain closure during a high vowel than

during a low vowel (by virtue of anatomical connections with the rear of the tongue). And movements of the tongue tip have to be specified from the baseline of concurrent tongue-body movements. Apart from these, a whole range of compensatory effects derive from this stage of processing; for instance, the ability that adults have (and which children appear to have to learn) to maintain vowel distinctions with teeth clenched together, or on an obstruction.

Motor-goal priorities

The next stage of processing is to set priorities on the various motor commands, such that those that must be *effected* fairly early are *initiated* with suitable chance of success. Recall that, in our discussion of perception, we had to invoke the concept of a processing window, of indeterminate dimensions; in production too, such a window is required. The underlying principle seems to be something akin to economy of effort: since *abrupt* transitions require more force, the general rule is for an articulator to start moving into position in good time. In practice, this may mean up to about six segments *ahead* of target (*anticipatory* coarticulation); but, since the principle holds good also for moving *away* from positions, it covers also a few segments *beyond* the target (*perseveratory coarticulation*). The result is that a coarticulation such as lip rounding prior to a rounded vowel occurs *wherever possible*, within this domain. In effect, this means that lip rounding in *Blackpool* will start even prior to /p/, during the voiceless velar-stop closure, but not earlier, since the vowel /æ/ is specified as unrounded. Such anticipatory coarticulations as these may conceivably carry certain perceptual advantages, cuing the advent of a forthcoming articulatory complex such as /u:/. The output of this *preplanning* phase of processing can therefore be described as a set of instructions for structure-specific coarticulations. What remains is to transpose these into actual motor commands, which is the function of the next component (fig. 4.12).

The motor-command centre

In neurological terms, the function of this component is to establish the precise firing patterns for the motor neurons (ch. 2). In order to achieve this, further transduction of the input is required. This could be achieved by a single-stage processor, wherein all the ncessary control parameters would be set at the required values. But it would be more realistic to think rather of a two-stage processor: this would consist of an upper command-centre, where moment-by-moment control of articulators is initiated, and a lower command-centre which executes these control signals and

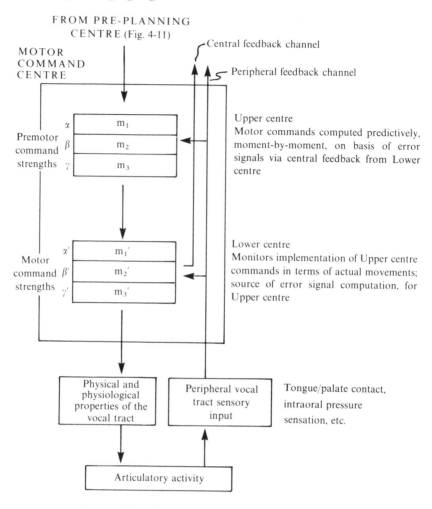

Figure 4.12 The lower components of the sensory goal model of speech production. (Based on Perkell 1980: fig. 3, p. 365.)

monitors their level of implementation. The lower centre would feed information back to the upper centre, so that on-line adjustments could be made at the initiatory level. In this way, such a system would allow for the accumulation (in some memory not shown in the model) of experience concerning the relationship between prediction (upper commands) and effect (lower commands). The output of the lower centre is the concept we referred to schematically at the beginning of this chapter, namely, the set of instructions to the articulatory organs.

The role of feedback

At various points of this discussion, we have referred to the controlling function of feedback, or upstream-oriented error signals in what is essentially a downstream command-signal model. Two types of feedback are hypothesised: *peripheral*, which is established via sensory pathways that are not directly involved in the downstream speech-processes, and *central*, which utilises the same pathways of the central command system.

There is actually not a great deal of direct evidence in support of the view that moment-by-moment feedback, of either type, is crucial to particular speech activities. Feedback disturbance, as in delayed auditory feedback (in the peripheral system) is certainly disruptive of normal speech production; but this is not quite the same as showing that undisturbed feedback is of crucial importance to current speech production. Again, long-term effects of feedback deprivation, as in the case of deafness, are known to be deleterious to the maintenance of speech control; but once more this says little about the moment-by-moment situation. There is evidence from studies of compensatory abilities that a considerable degree of *motor equivalence* is maintained in the face of obstructions of various sorts. By this is meant the ability to complete an articulatory goal in spite of a low-level disruption; the motor command is adjusted, on-line, to achieve the same goal by alternative means. For example, a sudden loading on the jaw may be applied just before labial closure is effected; the jaw can no longer complete the closure command, which is instantly routed via the lip muscles which show increased activity to achieve the closure (Oller and MacNeilage 1983). This sort of behaviour speaks very strongly of feedback in moment-by-moment use. But is it only functional in response to rather extraordinary moment-by-moment disruptions? It is noticeable, for instance, that it takes quite a long period of time, comparatively, for a speaker to adjust to the continued presence of an artificial palate. There may be here a distinction between adjustments that are mediated instantaneously via the feedback system, and those that necessitate a modification of what might be called the *central processing* patterns, which are available to the downstream command-signals. These patterns, or stored templates of neural activity, may well be necessary to accommodate routine fluent control of very rapid articulatory-event sequences, wherein the inter-event intervals may be simply too brief for a feedback system to operate.

These issues, clearly, are not easy to resolve. It is likely that feedback and central patterning interact, probably in rich and redundant ways. If this is so, it would explain why it is so difficult to isolate any one hypothesised feedback channel experimentally.

One very important consideration that may be of relevance here is the fact that speech is a mixture of *voluntary* activity (at the highest level of input) and highly *automatic* activity (at the lowest levels). To the extent that speech is centrally planned, it involves movements that seem to be comparable to anticipatory gestures (head turning or arm lifting) that have been observed in animal studies. The results of these much simpler studies suggest that such movements are the combined result of simultaneous *agonist* (acting) and *antagonist* (counteracting) muscle systems. The resulting movement is smooth, rather than step-like, as in the case of a gate with counteracting springs (Bizzi 1983). This sort of control seems to be typical of central programming (downstream influences). Perhaps rather closer to the situation of speech, swallowing is a complex coordinated activity involving about twenty muscles in the vocal-tract region which similarly represents a mixture of voluntary and automatic control. It can be initiated and accomplished with no feedback, but the presence of feedback pathways seems to facilitate the accommodation of variations in the size and consistency of the object being swallowed (the *bolus*). In speech, we may imagine a complex interaction between voluntary control (agonist and antagonist), central planning (stored templates) and on-line feedback (peripheral and central).

4.4.3 *Alternative views: coarticulation*

The model that we have just outlined serves to raise, as it is intended to, the major issues in speech production. Although it accepts an input that is segmental, it provides an output that is, in principle, compatible with the sort of behavioural phenomena we observed in the cine-fluorographic record of figure 1.3. It will be appreciated, however, that there is considerable debate about the way in which such an output is arrived at. In this section, we shall consider two alternative views, within which the problem of coarticulation is handled very differently.

Coarticulations as stored patterns

So-called *table models* have been proposed (Wickelgren 1969), which really extend the concept of stored templates or patterns to the general mode of speech production. Like the motor-command model, the input is hypothesised to be essentially segmental, but the individual segments are stored in a format like a table, or listing, which records all of their possible articulatory environments. Thus the consonant /k/ would be represented by listed patterns in the form 'X[k]Y', where X, Y are variables ranging over the whole class of preceding and following elements, respectively – including zero, in the case of initial and final /k/. The symbol [k] stands for the whole range of coarticulation variants of the input segment /k/ in these various environments.

It will be appreciated that in this sort of model the problem of coarticulation is radically disposed of, at the input level. But, of course, the cost, as measured in terms of sheer storage capacity, is considerable. And, since storage without retrieval is useless, we also have to consider the mechanism of gaining access to these patterns in an efficient and reliable manner. (We shall have something to say about an analogous problem to this below.) Furthermore, the number of stored forms has to be drastically revised upwards if more than just immediate environment is taken into account, as it surely must be; and then again, in respect of such suprasegmental factors as stress and rate of articulation. For these reasons, the table-model concept has been criticised as essentially unrealistic. But this is actually not a very convincing argument. If the table model is taken to its logical conclusion, it claims nothing more than that every single instance of speech sounds occurring in a larger context – for example, in a word – is stored and available to the speech-production system. This is, in other words, the same situation that we entertained as a possible basis for speech perception: namely, that the lexicon consists, in part, of the stored neural auditory/articulatory representations of the words of the language. Since in each such representation, each component is environmentally specified with respect to the others, we have a situation which is close to that of the table model. It seems likely that we have only to dispense with the concept of the linguistic *segment* and to talk more neutrally of the *components* of the neural representation; and then to replace the concept of 'table' with that of 'lexicon', and the rapprochement between these views is complete. Thus, the counterargument from astronomically large numbers may well fail, in the face of the prodigious capacities available in the human brain.

Coarticulations as synergistic effects

In spite of the brain's capacities, however, it may be argued that handling coarticulations at the highest possible level seriously misrepresents the properties of the speech-production system. If we observe coarticulations as a behavioural phenomenon, then they form part of the *external* requirements that any model has to satisfy. If we then achieve this by simply *internalising* the phenomenon – setting coarticulations up as part of some stage of planning in the model – then we run the risk of building in the very sort of behaviour that the model is supposed to account for. The test is: does the model *analyse* the phenomenon it generates? In the case of the table model, the answer appears to be no. To that extent, then, such a model stands condemned as being too powerful to be useful; it fails to characterise the nature of part of the primary phenomena it is set up to generate.

Along such lines as these, some researchers (Fowler *et al.* 1980; Tuller and Fowler 1980) have attempted to seek a middle way between the two extremes of, on the one hand, treating coarticulations as the result of a set of operations on an essentially segmental input; and on the other, treating them as 'given' in the input itself. As a result, increased attention has been paid to the existence of *synergies*, or muscle collectives, at the executive end of the speech-production process. The name for this sort of approach is *action theory*. One research strategy has been to investigate relationships between articulatory muscles under varying conditions of rate and stress. The results of such *electromyographic* (EMG) studies have to some extent modified the earlier interpretations of EMG findings. Originally, it was supposed that EMG evidence pointed up the variability of articulatory gestures; it was partly on such evidence as this that the concept of motor equivalence (or different means to the same end) was founded. Now, however, it seems that EMG evidence is beginning to uncover surprisingly constant *relationships between* muscle activities. In other words, although *individual* muscles show variable behaviour, muscle *groups* show relatively invariant internal relations. So far, this sort of evidence has been uncovered for five muscles controlling the lips, tongue and jaw in speech (Scott-Kelso, Tuller and Harris 1983).

This suggests that coordination is separately controlled from other variables such as rate. But where is it controlled from? Possibly it results from the proximity of the cortical control-centres for lips, tongue and jaw, in the motorstrip. If this intracortical influence is indeed responsible, then we should expect to find some manifestations of it in other types of relationship. One such is the relationship between manual and vocal control-centres, which are also proximally located in the motorstrip. Studies in this area have shown systematic and reciprocal effects to hold between speech rhythms (e.g. stressed and unstressed syllables in alternating pattern) and right index-finger movements (cyclic rotations). As the speech rhythm changed, the finger movement was also perturbed, and vice versa. In another study, speech was studied in relation to finger tapping; it was found that when the speaker paused for breath, the finger-tapping rhythm was also broken at just that point.

In a sense, investigations like these (see also J. G. Martin 1972) are extending an area which was first looked at in the last century, in relation to rhythmic influences on memory. It was quickly discovered that, for example, rhythmic structure not only aided recall of quite lengthy nonsense strings, but that it could actually be imposed by the subject on a string that was objectively arhythmic. Thus the sequence of twelve nonsense syllables:

bam fis lup tol gen ker dub naf mit pon sav niz

could be transposed into the rhythmic structure:

bám fīs | lúp tŏl | *gén* kĕr ‖ *dúb* năf | mít pŏn | *sáv* níz

(Ward 1920: 227)

Here we have ABA, repeated, where each of the units (or *feet*) consists of a *trochaic* (stress–unstress) pattern, with the A-feet showing extra heavy stress over the B-feet. It was also observed that such rhythmic structures could be imposed on regular stimuli like metronome ticks, and that subjects could, moreover, transform one such 'psychical rhythm' into another. As they did so, it was observed that such autonomic systems as heartbeat and respiration adapted to the change in rhythm. Rhythm, indeed, may turn out to be a fundamental concept in speech production. At the highest level, it has been suggested, for example, that 'phoneme' segments are inserted into rhythmic frameworks, to form the input to something like the motor-command model. Such rhythmic schemata would embody crucial suprasegmental factors as stress; and their regularity (which is psychological, rather than a matter of strict isochrony) is doubtless an aid to perception. Even at the lowest levels, rhythm may well turn out to be an important factor; for instance, it has been suggested that the natural opening and closing 'resonant frequency' of the jaw (which derives from its length, weight and hinge-point) controls the average range of syllable duration to between 160–200msec. (Lindblom 1983).

The point of all this, really, is to emphasise the point that coarticulation may be ill-conceived as simply a smearing of segment boundaries. It seems altogether more radical than that, and may result from fundamental dynamic properties of the neuromuscular systems underlying speech. Indeed, to look at the issue from entirely the reverse standpoint, the basic tendency of such a multi-channel system may be towards *synchrony* ('everything moves at once'). The control of speech timing, from this point of view, is a matter of *sequencing* and separating otherwise synchronous articulations. In this case, our motor-command model would have a complex, fully synchronised input, and the first stage of processing would be devoted to a temporal *linearisation* of this. Coarticulation would then arise as the result of a partial separation of over-lapping articulations. This view may have something to contribute to the assessment of how children acquire speech, and of what goes wrong in patients whose speech timing is abnormal.

4.5 Written language production

We may set our discussion of written language production within the same general framework as that used for speech in 4.4.1–4.4.2 above. We shall deal first with handwriting production, and for this purpose will return briefly to Hotopf's (1983) discussion of writing errors (see also ch. 3), before speculating on how handwriting processes might be organised in a Perkell (1980) type of sensory-goal motor-command model. We shall then consider typewriting production.

4.5.1 *Interpreting slips of the pen*

In interpreting this sort of data, we may start by referring to the concept of working memory, which, as in the case of speech, holds planned elements briefly, long enough for their relative ordering to be established and some degree of internal structuring, prior to execution. Some slips of the pen may be judged to arise from similarities between adjacent or nearby elements in this buffer, which may lead to confusion in selection. In the case of the pen slip illustrated in figure 3.8 for the target word *paradigmatic*, we may envisage a buffer sequence of letter features as in figure 4.13.

Here, the dotted lines indicate the normal output from this sequence of features (although the forms of the letters *a* and *d* have been kept apart, for clarity), and the solid lines show how the actual output may be described, in terms of omission of the second occurrence of feature F_1.

Now clearly, letter-feature slips can shed no light on our issue of the role of phonology in writing: they reflect a final output level that is necessary regardless of the nature of the input to it. We must accordingly look to our second, third and fourth types of slip for evidence. The second type, slips like *inhibtions*, may be taken as evidence that the buffer store is hierarchically, as well as sequentially, organised. Features F_1 to F_3 together underlie the output form *i*, let us suppose. The omission of this sub-sequence reflects the omission of a single underlying element (let us further suppose). The question then is: is this element graphological or phonological? (See fig. 4.14.)

The pattern of omissions suggests that orthographic rather than articulatory factors are involved. Most letters that are omitted are describable in terms of their status within the visual form of a word – generally word-medial, surrounded by prominent letters (having ascenders or descenders), not themselves being prominent, and so on. Factors such as presence or absence of stress, vowel quality, syllabic status, pronounceability of the output form and so on, are much less involved. The same holds true generally of additions, and substitutions. Contractions like *his is* (he is) can be interpreted either way. But what of *Freudiand &* (Freudian &)? This *might* be accounted for in terms of a phonological conversion of the ampersand *&* to /and/, prior to the slip; but it is just as plausible to think of interference from the *alphabetic* written form corresponding to the logograph.

Even cases of so-called 'phonetic spelling', such as *ridgid* (rigid) may reflect

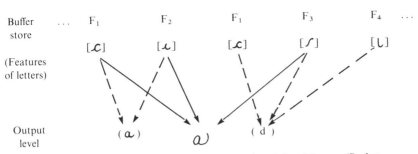

Figure 4.13 The production of a feature-based slip of the pen. (Broken arrows indicate normative relationships of hypothesised features to output letter forms)

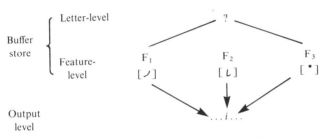

Figure 4.14 Possible hierarchical organisation of the buffer store in writing output

visual analogies rather than phoneme–grapheme correspondences as such: the pattern shown in *ridgid* may derive from that involved in *ridge, fridge, edge*, etc.; and *ques* (cues) may reflect the digraph group *qu-* rather than a sound substitution. Only in the case of single-symbol substitutions, as in *8* (H), *C* (3), etc. do we have clear evidence for the role of pronunciation. But these cases may be unusual, inasmuch as they do not involve written words, rather names of characters. There is likewise little comfort for a phonological hypothesis among slips of our third type, involving subword grammatical elements. Among the fourth type, whole-word slips, only *sound*-related substitutions are consistent with the hypothesis. One problem here lies in differentiating sound similarity from letter similarity. Proportionately, many more *form*-related (to use a more neutral term) substitutions are found in slips of the pen than of the tongue, in both closed- and open-class words. This may reflect the much slower rate of output in writing compared to speech (less than one syllable per second) which allows time for (a) buffer store decay and (b) the use of (phonotactic? graphotactic?) constraints for the construction of real-word output forms, thus accounting for the bias of pen slips to lexicality. It appears that,

231

taking into account the inherent relationship between letters and phonemes, and excluding the special case of *homophones* (which we shall deal with below), there is no evidence that phonemes, rather than letters, provide a superior characterisation of form-related slips of the pen.

At this point we should therefore turn our attention to homophone substitutions such as *sail* (sale). However, all that we can say about these is that they are consistent *either* with phoneme–grapheme recoding *or* with the operation of visual analogies. According to the graphological hypothesis, abstract graphological forms, in the lexicon, have to be converted into specific graphemic sequences prior to implementation. At the graphemic level, correspondences between analogic spelling patterns may be activated, and the wrong sequence may be set up in the buffer store as a result. Equally, there may be interactions between phonological and graphological factors: this may be required to account for *make* (may characterise). In contrast to the phonological hypothesis, which interprets writing output in terms of purely phonological underlying elements, the graphological hypothesis recognises the parallel activation of both output hierarchies.

We may conclude by stressing once again that the interpretation of slips of the pen differentially from those of speech is a difficult and controversial business, and that we have skimmed over many problems in this brief survey. But it seems fair to conclude that, so far, the case for a purely phonological basis of writing has not been established.

4.5.2 *Motor-control aspects*

Handwriting

We return here to aspects of the discussion in Viviani and Terzuolo (1983). As in the case of speech, output in handwriting is essentially continuous, with segments being definable within the continuum in terms of their centres rather than their boundaries. This raises once more the issue of whether input to the system is segmental, with subsequent smearing of segment boundaries, or essentially a continuous oscillatory wave form, with subsequent modulations for segment shapes. Either view is technically feasible, but description is probably clearer in terms of the first, which is the one adopted here. (It also has the advantage of allowing comparison with the model presented in ch. 3.) Within this approach, certain concepts and principles may be developed, as follows.

Sensory goals. The segmental sensory-goals form the primary input to the *pre-planning centre*, relating the (as yet poorly understood) features of letters to their eventual motor targets. The sensory goals are specified in terms of general settings such as 'linear distance *n* unit lengths', 'curvature of *n* degrees of arc', etc. There are also variably long suprasegmental goals, specifying the extent and rate of rightward sweep of the hand. This it is that *linearises* the consequences of the segmental goals, yielding letters that are either closer together or further apart, and establishing which letters occur within a suprasegmental sweep, and which are separated by sweep boundaries. As with speech, these sensory goals typically involve more than one muscle system for their execution. They are first converted into *sensory-goal scores*, which represent proportional temporal values for each of the segmental and suprasegmental goals of a given letter shape. This ensures the preservation of topological characteristics under changing conditions of output, e.g. in the size of letters required, or in the overall speed of execution. In other words, the basis for 'motor equivalence' is laid here, since, for quite large changes in letter size whole new muscle systems may be brought into play, to produce a given letter shape. Thus, arm movements may be employed in writing on a blackboard which are not at all involved in writing at a desk. Clearly, the sensory goals must be represented in quite an abstract manner for this spatio-temporal invariance to be possible. Probably also at this level is located the further global property whereby writing velocity increases with distance to be travelled. This means that execution time tends to be relatively stable for variations in letter size – a sort of invariant property of output, which actually involves context-sensitive setting at the sensory-goal score level for it to be maintained. The sort of time scale involved may be indicated by recalling (from ch. 2) that 500msec. is a typical execution time for the letter '*α*': the distance from start to finish is of the order 15–20mm in this instance. However, as we have noted, velocity along this distance is *not* constant, even for a given overall rate of handwriting. The sensory goal scores are next mapped onto *motor-goal scores* whose distinctive characteristic is that they are in one-to-one relationship with the manual 'articulators', e.g. 'thumb opposition, tension *i*', 'index-finger flexion, tension *j*', 'wrist flexion, tension *k*', etc. It is at this level that the local property governing variations in velocity through the letter shape is to be located, giving rise to marked decelerations at segments of highest curvature. The change in velocity is systematically related to the degree of curvature, in a way which may reflect specific interactions between muscle groups controlling articulators. There may be an additive relationship between this local property and the global property relating velocity to distance travelled (above). The result is a relatively invariant time to execute curves of unequal size, e.g. as in *α* vs *α*; speed increases with distance to be travelled (a global property, greater in the larger shape) and decreases with the degree of curvature (a local property, greater in the smaller shape).

These motor-goal scores are finally organised into *coordinated motor-goal sequences*, with internal segmentation erased, and priorities specified for certain motor goals to be initiated earlier than others. This constitutes the output from the preplanning centre, which is sent to the *motor-command centre*, whose function is to establish, maintain and adjust on-line the precise firing patterns for the motor neurons involved. For this purpose, it is convenient to think of a two-stage processor (as in the case of speech) thus allowing for *initiation* and *monitoring*, via *feedback*. This allows for compensating abilities under changing conditions of handwriting – relatively large mass changes (e.g. lighter or heavier writing implements) can be swiftly compensated for. However (as we have noted in ch. 2), it appears that increasing the frictional forces (e.g. by changing the quality of the paper) has the effect of reducing the size of writing, though time and shape characteristics are preserved. Such a system also allows for the long-term establishment of cause and effect relationships between upper and lower levels of motor command, essential to the development of largely automatic behaviour.

Typewriting

In handwriting, we have noted that the articulators form what may be called a *closed* system, with the pen held at the centre. In typewriting, the articulators do not act against one another in the same fashion, but operate rather in parallel, against a mechanical or electronic keyboard. In these ways, handwriting and typewriting appear to reflect different aspects of speech-production dynamics: in speech, articulators may bear on each other (e.g. labiodental and apico-alveolar contacts), but they may also operate in parallel (e.g. the tongue tip and the velum). For typewriting, as in speech, there is considerable overlap between successive movements, *finger strokes*, with the outcome events, *key pressings*, being more regularly timed than their initiations. This 'goal invariance' can be accounted for at the *coordinated motor-goal sequences* level of the model we have just been considering. In normal typewriting, we are dealing with movements of the order of seven to eight strokes per second, with intervals of 120–140msec. and reaction times (from letter choice to completion) of around 300msec. Purely biomechanical factors, as well as neuromuscular control factors, govern systematic differences in speed of key-pressing sequences depending on whether different hands are used, in alternation (around 110msec. intervals), or different fingers of the same hand (around 130msec.), or the same finger successively (the slowest, at around 160msec. intervals). Much of the advantage of the different-hands condition derives from overlapping control in the two parallel systems. This clearly has important implications for keyboard design.

Stability and variability of patterns. An experienced typist will produce the same sentence in a stable but non-isochronous rhythm on different occasions. This is partly reflective of the typist's 'hand', but it also has something to do with the nature of the structure of the sentence, in ways which we shall now briefly consider. It appears that, in contrast to speech, the temporal sentence pattern in typewriting is a simple function of its constituent word-patterns, i.e. that word patterns are the basic determinants of typing rhythm, and are relatively unaffected by their sentential contexts. Part of the word pattern is determined by the linear position of the letters within it: interstroke intervals are greatest word-initially and finally, leading to a slower–faster–slower rhythm, regardless of the constituent elements of the word. Overlaid on this basic word-rhythm is the effect of particular letter groups (that is, *after* keyboard/ hand-position effects have been taken into account): certain letter groups are more common in the language than others, and it is true of the less common ones (e.g. . . . *eau* . . .) that they have larger, and more variable, interstroke intervals. For any of the more common letter groups, the pattern of execution will not simply be a function of the constituent letters themselves (i.e. their transitional probabilities) but will also depend on their degree of embedding in the structure of the word. Compare -*th*- in *cathode* and *cathouse*, for example: the -*th*- in the first example will regularly be typed faster. The domain of this effect of context may be observed to extend up to three letters before, and two letters after, the letter group in question (and may cross word boundaries). All of these effects tend to produce similar patterns for the same sequences between different typists; but, as we mentioned earlier, there is also a discernible effect of the individual typist's 'hand'.

It is not easy to understand how the input to the preplanning component for typing production relates to that for speech and handwriting. The sensory goals are presumably in the form of finger-stroke initiations, but do they derive ultimately from their own lexical-form components? In other words, do experienced typists establish a new order of stored forms for their lexical entries? If not, do the sensory goals derive instead from graphological-form components for writing, or from phonological-form components for speech? As always, it proves difficult to disentangle the effect of having a lexical entry from pronounceability, and again from the effect of letter transitions. It *is* observed that typists slow down, and show loss of stable, repeatable patterns when they are faced with random letter strings to type, but that they can handle new words (for which they have no lexical entry) in a perfectly fluent and stable fashion. Perhaps we should appeal to the concept of legal graphotactic patterns in this respect. Perhaps too subword patterns are reflected in the typing 'sweeps' that may be observed for longer words; they tend to include four to five characters, and tend to be fairly uniform between typists, often having syllabic consequences (e.g. *fre-quent, char-act-ers*), although less common words may bring out more idiosyncratic strategies. The crucial thing about established word-patterns, however, is that they are invariant for a particular typist across changes in overall rate of typing, and prove highly resistant also to differences in mechanical loading (cf. the difference between pressing the keys on a manual vs an electric typewriter). But they do depend crucially on touch/pressure exteroceptive sensory feedback: 'imaginary' typing, with no keyboard, fails to maintain the stability of typing sequences. In all these major respects, a motor-control model of the sort referred to for speech and handwriting would seem to be applicable also to the control of movements in typing.

4.6 Conclusions

It will be apparent that, at various points in our discussion, we have assumed that there is a close relationship between the way the language signal is produced and the way in which it is perceived. This is particularly true of coarticulatory phenomena in speech production, and the context-sensitive nature of speech perception. Howell and Harvey (1983) address this relationship from the point of view that a model of speech perception must do more than seek to explain its problems away by reference to production issues, and vice versa. The relationship between perception and production must either be directly incorporated in the model proposed for each, or the two sorts of process ought to be modelled in ways that are essentially independent of each other. To understand what this means, we shall refer to the main points of their survey, which also provide a convenient summary framework for the issues we have dealt with in this chapter.

First, certain classes of model have been proposed within the approach that perception and production are to be modelled as independent of each other. Among these are included: (a) the feature model (see section 4.2.5 above), which proposes a set of abstract elements, smaller than the phonemic segment, which may be used either for perception, without reference to production, or vice versa (Perkell 1980; Stevens 1981); and (b) the template model (see section 4.2.5 above), as in, e.g. Wickelgren (1969), which attempts to provide for coarticulatory phenomena in speech production, in terms of a template of each segment-context possibility in the language, and which also envisages an independent set of perceptual templates. Howell and Harvey suggest that the template model can cope with basic coarticulatory and perceptual invariance phenomena, but appears to be unable to rise to the challenge of variations in speech rate, and in individual vocal-tract size, both of which would require a dramatic increase in the number of templates envisaged. The feature model really stands or falls on the basis of categorical perception, an issue which, as we have noted, is beset with methodological problems.

Among theories that posit a working relationship between perception and production, Howell and Harvey mention: (a) the motor theory of speech perception (Liberman *et al.* 1967), a brave early attempt which has attracted much criticism; and (b) action theory (see section 4.4.3 above; Fowler *et al.* 1980; Tuller and Fowler 1980), which is based on a concept of motor control of muscles being organised into interactive systems, and which essentially provides a new, more fully worked out 'motor theory of speech perception', in terms of this concept. Howell and Harvey conclude that, while action theory holds out much promise, it raises questions, e.g. concerning the large number of ways in which the brain can achieve the same production, or perceptual, end, which require more experimental evidence.

In reviewing issues in the processing of the language signal, we have also continually made reference to the lexicon. In perceiving the language signal, it is words that we are mainly concerned with, since these are the primary domains over which sound patterns are mapped onto meanings. Likewise, producing the language signal is a process that can be conceived of as essentially the representation of words. Multi-word utterances involve interword relationships that have their own manifestations in the language signal, but these are probably best approached as contextual modifications laid over sequences of words. Segmental units such as phonemes may be functional in processing the language signal, but it is not at all clear that such units have to be established in perception prior to lexical access, or in production prior to signal generation: indeed, a number of contextual-variation problems in production and perception may simply not arise, if we think of processing units as being non-segmental in nature. The case for grapheme segments having a processing role may be better founded, however. One possibility, in speech perception, is a mapping of subsegmental spectral templates onto word forms.

These issues take us on to the topic of the next chapter, which is lexical access (in perception and production). To prepare the way for this, consider the opening of B's contribution to the conversation discussed in chapter 3: 'erm I was reading in the paper this morning a a chap he's a director of a big company in Birmingham – who was th the world's number one football fan ...'. Our listeners' (A and C) first task is to catch it on the wing. It is available as an acoustic signal, presenting continuously varying dimensions of amplitude, frequency and intensity over time (ch. 1). It stimulates intense auditory-system activity (ch. 2), from the tympanic membrane situated in the ear canal of the outer ear, through the movements of the basilar membrane and the transducing responses of the cochlea, along the auditory nerve to the auditory centres in the brainstem and thence to the auditory cortex. The resulting percepts, within working memory, may be thought of as relating essentially to phonological segments plus associated contexts, or, alternatively, as non-segmental in nature (this chapter). At some point in this pattern-analysing process, contact is made with stored neurosensory elements whose peculiar property is that they are sufficiently large and stable in the language to support useful links between form and meaning: these are the elements of the lexicon. As we have seen in chapter 3, they are by no means all of the same type. To begin with, they are not all of the same size: in our discussion above, we referred to them simply as words: but some are multi-word sequences, of specialised meaning (idioms, such as *get browned off*, and compound forms, such as *league ground*), others are smaller than words (affixes, such as *un-*, *-ing*), and still others are frequently occurring fusions (such as *gonna*).

The importance of being large enough to support form–meaning relations lies in the often-remarked 'double articulation' of language: minimal-sized segments of language structure such as phonemes or graphemes are not sufficiently numerous to represent distinctively the meanings that have to be expressed, so they serve to make up the second-order sound-complexes that are sufficiently distinctive for this purpose. The elements of the lexicon are all at least syllable-sized, and many are multi-syllabic. On the other hand, the point about sufficient stability is that the longer sequences of a language tend not to be stably recurrent (e.g. *and he goes to all the matches away you know*), and hence are analysable into smaller units for form–meaning relationships to be stated, on a once-for-all basis. The elements of the lexicon thus represent a (language-specific) compromise between the two competing demands, of size and stability.

5
Accessing the mental lexicon

5.1 Introduction

5.1.1 *Preview*

The utterances that we produce and understand may be either single-word or multi-word in their structure. In this chapter we shall consider the sorts of processes that may be involved in accessing our mental lexicon, in both single- and multi-word utterance types, and both in speech and writing as well as in production and comprehension. In the first section, we consider what sorts of language forms may be stored as entries in our mental lexicon (5.1.2), and consider some general issues in lexical access (5.1.3). We then outline the form that lexical entries may take (5.2.1–5.2.2) and review some of the major experimental findings on lexical access (5.2.3). Sections 5.3 to 5.5 review some representative models of lexical access, highlighting the salient differences between serial and parallel types of processing. One of the longest-standing issues in the field of visual word recognition concerns the role of individual letter perception vs holistic word form perception in word recognition; in this context, we consider the status of units that are both larger than individual letters and smaller than words (5.6.1). Apart from the units of perception and production, we need to consider the role of context in lexical access (5.6.2). We also review the evidence on the status of stems vs affixes in lexical access (5.6.3). Finally, we draw some conclusions (5.7).

5.1.2 *Word units*

First, then, we return briefly to our three participants' discussion of football (the passage discussed in ch. 3, from Crystal and Davy 1975), and we pick up the beginning of B's monologue-ish section. We can look at it both from the point of view of B, who is trying to express his ideas in linguistic terms, and from the point of view of A and C, who are engaged primarily in the task of listening for understanding. As we join B's contribution, he has just explicitly responded to A's attempt to steer the conversation onto the topic of football, and is starting to develop his theme:

> erm I was reading in the paper this morning a a chap he's a director of a
> big company in Birmingham – who was th the world's number one
> football fan he used to spend about a thousand a year watching football

you know (C: coo) – he's he's watched football in every n . on every
league. ground in England all ninety two (A *laughs*) . . . (etc.)

We have not chosen this passage because of any particularly dramatic difficulties it might illustrate as far as lexical access is concerned: rather the reverse, since it appears to be entirely typical of a fairly fluent and rather well-
constructed spontaneous discourse on a coherent topic. As such, of course, it
has the property that, the further we go into the passage, the greater the supporting linguistic context will be for the understanding and production of any
particular word or construction.

Unfortunately, for our purposes, there is a problem in adequately representing the passage within the pages of a book. Since it is speech data, we need
to respect:

1. the continuity and breaks in the speech signal; as well as
2. the demarcating and highlighting function of intonation, which is,
    in the speech mode, at least as important as punctuation is to
    written language, but is a good deal more flexible and informative.

We may try to represent the data in conventional phonetic transcription:

[ɜːmaɪwəz | riːdɪŋɪnðə↑peɪpəðɪs'**mɔ̀ːnɪŋ** | ə ə | **ʧæp** | iː
zədɪ | **rèktər** | əvə | bɪg ↑**kʌmpənɪ** | jɪn | **bɜ̀ːmɪŋəm** | – huːwəzððə | wɜːldz
↑nʌmbə'wʌn ↑**fòtbɔːl'fæn**] . . . (etc.)

This representation of our data may serve to give some idea of the bases for
word recognition in continuous speech. On the one hand, it has nothing corresponding to the institutionalised word breaks of English orthography, so, in
this sense, the words are not 'given' in segmental structure as they are in
writing. But on the other hand, there is a variety of other, non-segmental,
cues, such as degrees of loudness and pitch, and durational features such as
prolongations and breaks, which are available for recognition processes to
work on (Cutler 1976). Some of these cues are relevant to linguistic units that
are larger than the word (phrases), and others to units that are smaller than
the word (syllables), so the question of initial word-segmentation for the purposes of word recognition is not a simple one. One of the issues that we have
to address is implicit in our discussion of 'larger' and 'smaller' units: exactly
what do we mean by 'word-sized'?

Words and higher-order structures

For the speaker/writer, accessing 'words' is a matter of mapping
ideas onto those stored meaning representations in the mental lexicon that are
associated with stable word forms, which can then be used to implement a

spoken or written output. For the listener/reader, the major task is to map portions of the linguistic signal onto the stored neurosensory traces in the mental lexicon; once activated, these will in turn stimulate their associated meaning representations ... and the beginnings of understanding will start to emerge. As far as the auditory signal is concerned, the potential cues may give rise to portion segments that are of various sizes, and which overlap considerably, for a given stretch of signal. It is clear, for example, that the words in the passage are organised into *higher-order constructions*, which are characterisable in grammatical–descriptive terms as *phrases* (e.g. noun phrases: *the world's number one football fan;* prepositional phrases: *in America*; verb phrases: *'s been*; and adjective phrases: *rather boring*) and *clauses* (e.g. *and he goes to all the cup matches away*). Generally, we may see the length of such potential sequences in the signal as inversely proportional to their internal stability and frequency of occurrence; on this account, the longer the sequence, the less beneficial it is to have it stored as a unitary entry in the mental lexicon. Thus, for example,

company

and

director

are plausible candidates for lexical access, whereas

director of a big company

is not. What this means is that processing the latter sequence will require a number of lexical-access operations, plus some computation of the relationships holding between the constituents (which we shall look at in more detail in ch. 6). It might appear, then, that such constructions have to be built up by the listener in understanding the passage, just as the meanings of individual words have to be recovered – for, after all, we know that constructional meaning is distinct from lexical meaning, and that structured utterances such as these contain both types. Against this view, however, it may be argued that the fact that such linguistic structure is 'there' does not necessarily mean that it must be processed, on-line, in the listener's understanding of such utterances – as with our perception of the phonological structure of words, it may arise from successful processing rather than be a precondition for it.

Leaving this consideration aside for now, we should note that the boundary between the two states of affairs in *company* vs *director of a big company* is not easy to determine, as may be seen by considering the example of

company director

This may be worth storing as a single entry, as against treating it as an instance of multi-word access plus relational computation. Individual mental lexicons may be supposed to differ in such respects, based on the life experiences of the individuals concerned. Quite long sequences may be represented as unitary to some degree in their entries, such as the idiom

getting browned off

however, it may not be the case that the parts of such constructional idioms are unconnected in the mental lexicon with their form-related counterparts (e.g. *get* in the sense of 'become', in the example above and as an individual lexical entry). Idioms may exist in the mental lexicon as sequences of individual entries which have particularly strong associative links holding between them.

We shall leave open for now the question of the boundary between lexical entries and sequences of lexical entries, i.e. whether *football fan, league ground,* etc. are 'words' or higher-order phrase constructions.

Words and lower-order structures

We also need to recognise a further issue, however, that arises from the fact that word units such as *world's, boring, matches,* and so on, have internal structure. Part of this internal structure concerns the sequencing of the sounds of speech, and the letters of the written language, and, as we have seen in chapter 4, the role of such structure in the word-identification process is not to be taken for granted: word recognition may take place *prior to* a complete phonological or graphological analysis, and our 'perception' of phonological or graphological structure (especially in respect of missing or distorted elements) may be a *function* of successful lexical access, rather than a precondition for it.

However, words are not merely to be thought of as sound or letter sequences: they may exhibit *morphological* structure also, which is described linguistically in terms of lower-order structures involving *stems* and *affixes*. Such structures are of various types, ranging from *derivational* to *inflectional*, from *lexical* to *grammatical*, from *non-productive* to *productive*, and from *abstract* to *concrete*. How far these dimensions of description relate to each other is a matter of debate, and different approaches will result in differing definitions of word units (see Matthews 1974; Bauer 1983; Jarvella and Meijers 1983; and Henderson 1985 for discussion in the context of word-recognition studies). Broadly, however, we may think of, e.g. *football fan* at one end of a continuum (a grammatical-type structuring of elements that are themselves of word status, and having independently specifiable meanings), and something like *world's* towards the other end (having one word-like element, and a bound grammatical marker suffixed to it). On the face of it, it appears likely that understanding two such different types of structure would involve rather different processes of recovering items from memory and providing a structural interpretation.

We should note that in some cases the analysis of morphologically complex forms will yield phonologically stable units, as in *walking* (*walk # ing*, where # marks a word boundary) while in others it will not, as in *opacity* (*opac + ity*, where + marks a subword morpheme boundary). In the latter case we might envisage composition rules which relate the varying stem forms to each other (Henderson 1985), but suppletion will presumably require rules mapping whole forms onto each other (e.g. *go, went*).

A further feature of morpheme identification is that, prior to the identification being made, there are forms that represent potential, but not actual, affixes, as in the *pre-* 'pseudo-prefix' of *premium*. It is sometimes a problem to know where the boundary between real and pseudo-affixes may lie: the linguist's traditional problem, concerning the status of affixes such as *-y* in *mighty, haughty,* etc. and of *-er* in *passenger, hammer,* etc. would appear to be reflected in possibly distinct organisations in individual lexicons.

Our questions concerning the status of morphological structure in lexical access are basically the following:

> Does perception of morphological structure play a role in access, or arise from it?
>
> Are stems and affixes stored and accessed in the same way, alongside each other, in the same lexicon, or are different stores and processes involved?

5.1.3 *Terms and concepts*

The general nature of the lexicon has been indicated already, in figure 4.1: very simply, it can be represented as comprising two components, stored word meanings and stored word forms, together with access paths that allow these components to communicate with each other, and with other elements in the processing hierarchy. We shall go into greater detail below, but for now we shall confine ourselves to two observations.

The first concerns word forms: the issue here is whether they are stored so abstractly in the lexicon as to obliterate the differences between written, spoken, read and heard forms of words. The advantage of having unitary, modality-neutral form entries for words in a lexicon is obvious: each lexical item may be specified more simply. The cost is found in the need to provide rules deriving, say, written forms from phonologically specified entries.

Whether the mental lexicon works on this principle is another matter, which depends, in a partly language-specific fashion, on the feasibility of formulating cross-modality derivation rules of sufficient generality and simplicity. The mind always has another option: to provide modality-specific word forms for each entry, whose advantage is that they are highly compatible with the systems that perceive and produce them. The cost is extra storage space in the lexicon, both for the more complex form-specifications and for the links between them. In our discussion below, we shall assume that modality-specific form components exist, since this allows us to respect the signal-based processing differences that we have reviewed in chapters 1 and 4, and to keep before us the issue: how far might the links between such distinct form components actually come to represent a statement of all that is common between them?

The second observation concerns word meanings: the issue here is whether these are represented in the mental lexicon in strictly linguistic-semantic terms, or in a way that also takes account of their more general cognitive attributes, such as associative and image-based properties. This is an issue that goes to the heart of what we consider the lexicon to be: does it consist, as indicated in figure 4.1, of a well-defined word-meaning component in systematic relationship with linguistic word-forms; or does it consist essentially of just those stored word forms, which are directly mapped onto a general knowledge base that is not specifically part of the lexicon itself? We shall adopt a compromise approach here, allowing for the representation of word meanings as well as word forms within the mental lexicon, but at the same time allowing for an open-ended relationship between word meanings and general cognition.

This provides us with a framework within which we may start to address the major issues in lexical access. We shall highlight the basic terms and concepts in the field here, before looking at some models of lexical access in the next section.

The lexicon

The diagram in figure 4.1 provides a broken line, labelled 'The lexicon', around two distinct components: word forms and word meanings. Is the lexicon to be thought of as a single entity, comprising all relevant stored form–meaning information? Or is it rather to be thought of as an assemblage of separate, but interconnected, specialist lexicons? Some researchers use the term 'the phonological lexicon', for instance, to refer to the mental inventory of the phonological word forms of the language, without their content specifications. This seems to be equivalent, in our layout, to entering and exiting the phonological forms of the lexicon without activating the links to meaning. In this connection, we should note that it is clearly possible and necessary to be able to store and reproduce newly encountered words, for which we may have as yet no proper meaning representation: thus we can say 'what is a (x)?' Also, we have to be able to convert an auditorily encountered (x) to a plausible spelled version, in order to look it up in a dictionary.

The concept of 'the semantic lexicon' is also encountered. This can be misleading. If it refers, in contrast to 'the phonological lexicon', to a system where meanings are stored *along with* their associated forms, then 'semantic lexicon' just means 'lexicon' in the wider sense of the term. Of course, it is occasionally the case that we have access to word meanings, without being able to retrieve their forms, as in 'What is the word for soaking meat in a mixture of liquids and flavourings before cooking?' (see the tip-of-the-tongue phenomenon, ch. 3). One interesting feature of such cases is our sensation of knowing that the meaning we wish to convey is word-sized (has a word to express it), even before finding the form.

A further, related, point is that reference is sometimes made to the possibility of a *direct* link between *visual perceptions* of words and their *meanings*. This too can be misleading: the most careful formulations of this view make it clear that the direct processing path that is actually envisaged leads from *visual analysis* of the letter array, resulting in, let us say, the representation of that array in terms of some abstract graphemic sequence, to the *graphological form* of lexical entries (and *thence* to their meanings). In terms of our layout above, it is not clear that any sense can be made of a truly direct link between the results of visual analysis and stored word meanings. Mention of direct access, however, takes us on to our next issue.

Access: direct and indirect

From the earliest investigations, it has been recognised that there are two possible ways of comprehending written language, and the difference between them really relates to the issue that we started out with in the preceding chapter, namely, at what point(s) do the written and oral language-processing paths converge? According to the *indirect access* view, they converge relatively early on in the processing sequence, *prior* to lexical access. If it is the case that all access in reading is indirect, then this amounts to the claim that we do not need to specify the input graphological form for lexical entries, on an access channel, and that all access is via phonological forms. As we shall see, this very strong claim is not tenable in the face of the available evidence, although an indirect route must exist (see 5.2.2 below). By contrast, direct access is so called because it is not mediated by mapping graphemes onto some point of the phonological input processing.

Prelexical versus postlexical

The possibility or otherwise of contact between orthographic and auditory processing paths is central to many models and theories, and it is all the more important therefore to distinguish whether one is dealing with pre-lexical or postlexical states of affairs. Prelexical refers to input processing up to the point of entry into the lexicon. Postlexical contacts may occur when, after a lexical entry has been accessed, its phonological and graphological form specifications become simultaneously available for responding. Thus, a written word may be *accessed* visually (no prelexical contact with phonologi-cal form) but responded to articulatorily, on the basis of the output phonolo-gical form specification (postlexical phonological encoding).

Words, non-words and response types

The experimental literature on which the models are based that we shall be considering in sections 5.2 and 5.3 below is fairly technical. We shall not go into it in great detail, since our purpose here is to interpret the main findings in terms of processing models. However, we clearly need to develop a general idea of the sorts of tasks that are involved, and the types of materials used, in these experimental investigations. Table 5.1 summarises the main tasks in terms of input types (stimuli) and output types (responses). It may be helpful to refer back to this table at points in the subsequent discussion. The main input types to bear in mind for now are the real and non-word items; and it is important to take note of the distinction between the more direct sorts of responses (naming, and pronunciation of words), and the indirect, or reflective judgements involved in lexical decision and evaluative responses.

5.2 Interpreting the findings

In this and the next section we shall consider the matter of model-ling the psycholinguistic processes that underlie the concepts we have intro-duced thus far, and the attempts that have been made to model the principal experimental findings. We shall start by setting out a preliminary framework within which the major processing issues may be located. (See fig. 5.1.)

5.2.1 *The lexical components*

The basic relationship in the lexicon is the arbitrary one between *content* and *form*. Words have meaning, and they have sound- or letter-struc-ture, and, at least in the case of simple words, there is no way of recovering the former from the latter by anything other than language-specific, acquired, associations. Starting at the top of the diagram in figure 5.1, notice the cloud-like shape, labelled 'content', which belongs within the lexicon box, but which

Table 5.1 *Input and output types in experimental studies of lexical access*

Input types

Real words	have entries in the lexicon
regular words	have regular spelling–sound correspondences, e.g. *rat, wave*, hence are in principle accessible either by grapheme–phoneme (G–P) conversion or by direct access
exception words	have irregular spelling–sound correspondences, e.g. *scissors, have*, hence can be accessed only directly; or, can be accessed faster directly, since they involve low-probability G–P rules
homophones	e.g. *sale* and *sail*, have identical phonological forms in their lexical entries, hence may be accessed only via graphological form. Or, if accessed via phonological form, it is non-unique and must be submitted to a postlexical scrutiny of graphological form
Non-words	have no lexical entries, hence cannot be said to be accessed; but can be responded to via G–P conversion
regular non-words	e.g. *mav, bix*, involve the most general G–P rules
exception non-words	showing similar spelling patterns to exception words, e.g. *scouk*, are pronounceable but involve less general G–P rules
illegal non-words	forms that are only nominally pronounceable, i.e. the illegality is defined in terms of phonotactic possibilities. The illegality may be complete, as in *sjmf*, or positionally restricted, as in *sjif, sijf*. These forms violate constraints on the input to the G–P rules
homophone non-words (pseudohomophones)	e.g. *freys, rufe*, may or may not look like natural mis-spellings (cf. *frays, roof*). No lexical access via graphological form (except possibly in the case of items that closely mimic slight mis-spellings), but G–P conversion yields a code which will permit access. NB: the access may be non-unique, as in /freɪz/ ↔ {*frays, phrase*}

Output types

Naming response	implementing the articulatory form of a visually presented real word, e.g. *thunder* → /θʌndə/. May be controlled either by lexical phonological output form, following lexical access, or by prelexical G–P conversion (if the word is regular)
Pronouncing response	as for 'naming', except the input form is a non-word, e.g. *mav* → /mæv/. Hence, the articulatory control does not derive ultimately from a lexical phonological output form
Lexical decision	deciding whether an input form is a lexical item or not. For real words, this must involve lexical access, either direct or indirect. In the case of homophone non-words, may be subdivided into *spelling* decision (*rufe* is not a word), which may be via direct or indirect access), and *pronunciation* decision (/ruːf/ is a word), where access must be via G–P conversion

Table 5.1 (*continued*)

Evaluation	e.g. as semantic category member (*rat* is a sort of animal), or as congruent with context (*tie the knot* vs *tie the not*). This involves lexical access, to make content specification available for the response. In the case of homophones, may be divided into *spelling* vs *pronunciation* evaluations (e.g. is *meet* a sort of food?). The pronunciation evaluation may represent postlexical phonology, and presumably *must* do so in the case of exception words, for which the G–P route is not available

Based on discussion in Henderson 1982.

also extends beyond it. This is a way of representing an area which is difficult to explore, containing everything that is relevant to word-based language processing which is not specifically boxed and labelled elsewhere in the diagram: thus grammatical knowledge, linguistic semantics, knowledge of the world, idiosyncratic associations – everything in human cognition; which certainly includes but also goes beyond the confines of even a psycholinguistic lexicon.

Running into and out from this area are the links to the *word forms*, which are components mediating access into and out from the content system. There are, to be sure, other entry and exit points for the content system: we can see a picture of a flower (visual non-lexical input) and name it (lexical-articulatory output), or hear the name (auditory–lexical input) and attempt to draw the object (manual non-lexical output). These other, non-lexical entry and exit points are not our main concern here, although we should note that, given the way the content system is organised with respect to the lexicon, they may play a role in certain contextual integration effects on lexical access. Thus, in a context where tulips are salient, even a degraded auditory or visual input signal representing the lexical entry 'tulip' may be perceived successfully, where it might not be in other contexts. Contextual effects, mediated via the content system, are provided for in links that lead out from the content system to the word-form components, 'readying' these components for certain types of signal-based input. Hence the two-way arrows in the diagram between *visual* and *auditory input* and the content system.

Among the word-form components, we recognise that in terms of its mental representation the way a word sounds is distinct from the way that it is written, and that there may be a more or less complex relationship between the two: i.e. there may be distinct representations in long-term memory for the *graphological* as opposed to the *phonological* forms of words. The latter are

248

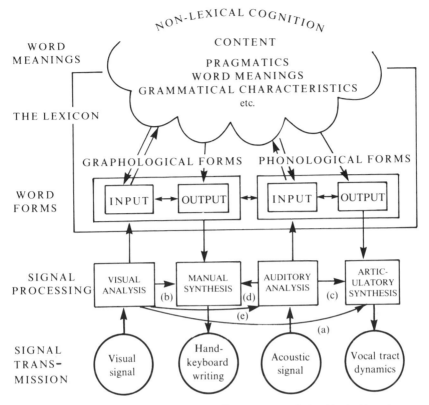

Figure 5.1 General framework of input–output relationships inside and outside the lexicon

acquired first, at least for that part of our vocabulary which is established prior to learning how to handle the written form of our language. In these terms, initial steps in learning how to read and write may be mediated through existing phonological word forms, but ultimately result in the laying down of separate, though related, written word forms (organised as letter structures).

Furthermore, since the observable processing differences in the input and output modalities are considerable (see ch. 2), we have to be in a position to disambiguate the concept of 'the way a word sounds' as between 'what it sounds like' (auditory perception) vs 'how to make it sound' (articulatory motor output); and so also for 'the way a word is read' (visual perception) vs 'how to spell it' (manual motor output).

Finally on connections within the lexicon, it should be noted that there is *some* evidence, albeit not very compelling, for the existence of auditory-to-articulatory and graphological-to-articulatory connections. Consider the case of exception words (words having non-simple grapheme-to-phoneme mappings) such as *nourish, conscience* and *beguile*: if we grant that these can be read aloud on visual presentation via something other than a grapheme-to-phoneme connection, then it is natural to assume that the link between input and response is mediated via full lexical access, i.e. involving activation of the content system. In other words, we read and understand the word that is visually presented; and we then mount a naming response. But it is often the case that the involvement of the content system may appear to be minimal: this may happen if our attention wanders as we are reading a passage, leaving us temporarily scanning print, and even reading aloud, with little awareness of what is on the page. And it has also been observed that some language-impaired individuals, suffering from a severe semantic disorder that leaves them apparently unable to access the meaning of certain words, can nevertheless read them aloud successfully (Morton and Patterson 1980). The conclusion from such instances may be that neither the grapheme-to-phoneme link nor that via the content system is effective, leaving the connections between word-form components as the only remaining possibility. The trouble with such arguments is that we cannot be sure that the content system is not operative, even in non-obvious ways, in spite of attentional neglect or apparent deficit.

5.2.2   *The perceptual and motor components*

This brings us to the level of *signal processing* in figure 5.1, outside the lexicon. We are less concerned here with what is in the analysis and synthesis boxes (auditory percepts and their graphemic equivalents may be assumed on the input channels, and sensory goals for speech and writing on the output channels), than with the possible links between them. The evidence for most of the links rests on the processing of regularly spelled forms, with minimal semantic involvement. As such, it derives in the main from *regular non-words*: these can be presented visually for a pronunciation response, via route (a) (note that 'pronunciation' is the term used where 'naming' would be appropriate for a lexically mediated articulatory response), or a writing response, via route (b). Note that route (a) must involve a grapheme-to-phoneme, or grapho-phonological (G–P), mapping. Auditorily presented non-words can also be pronounced ('repeated'), via route (c), or written, via route (d) ('dictation'). But there is also a very important link, via route (e), from visual to auditory analysis: this is a possible pathway for regularly spelled words also involving G–P mapping, and is the one that is appealed to in so-called *indirect lexical access*. We can, for instance, recognise that the non-word *phocks* sounds like a kind of animal (it is a pseudo-homophone).

This is because we can access the lexical item *fox* via the *phocks* → /fɒks/ G–P mapping.

5.2.3 *The major experimental findings*

Having now reviewed the general layout of lexical access, we shall turn to review the more important experimental findings.

The length effect

Does it take more time to access longer words than shorter ones? The question arises most obviously in relation to word recognition, though it has implications also for production (in the length of time required to organise an articulatory or manual implementation of a word). It has been traditionally addressed in the context of visual-word recognition, where, for a given fixation, all letters of a word are simultaneously available for processing. In the context of auditory-word recognition, the sequential nature of the signal, by virtue of which the early portion of a word may be sufficient to permit identification, to some extent short-circuits possible length effects. It will be appropriate to discuss the length effect here in terms of visual-word recognition only.

A basic version of the length hypothesis predicts that we process words letter by letter. A number of studies have obtained results that suggest that words are processed, at some early stage in the recognition process, in a letter-by-letter fashion. For example, Gough (1972) argues that letters are taken out of the visual buffer for processing at the rate of about 15msec. per letter, on average. If it is true that letters are involved in this way, then we should expect letter legibility to be important to word identification. Gough and Cosky (1977) present the results shown in figure 5.2 for 144 words read aloud by fifteen subjects. Although word-recognition latency increases linearly with length here, it appears that legibility is not a significant factor, casting some doubt on whether letters are the relevant unit involved.

Leaving this matter aside for now, we should note that Theios and Muise (1977) represent another school of thought on the length issue, explicitly rejecting the Gough (1972) estimate of 15msec. per letter, and recalling the experimental work of Cattell (1886) and Johnson's (1975) replication. Both of these studies involved a target-probe task, in which a subject is presented first with a visual letter-array (the target), and then with a sequence of other arrays (the probes), and has to identify which of the probe stimuli matches the target. Theios and Muise present the data shown in table 5.2 from one of Johnson's experiments. In this case, there is confirmation of Cattell's early results, and no support for the view that the letters of a word are processed sequentially. Forster (1976) also claims, on the basis of work done by Frederiksen and

Table 5.2 *Mean recognition latencies (msec.) for individual letters and words*

Type of target and probe	Response type		
	Yes	No	Mean
Single letter	537	499	518
1-Syllable, 5-letter word	529	517	523
2-Syllable, 5-letter word	533	510	521
Mean	533	509	521

From Theios and Muise 1977: table 2, p. 295; data from Johnson 1975.

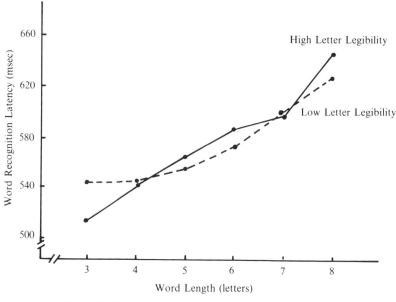

Figure 5.2 Word-recognition latency as a function of length and letter legibility. (From Gough and Cosky 1977: fig. 3, p. 284.)

Kroll (1974), Forster and Chambers (1973) and Chambers and Forster (1975), that there is virtually no effect of word length in word recognition.

What are we to make of such apparently conflicting evidence, on such an apparently basic physical property of words? Henderson (1982), reviewing the research field, finds that on pronunciation tasks average time per letter ranged

Table 5.3 *Word–non-word decision latency as a function of string type*

String type	Example	Mean decision latency (msec.)
Word	DESK	708
'Full' unpronounceable non-word	SJMF	607
'Left' unpronounceable non-word	SJIF	644
'Right' unpronounceable non-word	SAJF	680
Pronounceable non-word	SARF	746
Non-word homophonic with word	SAIF	810

From Gough and Cosky 1977: table 1, p. 278.

from 15msec. (as mentioned above, and also found in Cosky 1980) to 63msec. in Seymour and Porpodas (1980), for poorly developing readers. He suggests that 'as a rough generalisation, letter-length effects are reliably found in naming tasks but are usually, but not invariably, absent in lexical decision tasks' (p. 325).

If the letter-length effect is thought to reflect grapho-phonological recoding, then this task difference might hold interesting implications for processing models. But, as Henderson (1982) points out, the assumption of phonological recoding revealing itself in such an effect is not a necessary one. Theios and Muise (1977) and Gough and Cosky (1977) both usefully point up the issue of serial vs parallel processing: where a length effect is obtained, it is consistent with a serial-processing (letter-by-letter) account, and its absence is consistent with parallel processing (all letters at the same time, in parallel channels). It might be that length effects in naming responses reflect encoding rather than decoding strategies.

The legality effect

We have already briefly considered the legality of letter sequences in chapter 3, and suggested that in certain contexts it is hard to disentangle legality from pronounceability. To some extent legality might reflect purely visual constraints (such as the typical relative positions of particular letters in certain strings). But even here pronounceability remains an issue, as table 5.3 shows. The data in this table, from Gough and Cosky (1977), show the mean times taken for subjects to lexically decide certain types of string as words or non-words. It appears that a globally illegal sequence of consonants such as SJMF, which can have only a nominal pronunciation assigned to it, may often be rejected more rapidly than partially or fully legal sequences; further, partially legal sequences that show illegality early in the string (SJIF) are rejected more rapidly than those with later illegal substrings (SAJF).

Findings such as these are consistent with a two-step process (which may operate only because of the demands of the lexical decision task), which (a) at the first level discovers *globally* illegal sequences (presumably in terms of gross categories of letter structure), and (b) at a subsequent level discovers those strings which fail a more specific, left-to-right testing of letter transitions. Such a procedure would be consistent with the G–P mapping on route (e) in figure 5.1, and may indeed represent the first level of operations on this channel. So, going back to the case of the Gough and Cosky (1977) illustration, the extra time required to decide a legal non-word, such as SARF, over the globally illegal SJMF, may include the time taken to process all the letters of the legal string. But it must also include other processing too; for after G–P mapping has taken place, yielding the representation /saːf/, lexical access must be attempted, and must fail, before the item in question can be classified as a non-word. In other tasks too, legal vs illegal letter-strings may yield different findings, which may vary considerably from one task to another. Henderson (1982) notes that in cases where the subject, faced with lists of stimulus items, fails to become aware that some items are legal and others are not, the effect of legality may disappear. The relevant strategy may therefore depend to some extent on attentional processes.

The regularity effect

Regularity of letter–sound (or G–P) mapping is, as we have suggested in chapter 3, not to be thought of as an all-or-none property. It has been correspondingly difficult to isolate a pure regularity effect in experimental work; but the following passage, from Gough and Cosky (1977), will give an insight to some of the reasons why the effect might be important, and how careful the experimenter has to be.

> The most cogent test of the phonological hypothesis that we have yet seen was first proposed by David Fay; it was last conducted by J. D. Edgmon. Fay reasoned that if the printed word is converted into phonological form by means of grapheme–phoneme rules, then words which conform to regular rules should be converted (and understood) faster than words which constitute exceptions to such rules. Accordingly, Fay argued that we should compare the speed of comprehension of regularly and irregularly spelled (pronounced) English words. Edgmon was able to find 56 irregularly spelled words which met two criteria: that each word has a unique pronunciation (e.g. *bowl, gross*) which violates a grapheme–phoneme correspondence rule, and that there existed at least three words

> which exemplify the rule (e.g. *cowl–fowl–howl, boss–loss–moss*). Each
> irregular word was yoked with a regular control, matched in number of
> letters, syllables, form class, initial letter and phoneme, and frequency
> according to Kucera and Francis (1967). (To avoid any interactions,
> none of the examples of the rules which the irregular words violated were
> used.) The 112 items were presented in random order to each of 25
> subjects . . . who were asked to read them aloud as rapidly as possible.
> Each subject's median latency for regular and irregular words was
> computed. The means of these medians were 600msec. and 627msec.
> respectively, and the difference is highly significant. Evidently regular
> words are recognised and named faster than irregular. (pp. 280–1)

Henderson (1982), reviewing this and other studies, notes that, in addition
to this study's finding of a small but reliable regularity effect of 27msec.,
Stanovich and Bauer (1978), controlling for length, frequency and visual
appearance of stimuli, obtained a reliable 18msec. regularity effect:

> Furthermore, they were able to show that this effect was abolished in a
> task in which production latencies were measured without inclusion of
> orthographic decoding times. In this simple reaction time (RT) task, the
> words were presented for inspection and after a variable delay a signal
> was given to emit the word. Such RTs presumably reflect motor
> preparation times. The absence of a regularity effect in this task provides
> some assurance that the previous effect is truly related to orthographic
> decoding. (p. 125)

However, Henderson suggests that the regularity effect does not force us to
accept the prelexical G–P conversion route as the necessary source of this
effect. Most importantly, there is the work of Glushko (1979), in *lexical analogy theory*, which treats the difficulty of irregular words in terms of their
orthographic neighbours. For example, HAVE has a large number of neighbours whose G–P correspondence is inconsistent with it (SHAVE, SAVE, WAVE,
GAVE, etc.), and whose pronunciation pattern exerts an influence on the way
we process HAVE. This provides the basis for an account of G–P correspondences in terms of degrees of *consistency*, rather than discrete categories of
'regular' or 'irregular', and does so on the basis of *lexical relationships* (among
form components in the lexicon, in terms of fig. 5.1), rather than in *extra-lexical G–P rules*. Given that regularity and consistency have been conflated in
most experimental investigations, the nature of the so-called regularity effect
may need to be reinterpreted.

The frequency effect

Oldfield (1963) estimated the number of words that are both
known to educated English speakers and contained in the *Oxford English*

Dictionary at around 75,000, and to this we must add all those names of people, places and things that are sufficiently idiosyncratic or novel to escape the lexicographical process. We search this extensive mental lexicon very rapidly, and Oldfield (1966) further speculates that it would be efficient for such a system to conduct lexical search on the basis of frequency of items, so that high-frequency words were accessed earlier than low-frequency ones. The so-called word-frequency effect is commonly encountered in the literature; thus, Forster (1976) observes that 'words with a relatively high frequency of occurrence are classified [in a lexical decision task] faster than words with a low occurrence frequency e.g. *mildew, perspire, radiate*, although the latter are still perfectly familiar to the subjects of the experiment (e.g. Rubenstein, Garfield and Millikan 1970; Forster and Chambers 1973; Forster and Bednall 1976)' (p. 263).

In the Forster and Chambers (1973) study, an average difference of 71 msec. was found in favour of fifteen words having a mean frequency of 199 per million (in the Kučera and Francis 1967 count) over fifteen words having a mean frequency of only one per million. Theios and Muise (1977) point out that this is a small sample, and that the factor of letter–sound (G–P) correspondence was uncontrolled. They report on their own experiment in which

> we attempted to control for both phonology and the goodness of orthography by using pairs of homophonic words [e.g. *all* (high frequency) vs *awl* (low frequency)] and making within pair comparisons. This controls for phonology since the required response is identical for both members of the homophonic pair. With respect to orthography, the control is not as tight since the pair could differ on approximation to an optimal orthography. However both members of each homophonic pair are real words, and thus by definition each has a real orthography. It would be expected that in some instances, the lower frequency member of a homophonic pair would have a better orthographic structure than the higher frequency member. To the extent that this occurred, the correlation between word frequency and reading latency should be reduced, if indeed orthography has an effect on speed of word identification. (p. 305)

They used 600 homophones, and varied their presentation in upper- and lower-case letters. They found a difference of 11 msec. in favour of their high-frequency words (occurring an average of 600 times per million) over the low-frequency ones (at an average of thirty-two per million). What do we make of this? 'Whether the small 11 msec. difference is meaningful is open to question. It is quite possible that the difference is really due to differential orthographic

structure or letter-to-sound correspondence and not due to word frequency'
(p. 306).

Henderson (1982) notes that we might accommodate the frequency effect, if
it exists, within a model of the mental lexicon in more than one way. We could
arrange for high-frequency candidate words to be listed *before* low-frequency
ones, with respect to some serial-search procedure (Forster 1976); or we could
envisage high-frequency words as being represented in the store more *often*, in
respect of some random-access procedure (Landauer 1975); or as being
accessed more *readily*, in tems of degree of activation required (Morton 1979).
Henderson (1982) also cites Glanzer and Ehrenreich's (1979) finding that the
advantage of high-frequency words is diminished when they occur in lists of
words of various frequencies; this is a problem for models where the frequency
effect is fixed, in whatever manner. In conclusion, Henderson suggests that
'the word frequency effect has betrayed the trust invested in it by those who
believed it would serve to reflect in a rather direct way the working of the lexical access procedure. It seems likely that it is a composite of various factors
that influence various stages of word recognition' (1982: 336).

One can also investigate the frequency effect of stems in affixed words, independently of the frequency of whole affixed words. Taft (1979) found an effect
of stem frequency, whereby higher-frequency stem words (*re-proach*) were
faster to classify as words than the lower-frequency stem words (*dis-suade*)
(*reproach* and *dissuade* are of similar whole-word frequency). But he also
found an effect of whole-word frequency on inflected words that were
matched for stem frequency, which does not fit with the model. Nor is it clear
(Henderson 1982) that arguments from frequency can *in principle* support the
notion of morphological decomposition as a part of lexical access, since it is
possible that frequency effects may arise not out of the search procedure but
as a matter of response availability.

The lexicality effect

If we set aside the issue of pronounceability/legality of letter
strings, we can observe the advantage that real words have over non-words.
An example is provided in the comparison of lexical decision times for DESK
and SARF in table 5.3 above. Non-words take longer to reject than real words
take to be accepted, a finding which may suggest a lexical search which is prolonged, before being terminated as fruitless in the case of those non-words
that are not ruled out as non-lexical by virtue of their letter sequence.

There is also a lexicality effect on pronunciation of less common sound–
letter correspondences; so, *head* is not mispronounced as /hi:d/, by the
common *ea* → /i:/ rule (compare *bead*, *beat*, *seat*, etc.). This suggests an

advantage of input–output processing for items having a lexical entry over those that depend solely on extra-lexical machinery such as G–P correspondences. This leads to an assumption that the lexical route is inherently faster than the G–P route (at least for high-frequency words). Also linked to the lexicality effect, perhaps, is the observation that we can assign a pronunciation to non-graphemic items such as £ and idiosyncratically graphemic items such as *lb*.

But what actually is the basis for the effect of 'having a lexical entry'? The answer may be as complex as the notion of 'lexical entry' itself (which contains all the information, relating both to form and to content, that distinguishes one lexical item from all others in the system). Theios and Muise (1977) provide an illustration of the issues, in an investigation addressing the role of letter structure, sound structure and meaning on reading times for CVC letter strings.

> The population of CVCs can be partitioned into subsets according to semantic, phonetic, and orthographic properties. Some CVCs are in fact words, for example BAD ... and thus have a high semantic value as well as conforming to the phonology and orthography of the language ... The set of CVC [legal non-word] syllables may be subpartitioned into two sets: (a) CVCs that sound like real words (pseudohomophones) and thus have a high semantic value since they phonologically map onto real words, for example BAC ... and (b) CVC syllables which phonetically do not map onto real words and thus should have a lower semantic value, for example BAF ... Some CVCs ... do not occur in English words ... and yet they are homophonic to English words, for example ... DOH. In spite of their orthographic violations (or rareness) these CVCs presumably should have high semantic value since phonologically they map onto real English words. Other CVCs that do not occur in English ... are quite readable and pronounceable, for example, BEP ... These should be low on semantic and orthographic information but should be reasonably high on phonetic information since the letter-to-sound correspondence causes no problem for the reader. Finally there is the set of CVCs which most native English readers find difficult to pronounce ... for example ... XOL ... These CVCs should be low on orthography, phonology, and semantic meaningfulness. (pp. 301–3)

Imposing these six categories on reading–pronunciation data collected previously for 2,100 CVCs (Nodine and Hardt 1969), Theios and Muise were able to conclude that real-word CVCs exhibited a lexicality effect as illustrated by the following types (< means 'quicker than', / means 'not different from'):

$$\text{BAD} < \text{BAC}/\text{BAF}/\text{DOH} < \text{BEP} < \text{XOL}$$

Real words were on average 27msec. quicker to pronounce than the next non-word grouping; this group was on average 15msec. quicker than the pronounceable but non-occurring type; and the last category, of hard-to-pronounce CVCs, was 104msec. slower than the pronounceable type. The conclusion is drawn that, in this task, 'either good orthography and phonology or good phonology and meaning are equivalent in their contribution to reading and pronunciation speed ... [and that] ... good phonology (pronounceability) does not insure fast reading and pronouncing *unless* there is a good orthographic or semantic component to the CVC' (p. 303).

Henderson (1982), reviewing a range of studies, concludes that 'under appropriate testing conditions a lexicality advantage emerges reliably', but goes on to say: 'What cannot yet be decided is whether the underlying mechanisms serving the pseudoword advantage (over random arrays) ['pseudoword' is a convenient term for non-words having legal/pronounceable letter structure: see the legality effect, above] and the real word advantage (over pseudowords) [i.e. the lexicality effect] are totally distinct from one another' (1982: 274).

The homophone effect

We have noted that distinct letter strings may map onto the same sound as, or be homophonous with, others. This may hold between non-words (e.g. *zait/zate*), between real words (e.g. *sail/sale*), or between non- and real words (e.g. *rane/rain*; the non-word in such cases being referred to as a 'pseudo-homophone'). The fact that we can process the distinction between, say, *buoy* and *boy* in reading and writing is clear evidence for a distinct visual-processing path in the lexicon.

The homophone effect, however, refers to the finding of Rubenstein, Lewis and Rubenstein (1971) that in a lexical decision task it takes longer to reject pseudo-homophones, and to accept the less frequent member of a pair of real-word homophones than is the case for non-homophonous pseudo-words and real words. And they use this finding to argue (from the title of their article) for 'phonemic recoding in visual word recognition'. The argument runs as follows. The visual signal is processed, via G–P conversion, to yield a phonemic representation: this is then used to address the lexicon, which results in (a) a real word being accessed, in the case of a pseudo-homophone stimulus; or (b) more than one real word being accessed, in the case of a real-word homophone stimulus. In each of the situations, the appropriate lexical decision can only be made, it is argued, by running a postlexical spelling check, to establish, in case (a), that the pseudo-homophone must be rejected, and in case (b), that one of the words conforms in its spelling to the stimulus, and can therefore be accepted. In the latter case, the spelling check is assumed to run on the higher-frequency member of the homophonous pair first (e.g. *all* before *awl*; see the frequency effect, above).

As Marshall (1976) points out, however, such findings, which are intended to serve the phonemic-recoding view, 'rather conspicuously fail to rule out the parallel-processing version' (p. 113) by which sound structure and letter structure are activated together and allowed to interact. Henderson notes the poor control of the Rubenstein, Lewis and Rubinstein study, and reviews a number of others which either fail to find any effect of homophony, or find it in restricted conditions, suggesting that it results from the use of an optional strategy in certain situations (p. 326). As far as pseudo-homophones are concerned, any effect they may have hardly speaks to the way that real words are processed, in conditions that approximate to natural reading.

There is some evidence (Baron 1973; Doctor and Coltheart 1980) that homophones can slow, and make less accurate, the decision to reject a construction such as *she blue up the ballon*, compared to non-homophonous stimuli such as *she know up the balloon*. As Henderson (1982) points out, this is likely to reflect constructional processing as much as lexical access, and hardly constitutes evidence for prelexical visual-to-sound mapping (pp. 327–8).

5.2.4 *Modelling the findings*

Indirect versus direct processes

When considering the sorts of models that have been proposed for lexical access, it may be useful to bear in mind such familiar systems as a dictionary and a library. Each of these has internal organisation, for storing items, and access is achieved by a *search* procedure that exploits this organisation (e.g. alphabetic ordering of words in a dictionary, or the cataloguing system of books in a library). Where access is guided by search, we speak of *indirect* access, or two-stage access – *search*, followed by *matching*. By contrast, we might illustrate another sort of access procedure by reference to a word-processing package, in which we may have certain items stored by name, so that, on typing in the letters of the name (perhaps only the first few letters, sufficient to identify the item in question), the item can be accessed. There is no obvious search phase here; the procedure is *direct* access.

Forster (1976) provides a useful discussion of these procedures, which we shall follow below. We shall then continue with his account of a search model of lexical access (5.3), before turning to consider some direct models that have been proposed (5.4–5.5).

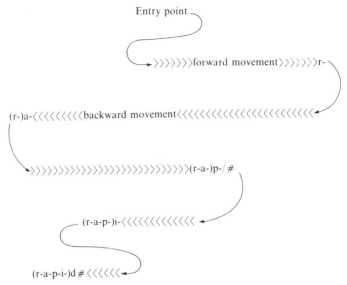

Figure 5.3 The configuration of a dictionary search for the word *rapid*

A search procedure for lexical access

Forster (1976) provides an illustration of consulting a dictionary, or other alphabetically organised listing. We scan the input word for its letter sequence, and then we enter the dictionary. In the case of a book dictionary, we open it at some page, and then move backwards or forwards through the pages till we find those entries that share the initial letter with the input word. For the word *rapid*, for instance, it is the letter *r*. The second letter in the input word is *a*, so we now move to those *r*-initial entries that have *a* as their next letter; the third input form letter is *p*, so we narrow the search down further to just those entries that have the initial sequence *r–a–p*; and so on. This (perfectly familiar) procedure may be displayed as in figure 5.3. The direction of our first movement is determined by the place of book opening in relation to the location of the initial target-letter; typically, we try to guide our place of opening by our knowledge of the alphabetic sequence, in relation to the thickness of the book. Subsequent movements, in both their direction and magnitude, depend on the fineness of the search strategies used: we can opt for large-sampling movements which must be quite predictive in nature ('I'll turn the next few pages together, because there must be a lot of *re-*'s'), or for more frequent, one-page-at-a-time sampling. Whatever method, or blend of methods, we use, the configuration of the search is one of narrowing down to a unique position, guided by a linear (left-to-right, letter-by-letter) analysis of the input word. It is the physical form (the letter structure) of the dictionary entry that determines the position that it occupies in the book; so a search mounted on the basis of physical-form analysis of the input word succeeds.

Now, if the dictionary is of the familiar sort, its purpose is not to store all possible physical forms of words but rather just those possible forms that actually occur as words in the language: hence we will not find several positions filled with possible but not actual words such as *ripad, parid, darip*, etc. Furthermore, in such a dictionary, the last letter of each entry must constitute a word-closing element, which we have signalled in the diagram above with - #. Note that there is such a signal after the -*d* of *rapid*; and also after the -*p* of *rap*, where, however, it is given as an alternative to treating this element as word-medial -*p*-. Inspection of the input-word letter sequence at this point tells us whether we have exhaustively scanned the input-letter sequence (and hence found our dictionary entry) yet, or whether we have to go on.

So much by way of illustrating the search procedure. But what might the organisation of the dictionary be like? We know that the normal sort of dictionary is in the form of a book, in which all the separately listed items are spelled out fully; but this involves considerable redundancy in the interests of ease of use in turning over the pages and scanning their contents; and it is possible that this sort of organisation is not required, and actually too costly, as far as the mental lexicon is concerned.

A transition-network formalism

Forster then considers an alternative, direct, procedure. We might state the initial letter, say *r*-, just once, for all the *r*-initial entries, and then spell out just their remaining letter sequence: *r*-, . . . -*ap*, -*apid*, . . . -*at*, . . . , etc. The same principle could then be carried through for the next letter in the sequence, and the next, and so on. In this way, each letter would be stated only once for each position in the word (initial, second, third, etc.), and we would build a retina of positional letter-elements through which search paths would define the existence of particular entries, as in figure 5.4. This is a type of transition-network formalism. Up to some determinate limit (say, twenty letters) it will permit all the words of the language to be represented, as pathways (sequences of letter-to-letter transitions) through the network.

It can achieve economy of representation in three ways:

1. because it allows pathways to merge: thus the independent words *rap* and *rapid* share the same path through the first three levels of the network, because they share the same letter structure up to that point. That happens to be the end of the word *rap*, but this is not necessarily the case for other shared words.

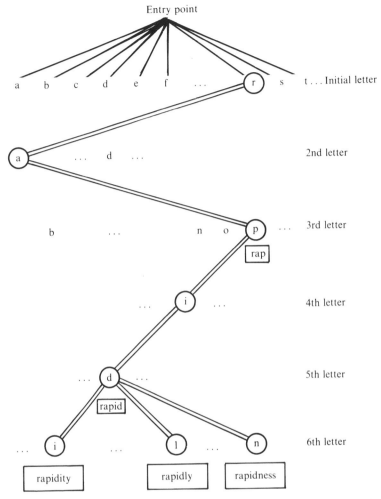

Figure 5.4 A transition-network representation of dictionary entries. (Based on Forster 1976: fig. 2, p. 261.)

Some words will share the same path through their whole extent, in which case they will be shown to be homonyms, e.g. *bank*.

2. because the number of specified pathways through the network is less than the number of all possible transitions: thus, after initial *r*-, the second-level letters *b*, *c*, *d*, etc. are not relevant.

3. because (as illustrated above), the letter structure may uniquely determine a word even before the end of the word is reached: word entries are

represented as boxed-in forms associated with various points in the network, and, while the word *rap* can only be associated with the end of its letter sequence (because of the existence of *rack*, *rat*, etc.), *rapidity* can be associated with a point in its pathway earlier than the end of the word.

We can quite conveniently think of such a mental lexicon being 'wired in', in some sense, in our memory. For the purpose of our present discussion, we need to transpose the terms of written language (suitable to our analogy with the book type of dictionary) into those of auditory perception. In auditory terms, the perceived properties of the stimulus, as delivered through the auditory system, would be required to match the stored properties of a particular pathway through the network. It is convenient to discuss this matching process as if the properties were segmental phonemes, for the purpose of illustration. Then, the presence of the phonemes /ra/- in initial and second positions matches the transition from /r/- to -/a/- between the first two levels in the network; the presence of -/p/ after this matches the transition to -/p/- between the second and third levels of the network, and so on. Given that the auditory signal is arriving at the ear in a temporally sequential fashion, it is natural to assume that the initial portions of it are available for processing earlier than the medial and final elements; and hence that the matching along the transition-network pathway takes place over the small amount of time that it takes the signal to come in. That is, the transition network is traversed *sequentially*; but note that 'sequential' does not mean 'serial' operation, since the mode of operation is actually parallel. This can be seen in the fact that each transition is carried out independently of all the others; if the input could somehow be made instantaneous, then all the transitions would also be carried out instantaneously in the lexicon.

Now, such a model makes two important predictions, as Forster (1976) points out:

1. non-words such as /ridap/, will be much faster to detect than real words;
2. longer words should take longer to access.

The first prediction is based on the fact that our lexical network has no place for non-words; so, encountering /ridap/ in the auditory signal, the attempt to traverse the lexical network fails at the point where its structure deviates from that of an actual word in the language – in this case, between /rid/- and -/a/ (note that the lexical item /rid/ associated with the third level in the network is not accessed because there is further structure in the auditory signal, inconsistently with the presence of this word). If all non-words deviated from real words only in their final phoneme, the earlier detection of non-words would not arise; but in an experiment involving non-words of varying deviation points, and real words, the nonword-detection effect would be predicted to appear. Unfortunately for our model, it does not. Forster (1976) states the position, as far as visual-word recognition findings are concerned:

> By means of the so-called *lexical decision* experiment, we can estimate the time required for lexical access to occur. In such an experiment, a letter sequence is presented visually for as long as the subject requires to classify the item as a word (in his vocabulary) or as a nonword as rapidly as possible ... in such experiments, it is typically found that familiar words are classified in around 500msec., but that nonwords require about 650msec. .... This is an extremely robust finding. (pp. 360–2)

Note that, if it were the case that the real words in such experiments were actually identifiable earlier in their letter sequence than all the non-words, according to our model, we would be able to challenge this conclusion: but care is taken in the design of these experiments to ensure that identification points on this basis are evenly matched as between non-words and real words.

The other prediction, that longer words will take longer to access than shorter words, is not borne out in other studies (e.g. Chambers and Forster 1975) also on visual-word recognition.

Finally, the model *fails* to account for an aspect of lexical access that *is* observed: the so-called 'frequency effect', whereby words of high frequency of occurrence in the language are generally accessed faster. As Forster says:

> There is simply no way of arranging the decision trees [another way of referring to the network pathways] so that frequency of occurrence of the word *itself* controls access time. It is of course possible to arrange matters so that *letter* frequency is a relevant parameter (e.g. by changing the order in which the paths are listed), but this typically has no detectable impact on processing time (e.g. Chambers and Forster 1975). (1976: 363)

A last-ditch defence might be mounted, by pointing out that these negative findings derive from studies of visual rather than auditory processing of words, and of words in isolation rather than in utterance contexts. Concerning the first of these points, we would be forced by this defence to postulate two entirely different access systems in the two modalities of language input, and hence would lose the possibility of a general model of audio–visual access. This is a sufficiently unwelcome outcome to prompt us to explore alternative models before accepting it. The second point needs careful consideration. At various points in the presentation of the transition-network model, it may have occurred to the reader to wonder about the logic of the argument that, e.g. 'we do not access /rap/ in the sequence /rapid/, because there is more to come in the auditory signal'. Such a statement seems to assume that word-boundary information is available in the auditory signal, at a point prior to lexical access; but this must either mean that there is some auditory clue to word boundaries, or that there is some circularity of argument. We shall return to this issue below; but we may note here that it does not obviously save the transition-network model from the findings that Forster cites. We shall take it, then, that this is actually a most unpromising model, and turn to consider the alternative that Forster offers us.

5.3 A search model of lexical access

Forster (1976) goes on to present a search model of lexical access. This is a type of two-stage processing model, where the first stage is completed before the second stage begins: as such, it is serial (rather than parallel) in its mode of operation. The first stage is the one in which the search is carried on: this search is ordered by frequency of the lexical items in the language, beginning with the most frequent items, then successively down through the listing until the lowest-frequency items are reached. Forster likens this stage to opening the right page of a dictionary, but finding the items on that page listed in order of frequency, with high-frequency items at the top, and starting the search from the top of the page down.

As with our first model, we have the analysed properties of the input word available, and our search through the frequency listing is for a match with those properties. Thus, we have been guided to the right 'page' by the initial /r/- (and possibly other aspects of the input signal as well), and we are now searching all the items on that page, not in terms of their further physical structure, but in terms of their frequency rank-ordering. But what happens when a match is found is very different from our first model: in the search model it yields, not access to the full lexical item itself (because the 'page' we are scanning lists word forms, not full lexical entries), but an abstract location marker, which tells us where the full lexical item is stored: having first retrieved the marker, we then use it to gain us access to the lexical item: this is the second stage.

A rather different sort of analogy may be helpful, based on a library, rather than a dictionary. We enter, looking for a particular book; we do not go straight to the main shelves where the books are located, since there are simply too many of them to permit efficient search of them in this direct fashion. So we go instead to the catalogue: this has entries which are ordered in a way which is different from the layout of the books on the shelves (e.g. alphabetically; it will have books listed together that belong to different topic areas which are housed on different floors of the building). Searching through the catalogue, we find something that matches what we are looking for; but we retrieve from this stage of the process, not the book itself, but an abstract location marker, telling us where to find the book on the shelves. Armed with this, we implement the second stage of the process, by using the marker to guide us to the right book on the shelves. The two-stage, or serial, nature of this procedure is highlighted by the impossibility of consulting the catalogue and going to the stack in a mixed, or parallel fashion; the catalogue search must be terminated, successfully, before the second stage is implemented.

5.3.1 *Access files*

Given that words have to be accessible in written form as well as in speech, and for producing language as well as receiving it, words must be stored in such a way that they can be searched for in a systematic fashion either by their properties as *message* elements (in the production of language) or by their linguistic *form*, either orthographic or phonological (their stimulus properties). The way this is achieved in the search model is to establish these distinctions of access in the search phase, or what we have likened to the catalogue system; so we have three catalogues, or *access files*, (a) orthographic, (b) phonological and (c) semantic–syntactic.

5.3.2 *The master file*

These access files are linked to a unitary *master file*, whose function is to represent all aspects of all the entries in the lexicon, their phonological, orthographic and syntactic–semantic properties, such that, once an entry in the master file is accessed, it is available for implementing any sort of response – speaking the word, writing the word, understanding the word. As a result, the access-file information on these entries is limited to the modality the access file is designed to serve: the orthographic access file has the letter structure of the words represented (so as to guide the search to the right place in the file), but has no phonological or syntactic–semantic information; and the other access files are similarly dedicated to their modality.

Within this framework, we can account for the intuition that an adequate lexicon must permit diversity of access, but unity of storage: whether we read *rapid*, hear /rapid/ or think 'rapid', it is the same word we are accessing in the master file. We may sketch the layout of this model as in figure 5.5. The model makes the following predictions:

1. High-frequency words will be accessed faster than low-frequency words – the so-called frequency effect (see also 5.2.3). It is accounted for in this model by the mixed nature of the search process. The stimulus properties of the

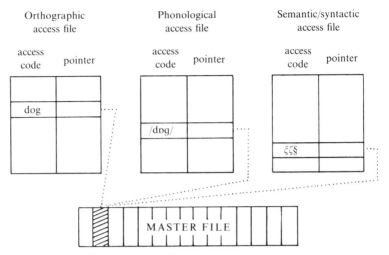

Figure 5.5 The search model of lexical access. (From Forster 1976: fig. 4, p. 268.)

auditory signal guide the search initially to the right area, or 'bin' of the relevant access file, but subsequent search of the bin is in order of frequency of the items stacked in it, from the topmost, high-frequency, items downwards. The exact nature of the stimulus-driven phase of the search is not clear; it might be based mainly on initial elements, or initial and final elements, or syllable structure, or stressed-vowel qualities, or some mixture of these. If we take the example of *bright* vs *blight*, we can see how two very similar items in the auditory signal, corresponding to the form /b/-liquid-/ait/, and hence located in the same auditory-access file bin, may be markedly different in frequency of occurrence: /bright/ will be encountered earlier in the bin search than /blight/, which will be located much further down.

2. In a lexical decision task (e.g. 'Is *darip* a word in English?'), it will take longer to reject non-words than to accept real words. In so far as the non-words concerned are structurally possible, in the phonotactic patterns of the language, this prediction derives from the so-called 'lexicality effect' (i.e. the advantage conferred on a real word by virtue of its having a lexical entry, unlike a non-word: see also 5.2.3). In this model it follows from the fact that, for non-words, (a) the phonotactically legal stimulus properties will direct the search to the 'right' bin in the auditory access file, but (b) the search through that bin will be exhaustive and fruitless, since the matching entry does not exist. As Forster puts it: 'it should be kept in mind that the overall system was designed for accessing *familiar* forms, not classifying unfamiliar forms. If

normal day-to-day language processing regularly required us to identify non-words as such, then no doubt we would have evolved more efficient procedures' [for dealing with them].

It is also possible, in this framework, to invoke the concepts of 'sufficient match' and 'post-access check', in the case of non-words that are highly similar to real words. This would allow that, in the visual mode, the non-word *obttle* would be quite likely to escape detection as such, particularly in running text (the proof-reader's problem); this would be the case if the match between the stimulus properties of the letter sequence *o–b–t–t–l–e* and the stored form *bottle* were sufficient to yield the abstract code to locate *bottle* in the master lexicon (no post-access check being implemented). By contrast, *ridap*, being unlike any real word, would be detected as a non-word more easily. It would also allow that in a lexical decision task, *obttle* would take longer to reject than *ridap*, since it would require a post-access check to highlight the discrepancy between the input and accessed forms.

5.3.3 *Cross-references in the master file*

So far, we have said very little about the master file, except that it must exist in order to represent what is common to all modes of language use concerning our lexical repertoire. But it is more than just a list or assembly of fully specified stored forms: there are inter-relationships between the constituent items. Lexicographers and semanticists have always recognised this, and psychologists too have made use of the concept of word associations. Meyer and Schvaneveldt (1971) showed this property in the context of a lexical decision task; they demonstrated that the time taken to classify a real word as such decreased if it was preceded by a real word that exhibited some semantic relationship with it. Thus, pairs like DOCTOR, NURSE, in a visual-presentation task, show reduced response latencies for the item NURSE, compared with pairs like TABLE, NURSE.

The search model accounts for this 'semantic priming' or 'facilitation' effect by postulating a series of cross-references in the master file, which are capable of acting as search paths. Thus, once the entry of DOCTOR is accessed in the master file, it is not necessary to go back to the orthographic access file for processing the next item, NURSE; rather, the system can allow for transfer immediately to the entry for NURSE in the master file, along the search path formed by the semantic cross-reference between the two items.

By this account, we would expect the frequency effect to operate only in respect of the first item in the pair, since only this is accessed through the frequency-ordered lists of the access file. Forster (1976) presents some results from an experiment that was designed to investigate this possibility. Four types of word pairs were constructed, according to whether both items were of high frequency (HIGH–HIGH), or of low frequency (LOW–LOW), or mixed, with the high-frequency item either first (HIGH–LOW), or last (LOW–HIGH). These four types were filled with words that were either semantically related pairs, or unrelated. The crucial predictions are that, in the mixed-frequency pairs, those where the first item is high frequency and related to the second item should be just as fast to process as the HIGH–HIGH pairs; while those that have the low-frequency member first, and related to the second word, should be slow to process, like the LOW–LOW pairs. For unrelated word pairs, the mixed types should have processing times that are a simple function of their combined frequencies, somewhere in between the HIGH–HIGH and LOW–LOW types, regardless of which item comes first.

However, the results reported in Forster (1976) do not fit easily with the predictions for related words (the findings for unrelated words are less important to our concern here, and are not reported fully enough for detailed comment). On the face of it, it would seem that the access file is being used for the second item in all cases, since all the pairs that have at least one low-frequency item are between 70 and 109msec. slower than the pair that does not. Forster suggests that it might sometimes be faster to use the access file for the second item in a pair, even where it is related to the first, depending on the sort of task that subjects are being asked to perform. Presumably, if the task was explicitly a semantic-relatedness judgement one, this would tend to encourage the use of cross-references in the master file, and would therefore be a better task to use if these cross-references are to be investigated.

Again, however, the findings that are reported are awkward for the model, in that the largest difference in response times occurs between the first two categories, which are predicted to be equivalently fast. Forster concludes that the semantic relations used in the experiment (e.g. between *fun* and *mirth*) are not of the sort that constitute cross-reference links in the master file.

The semantic task involved in the second of these experiments took on average about 140msec. longer than the lexical decision task in the first. This must relate somehow to the time it takes, having located a word, to scan its semantic representation. But it is not entirely clear how this is constituted, in terms of this model: whether it represents the total time to scan the semantics of both items, or just of the first item, with the semantic relatedness of the second being provided directly by the cross-referencing. At the bottom of this uncertainty is a question concerning the nature of the cross-references in the master file: do they effectively provide a separate search mechanism, and, if so, does this wastefully duplicate the function of the semantic access file? If there is no duplication, then what are the conditions under which one or the other search will be carried out? Are there sound-structure cross-references in the master file, and how far might these duplicate the operation of the phonological access file? A number of these questions really aim at the soundness of the basic distinction between the peripheral access files and the central master file. Let us recall that this distinction was established to account for *diversity of access* alongside *unity of storage*: we should ask whether this distinction necessarily involves a two-stage model of this sort. In particular, we need to ask whether it is really impossible to structure the same set of entries in distinct, modality-specific, ways, as the two-stage model assumes. If not, then we should consider whether a single-stage, or direct model can be formulated which might avoid the pitfalls of the transition-network version we considered earlier.

5.3.4 *Non-lexical and lexical pathways*

Before we leave the two-stage model, however, we should consider how it might accommodate our ability to pronounce, and make lexical decisions on, non-words as well as real words.

For our ability to pronounce spoken non-words, we may establish a non-lexical link between the auditory input and (articulatory) output: this follows from the impossibility of mounting a pronunciation response on the basis of the master-file entry in cases of non-words which, by definition, have no such entry. For lexical decision responses, we must use the auditory input to enter the phonological access file, in order to establish that there is no matching entry; this lack, established through exhaustive search, will then be assumed to trigger (through some connection not shown in the model) a NO response via the semantic–syntactic access file.

In the case of visually presented non-words, a pronunciation response must also be mediated via some non-lexical route involving a conversion of the results of letter perception into units of speech production, conventionally conceived of as grapheme-to-phoneme correspondence (GPC) (Henderson 1982). Lexical decision responses must involve entry into the lexicon at some point(s). Conceivably, this entry may be made via the phonological access file, on the basis of the phonological array that is the product of the GPC route, or via the orthographic access file, on the basis of the visual perception of the letter array (the grapheme sequence). Figure 5.6 shows these possibilities, in what Henderson (1982) refers to as a type of 'horse-race model'. We shall consider this formulation in a little more detail now.

The particular version of horse-race model that we are concerned with here assumes a serial type of lexical access on the visual-access channel (the right-hand branch from the grapheme sequence input box in fig. 5.6), to account for

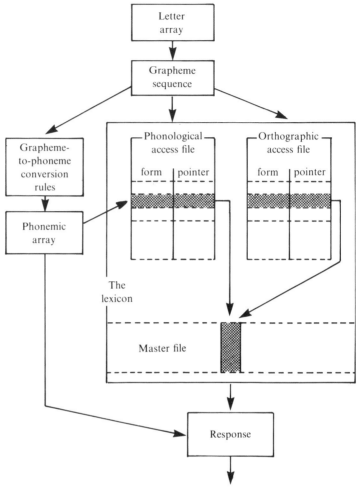

Figure 5.6 Lexical and non-lexical routes, in a search model for visual word recognition. (Based on discussion in Henderson 1982: 147–51, and fig. 5.5 above.)

the advantage of high-frequency words over those of low frequency, in terms of the frequency-ordered search in the relevant peripheral access file. This then leads to activation of the appropriate item in the master file.

The phonologically mediated access route (the left-hand branch in fig. 5.6) involves G–P conversion rules, whose specific nature is not at issue here. Most importantly, the following assumptions are made about the relations between these two channels:

1.   they are operationally parallel (i.e. this is a mixed model, with serial and parallel processing);
2.   the visual-access channel is intrinsically faster, *except for low-frequency words*;
3.   making a response, via either channel, inhibits all processing via the other.

Via the phonologically mediated channel, the G–P rules lead to a phonological output which can

1.   serve as the basis of a pronunciation response, and simultaneously
2.   address the lexicon via the phonological peripheral access file.

Note that, within this layout, no distinction is made between input vs output phonological components (compare our general scheme in fig. 5.1 above).

The outcomes of such a model are as follows:

1.   first, non-words can be pronounced, via the G–P route;
2.   real words can be pronounced, via either channel, with high-frequency words achieving access earlier via the visual channel than via the G–P route, and lower-frequency words being accessed earlier via the G–P route than the visual channel; this accounts for the overlapping response times of low-frequency real words with non-words;
3.   an effect of orthographic regularity will be found in those forms accessed via the slower, G–P, route, but will not be found in responses to high-frequency words, accessed via the visual channel;
4.   correct responses to high-frequency exception words will be faster, on average, than correct responses to regular words, some of which, in the low-frequency range, will be accessed via the G–P route;
5.   errors in pronouncing exception words will reflect failure of the visual-access channel, and hence will show longer latencies, on average, than correct responses to the same items (Henderson 1982: 150).

Thus far, we have considered how the model would account for various articulatory outcomes. But for lexical decision responses, entry into the lexicon is demanded at some point. This involves a connection between the output of the G–P rules box in figure 5.6 to the phonological peripheral access file. This at once comprises the operational parallelism of the two channels, since it allows for serial processing, first by the G–P rules and then by the lexical-access file. The picture that starts to emerge is more compatible, perhaps, with *one* pathway, serving *two* functions (one graphological, one phonological).

5.3.5 *Stems and affixes*

Henderson (1985) provides a review of the available research literature. As a result of their own and others' work in the early 1970s that showed some effect of morphological structure on word recognition, Taft and Forster (1975) suggested a testable version of a model of *written* word recognition that 'strips' affixes from stems *prior to* lexical access. Although the fact that the model was proposed for written word-forms is crucial to its operation, particularly in the matter of the identification of word boundaries, we may use it to illustrate the issues here, since it proved to be a highly influential model for a range of subsequent studies and discussions. The layout of the model, for prefix-stripping, is as in figure 5.7. Note first that this is a type of serial model, since it defines a set of stages each of which is implemented fully in an ordered fashion with respect to the other stages to which it is linked by arrows. Stages 2 and 4 relate to the (orthographic) access file of the search model we considered in section 5.3.3 above. Taft and Forster argue that such a decomposition model allows for economy of stored representations, since the stem for a number of (stem-)related words need only be specified once for all: thus *defensive* is reduced to (*de-*)-*fensive* by 'prefix-stripping', as in the model above; it is also subjected (presumably) to suffix stripping, to yield (*de-*)-*fens*-(-*ive*); and lexical search is then commenced, on the basis of the remaining, stem, element. However, it can be seen that in this case, the form, -*fens*-, is not quite canonical: we should expect -*fend*-. Possibly we should envisage, as Henderson (1985) suggests, a lexicon with a set of stem-morpheme entries, including -*fend*-, and a set of composition rules that are activated by the stripped affixes, and which determine the characteristics of particular word-formations. Thus, the activation of the suffixation rule involving -*ive* on the stem -*fend*- will lead to a match with the input form -*fens*-. Such a model predicts effects in word recognition that may be discussed under the headings of *affixation and pseudo-affixation, morpheme frequency* and *stem priming* (Henderson 1985, who also has a discussion of other types of effect).

Concerning affixation vs pseudo-affixation, the prediction from the model is that words like *lemon* will involve least processing, since they have no actual or potential affixal elements; that words such as *defend* or *trial* should be more difficult to process, since they have an affix to be stripped prior to stem access;

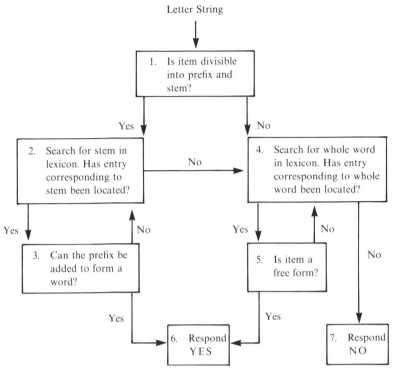

Figure 5.7 Morphological analysis in word recognition. (From Taft and Forster 1975: fig. 1, p. 644.)

and that words such as *premium* should be more difficult still, since they have a pseudo-affix (the *pre-* is not a prefix in this word).

This gives us three possible contrasts to investigate, as set out in figure 5.8. Henderson points out that most studies have concentrated on (c), in which the pseudo-affixed form follows the Taft and Forster model stages 1 → 2 → (no stem located) 4 → 5 → 6, while the affixed form takes the route 1 → 2 → 3 → 6: we then are forced to make an assumption about the relative times for processing steps 4 → 5 → 6 vs steps 3 → 6. Henderson reports Manelis and Tharp (1977) and Henderson, Wallis and Knight (1984) as finding no extra difficulty with pseudo-suffixed words, though he notes that most of the items used were derivational, and suggests that some effect might be found with pseudo-inflectional forms. Concerning pseudo-prefixation, Henderson, Wallis and Knight (1984) found no difference between pseudo-prefixed and clear monomorphemic words, although Taft (1981) found that pseudo-prefixed words took longer to name than their clear monomorphemic controls. So the results on

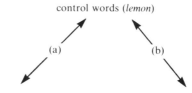

Figure 5.8 Contrasts for the investigation of possible affix effects in lexical access. (Based on discussion in Henderson 1985: 47–52.)

the comparison between words like *lemon* and words like *premium* are in conflict. The situation is not helped by the fact that, as we have noted, in cases such as *haughty*, it is difficult to decide on the status of the affix. Smith *et al.* (1984) have criticised Taft's (1981) choice of stimulus words on such grounds.

5.4 Word-detector systems: the logogen model

The transition-network model we considered earlier (section 5.2.4) was a direct one, in the sense that each element in the input signal contributed to part of the access process itself: this process was seen as cumulative, each phoneme in the input effecting one further step in the overall process, up to the point at which no further input was available, or was needed to identify the stored form. In a sense, this can be regarded as a type of *word-detector* model, since each phoneme in the input represents further evidence of the presence of a particular word, which, once the evidence has accumulated sufficiently, can be detected. But its operation, as we described it, was really on two levels: initially, it acts as a *phoneme* detector, and builds, or traces, a phoneme sequence, until the point at which a word matching that sequence is encountered. Arguably, a more truly direct mode of operation, as between the phonological analysis of the input and the lexical-access process, would be to have the device make probabilistic guesses about the lexical identity of the input sequence *at each point in the analysis*. Then it would truly be a *word-*detector model. Forster describes such a device as follows (although he illustrates from the visual mode, the nature of the description holds good for the auditory mode also):

> The essence of such a theory is that for each word there is a separate
> detector which is selectively tuned to the perceptual features
> characteristic of that word. Thus, the detectors for the word *dog* would be
> activated to some degree by any letter sequence having either an initial *d*,
> a medial *o*, or a final *g*. It would also be activated, although to a lesser
> degree, by sequences having letters *similar* to these. It might also be

activated by any sequence having exactly three letters and to a lesser
degree by two and four letter strings. Thus each detector has its own
tuning curve, and is responsive to a variety of inputs. (Forster 1976: 263)

Note that this extends the concept of analysers having selectively tuned response characteristics, which we have encountered in our discussion of the
auditory system in chapter 1, up to the level of the stored forms of lexical
items. There are two versions of this type of word-detector model which have
had considerable influence over the last few years: one, called the *logogen*
model (e.g. Morton 1969, 1970, 1979, 1980), derives in the main from work on
visual-word recognition (like the search model), although it aims to en-
compass auditory recognition also; the other, the *cohort* model (e.g. Marslen-
Wilson and Welsh 1978), has been formulated explicitly for the phenomenon
of spoken-word recognition. We shall consider each of them in turn, starting
with the historically older logogen model.

5.4.1 *Contextual influences in the logogen model*

For Morton (1979), the central issue in word recognition is the
role of *context*, because it is easier to recognise a word in some supporting
context than in isolation. This is important to us, because it suggests that word
recognition in running discourse, as is required of participants A and C while
B is talking in our passage in figure 3.1 above, is not simply a sequence of very
rapidly executed acts of isolated word recognition. Rather, isolated word
recognition, as investigated by many experiments in the field, is to be thought
of as a special case of processing, where contextual support is lacking. The
possibility exists that looking only at special cases of word recognition will
lead to a compilation of special effects, rather than of results that are indicative of the way the system normally operates.

Consider what happens if, for example, an external sound such as a cough,
or a door slamming, makes it impossible for us to perceive the acoustic structure of a portion of the input word-sequence, e.g. /dɪˈr§§tə/, in the sequence

/ ... ˈhiːz ə_____əvəˈbɪgˈkʌmpənijɪnˈbɜːmɪŋəm ... /

(§§ indicating the 'missing' portion of the signal). Listeners A and C are likely
to be (a) aware that an extraneous noise has occurred (typically recalling it as
having happened just before or just after the affected word); (b) unaware that
the sequence / ... ek ... / was not available for auditory analysis; and (c) con-
vinced that they have just heard the word *director* in the utterance *he's a direc-*
tor of a big company in Birmingham. This is what we referred to as the
'phonemic restoration' effect, in chapter 4.

There are really two sorts of context here, the local one of the word itself –

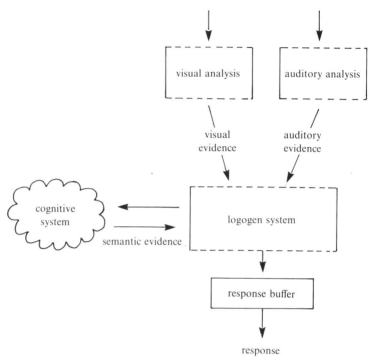

Figure 5.9 The main components and relationships of the logogen model. (Based on Morton 1979: fig. 1, p. 113; fig. 5, p. 138.)

how many words might /dɪˈr§§tə/ be? – and the larger one of the utterance. If we put the two together we would be asking something like: how many words could plausibly fit in the context *he's a* _____ *of a big company in Birmingham*, which begin with /dɪˈr/- and end in -/tə/, and whose missing middle section is about one syllable long?

The importance of context – linguistic and non-linguistic – as a practical support for what may be a degraded signal is an important consideration, and one that we shall say more about in chapter 6, section 6.1.2. In Morton's model, evidence about the occurrence of a particular word comes potentially from all modalities, and these inputs are in a 'conspiratorial' relationship with one another – deficiencies in one sort of input can be made good by reference to the information available in others, and they all combine to lower what Morton calls the *recognition threshold* of the relevant stored forms. We are dealing, then, with a word-detector system that does not just rely on the specific linguistic-signal properties, but is also able to pick up cues to the presence of a word from all available input channels, and sum their effects. It is a

278

system that looks for evidence, of any sort, that such-and-such a word has occurred.

Figure 5.9 illustrates the main components of the earlier logogen system (its later modifications do not concern us here, though we shall refer to them more fully in a moment). In the logogen system itself, at the heart of the model, are the logogens that give the model its name. These are not like dictionary entries (Morton 1979: 112), but rather constitute the tuned perceptual devices that respond to sensory and semantic input. It is here that sensory and contextual inputs interact, and give rise to outputs to the cognitive system, as well as to the response channel (in the case where the word is named; where the response is becoming aware of the meaning of the word, as in the case of understanding processes, this may be thought of as part of the output to the cognitive system; most discussions of the model assume a naming response). So we have a system that is basically tuned to the auditory and/or visual properties of words, and of their contexts of occurrence. The meanings of words, the fact that certain other words have recently occurred (see what we said earlier about the semantic priming effect), the knowledge that big companies have directors, etc. are all outside the logogen system itself. But there is a two-way connection between the logogen system and the cognitive system: what is happening in the logogen system at any moment forms part of the output to the cognitive system, and this, together with other types of knowledge, including knowledge of what the logogen system has recently been doing, can be fed back into the logogen system, to help regulate its performance.

5.4.2 *Thresholds and the frequency effect*

These delicate input–output balances are being adjusted and maintained dynamically all the time. Indeed, it is in this way that Morton approaches the frequency effect; Morton envisages that 'the threshold of a logogen is permanently [other discussions assume a long-term, rather than a permanent effect] reduced by some small amount every time that the logogen is active. This will, of course, happen whether the appropriate word is spoken, seen, heard, written or merely thought' (Morton 1979: 136).

This has the effect that higher-frequency words in the language have lower thresholds associated with them, and hence require less processing to yield access. Now, frequency actually involves at least two notions: (a) high-frequency facilitates recognition, and (b) where recognition is not possible, because of a degraded signal, or non-word status of the signal, then any response will reflect the ease of access of the 'nearest' matching item – i.e. it will tend also to be a high-frequency item, with a low threshold. To put it more simply, high-frequency items are more available both as correct and incorrect responses. The logogen model therefore predicts that, within a given frequency level, the best physical match will determine the response, but that, within a given range of physical matching, the highest-frequency item has an advantage over the others. There is thus a mixture of criteria for access here, just as there is in the access files of the search model, with physical attributes and frequency both playing a role. Errors will tend to show substitution of higher-frequency for lower-frequency items, as in *boule* → *ball*. But they will also show the effects of contextual influence, which may also operate to make certain responses more available, as in *saucer* → *table*, in the context *he put his cup on the* ____ .

Forster (1976) notes some problems with such a model. First, how do we prevent the higher-frequency item *bright* being more available than the target item *blight*, in response to the input signal /blait/? Secondly, in lexical decision tasks, it is noted that non-words having word-like properties, e.g. /bokl/ (auditory input) or *obttle* (visual input), take longer to reject than non-words that are not word-like, e.g. /ridap/ or *ridap* (Coltheart *et al.* 1976). This suggests a post-access checking stage (as we have already noted, in discussing Forster's model, above), and such an extra stage might take us out of the realm of purely *direct* access, and into the class of two-stage (or three-stage) models. Forster argues that 'If the term direct-access means anything, it means that the correct lexical entry is specified automatically without any other entries being specified as possible candidates' (Forster 1976: 266).

The first of these problems relates to the difficult-to-quantify nature of concepts like 'lowered threshold' and 'effect of context'; all we can say is that, to square with observation, the logogen system must operate with 'appropriately set' thresholds, in relation to the physical properties of the stimuli: but this is not testable. We might also point to the fact that *bright* is a more plausible error for *blight*, more so than vice versa; but this again does not derive from independently verifiable properties of the model.

The second problem is interesting in that it mirrors our query above about the soundness of the distinction between the stages in Forster's two-stage model. It may be that language processing in this area is not very comfortably to be described in terms of *either* clear-cut single-stage *or* two-stage models, and that operating with the former will suggest the need for more than one stage, while operating with the latter will indicate the breaching of the inter-stage boundary.

It may be that a resolution of this issue lies in the direction of distinguishing between what we 'normally' do (which may involve single-stage processing) and what we resort to in more artificial situations (of which the lexical decision task is arguably an example), where some back-up stage of processing may be necessary.

5.4.3 *Priming effects in the logogen model*

Morton (1979) took the view that 'since each logogen is appropriate for only one word, the [visual] occurrence of *phrase* would not affect the [visual] logogen for *frays*, even though they are spoken in the same way' (Morton 1979: 136). This would accommodate Neisser's (1954) finding that, after subjects had visually studied a number of words (e.g. *frays, ruff*) for a while, their ability to recognise them subsequently was facilitated, but they were not better at recognising their homophones when they were visually presented (*phrase, rough*). For Neisser, this represented a perceptual facilitation for specific visual patterns. Now, the question arises, would subsequent *auditory* presentation of /freiz/, /rʌf/ also show facilitation? If so, then visual input such as *frays* (and also *phrase*) or *rough/ruff* must go to the same logogen as the relevant auditory input /freiz/ or /rʌf/ (which happens to be the same in the case of each of these words).

The original form of the logogen system assumed that this was so; but some subsequent work showed that there was very little transfer (a) in the case of prior visual experience followed by auditory recognition, and (b) from auditory experience to subsequent visual recognition (Jackson and Morton, Clarke and Morton, both cited in Morton and Patterson 1980). Further, the degree of visual-to-visual transfer seems to be unaffected by whether the same word is used (as Neisser's hypothesis of a perceptual facilitation would require), or a strongly related one such as an antonym (Clarke and Morton). Much earlier, Winnick and Daniel (1970) had found that a naming response (e.g. to a pictured butterfly) had no facilitation effect on subsequent visual presentation of the word *butterfly*. These apparent independences, between modalities of input, are sketched in figure 5.10. Such independences, coupled with the principle that logogens are form-specific detector devices, leads to the splitting of the central logogen system into three subsystems (Morton and Patterson 1980), as in figure 5.11. The layout on the left (A) follows the same configuration as our original logogen model diagram above, for comparison; the version on the right (B) is broadly equivalent to this, but is arguably clearer and allows for compatibility with later discussion; the third version, (C), is also broadly equivalent, and conforms to the layout of our framework for discussion, in figure 5.1 above.

Although there are broad equivalences between these layouts, we should note that they actually embody different attitudes towards the concept of 'the lexicon'. In the original version of the logogen model, Morton was at pains to

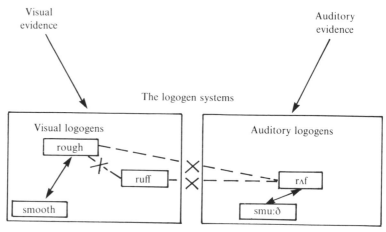

Figure 5.10 Modality-specific independences within the logogen system. (Arrows indicate existence of priming effects; broken lines mark little or no priming effect of one item on the other.) (Based on discussion in Morton 1979: 128; and Morton and Patterson 1980: 93–4.)

distinguish logogens from lexical items as such, since they were distinct from semantic–cognitive representations. This independence can more naturally be preserved, in the more recent model, in the form of layout A, in which a 'general logogen system' may be identified (by the dotted lines) which is distinct from the cognitive system, while layouts B and C permit the concept of a lexicon to be identified (again, shown by dotted lines). As between these latter two layouts, B treats the cognitive system as wholly within the lexicon, while C allows for the possibility that the cognitive system is partly within the lexicon, and partly outside it.

Using the later version of the logogen model, we may now turn to a consideration of non-lexical routes in reading.

5.4.4 *Non-lexical and lexical pathways*

Figure 5.12 shows how the B and C versions of the logogen model can be provided with non-lexical routes from visual and auditory input to articulatory output. From this, it will be readily apparent that the evidence-accumulating *logogens* correspond to the *lexical-form components* of our framework in figure 5.1, and thus embody a particular conception of the internal nature of these components. The main difference between figure 5.1 and version C in figure 5.11 is found in the absence of any direct link to *auditory analysis* from *visual analysis*, thus precluding lexical access by phonological recoding. In this way, the inputs to visual and auditory logogens are maintained as separate and parallel channels. There is output from the visual ana-

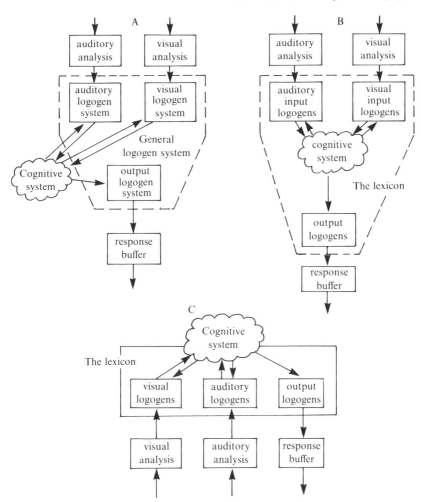

Figure 5.11 The later version of the logogen model (A, corresponding to the layout of the original; B, an alternative, equivalent layout; C, a further equivalent layout, similar to that in fig. 5.1). Non-lexical routes from input to response are not shown. (Based on Morton and Patterson 1980: fig. 4.2a, p. 93; fig. 4.2b, p. 95.)

lysis (and from the auditory analysis) to the *response buffer* (for speech; written *output* is not considered separately within this model). Thus, if we concentrate just on the outputs from the visual analysis, we find, as in the horse-race model of figure 5.6, two parallel and wholly independent channels, one to the visual logogens (direct access) and the other via G–P rules to the response buffer, to account for the ability to pronounce non-words. (The other link to

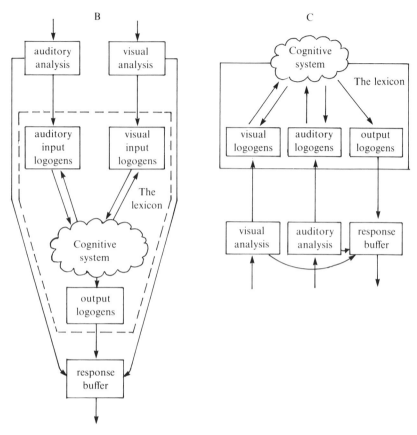

Figure 5.12 The later version of the logogen model (layouts B and C of fig. 5.11) showing non-lexical routes from input to response. (Based on Morton and Patterson 1980: fig. 4.2b, p. 95.)

the response buffer, from auditory analysis, is set up similarly to account for the ability to pronounce (repeat) auditorily presented non-words.)

Now, this G–P channel, unlike the one posited in the model of figure 5.6, clearly disambiguates the concept of phonological representation (is it for input? or for output?) by being purely for output. As such, it can hardly be called an 'indirect-access' route, since it can make no contact with lexical forms at all. This in turn means that these pathways in the logogen model exhibit the essential characteristics of a pure horse-race model, inasmuch as the two channels are wholly independent; but the finishing post in this case is not lexical access, but the naming/pronunciation response. All and only the words that are presented to this system follow the lexical route, through the visual logogens and subsequently to the output logogens. (We are not concerned here with the possibility of there being *two* variants of this route; the main route is via the cognitive system. See our remarks above on the status of the direct link from visual to output logogens, p. 250.)

It appears that this model can be used to account for the findings on naming/pronunciation responses, with the proviso that much depends on the critical activation levels of individual logogens, which are not formalised within the model. But what about lexical decision responses? Correct *yes* responses are mediated via the visual logogen system; but it is not apparent from what we have said thus far that correct *no* responses to legal non-words can be accounted for at all. One solution might be to build in an 'access clock', which would ring an alarm, signalling a *no* response, if no visual logogen were activated within some preset time. But this suggests that all such responses should be equivalently slow; it is therefore difficult to reconcile with the observed effect of homophone non-words (e.g. *sist*, resembling *cyst*). Such findings would seem to argue for a link between visual–auditory analysis (indirect access), but this, as we have seen, is explicitly rejected in the model.

5.4.5 *Stem priming*

Concerning the distinction between stems and affixes within the logogen model, Murrell and Morton (1974) found that when word 1 followed by word 2 sharing the same stem were visually presented, the priming effect of the first word on the second was as great as in the identical word-repetition condition. Stanners *et al.* (1979) found that a base verb was effectively primed by a derived form (e.g. *burned–burn*), but that only regularly inflected forms of a verb primed as effectively as identical repetition of the base form. They suggested that prelexical affix-stripping occurs only for regular inflections, while irregular formations activate their own detectors, linked also to the stem detectors, and hence yielding a partial facilitation effect. Of such findings, Henderson (1985) notes that

> The fundamental question that has to be posed for each of the
> experimental tests that we have considered is whether the effects which we
> obtain are attributable to morphological decomposition that occurs
> *prelexically*. In the previous section, we noted that morpheme frequency
> effects might well arise at a stage of decomposition that occurs after
> lexical access for the whole word. It is equally possible that morphemic
> priming effects rise due to feedback from morphological analyses
> supplied after lexical access. (Henderson 1985: 59–60)

285

5.5 **Word-detector systems: the cohort model**

We have noted the comments of Forster (1976) on the difficulty of making precise statements about individual thresholds and activation levels for items within the logogen framework. Another version of sophisticated direct-access model in which activation levels can be precisely stated was proposed by Marslen-Wilson and Welsh (1978). They used a shadowing task, in which subjects were listeners to a continuously read out passage from a novel and were required to reproduce it faithfully in their own speech as they heard it. Unknown to the subjects, certain words in the original reading were mispronounced. The shadowers generally followed the passage with fairly constant delays of about two to three words between input and output.

When a mispronounced word occurred in the original, they tended to treat it in one of two ways: (a) they fluently restored it (e.g. /trævədi/ → /trædʒədi/, *tragedy*) nearly 50 per cent of the time, with no disturbance to the shadowing delay pattern; or (b) they repeated it exactly, nearly 40 per cent of the time, with associated increase in the shadowing delay (e.g. /trævədi/ was reproduced in the output).

Now, the most interesting feature of the results from our point of view is that most of the fluent restorations were found when the following conditions were satisfied: (a) the phonemic distortion itself was slight (e.g. /trætʃədi/ for *tragedy*, where just the voicing feature is missing from the medial affricate); (b) the distortion was located in the final syllable; and (c) the word involved was highly predictable from context. By contrast, most of the exact reproductions of distorted forms took place when (a) the phonemic distortion was greater, and (b) the form was relatively unconstrained by its context. The difference between first and last syllable in the word was very slight in the case of faithful reproductions. Taking the word-position effect on fluent restorations into account, Marslen-Wilson and Welsh suggested the following amendment to the logogen model:

> At the earliest stages of the lexical access process, all lexical memory elements whose corresponding words begin with a particular acoustic sequence (defined, possibly, as the initial 150–200msec. of the input) will be fully activated. Each element in this initial cohort of word-candidates will then continue to monitor the subsequent input signals. Unlike logogens, these elements are assumed to have the ability to respond actively to mismatches in the input signal. Namely, at such point as the input diverges sufficiently from the internal specification for an element, then that element will remove itself from the pool of word-candidates ... the size of the original cohort will be progressively reduced, until eventually only a single candidate remains. At this point we may say that the word is recognised. (Marslen-Wilson and Welsh 1978: 56–7)

Thus, instead of *partial* and piecemeal activation of logogens in some unknown proportion to the degree of match with various types of input, we have only *two* degrees of activation to consider: zero, or full. Full activation of all members of a cohort occurs on the basis of the first element of the input. Thereafter, instead of the *summing* of the partial activations to individual threshold values, we have the progressive *elimination* of fully activated items, as the left–right processing of the stimulus continues. Thus, speed of recognition partly depends on the sequential sound-structure properties of the candidates in the cohort, and the point of recognition will be determined not by the end of the stimulus sequence but by the elimination of the last alternative candidate from the cohort.

Marslen-Wilson and Welsh suggest that a monosyllabic word in isolation can typically be identified about 300msec. after the stimulus sequence begins, and about 100msec. before it ends. Where a relatively slight signal distortion occurs early on in the word, the effect on reducing the cohort is relatively slight: initial pattern-matching is fairly rough and ready. Again, by the end of the stimulus sequence, the recognition of the word has generally been achieved, and even quite gross distortions may be fluently restored. It is in the early-to-middle part of the word sequence that the most intense activity in word recognition is located. Major signal distortions occurring at this point tend to interfere with this process: there is no real word of English that begins with /'trætʃ/-, so all cohort members are eliminated; so the reproduction of the signal /'trætʃədi/ at this stage in the shadowing task is associated with a faltering in the shadowing process. But there is one further, very important, implication: the response that is observed, /'trætʃədi/, cannot be mediated by lexical access, and hence must be achieved via some *prelexical access* route whereby the sound structure of the input can be converted into an appropriate set of instructions for the articulatory output system. This means that there are input–output relationships that do not involve the lexicon. We shall return to this point below, in section 5.7.

5.5.1 *The time course of word recognition*

An important feature of the cohort model is that it embodies the sequential nature of the auditory signal (cf. our discussion in 4.2.1 above) directly into the nature of the (auditory) word-recognition process: it makes sense within this framework to ask, not just *whether* a word has been recognised, but *when* (i.e. at what point in its transmission). We may illustrate with the case of *rapid*, adopting the simplifying assumption that the sequential nature of the signal can be represented by the segments /'r-æ-p-ɪ-d/. My dic-

287

tionary (to return for a moment to the book-type lexicon) contains about ninety entries having the initial sequence /'ræ/-; of these, about twenty were not known to me before I looked them up (being archaic, or from specialised knowledge areas); and of the remaining sixty, about half are related to each other in highly productive ways (e.g. *rapid, rapidity, rapidly; rat, rat-catcher*, etc.; note that we are here encountering the issues of stems and affixes, and one word vs two, which we noted in section 5.1.2 above, and which we shall say more about in 5.6.3 below). By the addition of -/p/, we reduce this cohort to around a dozen items (subject to the same indeterminacy about what constitutes distinct vs related forms). The arrival of -/ɪ/ in the stimulus sequence narrows the cohort to just the forms *rapid, rapidity, rapidly*, each of which involves recognition of the stem form /'ræpɪd/ (although, in the case of *rapidity*, this form is not in its canonical form, but shows stress movement to the second syllable). Let us grant that a purely stimulus-based ('bottom-up') cohort-type processing system will recognise the item *rapid* at this point. This is what is known as the 'uniqueness point' for this word; the point at which it diverges in linear structure from all other words in the language (and the cohort). The uniqueness point can be defined for any word by reference to an ordinary dictionary of reasonable size (bearing in mind the pronunciation, rather than the written form, of words, of course). A fair amount of experimental evidence suggests that the uniqueness point determines word-recognition performance, in a number of tasks (Marslen-Wilson 1984; Tyler and Wessels 1983; Ottevanger 1984).

However, we may wonder whether the processing is really this clear-cut. First, recall that the notion of segmental elements ('phonemes', in one sense of this term) arriving at the ear over time is certainly oversimplified (ch. 4), since any 'time slice' through the acoustic signal shows evidence of preceding and succeeding elements, as well as the current element. The auditory perception of this signal is therefore not susceptible of discrete judgements of a very precise nature concerning the point at which particular elements 'arrive'. The spirit of this objection tends in the direction of recognition points that might actually be in advance of the segmentally defined uniqueness point – by some very small factor. Secondly, however, we have to recognise the possibility that speech-sound processing is probabilistic in nature. Marcus and Frauenfelder (1985) say:

> In practice, it seems unlikely that such categorical decisions can reliably be made with the noisy and ambiguous signal which is speech. [Miller, Heise and Lichten 1951] have shown that words which are fully intelligible in sentences are often poorly understood when extracted and presented in isolation. Incoming phonetic information cannot always be

categorically recognised solely on the basis of the acoustic signal. More recent data further supports the idea that phonetic information is evaluated probabilistically rather than categorically during the process of word recognition (Frauenfelder and Marcus 1985; Massaro and Cohen 1983; Pisoni and Nash 1974; Streeter and Nigro 1979; Whalen 1983). (Marcus and Frauenfelder 1985: 164)

We have, suggest Marcus and Frauenfelder, three concepts to consider: (a) the *recognition point*, determined for any given word by empirical studies of human performance in word recognition, and being that point in the portion of the signal at which we can say that the word is recognised; (b) the *uniqueness point*, at which, for any given word, its initial string of phonemes diverges *by just one phoneme* from all other words sharing the same initial string; and (c) the point at which, some indeterminate moment *after* the uniqueness point, a probabilistic system of speech perception might be satisfied that word X had occurred. 'How is it then that there is good empirical evidence both for the probabilistic nature of processing and for the efficacy of the uniqueness point as a predictor of word recognition?' (p. 165).

To resolve this paradox, Marcus and Frauenfelder use the concept of *deviation*, defined as the number of phonemes that are different between any stimulus word and any item in the lexicon; and the related concept of *minimum deviation*, which is the number of phonemes that are different between the stimulus word and the nearest item in the lexicon. For a word sharing the same initial string as the stimulus, minimum deviation is zero up to the uniqueness point, and is one at the uniqueness point: what is unclear, and interesting to investigate, is whether minimum deviation continues to increase beyond the uniqueness point, and if so, how steeply. In other words, do all or most of the subsequent phonemes differ, between the stimulus item and its nearest match in the lexicon, beyond the uniqueness point? If so, then a probabilistic word-recognition system will be able to identify words only a short period of time after the uniqueness point; but if not, then it will need to process correspondingly more of the signal beyond this point in order to satisfy the criterion of recognition.

Marcus and Frauenfelder determined this issue by using a computerised phonetic dictionary of American English consisting of 20,000 words. Averaged data showed that over the first six phoneme positions after the uniqueness point, minimum deviation increased almost linearly at about 0.5 phonemes per phoneme position, suggesting that 'the efficacy of the uniqueness point is the result not of accident or fortuitous choice of stimuli, but of the statistical properties of the lexicon itself' (p. 165).

5.5.2 *Contextual effects*

Reference to the Miller, Heise and Lichten (1951) finding that speech intelligibility is better in context, again raises the issue in this discussion as to how far, and in what way, context might be used along with purely stimulus-based information in order to achieve word recognition. To go back to our cohort of a dozen items containing *rapid*, established on the basis of the signal sequence /rap/-, we should ask whether at this point available contextual information might permit the identification, probabilistically, of the target word. If so, then, the search for recognition points of words has to be conducted on the basis of particular words in certain contexts, with the possibility that recognition might occur earlier than the stimulus property of the uniqueness point. Marslen-Wilson and Welsh's (1978) findings suggest that context plays a role in the word-detection process; and Morton's (1979) model explicitly allows for this, in the input from the cognitive system to the logogen system. But does this input operate directly on the stored lexical items like the other types of signal input? Or, rather, does it indirectly enhance the effectiveness of these other types of input? This is an issue to which we shall return in section 5.6.2 below.

5.6 **Further issues**

5.6.1 *Lexical analogies*

Consider the non-word *sint*. It does not just *consist of* four graphemes, each of which has a (regular) grapheme-to-phoneme correspondence; it also *resembles* a number of real words, to some degree. Thus *sip, sit, sin; sink; simple, single; lint, flint; since*, all represent different sets of resemblances, which we have referred to generally as *grapho-phonological.* Note that they are not 'rules' in any sense; nor are they regularly based on such a consistent subword unit as the *syllable*. They consist rather in sequences of more-or-less arbitrary length within which *analogies* may be perceived, between one form and another (Glushko 1979, 1980; and see Henderson 1982 for discussion). Now, in this particular case, the grapho-phonological relationships are quite transparent, in respect of both *s*- and -*nt*. That is, all the analogies suggest that *s*- is pronounced as /s/ and -*nt* as /nt/. In this way, analogies can function rather like G–P rules. But the intervening element -*i*- is of less certain status. All the analogies just illustrated are consistent with -*i*- → /ɪ/; but other analogies exist, such as *pint, bind, find*, etc. (the homophone *wind* points both ways) which are consistent with the mapping -*i*- → /aɪ/. Let us grant the existence of a determinate set of analogies of each of these types; and let us further assume that a differential weighting can be established for these sets, which we may call the /ɪ/-set and the /aɪ/-set. The weighting will be a function of the *syntag-matic* (linear match) and *paradigmatic* (number of items in the match) aspects of the analogies with the input form *sint*. This would allow, in principle, for the *probability* that *sint* will be pronounced as /sɪnt/ rather than /saɪnt/. Thus, instead of G–P *rules*, we have statements of analogy – which may indeed be based on minimal units of single graphemes (-*i*- in this case), but with a par-ticular context. Hence, the analogic 'pressure' on -*i*- in *s–ght* would be differ-ent. Thus, G–P rules, as distinct from patterns that are directly available from *lexical* information, may not be required. Furthermore, the very notion of 'regular' vs 'irregular' turns out, in this approach, to be inappropriate, being replaced instead by a continuum of more-or-less general grapho-phonological correspondences.

We have already referred to the two dimensions of such analogies, the para-digmatic and the syntagmatic. Where the syntagmatic match is complete, between an input word and a stored lexical item, the 'quality' of the analogy will be maximal, even though the 'quantity', in terms of numbers of elements in the paradigmatic set, will be low. In most cases, it will be one, since *homo-nymy* is quite rare; in the case of input words like *bank*, the number of com-plete grapho-phonological analogies will depend on the number of lexical entries (the entries for *bank* 'of river', *bank* 'of earth' and *bank* 'of finance', let us assume). Partial homonymy, as *homography* (e.g. *lead, wind*) and *homo-phony* (e.g. *bale/bail*), representing lower degrees of syntagmatic resemblance, also involve quite small paradigmatic sets. Where the syntagmatic resemb-lances are of intermediate status, the paradigmatic sets are much more popu-lous, however, and a conflict between different grapho-phonological mappings may arise. Thus, in the case of *have*, there is only one lexical item that will make a full syntagmatic match; but there are many items – *wave, shave, save,* etc. – that will make a partial match, and set up a conflict in the nature of the -*a*- mapping (-*a*- → /eɪ/). By contrast, the input item *wave* will have intermediate matches (*shave, cave, save,* etc.), which are consistent with the identity match; only *have* will represent a different mapping (-*a*- → /æ/). The difference in these two situations allows for predictions to be derived regarding the difficulty of processing the two input forms, *have* and *wave*: forms will be difficult to the extent that they possess misleading analogies. An important point to notice here is that non-words as well as real words are sub-ject to this same principle. The only difference is that non-words, by defini-tion, lack an identity match (having no lexical entry). But the hypothesis is that they are nevertheless *processed by accessing lexical forms*. So pronunci-ation responses, as well as lexical decisions, in respect of non-words and real words alike, are held to be mediated via lexical access. This is the fundamental difference between the analogies approach and the others which we have considered above. In terms of this approach, we may recognise a class of *hermit* words: these have no near neighbours in the lexicon (Henderson 1982). That is to say, on all partial syntagmatic mappings, the number of items in the paradigmatic set is zero. In practice, hermit status is a matter of degree; but the real word *lynx* and the non-word *nerp* are substantially *hermit*-like. The prediction from analogy theory is that, because these forms have a minimal number of matching lexical items, they will take longer to respond to. This is found to be the case, and the effect is stronger for non-words as opposed to real words, as also would be predicted from the fact that real words by definition possess an identity match (e.g. the stored form *lynx*) that non-words lack.

Another class of words that can be distinguished in these terms is the *heretic* (Henderson 1982): so named from the fact that it is at loggerheads with all its neighbours. This is a property of specific and exceptional lexical phonology, and hence is only found with real words. *Have*, which we have already discussed, is one such; others include *comb*, and *sword*. To the extent that these show unorthodox grapho-phonological relationships which are shared by very few other items, they are predicted to be slow to respond to, and liable to over-regularised pronunciation.

Perhaps the strongest sort of evidence for analogy theory comes from such findings as that words having a misleading analogy, e.g. *wave*, take longer to name than those that do not, e.g. *haze* (Glushko 1979). Since they are both regular real words, of comparable frequency and internal structure, this seems difficult to account for; until the effect of the heretic *have* is considered (there being no corresponding heretic in the *haze, daze, faze, glaze* set). Conventional accounts of direct access and G–P rules find this sort of result very hard to accommodate.

5.6.2 *The contexts of lexical access*

Thus far, we have been considering the processing of isolated words rather than words in context; with evidence drawn from a variety of response types, of which only naming comes close to representing a fairly naturalistic sort of performance. In this section, we shall try to highlight some of the 'special' properties of what is really the 'ordinary' situation, of reading words in naturalistic contexts.

Fully acquired reading skills are, in normal circumstances, largely automatic. One advantage of this is that attentional control is thus freed for higher levels of processing, e.g. of syntax, semantics and pragmatics, which are presumably largely unaffected by the modality of the input. In this way, 'the eye' can be observed to run ahead of 'the mind'; and 'the voice', in the sense of the largely automatic levels of speech output, may safely bring up the rear. This sequence of processing constitutes the 'eye–voice span' that rightly attracted speculation from the earliest investigations of the reading process (Quantz 1897, cited in Henderson 1982). Where circumstances are not normal, e.g. where handwriting is difficult to read, attention is directed out to the level of visual analysis, and comprehension tends to suffer. Likewise, in beginning readers, the processing of letters tends to detract from the comprehension of the text.

The extent of the eye–voice span is thus controlled by the exigencies of the higher levels of processing, which are in turn affected by the momentary properties of the text. The eye–voice span, indeed, is just one reflex of these factors; we should also think of the 'eye–sense' span (if only it could be accurately measured), and of other types of 'eye–overt response' span. It has also been found that monitoring text for a target letter shows differential performance, depending on such text factors as position of the letter within a word, and the phonological, lexical and grammatical status of its environment. Letter monitoring is thus a useful, if artificial, way of shedding light on some of these contextual issues, much as phoneme monitoring has been used in the study of spoken-language processing.

A characteristic of such automatic skills is that they are vulnerable to interference from other attributes in the same processing channel. Thus, in the visual channel, Stroop (1935) demonstrated that subjects' naming of the colour of ink in which a word was printed was slowed, and made less accurate, if the word in question named another colour (e.g. red ink used to print the word GREEN). The so-called Stroop effect generalises to other forms of stimulus conflict; but the conflict is not so strong in 'reverse Stroop' situations, where subjects are required to name the colour word, printed in either compatible or conflicting ink colour (Chmiel 1984). Thus, as Henderson (1982) notes, certain associations, e.g. between the meaning of a word and its letter structure, are stronger than others, e.g. between meaning and ink colour. This is doubtless a reflection of the naturalistic circumstances within which we ordinarily encounter words. But the effects of such background associations may be altered, e.g. in experimental situations where the word GREEN is consistently written in red ink. See the discussion in Henderson (1982: 344), where this phenomenon is linked to the general property of local context establishing probabilistic strategies that may over-ride more long-term expectations, including semantic priming of one word by another.

Lexical priming

The interesting issue for us is how far such automatic processing of information in the visual channel may play a role in naturalistic contexts.

Our brief discussion of the evidence is based on Henderson (1982: 303–13), which should be consulted for further details. As far as processing in naturalistic contexts is concerned, it is suggestive that, where an ambiguous word like *palm* occupies the foveal field, it can apparently be reliably disambiguated by the presence of words like *tree* or *hand* in the peripheral field, even in cases where the disambiguating words are *subliminally* perceived, that is, *have not consciously been 'seen'* (Bradshaw 1974). In another type of demonstration, *visual masking* is employed (Marcel 1978). This technique involves sequential presentation of words in isolation, where the exposure of the first word is very brief, and is immediately followed by a *pattern mask*, e.g. a grid of lines, which activate the same areas of the retina as the letters of the immediately preceding word. This is possible because the transition from word to mask is too rapid for eye movements to take place. After the mask, a second word is displayed. Under these conditions, it is found that lexical decision on the second word is facilitated if the two words are semantically related (e.g. *doctor, nurse*). This semantic *priming* effect is observed even where the subject cannot report the existence or identity of the first, masked, word.

Subliminal automatic lexical priming of this sort typically occurs over short intervals (of around 50msec., extending up to 250msec.) between the priming and the primed words. It appears also to be based on lexical network relationships and is relatively unaffected by the size of the set of paradigmatic alternatives to the primed word. That is, it seems to prime a whole lexical field, regardless of the number of items within it. It likewise seems not to be selective: thus the priming effect observed in the sequence: *bank* + MASK + *money*, is unaffected by whether *bank* is preceded by *river*, or *day* or *save*. This is important: for, as a priming word, *bank* is ambiguous, and hence can only be effective on *money* if the appropriate semantic reading is activated. The results indicate that the 'financial' reading *is* activated (and presumably all other readings as well), regardless of the effect of prior occurrence of the semantically related word *save*. That this is a peculiar and significant property of what we are calling *automatic lexical priming* is underlined by consideration of a rather different effect, to which we shall now turn.

Lexical filtering

Another sort of contextual effect seems to involve selectivity, and even *inhibition* of *inappropriate* lexical access, and partly for this reason we shall distinguish it from *priming* by calling it *lexical filtering*. This is found in supraliminal conditions, such as the following sequences, where words are displayed successively, one at a time, and where masking is not involved (Schvaneveldt, Meyer and Becker 1976):

1. river   – date ⎫
2. river ⎫   ⎬ – money
3. day   ⎬ – bank ⎭
4. save ⎭

Compared to the unrelated condition (1), response latencies to lexical decision on *money* are here affected by the nature of the item that precedes the primer *bank*. Thus, in (2) the reaction time is slower than in (1), presumably because the wrong reading of the homograph has been activated by the preceding item *river*. And in the remaining cases, selective effects are observed in that while both (3) and (4) are faster than (1), (4) is fastest, presumably because the activation of the appropriate reading of the homograph primer is greater by virtue of the semantic reinforcement from *save*. Such supraliminal lexical-filtering effects, both facilitatory and inhibitory, may be based on perceived *interpretive* expectations and weightings, and we may wonder how far they are revealing of issues involved in the processing of syntactically organised utterances.

Naturalistic contexts

The two sorts of contextual influence that we have just discussed presumably operate together in normal reading, with the filtering effect routinely obscuring the priming effect. In particular, the nature of the filtering effect prompts the question whether this is the basic mechanism of contextual interpretation in orthographic language processing. It would seem, however, that this is not the case.

First of all, it should be understood that purely lexical (word-to-word) effects are distinct from those that are specific to the particular syntactico-semantic *orderings* of words in sentences. Lexical priming and filtering occur in certain *strings* of words, regardless of their syntactic status. So, to take Lashley's (1951) example, we are still left with the question of what it is that affects the access of *canoe* in (*Rapid* { **writing* / *righting* } *with his uninjured hand saved from loss the contents of the*) *capsized_____*. In spite of the relationship between *capsized* and *canoe*, it can hardly be relevant that *capsized* subliminally primes and supraliminally filters *canoe*. The conclusion seems to be forced on us by the consideration that the appropriateness of *canoe*, and the inappropriateness of, say, *tulip*, in this context is unaffected by replacing *capsized* with *overturned*, or *damaged*, or by nothing.

If the contextual determinants of lexical access are not to be found in the preceding word(s), then do they consist in the whole of the preceding context? Fischler and Bloom (1979) found facilitatory effects (in the form of short latencies to lexical decision) only on words which are more than 90 per cent *predictable* in particular contexts (i.e. are reliably chosen more than 90 per cent of the time in a sentence-completion task). Given that in most cases words are not this predictable (apart from the special closed-class items such as determiners and prepositions), the finding seems to dispose of this possibility, therefore, as a general factor in contextualised lexical access. The vast majority of words that we encounter are plausible, rather than predictable, in their contexts.

This observation probably holds the clue to the normal situation; there is no *pre*lexical *advantage* from context, but rather a *post*lexical *disadvantage* for those words which do not integrate readily with the interpretation that has been previously established. This therefore does not involve us in hypothesising contextual facilitation of thousands of lexical items just prior to the access of *canoe* in our example; but rather a difficulty, just after lexical access, if it appears that the word in question does *not* fit the context. In this connection, we should note that part of Lashley's point was that, auditorily presented, his example tended to force most listeners to reassign the lexical interpretation of /raɪtɪŋ/ from **writing* to *righting*. This is an interpretive procedure that can only be initiated subsequent to successful access of *canoe* and the perception that it fails to mesh with the preceding context. The issue of contextual integration of words with preceding utterance-organisation is one that we shall pursue further in the next chapter, and which would appear to belong to those levels of language processing that are essentially the same for both spoken and written forms of input.

The nature of 'lexical access'

We should conclude this section by underlining the highly differentiated nature of the concept 'lexical access'. In its widest sense, it appears to be involved in both subliminal and supraliminal perception, and is further fractionated along the lines of the major dimensions of figure 5.1 above. We can 'think' words (accessing content without form), as well as read them, write them, speak them and hear them. And possibly, we can 'rehearse' them in the sense of treating them as purely formal objects, without (conscious) reference to their meaning, in situations where rote learning is called for.

5.6.3 *Stems and affixes*

We have outlined some recent and current approaches to lexical storage and access and have at certain points in our discussion taken up the issue of morphological structure of words as a possible factor in lexical access (5.1.2, 5.3.5, 5.4.5). Are stems and affixes stored and accessed in the same way, alongside each other, in the same lexicon? Or are different processes and memory stores involved?

We may conclude that we are not yet in a position to say definitely how morphologically complex word forms are recognised. It appears that their morphological structure becomes available quite early, particularly if it is regular in formation; but whether it is a *means of access* is not clear. Henderson (1985) points out two advantages of a system which yields morphological analyses fairly rapidly in the word-recognition process:

1. morphemes tend to be stable elements – although this tendency is not completely reliable, as we have seen in the alternation – *-fend- / -fens-*;

2. inflectional and derivational affixes are useful to the interpretation of the role of word forms in higher-order groupings such as phrases and clauses – as illustrated (so often in such discussions) by the syntactic information that can be derived from Lewis Carroll's Jabberwocky verse.

However, Henderson also points out that it is not just the affixes that permit interpretation in such near-English passages: nonce words such as *slithy* evoke meaning responses on the basis of non-morphemic elements of their structure, e.g. the initial *sl-*. To this observation, one might add the perplexing reliability of Brown, Black and Horowitz's (1955) finding, that people can match semantically close meanings with word form-pairs in languages they have never encountered before, if the pairs are introduced along with the relevant semantic dimension. Thus, for example, which of these Tamil forms means 'this' or 'that' – /aː/- vs /iː/-? (See the end of the next paragraph for the answer, after you have first tried to guess.) There would appear to be sound–meaning connections in the lexicon that do not depend on morphological status in the language, and which may reflect tendencies, which even different language families share, in the relation between certain basic phonological contrasts and certain basic meanings.

Finally, we may shift the discussion back to spoken-word recognition in continuous discourse and observe that the argument for affix stripping prior to lexical access here faces additional hurdles in the lack of both institutionalised word boundaries and conventional shapes of morphemes: [... in'tents ...] may represent *in tents, in tense* or *intense*, and hence the auditory analogue of the 'Letter string' input to the Taft and Forster model does not have word status as a 'given' property. Considerations such as these may usefully heighten our sense of the complexity of the operations involved in the auditory perception of words and their associated (higher- and lower-order) structures. (Answer to the Tamil question above: /a:/ = 'that', /i:/ = 'this'.)

5.7 Conclusions

We may start our conclusion to this survey of word recognition by noting Morton's (1979) advice regarding the models that have been proposed: 'don't become too attached to any of them'. But there can be no doubt that they are essential to our understanding of an important aspect of spoken-language understanding. The models deliberately represent extreme positions along the serial- vs parallel-processing dimension, and provide a perspective on human abilities by their degree of fit with the data derived from subjects' performance. Among the more important points are the following:

1. input to the lexicon may be processed in modality-specific ways, to a degree; but at some level the system represents items in a modality-neutral fashion;

2. input–output relations may be mediated without involving the lexicon directly, although an attempt may be made to find a lexical form in the process, as in the pronunciation of a non-word. For this, both Forster's (1976) model and that of Morton (1979) require the addition of a route that connects the auditory analysis of the input to the response buffer. We have seen, in our discussion above, that there are further connections to be made across components outside the lexicon (master file or logogen), mediating written- and spoken-language forms of input and output. The provision of these routes allows for the possibility of speech- and visual-signal processing both outside the lexicon (stimulus-faithful, able to handle non-words) and within the lexicon (highly normative, responsible for phonemic restoration effects);

3. the system is set up in such a way as to handle real words better than non-words, and high-frequency words better than low-frequency ones;

4. the operation of the system is also facilitated in some fashion by supporting context for the target word; but whether this constitutes an independent access system, from cognitive input, or not remains unclear.

To these points we should also probably add the following:

5. almost certainly the lexicon allows for *degrees* of involvement of its component parts in the process of lexical access: in some situations we are processing for meaning rather than form (as in participating in a normal sort of conversational interaction), but in others we can reverse this setting (as, for instance, in a speech-shadowing task). This has the important consequence that

the concept 'lexical access' is not an all-or-nothing affair, and it may be that asking subjects to perform certain tasks will involve different degrees of access, which might lead to difficulties in interpreting the results that are obtained. We might also wonder how far degree of activation (in the logogen model), or persistence in the cohort (in the cohort model) might 'leak' into the understanding system, in covert fashion, in cases where contextual support permits. For instance, in the case of the word *rapid* in Lashley's famous example sentence

rapid righting with his uninjured hand saved from loss the contents of the capsized canoe

it is noticeable how many listeners, when pressed to give details of what they understand by this sentence, give descriptions involving a canoeist struggling in *turbulent* waters. The 'turbulence' of the waters may result from a straightforward bridging assumption from the (assumed) existence of the water to the apparent predicament of the contents of the canoe; but one also wonders whether *rapid* in the sense of 'swift flowing water over a rocky river bed' has not somehow 'leaked' through into the cognitive system from the lexicon. If so, then a good deal of polysemy (one form, with linked but distinct meanings) may be associated with such leaks in the system.

6. We may also note what appears to be a related problem, particularly for the model which attempts, like the cohort model, to grapple with the issue of the sequential nature of spoken-language input. In the case of /'rapid/, the first syllable takes us far enough into the word for intense activity among the cohort members to be taking place. Around the time that the -/p/- segment is encountered (if we may simplify speech-signal processing in this way), we are not in a position to identify the word that has actually occurred (see also Grosjean 1985). This is because, depending on the nature of the input, we may have to allow for word recognition to take place at a point *after*, as well as *before*, the end of the relevant input sequence. Is it the case that some part of the system calls out the existence of the word *rap*, or the word *wrap*, as at the start of an utterance such as *rap it* ... or *wrap it* ..., or *rapping* ... or *wrapping* ...? We have no awareness of such decisions, clearly; but this does not mean that they may not take place. Possibly they are made in some probabilistic fashion, pending further support in the rest of the signal; perhaps they are not made at all until the point in the signal where a clear decision *can* be made. The distinction represented here is essentially one between *non-deterministic* and *deterministic* types of *parsing* strategy, and usefully serves to remind us, at the end of this chapter, that word recognition and the perception of the

structural properties of utterances must proceed in some intimately related fashion. We shall take up the latter topic in the next chapter.

Since this chapter was prepared, Aitchison (1987) has appeared, providing a comprehensive introductory survey of the issues and models. Further, Frauenfelder and Tyler (1987) updates research into spoken-word recognition, concentrating in particular on the microstructural phases of word recognition, from acoustic cues to meaning representations, and the types of contextual influence on these phases. The articles in this collection provide particularly useful further reading in relation to the present chapter, in their representation of certain approaches and models that we have left out of our account. Finally, we should mention the benchmark-publications within the parallel-processing approach represented by the Parallel Distributed Processing (PDP) Research group, Rumelhart and McClelland (1986, being volume 1) and McClelland and Rumelhart (1986, being volume 2). The latter volume in particular contains many references to lexical access, within an attempt at an integrated theory of processing on parallel principles, encompassing both psychological processes and biological mechanisms.

6
Understanding utterances

6.1 Introduction

6.1.1 *Preview*

In this chapter, we are concerned with the processing that is involved in our understanding of utterances. Now, 'utterances' can be of many different kinds, ranging from marginally linguistic vocalisations of emotions, through social gambits and stereotypes, to lexical elements (which may appear as single-word utterances) and structured grammatical sequences. The concept 'utterance' is thus a pretheoretical one, which will defy any attempt to provide an all-embracing characterisation in terms of linguistic properties. We shall, however, characterise it for our purposes here as any signal-based implementation of the abstract language system. This provides for written as well as spoken utterances, but excludes covert use of language as in silent verbal reasoning.

In the preceding chapter, we have examined some issues in lexical access, in a way that has not really considered the role of words *in* (*single- or multi-word*) *utterances*: for it is one thing to gaze at letter arrays flashed briefly on a screen, in order to pronounce them, or decide whether they constitute a word, etc., but quite another matter for us to read words in written utterances. And so also for speech perception in artificial situations vs listening to utterances for their communicative potential. In this chapter, we shall attempt to review what is known about processing linguistic utterances, of the multi-word type, since they afford us evidence of lexical and structural processing proceeding in some relationship to each other (see Scholes 1978; Cutler 1983). We are therefore not simply leaving the issue of lexical access and turning to a new one; but rather broadening the scope of our considerations. In the next chapter, we shall review the situation, in the same spirit, regarding utterance production.

We shall begin with a review of the nature of understanding: what sort of construct might this be (6.1.2)? We shall then consider the issue of parsing, which is fundamental to the processing of word–word relationships in structured utterances (6.1.3). We shall then turn to some models that envisage a serial relationship between lexical access and parsing – basically, 'collecting words' before 'computing sentences' (in section 6.2), and contrast them with the sort of approach that sees lexical access proceeding in parallel with other levels – syntactic, semantic and pragmatic – of analysis (6.3.1–6.3.3), which may be thought of, very broadly, as operating in a way that is compatible with a transition network of grammatical categories and relationships (6.3.4). This takes us to the issue of how far a syntactic analysis may be seen as criterial to utterance interpretation – the so-called 'syntax vs semantics' issue (6.4.1–6.4.2). From here, we are able to address the phenomenon of ambiguity (6.4.3), and further issues in interpretation, concentrating on how the listener arrives at a reconstruction of what the speaker wishes to communicate (6.4.4).

6.1.2 *The nature of understanding*

Processing towards understanding

Perhaps the most striking feature of linguistic understanding of spoken input is its apparent speed; we get glimpses of this in the ability of participants A and C, in our example passage (fig. 3.1), to interject, laugh at and react to aspects of B's message (and/or the way he says it), appropriately and at very short latencies (imagine the problems that would be, and sometimes are, caused by laughing just a moment too late in a spontaneous dialogue). It is nevertheless a feature that, because it comes so naturally, we tend to take for granted. The necessity for speed is matched only by the requirement for *consistency* of performance; for, in the original conversation, B's words (to illustrate with those units, for convenience) were succeeding each other into oblivion, acoustically, at the rate of about one third of a second, each, and there were around 280 attempts at word recognition to be made (some requiring negative returns, as the forms involved turned out to be fragments, or filled pauses) over a period of about a minute and a half. Not only that, but A and C were, at any given moment, up to and including the end of B's contribution, ready to react to, and ask questions on the basis of, what B had been saying; that is, as listeners, they were also potential speakers and could switch from one role to the other on the basis of not only very swift, but also very complete analysis of B's message.

Much normal reading for meaning is also accomplished at speed; but a feature of written language is that, as in the case of the passage laid out for our inspection (e.g. in ch. 3), it is timelessly coextensive in all its parts, and we can retrace our earlier scans of parts of it at leisure if we wish. Such a difference would appear to be of the very essence in considering the distinction between the early stages of processing the spoken- vs written-language signal (ch. 4). In this chapter, we shall concentrate on spoken language understanding, from the point at which lexical access becomes possible. From this point on, it may be that certain differences remain between spoken- vs written-language under-standing, but the issues that we shall explore are common to both.

However astonishing this feat of rapid spoken-language comprehension may be, which we perform with little or no conscious effort, we should not feel unduly tentative in our efforts to understand our abilities in this regard. If we look a little closer at the end product of these abilities, we may come to the conclusion that, after all, understanding is an understandable human construct, subject to gaps and imprecision, and even downright misunder-standing. Fast, effortless and astonishing as it may be, spoken-language understanding is by no means perfect; and, just as in language production, naturally occurring errors (see ch. 3, sections 3.4.2 and 3.4.4) may yield im-portant information about the nature of the processes involved. We should ask, concerning our example passage: what sort of understanding do A and C construct on the basis of B's discourse?

Of course, it is not very easy to get a satisfactory answer to this question. We might ask native speakers to listen to the passage on tape and then tell us everything they think they know as a result of it. However, some people are better than others at this apparently rather unnatural task, and it would be unsafe to conclude from this that they are better spoken-language under-standers. Further, such a task takes time over and above that involved in natural spoken-language understanding, and further 'understanding' may take place during its completion; such secondary understanding may be im-possible to disentangle from primary understanding, and may be another source of difference between subjects' performances on the task. Yet another problem arises from the fact that such 'eavesdroppers'' understanding of a conversation that was not constructed with them in mind, and in which they were not involved, might not accurately reflect the understanding that the par-ticipants A and C arrived at; such a situation would come about if speaker A makes some allusion to private knowledge that B and C, but not our eaves-droppers, were party to. But, generally, we might suggest that a typical under-standing of this passage would involve:

1. a Birmingham company director
2. who is a keen follower of English football, and especially of West Bromwich Albion,
3. who has regularly travelled abroad in this pursuit,
4. but his enthusiasm is waning now
5. compared to other sorts of entertainment, such as night clubs,
6. football grounds are too uncomfortable,
7. the matches themselves are not so enjoyable as they used to be
8. and the ticket prices have gone up.

In practice, however, an individual's understanding of the passage would specify more detail, at least in some points; it might downgrade certain other points; and it might build in certain elements that are not actually specified at all.

Some of what is built in might be factual, drawn out of the listener's own knowledge (which maybe even the speaker does not possess), such as that West Bromwich Albion is a local football team for someone who lives in the Birmingham area. But other types of background knowledge that might be brought to bear on what B is saying tend to be general, and more stereotypic (see the notion of 'scripts' for understanding conventional situations: Minsky 1975; Schank and Abelson 1977). For example, we 'know' about company directors: they sit in plush offices and board rooms; they drive, or are driven, in comfortable limousines; they travel abroad by air in preferential seats and use exclusive airport lounges between flights; and so on. Consistent with this stereotype is the mention of the plush surroundings of nightclubs and sophisticated entertainment. Small wonder that such a man is getting increasingly fed up with the discomfort of going to football matches to support his team.

On the other hand, we also 'know' about football fans: they follow a winter game, stamping their feet and blowing on their hands to keep warm on windswept terraces, before walking home to have their tea; they are highly knowledgeable of the game and critical of boring, unimaginative play and of the referee's decisions; they travel to away matches on football coaches or special trains in company with other fans; and they are sensitive to the cost of getting into the grounds.

There is often a contrast between many aspects of such stereotypes, and, where more than one is invoked by a discourse, as here, a listener has to construct an understanding that will somehow cope with certain aspects of each. For instance, in this case, one listener may adjust his version of the company director: he may, after all, be quite young; from a working-class background; still walk with the fans to the local matches; stand on the terraces; travel in the football coaches to away matches; and so on. Another individual may adjust his version of the football fan, putting him in the setting of the more comfortable, season-bookable, seats in the football ground, travelling as a businessman when he follows his team abroad, staying in good hotels, and perhaps combining football and business on many of the trips, and so on.

The important point to notice about this sort of account is that:

1. the understanding of individual parts of the linguistic message takes place in the context of the understanding of other parts;
2. it also takes place in the context of our general knowledge about the events and objects being talked about;

3. as a result, one individual's understanding may incorporate elements that were not actually specified in the linguistic message;
4. this in turn may lead to certain differences between individuals concerning the exact nature of their understanding of the same discourse.

There is no need here to develop each of these points at length. Researchers in this area of understanding (see Brown and Yule 1983; Levinson 1983) have pointed to the nature of the social contract that is *implicit* in the act of holding a conversation, in terms of which listener(s) and speaker assume that they are speaking the same language, that they are competent in the language, that the speaker has an intention other than deception, that listeners have the willingness to make the usual 'bridging' assumptions that relieve the speaker of the need to be grindingly specific, and so on. Central to this contract is Grice's (1975) notion of *conversational implicature*, which derives from the *cooperative principle* and certain *maxims*, of which arguably the most important (and the one that Grice says least about) is *be relevant* (see section 6.4.4 for further discussion of this).

But we should underline the significance of point (3) above, because it offers a possible parallel between what we may crudely describe as 'linguistic' and 'non-linguistic' understanding. If we recognise words, and perceive speech generally, via our stored memory for linguistic forms, it may also be true that we perceive aspects of the world around us, as presented to us through non-linguistic means, via our stored knowledge of the way the world works. In our understanding of extended linguistic discourse, we may engage both linguistic and non-linguistic modes of perception and knowledge, in a way that makes it impossible to discern the boundary between the two. It may also be useful in this connection to note the fairly extensive set of terms available for use in describing what happens during 'input processing': *perception, interpretation, comprehension, understanding* and *recognition* are all found, in varying contexts, and with greater or less definition. *Perception* is probably best reserved for initial processing of the input; *understanding* is most usually regarded as the end product, at the other end of the peripheral/low-level vs central/high-level dimension. *Recognition* is used where the assumption of processing via stored forms in memory is strong; *interpretation* more usually carries with it the implication of creative processing, going beyond the strict properties of the signal. *Comprehension* is a frequently used term, which appears to act as a cover for both *interpretation* and *understanding*. But it should be emphasised that there is no generally agreed usage for these terms, because of the preliminary nature of our knowledge.

In this discussion, we have referred more than once to 'input'; in the next section we shall try to clarify what this means, in the context of the sort of conversation that our participants were engaged in, and we shall try to clarify also how it relates to such notions as peripheral vs central processing.

The nature of input

We know, of course, that we could take many utterances out of our passage, and present them, isolated from context, as linguistic units such as sentences, and have them understood. For example,

> (1)   He used to spend about a thousand a year watching football you know

can be understood in this way. But we should be careful what we mean when we use expressions such as 'can be understood'. One interpretation, which seems not to be appropriate, is that there is a fixed value for this expression in the language, which can be determined by any competent user of the language whenever he or she encounters (hears, or reads) the expression, in any context, including zero context (isolation). The other interpretation is that 'can be understood' means something like 'can be subjected to processes of understanding that are viable for this language', and this version leaves open the possibility that the end product of understanding will not always be quite the same, depending on who is doing the understanding, and what context the utterance appears in. The fixed value interpretation has its use, in defining that part of the meaning of the utterance which is independent of its context and interpreter; it is the business of linguistic semantics to make statements of this sort. But we are concerned here with meaning more generally, as it is arrived at through psycholinguistic processes of understanding. In the ordinary situation, these processes make use of not just the linguistic structure of the message, but all other available information; 'available', both simultaneously, on other channels (e.g. facial expression, gesture, and so on), and also from preceding information on the same channel (the context of prior linguistic messages), and the other channels (the context of prior, relevant, non-linguistic speaker behaviour). In these terms, then, the case of understanding the linguistic sentence presented in isolation, as in (1) above, is best regarded as a special instance of our ability to understand linguistic messages *in context*; that is, even where the context is zero.

Therefore it would be a dangerous oversimplification to talk as if there were acoustic input in the conversational channel, and no other; in the typical situation of utterance, there is information from extra-linguistic context coming in via all our senses (including our hearing, alongside the auditory linguistic signal), and there is input too from our knowledge, stored in memory, of 'how the world works', and 'what has happened recently'. Using the case of *spoken*

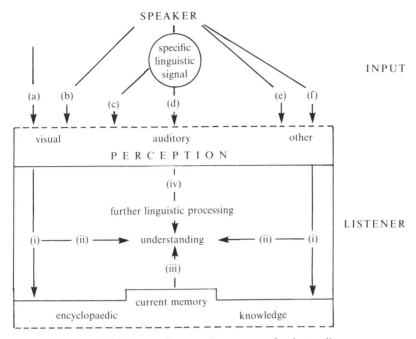

Figure 6.1 Sources of input to the processes of understanding

language comprehension for illustration, we may set the situation out schematically, as figure 6.1. In this simplified format, we can illustrate the following types of input:

(a) This is visual input which is independent of speaker and listener, containing information about objects and events in the situation of utterance; not all of it will be relevant, at least not all the time, but it may be necessary to monitor this channel for potential referents of linguistic expressions, for example.

(b) This is visual input from the speaker which is independent of the linguistic message; gestures, facial expressions, posture, etc. may carry information that is relevant to the linguistic message, indicating irritation, amusement, and so on, and the speaker may actually rely on this channel in determining the form that the linguistic message takes (e.g. to signal ironic intent).

(c) This is visual input from the speaker that is dependent on the form of the linguistic expression; lip, jaw, tongue and associated facial movements

307

accompany the articulatorily executed auditory signal, and may modulate auditory perception (McGurk and McDonald 1976). So-called 'lip-reading' by hearing-impaired listeners involves all these facial features, and not just lip-movements alone.

(d) This is the auditory input from the speaker that is formulated specifically as constituting the linguistic signal.

(e) This represents auditory input from the speaker which is not dependent on the articulation of the specific linguistic signal; it includes voice quality and rate, as well as precision of articulation, and the speaker is at liberty to control information on this channel, as in (b); but it may also signal involuntary aspects of the speaker's state.

(f) This represents other sensory information from the speaker, such as a light tap on the arm, or some conventional contact like a handshake.

As far as the listener is concerned, our diagram indicates the main hypothesised processing routes and interactions for these types of input. We have used the term *perception* for the peripheral level of visual, auditory and other sorts of processing, and have shown the routes from these processes as (i) to (iv); but we should bear in mind that interactions between, for example, visual and auditory perception processes exist even at the peripheral level.

The routes numbered (i) take information from outside the domain of the specifically linguistic signal to memory, which we have divided into two general areas, or *current memory* and *encyclopaedic knowledge*; those numbered (ii) link this information into the understanding of the utterance (where this information is relevant to it); the route (iii) allows information from recent experience to play a role in understanding, and we may also think of older-established knowledge as bearing on the understanding process through being loaded into current memory ('foregrounded') first; and the route numbered (iv) represents the result of processing the specific linguistic signal itself – note that the information available from this route may embody the results of processing interactions from more than one input channel.

Finally, we should point out that, in this 'box and arrow' sketch, the location of *understanding* is not a 'box', as in the case of the memory 'box', or the perception 'box', but rather a merging of arrows: it is not a place to be reached, or a set of processes, but the result of a number of interactions, in dynamic balance.

The nature of memory

The diagram in figure 6.1 is a fairly classical one in respect of its treatment of memory. It recognises that the contents of memory can interact with the results of perception, but it holds memory and perception apart, as distinct components of the processing system. It also embodies a typical distinction between 'current memory' (other terms used are 'working memory' and 'short-term memory') and 'encyclopaedic knowledge', the contents of some 'long-term memory' store (see Baddeley 1976).

Some recent work on memory suggests that this picture may be fundamentally misconceived. Allport (1985) provides a non-technical survey of theories of 'distributed memory' systems, from the viewpoint of language processing, in which he stresses the following points:

1. Memory is crucial to language use, in all aspects, and at all levels (i.e. from speech perception to semantics).

2. Traditional accounts of language processing tend either to be highly abstract (the 'cognitive' approach), as evidenced in models of the lexicon such as we have been considering in chapter 5, or to be neurophysiologically concrete, in the sense of our survey in chapter 2; there is, at first sight, little relation between the two approaches, such that one can constrain the other, and this has been true also of the role of memory in language use.

3. The distinction, within the classical approach, between a central, long-term vs peripheral, short-term memory has been effectively criticised; most importantly, so-called evidence for short-term memory has been argued to split into separate pieces of evidence for various 'processing span' capacities, *dependent upon the nature of the material to be processed.*

4. If we look at lexical access, for example, we might appeal to the notion of a 'network' type of representation (see our discussion of utterance production below, in ch. 7, section 7.3.3), in order to model lexical storage and interrelationships at both the levels of sound-structure forms and of meanings.

5. Instead of interpreting the nodes in such a network as corresponding to different physical elements, such as neurons, cell assemblies and the like, we may see them rather as corresponding to distinct *patterns of activity* in the neurophysiological substrate. This has the important result that different nodes can be represented by distinct activity patterns within the *same* set of neural entities. In this sense, the representation of different abstract elements (meaning concepts and sound-structure forms) within the network is *distributed* over the same physical elements in the network.

6. The inputs to such a system will give rise to certain activity patterns occurring and recurring repeatedly, resulting in stronger and stronger associations between the activated elements in each pattern.

7. Eventually, individual patterns will require only a subset of their elements to become activated for the other, inter-associated, elements also to become activated; this type of pattern is said to be *auto-associated*, and represents one of a set of stable responses in the system.

Allport then outlines a number of characteristics of distributed memory:

1. *Stability*: once established a stable pattern will tend to maintain itself.

2. *Part-to-whole retrieval*: as a result of (7) above, the phenomenon of 'phonemic restoration' (see chs 2–3) is a natural consequence of the auto-associated pattern response.

3. *Retrieval dynamics*: an input that stimulates more than one auto-associated response pattern (e.g. a word that shares a number of stimulus properties in common with other words) will result in the system taking longer to derive a single, stable response. Presumably, this may be observed, in the case of word recognition, at the level of form resemblances, or at the level of meaning resemblances.

4. *Categorical perception and 'capture'*: an input pattern that is similar to an auto-associated one will tend to evoke it, and thus be perceived as, or 'captured by' it. (See the discussion of categorical perception in ch. 4, section 4.2.4.)

5. *Superimposition of patterns*: since patterns of activity are distinct from the interconnected elements involved in them, more than one pattern can be sustained that involves exactly the same elements, and there will be no interference between them.

Finally, we shall assume that, within this general approach, provision is made for a number of distinct but interconnected networks. We have already suggested above that there will be one for word forms, and another for word meanings; but this is probably far too simple. It is more plausible to think of distinct word-form networks for auditory perception vs visual perception vs articulatory production vs written production (further distinctions being made between handwriting vs typewriting, for example); and the complex area of word meaning is probably to be thought of as divided into various sub-areas of kinaesthetic, visual, auditory, tactile, and other domains of perception and experience. In this sense, the term *distributed* is most compelling, as a description of the envisaged system: instead of 'perception' at one end of our 'listener-box' above, and 'memory/knowledge' at the other, we would envisage memory capacities as linked to every aspect and level of activity within the

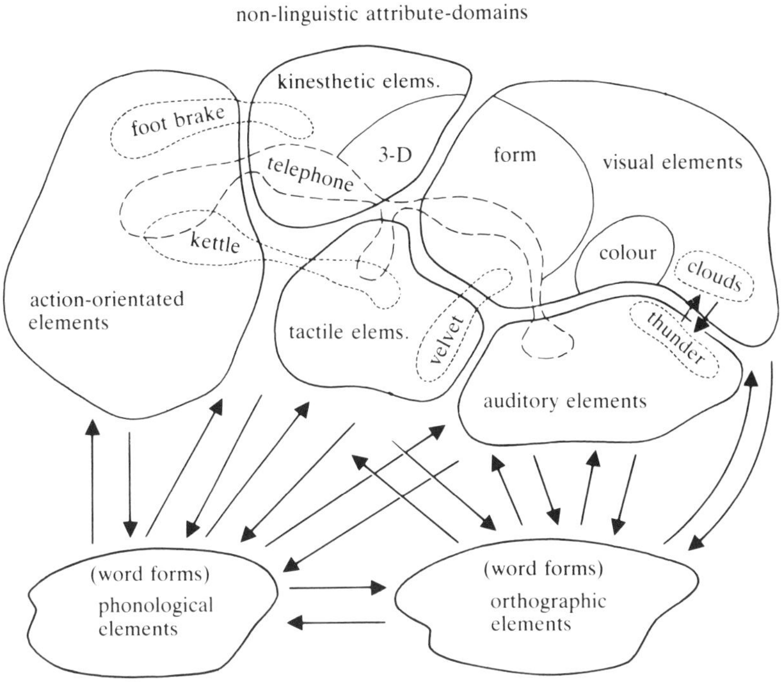

non-linguistic attribute-domains

Figure 6.2 A schematic illustration of distributed memory. (From Allport 1985: fig. 2.4, p. 53.)

box, and interlinked with each other. Allport (1985) provides the schematic illustration in figure 6.2, as a way of highlighting the sensory and motor aspects, as well as the higher cognitive aspects, of distributed memory. We should note the systematic relationship that exists between this sketch and the generalised layout of functions within the cerebral cortex of the left hemisphere (ch. 2, section 2.4.1). Our memory for an object consists in part of what it looks like (involving the visual cortex), what it sounds like (the auditory cortex), how it may be used (involving parts of the motor cortex and the parietal area), and so on.

6.1.3 *Parsing*

We have noted the obvious point that in understanding multiword utterances we have not only to access individual words but also to take account of the relations holding between them (corresponding to the time-honoured distinction, within linguistic semantics, between lexical and sentence meaning – see Fodor 1977). It is generally acknowledged that these relations are not 'accessed' or 'recognised', with the implication that they are 'stored' in some way prior to an utterance, and can be activated via some matching process (as lexical items can be). Instead, we think of 'accessing' words, but 'processing' or 'computing' relationships between them. The most usual term for this processing is *parsing*.

What sorts of relationships are parsed in human understanding of utterances? The answer may be 'essentially syntactic' or 'essentially semantic', or a mixture of the two, depending on the type of parser envisaged. For example, by syntactic parsing we might understand how *a big company* is parsed as consisting of an article, an adjective and a noun in suitable linear order for forming the internal constituents of a noun phrase of English. By semantic parsing we might characterise the same phrase as an indefinite referring constituent of some larger proposition. (We might also extend the term to phonological parsing, which would involve the processing of the whole sequence as constituting a single phonological unit, with the main stress falling on '*company*, or on '*big*, as the case may be.) We shall not go into further details here, but we shall see that syntactic parsing forms the major focus of our discussion below, with some comments towards the end on the matter of semantic parsing.

Current work on parsers owes much to work in computational linguistics, within the context of the wider field of artificial intelligence: Grishman (1986) defines a parsing device as 'a program which determines the derivation(s) of a sentence (according to a particular grammar)' (p. 14). Within this sort of approach we must recognise three general concepts: the human capacity for language, which is the object of psycholinguistic enquiry; the linguistic grammar, which is understood here as a body of description and theory providing insight into the nature of this capacity; and the parsing device, which is a formal means for implementing a grammar. Bever (1970) proposed a set of operating principles, or heuristics, which the mental grammar might employ in understanding linguistic input – these are, then, possible parsing procedures for the mental grammar (MG). Parsing procedures (PP) have also been proposed, within computational linguistics, for particular versions of linguistic grammar (LG). We may set out these elements as in figure 6.3. In these terms, we can ask how far the LG–MG correspondence is a direct one, and how far a body of parsing procedures is directly related to either the MG or the LG. Since the MG and its operating principles constitute the unknown, we may start by considering parsing from the point of view of the PP–LG relationship. We have noted (ch. 3, section 3.1.2) that, at least since the review of Fodor and Garrett (1966), the relationship between the LG and the MG appears to be indirect, and Bever's (1970) proposals for heuristics in human linguistic understanding were made in explicit rejection of the view (Brown and Hanlon 1970)

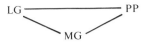

Figure 6.3 Relationships between the linguistic grammar (LG), parsing procedures (PP) and the mental grammar (MG)

that the LG provided a direct reflection of the MG. Essentially, we are looking for a set of procedures that will relate the linear form of utterances (i.e. as they appear in the language signal) to their relational structure within grammar (ultimately, the MG): as such, parsing may be envisaged as involved in either output or input mode, but our concern immediately will be with input.

The essence of parsing, as opposed to lexical identification, is that the listener is working with input that consists of lexically identifiable elements, temporarily sequenced; and is working towards determining the interrelationships of those elements as a part of the understanding process. In illustration of this, let us now return to our example passage, to raise the question of how a lexical recognition and parsing system might tackle an input sequence such as:

> (2) erm I was reading in the paper this morning a a chap he's a director of a big company in Birmingham . who was th the world's number one football fan . . .

We know that the speaker goes on for much longer than this, and we have arbitrarily stopped our example short at this point. Even so, there are as many as thirty-one elements within this sequence which will require decisions regarding lexical access, if we include the conventional 'filler' form *erm* (is this a non-word? or is it represented in the lexicon as one of a fairly small set of forms, empty of content but nevertheless serving a definable function?), the repetition of *a*, the cliticised form *'s* of *is*, the partial anticipation of *the*, and the possessive *'s* on *world's* (which is not a cliticised verb, although it has the same form as one). Even without these, there are twenty-eight occasions of lexical access, within 8–9 seconds. But our main concern here is with how it might be parsed.

Parsing strategies

A first step into the issues of parsing is to consider that one is working from (a) observed sequences of elements and (b) knowledge of one's language, to (c) conclusions about the hierarchical organisation of those elements. Given the indirect relation between linear sequence and hierarchical organisation, problems arise. To some extent, they may be addressed by reference to known patterns or trends in the indirect relationship: for instance (to take a very simple example), the pattern that subjects of clauses, which are definable hierarchically as the NP immediately dominated by S (Chomsky 1965), tend to precede the verb in the linear ordering of English. By capitalising on such patterns, a parser may be equipped with *strategies* for coping with the input. To some extent, these may reflect *parameter settings* in the LG (Chomsky 1981). Such strategies are of psycholinguistic interest to the extent that they account for how and why things go wrong in human parsing, as much as for what they get right.

At this point in our exposition we must acknowledge that we have reached an area of difficulty. We shall mark it with a paragraph that we may describe as containing an important digression. In an ideal world, and at our current state of knowledge, we should wish to make use of approaches from the fields of *computational linguistics, theoretical linguistics* and *psycholinguistics,* to constrain our understanding of how language comprehension proceeds. Very briefly, and crudely, we would expect computational approaches to be concerned with *getting parsers to work,* in terms of some program, with respect to some restricted subset of sentences of the language; however, while this is right, it is also the case that workers in this field have been interested in providing parsing procedures that are *plausible,* from a human-processing viewpoint. Not surprisingly, the degree of commitment to, and of success in, the latter objective has varied a good deal between different researchers. Just as crudely, we may say that linguistic approaches have generally been from the point of view of *what parsing must be like,* given some theory of grammar; but here too, there has also been a concern with what is plausible, and with possible counterevidence from human performance. Psycholinguistic approaches are, we may say, those that take the data from empirical human processing as their starting point; but they have, by virtue of this, also been acutely aware of the methodological difficulties involved in defining what is 'plausible' in the realm of parsing, and have shown a willingness to consider computational and linguistic principles of parsing as clues to the principles that might be involved in human performance. We shall therefore be eclectic in our review of parsing research (though certainly not exhaustive). But we should advise the reader to ask, of these and other approaches, how far they have been established with respect to empirical data on human performance. We shall refer to 'the parser' at many points in the following discussion, without wishing, or indeed being able, to say very precisely whether this is to be understood as the *human* parsing system or not. With this caution, we shall proceed.

The idea that humans understand sentences by parsing them according to certain strategies was proposed by Bever (1970), in explicit contrast with some contemporary and earlier approaches. What he wanted to call into question was the view that the *derivational complexity* of sentences (as measured in terms of their derivation according to a set of rules in grammar) entered directly into the parsing process (see, for instance, Bever's 1970 comments on Brown and Hanlon 1970; and Levelt 1978, for a review of studies in the subsequent period of research).

Bever suggested that the listener tests an input sequence for the goodness of fit it offers with certain *canonical schemas* such as 'Actor ... Action ... (Object)'. Word strings that readily yield to this sort of analysis are predicted to be easier to process than those that do not; for these latter, the processing system has to refer to further canonical schemas in order to determine their status. This suggests a hierarchy of canonical schemas, with those at the top being the ones that are most often required in the language, and those towards the bottom serving as fall-back devices, used only when necessary. The virtue of this approach is that it provides for a characterisation of how easy or difficult it is for the listener to process an utterance, independently of the terms in which the utterance may have been produced by the speaker. Thus, in the example

(3)   The horse raced past the barn fell

we can say that the construction is, from one point of view, a restricted subject–relative clause type, with passivisation of the relative clause and deletion of the optional relative pronoun and passive auxiliary verb (*the horse (that was) raced past . . .*). But we may also note that, from the listener's viewpoint it presents peculiar difficulties, because of the high-priority canonical schema that powerfully operates to treat the initial sequence *the horse raced past the barn . . .* as 'Actor ... Action ... Modifier', in the main clause of the construction. This, furthermore, appears to represent fairly directly what people report after hearing this construction; there is a feeling of suddenly being stranded when the word *fell* is reached, since it is not catered for in terms of the analysis applied up to that point. There is a sensation also of being forced back to re-analyse the initial sequence, this time equipped with the knowledge that *fell* occurs where it does.

This sort of phenomenon is known, picturesquely, as a *garden path effect*, and it can be quite naturally accommodated in a system with a hierarchy of canonical schemas, or processing strategies. Grammatical garden paths frequently arise through a mixture of lexical and constructional factors, as here: we can dispel the effect in this example by inserting the relative pronoun, *or* by using a suffix on the verb such as *-ing*, which is not homonymous with a finite tense form, or by using a different verb, such as *dragged* (which causes the processing system some difficulty inasmuch as it requires a passive interpretive schema, but avoids the classic garden-path property of withholding crucial information till the last possible moment).

An example of a pervasive parsing problem is found in the way that modifying phrases such as *this morning* and *in Birmingham* are attached to the rest of the utterance. Broadly, the problem concerns where in the structural hierarchy such constituents should be attached, given that in some constructions they seem to belong most naturally with the whole verb phrase constituent (as in *this morning*), in others with the most recent phrase constituent (as with *in Birmingham*), and in other cases may equally be attached to more than one node.

Kimball (1973) addressed this issue, among others, and we may review his *parsing principles* briefly here, particularly since they have been referred to by many researchers since.

Principle One (Top-down): Parsing in natural language proceeds in a top-down manner. This means that, as soon as the first word is encountered, the parser constructs a high-level category, such as S (for sentence) to accommodate it, and supplies such intermediate structure between S and the immediate word category (say, Article) as the grammar requires. For our example, we would have:

(4)

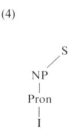

where the Pronoun category is interpreted as an NP under S.

Principle Two (Right Association): Terminal symbols optimally associate to the lowest non-terminal node. It appears that this means that the parser will try to attach *in the paper* to the VP mode and *this morning* to the NP node dominating *the paper*, in example (5):

(5)

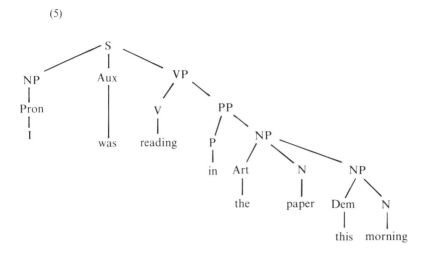

thus producing the right-branching structure shown above. But it may be argued that a preferable attachment for *in the paper* is to the S node, rather than the VP node, since *read* does not require such modification as a condition of its occurrence; and it is certainly preferable to have *this morning* as a modifier linked to the S node direct. This is not to say that the parser *cannot* yield such structures as:

(6)

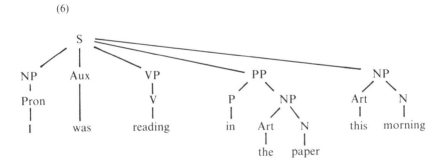

but it does mean that it must rely on other than purely categorical (PP, NP) information to do so. Among such information would be the lexical content of PP and NP, as well as of the VP, and the real-world knowledge thus mediated. By contrast, the principle would lead to the appropriate attachment in the case of *in Birmingham*, in (7):

(7)

```
              S
          /       \
       NP          VP
        |         /   \
      Pron       V     NP
        |        |    /  \
       he       's  Art   N
                     |    |        PP
                     a  director  /  \
                               P      NP
                               |    / | \
                               of Art Adj  N        PP
                                   |   |   |       /   \
                                   a  big com-    P     NP
                                          pany    |     |
                                                  in  N prop
                                                        |
                                                   Birmingham
```

Principle Three (New Nodes): The construction of a new node is signalled by the occurrence of a grammatical function word. By this principle, the parser will find it more difficult to assign structure to the input sequences where optional deletion of elements such as complementisers and relative pronouns has taken place. Part of the difficulty of the example *the horse raced past the barn fell* arises from the violation of this principle.

Principle Four (Two Sentences): The constituents of no more than two sentences can be parsed at the same time. This principle is set up to account for the sudden increase in computational load in examples such as

(8)   The question the girl the lion bit answered was complex

compared to either

(9)   The question the girl answered was complex

or

(10)   The girl the lion bit answered the question

Principle Five (Closure): A phrase is closed as soon as possible, i.e., unless the next node is parsed as an immediate constituent of that phrase. This also helps to explain the complexity of *the horse raced past the barn fell*; the parser, taking the sequence *the horse raced past the barn* as a sentence, assumes that the sentence is closed. The Bever strategy, to take the first N ... V ... (N) sequence as a main clause, is a special case of Closure, according to Kimball.

Principle Six (Fixed Structure): When the last immediate constituent of a phrase has been formed, and the phrase has been closed, it is costly in terms of perceptual complexity to go back and reorganise the constituents of that phrase. Since, by this principle, it is costly for the parser to backtrack, in cases such as *the horse raced past the barn fell*, it would be advantageous for the parser to have some 'look ahead' facility, to minimise the occasions for such backtracking. This facility would be limited – it is not enough, for instance, to cope with this example – but would nevertheless help in cases such as sequences beginning with *that*, which could continue in the following ways:

(11) (a) That chap is a company director
      (b) That is a strange story
      (c) That he is a football fan is rather strange

Principle Seven (Processing): When a phrase is closed, it is transferred into a syntactic (possibly semantic) processing stage and cleared from short-term memory. This is essentially the principle that governs the relation between the two stages of a serial processing-device such as we shall be considering below. It says that initial processing will be in units such as NP, VP and PP. In centre-embedding constructions such as (10)

(10) The girl the lion bit answered the question

the NP *the girl the lion bit* cannot be closed until after another NP, *the lion*, has been opened and closed, and another VP, *bit*, has also been opened and closed: hence, a good deal more structure must be held in short-term memory before it can be cleared.

Kimball points out that these parsing principles are closely connected to each other, and envisages that they interact with each other in the processing of input sequences. As we have noted, one of the important underlying concepts is that of short-term memory, a limitation which distinguishes natural-language parsing from computer-language parsing: a further important concept which distinguishes natural-language parsing, according to Kimball, is that it is not *deterministic*:

> a parser for a programming language yields a unique tree for each string. Not only this, but also the behaviour of the computer parser must be deterministic. That is, its action at any given string of input terminals and stack configuration [i.e. a given part of the input string which it is scanning at a given moment, and what it has stored in a memory 'stack' regarding its operations up to this point] must be uniquely determined. A model of parsing in natural language must allow for more than one parse

> and should predict on the basis of considerations of surface structure complexity which parse will most likely be offered as the first choice by a native speaker. (1973: 20)

This point, and Kimball's principles, set the stage for much of the later work that has been done in this tradition, including some that explicitly rejects the claim about the non-deterministic nature of natural language parsing. But first we must return to consider the serial and parallel possibilities, considering the serial types first.

6.2 Serial models

Given that parsing and lexical access are distinguishable aspects of the processing of multi-word utterances, we should ask in what way each is carried on in relation to the other. There are, logically, the following possibilities:

1. parsing is completed before any lexical access takes place;
2. all lexical items are accessed before any parsing is attempted;
3. lexical access and parsing occur together, in some way.

We shall consider each of these possibilities below. It may appear that (1) is at first sight rather unlikely, since lexical access is so rapid and automatic; as we shall see, however, in a restricted sense, it is a possibility that has to be considered. It should be clear that (1) and (2) represent serial accounts of what happens, while (3) may have either continuously parallel processing, or (1) and (2) alternating in close serial fashion. We should also note here that there is no reason, *a priori*, why the human linguistic understanding system should not exhibit, say, parallel processing in the matter of lexical access, and serial processing in parsing, or vice versa. After all, different processing tasks may call for distinct types of processes, yielding an overall system that is a hybrid.

6.2.1 *Parsing before lexical access?*

As we have noted above, in the usual case, this order of processing does not arise, since (a) utterances we are exposed to usually have familiar words in them, and (b) these words trigger automatic lexical recognition that is extremely rapid. It is extremely difficult, if not impossible, to attend to an utterance sufficiently to carry out a syntactic parse without recognising the familiar words it contains.

However, in the case of Jabberwocky, we have a limited example of the type, where certain elements in the string to be parsed are non-words, while others, including articles, prepositions and suffixes, are in appropriate positions and form the basis on which a parse can be successfully attempted:

(12)   A morpish foll has varely glempsed the rass

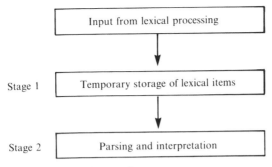

Figure 6.4 A simple type of two-stage parser

Further, in the case of utterances which have substrings containing words which we have not heard before (hence have no lexical entry for), by definition the parsing (in that part of the substring) must take place without lexical access. The parse is a means of starting the process of building a representation (phonological, grammatical and ultimately semantic) of the newly encountered word in our mental lexicon. However, it is clear that in this case also, the parse is based on information from surrounding lexical items (including morphological elements such as affixes) that are successfully accessed. We may conclude that parsing prior to lexical access is possible in limited contexts (where there is sufficient parsing information from surrounding lexical items) and in less usual situations. We shall now turn our attention to the other main types of processing order.

6.2.2 *Lexical access before any parsing*

The simplest model of this type, involving a strict separation of lexical access from subsequent parsing, may be envisaged as in figure 6.4, where we envisage that all of stage 1 ('word collecting') is complete before stage 2 is initiated. This raises the issue of the processing capacity of stage 1: *how many* lexical items can it store? There is reason to believe that such a system would need to have more than one 'bite' at our example above, because twenty-eight (or thirty-two) lexical items would simply overload the capacity of the stage 1 store.

The reason for this may be illustrated by the following example. If telephone numbers normally consisted of thirty digits, we should always expect to have to write down a number on first hearing it, even if we wished to retain it only for just long enough to dial it. As it is, with numbers that are generally up to around six or seven digits long, we can normally perform this task without resorting to pen and paper; we can 'catch' it for long enough to dial it, and perhaps rehearse it mentally, to aid longer retention in memory, engage in mnemonic strategies of various sorts, or, eventually, to be on the safe side, decide to write it down.

In this analogy, it is the initial 'catching' that concerns us, rather than subsequent rehearsal. The limitations of what has often been called *short-term memory* (STM) have been documented over many years, especially since the work of nineteenth-century psychologists; but the classic study in recent times is that of Miller (1956), reviewing a whole range of experimental findings. Miller estimated the capacity of STM as 'the magical number 7' (plus or minus two), which in the case of our simple model would lead us to expect a capacity for stage 1 memory of up to around seven lexical items at a time. Consider being asked to listen to the following list of digits (fourteen in all), *just once*:

(13)   nine seven three six eight five one four nine five seven two eight six

You would not hope to recall them all, even immediately. Whereas, if there were only seven digits:

(14)   nine seven three six eight five one

your success rate would be much higher. As this implies, if you handled the fourteen-digit list in two successive sweeps, recalling as many words as you could after each sweep, your combined total of recalled words would be much greater than that for a single sweep. If such immediate recall ability is at all reliable as a guide to the sort of storage that goes on in language processing, it would suggest that language processing is carried out in sweeps of around seven words at a time, with stage 1 alternately collecting the words and handing them on for further analysis, as 'packages', to stage 2; and stage 2 alternately parsing these packages and then waiting for the next package to be received. In our example, the packages might be something like the following:

Sweep   Package
1.   erm I was reading in the paper
2.   this morning a a chap he's
3.   a director of a big company in
4.   Birmingham who was the world's number one
     etc.

Two points immediately arise out of what we have said thus far: we shall take each of them in turn. First, surely language processing is different from recalling telephone numbers? Unfortunately, our model is so simple that, as far as stage 1 is concerned, the answer to this point must be no. Until the operations of the second stage have been implemented, there is no way that the system can distinguish between grammatically structured and unstructured sequences of words.

Secondly, our illustration of packages has surely been unduly rigid in making each package exactly seven lexical items (as envisaged above) in length. Might we not expect actual language processing to be more *flexible* than this? Now, it would be an advantage, presumably, if the first stage could somehow 'tailor' the size of its packages to the needs of the second-stage processor, e.g., by stopping just short of seven words, or going just beyond seven words, in one package, if by doing so it could respect a phrase boundary that the second stage will find relevant. Unfortunately, again, this sort of intelligent flexibility is beyond the capacity of the first stage as constituted in this model. Even if it were constructed in such a way as to permit variation in the number of words in each package, say, between five and nine words, this alone would not guarantee that these variations will be related to the grammatical properties of the input sequence.

6.2.3 *Modified serial approaches*

One way to enable the first stage device to meet the needs of the second stage is to build in some preliminary processing abilities to the first stage. To some extent, this compromises the strict separation of the types of work that the two stages perform: hence we shall refer to these approaches as *modified serial*. There are a number of ways in which this sort of approach can be implemented. We shall now consider three versions, the first two of which are related explicitly to particular versions of LG, while the third is better described as related to speculation regarding the MG.

The sausage machine

The rather curious name for this model harks back to our description of 'packages' in section 6.2.2 above; Frazier and Fodor (1978) liken this packaging procedure to the way a sausage machine makes units (sausages), of a given size, which are linked to each other, out of continuous input: 'the human sentence parsing device assigns phrase structure to word strings in two steps. The first stage parser (called the PPP) assigns lexical and phrasal nodes to substrings of roughly six words. The second stage parser (called the SSS) then adds higher nodes to link these phrasal packages together into a complete phrase marker' (p. 291).

Note that the first-stage limit of up to six words suggests a conservative estimate of short-term memory capacity, prior to any phrasal chunking. It is the task of the PPP to achieve this chunking (preliminary parsing), and of the SSS (which works only on the output of the PPP) to sweep along behind the

PPP, picking up the chunks and organising them in terms of a more global view of 'dependencies between items that are widely separated in the sentence and of long term structural commitments which are acquired as the analysis proceeds' (p. 292).

By way of illustration, let us return to the issues addressed by Kimball's principle of Right Association. The following sentences have two interpretations: (a) with the phrase *for Susan* attached to the VP *bought the book*; and (b) attached to the NP *the book*:

(15)   Joe bought the book for Susan
(16)   Joe bought the book that I had been trying to obtain for Susan

Frazier and Fodor suggest that Right Association as put forward by Kimball is actually insufficient for all the relevant data, and offer a revised version, which they call Local Association. They go on to say that the principle of Local Association sets in only at some distance, since the (a) interpretation appears most plausible for the shorter version (15), while it is the (b) version that is plausible for the longer (16). They argue that the preference for (a) over (b) in the shorter version is a case of a parsing principle that they call *Minimal Attachment*: by this, an item 'is to be attached into the phrase marker with the fewest possible number of nonterminal nodes linking it with the nodes that are already present' (1978: 230). Since attachment to the VP involves no extra nodes, while attachment to the NP *the book* involves the creation of an NP node to dominate the whole sequence *the book for Susan*, this principle accounts for the facts as set out above. Further, they link this principle, and the distance factor in Local Association, to the design of their parser:

> Let us suppose for the sake of argument that the first stage parser has the capacity to retain six words of the sentence, together with whatever lexical and phrasal nodes it has assigned to them. Then in processing [*Joe bought the book for Susan*], it will still be able to 'see' the verb when it encounters *for Susan*. It will know that there is a verb phrase node to which the prepositional phrase could be attached, and also that this particular verb is one which permits a *for*-phrase. But in [*Joe bought the book that I had been trying to obtain for Susan*], where a long noun phrase follows the verb *bought*, the first stage parser will have lost access to *bought* by the time *for Susan* must be entered into the structure; the only possible attachment will be within the long noun phrase, as a modifier to *trying to obtain*. (1978: 300)

Locality constraints on parsing: the Berwick and Weinberg model
Berwick and Weinberg (1984) also offer a two-stage parser, the first stage of which builds structures, and the second of which scans the output

of the first stage for relationships at a distance. But their parser is of the 'bottom-up' variety (thus violating Kimball's Top-down principle, which he characterised as 'the process employed by speakers of natural languages' (1973: 16)), which does not seek first to establish the highest-level node, but rather some intermediate node dominating the first *n* elements in the input sequence. Further, it is a *deterministic* parser, thus contradicting Kimball's view of the difference between natural- and computer-language parsers. To achieve its deterministic operation, the first stage has a 'look ahead' ability of a restricted type; thus, it can delay analysis of a substring in the input until such time as it can state the analysis deterministically, i.e. in a unique way (although it may still 'get things wrong').

The function of the second stage is to link (by coindexing) pronouns, anaphors (e.g. *the boy*, referring back to some named individual), and *traces*, as used in current versions of transformational grammar (e.g. Chomsky 1981; Radford 1981).

Berwick and Weinberg further take the position that there is a particularly close relationship between human parsing (as modelled in their parser) and the theory of transformational grammar (see our discussion of fig. 6.3, above). Within this theory, there are a number of constraints on which constituents may be moved to which positions in sentence structure, and it has been proposed, notably, that a number of constraints that were formerly thought to be more or less independent of each other (requiring separate statement) are in fact examples of a single constraint, called *subjacency*.

We may briefly illustrate subjacency, from one area of grammar, as follows (see, e.g., Radford 1981 for a fuller discussion). Suppose we take a *wh*-question of the 'echo' type, as in:

(17)   Bill would eat what?

we can relate this to the corresponding non-echo type by positing a rule of *wh*-movement, whereby the *wh*-element moves to the front, and leaves a trace of itself behind:

(18)   What would Bill eat *t*?

In an indirect question, such as:

(19)   What did you believe that Bill would eat?

the *what* occurs in initial position, even before the main clause, and, without the subjacency condition, it might be supposed that it got there by a single movement, as in:

(20)   What [$_s$did you believe that [$_s$Bill would eat *t*]]?

325

But this sort of movement possibility, if allowed generally in the grammar, would yield a number of ungrammatical strings, as in:

(21)   (For Bill to eat that would be dangerous →)
       *What [s[NPfor Bill to eat *t*] would be dangerous]?

Hence, it is supposed that there is a constraint (subjacency) on *wh*-movement such that it can move a constituent across only one S- or NP-boundary; these are the so-called 'bounding nodes'. But, since this leaves *what did you believe that Bill would eat t?* as non-generatable, it is allowed that *successive* movements of *wh*-elements may occur that cross more than one bounding category, *as long as only one such boundary is crossed on each movement.* This effectively blocks our ungrammatical example above, but allows for:

(22)   What did you believe *t* that Bill would eat *t*?

where the cycles of movement are indicated. For this reason, such movement is called *successive-cyclic* (Radford 1981).

The concept of subjacency is then an important one within current transformational grammar (TG) theory, and Berwick and Weinberg claim that it governs the operation of their first-stage device. Putting it another way: their parser needs subjacency to operate in English, because only in this way will the input string be structured in such a way as to allow the parser to link traces to their antecedents.

Now, if the linking of traces to their antecedents (or *trace-binding*, as it is called) is subject to the locality constraint of subjacency, it follows that it must be an operation of the bounded first-stage device. But, as we have seen, other antecedent-to-element links (to pronouns and anaphors) are said to be performed by the second-stage device. Why is there this difference? The answer is that traces are special in that they are not overt entities in the input string, but rather have to be hypothesised by the parser. Since it is the function of the first-stage device to *build*, and the second-stage device to *link*, it seems reasonable to conclude that trace insertion is part of the building process, and hence is part of the first stage.

The next point is that, in *deterministic* parsing, a trace should not be built into the analysis of the input sequence unless it is fully determined in context – that is, unless there is an antecedent available to bind it. In this light, the following sentences pose an interesting contrast:

(23)   Did John say that Frank believed ... that Bill would eat?
(24)   What did John say that Frank believed ... that Bill would eat?

In the first, *yes–no*, type of question (23), the parser can straightforwardly take each *that*-clause as the object of the preceding verb; but in (24), *wh*-type, there is, as well as this interpretation, the possibility that *what* is the object of the first verb, *say*, as in:

(25)   John said what (that Frank believed)...?,

or of the second verb, *believed*, as in:

(26)   John said that Frank believed what?...

In the interpretation where each succeeding clause is the object of the preceding verb, *what* is the object of the last verb, *eat*, as in:

(27)   John said that Frank believed ... that Bill would eat what?

To put this, informally, in trace-type notation, we have:

(28)   What did John say (*t*) that Frank believed (*t*)... that Bill would eat (*t*)?

where each interpretation that is possible *up to that point of the input* is represented by a *t*-element, in parentheses. By the end of the sequence, it is clear that only the final *t*-position is possible: thus, for example, it is ungrammatical to have structures such as:

(29)   *John said much that Frank believed ... that Bill would eat

The parser, being deterministic, cannot do as we have done here, and 'hedge its bets' by putting *t*-elements into parentheses, pending further analysis of the input sequence. Rather, it must build a *t*-element into each possible position in the sequence, as these occur. Putting this another way: given the antecedent *what* as the first word, the parser 'knows' that a trace must be found for it in the subsequent sequence; since trace binding is said to be a function of the first-stage device, and since this is limited in its operation, it 'finds' the first ('locally' available) position for the trace, i.e. after the first verb, *said*, yielding the structure:

(30)   What did John say *t* ...

Then, as further input becomes available, it constructs the trace locally again,

(31)   What did John say *t* that Frank believed *t* ...

where the second *t* is not taken as representing an alternative interpretation to the first, but as linked to it, in one and the same interpretation. As further input is scanned, it goes on providing locally constrained traces,

(32)   What did John say *t* that Frank believed *t* ... that Bill would eat *t*?

Then the second-stage device, faced with a succession of traces in the string as analysed by the first-stage device, coindexes them all (i.e. treats them as all bound to the antecedent *what*):

(33)   What$_i$ did John say t_i that Frank believed t_i ... that Bill would eat t_i?

This analysis, then, represents a faithful record of the movement of *what* from its position as object of *eat*, via the successive-cyclic intermediate movements required by the subjacency constraint, up to its initial position in the sentence. As such, the analysis may be said to recover the processes involved in the generation of the sentence, and, by implication, the processes by which the speaker produced it.

Berwick and Weinberg's parser contributes to theories of the human parsing capacity by making an apparently testable claim, that subjacency constitutes an important structural feature in natural language from the point of view of parsing processes. Their parser needs subjacency because it is deterministic and has only a limited ability to search through what has been parsed to locate antecedents. As such, their parser, and their claim, has been criticised (Fodor 1985) as being too wedded to one particular linguistic theory; for example, subjacency has no status in Generalised Phrase Structure Grammar (GPSG; see Gazdar 1981), so the Berwick and Weinberg parser seems to require, from this point of view, a premature assumption regarding the unassailable position of current TG theory as far as language processing is concerned. Further, there are parsers (GPSG-based; and Augmented Transition Network (ATN) types – see section 6.3.4 below) that are not limited in their capacity to search for antecedents. We shall return to this issue, after first reviewing some criticism of the serial-processing viewpoint in general.

Functionally complete units

We have already referred to Bever's (1970) concept of canonical schemas in parsing (section 6.1.3 above). In relation to these, the question that arises is: How do input sequences get matched, or tested, against stored canonical schemas? It is not just word-type and order information that is available for use, but a host of other potential cues as well, including affixes and prosodic contours. A study by Carroll, Tanenhaus and Bever (1978) provides a convenient illustration of this approach (building on Bever's earlier work). They first of all address the issue of setting the boundaries on the domains of processing (see 6.2.2 above) by setting up units that they argue to be realistic for this purpose. They refer to the earlier attempts in this regard, e.g. the notion that the listener chunks the input sequence into *linguistic clauses* (Bever, Lackner and Kirk 1969; Fodor, Bever and Garrett 1974) or into *major surface-structure constituents* (Fodor and Bever 1965; Chapin,

Smith and Abrahamson 1972), and criticise them as being too *structural*, 'at the price of overlooking potentially important *functional* segmentation variables' (p. 190).

They point to the fact that major constituents may be arbitrarily long (necessitating some internal chunking prior to the major constituent boundary) and, conversely, that linguistic clauses may be excessively short (necessitating immediate recoding in order to yield effective chunks for processing). These two problems are illustrated in their example:

(34) Walking, talking, eating, ... and sleeping were the preferred activities of the lazy, fat, old, ... man with the flea-bitten dog.

Here, (a) each of the subjectless gerunds in -*ing* represents a separate linguistic clause (in terms of their approach), and (b) the NP occurring immediately after the verb *were* can be indefinitely long. The proposal that Carroll, Tanenhaus and Bever put forward is introduced as follows:

> a sequence of words will comprise a better segmentation unit if it is potentially recodable into an independent memory structure. Current views of memory have identified such memory units with propositional structures (e.g. Kintsch, 1974; Rumelhart, Lindsay and Norman, 1972). Thus, we make the assumption that linguistic sequences which can be directly mapped onto complete propositional structures are the ideal segmentation units in sentence perception. We refer to such sequences as *functionally complete*. (1978: 192)

The following examples from their study should help to illustrate what these functionally complete units (FCUs) look like, by underlining them:

(35) (a) After John spilled the beans, everyone ignored him
      (b) The town's construction of a new school cost the taxpayers a mint
      (c) Fleeing was John's alternative to fighting

Both (35a) and (35b) have two FCUs; in (35a) they are non-overlapping, while in (35b) the smaller is wholly contained within the other. The presence of a verb is no guarantee of FCU status, since *construction* in (35b) helps to define *the town's construction of a new school* as an FCU, even though it is not a verb, and (35c) contains two verbs, *fleeing, fighting*, which do not represent FCUs.

If we grant that FCUs are the segmentation units that this serial processing system is attempting to work with, we must ask what potential cues there might be in the input signal that could serve to inform the system about their presence. Carroll, Tanenhaus and Bever suggest the following cues:

1. 'noun-verb-noun' configuration;
2. copula deletion;

3. subject deletion;
4. presence of noun/verb;
5. presence of noun/verb morphemes;
6. sequence length.

The first of these is essentially the formal basis of the original Bever canonical schema, that a Noun ... Verb ... (Noun) sequence is a unit (here, an FCU) that can be interpreted (as 'actor ... action ... object'). The next two cues illustrate what Carroll, Tanenhaus and Bever refer to as contextual and inferential cues: it is suggested that *the big dog* can be contextually supplied with the 'missing' copula of the proposition 'the dog is big'; similarly, we can supply *John* as the subject of *fleeing*, and *fighting*, in (35c). The point of these cues seems to be that, while the constructions they immediately occur in are not FCUs, they can be mapped onto full propositional structures, presumably in the second, interpretative, stage of the system. So they are cues to non-FCUs of an interesting type, and hence indirectly cues to the larger FCUs that contain them. The next two cues, (4) and (5), are what Carroll, Tanenhaus and Bever call *real sign cues*; the mere presence of a noun, or a verb – as elements that are essential to functional completeness – is taken to provide evidence of an FCU. In the same way, affixal morphemes, such as a plural or tense suffix, are taken as cues to noun and verb stems below the level of the word. The last cue, sequence length, takes us back to examples like (34) *walking, talking, eating, ... and sleeping*, etc., since we are told that, where sequences are excessively long, they may function as segmentation units in themselves, even though they are functionally incomplete. So length itself serves as a cue to set a unit boundary – Carroll, Tanenhaus and Bever call it a *processing capacity* cue, as opposed to an *internal structure* cue.

Armed with these cues, Carroll, Tanenhaus and Bever seek to show that they are effectively observable in various experimental findings. They conclude that there is a 'cost hierarchy' of cues, ranging from the low-cost cues (where the listener need only consider a single word in the input sequence, e.g. local sign cues), and high-cost cues such as the 'noun–verb–noun' configurational cue. One possibility, of course, is that these hierarchically organised cues are deployed in a serial processing fashion: Carroll, Tanenhaus and Bever suggest, however, that 'while the effectiveness of local sign cues in segmentation processing may typically *precede* that of configurational cues, the former may not necessarily construct the input to the latter. Another way of putting this is to say that we doubt that the hierarchy of cues reflects a serially structured segmentation process' (1978: 215). They conclude that we actually know very little about the most fundamental question, which is 'how these relational structures are recognised and integrated into percept and concept' (p. 216).

We may conclude this section by examining how the Carroll, Tanenhaus and Bever cues would apply to our example from the conversation about football. In the sequence:

(36) *I was reading* in the *paper* this *morning* a *chap he's* a *director* of a big *company* in *Birmingham*

we have the following pattern of noun(N)–verb(V) occurrence, assuming that pronouns such as *I* count as nouns, and that auxiliary verbs such as *was* in *was reading* count as verbs, for this purpose (i.e. the elements underlined in our example):

(37) N V V N N N N V N N

We have underlined here the potential FCU that can be identified according to this criterion. Possibly we ought to include the initial N V V N sequence also (marked by broken underlining), with some other strategy to tell us that ... V V ... ought to be attempted as a sequence of premodifying verb (e.g. auxiliary) followed by main verb, constituting a complex-verb element. This would leave two Ns (*morning, chap*) unaccounted for in the middle of the sequence, and two at the end (*company, Birmingham*). We should actually want the noun *chap*, in its phrase grouping *a chap*, to be identified as an element that 'hangs loose' between the preceding and following sequences; but the other three Ns occur in phrases that, by contrast, have to be integrated into their FCUs.

Under the heading of noun/verb morphemes, we should also probably include elements such as prepositions, which have a grammatical marker function with respect to following noun phrases, as well as articles, which help to define the onset of the noun phrase. This would allow us, let us say, to group structures such as *in the paper*, *of a big company*, and *in Birmingham*; and we might envisage some strategy that would try to attach such phrases to the preceding, rather than the following, FCU first. Further clues to structure would come from the tensed forms of *was* and *'s*, and from the *-ing* suffix on *reading*.

This would give something like the situation in figure 6.5. If this is the output of the first stage, then we would have two sweeps (at least) through this portion of the input, one for each FCU; the as yet unconnected phrases *this morning, a chap* may perhaps be thought of as they are set out here, tagging along behind the FCU in the first sweep, pending the further processing of the second stage. Each of these sweeps has ten lexical items, i.e. is longer than a purely word-based processing account could handle, but is not so long as to

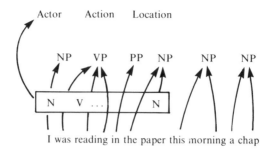

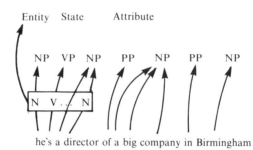

Figure 6.5   The internal cue structure of Functionally Complete Units. (Based on discussion in Carroll, Tanenhaus and Bever 1978, pp. 192–5.)

exceed the required length constraint of FCUs. Stage 2 processing would follow each of these FCUs, mapping their contents onto propositional representations, and deriving further aspects of their meaning from there.

6.3   Parallel models

6.3.1   *Parsing and lexical access together*

In contrast to the serial processing models we have just been reviewing, parallel processing of constructional sequences involves an exhaustive analysis of the input string from the very first word. Interpretation of the rest of the input sequence builds on (a) the properties of that input, in the light of (b) what has been analysed thus far. It is therefore essentially *interactive* in nature.

Two important consequences flow from this. First, while there is a need to define a preliminary input domain, or 'processing window', this may be done without reference to the immediate time-pressures on storage. The simplest type of parallel model will work on the basis of an input sequence that is processed one lexical item at a time. That is to say, it will operate in step with the results of lexical access, as they become available.

Secondly, the analysis is highly predictive: given what has been discovered thus far, certain expectations are set up regarding the further properties of the input sequence. This allows for rather precise microgenetic 'fine-tuning' of the analysis as it proceeds, and provides a natural framework for the effect of constructional context on processing, both at the lexical and the constructional levels.

This 'real-time' or 'on-line' approach is well suited to bringing out the temporal characteristics of spoken-language understanding, since it says that, at any given point in the input sequence, all that is available to the syntactic processor is to be found in (a) what it has already analysed, together with (b) what it 'knows' about the language. This state of affairs persists right to the end of the sentence, with the body of available knowledge about the current utterance increasing until, at some point (not necessarily always the last word), the analysis is complete. Contrast this with the serial approach, where, with the last word (of the processing domain, however defined), the main analysis *begins*.

6.3.2 *Parallel processing versus FCUs*

Marslen-Wilson, Tyler and Seidenberg (1978) propose a model of the parallel type which they call the 'on-line interactive' model, and they offer it in explicit contrast with the FCU model of Carroll, Tanenhaus and Bever. They say:

> Our purpose here will be, first, to show that the correctness of the claim that speech is structured into clause-like processing units does not necessarily depend on the correctness of the clausal processing hypothesis as well. We will then go on to propose a rationale for the clausal structuring hypothesis that is more compatible with the on-line interactive approach. In particular, we will try to show experimentally that to the extent that there is 'clausal' segmentation of the speech input, it is a function of what we will call the interpretative informational structure of the utterance, and not simply of its syntactic structure. (1978: 220)

The first point here is that evidence for clausal segmentation, which Carroll, Tanenhaus and Bever cite, does not necessarily constitute evidence that such segmentation occurs as a *precursor* to the analysis; it may be a *product* of it. (This line of argument resembles the point concerning the role of speech-sound segments in lexical access in ch. 5, section 5.1.3.) The second issue here concerns the nature of the on-line interactive model. The third issue relates to the distinction between 'informational' vs syntactic structure.

The on-line interactive model

Marslen-Wilson, Tyler and Seidenberg note that there is evidence from *word-monitoring* and *speech-shadowing* experiments 'that the listener can begin his structural interpretation from the first word of a sentence, without having to wait until a clausal unit has been completed (Marslen-Wilson 1973a, 1973b, Marslen-Wilson and Tyler 1975, Tyler and Marslen-Wilson 1977)' (1978: 221).

We have already described speech shadowing, in the context of lexical access (ch. 5); word monitoring is a task where subjects have to listen for the occurrence of a particular word, specified in advance, in some experimental context, and a usual sort of measure of this performance is a response-latency one: subjects press a button as soon as they have detected the word; this stops a timer, which allows their reaction time to be measured. The assumption is that reaction times will be longer for words that are processed in more difficult contexts.

Marslen-Wilson, Tyler and Seidenberg argue that while this evidence alone rules out a *strict* serial model, in which no processing at all takes place during the first stage (purely passive 'word collecting'), it is not inconsistent with a modified serial approach such as Carroll and Bever (1976) and Carroll, Tanenhaus and Bever (1978), as considered above. They therefore sought to bring experimental evidence to bear specifically on this latter type of serial model.

They asked subjects in a further word-monitoring experiment to listen for a word that *sounds like* a target word (rhyme monitoring), or *means* such-and-such (category monitoring), in sentences like:

> (38) (a) Although Mary very rarely cooks *trout*, when she does so it tastes delicious
>
>   (b) Although Mary very rarely cooks, *trout* is one thing she prepares well

The target word is *trout* in each case, and each of these sentences consists of identical word-sequences up to and including this target. Any difference in subjects' performance must therefore be ascribed to the syntactic and prosodic structures involved. Crucially, the syntactic difference is that in the first sentence the word *trout* is (the last word) in the first clause, while in the second sentence it is (the first word) in the second clause. We could substitute for 'clause' here, 'functionally complete unit' as defined in Carroll, Tanenhaus and Bever (1978) and the situation would be the same.

Now, we shall assume that word monitoring in sentences requires two processing steps: first, lexical access; then checking the word against the monitoring specification – does it have the right sound, or the right meaning? Clearly, making a rhyme check does not require access to meaning, but making a category check does. Because of this, both serial and parallel models would predict that rhyme monitoring should be unaffected by whether the word appears in a random word string, where meaning interpretation is not possible for the word context, as in sentences. The two sorts of model diverge, however, in respect of predictions about category monitoring: if the first stage of a serial model is a strictly word-collecting device, with no parsing capacity, then no difference should emerge between random and syntactically structured sequences of words, but if a parallel, on-line interactive model is operative, then category monitoring is predicted to be facilitated in the context of a word string where there is syntactic and semantic structure. This facilitation effect is what an earlier study, Marslen-Wilson and Tyler (1975), claimed to find. However, while this finding appears to rule out a strict serial model, in which the first-stage device does not 'know' the difference between random and syntactic strings, it does not touch so directly on the prediction of a modified serial model of the sort proposed by Carroll, Tanenhaus and Bever (1978). What Marslen-Wilson, Tyler and Seidenberg (1978) sought to do was to bring this sort of evidence to bear on the modified clausal processing hypothesis that Carroll, Tanenhaus and Bever proposed.

According to such a serial approach, category monitoring should be easier in sentence (38a) above, where the target is located late on in the first clause/ FCU to be processed, than in (38b), where it occurs early on in the last. This is because *some* constructional analysis has been made of the first clause by the time *trout* is encountered within it, and the processing unit is about to go to the second-stage device for further processing, which will reveal the properties of the target that the task demands. By contrast, in the second sentence, *no* structural analysis is available for *trout* until the operation of the first stage has progressed to the point where it can hand over to the second stage. But, as far as rhyme monitoring is concerned, the relevant information is contained in the specification of the word form alone so that performance should not be affected by this difference in the position of *trout* in relation to the clause (or FCU) boundary.

However, an on-line interactive model is able to make syntactic and semantic judgements, word by word, on the basis of the information gathered so far about the input sequence: thus it would appear that it predicts no effect of target-word location *vis-à-vis* the boundary between first clause and second clause, for either rhyme or category monitoring. We shall go further in a moment, but we may set out the predictions of the two models thus far as in table 6.1. For sentences like those given above, the results were as set out in table 6.2.

Table 6.1 *Serial and parallel model predictions for the target-monitoring tasks*

Model	Prediction			
Serial (FCU) model	Target located in			
	First clause		Second clause	
Monitoring for	early	late	early	late
Rhyme		no difference		
Category	slow	fast	slow	fast
Parallel (on-line) model	Target located in			
	First clause		Second clause	
Monitoring for				
Rhyme			no difference	
Category			no difference	

Based on discussion in Marslen-Wilson, Tyler and Seidenberg 1978: 228.

Table 6.2 *Mean response latencies for the monitoring tasks*

Task	Mean response latencies (msec.)	
	Target located in	
Monitoring for	First clause	Second clause
Rhyme	419	482
Category	399	481
Mean	409	481

From Marslen-Wilson, Tyler and Seidenberg 1978: table 7.1, p. 231.

There are two observations to be made here. The first is that the lack of any difference in monitoring-reaction times as between rhyme vs category monitoring is just what the parallel model would expect and the serial model would not: semantic and phonological information appear to become available together. But the second observation is more problematic for the parallel model: there appears to be an effect of location *vis-à-vis* the clause boundary, with the second-clause target being slower to respond to. Actually, this does not quite suit the serial model either, since it would expect such an effect for category monitoring only, whereas it is observed to occur equally for both types of monitoring. What might constitute the basis for this unexpected increase in the rhyme performance in the second clause? And how might the parallel model account for the corresponding increase in category monitoring also? To find the answer to both these questions, Marslen-Wilson, Tyler and Seidenberg make an appeal to what they call 'informational structure'.

Informational structure

Consider what happens, on line, beyond the first four words of the examples in (38) above. In (38b), where the fifth word *cooks* is final in the first clause, we shall say that it fits certain structural expectations set up on the basis of the analysis thus far – it is a main verb, marked by -*s* for concord with the subject NP *Mary*, and so on. It also bears the prosodic contour, *cŏoks*, which fits a structural expectation set up by the first word, *although*, that a subordinate clause boundary will be encountered before the end of the sentence. By contrast, in (38a), *cooks* only fits the first type of these expectations, and it is *trout*, prosodically *trŏut*, that fits the second.

These considerations illustrate the *interactive* nature of parallel processing: analyses at different levels are performed separately on the same input sequence, and may affect each other. Marslen-Wilson, Tyler and Seidenberg discuss other examples, showing what they call 'informational relationships *between* clauses'. Consider, for example, the following:

(39) (a) *Because he didn't like it*, John threw the book away
      (b) John threw the book away *because he didn't like it*.

Here, the identical italicised portions must be processed rather differently by an on-line model, since *he* can instantly be integrated with an already analysed *John* in (39b), but not in (39a). Such differences, which are quite independent of clause-internal syntax, arise from, and help to highlight, between-clause syntax. Hence, processing below clause level will interact in some respects with processing above clause level, which is taken to be a part of informational structure.

The implication of these considerations is as follows: an on-line model cannot expect target-word location to have no effect at all on sentence processing in situations where such interactions are taking place. Specifically, an on-line *interactive* model, as far as our original examples are concerned, will predict that in (38) *trout* in the first position of the (second) clause will yield rather longer response latencies than *trout* in the final position of the (first) clause, by virtue of the fact that it is relatively unconstrained by the preceding context. Further, it is suggested that both the rhyme- and the category-monitoring tasks should be affected by this factor, since, in an interactive system, preceding context can facilitate, or fail to facilitate, word-form access as well as meaning-representations. Thus, we should revise our predictions (those for

Table 6.3 *Revised predictions for the target-monitoring tasks*

Model	Predictions			
Serial (FCU) model	Target located in			
	First clause		Second clause	
Monitoring for	early	late	early	late
Rhyme			no difference	
Category	slow	fast	slow	fast
Parellel (on-line) model	Target located in			
	First clause		Second clause	
Monitoring for	early	late	early	late
Rhyme	slow	fast	slow	fast
Category	slow	fast	slow	fast

Based on discussion in Marslen-Wilson, Tyler and Seidenberg 1978: 229.

the serial model remaining unaltered, but repeated here for convenience), as in table 6.3.

Thus, taking informational structure into account (rather than clause structure, or FCU structure), the parallel model predicts, crucially, that performance on the *rhyme*-monitoring task will not be impervious to target-word location effects, and will show the same sort of effects as are found on the category-monitoring task.

But what about the effect of differing sorts of informational structure across a clause boundary? Marslen-Wilson, Tyler and Seidenberg argue that the *trout* example-type (38) represents a situation where the two clauses are relatively complete and independent of each other. There is nothing like the antecedent- and anaphoric-pronoun relationship that holds between *John* and *he* here. But a less informationally complete first clause, within the same sort of structure as our original examples, would be found in (40):

(40) (a) Even though they are quite small *cats*, they need a lot of living space
      (b) Even though they are quite small, *cats* need a lot of living space

In this sort of case, the on-line model would predict that the apparent 'clause boundary' effect should be damped, since it is not clause boundaries as such, but processing links with preceding context, that determine how readily elements can be integrated in the overall analysis. The clausal-processing model, viewing the clause boundary as the crucial factor, would not make this prediction. Again the on-line model (but not the clausal) would predict the same pattern of findings for both monitoring tasks. The results appear in table 6.4.

Table 6.4 *Mean response latencies for the monitoring tasks, new data*

Task	Mean response latencies (msec.)	
	First clause	Second clause
Monitoring for	last word	first word
Rhyme	436	439
Category	437	451
Mean	437	445

From Marslen-Wilson, Tyler and Seidenberg 1978: table 7.1, p. 231.

There is, obviously, much more even performance here, around midway between the fast and slow response latencies with the original sentence type. This supports the on-line model's prediction that the two tasks will show comparable performance, and that there will be 'a reduction in clause-boundary demarcation effects when the first clause ... is dependent on the second clause for its full interpretation' (Marslen-Wilson, Tyler and Seidenberg 1978: 229).

However, as Marslen-Wilson, Tyler and Seidenberg point out, it is not immediately clear what the nature of this dependence is, nor how it varies with different instances of informational incompleteness. Their own interpretation is that it is essentially a non-syntactic matter, and they go on to sketch out quite a strong view against the role of syntax in sentence processing:

> it is not clear ... what function a syntactic level of representation would serve in a truly interactive parallel processing system. If a distinct syntactic level is being computed, then the data show that it would run concurrently with a level of semantic interpretation with which it would be in continuous interaction. But if the listener can draw simultaneously on both syntactic and semantic knowledge to construct two such closely interdependent processing representations, then these two representations would hardly be functionally distinguishable, and the separation between them appears to serve no obvious purpose for the processing system. (1978: 242)

However, some further work within this general approach suggests a modification of this view, as we shall now see.

6.3.3 *The temporal structure of spoken-language understanding*

A further study, Marslen-Wilson and Tyler (1980), provides the title for this section, and addresses the issue of syntax vs semantics, as well as lexical access in relation to constructional interpretation. In this study subjects were asked to monitor for a target word that was located in the second member of a pair of sentences, the first providing for prior context, as in:

(41) (a) The church was broken into last night
(b) Some thieves stole most of the *lead* off the roof

where the target word, *lead*, is italicised.

The following variables were introduced into this task:

1. Monitoring type; this was split into three:

   (a) identical word monitoring: subjects were, e.g., told to monitor for *lead*;
   (b) rhyme monitoring: subjects were told to monitor, e.g., for a word that rhymes with *bread*;
   (c) category monitoring: subjects were told to monitor for, e.g., a word that is *a kind of metal*.

By this means, it was possible to establish a base-line response latency, for the identical word task, against which the rhyme and category latencies might be compared.

2. The target word location was varied between nine positions within the second sentence, from the second word onwards. Example (41b) above shows *lead* in position 6. The preceding, context, sentence is particularly important in providing for prior context even where the target-word locations is early in the second sentence of the pair.

3. The nature of the context was split into three types:

   (a) normal, as illustrated above;
   (b) syntactic prose: this term refers to word sequences that are syntactically legal, but semantically ill-formed, e.g.:

   (42) (a) The power was located into great water
   (b) No buns puzzle some in the *lead* off the text

   (c) random: where no syntactic cooccurrence constraints are observed, as in:

   (43) (a) Into was power the great located
   (b) Some the no puzzle buns in *lead* text the off

The point of this variable was to separate the effects of syntactic and semantic structure.

The predictions, according to serial and parallel models, can be stated as follows. For the serial model, word recognition is based solely on acoustic–phonetic input (plus frequency ordering in the search bins), so no effect of context or position should occur, within a processing domain; since rhyme and category monitoring both involve search plus match, they should be slower than identity monitoring (involving search only); and since rhyme monitoring is carried out only on the basis of acoustic–phonetic properties, which become available a stage earlier than semantic properties, rhyme monitoring should be faster than category, yielding a predicted order of (fast) identity < rhyme < category (slow), across all other factors.

For the parallel model, word recognition is based from the start on acoustic–phonetic input plus whatever syntactic–semantic information becomes available; the lead-in sentence provides background context, in which normal prose will facilitate most, and random prose least; later position in the sentence will also facilitate, by allowing for further contextual effects; in normal prose, all types of monitoring will use all types of information, so only identity monitoring should be faster (involving word recognition without subsequent matching) than both rhyme and category monitoring, yielding the order: (fast) identity < rhyme = category; in syntactic prose and random, category monitoring should be slowed, since there is no semantic information from context, yielding the order: identity < rhyme < category.

The main results may be briefly summarised here. Taking just task and context variables for the moment (i.e. ignoring position), mean response latencies (in msec.) were as in table 6.5. This shows an expected overall ordering of identity-, rhyme- and category-monitoring times; and corresponding values for the rhyme and category tasks just in the normal prose context, as predicted by the parallel model. It also reveals a difference between normal- vs syntactic-prose contexts, with the normal showing faster response times, as expected in the parallel model, by virtue of the fact that in this model semantic information (the distinguishing factor between syntactic prose and normal) can be used from the start, where it is available. Finally, there is a smaller but observable effect of syntactic form, as observed in the faster times for syntactic prose over random; this is predicted in the parallel model, *if* syntactic and semantic information are distinct and separable levels of information in processing.

These two effects, of semantic information and syntactic information, also turn up in the data on the variable of target-word location in the sentence. Mean response times decrease steadily from the earlier to the later positions for normal-prose contexts, and for all three monitoring tasks. This reflects the steady increase of contextual information, as it becomes available during the processing of the sentence, as predicted in the parallel model.

The semantic-information effect shows up in the data from syntactic-prose

Table 6.5 *Mean response latencies for the monitoring tasks: data from two sentences*

Context	Mean response latencies (msec.), by task			
	Identity	Rhyme	Category	All
Normal	273	419	428	373
Syntactic	331	463	528	441
Random	358	492	578	476
All	321	458	511	

From Marslen-Wilson and Tyler 1980: fig. 1, p. 20.

contexts, where this decrease in response times with later word location is observed for only the identity- and rhyme-monitoring tasks, and not the category monitoring. This derives from the fact that in syntactic prose, information about *form* is used, but semantic information is lacking.

Finally, the syntactic-information effect is found in the difference between the syntactic-prose and random contexts; these are not identical as far as the word-location variable is concerned, since there is no effect of word location in random prose, while syntactic prose shows decreasing response times with later word location in the sentence for both identity and rhyme matching; it does not show this decrease in category monitoring, however, suggesting that syntactic information is not being used directly in this task.

Marslen-Wilson and Tyler conclude that:

> First, there is clearly a sense in which 'words' have a psychological reality ... We group together here not only words as phonological objects, but also as clusters of syntactic and semantic attributes. It is clear from the kinds of interactions that take place during word-recognition that all these aspects of the internal representation of words must be very closely linked.
>
> Secondly, the present data provide good evidence for the psychological reality in processing of a form of 'non-semantic' structural analysis. (1980: 60)

They then go on to say that they find no evidence in their data for a distinction between 'semantic' vs 'interpretative' knowledge sources: they see instead one meaning-based knowledge source, and label it 'interpretative', yielding a system that has the following three knowledge sources: *lexical, structural* and *interpretative*. Of these, we have covered the first two in some detail, and the last remains to be considered (in section 6.4, below). First, however, we shall

consider a much-discussed type of formalism for the sort of parallel processing that we have looked at here, namely *transition networks* for syntax.

6.3.4 *Transition networks in syntax*

It will be useful at this point to consider a formalism that would
allow for the point-by-point building of structure, in relation to sequential
input, as the on-line interactive model requires. One of the earliest
approaches, and one of the most influential within psycholinguistics, has been
based on a family of systems developed within computational linguistics, and
known as *transition networks*. While these turn out to have some serious
inadequacies as plausible models of the MG, they serve to highlight some important issues that we need to raise. We shall consider why they are unsatisfactory, and briefly indicate the nature of some current formalisms, at the end
of this section.

We have already encountered the concept of 'transition network', in discussing word-recognition models (ch. 5, section 5.2.5). If we assume that a
recognition device exists that can cope with simple and complex word forms,
and can identify stems and affixes within the latter, we may approach the task
of accounting for the processing of multi-word constructions by considering a
transition network that scans the input sequence in terms of the elements
(words, stems, affixes) that are stored in the lexicon, and reaches conclusions
about the constructional properties of the sequence on this basis. This is a type
of parsing device which, unlike those we considered earlier (sections 6.2.2,
6.2.3 above), does not have a distinction between two stages of operation.

A basic transition-network system for syntax is considered in Chomsky
(1957), and is illustrated by the very simple layout in figure 6.6. Here, we
assume for simplicity that the scanned elements are whole words. Calling this
network a 'state diagram' (since it contains a number of processing states),
and describing it from the point of view of the speaker rather than the listener,
Chomsky describes its operation as in figure 6.6.

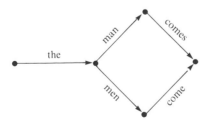

Figure 6.6 A simple transition network. (From Chomsky 1957: example (7),
p. 19.)

> Given a state diagram [as illustrated here], we produce a sentence by
> tracing a path from the initial point on the left to the final point on the
> right, always proceeding in the direction of the arrows. Having reached a
> certain point in the diagram, we can proceed along any path leading from
> this point ... Each node in such a diagram thus corresponds to a state of
> the machine ... In producing a sentence, the speaker begins in the initial
> state, produces the first word of the sentence, thereby switching into a
> second state which limits the choice of the second word, etc. Each state
> through which he passes represents grammatical relations that limit the
> choice of the next word at this point of the utterance. (1957: 20)

We should point out at once that nothing hangs on the choice of the speaker
viewpoint in this passage: such devices are particularly suitable for running in
either production or reception mode, and we can replace phrases such as 'the
speaker produces' with 'the listener perceives or constructs', with no difficulty
at all.

Recursive transition networks

One of the points of Chomsky's discussion, of course, is that the
limits on such a device are too great to make it applicable to natural language
processing. It is a simple kind of finite-state device that cannot cope with the
feature of recursion, for instance. It is possible to add closed loops to the
network, however, as in figure 6.7 (again from Chomsky 1957). This is now a
recursive transition network (RTN), allowing in principle for non-finite
output (*the man comes, the old man comes, the old old ... man comes*, etc.) from
a finite-state network. But, in spite of the increased power of such a device,
Chomsky argued that it is '*impossible*, not just difficult, to construct a device
of [this] type ... which will produce all and only the grammatical sentences of
English' (1957: 21–5). This is true of RTNs, and they are just as inadequate for
modelling the listener as they are the speaker. Chomsky went on to consider
phrase-structure grammars for the representation of natural languages, and

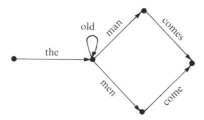

Figure 6.7 A simple recursive transition network (RTN). (From Chomsky
1957: example (8), p. 19.)

eventually concluded that these required supplementation by *transformational rules* for this purpose. Within this grammatical tradition a number of researchers approached the issue of modelling human parsing abilities by supposing that these could be visualised as strategies for relating a sequence of words in the language to a *surface-structure phrase marker*, and thence, by known properties of transformational rules, to a *deep-structure phrase marker*; it was further envisaged, within this approach, that the deep-structure configuration was intimately linked to the meaning of the word sequence. It was within this approach that Kimball (1973) reviewed the proposals that had been made, and established his own set of principles of surface-structure parsing in natural language (see above, section 6.1.3), and the work of Berwick and Weinberg (1984), though it differs, as we have noted (section 6.2.3 above), in some fundamental ways from Kimball's, may be seen as continuing the tradition of a parsing procedure that is closely allied to transformational generative grammar.

Augmented transition networks

But work in transition-network formalisms by a number of researchers whose immediate goals had more in common with *artificial intelligence* than with linguistic description (Conway 1963; Thorne, Bratley and Dewar 1968; Bobrow and Fraser 1969; Woods 1970) led to further types of transition-network devices that overcome the inherent limitations of RTNs. These are the so-called *augmented* transition-network (ATN) systems that have stimulated considerable interest in psycholinguistics for more than a decade (Kaplan 1972, 1973; Woods 1973; Stevens and Rumelhart 1975; Wanner and Maratsos 1978; Wanner 1980). Basically, what is special about the ATN class of systems is that (a) it has *conditions* attached to its operations, and (b) these operations are extended by the addition of certain *actions*. In order to illustrate these properties, we may refer to the proposals in Wanner and Maratsos (1978).

Principles of ATN operation

If we start from the type of RTN discussed in Chomsky (1957), we can recognise that an obvious increase in processing capacity can be achieved by having the model operate in terms of *form classes* (e.g. article, noun, preposition, etc.) instead of *words*. This, in turn, requires a lexicon where individual words can be stored and accessed together with their form-class properties. At once, we are now dealing with whole classes of (lexically diversified) sentences where before we were limited to particular sentences. Figure 6.8 provides an illustration of a class-based RTN. This will allow us to handle not

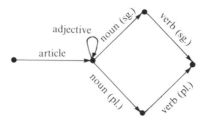

Figure 6.8 A word-class RTN

only *the man comes*, etc., but also *the apple drops*, and a whole range of lexically specified constructions. This feature is common also to all the ATN systems that we would be interested in. As far as ATNs are concerned, Wanner and Maratsos make the following additional points:

1. ATNs are flexible: within a general ATN formalism or notation, different types of grammatical capacity can be built in and compared.

2. ATNs are sensitive, providing for variation in the exhaustiveness of syntactic analysis during sentence processing:

> The system is capable, in principle, of performing a complete syntactic analysis of any sentence, providing information about the contextually appropriate syntactic categorisation of each word, a proper bracketing of each phrase and clause and specification of the grammatical function of every word, phrase and clause. These functional specifications are rich enough to provide at least as much semantically relevant grammatical information as Chomskian deep structures (Chomsky 1965). However, unlike earlier models of comprehension, which performed complete syntactic analyses, an ATN can make intermediate results available for semantic analysis in a natural way. (1978: 120–1)

3. ATNs work directly from the input: they build functional information (such as 'subject of', 'object of') as well as processing syntactic form, providing a natural formalism for linking structural sequences such as … *noun* … *verb* … *noun* to functional schemas such as *actor – action – patient*.

4. ATNs are suitably powerful: they have the power of transformational grammars (Woods 1970), but they do not make use of a transformational component intervening between the 'surface' (input) structure and the interpreted output.

5. They have processing characteristics that appear to lend themselves to the application to human language processing, viz.:

(a) Sequential operation: Wanner and Maratsos actually use the term 'serial', but in the sense that we have reserved for 'sequential' acceptance of the input. The mode of operation of ATNs is properly to be described as parallel processing.

(b) Active processing: in principle, the input sequence may be structured in more than one way by the listener. In other words, the analysis is not wholly driven by the specific linguistic signal: 'The listener can use his knowledge of linguistic structure and his appreciation of surrounding sentence context to impose a phrase-structure analysis on the input sentence. An ATN can do the same, and in doing so it provides an explicit characterisation of how linguistic and contextual knowledge are employed' (1978: 122).

(c) Organisation of procedures: ATNs allow for the decomposition of sentence processing into subprocesses that can be made to reflect the linguistic organisation of sentences (linguistic units and levels of structure). They basically consist of a *processor*, which compares the input with the stored patterns which make up the transition network, and the *transition network* itself. This network can be partitioned into *clause* and *phrase* networks which are separate from each other in that no transition path or *arc* connects them. But the processor can be instructed to shift from a point in the clause network to a phrase network, and back again, by certain *conditions* that are built into the networks. These conditions form part of the 'augmented' capacity of ATNs. Wanner and Maratsos label these conditions, or instructions, SEEK (instructing the processor to suspend operations on the clause network and 'seek' out a suitable phrase network) and SEND (instructing the processor to leave a processed phrasal subnetwork, and to carry the results of this processing back to the main network). As it goes, the processor can also be instructed to assign functional labels to the structures it is building: 'this noun phrase (the result of a subnetwork traverse) is SUBJECT (in the main network)', for example. This ability forms part of the *actions* that further characterise the augmented nature of ATN capacity.

ATN illustration

Let us now consider some network fragments of the sort that Wanner and Maratsos envisage, to see how an ATN would handle a construction taken from our passage where B is talking about the company director football fan. Wanner and Maratsos' networks have arcs that are labelled with the following types of information:

> SEEK, and SEND, as just discussed, transfer processing from clause networks to phrase networks, and back again;

Clause

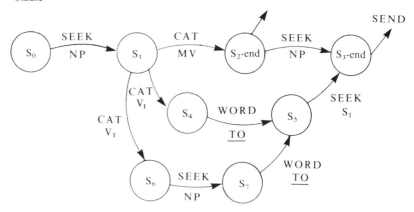

Noun Phrase

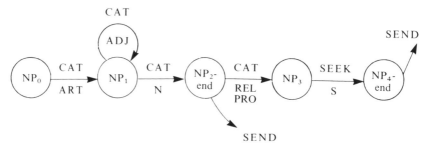

Figure 6.9 Sample transition networks. (Based on Wanner and Maratsos 1978: fig. 3.4, p. 150.)

CAT, for 'category', where the arc is associated with an input element that belongs to a recognised grammatical category such as Noun, Article, etc.;

WORD, for those input elements that are specified as particular word forms, e.g. the form *to* in verb structures such as *want to go*.

The relevant networks are set out in figure 6.9. Starting from the initial state S_0 in the clausal network, the processor can only move to S_1, and this transition or arc is associated with the instruction to transfer the processing at once to the noun-phrase network (SEEK NP).

Accordingly, the clausal analysis marks time at S_1, while the phrasal analysis is initiated by a transition from NP_0. In other words, this fragment of

English network structure is good for processing sentences that begin with a noun phrase of some sort. As soon as the input sequence starts, then, the ATN attempts this transition, while scanning the first word, *he*. Note that this assumes that the input has some way of extracting *he* from *he's*, or from *he's a*, etc.; we shall regard this as the function of the lexicon in the initial processing of the speech signal. We can represent this state of affairs as follows:

(44)　　*Input word　Processing　Analysis*
　　　　　he　　　　　$S_0 \rightarrow S_1$　　　$[_{c/decl}$

Here, the analysis indicates the start of a clause (shown by the opening of a square bracket labelled 'c'); but it is also possible for the system to recognise this clause as belonging to a particular functional type, namely 'declarative', since it does not begin with an auxiliary or copular verb (*is he . . . ?*) nor a question word (*who is he . . . ?*), nor a full verb (*sit . . .*), which would allow the system to label the clause as 'interrogative' or 'imperative'. The functional information is represented in the analysis as a slash-demarcated symbol, in this instance 'decl' for declarative. The results of the $S_0 \rightarrow S_1$ arc also include the following:

(45)　　*Input　Processing　Analysis*
　　　　he　　NP$_0$　　　$[_{c/decl}[_{np/subj}$

which represents the fact that a noun-phrase constituent has been opened ($[_{np}$), functioning as subject ($_{/subj}$).

The presence of the first word of the input also drives the analysis a further step, however; it is recognised (via the lexical-access system) as a pronoun ($[_{pro} he]$), along arc $NP_0 \rightarrow NP_2$ (not shown in fig. 6.9):

(46)　　*Input　Processing　Analysis*
　　　　he　　$NP_0 \rightarrow NP_2$　　$[_{c/decl}[_{np/subj}[_{pro}he]$

But this step takes the processor to an end state in the NP network, associated with the instruction SEND; this returns the processor to where it left the clause network, at S_1, with a closed NP constituent as the fruits of its analysis thus far:

(47)　　*Input　Processing　Analysis*
　　　　he　　NP_2 SEND: S_1　$[_{c/decl}[_{np/subj}[_{pro}he]]$

From S_1, it is in a position to scan the next element in the input, *'s*:

(48)　　*Input　Processing　Analysis*
　　　　's　　$S_1 \rightarrow S_2$　　$[_{c/decl}[_{np/subj}[_{pro}he]][_{vp}[_{mv}$'s$]$

Notice that here we have the category main verb recognised in this transition, but that we have also built in the opening of a verb-phrase constituent ($[_{vp}$). This is a type of 'structure-building' operation that is also possible in such systems, where a sequence of particular categories may carry structural implications in the language (in this case, the structural implication is that a verb element following a closed subject NP constituent is the first element of a VP constituent). (One may wonder whether it would not be better to have a SEEK VP instruction associated with the arc $S_1 \rightarrow S_2$, so that processing may be transferred to a subnetwork that would be able to handle not just main verbs but also constructions of auxiliary and catenative verb types, as well as verb-particle constructions; but we shall not pursue this here.)

S_2 has two exits, SEND and an arc to S_3; SEND provides the option to end the clause processing at this point (and transfer the results to further, semantic-level processing), if there is no further element in the clause sequence. But there is, in this case; it is the word *a*, the first element of a postverbal noun phrase. The ATN system attempts to handle this in terms of the alternative exit, to S_3. This arc is associated with an instruction to SEEK NP, so the processing is transferred to the NP_0 state of the noun-phrase subnetwork; and the grammatical properties that are accessed in the lexicon for *a* identify it as a member of the category *article*, thus permitting the transition to be made from NP_0 to NP_1. These steps may be summarised as follows:

(49) (a) *Input*   *Processing*   *Analysis*

       a $S_2 \rightarrow S_3$ clause continues, with a postcopula noun phrase

    (b) a NP_0 $[_{c/decl}[_{np/subj}[_{pro}he]] [_{vp}[_{mv}'s][_{np/compl}$

    (c) a $NP_0 \rightarrow NP_1$ $[_{c/decl}[_{np/subj}[_{pro}he]] [_{vp}[_{mv}'s][_{np/compl}[_{art}a]$

The next word is *director*, which satisfies the next arc from NP_1 to NP_2; this is a possible end point for the noun phrase, but there are two further possibilities, depending on what the next word in the sequence is. One is a relative-clause continuation, which would be attempted if the next word was a relative pronoun such as *who*; the other is a postmodifying prepositional phrase, signalled by a preposition occurring after *director*. This is itself followed by a noun phrase, so, rather than build a duplicate noun phrase network at this point, the preposition-based continuation takes the form of an arc which transfers the processing back to NP_0:

(50)   *Input*   director

       Processing $NP_1 \rightarrow NP_2$

       Analysis $[_{c/decl}[_{np/subj}[_{pro}he]] [_{vp}[_{mv}'s][_{np/compl}[_{art}a][_{n}director]$

(51) *Input*   of
      Processing $NP_2 \to NP_0$
      Analysis $[_{c/decl}[_{np/subj}[_{pro}he]]$ $[_{vp}[_{mv}$'s$][_{np/compl}[_{art}a][_{n}director]$
                     $[_{pp}[_{p}of][_{np}$

The next sequence of words, *a big company*, drives the processing through arcs NP_0 to NP_1 to NP_2 again, with the additional feature of the adjectival arc which 'loops' the processing from NP_1 to NP_1 on the way:

(52) *Input*   a
      Processing $NP_0 \to NP_1$
      Analysis $[_{c/decl}[_{np/subj}[_{pro}he]][_{vp}[_{mv}$'s$][_{np/compl}[_{art}a][_{n}director]$
                     $[_{pp}[_{p}of][_{np}[_{art}a]$

(53) *Input*   big
      Processing $NP_1 \to NP_1$
      Analysis $[_{c/decl}[_{np/subj}[_{pro}he]][_{vp}[_{mv}$'s$][_{np/compl}[_{art}a][_{n}director]$
                     $[_{pp}[_{p}of][_{np}[_{art}a][_{adj}big]$

(54) *Input*   company
      Processing $NP_1 \to NP_2$
      Analysis $[_{c/decl}[_{np/subj}[_{pro}he]][_{vp}[_{mv}$'s$][_{np/compl}[_{art}a][_{n}director]$
                     $[_{pp}[_{p}of][_{np}[_{art}a][_{adj}big][_{n}company]$

At this point a further prepositional element, *in*, is encountered in the sequence, again taking the processing back to NP_0. It is followed in turn by a proper noun, *Birmingham*, which satisfies the arc to NP_2, which represents the fact that a proper noun constitutes one type of whole noun phrase:

(55) *Input*   in
      Processing $NP_2 \to NP_0$
      Analysis $[_{c/decl}[_{np/subj}[_{pro}he]][_{vp}[_{mv}$'s$][_{np/compl}[_{art}a][_{n}director]$
                     $[_{pp}[_{p}of][_{np}[_{art}a][_{adj}big][_{n}company]$ $[_{pp}[_{p}in][_{np}$

(56) *Input*   Birmingham
      Processing $NP_0 \to NP_2$
      Analysis $[_{c/decl}[_{np/subj}[_{pro}he]][_{vp}[_{mv}$'s$][_{np/compl}[_{art}a][_{n}director]$
                     $[_{pp}[_{p}of][_{np}[_{art}a][_{adj}big][_{n}company]$
                     $[_{pp}[_{p}in][_{np}[_{nprop}Birmingham]$

Now the processing is back again at NP_2, and the system provides for the possibility that the noun phrase may end here. Let us suppose that it does, and that the whole utterance ends here. What would we require our parsing system to do?

Starting with the most recently opened constituent, the NP *Birmingham*, we would want this to be closed, as $[_{np}[_{nprop}$Birmingham$]]$; next, the PP *in Birmingham*, we would also want to be closed, thus:

(57) $[_{pp}[_{p}$in$][_{np}[_{nprop}$Birmingham$]]]$

After this, the NP *a big company in Birmingham*, and the PP *of a big company in Birmingham*, would likewise need to be closed, thus:

(58) $[_{pp}[_{p}$of$][_{np}[_{art}$a$][_{adj}$big$][_{n}$company$][_{pp}[_{p}$in$][_{np}[_{nprop}$Birmingham$]]]]]]$

Finally, we should need to close the whole NP constituent *a director of a big company in Birmingham*, as follows:

(59) $[_{np/compl}[_{art}$a$][_{n}$director$][_{pp}[_{p}$of$][_{np}[_{art}$a$][_{adj}$big$]$
$[_{n}$company$][_{pp}[_{p}$in$][_{np}[_{nprop}$Birmingham$]]]]]]]$

This would complete the noun-phrase analysis, with the SEND function transferring the processing back to the main, clause network; here, the VP constituent would need to be closed, as would the whole clause, giving:

(60) $[_{c\ decl}[_{np\ subj}[_{pro}he]]$
$[_{vp}[_{mb}$'s$][_{np/compl}[_{art}$a$][_{n}$director$][_{pp}[_{p}$of$][_{np}[_{art}$a$][_{adj}$big$][_{n}$company$]$
$[_{pp}[_{p}$in$][_{np}[_{nprop}$Birmingham$]]]]]]]]$

These closures can be effected by allowing the system to keep track of all constituents that are opened, in the order that they are opened; this is conveniently done by means of a 'pushdown store', a sort of memory that operates on the principle of 'first in, last out'.

This completes our illustration of a transition-network formalism for parsing the between-word structure of the input, and we have seen how this formalism permits the point-by-point building of structural representations in a way that is quite distinct from the other, two-stage parsing systems that we have considered. As an illustration, it has its limitations. Among these are the fact that, by choosing this example, which has right-branching structure, we have avoided the problem of how to effect other sorts of attachment, as discussed in section 6.1.3 above (see further below). Another is that we have assumed the relevance of *syntax* in the parsing process. We shall go further into the latter issue in the next section. First, however, we should consider some of the perceived limitations of ATNs as models of the human parsing system.

Limitation of ATNs

We should stress that, in the course of our example, the word-by-word parsing approach throws up a number of decision points, which we have ignored till now. Thus, at:

(61)   he's ...

the *'s* element might be an auxiliary verb, as in:

(62)   he's been to ... ,

instead of the main verb. And at the point:

(63)   he's a director of ...

we might have to close the NP at the end of *director*, as in the case where, e.g. the *of* initiates a phrasal category such as in this continuation:

(64)   he's a director of sorts ...

Finally, at:

(65)   he's a director of a big company in ...

we might have to close the PP at the end of *company*, if the *in* opens a category such as in the following continuation:

(66)   he's a director of a big company in constant touch with his employees ...

where the *in*-constituent clearly refers to the director rather than the company.

Let us take up an aspect of the last observation first. As we noted above, we have assumed that right association (Kimball 1973)/minimal attachment (Frazier and Fodor 1978) give the desired parse for the sequence *a big company in Birmingham*. But such assumptions are not inherent to ATNs, unless they are specifically built in, as desirable characteristics of their operation. In fact, Wanner (1980) proposes just this, by scheduling all SEND arcs after every other type of arc (right association: 'add as many nodes to the current constituent as possible'), and all CAT arcs and WORD arcs before all SEEK arcs (minimal attachment: 'the parser should never add an additional non-terminal node to the parse tree unless it is forced to by the grammar'). In such ways, ATNs can be specified in order to reflect certain strategies which may be regarded as characteristic of human performance.

More generally of decision points, we can say that, in some cases, they throw up competing analyses which can be settled with the very next word in the input sequence; in other cases, the decision must be postponed. Lashley's example

(67)   rapid *writing/righting* with his uninjured hand saved from loss the contents of the capsized *canoe*

shows a dramatic instance where the postponement of important information is delayed to the end of the utterance. In still other cases, the information required will not be contained within the bounds of the utterance, and the

Figure 6.10 Illustration of a chart structure in parsing. (From Varile 1983: example (17), p. 79.)

utterance, by virtue of this fact, will be said to be ambiguous. The ambiguity may be resolvable by reference to *contextual* information, or it may not. The decision point itself may arise as a result of *lexical* ambiguity, or *structural* ambiguity. Whatever the circumstances, the important question is: what does the parser do? We shall answer this question in terms of an ATN parser here, and return to consider what the human parser might do later.

If an ATN happens to compute a 'dead-end' interpretation first, it must backtrack, keeping a record of what it has just done, and try an alternative interpretation. Unfortunately, the structure to be interpreted on the next attempt will be treated as if it were being encountered for the first time, even though parts of it may be common to both interpretations (e.g. NP and PP structure, in attachment decisions). Johnson (1983) cites the proposal of Woods (1973) to allow for the construction of a table of 'well-formed symbols', even during unsuccessful parses, which can be consulted on reparsing. Johnson notes that this 'involves a trade-off of computation time against storage space and retrieval time for all possible partial constituents which may be unacceptable in some environments' (1983: 70), and refers to an alternative approach, in terms of *chart*-parsing (Kay 1976), which may be used with ATNs as well as other systems. Varile (1983) provides a brief introduction to charts. Essentially, they are ways of representing hierarchical syntactic relationships in terms of a set of ordered and oriented arcs linking a set of nodes, having unique entry and exit points, unique labelling, and no loops (e.g. for Adj). An idea of what this might mean, in terms of our example above, is provided by Varile's illustration of one chart (fig. 6.10) which suffices for representing the sequence *a big company*. The 'NP' is the labelling (on the broken line), to be distinguished from the solid lines representing the arcs between the nodes. Another chart will provide the representation of the PP in the sequence *in Birmingham*. And each of these charts will be embodied in the chart for the NP *a big company in Birmingham*. Varile points out that economy is achieved in this way:

Economy of space in that common subparts of families of strings of trees are represented only once. And economy of computation because rules which involve common parts of families of strings of trees need not be applied as many times as there are members in the family. And also because on back up after failure, well-formed substrings need not be recomputed (as for example in ATNs). (1983: 86)

6.4 Interpretative processes

So far, we have discussed some of the syntactic processing that might take place, in serial and parallel models of comprehension. We have also made reference to further, interpretative, levels of processing, and have noted how in the serial model interpretative processes are set in train once the first stage of preliminary collecting/grouping is over, and that in the parallel model, they start to operate as soon as the first word has been recognised. Our concern in this section is to address some of the interpretative issues more directly. We are now making contact, therefore, with the points raised in section 6.1.2 above.

6.4.1 *Syntax versus semantics*

As our discussion of some of the work in utterance understanding has shown, an issue that has been raised is the extent to which two levels (at least) of processing can be distinguished and justified in understanding the relations between words in multi-word utterances. This is, as may be appreciated, a rather cumbersome way of stating the issue, and the section heading puts it in the more succinct and usual terms: do we need to recognise an independent level of syntax as well as semantics in utterance understanding?

The first point to be made is a general one, relating to the terminology. We shall assume that, by 'syntax', we refer to the grosser constructional properties of utterances, in which sense we may speak, for instance, of utterances having particular realisations of definite noun phrases, tense-, mood- or aspect-marked verb forms, verb-complement structures, and so on, in which these categories are signalled by certain morphemes in construction with each other (e.g. determiners with head nouns, auxiliary verbs with head verbs, and noun phrases, adjectival phrases or adverbial phrases in construction with verbs, etc.). We shall further assume that by 'semantics' we refer to both lexical and constructional aspects of utterance meaning, including the sort of knowledge-based level of representation known as pragmatics (Levinson 1983).

In these terms, one version of the opposition between 'syntax' vs 'semantics' reads like 'constructions' vs 'word meanings'. On this view, an utterance containing the words *dog, eat, biscuit* will bear only one plausible way to construe them, so that the meaning of the utterance is likely (so the argument runs) to be derived by a probabilistic strategy (Bever 1970) based on processing the word meanings alone. The finding that 'reversible' passive constructions are harder to process than 'non-reversibles', such as

(68)· The biscuit was eaten by the dog

and that non-reversible passives are no harder than their active counterparts (Slobin 1966) was an early indication that word meanings, and the real-world knowledge they reflect, were factors to be taken account of in studying utterance understanding. Accordingly, we might envisage 'syntax' as irrelevant to the determination of the message structure of particular utterances.

Another version of the opposition would say that, while surface signals such as word order, grammatical morphemes, etc. are processed, along with word meanings, there is no exhaustive determination of a syntactic derivation prior to message structure being arrived at.

Other versions would draw the distinction between syntax and semantics in other ways, and, for each one there may be debate over whether 'syntax' is involved as an independent level of processing as well as 'semantics'. Given the centrality of transformational grammar models at various stages in the development of modern psycholinguistics, it is not surprising that 'syntax' has frequently been taken to be synonymous with 'transformational operations'. Thus, the debate over 'syntax vs semantics' within psycholinguistic accounts of language comprehension has been understood by many, on each side of the debate, to be essentially concerned with whether or not there is evidence of transformational operations, or related concepts such as transformationally linked levels of description, or constructs such as traces, in the data on human natural language comprehension.

It may be appreciated from this that there has not been a very clear debate of these issues in psycholinguistics: the status of the argument is not helped by cheerful slogans such as 'psycholinguistics without linguistics' (which may be glossed as the study of mental operations in language processing independently of formal linguistic theories), and analogies such as 'if you can read the signposts, you don't need a map' (which must mean something like if you know the word meanings, you don't need to compute the syntactic representation) (both these quotes can be found in Johnson-Laird 1983: 339–41). The old issue of how far 'linguistic' concepts (such as syntax) might be directly involved in psycholinguistic processes (Watt 1970; Fillenbaum 1971) has also been caught up in the debate. And, of course, we should note that the opposition between serial and parallel models may be involved, inasmuch as an autonomous level of syntax, exhaustively computed prior to the derivation of a meaning representation, fits particularly well with the demands of a serial, rather than a parallel, account of processing.

This leaves open, of course, the issue as to how far 'constructional' and 'meaning-related' factors are separately involved in language comprehension: we have seen that Marslen-Wilson and Tyler (1980) use the terms *structural* and *interpretative*, respectively, in these senses, and conclude that they are both involved, although structural effects are smaller (at least, in the tasks their subjects had to perform).

6.4.2 *Conceptual-dependency models*

Within the field of Artificial Intelligence (AI, which we may briefly describe here as the common ground between computing and psychology), some computer-implemented parsers have been developed which work on the 'conceptual-dependency' principle (Schank 1972, 1973, 1975), i.e., where the immediate goal of processing is a *semantic* (in the wider sense) or *interpretative* (in Marslen-Wilson and Tyler's sense) level of representation, and where 'syntax' is said to play no necessary role at all. Such a system is Riesbeck's *English Language Interpreter* (ELI) parser (as described in Riesbeck 1975), and we may conveniently consider its underlying assumptions here.

In considering the fruits of AI research generally, it is necessary to bear in mind that the first requirement is to 'save the appearances', i.e. to establish *what* the computational system can respond to, in relation to a given input. The issue of *how* it does this, and what relation this bears to processes of human understanding, is one that deservedly attracted much discussion within the field (much as has the relation of the LG to the MG within psycholinguistics; see 3.1.2 above). Having said that, however, let us briefly consider the six principles that Riesbeck and Schank (1978) set out for ELI as a 'conceptual analyser'. They are as follows:

1. parsing must be done in context;
2. parsing does not notice ambiguity;
3. parsing uses syntax only when semantically required;
4. parsing is expectation-based;
5. parsing takes multiple word-meanings as ordered with respect to context;
6. parsing is really a memory process.

Principles 1 and 4 coincide with considerations that have already been raised and illustrated at various points in our discussion, and need not detain us further here; but we might wonder whether Riesbeck and Schank materially overstate the case with respect to principle 1, when they say that:

(69)   I just came from New York

is 'wildly ambiguous' when it is placed in contexts such as providing the answer to the following questions:

(70)   (a)   Would you like to go to New York today?
       (b)   Would you like to go to Boston today?
       (c)   Why do you seem so out of place?
       (d)   Why do you look so dirty and bedraggled?
       etc.

While it is true that utterance meanings have to be determined in context, it may also be the case that utterances have meaning in zero context and that, in spite of what Riesbeck and Schank say, this 'zero-context meaning' may be part of the interpretation of the utterance when it is answering questions such as (70a) to (70d).

We should also note that, with prosodic structure in speech, some of the 'ambiguity' of such examples is reduced. Further, it is necessary to distinguish between:

1.   utterances that have vagueness (illustrated in the example above), or indeterminacy;
2.   utterances that have 'n-determinacy', where n is some small number of determinate constructions that can be parsed for an utterance;
3.   utterances that are ambiguous, in which cases the 'n-determinacy' is not resolved by the end of the utterance (see our discussion of the ATN illustration above).

Principle 6 raises a rather different issue. Riesbeck and Schank provide the following example (referring to Hemphill 1975):

(71)   John went to the store for Mother

in which it is claimed to be necessary for the analyser to retain in memory the current location of Mother; if she is in the store, then the interpretation of *for* is something like 'go to get', whereas if she is elsewhere the interpretation is 'on behalf of'.

Riesbeck and Schank ask: 'How can we hope to parse [this utterance] without the ability to ask these questions about Mother's location?' (1978: 254). But part of an answer may be that it is precisely *syntactic* parsing that is possible, while semantically there are two interpretations for the lexical item *for*, which (a) may be resolved, if the information on Mother's location is to hand, or (b) may not be resolved, if it is not.

This takes us on to the principles 2 and 5, which are concerned with *ambiguity*. But first, we should note, with respect to the remaining principle 3, that something like syntactic parsing in lieu of semantic is allowed for in ELI. Riesbeck and Schank say 'For one reason or another, we have often been reported as advocating the abandonment of any syntactic analysis in a parser. This has really never been our position. Rather, we simply believe that syntactic considerations should be done only when they are needed, i.e. after other more highly ranked considerations are used' (1978: 252).

6.4.3 *Ambiguity*

Most of the earlier studies of ambiguity appear to have been motivated in part by the attraction of inquiring into a special phenomenon, to observe how the processing system operates in exceptional circumstances: e.g. MacKay (1966, 1970a); Foss, Bever and Silver (1968); Garrett (1970). Gradually, however, it has come to be appreciated that, as we have seen, decision points and multiple analyses may be of the essence in natural-language processing.

Serial versus parallel processing

Most of the early studies of the processing of ambiguous constructions show clear commitment to fairly extreme serial or parallel processing accounts.

The serial view (e.g. in Foss, Bever and Silver 1968) is that a *decision* is made at the point of ambiguity, and that one interpretation only is proceeded with ... until it is shown (by later context) to have been wrong. According to this account, processing of the input beyond the point of ambiguity should show no complicating effect of the ambiguous item, since the processor has made its unique interpretative decision: the input is, effectively, unambiguous.

By the parallel-processing account (e.g. in Mackay 1970a), however, the processor is loaded with the task of pursuing more than one interpretation, from the point of ambiguity onwards. Therefore, it is predicted to show the complicating effect of ambiguity in processing this part of the input sequence, until some point at which sufficient context has accrued to permit the elimination (Mackay 1970a sees it in terms of 'perceptual suppression') of the unwanted interpretation.

However, the opposition between these two models in respect of ambiguity is not quite as clear-cut as stated here, by virtue of the presence of *bias*. This reflects the degree of strength of one possible interpretation over another, for a given ambiguous sequence. Mackay (1970a) provides for the quantification of bias as an important variable in his experimental design. In terms of this sort of approach, the difference between processing a sequence with two interpretations, where one of them has a 90 per cent bias, and the other a 10 per cent bias, may appear to approximate to the serial position where just one interpretation is pursued.

Thus, *each* of these models can account for the 'garden-path' phenomenon that we referred to earlier (section 6.1.3). But they make different predictions. The serial model predicts no computational difficulty in respect of ambiguity *as long as the appropriate interpretation is chosen*, and considerable computational difficulty *if the inappropriate interpretation is chosen, and the processor eventually has to backtrack and recompute* (this is the garden path). The 'perceptual suppression' model of Mackay predicts that computational difficulty for ambiguity will be directly proportional to the strength of the bias of the interpretation that has to be rejected (or suppressed), so that, the more likely is the *inappropriate* interpretation in some context, the greater will be the computational difficulty *because it is harder to suppress the undesired interpretation* (this is the garden path).

Nevertheless, some important, and testable, predictions remain between the two models, particularly where the appropriate interpretation is the most likely one in context; in this case, the serial model predicts no computational difficulty (because no backtracking is required), while the parallel model predicts some degree of extra processing load, proportional to the probability attached to the inappropriate interpretation (which will have to be suppressed).

So far, so good; but, as Garrett (1970) pointed out in his review of experimental findings, *there appears to be evidence in support of both models*. He proposed to resolve this paradox by observing that experiments supporting the parallel model involve tasks that seem to tap immediate or on-line processing, whereas those that support the serial model appear to call for judgements after the construction has been processed and stored in memory.

This allows for the possibility that what actually happens is that there is an *initial* increase in processing load, as the interpretative system attempts to pursue more than one interpretation, from the point of ambiguity, and that this is then followed by a more-or-less rapid resolution of such a complex state of affairs. In the case of lexical ambiguity, this implies that lexical access is initially productive of all meanings of a word.

A study by Cairns and Kamerman (1975), involving a phoneme-monitoring task, appears to support this view. When the target phoneme was located immediately after a decision point, such as an ambiguous word, reaction times were slower than they were in unambiguous control sentences. But where the target phoneme was located some way 'downstream' of the point of ambiguity, reaction times were found to be of the same order as in the unambiguous controls, even though the intervening words appeared to contribute nothing explicitly to resolve the ambiguity. Onifer and Swinney (1981) used a cross-modal (auditory–visual) task, to get at the same issue. Subjects had to listen to sentences, and, at variable intervals after a decision point, were visually presented with words. When these visual stimuli occurred immediately after an auditory point of decision, subjects responded more quickly to those visual words that related to *either* of the possible interpretations of the sentence than to control (unrelated) words; but after 1.5sec., subjects responded most quickly to just those visual words that corresponded to sententially appropriate readings.

In so far as decision points are thrown up by *structural* properties of utterances, such as decisions regarding attachment of constituents, we may find two views in the field. One holds that we are dealing with a distinct processing phenomenon, reflecting a level of autonomous syntax within a *modular* processing system (Fodor 1983; Ferreira and Clifton 1986). The other view is more compatible with those linguistic accounts that stress the interdependence of lexical with structural factors. Thus, as we have noted in our ATN illustration above, decisions regarding attachment of constituents may depend on their lexical content. The issue for modularity is whether initial processing is carried out in terms of syntax alone. It may be that, from the outset, lexical, structural and contextual factors interact (Crain and Steedman 1985). A strongly interactive system would make decisions on a word-by-word basis, and pay the price in frequent revision; alternatively, a system that avoided all such decisions would have to carry forward a complex set of interpretations until some to-be-determined point.

In response to this sort of problem, the serial-processing account is to separate the stage of *sequence scanning* from that of interpretation, so that interpretation may be constrained by knowledge of the subsequent as well as the earlier portions of the input: in effect, the first stage operates in order to relieve the second stage of the problem of sequentially ordered input.

The response of the parallel model is to have probabilities attached to the alternative interpretations that arise at decision points in the sequence, reflecting the degree of correspondence there is between certain structural patterns and certain interpretations (e.g. there is a high probability that the first NP of a sequence will be the actor, especially if it is animate). Fodor (1985) and Berwick and Weinberg (1985) discuss these problems within a two-stage approach, and Wanner (1980) and Fodor and Frazier (1980) discuss the issues as they relate to two-stage vs single-stage approaches.

6.4.4 *Further issues in interpretation*

Parsing research such as we have reviewed typically deals with issues in the computation of lexical and structural aspects of individual clause-utterances. But this is not all that is involved in language comprehension, as the discussion of Marslen-Wilson, Tyler and Seidenberg (1978) shows (section 6.3.2). Their concept of 'informational structure' involves *prosodic* organisation and *anaphoric* relations: at least these, and possibly other aspects of discourse, need to be taken into account, therefore, in a study of language comprehension. Cutler and Ladd (1983) provide an overview of issues in the measurement of prosodics, and ways in which the data may be modelled. Prosodic organisation does not simply reflect syntactic structure (Gee and Grosjean 1983), but may also be determined by, and cue, pragmatic aspects such as predictability of elements in sequence (Buxton 1983) and new vs given information (Brown 1983). Anaphoric relations likewise reach out from syntactic to discoursal domains, reflecting meaning as well as syntactic constraints. Garrod and Sanford (1985) examined the interpretation of anaphoric expressions in written discourse, by measuring the time taken to detect mis-spellings on verbs which were either consistent or inconsistent with a full contextual interpretation of the prior anaphor. Performance indicated that subjects were interpreting the anaphoric expressions as soon as they were encountered, as long as they referred to main characters in the narrative. Malt (1985), also using written material, looked at degrees of relation between utterance pairs in discourse, and found that subjects were faster to understand anaphoric links cued by verb-phrase ellipsis when the utterance containing the antecedent expression was marked in some way (e.g. a question expecting an answer) as being related to subsequent discourse. This suggests that readers can selectively store on-line information that may help in the immediate interpretation of subsequent anaphoric expressions. Such findings are of interest in suggesting how discoursal relations may be understood. Instead of the 'story-grammar' approach (Mandler and Johnson 1977), which essentially seeks to find in discourse the sort of hierarchical structuring that is characteristic of sentences, we may need to consider a distinct sort of structure, within which plausibility of reference, between antecedent expressions and their lexical and other (pronominal, elliptical) anaphors plays a major role.

We now turn to consider those aspects of interpretation which interface with our existing knowledge systems.

The intentional view

Clark (1978) distinguishes the following views of language comprehension:

1. the 'independence' view by which the literal or direct meaning of a sentence is arrived at by such computational processes as we have reviewed so far, which do not extend to supplying such referential and real-world knowledge as that, for example, *he* in *he's a university lecturer* might refer to the person who has just walked into the room, etc.;

2. the 'constructivist' view, by which 'elaborate mental edifices' are built up for the situation a sentence describes; Clark cites Bransford and Johnson (1973), Bransford and McCarrell (1974), and we might well suspect that mental models (Johnson-Laird 1983) fall within this category also (see section 7.2 of chapter 7);

3. the 'intentional' view:

> one that lies between the independence and constructivist views. In it comprehension is conceived to be the process by which people arrive at the interpretation the speaker *intended* them to grasp for that utterance in that context (see Grice, 1975; Schiffer, 1972; Bennett, 1976). Unlike the independence view, this view requires listeners to draw inferences that go well beyond the literal or direct meaning of a sentence ... But unlike the constructivist view, it limits the inferences to those that listeners judge the speaker intended them to draw. It excludes stray thoughts about mad uncles. In this view the speaker's intentions are critical, but they can ever only be inferred. (Clark 1978: 295–6)

Indirect requests constitute a ready example of how a listener, to be said to have comprehended the speaker adequately, must get behind the literal meaning of, e.g. *it's cold in here, isn't it?*, to an awareness that the speaker's *intention* is that someone, very possibly the listener, should either close the window, or suggest that it would be a good idea for it to be closed. Clark suggested that indirect requests might be processed as follows:

Step 1   compute the direct interpretation;
Step 2   check for possible indirect force;
Step 3a if there is none, go to step 4;
Step 3b if there is such, compute an additional interpretation in terms of the known conditions of the speaker–hearer contract;
Step 4   assume that the final interpretation arrived at is 'the ultimate reason for the utterance'.

Now, if indirect requests are truly indirect in this processing sense – i.e. of involving an extra processing stage (in step 3b) – then this might appear in performance measures such as subjects' reaction times in a task involving the comprehension of such requests. Clark found that subjects took longer to judge indirect requests such as *can you open the door?* and *must you open the door?* 'true' or 'false' of a pictured situation than corresponding direct requests, such as *please open the door*, and *please do not open the door*. He also found that the more time it took to compute the direct meaning of an utterance (step 1), the longer it took, overall, to arrive at the contextually appropriate indirect meaning – consistently with the view that step 1 is a direct component of the processing of indirect requests.

Definite reference is another area where the speaker–listener contract is involved: basically, a definite referring expression, such as *the knife*, can only be used by the speaker when (a) the speaker has a specific referent in mind, and (b) has good reason to expect that the listener can identify it without undue difficulty. Clark suggests that listeners go about this task as follows:

Step 1 compute the description of the intended referent;
Step 2 search memory for an entity that (a) fits this description and (b) satisfies the criterion that the speaker could have expected you to find it; if successful, go to step 4;
Step 3 use the simplest assumption to posit the existence of such an entity under conditions (a) and (b) of step 2; if successful, go to step 4;
Step 4 identify this entity as the intended referent.

By this view, identifying referents should take longer when listeners have to add bridging assumptions. Haviland and Clark (1974) found that it took on average about 200msec. longer for listeners to comprehend the sentence *the beer was warm* in (72b) compared with (72a):

(72) (a) Esther got some beer out of the car. The beer was warm.
      (b) Esther got some picnic supplies out of the car. The beer was warm.

Shorthand expressions are also identified by Clark as a type of expression involving problem solving by the listener (and, of course, contractual good behaviour on the part of the speaker); the expression *three Picassos* might refer to works of art by Picasso, to people named Picasso, people with the characteristics of Picasso, or (ironically, perhaps) to artists striving to achieve their own styles, and so on.

In conclusion, Clark links all these types of computation with a general ability to solve problems:

> to set up goals, search in memory for pertinent information, and decide

when the goals have been reached. Indeed, in inferring what is meant, people consider non-linguistic factors that are far removed from the utterance itself, and their skill at solving this problem is sometimes taxed to the limit. Comprehension is a form of thinking that should not be set off from the rest. (Clark 1978: 320)

More recently, Clark (1983) has argued the case for 'intentional interpretation' further, by referring to a ubiquitous phenomenon which he calls *nonce sense*. An example of this would be found in the well-known type of waiters' parlance *the steak and two veg. in the corner is getting impatient*, where, as Clark argues, a traditional syntactic parser and a traditional lexical-access model (i.e. as described in earlier sections) would simply fail on the noun phrase *the steak and two veg. in the corner*. For instance, such a parser would fail to link *he* in a continuation like *... and he's not too happy with the house wine either*, with the antecedent noun phrase *the steak and two veg. in the corner*. Clark suggests that such nonce-sense expressions are an example of the general type of indirect uses of language. We can set out the intention of the speaker quite straightforwardly, as (73a):

(73) (a) The speaker wants the listener to recognise that he is using 'steak and two veg.' to denote a particular customer who has ordered a meal of that description.

We can also set out the incorporated literal or direct processing step that is involved, as (73c) (we shall come to (73b) in a moment):

(73) (c) The speaker wants the listener to recognise that 'steak and two veg.' is an expression denoting a meal.

But in addition, argues Clark, we must have an intermediate goal in this 'goal hierarchy', as (73b):

(73) (b) The speaker wants the listener to recognise that the description of the person who is getting impatient is one that the listener can identify uniquely without difficulty, on this occasion and in this setting.

The addition of (73b) is essential, Clark argues, for an *intentional parser*, even if we do not understand much more than this about how they can be made to work, and how they create the speaker's intended senses. He concludes that: 'the current conception of parsing needs revision. It ought to be thought of not as the analysis of the sentence uttered, but as the analysis of the speaker's intention in uttering the sentence' (1983: 32–8).

We may therefore seek to bring the speaker into our account of natural language interpretative strategies; but what of the listener?

The case of more than one listener

We may recall, at this point, our participants in the discussion of football. The speaker, for the extract that we have intermittently considered, is participant B; and what we have been reviewing here is a set of arguments for the view that what the listener does is to arrive at an analysis of B's intentions, via not just the specifically linguistic signal and the processing of this, but also the non-linguistic information that is available on all input channels, and general reasoning abilities. The result, according to Clark, is *shared*, or *mutual*, knowledge, as between speaker and listener. But, in our passage, we should not lose sight of the fact that there are *two* listeners, A and C, who, we must assume (e.g. from the evidence of their appropriate interventions from time to time), are each in a state of mutual knowledge with B as the conversation progresses, and *hence with each other*.

Clark and Carlson (1982) have addressed this issue, and argued that it requires a revision of standard speech-act theory. Where there is more than one listener (for some stretch of conversational discourse), these listeners may be addressees rather than participants (as in the case of transgressing pupils in the headteacher's study), participants (as A and C in our passage), or overhearers; and the speaker's intentions with reference to these different types of listeners must be different. Clark and Carlson propose a set of new illocutionary acts, which they call *informatives*, and which they regard as appropriate to the case of a speaker in relation to *participant* listeners. Thus, standard illocutionary acts such as *requests* may be made to more than one listener, simultaneously, if, and only if, the speaker *intends to inform* each listener (i.e. to treat each as a participant). Thus *listeners*, as well as *speakers*, have to be taken into account when considering the nature of speech acts.

Mutual knowledge versus relevance in interpretation

The refinement of the speech-act approach, in this and other ways, is not the only way forward, however, and Sperber and Wilson (1982) present arguments that it is misconceived. They query the processing role of *mutual knowledge*, suggesting that (here we might recall the arguments concerning the status of phonological segments in lexical access, and clause-like units in syntactic processing) it arises as a result of comprehension rather than as a precondition for it. Specifically, they present three main arguments against the mutual-knowledge approach:

1. 'first, the identification of mutual knowledge presents problems which, contrary to the predictions of the mutual knowledge framework, do not give rise to corresponding problems of comprehension';

2. 'secondly, mutual knowledge is not a sufficient condition for belonging to the context: a proposition may be mutually known without being part of the context';
3. 'thirdly, it is not a necessary condition either: a proposition may belong to the context without being mutually known' (1982: 62).

We shall take (1) first. Clark and Marshall (1981) pointed to *physical copresence* of an object, e.g. a candle, on a table at which participants A and B are sitting, staring at each other and the candle between them, as the sort of evidence that people tend to rely on when inferring mutual beliefs: we should say that A and B each may reasonably infer mutual knowledge of the candle, with only such minimal assumptions as that the other is attending to the candle, and is a rational person. Another type of evidence is found, they suggested, in *linguistic copresence*, as when A tells B *I bought a candle today*. A third type is *community membership*, from the most general level (e.g. that both A and B are adult humans), down to quite specific levels (e.g. that they are both members of the same club, know certain people and events in common, etc.). Typically more than one of these types of evidence may be present: in our football conversation, participants A, B and C, while they do not have physical copresence at a football match in common (at the time of speaking and listening), nevertheless would be said to have linguistic and community membership sources of evidence for mutual knowledge.

On this point, we may ask, in the spirit of Sperber and Wilson, how far the knowledge that is called on by the linguistic expression *football today* (from A, at the outset of our extract) may be regarded as mutual as between A, B and C. It might take considerable and detailed investigation to uncover exactly what is held in common by three participants in the matter of 'knowledge about football' (see also our introductory discussion of problems in determining what is understood by different people from one and the same linguistic expression, section 6.1.2 above). The point here is not that this investigation might prove ultimately to be impossible; rather, it is sufficient to suggest that such determination of mutual knowledge is more complex than, and is not required for, the understanding that participants A, B and C have of their conversation.

Concerning (2), we must ask, how it is envisaged that context plays a role in comprehension. Presumably, it involves recovering from memory certain specific items of information, in which case we need some way of constraining this activation of knowledge – or else we should be supposing that our entire knowledge systems, say, of football, company directors, Birmingham, nightclubs, and so on, are involved in understanding a conversation. Mutual knowledge, Sperber and Wilson suggest, is smaller than our total encyclo-paedic memory, but larger than the 'actual context used in comprehension' (1982: 66).

On (3), Sperber and Wilson cite Clark and Marshall's example of partici-pant A saying to B *have you ever seen the movie showing at the Roxie tonight?* Clark and Marshall's point is that, unless A and B's knowledge is *fully* mutual, comprehension may fail. Thus, let us suppose that A knows that a late change in the film programme has occurred, and also knows that B knows about this; but A knows that B does not know that A is aware of it. B is there-fore likely to assume that A's definite expression *the movie showing at the Roxie tonight* refers to the originally scheduled film, whereas in fact this is not the case. This is an example of knowledge that is only shared to some degree, and is likely to yield misunderstanding: hence, it shows that full mutual know-ledge is necessary to comprehension. Of this sort of example, Sperber and Wil-son say: 'We believe that the unnaturalness of these examples is not accidental ... In real life, if any such unnaturally complex situation arose, either the hearer would ask for clarification, or, as likely as not, misunderstanding *would occur*' (1982: 68).

They go on to suggest that real-life language use displays a willingness to risk such less-than-complete mutuality of knowledge, in all sorts of much simpler situations: for instance, when an English speaker in a foreign country goes up to a stranger and asks *do you speak English?* Equally, though less obviously, perhaps, our participant A in the football conversation takes the risk of steering the discussion onto the topic of football even though he may be unsure of the mutuality of B and C's knowledge with his on this matter.

Relevance

Sperber and Wilson then propose that, of Grice's (1975) maxims, it is that of *relevance* which is necessary and sufficient for comprehension in context. In their approach,

1. the listener searches for that interpretation of an utterance which will make the utterance most relevant, in a particular situation;
2. this involves a search for the context which will make this inter-pretation possible;
3. initially, the context consists of the immediately preceding utter-ance; the listener tries to arrive at an interpretation which is con-sistent with implications derivable from this context; if this fails,
4. (a) the listener can widen the context by adding what he remem-bers of utterances further back in the conversation; or

(b) he can recruit encyclopaedic knowledge to flesh out the concepts present in the utterance or the preceding context; or

(c) he can add to the context information that is available through nonlinguistic input channels, e.g. from watching a football match that speaker and listener are spectators at.

Of stage 4 generally, Sperber and Wilson say: 'The hearer does not have to worry at this stage whether the additions he is making to the context belong to the common ground or not' (1982: 76).

They envisage that these additions increase the processing cost. Given this, the speaker tries to avoid putting this burden on the listener, and the listener may assume that the speaker has made this attempt. The speaker must believe that the listener has a good chance of finding the context that will maximise the relevance of what the speaker says. Mutual knowledge may be the basis for this belief, but not always: 'For instance, if someone walks up to you in the street and asks "What time is it?", you assume that the answer you give is relevant to him, that is, that it has a number of contextual implications, without knowing at all what they are and what the context may be' (1982: 77–8).

We may conclude this brief discussion of the debate by noting that the empirical consequences of such theoretically distinct approaches remain to be investigated. It is not yet clear, given our lack of detailed knowledge of comprehension processes, how far different approaches are actually competing or complementary: nor to what extent they can be modelled by the sort of mechanisms that have been proposed for other levels of processing. What does seem clear, however (and part of the difficulty lies in this), is that language understanding ultimately merges with general understanding, however this may be conceived, at some level.

7
Producing utterances

7.1 Introduction

7.1.1 *Preview*

In this chapter we shall see how far the naturally displayed evidence from language production (which we reviewed in ch. 3) can be used to establish components of a model of language production.

In our exposition, we shall start with the model proposed by Garrett (1982): this is a convenient starting point for us because it represents the culmination (thus far) of the error-based model discussed in Garrett's earlier work, but also attempts to pull together insights from the work of Fromkin, also based on error data, and that of Goldman-Eisler and her associates (Goldman-Eisler 1968; Beattie 1980; Butterworth 1980b) on the evidence of hesitation phenomena. In section 7.2 we start looking more closely at the topmost, or 'message-structure' level. In this, we make contact with the meaning-representation issues that we arrived at in the last chapter, in considering comprehension processing. Much of what we have to say about possible mental representation here derives from the work of Johnson-Laird (1983). We return to the matter of lexical access in production, briefly touched on in chapter 5, in section 7.3, and consider the form in which word meanings may be represented in the mental lexicon. Garrett's model recognises two levels of sentence structure, a deeper as well as a more superficial one, and their organising characteristics are investigated in the next section (7.4). Finally, we consider the serial nature of Garrett's model and examine some arguments (Dell and Reich 1981; Stemberger 1985) relating to the possible interactions between levels in such a model (section 7.5) which would lead to a parallel interpretation.

7.1.2 *Assumptions and preliminaries*

The Garrett model is based on a number of considerations and assumptions, as follows.

1. *Computational decomposition reflects the grammatical decomposition of the language faculty.* This is an hypothesis according to which observations such as '*a* is adjusted to *an* after the anticipation error in

(1)   I deserve *an around* of *plause* for that'

370

are held to tell us something fairly directly about the nature of the psycho-linguistic processes involved in speech production. The statement is a 'computational' one, inasmuch as it assumes that one sort of process is dependent on the output of another – a type of 'information-flow' account.

These processes can be thought of as operating at familiar levels of linguistic description, so the hypothesis really involves a fairly direct relationship between these levels (as established by formal, reflective linguistic analysis) and stages of speech production.

As Garrett points out (1982: 21), the hypothesis might prove untenable if the exacting effects of producing (planning and executing) speech under normal time pressures force the language faculty into patterns of behaviour that are radically different from those involved in yielding contemplative linguistic analyses. As we shall see, the linguistic levels that are implicated in current models of production are fairly general ones – message formulation, lexical specification, syntactic configuration and so on – so we can say that the hypothesis is not yet tested in very great detail.

2. *The processes of speech production are independent of, and may interact with, general cognitive and motor-control factors.* This is really the same principle, on a larger scale. We assume that, just as there are, for example, (foreign) language articulatory targets that we cannot normally achieve without training, even though our motor control system is in principle capable of them, so there are certain language-specific grammatical properties that are not simply determined by the ultimate form of the cognitive plan that forms our intention to say something. That is, a foreign-language learner must learn not only speech sounds in the target language, but also specific grammatical properties, which are nevertheless within the general capability of the learner by virtue of their existing faculty (their ability to speak their native language).

This seems a reasonable assumption, notwithstanding the possibility that certain modes of thought, 'ways of viewing the world', may be characteristic of one language community rather than another. This assumption also allows for the possibility that cognitive factors may influence speech processes in ways that may be observed to hold across languages (Gazdar 1980).

3. *Speech errors may be revealing of levels of processing.* This assumption is basic to the research traditions involved in analysing naturally occurring speech errors. The sorts of levels envisaged may be summarised as: (a) the form of the utterance may fail to represent the intended message-level structure; (b) less commonly, the abstract form of the utterance may not be appropriately represented in its expression; and (c) at the level of abstract forms, we

may occasionally have the experience of 'talking ourselves into a syntactic corner' a form of what may be called a 'maze'.

Thus we have: message vs form; and abstract form vs concrete expression.

4. *Speech production is subject to real-time constraints.* At the output end of the process of production, the rate must be sufficiently rapid that our memory for what has been planned, and what has been excluded, is still available.

Memory for topic is relatively long, and even a slow output rate rarely exceeds its limitations – although most speakers have experienced the 'Where was I?' phenomenon, and not only after some extraneous interpolation.

Memory for specific grammatical form is much shorter, and we more frequently encounter a point in output where one's choice of how to continue an utterance may be in doubt because memory for the initial form has been lost. A common speaker-strategy in such cases is to restart the utterance; but if this does not happen, the latter part may be output and may fail to construe with the earlier, in violation of grammatical (but not message-level) constraints. The speaker may be unaware of this failure, or may carry on regardless.

Equally, however, output must not exceed the rate at which planning decisions are made, at any level. To the extent that this does happen, we would expect the output to be 'contentless' to some degree, at those points where the outrunning occurs; this may take the form of pausing, or of using stereotyped phrases, or of lexical forms such as proforms, lacking in specificity. Combinations of all these types would be expected to occur, for example, in fluent aphasic speech (see ch. 8); in normal speakers, the most usual response, e.g. to games where one is forced to keep speaking without undue pausing or hesitations, is to slow the rate of output so as to match that of planning, marked by longer durations given to articulation of words and syllables.

The nature of real-time constraints may be quite exacting, and their effects are found in the 'naturally displayed' evidence that we started considering in chapter 3. Normal speech errors and non-fluencies are therefore not merely evidence of how the system can go wrong (with the assumption that it will go wrong only in exceptional circumstances) – the assumption is rather that they are more directly evidence of how, and under what conditions, the system normally operates.

7.1.3 *The hesitation model versus the speech-error model*

In the following general terms, Garrett contrasts the hesitation model of Goldman-Eisler (1968) with the speech model of Fromkin (1971).

The nature of the evidence

For Goldman-Eisler the evidence comes mainly from the phenomena of hesitation, and is interpreted in terms of cognitive psychology (the planning phases of speech). For Fromkin, the primary source is speech errors, interpreted in terms of formal linguistics (the levels of structure in speech). These evidential distinctions are significant inasmuch as they direct attention to distinct aspects of the speech-production process.

Aspects of the speech-production process

Hesitation data are quite straightforwardly interpreted in terms of message-level planning. Goldman-Eisler envisaged creative planning at this level as a dynamic process involving conceptual relations (e.g. Actor–Action), lexical selection and generalised syntactic form. Syntactic-to-articulatory mapping was seen as *routine* planning, this term referring to processing that is not under direct planning-control. Thus, a traditional sort of dualistic psychological theory is involved, with inner 'cognitive' processes being distinguished from outer 'automatic' ones (see Campbell 1986 for a discussion of such a distinction in the context of language acquisition). The demands of the creative planning level reveal themselves in the way they force the operations of the routine level to wait for further instructions at certain points.

In Fromkin's model, data from the non-articulatory-based speech errors are interpreted mainly at sentence level, with certain assumptions (e.g. that semantic primitives are features rather than word-sized) being made about the nature of the meaning-level representation.

The difference in focus between the two approaches can be illustrated as in table 7.1 (from the discussion in Garrett 1982: 28–36). It is not very easy to make comparisons between two such very different sets of stages. What we are calling stage I for Goldman-Eisler could be argued to correspond to stages I–IV in Fromkin, but the fit is not complete. The important point to notice, at this step in the exposition, is that it is stages I for Goldman-Eisler, II for Fromkin that represent the major aspect of the production processes that we are concerned with here.

The place of lexical selection

In Goldman-Eisler's model, lexical selection is found both before and after syntax; presyntactically, it is involved in content-specification; and post-syntactically, under the control of abstract syntactic form, certain other lexical choices are made.

For Fromkin, lexical specification, but not selection of lexical items, is embodied in syntactic form, as bundles of syntactico-semantic features; it is not until stage IV that lexical insertion takes place.

Table 7.1 *Comparison of the Goldman-Eisler and Fromkin models of language production*

Goldman-Eisler	Fromkin

I Creative aspect (under voluntary control)
  (a) Content
  (b) Abstract syntactic form
  (c) Lexical specification
	I Meaning representation
	
	II Syntactic structure, with semantic features at lexical sites
	
	III Intonation assigned
	
	IV Lexical insertion, by
	  (a) meaning, then
	  (b) form

II Routine aspect
  (a) Syntactic organisation details
  (b) Articulatory output
	V Morphophonemic processes, and Articulatory output

Based on discussion in Garrett 1982.

The sources of non-fluency

Goldman-Eisler's model, as we have seen, traces hesitation phenomena in the routine aspects of speech production back to sources in the creative aspects. There are three such sources, as can be seen from our discussion above:

1. conceptual sources (content);
2. abstract syntactic form;
3. lexical choice.

In Fromkin's model, if we take the assignment of the intonation contour (stage III) as the initiation of the temporal configuration of the utterance, then only processes subsequent to this can be disruptive of it – principally, lexical insertion (stage IV).

The scope of non-fluency in the hesitation model

Because conceptual structure is recognised as a potential source of non-fluency in the Goldman-Eisler model, it is possible to accommodate the distal effects we described in chapter 3, under the heading of 'the encoding cycle'. We have noted that the work of Butterworth (1980b) has provided evidence of a correlation between fluent and non-fluent phases in spontaneous speech on the one hand, and 'idea groups', as judged by naive subjects, on the other. It is argued that non-fluent phases precede the onset of new idea-groups, and may thus be interpreted as points of long-range forward planning. Further work by Beattie (1983) has argued that gestural and gaze behaviour occurring during pauses in spontaneous speech is also linked to the encoding cycle: gestures in the fluent phase tend to be iconic, i.e. expressive of the message in the idea group currently being communicated, and emphasise or extend the linguistic means of expression; but gestures in the non-fluent phase tend to be non-specific in their content. Similarly, speaker gaze tends to be differentiated in the two types of context: it tends to be listener-orientated during the fluent phase, but averted during the non-fluent. Such evidence points to a distinction between fluent phase (FP) pausing and hesitant phase (HP) pausing. The natural interpretation of HP pauses is that they are markers of the loci of planning over very large domains – represented by whole fluent phases (perhaps one or two dozen clauses) in the encoding cycle.

It is a more difficult matter to establish exactly what planning takes place at such loci, however. It seems least likely that lexical selection for the upcoming fluent phase is involved, since this may constitute several clauses, and lexical selection is usually regarded as a more local type of process. More likely, then, the planning at HP pause-loci is for content (which does not exclude some lexical selection), but this is still a vague notion. How much abstract syntactic form is processed at such loci? Indirect evidence comes from the observation that syntactic complexity in the later part of the non-fluent phase does not appear to correlate with length of the preceding HP pausing, suggesting that syntax is planned more locally.

Beattie (1980) has found evidence in the HP pauses for a relation between pause length and length of following clause in the HP pauses, suggesting that syntactic planning is taking place fairly locally there. That no such relation emerges in the fluent phase is consistent with the view that some syntactic planning may take place before these phases are initiated, i.e. in the HP pauses.

So the picture is quite complex. In the FP pauses, there is probably a mixture of lexical selection and syntactic planning. Syntactic effects appear to emerge in the way pauses gather at clause and constituent boundaries (see ch. 3), when pause incidence is being considered. Pause duration and pause incidence may be telling us different aspects of the same complex story.

If lexical selection is not the major activity that is carried on in the sorts of pauses we have been considering, it is nevertheless an obvious determinant of much non-fluency. It may account for certain aspects of pause behaviour during both the hesitant and fluent phases, and it is most likely to be solely responsible for pauses immediately preceding major lexical items within clause and phrase constituents. Consistent with this view, Goldman-Eisler (1968), Butterworth (1980b) and Beattie (1983) have reported prelexical pausing to be related to the predictability of following words in spontaneous speech. Butterworth has suggested that, where prelexical pauses are accompanied by iconic gestures, form-based lexical retrieval processes may be distinguished from meaning-based selection (see our discussion of the tip-of-the-tongue phenomenon in ch. 3).

The mechanism of nonfluency in the hesitation model

To conclude, Garrett (1982) suggests that we may relate the three sorts of pause determinants just outlined to their respective mechanisms.

1. *Overload*: distal pauses, linked to the encoding cycle, arise from the demands of conceptual planning which momentarily overload the system, yielding pauses that are associated with non-specific gestures, averted gaze, a break between idea groups and the onset of a fluent phase.

2. *Establishing frames*: a frame, as distinct from a plan, is specified for certain syntactic properties, and generally (we assume) corresponds to a clause. Establishing a frame yields pauses that, in terms of their incidence, tend to gather at major constituent boundaries (frame-joints), particularly those that are clause-initial (between frames).

3. *Filling the frames*: if a plan is a sequence of frames, specified locally on a frame-by-frame basis, then a frame is a sequence of elements of which some, particularly the major lexical items, are also specified locally. Filling a frame, word by word, yields pauses that tend to gather at prelexical points.

Finally, let us recall, first, that 'pause' in this discussion is a quite general term covering a range of distinguishable phenomena, filled and unfilled hesitations, and also phrase- and word-final segment lengthening; secondly, that all three mechanisms may combine, in complex determination of individual pauses; and, thirdly, that not all such planning mechanisms may occur actually during such pauses, since stereotypic stretches of speech, including such 'filler' words and phrases as *actually, well, I suppose, you know*, etc. may afford the speaker planning opportunities that would escape a traditional type of pause analysis.

7.1.4 *The speech-error model*

Levels of representation

We need, then, to recognise a number of potential levels of processing, which Garrett (1982) refers to as *the message level, the sentence level* and *the articulatory level*.

376

The message level

This is described as a real-time construct, compositionally built up from simple concepts that are linked to the speaker's perceptual and affective states and encyclopaedic knowledge, according to some 'conceptual syntax'. It is related to the pure-linguistic level of an utterance; but, unlike semantics in formal grammars, it embodies non-linguistic encyclopaedic knowledge as well. 'Pragmatic–semantic' might be a closer description.

Garrett also suggests that the word meanings, as found in the lexicon of a language, might form the basic vocabulary also of message-level structures and processes. Thus, when the message level is described as (de)compositional, this means that individual messages can be thought of as being built up out of, or decomposable into, meaning components that essentially map onto the word meanings in the lexicon. These word-sized meaning components are themselves, in certain semantic descriptions, seen as decomposable into *semantic features*; but Garrett is at pains to suggest that these features seem to play no role in speech production. One reason for this is that there is little or no evidence in speech production data for the view that 'bachelor', 'die', 'empty', etc. involve a negative feature, as in 'not + married', 'cause + not + live', 'not + full', etc. Clearly, the assumption that the basic building blocks of the message are 'word-sized' rather than atomistic elements such as semantic features prepares for the stage in the model where message-level formulations are mapped onto word meanings in the lexicon.

The sentence level

This is described as the real-time construction of representations wherein lexical items (selected through their meanings) and abstract utterance-markers such as tense, number, mood, etc. are grouped into phrasal constructions. These elements all have phonological forms, so that this level establishes a mapping between message structure and articulation.

The articulatory level

This is the level which is addressed in the model we have already discussed in chapter 4, working from sensory goals for articulatory targets down to monitored innervation and control of specific muscle groups in the articulatory system. We shall not consider it further in this chapter.

7.2 The internal structure of the message level

Our discussion of the Garrett model has introduced certain levels of representation. Of these, Garrett's own discussion focusses particularly on the sentence level, but we shall start with a closer consideration of the message level, and its relationships with the internal structure of the lexicon. For this purpose, we shall not pursue further the line of evidence that derives from hesitation phenomena, but turn to consider a different body of evidence, from certain sorts of conceptual operations. In this connection, we shall refer to the work of Johnson-Laird (1983) which, while it owes no allegiance to the Garrett model, serves as a useful framework within which some of the important issues may be raised.

7.2.1 *Models of meaning*

We have earlier (ch. 3) made reference to the relatively inaccessible nature of meaning; but having pushed the problem aside in this way for the intervening discussion, we now have to face it more squarely. We have, according to Garrett (1982), to deal with a message level having the following properties:

1. it is a real-time conceptual construct;
2. it is compositionally built up from simple concepts by some sort of 'conceptual syntax';
3. it uses pragmatic (i.e. real-world knowledge) as well as semantic input;
4. the primitive elements that constitute its basic vocabulary are word-sized units rather than semantic features.

While these points help to set the scene, they do not take us very far towards an understanding of the structures and processes that might underlie the linguistic forms of representation in the Garrett model.

The issue that confronts us concerns the nature of thought processes, and how they are related to the sorts of representations that constitute the linguistic bases of language production. Johnson-Laird (1983) provides a wide-ranging review of the problems and approaches to this area in a form which allows contact to be made, in general terms, with the sort of model we have been discussing. In particular, Johnson-Laird has been interested in *reasoning*, the sorts of thought processes that are said to be 'logical', moving from evidence to conclusion. Of all the various types of thought processes, these might appear, by their apparent systematicity, to be among the most amenable to description and analysis. The steps in reasoning involve *inferences*, and these may be studied most easily in fairly formal conditions, as in *syllogisms*, such as:

(2) (a) Some of the artists are beekeepers
     (b) All of the beekeepers are chemists

(a) (b)

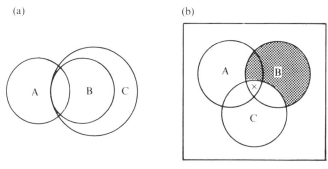

Figure 7.1 (a) Euler circle and (b) Venn diagram representation of 'Some A are B, all B are C'. The Euler circle representation is not the only one possible. The shaded area of the Venn diagram indicates subsets that are ruled out by the premises, and x marks the area that conforms to the conclusion '∴ some A are C'. (Based on discussion in Johnson-Laird 1983: pp. 77–93.)

(ci) Therefore some of the artists are chemists
(and (cii) Some of the chemists are artists)

but they may also be found in more everyday situations, such as:

(3) A: Do you know where the squash courts are, please?
     B: I think that's the sports hall over there.
     A: (goes to indicated building)

7.2.2 *Mental models versus mental logics*

A traditional view of the sort of reasoning just illustrated – at least in its more successful moments – is that it proceeds according to universal laws that hold just as well for that part of the universe that lies inside our heads as for everything outside. The laws governing thought are essentially those that govern the operation of physical machinery, whether (as in a typical nineteenth-century analogy) steam engines or (more recently, and more compellingly, perhaps) computers. Particular systems of such laws have been proposed, e.g. 'reasoning is nothing more than propositional calculus itself' (Inhelder and Piaget 1958: 305, quoted in Johnson-Laird 1983). For syllogisms, it has been suggested that mathematical notations such as Euler circles or Venn diagrams provide an insight into the nature of the reasoning processes involved, as illustrated in figure 7.1. Johnson-Laird notes that this 'mental-logic' approach has a number of problems:

1. it has difficulty with quantified expressions, such as '*every* X has *some* Y';

379

2. a very high number of formal representations typically have to be computed and evaluated to arrive at the set of possible outcomes – sufficiently large to raise suspicions about their psychological plausibility;

3. it cannot account naturally for certain aspects of human performance, e.g.

   (a) the extent and varieties of normal errors made on particular syllogisms;

   (b) certain 'figural effects', as in the clear preference for (2ci) above over (2cii) (though each is equally valid; see below for further discussion);

   (c) the effect of content, by which it is easier to arrive at conclusions when the elements in a syllogism are represented by familiar, imageable words rather than by the abstract symbols A, B, C.

Johnson-Laird refers to the work of Craik (1943) for an alternative concept of a 'mental model'. This has the following general properties:

1. it is a small-scale, internal, model of external reality;
2. it has a *direct* relationship with its external counterpart;
3. it is a *functional* rather than a physical entity;
4. it is not necessarily complete or accurate;
5. it has *recursive function*.

Some of these points require some comment.

Direct representation of reality: What is emphasised here is that, for example, an engineer's mental representation of a particular bridge, or a sculptor's idea of a statue, is couched in terms of the materials and proportions of the actual object. Model stresses will run through the model bridge (guided by the engineer's knowledge) like real stresses through the real bridge; and the spatial relations between different parts of the idea of the statue will appear in the final result.

Functional representations: Nevertheless, the model is essentially a relational structure rather than a physical entity. We must assume that the mental model, as a complex neurophysiological entity, or state of affairs, exists in the brain, but it is not this brain construct, in terms of the cells and pathways involved, that models the real world in a direct way. The mental model is a construct of the mind, rather than the brain. So, just as in part I, chapter 2 we were able to discuss the architecture of the brain from the point of view of language, without making contact with language itself, so here we assume that thought processes are not simply reducible to brain states. In this sense, the mental model is abstract: Johnson-Laird likens this abstractness to that involved when we say that a particular computer program (in the abstract sense) is available in different versions (the physical sense), to run on different pieces of hardware.

Completeness and accuracy: Human beings are constantly manipulating objects that they barely understand, both natural (e.g. garden plants) and artificial (e.g. cars and television sets). Hence, we cannot require people's understandings to be utterly faithful representations of these objects. Also, there must be individual differences in degree of understanding: the television set is a box with knobs on to most people, but much more than this to the repairman.

Recursive function: We can illustrate this properly by reference to one of the earliest modern attempts to understand the conceptual structuring that underlies complex behaviour, presented in Miller, Galanter and Pribram (1960). They envisaged such behaviour as governed by *plans*, which are built up from basic units that can be likened to simple flow-charts of information control – Test–Operate–Test–Exit (or TOTE) units. (See fig. 7.2.) Aspects of complex performance, such as hammering a nail into a block of wood, can be viewed as sequences that are guided by *plans*: it is such guidance that distinguishes complex activities from random acts. Further, it is not just the succession of individual acts of hammer striking that is complex: each hammer strike has its own components, viz. of raising, then lowering, the hammer. The complex plan thus allows for recursion in two senses: first, operationally, it allows for recirculation of control around the TOTE structure any number of times prior to Exit; secondly, in its structural configuration, it allows for TOTE units to be embedded inside larger TOTE units, thus enumerating a hierarchy of control processes that is dominated by a single plan. The essence of such an arrangement is captured in the following:

> More complicated Plans ... can similarly be described as TOTE units built up of subplans that are themselves TOTE units. A bird will take off, make a few wing strokes, glide, brake with its wings, thrust its feet forward and land on the limb. The whole action is initiated as a unit, is controlled by a single Plan, yet is composed of several phases, each involving its own Plan, which in turn may be composed of subplans, etc. (Miller, Galanter and Pribram 1960: 37).

7.2.3 *Propositions, images and models*

There are basically three ways in which abstract problems or properties can be represented in terms that are compatible with what is

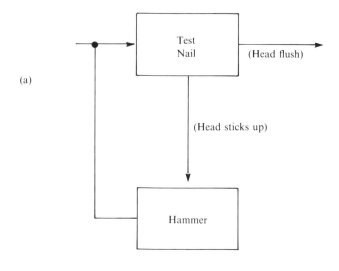

(a)

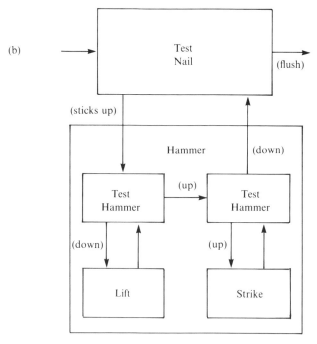

(b)

Figure 7.2 TOTE-units (a) simple, (b) hierarchical. (From Miller, Galanter and Pribram 1960: figs 3, 4, 5, pp. 34–6.)

observed of human performance (as opposed to abstract systems of logic): mental *propositions*, *images* or *models*. What we have said thus far does not address the issue of how far they are to be distinguished from each other, so we shall briefly compare them here.

Reasoning with propositions

Propositions have the virtue, from our point of view, of being compatible with and close to the utterance of language. They are, in Garrett's terms, the ultimate product of the message level in language production, available for fairly straightforward mapping into the first linguistic level, the functional level of representation. Propositional vocabulary is close to the surface vocabulary of language; propositional syntax is close to the functional-role frames of the functional level. If a speaker wants to describe a sequence of related events, then the sequencing, and the relation between the events, must be part of the message-level structure (Garrett 1982) or plan (Miller, Galanter and Pribram 1960), or propositional representation (Johnson-Laird 1983) that underlies the utterance.

Reasoning is involved in the exercise of the speaker's judgement in how much detail to put in, or leave out. For instance, in the utterance sequence (adapted from Johnson-Laird 1983: 52):

(4) (a) The victim was stabbed to death through the throat
     (b) The suspect was on a train to Edinburgh at the time

the speaker has judged appropriately if we are intended to infer that the suspect has an excellent alibi. But we shall feel deprived of information if it is revealed subsequently that the murder in question took place on that train. Johnson-Laird reports that listeners who are asked whether the suspect's alibi is really a good one will try to reinterpret the utterance sequence in an effort to examine certain (possibly erroneous) assumptions that may have been involved in their understanding (see our discussion at the beginning of ch. 6), even to the extent of speculating about extremely long knives. In this process, Johnson-Laird suggests that what they have been doing is going back and forth between the original utterance and their *propositional representation* of it; the latter is sufficiently close to the former to permit accurate verbatim recall of the utterance sequence, at least over short periods of time. Also, they have been attempting to eliminate those possibilities that are ruled out by the premises, until only one (apparently) is left.

This suggests that propositional representation enables reasoning to proceed without recourse to mental logic and formal rules of inference; but it does

Table 7.2 *A 'tableau' representation of the premises 'Some A are B', 'All B are C', with the conclusion 'Therefore some A are C'*

	artist			
'some,	artist =	beekeeper =	chemist	'therefore some
but not	artist =	beekeeper =	chemist	of the artists
all of		beekeeper =	chemist	are chemists, and
the artists	'all the	beekeeper =	chemist	some of the
are bee-	beekeepers		chemist	chemists are
keepers'	are chemists'			artists'

Based on Johnson-Laird 1983: 95.

not establish the relation between propositions and mental models, to which we now return.

Mental models

To go back to the artist/beekeeper/chemist syllogism in example (2): a way to reason without Euler circles or Venn diagrams is to set up what Johnson-Laird (1983: 137) calls a 'tableau', as illustrated in table 7.2. If we set the tableau out like this, using pen and paper, we are going straight from propositional representation to a pen-and-paper model in the real world; if we eliminate the pen-and-paper version, the tableau is set up in the mind – it is a mental model.

Such a model could account for the figural effects that derive from the order of its construction: artists come before beekeepers in the tableau, so the response bias towards (2ci) *some of the artists are chemists* (rather than the equally valid (2cii) *some of the chemists are artists*) derives from properties of the mental model (the term 'figural' refers to the *configuration* of the tableau or model used); these in turn can be argued to derive from properties of the propositions constructed from the utterance sequence embodying the syllogism.

But what of naturally occurring discourse? This can also be seen as involving speaker-judgements/listener-inferences, but they are not so explicit as those found in syllogisms, of course. Consider (again adapted from Johnson-Laird 1983: 128):

(5) The victim was stabbed to death through the throat. The pilot put the plane into a stall just before landing on the strip. He just got it out of it in time, and ran off in the confusion as soon as it had come to a halt. Wasn't he lucky?

In this constructed example, the speaker, we shall say, is describing a complex sequence of events, forming a complex whole. This is represented as a single mental model of the whole incident. It is the speaker's judgement that the fact that the victim was a passenger on the plane, the fact that the plane had a pilot, etc, need not receive explicit propositional representation. Such judgements depend on the speaker's awareness of the listener's knowledge. Equally, the intended meanings of the ambiguous items *pilot, plane, stall, strip,* are judged not to need explicit marking. The specific referential links, from the first *he* (*the pilot*), the first *it* (*the plane*), the second *it* (*a stall*), the ellipted subject of *ran off* (*the pilot*), the third *it* (the plane) and the second *he* (*the pilot*) are all likewise not explicitly marked. Finally, the force of the question *wasn't he lucky?*, which is 'rhetorical', more like a statement, is not explicitly marked.

What this suggests is that *certain* aspects, over others, of the mental model are being extracted and embodied into propositional form by the speaker; the propositions carry certain explicit markers of gaps, where the listener must build inferences – e.g. definite noun phrases (*the pilot*), pronouns (*he*), ellipsis (*ran off*) – but the nature of the links across these gaps is left implicit rather then explicit.

There is thus, underlying a linguistic utterance, a mental tableau within which everything is explicitly related to everything else (up to the limits of the speaker's knowledge), but not all these relationships appear in the propositional representation. Some relationships do not appear at all; others do appear, but implicitly. The nature of a propositional representation of a given mental model will vary, depending on the speaker's judgement of the listener's knowledge, the context and the earlier discourse. A mental model, for Johnson-Laird, appears to stand in the same sort of relationship to propositional representations as does Miller, Galanter and Pribram's (1960) master-Plan to the subplans that it dominates. But whereas subplans might simply be regarded as more locally determined specifications of aspects that are only covertly embodied in the master-Plan, the mental model is the construct that contains all the available detail, and the speaker's task is to judge how and what to select from it for building a propositional representation.

Images

It might appear from what we have said thus far that Johnson-Laird is using the term *mental model* essentially to refer to what are more generally called *images*, about which there has been a great deal of psychological research. It is well established that images are conscious phenomena, that they aid memory, can encode spatial information and be rotated in 'the mind's eye' at a certain speed, etc. But what the nature of images might be is less clear. They cannot be 'pictures in the mind' (as the expression 'in the mind's eye' suggests), because this would require an homunculus (possessing the 'eye') in the mind, whose mind receives the pictures by means of having an homunculus . . . and so on, *ad infinitum.*

Johnson-Laird distinguishes two views on the nature of images: one, attributed to Paivio (1971) and Kosslyn (1980), is *realistic*, inasmuch as it assumes that mental images share certain perceptual processes that are involved in the visual perception of external objects, that mental-image rotations are gradual, and analogous to the visual perception of rotating objects, and that images are representational of (temporarily absent) objects.

The other view, associated with Pylyshyn (1973, 1981), also regards images and the results of visual perception of objects as similar, but sees them each as being mediated by propositional representations, such as we have discussed above. According to this, *propositional*, hypothesis, there is a many-to-one propositional-to-element relationship in visual arrays, rotations are incremental rather than gradual and images are *epiphenomenal*, i.e. they may be constructed from propositional representations of (absent) objects, but they do not have to be, and, unlike propositional representations, they are not our primary means of reflecting upon those objects.

For Johnson-Laird, mental models can be seen as underlying not only propositions (as discussed above), but also images. Propositions are distinct from mental models, as we have seen, in having an arbitrary conceptual syntax, i.e. they are linearised, in real time. By contrast, mental models are multidimensional, non-linearised constructs; and images may be thought of as particular, two- or three-dimensional 'views' of mental models. Whereas we may have a mental model of *planes* (aircraft) or *pilots* (of aircraft) in general, we may also have *images* of particular examples of these.

Finally, we may put mental models, images and propositions in relationship to each other by adapting an observation of Pylyshyn (1973): we may rotate a mental model of, say, a room, by adopting a particular *imaginary* standpoint from which it is to be viewed; this establishes the spatial representations in the model in a fixed way – the bed is now to the left of the cupboard (from the opposite viewpoint, it would be to the right). Such a specification is not a fixed property of the mental model, but it is consistent with the multi-dimensional nature of that model. A propositional representation of this image may leave this spatial relationship between the bed and the cupboard relatively unspecified – using a spatial term such as *next to* or *beside*. Thus, in principle, a propositional representation may encode aspects of the mental model as formed in a particular mental image of it, or directly from the mental model itself, or

Mental Model

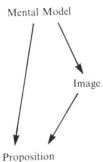

Image

Proposition

Figure 7.3 Possible encoding relationships between mental model, image, and propositional representation of meaning. (Based on discussion in Johnson-Laird 1983: pp. 146–66.)

both: see figure 7.3. We may say, in these terms, that where the contribution of the mental image is minimal, the resulting description may be radically indeterminate, as in:

> I have a very small bedroom with a window overlooking the heath. There is a single bed against the wall and opposite it a gas fire ... The room is so small that I sit on the bed to cook. The only other furniture in the room is a bookcase on one side of the gas fire next to the window ... and a wardrobe. It stands against the wall just near to the door, which opens almost directly onto the head of my bed. (Johnson-Laird 1983: 162)

A passage like this, low in image-based elements, is construable in many different mental representations; the listener will have no difficulty in constructing a propositional representation, but may find it difficult to go beyond this. Different listeners would vary a good deal in their attempts to draw the room from their (perfectly competent) understanding of the passage, and memory for such a description will be less good than for one which permits the construction of a single mental model. In terms of Grice's (1975) conventions, the speaker (or writer) has saddled the listener with an unfair burden of understanding.

Thus far, we have been considering the 'syntax' component of our general processing-model in figure 4.1. Propositional representations of meaning are essentially syntactic in nature, since they are linearised structures involving classes of elements (i.e. the syntax of semantics). We shall now turn to the nature of the elements concerned, which comprise those aspects of meaning for which the language in question provides *lexical* representation.

7.3 Lexical access: the nature of stored word-meanings

In a propositional representation of meaning in message structure, such as might be derivable from a mental model, there are 'elements' as well as 'relations between elements'. The existence of elements raises the issue of access to those meaning complexes that are subparts of the message structure and stored as stable representations of word meanings in the mental lexicon.

7.3.1 *Semantic features or meaning components*

On this matter, we have observed that Garrett (1982) views with scepticism the possible role of atomistic semantic features or meaning components – and Johnson-Laird (1983: 207) is equally dismissive of them. Before we move on, however, a word about the terms used for these atomistic primitives may be in order. 'Semantic features' and 'meaning components' are two terms that are often used together; we should bear in mind, however, that our primary concern is with meaning, and linguistic semantics is best thought of as a particular approach to the study of meaning. Thus 'semantic features' strictly means features that have been proposed within semantics, whereas 'meaning components' may be thought of as those entities which semantic features are set up to elucidate.

We shall not go into the arguments against such primitives here, except to note that Garrett's scepticism is supported by Johnson-Laird's (1983) report of a failure to find any effect of semantic-feature complexity in pairs of verbs such as *get/take, move/throw*, etc. We may also observe that semantic features have been criticised on theoretical–descriptive grounds within linguistics – e.g. Bolinger (1965) and Palmer (1981). While it is true that most psycholinguistic studies casting doubt on the validity of meaning components in lexical entries derive from comprehension tasks, rather than production, it is unlikely that representations of meanings are basically different between these two modes of performance.

An alternative way of capturing relations between words in semantics is the use of *meaning postulates* (Kempson 1977; Biggs 1982; Johnson-Laird 1983); as such, we should consider how far they may provide a suitable alternative for the representation of meaning in the mental lexicon. Meaning postulates may be thought of, in a preliminary fashion, as similar to the *redundancy rules* that are associated with semantic analysis in terms of features. Such rules specify that, for example, the semantic features of 'husband' may be reduced in the way illustrated in figure 7.4 (after the discussion in Kempson 1977: 88–92, 188–91). This achieves economy of representation in two ways: first, by putting certain semantic features into relationship with each other in a way that is stated once for all in the lexicon; and secondly, by allowing for a con-

'husband'

(a) Feature specification   (b) Redundancy rules + Feature specification

[Human]	Redundancy rules (of general application)
[Animate]	[Human] x → [Animate] x
[Adult]	[Adult] x → [Animate] x
[Concrete]	[Animate] x → [Concrete] x
[Married]	[Married] x → [Adult] x
[Male]	[Married] x → [Human] x

Resulting feature specification
[Married]
[Male]

Figure 7.4 Two feature specifications of 'husband', (a) without, (b) with redundancy rules. (Based on discussion in Kempson 1977: pp. 88–92.)

sequent reduction in the complexity of the semantic representation of individual lexical items.

The use of meaning postulates essentially extends this approach, to the point where *all* elements of semantic representation are stated in terms such as:

$$(A) x \rightarrow (B) x$$

In principle, A and B may be semantic features [A], [B], just as in redundancy rules, but an alternative (in view of the difficulty with these primitives) is to have A and B representing the *lexical items* themselves of the language concerned. That is, the lexical items are treated as semantically primitive, and are set into relationship with each other by these rules. It is this type of meaning-postulate approach that we shall consider here.

Accordingly, the meaning of 'husband' may be specified as:

'husband' x → 'married' x
'married' x → 'adult' x
'adult' x →

At this point, our formalism proves unhelpful, for the word 'husband' must be put into relationship with 'male', but the word 'adult' is in relationship with both 'male' and 'female'. So we can state meaning postulates more conveniently as:

'husband' x → 'married' x
AND 'adult' x
AND 'male' x, etc.

As Kempson (1977) points out, meaning postulates provide for a weaker representation of word meaning than semantic features; they do not try to capture all aspects of a word's meaning, such as what defines a 'waitress' vs a 'woman', but simply seek to represent the full set of lexical relationships between these words and others in the lexicon. To the extent that these words have similar relationships with other words, they will be shown to have similar meanings; postulates do not go beyond this.

A further consequence of this approach is that the concept of a semantic entry is dispensed with entirely. This may appear to be a startling result, but it follows quite straightforwardly from what we have said. If we wish to point to the formalised semantic specification of a particular word, we can no longer point to some internal set of features; the semantic specification lies word-externally, in the relationships that the word in question contracts with the other words around it in the lexicon. Words, that is, derive their semantic value from the organisation of their semantic space.

7.3.2 *Lexical access via meaning representations*

If we now bring the discussion back to psycholinguistic issues, we can consider the implications of relying, as Garrett's model does, on message-level elements that are basically lexical, or 'word-sized'. Their corresponding entries in the mental lexicon are unanalysed, stored elements of lexical meaning; their meaningfulness derives from their being set in many-to-many relationships with each other. As such, the individual items in this lexicon have nothing corresponding to an internal meaning-specification. It is difficult to see, then, what information could possibly be contained about such items in the 'semantic-access' file of Forster's indirect model of lexical access (5.3.2).

It is as if we were to walk into a library with no catalogue system, but with a set of guidelines to the effect that books on topic A are shelved alongside books on topic B, and so on. In other words, we are led directly to the main stacks, and the preliminary stage of consulting the catalogue is eliminated. If this seems a rather unlikely, and inefficient, way of organising access to books in a library, we should not conclude that it is equally unsuitable as a model of human lexical access. After all, the analogy between a library and a mental lexicon is not perfect. If a message-level element having the properties of being human and female 'calls up' or 'activates' all such entries in the lexicon – 'woman', 'waitress', 'actress', etc. – this may naturally allow for such activated entries to interact with further properties of the message level, such as that the mental model involves a kitchen or restaurant event, in which case 'actress' is not further activated, but 'waitress' is.

In this way, the model is not only direct; it is also interactive and parallel in processing mode, since it allows for different elements and properties of the message level to enter into and guide, or constrain, the search process, along a number of different pathways through the lexicon, and activating a number of lexical items as it proceeds.

7.3.3 *Semantic networks*

The sort of approach we have been considering here is frequently represented as a distinct type of theory, *semantic-network theory*; but Johnson-Laird (1983) is right to suggest that it is better thought of as a notation or formalism. As such, it derives from work (Collins and Quillian 1972) in artificial intelligence, where the meaning of a word is set up in terms of a network of 'is a' relationships, as in:

'husband' → is a → 'man' → is a → 'human' → is a → 'animal'...
→ is a → 'adult'...

Network formalisms have been proposed, on the boundaries of psychology, linguistics and artificial intelligence (e.g. Hinton 1981), which attempt to model human performance in terms of *network hierarchies* of lexical items, *network distances* between lexical items and *network transitions* associated with faster or slower links between points in the network. Modelling human performance in these terms is complicated (Collins and Loftus 1975; Anderson 1984); individual properties, such as distance, seem not to be reliable determinants of lexical access (as Johnson-Laird notes). Interactions between various network properties seem generally plausible, but are difficult to quantify and express as specific, testable hypotheses.

Johnson-Laird's own proposal (1983: 217) introduces another possible determinant of lexical access; he distinguishes between words that are basic, not defined in terms of any other words of the network, e.g. 'be', 'go', 'move', 'at', etc, and words that can be defined in terms of others, particularly the basic set, e.g. 'cost', 'weigh', 'fly', 'emigrate', 'behind', etc.

We shall not go into these issues further here. We shall return to the concept of a lexical network below, in considering some alternatives to the standard interpretation of Garrett's model.

7.4 **The internal structure of the sentence level**

Thus far, we have been concerned with the message level and the ways in which it might be mapped onto lexical and syntactic aspects of the language system. This brings us to consider the nature of the sentence level in more detail, and Garrett argues that it is possible to delineate its internal structure by looking closely at movement errors (exchanges and shifts) and replacement errors (substitutions and blends), of the sort that we reviewed in chapter 3.

7.4.1 *The sentence sublevels*

Garrett proposes the terms *functional* and *positional levels* for sublevels within the sentence level. They are distinguished by the nature of the elements involved, their qualitative inter-relationships and the domains over which they operate.

The functional level

Movement errors at this level typically involve word elements, of corresponding grammatical categories (noun and noun, verb and verb, etc.), playing similar roles in phrases (modifier and modifier, head and head, etc.), and the movement domain traverses a phrase-constituent boundary. We may note that this has the secondary effect of yielding rather extensive domains of movement, compared to those of the positional level:

(6)   As you *reap*, Roger, so shall you *sow*.

The positional level

This involves subword elements, syllables, segment clusters, singleton segments and, occasionally, subsegmental features (see part I, chapter 3, section 3.4.1) with no grammatical-category or phrasal-role correspondence, but frequently with similar phonological roles (onset and onset, coda and coda, etc.) frequently within the same constituent phrase (which may better be characterised in terms of phonological criteria – a phonological phrase), and hence over rather shorter distances than word movements at the functional level:

(7)   *show sn*ovelling

In an earlier study, Garrett (1980a) provided a tabular demonstration of some of these distinctions for exchange errors, as in table 7.3. From this it will be seen that word exchanges are set apart from both stranding and sound exchanges, with most (not all) stranding exchanges belonging to what is here referred to as the positional level. There is claimed to be no effect of subword segmental structure in functional-level word exchanges, and a strong segmental effect in positional sound exchanges.

The picture thus far may be set out as in figure 7.5.

7.4.2 *The internal structure of the syntactic component*

It remains for us to ask how the mapping from the functional level to the positional level might take place, via some syntactic component that the

Table 7.3 *Constraints on exchange movement errors – phrasal membership and grammatical category*

Exchange error	Phrasal membership		Grammatical category[b]	
	Within[a]	Between	Same	Different
Word (N = 200)	0.19	0.81	0.85	0.15
Stranding (N = 100)	0.70	0.30	0.43	0.57
Sound (N = 200)	0.87	0.13	0.39	0.61

[a] Internal to a simple NP or VP, where VP is taken to include main verb plus obligatory phrasal constituents such as direct object NP.

[b] All types of exchanges, word, stranding and sound, are almost entirely confined to the major lexical categories Noun, Verb, Adjective, Preposition.

From Garrett 1980a: tables I, II, p. 189.

Garrett model does not specify. Lapointe (1985) has addressed this issue directly, in the context of a study of language pathology, specifically, agrammatism in Broca's aphasia (see ch. 8, sections 8.2.3 and 8.4.2 for further information on these concepts). His conclusions are not restricted to the field of language pathology, however, and it will serve our purpose here very well to consider them.

Lapointe is concerned just with verb phrases in language production, and therefore his discussion provides an illustration from this area of how the syntactic component might work. He calls his model a *syntactic processor*, and discusses it in terms of (a) what sort of input it receives from the functional level; (b) the means by which positional-level frames are stored in the system; and (c) the nature of the output from the processor.

The input to the syntactic processor

Concerning the input from the functional level, much currently remains unclear. It may be thought of as specifying underlying grammatical relations, or as basically semantic in nature, or both (depending on one's view of how distinct these concepts might be). Lapointe assumes, for the sake of convenience, that input to his syntactic processor will include information such as, e.g.,

(... indicative, active, durative, present, sing-3 ...)

where the dots indicate information from the functional level about elements preceding and following the verb phrase in the utterance.

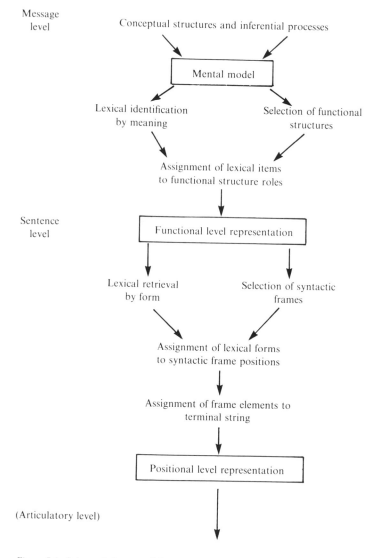

Message
level

Conceptual structures and inferential processes

Mental model

Lexical identification
by meaning

Selection of functional
structures

Assignment of lexical items
to functional structure roles

Sentence
level

Functional level representation

Lexical retrieval
by form

Selection of syntactic
frames

Assignment of lexical forms
to syntactic frame positions

Assignment of frame elements to
terminal string

Positional level representation

(Articulatory level)

Figure 7.5 Schematic layout of the message and sentence levels in the Garrett model. (Based on Garrett 1982: pp. 67–8.)

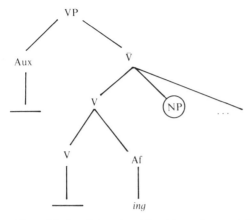

Figure 7.6 A verb-based positional frame fragment. (From Lapointe 1985: example (30), p. 130.)

The positional frames

Lapointe considers the positional frames to have the sort of structure represented in figure 7.6. He refers to this type of structure as a *fragment*: it represents the maximal phrase structure associated with a particular head category (here, it is V), both higher than the V-node (up to a VP node) and lower, down to the *stem + affix* morpheme structure; and it also includes slots, defined as empty spaces under certain nodes, where the head lexical element (a suitably specified verb from the lexicon), and dependent function-words (such as auxiliary verbs) may be inserted, and circled symbols (e.g. the NP in this example), representing positions where other constituents (having their own internal structure) may be attached.

The fragment and function-word stores

As far as storage is concerned, Lapointe envisages two distinct types of stores: one, for lexical head categories (an N-store, as well as a V-store, and others), and another type for 'dependent function' (or grammatical) word elements (e.g. determiners, auxiliary verbs, and so on). This distinction is well attested in both descriptive linguistics and in performance data from both normal and abnormal language use, and, in spite of difficulties associated with it (see 3.3.2), it is natural to embody it, within this type of model, in terms of different types of store. Thus, the basic function of the processor is to access fragments from these stores and to combine them in grammatically appropriate ways.

Table 7.4 *A partial V-fragment store for English*

English V fragment store

V	Aux V + ing	Aux V + ed″	Aux being V + ed″ …
V + s	Aux been V + ing	Aux been V + ed″	Aux been being V − ed″
V + ed			
Aux V + ed′			

From Lapointe 1985: table 6, p. 132.

The internal organisation of these fragment stores is obviously an important issue. Lapointe argues, on the basis of a dimension of morphosemantic complexity (the details of which need not detain us here) that a partial V-fragment store for English might look like the arrangement of table 7.4. The least complex phrase-structure type is located in the leftmost column, with increasingly complex structures arranged in columns to the right of this; and the least complex forms within each structural type are located at the top of the columns.

The organisation of the auxiliary-fragment store is more unsettled, but Lapointe suggests an arrangement with *be* forms in the leftmost column (least complex), then a column with *have* forms, then *do* forms and finally (most complex) the modal auxiliaries.

The operation of the syntactic processor

Turning now to the operations performed by the syntactic processor, we may first refer to the diagram in figure 7.7. This shows the syntactic processor to have three subcomponents: a *control* mechanism, a store *locator* and a stem *inserter*, as well as three types of store: the two fragment stores mentioned above, for fragments and function words, as well as an *address index* containing the addresses of cells in the fragment and function-word stores, where specific information may be found.

The control mechanism receives input from the functional level, activates the address index to find the location of the required cells in the fragment and function-word stores and passes this information to the locator.

The locator may be thought of as a set of *read/copy devices* (see our discussion of Shattuck-Hufnagel's (1983) scan-copier model at the level of sound structure, in section 4.4.1), one for each fragment store (N-store, V-store, etc.), and each function-word store (determiner store, auxiliary-verb store,

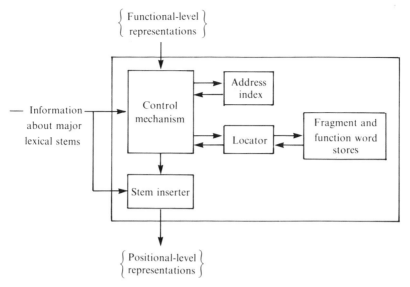

Figure 7.7 Schematic diagram of the syntactic processor. (From Lapointe 1985: 133.)

etc.). Each read/copy device is constrained in the way it can move through its store, along tracks defined by the rows and columns; in this way, it is possible to operationalise the concept of 'complex form' by making it more distant from – hence, less easily accessed by – the read/copy device, which is assumed to be 'at rest' in the top left-hand corner of each store. It is also assumed that the read/copy device can only access one cell's information at a time, between returns to its resting place.

Once the locator has activated the relevant set of read/copy devices and has received input from their operation, its task is completed by handing this information back to the control mechanism, in the form of fragments and function words. The control mechanism's task then is to combine these in grammatically appropriate sequence, and to pass the result on to the stem inserter.

The stem inserter, finally, inserts the phonological representations of the lexical items that have been activated in the lexicon (a parallel process to the one we have just been following through the syntactic processor) into the appropriate positions defined in the output of the control mechanism. It may be thought of as a copying mechanism, and here we make contact with our discussion in chapter 4 (Shattuck-Hufnagel's scan copier is a type of mechanism that performs this function).

397

7.4.3 *Movement errors*

Exchange errors

These are assumed to arise as representations at a higher level are mapped onto representations at the next lower level (refer back to fig. 7.5). They are a consequence of a failing to preserve ordering relations between elements across the interlevel boundaries. Thus, word exchanges arise from mismappings of message-level elements onto functional-level elements, and sound exchanges from mismappings of functional-level elements onto positional-level elements. Stranding errors, or most of them, belong to this latter area, too.

Since exchanges of all types almost exclusively involve major lexical categories (see note (b) in table 7.3, above) we may draw a distinction, valid for each of these two interlevel mappings, between frame elements (at message, functional or positional levels), which do not exchange, and lexical elements, which do.

As we have seen (in 3.4), Shattuck-Hufnagel (1983) envisages a segmental and stress-specified skeletal frame for each lexical item, in order to account for the distinction between those sound elements that move and those that do not: movable elements are articulatory specifications, more usually as complexes than single features, while stable elements are syllable patterns, and stress patterns, constituting the lexical frame.

We may assume a similar distinction in respect of the assignment of major lexical items to phrasal-planning frames, at the functional level. Between these types of exchange, we may consider stranding errors to arise early on in the mapping from the functional level to the positional level, where word forms as minimal grammatical elements (e.g. *fool* in *foolish*) are retrieved and copied into erroneous positions in the positional frame. This is prior to their specification as phonological units (e.g. the syllables /fuː/ and /liʃ/), from which sound exchanges may arise.

Shifts

Interestingly, the distinct category of shift errors can fit into this account of the error mechanism for exchanges. Shifts tend to involve inappropriate ordering of adjacent elements relating to major and non-major lexical items:

(8) (a) unless you got somethin' to bétter do
     (b) easy enoughly

Assuming that non-major items are part of the planning frame, Garrett suggests that 'shift errors are understandable as a consequence of the processes which determine the siting of such elements in the (lexically interpreted) terminal string of the positional representation' (1982: 51).

Taken together with the observation (Cutler 1980) that shifts typically show stresses that move with their intended sites (as in example (8b)), this tends to support the view that shifts are best interpreted as movements of lexical items *vis-à-vis* certain stable frame-elements (see 3.4.1).

Thus we extend the statement of principle regarding frame elements generally from 'they do not exchange' to the stronger claim 'they do not move'.

7.4.4 *Lexical factors*

We have distinguished between major lexical items, which are subject to exchange errors in the formulation of the functional-level representation, and frame elements, including non-major words and affixes, which form part of the positional-level frame. We shall now examine a little more closely the nature of errors involving major words. One of the striking observations to be made is that nearly all such errors appear to fall into either meaning-related or form-related types, and hardly ever into both at once.

Meaning-related errors

Substitution errors tend to involve antonyms (*hot/cold; love/hate*) and cohyponyms (*wash/brush your hair*), while blends are more common with synonyms, as in *dinner is ret* (*ready/set*), or, more occasionally, hyponym/superordinate pairs, as in:

(9) They have more protein than *meef* (meat/beef)

However, the last two types may be difficult to distinguish, since, in context, hyponym/superordinate pairs may be synonymous (*bitch/dog*).

These errors are presumably to be located in mapping the message-level representation onto the functional level. Consistently with his scepticism regarding the role of semantic features at the message level, Garrett observes cases of substitution where the meaning relationship is associative or inferential rather than decompositional, as in example (10) (Garrett 1984: 56):

(10) I just put it in the oven at very low *speed*
      (the idea to be communicated was that the ham had to cook slowly)

Form-related errors

Substitution errors involving form similarities tend to show initial-position effects, as in:

(11) (a) because I've got an *appartment* now (appointment)
      (b) they haven't been *married* ... uh, measured ...

Table 7.5 *Levels and processes involved in major lexical-class errors*

	Processes
Message level → functional level	
word substitution, blends	Lexical selection on basis of message-level properties, insertion into functional-level representation; meaning relevant, form irrelevant
word exchanges	Lexical assignment by functional role to positions in functional-level representation; grammatical category preserved, meaning, form irrelevant
Functional level → positional level	
word-substitutions, sound exchanges, stranding errors	Selection of word forms; meaning irrelevant, grammatical category irrelevant; position in word (e.g. initial, stressed syllable) relevant

Based on discussions in Garrett 1980a: 206–17.

and one may also observe some stressed-syllable effects (which may play a role in each of these examples). Unfortunately, the issue of computing word-final similarities between elements in a substitution is confused by the limited range of variation in inflectional and derivational suffixes in English. We have noted initial-position and stressed-syllable effects before (in 3.4.1, on sound exchanges and tip-of-the-tongue phenomena, and in 5.5, in the cohort model of word recognition).

Lexical retrieval

We may start to put together some of these observations concerning substitution and exchange errors involving major lexical items, within the framework of figure 7.5, as set out in table 7.5. The mapping of message-level onto functional level representations may be thought of as initiated through meaning relationships (as we have noted, involving more than purely semantic parameters). Word substitutions and word blends involving meaning similarity have their source here. Form characteristics are irrelevant, if by these we mean morphophonological forms. However, functional roles are also implicated in this selection process, so it would seem reasonable to expect some correspondence of grammatical class among such errors, inasmuch as there is some relation between grammatical and meaning categories. Thus, for example, *hot/cold* are more natural antonyms than *heat/cold*, at least in those contexts where *cold* is used as an adjective (*it's cold/hot in here*), since *heat/cold* in such a context would represent different grammatical classes. In so far as grammatical class, reflecting functional role, represents abstract form, this may therefore be relevant.

Word exchanges seem to derive from a stage where initial, meaning-based, selection has been made, and processes of assignment of lexical items to sites in the functional-level frames are operative. Garrett suggests that 'sentence-level processes, once set in train, are neither monitored for nor couched in terms of meaning parameters' (1982: 57). Hence, grammatical category is preserved, but meaning, as well as morphological form, is irrelevant.

Word substitutions involving formal similarity, sound exchanges and stranding errors are all characterised by their independence of meaning and grammatical class, and by the influence of form. The word substitutions of this type arise from that phase of the word-retrieval process in which word forms are selected for subsequent insertion into the positional-level planning frame. Sound exchanges and strandings derive from processes which assign segmental specifications to sites in the positional-level frame. There is thus a parallel between these errors at the positional level and word exchanges at the functional level.

Closed-class items

Thus far we have concentrated mainly on major-class lexical items, and have merely noted that non-major words and grammatical affixes, or closed-class items, seem to be specified as part of the frame, and not to be subject to movement. Unlike major-, or open-class, items, there is an intimate link between closed-class elements and the phrasal configurations in which they occur. Garrett suggests that we regard them as specified, not by lexical retrieval, but rather by 'the (unknown) processes which select phrasal frames' (1982: 61) at the positional level, under the influence of functional-level constraints.

Segmental errors are very rare in these items, which may indicate that they are not specified for their segmental phonological structure until some point after open-class items have been so specified. This situation would then also account naturally for the form of the closed-class item {indefinite article} → *an* in:

(12)   an _anguage *l*acquisition problem

and of the closed-class item {past} → /id/ in:

(13)   Well, I *wait*ed him to *warn*.

The status of prepositions

A particularly interesting situation is found with prepositions. These behave like major-class items (noun, verb, adjective) in respect of their occurring in exchange errors, at the message-to-functional-level mapping: but, like frame elements, at the positional level they do not get involved in sound-exchange errors. Garrett addresses this situation by treating prepositions in a systematically ambivalent way: as lexical elements at the functional level which become 'demoted', through a cliticisation process, to the status of frame elements at the positional level. The notion of a clitic is basically a phonological one, so Garrett argues that the positional level be regarded primarily as phonological in nature. In this sense, 'phonological' does not exclude syntactic factors such as constituent boundaries and categories: 'phonological phrasing' and 'syntactic phrasing' coincide, to some important degree.

7.4.5 *Summary*

Garrett's model, as far as concerns us here, may be regarded as essentially embodying the distinction between two levels: the functional, consisting of abstract syntax and meaning-specified lexical items, vs the positional, consisting of phrasal groups of a syntactico-phonological kind, affixed elements and form-specified lexical items.

Further, the model claims that, by the criteria of

(a)   grammatical class,
(b)   phonological similarity, and
(c)   domain of movement,

naturally occurring speech errors can be assigned to one or other of these levels. Errors that (a) respect grammatical class, (b) ignore phonological similarity, and (c) operate over relatively large domains, can be located at the functional level; those that (a) ignore grammatical class, (b) respect phonological factors, and (c) operate over relatively small domains, can be located at the positional level.

This situation reduces to two simple claims:

1.   the positional level is blind to functional-level information;
2.   the functional level is blind to positional-level information.

A model like this, having such independence or autonomy between levels, lends itself naturally to interpretation as serial in operation. According to this interpretation, both the functional- and positional-level representations are real-time constructs – that is, they have sequentially ordered constituents along the time dimension, and cannot communicate with each other because, for a given domain of processing, the functional level must be completed prior to the initiation of the positional level.

7.5 Serial versus parallel interpretations

A serious challenge to the serial-processing view, however, has been made in a study by Dell and Reich (1981). Working within the same framework as Garrett, they wish to recognise more complex flows of information between these levels than the serial model allows.

They took the claims of the serial model and operationalised them as follows.

1. Sound errors (i.e. of the positional level) should show no lexical bias. That is, in errors such as

> (14) *f*itch *p*ork (pitch fork)

the fact that the exchange yields one non-word, *fitch*, and one real word, *pork*, is totally coincidental. The result could just as easily, and irrelevantly, been two real words or two non-words. Notice that what we may call the lexicality effect (see also ch. 5, section 5.2.3) here is taken as deriving from outside the positional level, specifically, from the functional level.

2. Word errors (i.e. of the functional level) should show no phonological bias. That is, in errors such as

> (15) no-one is *taking* you into *talking* ... (a nap)

the fact that two phonologically similar word forms are involved is purely by chance. This follows from the interpretation of the positional level as phonological, and autonomous from the functional level.

Dell and Reich set out to test each of these versions of the claims embodied in the serial model.

7.5.1 *Is there a lexical bias in sound errors?*

Garrett himself addressed this issue. He made an estimate of how often sound exchanges could be expected to create words by chance, by sampling word pairs from published interview data and exchanging their initial sounds. This suggested that words could be created by chance in this way about 33 per cent of the time.

Looking at Fromkin's (1973) corpus of errors and the MIT data up to that point in time, Garrett found word outcomes from initial-sound exchanges running at 40 per cent and 38 per cent respectively – not sufficiently above estimated chance level to provide evidence for a lexical bias.

Another point Garrett made was that, since real words are characterised by some very striking differences in their frequency of occurrence (*fife* is very much less frequent than *wife*), the lexicality effect should reveal itself also in terms of a frequency effect (see also ch. 5, section 5.2.3). In other words, if for example *pork* arising from an error such as *fitch pork* is actually the lexical item *pork* as in *I like apple sauce with my roast pork*, then the production of *pork* in error contexts ought to match the known frequency characteristics for the real word. More generally, most of the apparent-word outcomes from sound errors should consist of the more frequently occurring words in the language.

However, there seemed to be no relation between frequency of word outcomes from sound errors and frequency of words in the language, in the data Garrett examined: more than 60 per cent of the apparent-word outcomes had fewer than twenty occurrences in the Kučera and Francis (1967) word-frequency lists. This suggested that *pork* from *fitch pork* is not the real word *pork*, but a non-word that is homophonous with it.

However, this still leaves the issue as to whether there is what we may call a lexical-form effect, according to which error outcomes are more likely to converge on, or be homophonous with, actual words in the language. Does the existence of certain actual word-forms in the language 'pull' the errors into certain phonological patterns?

Garrett's finding that apparent-word outcomes occur at 38–40 per cent of the time in the data might seem to rule this out, in view of the estimate of chance level at around 33 per cent. But, in considering chance levels of homophony, we must take into account the phonological nature of what Dell and Reich call the *source* words: e.g. *red* has many phonological neighbours, and hence can easily slip into the apparent words *head*, *bed*, *fed*, *shed*, etc., while *pipe* has many fewer neighbours (if we just consider outcomes from initial-segment exchanges). Unless we take this factor into account, our estimates for chance levels, for particular word pairs, are going to be wrong.

Concentrating on examples of this type, word-initial consonant errors, before a following vowel, Dell and Reich found 363 instances in approximately 4,000 naturally occurring speech errors in their corpus at Toronto University (the Toronto corpus). Of these, 196 were exchanges, ninety-nine were anticipations (including some, e.g. *leading ... uh, reading list*, that were potential exchanges which the speaker caught in time), and sixty-eight perseverations.

Estimating chance level

The framework for discussion is as shown in table 7.6. In these terms, we can say that the first outcome-string provides the crucial test of the lexical-form effect, as far as exchanges and anticipations are concerned.

Table 7.6 *The framework for the analysis of exchange errors*

Intended words		Outcome string		
1st	2nd	1st	2nd	
pitch	fork	fitch	pork	exchange
		fitch	fork	anticipation
		pitch	pork	perseveration

Based on discussion in Dell and Reich 1981: 616.

This is the initial, and arguably the initiating, part of these errors, and the remainder, the second outcome-string, may be regarded as a residual or default element.

We have seen how Shattuck-Hufnagel's (1983) scan-copier model also embodies this view. In the case of an exchange, the scan-copier monitor, after the initial error yielding *fitch*, places the unassigned /p/ segment in the gap left by /f/ (in the schema for the second word). In anticipations, it ensures a second copying of the appropriate segment, /f/, in that slot.

But in perseverations, it is the second outcome-string that should be tested for lexical-form effects, since here the status of the first outcome-string is guaranteed (no error, hence a real word).

For each of the first two types of error, exchanges (n = 196) and anticipations (n = 99), a five-step procedure was carried out to estimate the appropriate chance level of word-form creation. This procedure is illustrated in table 7.7, for an illustration corpus of exchange errors (n = 4), from Dell and Reich (1981). The criterion for lexicality of the outcome string was whether it appeared in *Webster's seventh collegiate dictionary* either as an entry, a grammatical form of such an entry or a proper name from one of the appendices. The procedure was followed through for both first and second outcome-strings.

Dell and Reich point to two advantages in using such a procedure. First, because it uses the phonological properties of the 'sound-slipping' words themselves in the estimate, the result is sensitive to the average length, phonological structure, grammatical class and other properties of the words involved. Secondly, because all the slips studied involved initial prevocalic consonants, all the strings created in the matrices of steps 4 and 5 of table 7.7 were phonetically possible. So the estimate is not skewed at the outset by being based on combinatorially impossible instances.

Table 7.7 *Calculating chance expectations for lexical bias in sound errors*

===

Sample 'corpus' of four exchanges

> pitch fork → fitch pork
> Lawrence and Warden → Wawrence and Larden
> postal code → coastal pode
> chin tickled → tin chickled

Step 1   Create two lists

list one	list two
pitch	fork
Lawrence	Warden
postal	code
chin	tickled

Step 2   Determine the proportion of each initial phoneme in each list

list one		list two	
/p/ = 0.50		/f/ = 0.25	
/l/ = 0.25		/w/ = 0.25	
/č/ = 0.25		/k/ = 0.25	
		/t/ = 0.25	

Step 3   Strip each word of its initial consonant

list one	list two
-itch	-ork
-awrence	-arden
-ostal	-ode
-in	-ickled

Step 4   Combine stems from list one with initial consonants from list two; determine if the resultant strings are words

	/f/	/w/	/k/	/t/	row
	0.25	0.25	0.25	0.25	sum
-itch	0	1	1	0	0.50
-awrence	0	1	0	1	0.50
-ostal	0	0	1	0	0.25
-in	1	1	1	1	1.00

0 = non-word   average of row sums = 0.56
1 = word

The probability that the first outcome of an exchange will create a word is 0.56

Step 5   Combine stems from list two with initial consonants from list one; determine if the resultant strings are words

	/p/	/l/	/č/	row
	0.50	0.25	0.25	sum
-ork	1	0	0	0.50
-arden	0	0	0	0.00
-ode	0	1	0	0.25
-ickled	1	0	0	0.50

0 = non-word, 1 = word   average of row sums = 0.31

The probability that the second outcome of an exchange will create a word is 0.31

===

From Dell and Reich 1981: table 2, p. 618.

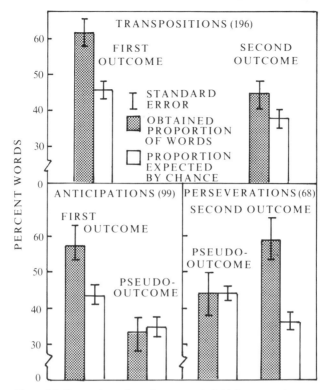

Figure 7.8 Proportions of word outcomes in initial consonant errors and chance estimates. (From Dell and Reich 1981: fig. 1, p. 619.)

The results are set out in figure 7.8. They indicate a strong lexical-form effect in the first outcome-string (note the gap between the range of the standard error for expected vs obtained proportions of words), but not in the second outcome-string. This is true for both exchange errors (transpositions) and anticipation errors. Concerning the perseveration errors, it was felt that their low number (n = 68) rendered the standard calculation procedure unreliable. Instead, the mean of the expectations derived from exchanges and anticipations was used (45 per cent and 44 per cent respectively for first outcome-strings, and 35 per cent and 36 per cent for second outcome-strings).

Dell and Reich conclude that there is strong evidence here that:

1. the mechanism of exchanges and anticipations is to be sought in the first outcome-string, and of perseverations in the second; and
2. this mechanism preferentially gives rise to word forms.

The answer to the question, 'Is there a lexical bias in sound errors?', would seem to be:

1. no, so far as we can tell, if by 'lexical bias' we mean that *pork* in *fitch pork* is the same item as the real word *pork*; but
2. yes, if by lexical bias we refer to the tendency for such errors to slip into patterns that are created in the language by existing phonological word-forms of the stock of lexical items.

7.5.2 *Is there a phonological bias in word errors?*

We now turn to the possible role of phonological (i.e. positional-level) factors in word errors. Following the outline of Garrett's model, we can deal with this under two headings: identification of words as complexes of meaning properties; and assignment of words as meaning complexes to roles in the functional-level structure.

Phonological factors in word-identification processes

How far might semantic substitution errors, e.g. *wash* for *brush* in the context ____ *your hair*, be contingent upon dimensions of phonological similarity, such as C(C)V/ʃ/? We have seen that Garrett's model (fig. 7.5) distinguishes meaning-based word-substitution errors as deriving from message-to-functional-level mappings, and form-based word-substitution errors as deriving from functional-to-positional-level mappings. If these are discrete, serially ordered stages, then word-substitution errors will be either of one type or the other. Apparent phonological similarities in target/outcome semantic substitutions will be there by chance only; so, obviously, we must again address the issue of obtaining reliable estimates of chance levels.

Dell and Reich (1981) identified 289 word substitutions, and 63 word blends, in the Toronto corpus, all involving content words. They determined the phonological similarity of the target/outcome pairs in each case by considering the identity of individual phonemes in first, second, third and fourth positions, and comparing them with chance estimates computed from the same corpus of substitutions and blends. These estimates, as before, are derived from all possible pairings of target words with outcome words in the corpus, and by marking the resulting percentage of identical phoneme matchings for each position in the word individually. The results show that *for word substitution and blends in general* there is a clear and sequential effect of phonological similarity: the actually occurring errors tended to share identical phonemes with their targets, especially towards the beginning of the word (see fig. 7.9).

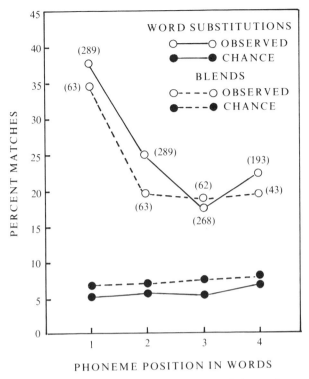

Figure 7.9 The phonological similarity between the interacting words in word-substitution errors and blends. Numbers in parentheses are the number of cases on which each percentage is based. (From Dell and Reich 1981: fig. 2, p. 623.)

Now, the question arises as to how far this is true of the subgroup of substitutions and blends that are meaning-based. Accordingly, Dell and Reich identified those cases where a meaning relationship such as antonymy, cohyponymy or superordinate–hyponym could be discerned. In this process, morphologically and associatively linked words such as *optician/optometrist*, and *Hungarian rhapsody/restaurant*, were excluded, to avoid possible unwarranted phonological effects. This yielded 130 'semantic' errors and 159 'non-semantic' ones (see fig. 7.10). It appears that, while the phonological effect is less marked on the semantic group, it is still greater than would be expected by chance, and hence runs counter to the serial-processing model. It is also greater than the percentage of phoneme matches found on a set of 464 near-synonyms (Whitten, Suter and Frank 1979), so the possibility that this result might be influenced by a coincidence of semantic and phonological dimensions in the language itself must be ruled out.

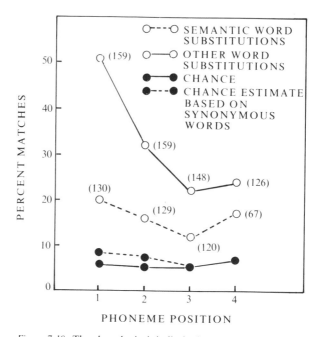

Figure 7.10 The phonological similarity between the interacting words in semantic and other word-substitution errors. Numbers in parentheses are the number of cases on which each percentage is based. (From Dell and Reich 1981: fig. 3, p. 624.)

Dell and Reich make the point, also, that nearly all the phonological matches in the semantic group were from target/outcome pairs that showed only a partial similarity: so the overall phonological effect is partial and pervasive (contributed to by all the items to some degree), rather than strong and intermittent (as would be the case if just a few items had shown near-identity as between target/outcome). This is exactly the wrong sort of result for a serial model of the Garrett type.

Phonological factors in word-assignment processes

Dell and Reich (1981) also looked at 155 content-word misordering errors from the Toronto corpus, and divided them into functional-level errors (n = 81) and others (n = 74), on the criteria of shared grammatical class and error domains of at least two intervening words (see 7.5 above). Phonological similarity of words participating in each error was assessed as before. The functional-level type errors showed a greater degree of phonological relationships than would be expected by chance, and the functional-level and other types of error were not different from each other in this respect. Once

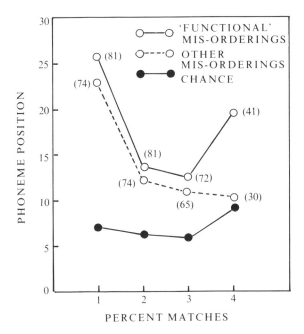

Figure 7.11 The phonological similarity between the interacting words in 'functional'-word mis-ordering errors and other word and morpheme mis-ordering errors. (From Dell and Reich 1981: fig. 4, p. 626.)

again, the functional level appears to be significantly influenced by positional-level phenomena (see fig. 7.11).

7.5.3 *Interpretation of the evidence*
The Dell and Reich study therefore makes three observations:

1. sound errors (involving prevocalic initial consonants in content words) tend to yield word forms;
2. meaning-based word-identification errors (substitutions) are open to phonological influences;
3. meaning-based word-assignment errors (exchanges) are open to phonological influences.

We must now ask how this information is going to be used in our understanding of production processes. We shall consider a number of possibilities, in turn.

1. Are the findings relevant? The Toronto corpus was collected, quite rapidly, by students of psycholinguistics at the University of Toronto. They were

instructed to carry a notebook at all times and to write down every little slip they heard over a one-month period, together with its context. This was repeated for five one-month periods.

Does this method lead to a lack of comparability between the Toronto corpus and other corpora? It is difficult to see how it might. Using a large number of collectors would reduce the possibility of a collector-perceptual bias (some individuals may be more sensitive to certain types of error), and the possibility of a sampling bias (relying on a few individuals to collect the data tends to narrow the range of conversational partners, topics and settings). But it is not clear that these advantages would lead to a data-base sufficiently different from the established corpora at UCLA and MIT, particularly since the Dell and Reich study is limited to easily detectable and central types of error. Possibly their decision to look just at prevocalic consonants in initial position of content words is a distorting factor; but they performed the same analysis on Fromkin's (1973) corpus and, although only sixty errors of the same type could be found there, they report essentially the same results. We have to conclude that the results are relevant.

2. Do we abandon the Garrett model? The demonstration of interactions between processing levels in Garrett's model is not, by itself, evidence against these levels. Dell and Reich distinguish between *constraints* (e.g. shared grammatical class, phonological-structure properties, domain of error, etc.) on the basis of which the levels are established, and *probabilistic tendencies* for interactions to take place between these levels. The evidence thus far is that we keep the model but abandon the strictly serial interpretation of the information flow within it.

3. How do we interpret the lexical-form effect? There are two parts to the answer. The first has to do with the claim that the effect has to be sought in the initiating part of the sound-based error, the source of the exchange, anticipation or perseveration. To go back to the *fitch pork* example, we would have to conclude that, whatever the formal similarities between the second element here and the real word *pork*, there is no lexical-form effect operative here, since the error is triggered by the first element, *fitch*. But in exchanges like *coastal pode*, we should conclude that the first element, *coastal*, shows a lexical-form effect.

The second part of the answer is that we are talking here about lexical *form*, rather than simply about *lexical* effects: this is because there seems to be little or no evidence that it is the real word *coastal*, as a form–meaning complex, that turns up in the first-element position here (complete with associations of white cliffs, mewing seagulls and the sound of waves on rocks, perhaps).

412

To the extent that this is true, we may not be dealing here with interactions between the functional and positional levels as such. Rather, we should perhaps think in terms of links between different factors in the generation of the positional level: (a) the existence of word forms in the lexicon; and (b) the filling of phonological segments in the articulatory memory, or buffer store, that controls the articulatory output of speech.

4. How do we interpret the phonological effect? This might well be thought of as a word-form effect as well, since the phonological dimension that is observed in semantic errors may derive from the stored phonological properties of the language, as found in the word forms in the lexicon.

This effect is truly one that links the functional and positional levels. A strict serial approach effectively looks on 'the lexicon' as two distinct lexicons, the semantic lexicon, activated by message-level factors, and consisting of word meanings; and a phonological lexicon (a better term perhaps is a word-form lexicon), consisting of stored word-strings.

The evidence from Dell and Reich's study is more consistent with a single lexicon, with connections between stored word-meanings and stored word-forms. Activation would occur in parallel at both the meaning and the sound-structure levels in such a lexicon. It would be a type of network memory-store (see section 7.3.3 above), with links also to non-linguistic, encyclopaedic knowledge. As Dell and Reich envisage the situation,

> retrieval processes in this lexical network occur by spreading activation
> with each activated node sending a proportion of its activation to all
> nodes connecting to it . . . In the mapping from some unspecified
> representation to the functional representation it is assumed that
> semantic nodes in the lexicon are activated. This activation then spreads
> throughout the lexicon. The functional representation is built up as
> grammatical rules select and order word constituents . . . However, the
> words that are available for selection (those that are highly activated) will
> have been influenced by nonfunctional factors as a result of spreading
> activation. In particular, words that are phonologically related to
> intended words will have become activated because activation spreads to
> them via phoneme nodes shared with intended words. (1981: 627–8)

The sort of network they are assuming is depicted in figure 7.12.

7.6 Conclusions

In this chapter we have reviewed, quite selectively, some current approaches and suggestions regarding the components of a production model. It must be emphasised that there is no settled view on these matters, and that much research remains to be done. The treatment of models of meaning, the

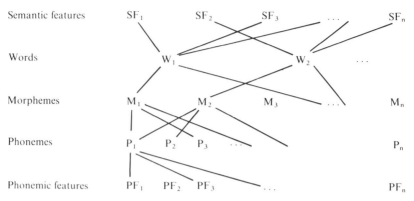

Figure 7.12 A network for the semantic and form properties of words. (Based on discussion in Dell and Reich 1981: pp. 627 8.)

lexicon and syntax here are offered as glimpses of how things might be organised, but obviously much of this area is controversial and open to further developments.

To tie things together a bit, let us return briefly to the layout envisaged in figure 4.1. Questions have to be raised both about the relations between the various components, and their internal structure. Concerning relations, we may pick out for mention here those between: (a) the message level and the lower levels, within both the syntax and the lexicon hierarchies; (b) the upper and lower levels within each of these hierarchies; and (c) the two major hierarchies themselves, of the lexicon and the syntax. We have outlined both serial and parallel positions in respect of (a) and (b), and it is not difficult to envisage how they might be extended to (c): given that the message level controls both lexical access and syntactic structuring, it could be that either the one is dependent upon the other, or that the two processing hierarchies interact, with lexical decisions affecting syntactic choices, and vice versa.

We may also recall the point made earlier regarding the level of signal production, namely that it characteristically reflects coarticulatory processing. Within the abstract language system, discrete linearisation of elements (phonological segments, lexical items and phrasal and clausal categories) is of the essence: but we have seen that not only does this not rule out the possibility of parallel, interactive processing, but that, indeed, certain effects appear to make this likely. What is still not clear is the level or levels at which linearisation takes place (given some non-linear concept of message structure, such as the mental model). One possibility is that 'given' topics tend to precede 'new' ones by virtue of their familiarity to the speaker and hence their relatively easier lexical access; such a view would be consistent with the lexical hierarchy taking the lead, but interacting with the syntactic (Bock 1982).

More detailed working-out of interactive accounts of language production may be found in Stemberger (1985) and Dell (1986). In addition, it is naturally the case that message structures may be encoded both through the language-production hierarchy and through other communicative means, such as gesture: McNeill (1985) provides a view of the inter-relationship between these encoding hierarchies which emphasises their ability to be regulated by a unitary system of linearisation and rhythmic timing. Aspects of message-level structuring are discussed within the Parallel Distributed Processing (PDP) framework in Rumelhart, Smolensky, McClelland and Hinton (1986), from whom we may take the following observation with which to close not just this chapter, but also our main account of the issues in modelling normal language-processing (chs. 4 to 7):

> We believe that processes that happen very quickly – say less than 0.25 to 0.5 seconds – occur essentially in parallel and should be described in terms of parallel models. Processes that take longer, we believe, have a serial component and can more readily be described in terms of sequential information-processing models ... We would caution, however, that when one chooses a formalism such as production systems and attempts to use it ... to describe the conscious sequential processes that occur at this slow time scale, it is important not to fall into the trap of assuming that the microstructure of these sequential processes should also be described in the same terms. (pp. 56–7)

8
Impairment of processing

8.1 Introduction

The preceding chapters have attempted to survey language functions in the individual, including the more peripheral structures and processes as well as the more central ones. In this chapter we shall be asking in what ways this spectrum of functions may be impaired as a result of damage to the neurophysiological substrate. This takes us into the field of *aphasia* research, or aphasiology. Because language is a complex of functions, its manifestations of impairment are not all the same, leading to a situation which some authorities characterise as different types of aphasia, and which others see rather as different forms of a single condition.

As distinct from the study of normally occurring, transient errors, we are dealing here with long-term, systematic impairments, though to some extent there may be change in certain of their characteristics over time, as a result of spontaneous recovery, or specific treatment, or both together. Naturally, enough, since we are dealing with linguistic consequences of damage to bodily tissue, medical influence in this field has been traditionally strong. Moreover, issues in this field have proved very complex, with problems in diagnosis and interpretation. This is perhaps what should be expected, given the already complex nature of normal language-processing. As a result, students have often found the field a difficult one to approach for the first time. Medically trained students find the linguistic terminology just as difficult as those from a linguistic background find the medical terms; and hotly contested issues have been debated over the years by authorities espousing radically different approaches and assumptions, not infrequently using similar or identical terminology in rather distinct senses.

8.1.1 *Basic concepts*

Traditionally, aphasia has been defined as the (a) *impairment* of (b) *central language abilities* in (c) the *speech* modality following (d) *brain damage*. Taking the italicised elements in this definition in turn, we should note that the impairment may be more or less complete; second, it is differentiated from impairment of both non-verbal cognitive functions (i.e., intellectual vs language abilities) and peripheral functioning (i.e., speech vs language

416

abilities); third, it is not strictly involved in the impairment of written-language functions. The terminology that derives from this tradition thus distinguishes, at least in principle, between aphasia (total loss) vs *dys*phasia (some degree of loss); aphasia vs *alexia* and *agraphia* (loss of reading and writing functions, respectively – and there are also the terms *dysgraphia, dyslexia*); and between aphasia and *agnosia* (literally, loss of knowledge), and *anarthria* and *apraxia* of speech (the latter two referring to aspects of articulatory disorder – for which there are also the terms *dysarthria, dyspraxia*).

There is a growing modern consensus that some of these terms, if strictly interpreted, actually carry undesirable and problematic assumptions regarding the underlying nature of language abilities and hence of their impairment. The distinction between *a*- vs *dys*- terms has long been over-ridden by practical considerations: thus, e.g., aphasia and dysphasia are used quite interchangeably, usually in the sense of some degree of loss (since total loss is a relatively uncommon and transitory condition), while in many cases one or the other prefix is preferred, depending on usage rather than any meaning distinction. There is asymmetry in the lack of a distinction within aphasia corresponding to that between alexia (input) vs agraphia (output). The term 'aphasia' is frequently used, as in the opening paragraph above, as a superordinate, to cover alexia and agraphia as well. Dysarthria, however, usually stands outside, as an impairment of muscular function, affecting non-linguistic as well as linguistic control of the vocal tract. Dyspraxia of speech, referring to more central speech-control dysfunction, is more problematic, as we shall see.

In the following sections, we shall attempt first to review the bases of aphasiology and to relate this approach, wherever possible, to the psycholinguistic perspective that has been presented in the earlier chapters (see also, e.g., Saffran, Schwarz and Martin 1980; Cooper and Zurif 1983). We shall then examine in a little more detail some problematic issues in linguistic interpretation: this is an important undertaking, if we are to be able to use the evidence from language impairment to shed light on the normal system, and vice versa. In our discussion of the traditional concepts we rely particularly on Albert *et al.* (1981), Benson (1979) and Kertesz (1979).

8.1.2 *Damage versus other bases of impairment*

We shall follow the traditional definition of aphasia in restricting our survey to impairments that are associated with *damage* to the brain, as opposed to abnormal (psychotic) *states*, or *congenital* or *developmental* structural abnormalities. Here again, though, we should not be blind to the possibility that such a distinction may be artificial. Language impairment, arising

417

in association with various abnormalities, not all involving damage to previously normal brain-functions, is a phenomenon that calls properly for its
own analysis, and there may prove to be certain similarities between the sort
of language impairment that is associated with more than one radically different *aetiology* or assumed causative condition. In general, though, it seems wise
of some aphasiologists to question the *uncritical* acceptance of the term 'aphasia' in the case of language disorders of children, unless there is evidence of a
substantially established normal language-system in the child prior to the
onset of the disorder. Not surprisingly, such evidence is usually hard to find,
and this makes interpretation of such disorders exceedingly difficult; it may be
impossible to know, in the presence of certain aspects of language difficulty in
such cases, how much may be safely attributed to damage to a previously
acquired system, and how much to the immaturity of the system prior to
injury. Similarly, at the other end of the chronological scale, there is the problem of impaired language-functions in association with natural aging-
processes. We shall exclude these for our convenience now, but we must recognise that there may be similarities as well as differences between geriatric and
non-geriatric populations in respect of certain aspects of language impairment. Finally, as far as abnormal psychological states are concerned, we must
acknowledge that the distinction between 'structural damage' and 'altered
state' may be artificial, particularly as our viewpoint becomes more detailed,
focussing on the neurochemical exchanges in the *cytoarchitectonics* or cell
structure of the central nervous system.

There is, then, a good deal taken rather for granted in the way that we have
defined our survey, but a sufficient awareness should go some way to averting
the dangers of this fairly traditional approach.

8.1.3 *The framework of psycholinguistic functions*

As we have seen in earlier chapters, language has many psycholinguistic aspects, and we therefore have to assess language impairment in
terms of some commonly tested language functions in the assessment of aphasia, as set out in table 8.1. We shall refer back to these language functions in
our characterisation of the main types of aphasia, in section 8.2; but first we
shall address two further topics: the nature of the physical ills that brain-based
language abilities are vulnerable to, and the problem of determining what sort
of brain damage results from them.

8.1.4 *Causes of brain damage in cases of language impairment*

This is the more straightforward of these last two topics,
although, as table 8.2 shows, there are overlapping effects between the major

Table 8.1 *Some commonly tested psycholinguistic abilities in aphasia examination*

Conventional label	Description of activities involved
1. Spontaneous speech	Message structure encoding, to articulatory output: description of interests, hobbies, etc., or picture description, or narrative of well-known story, or personal event
2. Auditory comprehension	Responding in a meaning-appropriate way to what is presented, from individual words up to full discourse
3. Auditory repetition	Immediate recall and reproduction of utterances, with full comprehension
3a.	As above, but with less than full comprehension
4. Spontaneous writing	As for (1) above
5. Reading comprehension	As for (2) above (silent reading)
6. Copying	Reproduction of written material, from individual words to full text, with full comprehension
6a.	As above, but with less than full comprehension
7. Writing to dictation	Reproduction in graphic form of continuously presented auditory input; with or without full comprehension
8. Reading aloud	Reproduction in articulatory form of continuously presented written input; with or without full comprehension
9. Confrontation naming	Articulation of lexical forms in response to visual, auditory or tactile presentation of word referents
10. Written-word to object matching	Gestural identification of word referents in response to visual presentation of word forms

Table 8.2 *Major types of cerebral damage associated with language impairment*

Cause	Vascular disease (CVA)					
Damage	Embolism	Thrombosis	Haemorrhage	Tumour	Trauma	Infection
Infarct	√	√				(Abscess) √ (Inflammation of vessels)
Compression		√	√		√	(Abscess) √
Severation			(Herniation) √		√	
Micro-organic invasion						√

Based on discussion in Benson 1979: 18–29.

consequences of four sources of disruption to brain tissue: *vascular disease* (disease of the blood-supply vessels, in particular the main cerebral arteries); *tumour; trauma* (sudden injury, e.g. from gunshot, road-traffic accident or the controlled excision undertaken in surgery); and *infection*. These give rise to four main types of damage: *infarct* or local loss of blood supply, leading to an area of cell death (surrounded by less severely affected tissue, and further out by normal healthy tissue); *compression; severation;* or micro-organic *invasion* of brain cells.

Vascular disease, probably the most common cause of brain damage, is generally referred to as 'CVA' (for cerebral vascular accident), or, more simply, as 'stroke'. Three basic kinds are recognised: *embolism* refers to blockage of an artery or vein by blood clots or other bodies, transported to the point of blockage by the blood current from other regions of the vascular system; *thrombosis* is the blockage of an artery or vein *in situ*, by processes which lead to a build up of material on the inner walls, or to a thickening of the vessel walls through inflammation; *haemorrhage* is the shedding of blood directly from a vessel into the surrounding tissues. It may proceed from an *aneurysm*, which is a bulbous protrusion formed by weakening and dilatation of a vessel wall, or from an *angioma*, which is a sort of tumour consisting of blood vessels, or from excessively high blood-pressure within an otherwise normal vascular system.

Tumours, not as frequent as strokes, often infiltrate cerebral tissues quite widely and microscopically before they start to produce focal, or highly specific and identifiable, effects: the early effects may therefore be relatively mild and widespread. Later effects, as the seat of the tumour distorts with its growth, may be more or less direct. There may be haemorrhage into, or pressure upon, the surrounding tissues, but there may be also more distant effects, for example as distortion by pressure in one place causes herniation of tissue at some vulnerable spot elsewhere. Where surgical excision is undertaken in treatment, the effects of trauma as well as tumour may be observed.

Trauma is often thought to yield relatively neat focal injuries, but this is almost never the case with low-velocity penetrations (e.g. shrapnel) and even high-velocity projectiles tend to have marked and diffuse pressure-effects outside their immediate path through the tissue. Civilian trauma is most often the result of road-traffic accidents (RTA) which frequently yield non-penetrating, so-called 'closed-head' injuries. These typically involve quite extensive damage as a result of sharp deceleration and rotational forces, resulting in a compression and shearing of the brain (whose consistency may be likened to a fairly well-set blancmange).

Infection, with the use of modern antibiotics, has much decreased in incidence as a source of brain damage. Temporal lobe abscess, as a complication of chronic middle-ear infection (e.g. otitis media) used to be a commonly encountered, relatively focal type of damage in association with language impairment. Nowadays it is the infection of herpes simplex encephalitis that may typically be involved in aphasic symptoms, in association with loss of established memory and of the ability to learn new material. Other, degenerative disorders, such as Huntington's chorea and multiple sclerosis, should be mentioned in this context: in many cases, any aphasic symptoms arising in association with these diseases usually prove to be secondary to impairment of more general memory and intellectual processes, and are correspondingly more difficult to evaluate.

8.1.5 *Determining the site of brain damage*

It might seem a straightforward matter to localise at least the more focal types of brain damage, but the task is in practice extremely difficult. One reason for this is that differences of about 1cm can be significant for establishing an association with language impairment, so the precision of location that is required for neurolinguistic correlations is of a fairly high order. Another reason is that an area of damage may be both focal and large: a typical infarct may appear to direct inspection (as at autopsy) as an irregular cavity with an aperture of several square centimetres where healthy cortical tissue had once been, and extending more or less deeply into the central regions. The walls of this cavity may be lined with a layer of damaged cell-tissue which is abnormally softened and whose functional integrity is difficult to determine: soon after the injury, this area may be completely non-functional, but it may gradually recover to some extent (perhaps contributing to the often observed spontaneous period of partial recovery in the acute phase of many aphasic conditions). Later on, it may develop a *sclerotic* or scarred surface. For purposes of localisation, this zone represents an uncertain quantity. Consider also the difficulty of reconstructing the 'epicentre' of such an infarct, in relation to established case-history prior to autopsy. Figure 8.1 indicates the sort of cavity that may be encountered, illustrated in *Broca's area* (see 2.4.1 above, and 8.2.3 below). The coronal section view shows the front part of the cavity as viewed from the rear. Note that considerably more damage has occurred, particularly to the temporal lobe, than appears from the lateral view alone. There, what is seen most directly is damage to the cortex or 'grey matter' comprising the cell bodies that lie along the surface of the cerebral hemispheres. A good deal of the medial or inner surface of cortex, and the

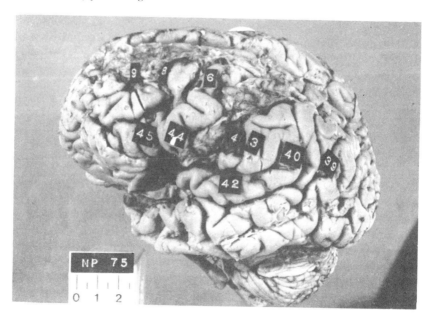

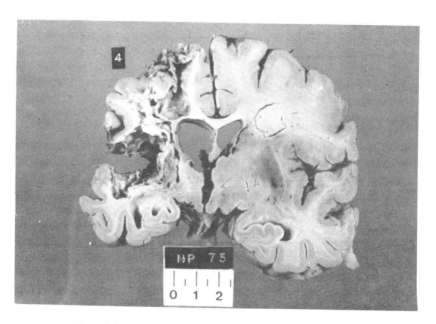

Figure 8.1 (a) Lateral and (b) coronal section of the brain, showing damage to Broca's area and surrounding tissue. (From Kertesz 1979: figs 8.2, 8.3, pp. 139–40.)

underlying white matter, of the temporal lobe has been destroyed in the illustration in figure 8.1, as well as the frontal-lobe white matter, quite deep to the inner ventricles.

So much for the illustration of one sort of damage; we shall now review the techniques that are available for determining the nature of such injuries as these, in ways that are potentially helpful to understanding the bases of language impairment.

Autopsy. We have already mentioned this, and it is perhaps the most obvious and certainly the most direct means of inspection, allowing for greatest accuracy of measurement. However, it has some disadvantages for our purpose, since it is not regularly available for a balanced cross-section of language impairment case-histories – rather, only for those where death occurs while the patient is still sufficiently within reach of sufficiently interested neurological specialists (and also, of course, where permission of relatives has been obtained). Many patients go on living for years after the onset of impairment, and may die, from delayed or unrelated causes, beyond reach and knowledge of those involved in treatment of the disorder in its acute phase. Even in cases where autopsy is performed, death may have occurred before the nature of the language impairment could be adequately assessed, either because of insufficient testing, or because of changes in the patient's condition. In many cases also, the language-related injury may be difficult to disentangle from early pathological conditions that may not have led to symptoms, and from subsequent strokes or other injuries which may have compounded the original language impairment. In spite of all these difficulties, however, autopsy examination formed the foundation of aphasiology in the last century, and has remained the classic method during the formative phases of aphasiological research.

Direct neurological examination. The advantage of this method is that it can be performed on a living patient and can form part of an integrated clinical picture, along with assessment of the language impairment itself. The examination may be performed in the treatment of *haematoma* (swelling caused by haemorrhage), abscess or tumour, prior to surgery. The recording of the surgical excision itself can be very precise, including depth information; but it may be difficult for the surgeon to identify landmark regions of the brain in a situation where the cranial opening is kept as small as possible and the brain itself may be distorted in shape or position by pressure effects in the locality of the abnormality.

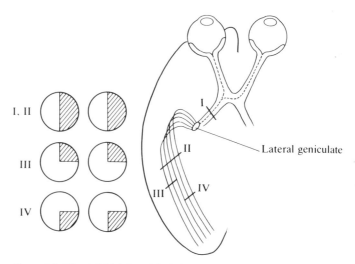

Figure 8.2 Visual-field defects (shaded areas) associated with certain lesion sites (I–IV), illustrated for the left hemisphere. (Based on Walsh 1978: fig. 7.4, p. 226.)

Indirect neurological examination. This is the best-established, most straight-forward and most routinely performed examination; it provides the bulk of the neuroanatomical information on language disorders that are encountered outside specialist research centres (i.e. in referrals to speech-therapy units from neurological wards in general hospitals). It consists of assessing the patient's general sensory and motor abilities in association with the language disorder, and much of it may be carried out at the bedside. Thus, in the motor examination, a right-side *hemiplegia* (paralysis) indicates a deep lesion in the left-hemisphere motor cortex, while right-side *hemiparesis* (partial or incomplete paralysis) indicates a less severe lesion: a right-side *crural* paralysis, affecting leg and shoulder but sparing arm and face, is associated with damage to the areas served by the anterior cerebral artery. In the sensory examination, an important component is the testing of the visual field: a right-field *homonymous hemianopia* (see fig. 8.2) is commonly associated with lesions in the left parietal-occipital lobes, quite deep to the lateral geniculate nucleus or the geniculo-calcarine pathways (see also ch. 2). Without going further into the scope of this type of examination, we can note that it requires inferences to be made on the basis of established neurobehavioural correlations, and that it is open to the usual experimenter effects – lack of thoroughness and subjective bias. Additionally, it can only be effective where the language impairment is accompanied by significant (i.e. testable) general neurological deficits, which is not always the case. Finally, because it is indirect, it may not be sufficiently discri-

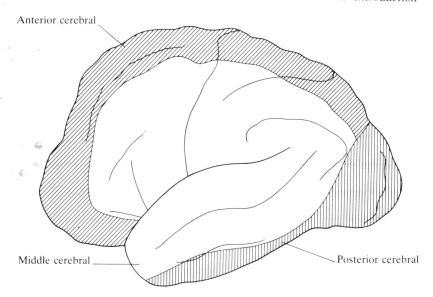

Anterior cerebral

Middle cerebral

Posterior cerebral

Figure 8.3 Lateral view of the left cerebral hemisphere showing the areas served by the three main cerebral arteries. (From Benson 1979: fig. 3.4, p. 25.)

minating where the brain damage takes the form of multiple lesions over different sites.

Instrumental examinations. There are a number of instrumental techniques currently available. One of the uses of *electroencephalography* (EEG) is for this purpose: electrodes are placed at points over the scalp and a continuous reading is taken from them, in parallel, as they monitor different parts of the brain for local electrical activity. Brain damage shows up as abnormal patterns of activity recorded by some electrodes but not others. A somewhat similar technique is used in *regional cerebral blood flow* (rCBF) investigations, where again simultaneous counts are taken from points over the scalp, this ?cording the passage of radioactive isotopes injected into the blood supply to the brain. The record can show increases and decreases in the blood flow to certain regions of the brain in relation to certain tasks being performed by the patient at the time (e.g. word-finding, or spontaneous speech). Brain damage shows up, again, as perturbations in the normal patterns. Both of these techniques suffer from similar difficulties for our purpose: neither can provide accurate depth information, and the precision of local surface information is limited by the distribution of sampling points over the scalp.

Other approaches aim at a pictorial scan of the brain. *Cerebral angiography*

425

involves injecting radiopaque material into the cerebral vessels and then taking X-ray pictures: this has been used quite often after stroke, to determine the site of an embolism or thrombosis, which in turn is suggestive of certain areas of damage in the brain (see fig. 8.3). But this is essentially examination of the cause of damage, rather than of the damage itself, and it is also done at some risk to the patient. It is not so commonly used these days. *Radionucleide* (*RN*) *scanning* provided the first really safe and effective means of determining site of lesion in the living brain: RN scans have proved effective in providing three-dimensional information on tumours and in locating relatively recent (up to ten weeks) stroke damage. *Computerised axial tomography* (*CAT*) scanning is a possibly even more important development, which usefully complements the information available from RN scans: CAT scans tend to pick up early infarcts before RN scans are positive, and to show older infarcts more sharply than RN scans do; while acute infarcts of more than one week old tend to show best on RN scanning. Thus, these two methods, used together, can differentiate between recent and more established infarcts. Such developments undoubtedly hold the greatest promise for improving the quality of information on the neuroanatomical bases of language disorders.

8.2 The main aphasic syndromes

In this section we shall briefly review each of the more commonly recognised patterns of language impairment that have been discussed by aphasiologists. In so doing, we shall be drawing on the results of more than a century of intensive research and information gathering which has been carried on in the face of two major difficulties: first (as we have just seen), it has not been a straightforward matter to identify the nature of underlying pathology; and second, there has been the problem of developing sufficiently refined, yet clinically practicable, methods of assessing impaired and residual language functions in objective yet non-artefactual terms. In a sense, the preceding chapters of this book have been concerned with this latter difficulty alone. There is, then, not surprisingly, no single consensus view on the nature of the disorders we are about to review. But there has gradually emerged a mainstream tradition within which these disorders can be described: the descriptions can be recognised, even where differing interpretations are proposed. It is this sort of tradition that we shall draw on here.

The term *syndrome* is part of this tradition. Clearly, it shows the influence of the medical model that we have already mentioned. It will need to be discussed in more detail in section 8.3, but for now we can characterise a syndrome as a cluster of symptoms that occur together with greater than chance frequency. It is a concept that exists at the level of clinical symptoms rather than the under-

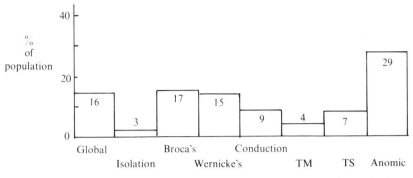

Figure 8.4 Incidence of aphasic syndromes in a population of 150 aphasics. (Based on Kertesz 1979, p. 71.)

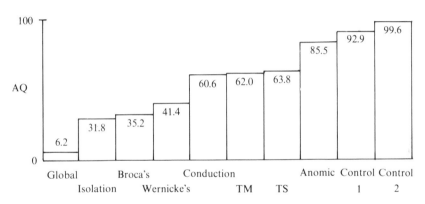

Figure 8.5 Level of functioning, as measured by the Aphasia Quotient (AQ) by aphasic syndrome. (Based on Kertesz 1979: table 4.9, p. 72.)

lying pathology, though of course the syndromes have been taken by many as statements of *effects* which are in search of corresponding statements of causation, in terms of information from site and nature of lesion. Figures 8.4 and 8.5 set out the relative incidence, and severity, respectively, of the syndromes we shall be reviewing first. The study from which these data are derived contains 150 language-disordered patients of whom a majority represented an acute aphasic group, mainly suffering from stroke; trauma, haemorrhage, aneurysm and degenerative disease, are also represented, in decreasing order of incidence. The categories represented in the figures are those derived from a preliminary standard clinical diagnosis, such as most clinicians would either subscribe to or at least recognise.

Figure 8.6 shows, from the same study, which lesion sites are involved; and table 8.3 provides an outline of the major characteristics of the syndromes in

427

Table 8.3 *The comparative symptomatology of the main aphasic syndromes*[a]

The more common syndromes							
Global		Broca's		Wernicke's			Anomic
The less common syndromes							
	Isolation		Trans-cortical motor		Trans-cortical sensory	Conduc-tion	
Fluency							
----------------------------0–4--------------------				---------------------------5–10---------------------			
Comprehension							
-------------0–3.9 ----		------------4–10 -----		------------0–6.9 ----		-------------7–10 -------	
Repetition							
0–4.9	5–10	0–7.9	8–10	0–7.9	8–10	0–6.9	7–10
Naming							
-------------0–6-------		------------0–8-------		--------------------------0–9----------------------			

[a] The scores reflect performance out of a possible 10 on a standardised aphasia test, the Western Aphasia Battery (Kertesz 1979, table 4.2, p. 58; see 8.3 below). The cut-off points in the table represent the ranges that appeared to classify 150 aphasics unequivocally into traditionally recognised clinical syndromes

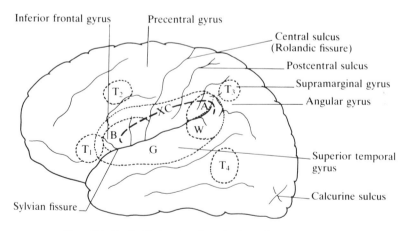

Figure 8.6 Typical lesion sites for aphasic syndromes: A, anomic; G, global; B, Broca's; W, Wernicke's; C, conduction (the position of the letter X indicates a subcortical lesion in the arcuate fasciculus represented by the thick dotted line); T₁₋₂, transcortical-motor; T₃₋₄, transcortical-sensory. (Based on Kertesz 1979: figs. 9.2 to 9.21, pp. 147–62.)

relation to each other. It should be emphasised that figure 8.6 is based on group data, from the observed distribution of lesion sites in individual cases of diagnosed syndromes. It therefore reflects to some extent individual differences in the exact nature of particular lesions, in the location of brain function within individuals, and in the way that particular syndromes are manifested. The first two points are consistent with what we have covered already; the latter point is important, inasmuch as there are, for example, observed differences among patients who are classified as having the same syndrome – see Howard (1985) for differences within so-called Broca's aphasics – and there are also points of similarity between syndromes, as table 8.3 shows. Figure 8.6 is also simplified in the sense that it attempts to show the more central, non-overlapping areas of lesion/syndrome correlation. It follows that, for all these reasons, a lesion in any particular site may have symptomatic consequences that cannot be predicted from the information provided in figure 8.6 and table 8.3. But at least they provide a useful framework for discussion, as well as for clinical purposes.

An important feature to notice in figure 8.6 is the central area of language functions, extending from Broca's to Wernicke's areas, above and below the sylvian fissure. Extensive damage within this area is consistent with global aphasia, and within it particular lesion sites are associated with Broca's, Wernicke's, anomic and conduction syndromes (which we shall be discussing shortly). But, outside this area, are the lesion sites associated with the so-called transcortical syndromes, the anterior or motor types (T1 and T2) and the posterior or sensory types (T3 and T4), whose significance in aphasic typology lies in the disturbance of connection between the central language-area and surrounding areas of brain function.

We shall now turn to consider the syndromes individually. The largest group in figure 8.4, and the least severe, in terms of figure 8.5, is represented by anomic aphasia, and we shall start with this syndrome.

8.2.1 *Anomic aphasia*

This is not a very easy syndrome to categorise. The *symptom* of *anomia*, or general word-finding difficulty, is recognised in other syndromes, and therefore a distinction is drawn between the state of affairs where the anomia is part of a larger syndrome which usually has more dominant symptoms, and anomic aphasia which is where anomia exists as the dominant symptom, in a relatively 'pure' form. In this sense, the syndrome of anomic aphasia may be said to consist of marked anomia plus the absence of other severe symptoms. But a further difficulty is that anomia is a vague concept, so that clinical subtypes, *word-production anomia*, *word-selection anomia* and different types

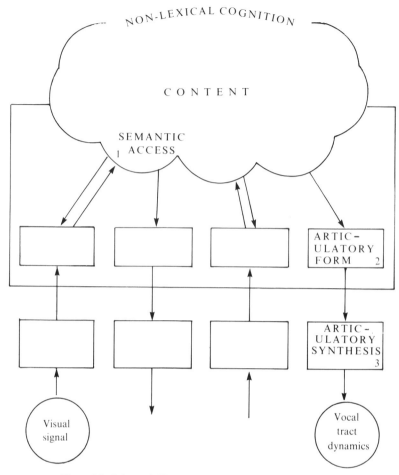

Figure 8.7 Schematic illustration of hypothesised location of processing impairments in (1) semantic anomia, (2) word-selection anomia (articulation) and (3) word-production anomia (articulation). (Based on discussion in chapter 5, above, and Benson 1979: 101–4.)

of *specific anomia* (depending on which sort of words are most affected), are usually distinguished (see fig. 8.7). Spontaneous speech is described as fluent but empty of specific content-words (particularly nouns, but other major lexical categories also, including main verbs other than *be*, adjectives and adverbs), and full of proforms such as pronouns, *thing*, *someone*, *suchlike*, etc. Although said to be fluent, spontaneous speech is frequently interrupted by pauses for word finding and is marked by circumlocutions. Occasionally *semantic paraphasias* or substitutions linked to the meaning of the assumed target word are noted (see the discussion of substitutions in ch. 3). Auditory

430

comprehension is reported to be generally good or mildly impaired, and auditory-oral repetition abilities are excellent, with full comprehension. Written language abilities – depending on whether the person doing the assessment sees these as relevant to the syndrome or not – may be good: in general, free writing, or writing in response to a picture stimulus is characterised by the same word-finding difficulties as speech production, and hence tends to be rather worse than the more constrained activity of writing to dictation, or copying a written sentence. Spelled-word recognition is also good. Performance on selecting an object in response to its written name may be excellent. Conversely, when confronted with an object and asked for its name (so-called 'confrontation naming'), the patient may perform quite poorly, though this depends on the severity of the syndrome. Generally, prompting with the initial phoneme or syllable does not help, and the patient may even fail to accept the correct name when it is provided by the examiner ('No, it's not that ... I was trying to get ... no, it's gone.').

The picture emerging here is of a difficulty in activating the appropriate *output-form component* of the lexical item (see ch. 5), when provided with an adequate *content specification*. The subtype of word-production anomia is consistent with this difficulty being associated with the implementation of the output form itself: the patient, we shall say, appears to have the meaning of the word but is unable to initiate the motor production of it. *Phonemic paraphasias*, or sound substitutions within the appropriate syllable-structure, may be noticed, and in this type of anomic aphasia prompting with the first consonant or vowel may be helpful. In word-selection anomia, the appearance is that the patient knows the *concept* (e.g. can describe the function of the object) but cannot find the *word*. This is consistent with an inability to activate the *lexical-form component*. Non-verbal identification, e.g. by matching the stimulus object with related objects, making pairs such as fork–plate, matchbox–ashtray, etc., is usually well preserved. In *semantic anomia*, the presumption is that the patient cannot be said to have the concept itself (a sort of *asymbolia*, in traditional terms) so he cannot perform non-verbal selection appropriately and confrontation naming is failed, with little or no help from prompts ('It begins with /sɪz/ ...') or cues ('You cut your fingernails with a pair of ___ ').

The occurrence of *modality*-specific anomia is usually marked by such terms as *visual agnosia* and *auditory agnosia*: a condition on the use of these terms is that at least one modality should be relatively spared, so that, e.g. in visual agnosia, auditorily presented stimuli, such as the sound of a waterfall, can be named, while visual stimuli, such as a picture of a waterfall, cannot. The use of the term 'agnosia' in such cases is intended to reflect the likelihood that there is some impairment within the content system preventing one non-verbal sensory modality, but not another, from achieving comprehension (see also remarks on modality-specific effects on priming in ch. 5). In such cases, as also with *category*-specific anomia (e.g. where colour words, or body-part words are selectively impaired), lesions are suspected to interfere with the connections from the relevant sensory areas to the assumed semantic area. Figure 8.6 illustrates some evidenced sites of lesion, but this syndrome, partly because of its variably defined symptomatology, is perhaps best thought of as a relatively 'non-localising' impairment. There are usually few localising indications from the general neurological examination. Some authorities recognise a syndrome (or hypersyndrome) consisting of anomic aphasia, *alexia with agraphia* (i.e. impairment of both reading and writing abilities in at least some respects) and the *Gerstmann syndrome* (itself a syndrome, of fairly controversial status, comprising left–right disorientation, *acalculia* or the loss of numerical abilities, agraphia – note here the overlap with the loss already mentioned – and *finger agnosia*, a condition where the patient is unable to discriminate one finger from another). A localisation for this syndrome has been proposed in the angular gyrus (see fig. 8.6). However, whether this situation represents anomic aphasia as such, or a different syndrome in which the symptom of anomia plays a part, is open to question. Anomia as a mild symptom may be evidenced from lesions anywhere in the brain, even in the right (non-dominant) hemisphere.

8.2.2 *Global aphasia*

Among the syndromes at the next level of incidence (around half the frequency of anomic aphasia) we find one which is at the other extreme of the severity scale, *global aphasia*. In this syndrome, all testable parameters of language function are severely impaired, so much so that many other non-language abilities are simply not testable. Spontaneous speech-output is severely limited, though frequently not to the level of complete *mutism*; generally, a few words or phrases are found, though often they do not appear to be contextually motivated, or even appropriate to the situation of utterance. The patient may be able to utter only a few syllables that are recognisable when they occur again but not as words or portions of words. However, prosodic contrasts may be observed even on these unintelligible utterances. Even stereotyped phrases and sequences such as the patient's name, standard greetings, the days of the week, etc. may be impossible to elicit. Auditory comprehension may be slightly better, though possibly estimates of this are inflated by not discounting the role of non-verbal interpretation (e.g. of gesture, facial expression, and so on). The patient is severely disabled in repeating (auditory–oral) and in copying (written material). Reading comprehension is severely impaired, although the fact that any measurement is possible in this at all suggests that comprehension may be genuinely better than output abilities in this syndrome. Writing, in response to a picture stimulus, is not possible; some measurable performance may be found on writing words to dictation, and even on spelled-word recognition. Best performance (at around one-fifth of normal scores) is found on matching written names with objects. By contrast, confrontation naming is severely impaired. The syndrome has been characterised as one of 'phonemic disintegration' in view of the remarkably reduced sound-structure inventory of speech output, and the limited speech comprehension. It may be that this term simply captures a fairly superficial aspect of the syndrome, however, and it has not gained wide acceptance. There is a real doubt as to whether there is a single consistent syndrome in this impairment pattern, where all parameters of functioning are at such low levels. Certainly, it has been observed that recovery, in so far as it occurs at all, is frequently towards another syndrome, such as *Broca's aphasia* (8.2.3). This raises the possibility that there is a 'true global' aphasia, which shows no trans-syndromic recovery pattern, and various 'pseudo-global' conditions which are actually very severe early stages of other syndromes. (It will be appreciated that such considerations as these go to the heart of the problematic status of the concept of 'syndrome', and we shall not pursue them here.) Global aphasia has been evidenced in association with a variety of left-hemisphere lesion-sites, usually of fairly massive extent. Localisation is, therefore, not always thought to be a very realistic undertaking, but where focal damage can be ascertained, it usually occupies the edges of the *sylvian fissure* (fig. 8.6), together with the surrounding (*perisylvian*) cortex. In contrast to language, the neurological examination may show severe general impairments, but also, surprisingly, minimal loss. For this reason, the focal damage-areas are thought not to extend to the motor- or sensory-association areas. What this means, simply, is that where, in a particular patient, the damage does so extend, and sensory/motor impairment is accordingly found, this is interpreted by some authorities as 'global aphasia with sensory/motor involvement'.

8.2.3 *Broca's aphasia*

Now we turn to one of the classic syndromes, one that is generally thought to be sufficiently well defined to function as a benchmark or cardinal syndrome in relation to which certain other syndromes may be more clearly assessed. It occurs about as often as global aphasia in the data of figure 8.4, but is not so severe, since certain abilities tend to be relatively well preserved. It was first described by the French neurologist Paul Broca in 1861, supported by clinical case-history and autopsy. Since then, questions have been raised about its neuroanatomical basis, and even about its status as a true 'aphasia' at all (see sections 8.5.1, 8.5.2); but what is most noticeable is that it has become a firmly established *clinical entity*. As such, it refers to the following cluster of symptoms. Spontaneous speech is described as non-fluent: the output rate is very low and there are articulatory difficulties which give an impression of effortful stumbling. Segmental substitutions are observed, as well as *dysprosody*, the disruption of normal intonational patterns. Utterances produced in this way are typically short, many consisting of one word, with a maximum of around three to four. Such utterances also show what is frequently described as a syndrome (or sub-syndrome) of *agrammatism*: apart from being consistently short, utterances are constructed around major lexical-class words such as nouns, main verbs and adjectives, and other elements such as determiners, prepositions and auxiliary verbs tend to be omitted. The result gives the impression of 'telegrammatic' output. In severe cases, all output may be reduced to nouns, and in most cases nouns appear to be more readily used than verbs. Against this, however, stereotype phrases, including overlearned sequences such as the days of the week, or bits of verse, appear as strikingly normal. The patient may end a prolonged unsuccessful attempt to utter a word with a fluent 'Oh! I don't know', and may in general be able to punctuate his or her efforts with fluent control of social utterances such as *I see, no, yes* and sequences of these, all with strikingly good intonational control.

Auditory comprehension is usually reported to be better than speech output, but there is wide variation – and some doubt – in just how good it is. Possibly it is better for short utterances and for highly referential words, and much less good for longer structures and relational terms such as directional prepositions and adverbs. The good control of social utterances may contribute to the clinical impression of a patient who knows much more than he or she can express. Generally, there appears to be difficulty in responding to multiple sequences such as 'give me the ball, the pen and the brush'. Repetition is impaired, showing quite straightforwardly the effects of whatever comprehension loss may be present, and some of the impairment of spontaneous speech; however, the speech-output characteristics are generally rather better than in spontaneous speech, even though the types of impairment (segmental substitution, agrammatism) are the same. Where the stimulus material clearly stretches the residual comprehension abilities, the output may be as severely affected as spontaneous output. Confrontation naming is impaired, though it may be more fluent and successful than spontaneous speech. A word-finding difficulty, or word-selection anomia, frequently appears as an obstacle to later stages of recovery.

Reading comprehension is variable – it may appear fairly normal, but is again subject to problems in handling longer, more complex sequences, even where the individual words can be read. Reading individual words aloud yields rather better speech output than does spontaneous speech, in most cases. Written word–object matching may be quite good. Written output, however, is always poor. Letters are large, messy and poorly formed, and it is important to note that this is not simply to be accounted for by the fact that the patient typically has to use the non-preferred hand for this task, as a result of associated motor deficit (see below). Sequencing difficulties are also found in writing, with many letters omitted and numerous reversals and other misspellings. Sentence copying is severely impaired largely because of this output problem, as is dictation writing of individual words. Spelled-word recognition is extremely poor.

Neurological examination normally reveals a right-side hemiplegia or hemiparesis, accompanied by a usually milder sensory loss. Additionally, there may be a difficulty, not attributable to muscle weakness, that impairs the initiation of well-comprehended commands to move parts of the left side of the body. Thus, the command to take guard with a cricket bat may be hard to carry out, even where it can be performed spontaneously. This phenomenon is referred to as *apraxia*. The visual field may be affected, with a right homonymous hemianopia usually indicating more posterior damage (see fig. 8.6). There may be a tendency for the eyes to wander off to the left of centre during fixed gaze (*conjugate left deviation*), due to extra-ocular muscle-control impairment. Figure 8.6 indicates a typical focal localisation for this syndrome, although the extent of the damage can vary widely. Many of the issues that have caused debate about the neuroanatomical basis of this syndrome can be found in the following graphic and succinct account of Broca's original patient:

> Broca's first case, Leborgne (Tan), was 51 when he died, and lost his speech at 30 (it is not known whether gradually or suddenly). He understood everything, but he only answered 'tan, tan' rather expressively. He would lose his temper and supplement his vocabulary with expletives. He had gradually increasing right arm and leg paralysis, ten years after the onset of the illness. Broca examined him on several occasions, and noted erroneous responses; these he attributed to impaired intelligence, due to his expanding cerebral lesion (a stroke in evolution?) or his fever (he was admitted with cellulitis of his right leg). Broca predicted that a slowly progressive, chronic softening would be found in the left frontal lobe, with extension into the corpus striatum (because of the hemiplegia). The autopsy showed a cyst over the left sylvian fissure. When this was punctured, an egg-sized cavity was found,

435

separating the frontal and temporal lobes, representing the loss of cerebral substance. Softening extended beyond the limits of this cavity and a considerable portion of the left hemisphere had been gradually destroyed by this process. The posterior half of the third frontal convolution (F3), and the second frontal convolution (F2), the inferior marginal convolutions (T1) and the insula had been eroded ... Broca assumed that the illness progressed in a biphasic manner: first, one of the frontal convolutions, 'probably the third', was affected (loss of speech), then the other areas as well (paralysis). He then said that generalized atrophy was responsible for the disorder of intellect. (Kertesz 1979: 124)

We shall return to consider some of these issues below, in section 8.4.

8.2.4 *Wernicke's aphasia*

Of comparable severity and frequency of occurrence to Broca's aphasia, *Wernicke's aphasia* represents another classic syndrome. Described by the German neurologist Carl Wernicke in 1874, it provided in many ways a complementary pattern to Broca's aphasia, and the two syndromes together formed the foundation of ensuing aphasiological research efforts. In the subsequent debates, those who called the 'aphasic' status of Broca's syndrome into question usually pointed to Wernicke's syndrome as an example of 'pure aphasia'. They seem to have had in mind a distinction between speech output (markedly reduced in Broca's, but quite fluent in Wernicke's) vs comprehension (largely spared in Broca's, but severely impaired in Wernicke's).

Spontaneous speech is characterised as fluent, with a high (even abnormally high) rate of output and a tendency to run on even in the face of efforts on the part of the examiner to intervene (*logorrhea*). Phonological phrase-length is normal, with good control of intonation and articulatory targets. Grammatical structure may appear normal at first sight but is sometimes marked by inappropriate stem–affix formations, such as *is louding* for *is loud/is talking loudly*. It is also usually lacking in specific content-words and is therefore described as 'empty'. These features together constitute the subsyndrome of *paragrammatism*. The emptiness of the output derives largely from substitutions at the sound segment level (so-called *literal* or *phonemic paraphasias*) and of one word for another (so-called *verbal paraphasias*). Frequently the target word is not determinable from the paraphasic error, and the resulting form is called a *neologism*. Where neologisms predominate, the output is described as *jargon*; the term *jargon aphasia* should, therefore, probably be thought of more as a symptom than as a syndrome, though this is a contested issue.

Stereotyped phrases are observed, as well as overlearned sequences such as the days of the week, and they may be produced fluently once 'set'; there may be some difficulty in breaking one set and establishing another. Auditory comprehension shows a severe loss, often restricted apparently to certain single-word utterances or stereotyped expressions. In some patients there is a question of impaired auditory discrimination, but in most cases a semantic problem is assumed to exist. The patient may be able to respond to whole-body commands (e.g. 'Show me how you dig the flower beds') better than anything else. Frequently a fatigue or 'jamming' effect builds up; examiners report a sense of 'doors closing' that had previously been 'open', as the patient starts to fail on items that had been successfully managed earlier in the session. Repetition is always impaired, usually in parallel degree to auditory comprehension. Confrontation naming is usually bad, marked by paraphasias; but in some patients who are otherwise diagnosed into this syndrome it may be relatively good. It is frequently better than the ability to act out verbal commands.

Reading comprehension is always impaired and may be severely affected; but it is not always in parallel with auditory comprehension, and some rather striking dissociations between auditory and reading comprehension have been reported. Reading aloud is variably performed, depending on the level of reading comprehension; written word–object matching is generally rather better.

Written output consists of well-formed letters, in fluent sweeps, but an attempt at picture description typically contains largely unintelligible sequences mixed with recognisable words: in many ways a written analogue of the spontaneous-speech output. Dictation of words is also poor, with many paraphasias. Copying a written sentence is rather easier. Finally, spelled-word recognition is severely impaired.

The usual interpretation of these symptoms is one of a semantic disorder, which may affect spoken- and written-language processing differentially. Speech and writing output are described as semantically empty, which seems to reflect a presumption that semantic control over output is somehow blocked, or disconnected. This by itself, however, would not explain the loss of comprehension, which seems to require an impairment within the semantic system itself, or possibly a disconnection of input to the semantic system. The most parsimonious hypothesis is of a semantic impairment which is central, so as to affect both input and output processing; but it may apparently spare written language relative to speech, or vice versa. Some authorities, doubtless mystified by this, have proposed an auditory deficit as the essence of the syndrome, but it is not entirely clear that this accounts for the output features nor for the frequent loss in written-language abilities. The interpretation of the syndrome is thus quite problematic. This is compounded by the variable role of word-finding difficulty within the pattern; the best view seems to be that this should not be considered an essential symptom within the syndrome, but rather as a frequently occurring concomitant.

The neurological examination may show rather little: generally little or no paresis; exceptionally, some cortical sensory loss; and sometimes an upper-right quadrantanopia, reflecting involvement of temporal-lobe radiations of the visual system (see fig. 8.2). The site of lesion is placed in the superior temporal lobe, close to the temporal–parietal junction, and extending into the infolded surface from the sylvian fissure, out of sight from a lateral view of the brain. This area (known as *Heschl's gyrus*) also contains the primary auditory cortex, and Wernicke's area is usually somewhat posterior to this. Posterior and inferior involvement from this site is usually associated with anomia as a complicating symptom. Most Wernicke patients have lesions that extend considerably beyond the focal site, and parietal-lobe involvement is not uncommon, particularly in association with more severe loss of reading and writing abilities. The patients are frequently unaware of their incomprehensible output and do not understand why they cannot understand what others say to them. This may result in paranoid attitudes, which may in turn have an adverse effect on the assessment of the disorder.

8.2.5 *Conduction aphasia*

Discussion of Broca's and Wernicke's syndrome sets the context for this syndrome, which is less frequent than either and also less severe overall (see figs. 8.4 and 8.5). Spontaneous-speech output is somewhat like Wernicke's aphasia, being fluent and paraphasic, with good articulation. But the rate of output is not so high, and there are hesitations – which may be associated with word-finding – and less good control of intonation. Sound-segment substitutions are particularly noticeable. Overlearned sequences and verses are well retained in production, once they have been set.

Auditory comprehension, even more so than in the case of many Broca's aphasics, is rather good, or normal – certainly sufficient for carrying on a fairly undemanding conversation. Complex grammatical structures, however, are generally not understood.

The crucial feature of the syndrome is that repetition, in spite of the presence of output and input abilities, is severely impaired. Attempts to repeat are marked by multiple substitutions of sound segments, and also of lexical items, particularly in closely structured semantic fields such as kinship terms, colour names and numerals. In this pattern of deficit, comprehension of the required word is frequently revealed, in the form of some appropriate circumlocution or semantically related error word. There is a suggestion that the repetition impairment is particularly severe for closed-class items (e.g. prepositions, determiners, etc.). Confrontation naming is usually bad as well, with word-finding problems and paraphasic output.

Reading comprehension is good to normal, parallel with the auditory mode; reading aloud is rather better than repetition of auditory input, though it too is substantially impaired. By contrast, written word–object matching is performed at or near normal levels.

Spontaneous-writing output is parallel to Wernicke's in many ways: some individual words are recognisable and letters are well formed, but there are many irregularities in the sequencing of letters within words and of words in constructions.

Copying a sentence may be performed rather well, in contrast to the severe auditory–oral repetition deficit. But writing words to dictation and recognis-ing orally spelled words are both substantially impaired. The striking symp-tom here, as we have noted, is bad repetition in the face of fluent (if paraphasic) production and spared comprehension. The most usual interpre-tation of this remarkable finding has been in terms of a disconnection between auditory input and oral output, specifically arising from damage to known conducting pathways linking from the former to the latter (hence the term 'conduction aphasia'). The presence of relatively well-preserved written-language copying, in some patients at least, suggests a disconnection that is specific to the auditory–oral mode. However, Kertesz (1979) suggests that the auditory–oral connection may be severed in two rather distinct ways: one would imply a disconnection of auditory processing from production; the other would imply the reverse. For most assessment purposes, this may seem a distinction without a difference; but it may be relevant to localisation of lesion (see below) and other behavioural evidence (see section 8.3).

The neurological examination may have quite variable findings. There may be some right hemiparesis (more usually of the arm than the leg), or none; there may be some sensory loss, sometimes a bilateral loss of pain, or none. (Some patients experience a rather intense pain in the later stages of recovery, called *pseudothalamic pain* to suggest its severity, akin to that associated with certain thalamic lesions.) There may be a right visual-field quadrantanopia, either upper or lower, or hemianopia, or no loss.

Two lesion sites are suggested: the basic one is shown in figure 8.6 as a cross above the sylvian fissure, which is actually supposed to represent a subcortical lesion to the *arcuate fasciculus*, a bundle of white-matter pathways running from Wernicke's area to Broca's area. An alternative site has been proposed, close to Wernicke's area, below the sylvian fissure. In each case, the lesion may be quite small. The two sites may be associated with two distinct varieties, as mentioned above (and taken further in section 8.3).

In conclusion, we may note that conduction aphasia, together with Broca's and Wernicke's, completes the set of syndromes that are commonly associated with focal lesions in the 'language area' that we referred to above (p. 429) – also known as the 'perisylvian region'. The syndromes to which we now turn are generally associated with focal lesions around the outer margin of this area, and hence, from a neuroanatomical standpoint, may be seen as involving connections into, and out from, more central language-processing regions. We should note that, as figure 8.3 indicates, stroke damage associated with just the middle cerebral artery would involve the perisylvian area, while the outer margins are served by combinations of the middle and anterior, and middle and posterior cerebral arteries.

8.2.6 *Transcortical motor aphasia (TM)*

Transcortical here refers to the assumed border-zone status of the syndrome, at least with respect to its neuroanatomical basis. Transcortical *motor* aphasia is a relatively rare, moderately severe syndrome in which the motor-production aspects of speech are markedly impaired. We must bear in mind the characteristics of Broca's aphasia, and ask how this syndrome is to be distinguished from it.

Spontaneous speech is non-fluent, with particular difficulties in initiating articulations, leading to a more stumbling, repetitive or stuttering output than is usual with Broca's speech. *Perseveration*, where the output seems locked in to a cycle of identical syllables, may be observed. Like Broca's speech, articulatory effort is noticeable, but overlearned sequences and stereotypes may be fluently and accurately produced, once set. The patient responds well to sound-structure prompts and contextual cues. Also, as in Broca's syndrome, agrammatism is present.

Auditory comprehension appears relatively well spared, at least in casual demands, but, as with Broca's, weakness becomes evident in multiple sequencing and relational terms. The contrast between affirmative and positive, as represented in responding to *yes/no* questions, may be lost; this, together with perseveration of non-verbal response, tends to make accurate assessment of comprehension extremely difficult. There may also be apraxia in non-verbal responses.

Repetition is good to normal, and here lies the criterial difference between this syndrome and Broca's aphasia. The patient can detect and correct grammatical errors in stimulus materials, and distinguish non-words from real words.

Confrontation naming is poor, showing the same sort of articulatory problems as spontaneous speech, which may be alleviated by prompting. Some word-finding difficulties are also observed routinely.

Reading comprehension is often rather good – better than Broca's, on the whole – though some patients are described as having significant *alexia*, or reading difficulties, also. Reading a complex sentence aloud is moderately difficult for these patients, though, because of the grammatical complexity of the stimulus material. Written word–object matching is rather good.

Spontaneous writing, again like Broca's, shows large, messy letters, poor letter-sequencing, and the features of agrammatism. But copying a sentence is much better, generally impaired only by letter ill-formedness. Dictation of words is rather poor as is spelled-word recognition: in each case, sequencing difficulties, in output as well as input processing, may be the main reason, since each of these tasks involves a shift between modalities.

As we have seen, these symptoms are rather closely aligned with those of Broca's aphasia, apart from the relatively spared abilities to reproduce input in terms of output where no shift in modality (speech, writing) is involved. But even in Broca's aphasia it has been suggested that this ability may be retained rather better than spontaneous output, and the two syndromes may accordingly be held to differ primarily in degree rather than in kind. The neurological examination may also yield findings that are very similar to those of Broca's aphasia, and figure 8.6 demonstrates the two evidenced focal sites of lesion $(T_1 T_2)$ – both, it will be observed, rather close to Broca's area in the perisylvian region. Recovery from Broca's aphasia may take the form of transcortical motor aphasia, if repetition abilities improve sufficiently in relation to the others.

8.2.7 *Transcortical sensory aphasia (TS)*

In this syndrome we find a parallel situation with respect to Wernicke's aphasia to that just noted between transcortical motor and Broca's syndromes. In other words, the transcortical sensory syndrome is broadly similar to its perisylvian counterpart, Wernicke's, but is distinct in showing spared repetition abilities. It is fairly rare, and moderately severe (also like its motor counterpart).

Spontaneous speech is fluent, with many paraphasias and neologisms; but it is also striking for its *echolalia*, or strong tendency to repeat faithfully what has just been said by the examiner. In this respect, strength in repetition is actually more of a defect.

Auditory comprehension is severely impaired, showing a difficulty with *yes/*

no questions (as in transcortical motor aphasia), indicating named objects and performing actions to command.

By contrast, repetition is excellent, at least in terms of an assessment which does not take comprehension (it may be entirely lacking) into account in this respect. Whether this is actually to be taken as the same ability that is assessed where comprehension is present is extremely unlikely from a psycholinguistic point of view, of course. Nonsense sequences are repeated as faithfully and readily as meaningful ones, up to the limit of auditory memory-span (which may be rather restricted). Confrontation naming is very poor, frequently leading to a long, unrelated utterance.

Reading comprehension also shows a severe impairment, although reading aloud may be spared as an uncomprehending transposition skill. But it is noticed that, for many patients, reading aloud a complex sentence is very difficult. Written word–object matching is bad, on the whole rather worse than in Wernicke's aphasia.

Spontaneous writing is severely affected, as in Wernicke's, and even the task of copying a sentence is poorly performed. However, while writing words to dictation is similarly impaired, spelled-word recognition is vastly better than in Wernicke's aphasia, and, next to auditory repetition, may be the best preserved ability (i.e. to a moderate degree).

The picture that emerges from these findings is one of differentially spared auditory reproduction, albeit within a limited span. The contrast with Wernicke's aphasia seems quite marked.

The neurological examination may show mild, Wernicke-type symptoms, or no deficits, though there is frequently some right-field visual loss (upper or lower quadrantanopia, or hemianopia). The mildness of these signs, together with the striking echolalia, may lead to misdiagnosis of these patients as psychotic. Figure 8.6 indicates the two evidenced focal sites of lesion for this syndrome (T_3, T_4), posterior to the perisylvian site of Wernicke's aphasia, and either slightly superior or inferior, in the posterior parietal or temporal lobes.

8.2.8 *Mixed transcortical aphasia*

Placing the two transcortical aphasias together in Figure 8.6 has anticipated an advantage in presenting this syndrome, which is a remarkable, and rare, combination of both types. Its effects are very severe, since it effectively cuts off the central language abilities from the surrounding areas of brain organisation; for this reason, it is frequently referred to as the *isolation syndrome*.

Spontaneous speech may hardly be said to exist, since these patients do not speak unless spoken to, and then produce highly echolalic, stereotypic speech.

Overlearned sequences may be responded to readily, and fluently copied and/ or completed. Once a particular set has thus been established, it may be difficult to turn the patient to another task. Auditory comprehension is severely impaired, and may be non-existent, even when assessed through non-verbal responding. Repetition is well preserved, in the uncomprehending sense of the term, within a limited auditory span. Confrontation naming is severely impaired, with frequent failure to respond, neologisms and paraphasias. Reading comprehension is very poor, as is reading aloud, but written word–object matching may be relatively spared, in some patients at least. Spontaneous writing is virtually non-existent; there may be some residual ability to copy, but writing to dictation is more severely impaired. Spelled-word recognition may be relatively spared, as in transcortical sensory aphasia.

The picture that emerges is one of relatively low-level (i.e. non-comprehending) input–output relations, generally better preserved in spoken- rather than written-language input. But we should note the relatively good non-verbal responding to written names of objects; this seems to represent an interesting input–output relation where comprehension is involved. It is difficult to know whether this is achieved on the basis of grapheme–phoneme conversion, direct visual access, or a mixture of both. We should recall that this task is also reported as well performed in the transcortical motor syndrome. The neurological signs are quite variable, and indicative of rather widespread damage. There is often right hemiplegia or even bilateral quadriparesis (i.e. affecting all four limbs), accompanied by significant sensory loss. Frequently a right homonymous hemianopia is present. The sites of lesion that have been determined generally correspond to simultaneous damage in both the frontal and temporal-parietal areas that are associated with the other transcortical syndromes separately (see fig. 8.6): the damage is usually more widespread than just these regions, however.

8.2.9 *Alexia and agraphia*

We may conclude section 8.2 with some remarks on the apparent status of the disorders that are grouped under the labels of *alexia* and *agraphia*. We have routinely included symptoms relating to reading and writing abilities in our discussion of the eight major syndromes above, and in so doing we have departed somewhat from many traditional treatments of them. There has been an assumption that aphasia is primarily to be identified in the area of speech input and output abilities, in relation to which alexia and agraphia may appear as extraneous complicating involvements. In this sense, perhaps, traditional aphasiology and many structural-linguistic approaches have been in rather close agreement, though for different reasons. To the extent that

Table 8.4 *The comparative symptomatology of the syndromes of alexia and agraphia*

	Frontal		Parieto-temporal	
	Alexia	Agraphia	Alexia	Agraphia
Reading comprehension	Partial, mainly for nouns and action verbs; anomia for letter names		Bad on words, letters; tracing letter shapes does not help	
Reading aloud	Isolated substitutions; Sentence meaning may be guessed; Spelling aloud may be poor, better on nouns		Bad Cues of little help	
Written-word to object matching	Partial		Bad	
Spontaneous writing		Poor spelling; large messy letters little output, omissions		Letter mis-sequencing; well-formed shapes; low content
Copying		Omissions, insertions of letters and parts of letters; worse than hemiplegia can account for		Adequate, but poor comprehension
Dictation		As for spontaneous writing		As for spontaneous writing

Based on discussion in Benson 1979: 107–28.

written language impairments have been recognised, they may be set out as in table 8.4.

We have already noted that the terms 'alexia' and 'agraphia' mark a distinction of input vs output that is neutralised in the more general term 'aphasia': hence the empty areas of the table represent symptoms that may be associated with, but are not essential to, the disorder indicated for a particular column. Four types of disorder are set out in this way; they are distinguished (on the basis of evidenced focal-lesion-sites) as *frontal* vs *parieto-temporal*. It is also strikingly apparent that frontal alexia/agraphia align themselves, in symptomatology, with each other, and to Broca's aphasia (table 8.3); and that parieto-temporal alexia/agraphia are similarly aligned with each other and with either Wernicke's or anomic aphasia, depending on the specific pattern of symptoms. From these considerations it would appear that, for these main types of written-language impairment at least, the distinction between symptom and syndrome may be problematic (as we noted earlier, in the case of anomia vs anomic aphasia). Clearly, from a clinical point of view, it is sensible to label distinctly those disorders where speech is primarily affected from those where written-language abilities are mainly impaired. However, the use of different labels should not blind us to the possibility that it is the balance of symptoms, rather than radical syndromic distinctions, that may be involved. In essence, we may be dealing with either agrammatism, or paragrammatism (however these may best be defined), in one or the other of the principal alternative modalities of language. Such consideration receives support from the focal lesion-sites involved, in the area of the angular gyrus (fig. 8.6). We shall return to alexia and agraphia in rather more detail in section 8.4, below.

Thus far, we have briefly reviewed the results of more than a century of research concerned with the establishment of syndromes and the possible localisation of their lesion sites (though we have not done justice to the nature of the debate over 'localisationism' that has attended this development). Two further steps are essential in the progress of aphasiology: one is the development of objective taxonomies of aphasic performance; and the other is a closer examination and interpretation of the linguistic characteristics of aphasic impairments, in terms of some viable model of language processing. We shall consider the first of these steps now, and turn to the second in section 8.4.

8.3 The validation of aphasic syndromes

It is essential to try to go beyond the essentially subjective assessments that form the basis of the syndromes we have discussed, since only in this way can the clinical picture be brought into line with recent advances in

445

Table 8.5 *Scoring items on the Western Aphasia Battery*

Performance category	Measure
1. Spontaneous speech	Information content
2.	Fluency
3. Comprehension	Yes/no questions
4.	Auditory word recognition
5.	Sequential commands
6. Repetition	
7. Naming	Object naming
8.	Word fluency
9. Responsive speech	
10. Sentence completion	
11. Reading	
12. Writing	
13. Praxis	
14. Drawing	
15. Block design	
16. Calculation	
17. Raven's matrices	

Based on Kertesz 1979: table 7.5, p. 110.

the investigation of the neuroanatomical bases of aphasia (see 8.1.5 above). This is not to say that traditionally recognised syndromes such as those we have just described have not been, or may not continue to be, highly useful as a framework within which the individual impairment and needs of particular patients may be most sensitively addressed. It would be impossible to try to devise a clinically useful, objective, standard testing-procedure intended to cope with the full range of aphasic patients referred to a typical speech-therapy clinic: most aphasics have little stamina for the prolonged testing of their impaired language-abilities, and a monolithic testing procedure would be a hindrance, rather than a help, to routine clinical practice as it is carried on today. Most clinicians, whose first concern is for the patient, work from their training and experience in recognising the major syndromes, or approximations to them, on the basis of 'touchstone' testing, and they proceed from there to investigate the individual patient's needs.

Notwithstanding all this, however, there is a clear need for research interests to go forward, and for these purposes a class of standardised testing-procedures has been developed within the last few decades, offering reasonable hope of providing objective tests of clinical syndromes. As yet, however, these tests are still not sufficiently refined in their elaboration of linguistic-

Table 8.6 *Fluency scoring on the Western Aphasia Battery*

Score	Description
0	No response or short, meaningless utterances
1	Recurrent utterances used in a meaningful way, with varied intonation
2	Single words, mostly inappropriately used
3	Fluent, stereotypic utterances or mumbling, very low volume jargon
4	Predominantly single words, often appropriate, with occasional verbs or prepositional phrases; automatic sentences only: 'Oh, I don't know'
5	Predominantly telegraphic, halting speech, but some grammatical organisation; paraphasias may be prominent; few propositional sentences
6	More complete propositional sentences; normal rhythmic patterning may be present within phrases
7	Phonemic jargon with semblance to English syntax and rhythm, with varied phonemes and neologisms
8	Circumlocutory, fluent speech; marked word-finding difficulty; semantic jargon; often complete sentences
9	Mostly complete sentences; hesitation over parts of speech, auxiliary verbs, or word endings; some paraphasias; some word-finding difficulty
10	Sentences of normal length and complexity, without perceptible word-finding difficulty

From Kertesz 1979: 41–2.

performance categories or in their scoring of performance in these categories. Table 8.5 lists the categories recognised in a good modern test, the Western Aphasia Battery (WAB), in relation to which factors such as word frequency, imageability of words, contextual probability of words in constructions and grammatical, semantic and phonological complexity are taken account of in selecting the stimulus materials to be used. Nevertheless, there are weaknesses. For instance, the analysis of writing performance is as yet less well developed than one would wish, to take account of both mechanical and non-mechanical aspects of this highly complex modality. And the scoring system provided for the dimension of *fluency* under the heading of *spontaneous speech* shows how difficult it may be to provide an objective, sensitive and reasonably comprehensive assessment of the major aspects of language samples elicited under relatively unstructured conditions (see table 8.6).

Without going further into these problems here, we shall now follow some research that has been based on the WAB, directed towards the goal of objectively evaluating the clinical syndromes we reviewed in section 8.2. There is currently no better available indication of how successfully these clinical syndromes represent what we might call the 'natural taxonomy of language disorders'.

8.3.1 *The numerical taxonomy of aphasic syndromes*

A step towards the goal of a natural taxonomy is to quantify aphasics' performance on a test like the WAB and then to apply some objective grouping-procedures to the scores they achieve across the individual items in the test battery; Kertesz and his colleagues (Kertesz 1979) have used a type of clustering procedure as a preliminary test of the data, where similarity–dissimilarity of performance over the test items is represented in terms of hierarchically organised clusters of individual patients. The more similar two patients' score profiles are, the closer they are clustered in the resulting tree structure (or *dendrogram*). These clusters are then subjected to a further test of relatedness, the *nearest-neighbour network analysis*; this looks at the clusters which are closest together, and tests them to see if their distance apart, from centre to centre, is greater than the variation of individuals around their centres. If not, then the clusters effectively have overlapping boundaries, and are best treated as not truly distinct. Taking just the patients with infarcts (N = 142), on a selection of five spoken-language items from the WAB, the cluster analysis as set out in the dendrogram of figure 8.8 emerged. Ten clusters were found, of which I and II correspond well to the clinical categories of global and Broca's aphasia, respectively, and v, VII and x correspond perfectly with the clinical syndromes of transcortical sensory, Wernicke's and anomic aphasia, respectively. As Kertesz (1979) notes, this constitutes impressive justification of clinical categories. The main discrepancies were found with the clinical categories of mixed transcortical and transcortical motor aphasia, neither of which turned up more than a quarter of the time in any numerically established cluster. Interestingly, clinically diagnosed conduction aphasics fell into two distinct *taxa*, or groups, which Kertesz, on inspection, proposed to label 'afferent conduction' and 'efferent conduction' – a distinction which recalls the suspicion referred to in 8.2.5 above that there may be two distinct types of this syndrome, linked to different sites of lesion. The afferent type is closer to Wernicke's, both in clinical symptomatology and in the dendrogram (with lower repetition, naming and comprehension, but higher fluency), and the efferent type is closer to the anomics (with higher naming and lower fluency).

The two anomic clusters are distinguished by degree of severity; IX shows relatively high performance on most measures apart from naming, but x has nearly normal performance, with relatively mild anomia. A nearest-neighbour analysis supports all of these clusters except for I and II, which turn out to be not truly distinct, although the relatively good comprehension of II (Broca's) keeps them clinically apart.

A taxonomy of post-trauma patients (N = 25), drawn from a civilian population (none with penetrating missile injury) within thirty-five days of head

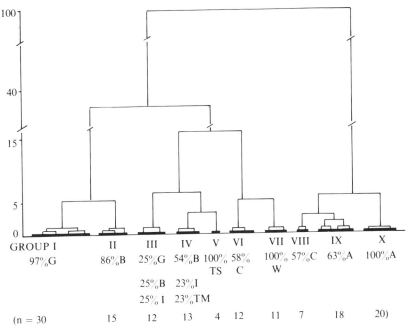

Figure 8.8 Cluster analysis, with percentage composition of groups by aphasic syndrome, for 142 aphasics with infarcts, on the WAB. (Based on Kertesz 1979: fig. 6.1, p. 86, table 6.1, p. 87.)

injury yielded essentially similar results, based on a total of twelve out of the seventeen items from the WAB. But a taxonomy of patients with tumour (N = 34) revealed a very different pattern, with few patients in clusters corresponding to global, Broca's or Wernicke's syndromes, and a high proportion of anomics. These patients were seen at the time that their tumours were discovered, a highly variable time from the onset of their aphasic symptoms. The low incidence of global aphasics and high proportion of anomics may reflect the fact that tumour symptoms tend to be mild and diffuse (via pressure effects) at all stages up to the last. These exploratory analyses tend to lend support to the traditional clinical picture and to extend and refine the categories in ways which document the effect of *aetiological* (or causative) factors in the emerging syndrome (e.g. tumour aetiology vs other types).

Another obvious question to ask is whether there is any real difference between acute- and chronic-aphasic populations. Looking at a group of 147 patients with infarcts, on the spoken-language measures 1–5 only, the acute population (N = 64) yielded eight clusters, confirmed by nearest-neighbour analysis, and the chronic population (N = 83) yielded the same number (see

449

Table 8.7 *Cluster analysis, with percentage composition of groups by biphasic syndrome, for aphasics with infarcts, in acute and chronic phases*

Clusters	Chronics	Acutes
I	10 global 5 Broca's	15 global
II	2 Wernicke's	5 Broca's 1 other
III	6 Broca's	10 Wernicke's 1 Broca's 1 conduction
IV	2 isolation 1 transcortical motor 1 Broca's	4 Broca's 2 conduction
V	4 Broca's 1 Wernicke's 2 conduction	3 conduction 1 anomic
VI	10 mixed, mild, low fluency 1 Wernicke's	2 isolation
VII	24 anomics	3 transcortical sensory 2 Wernicke's 1 conduction 1 transcortical motor
VIII	12 anomics 1 conduction	11 anomics 2 transcortical sensory

Based on Kertesz 1979: Figs. 7.1, 7.3, and discussion, pp. 100–6.

table 8.7). Inspection of the composition of comparable clusters between the two groups yields certain findings, of which we may mention here the following: (a) that there is considerable recovery from the cluster corresponding to Wernicke's aphasia is indicated by comparing acute III with chronic II; (b) the fact that many different syndromes ameliorate to a clinical anomic syndrome emerges from a comparison of acute VIII with chronic VII and VIII; (c) the rather pessimistic prognosis for Broca's aphasia is shown by the comparability of acute II with chronic III; and (d) the suggestion that global aphasics may recover to a symptomatology akin to Broca's is supported by comparing acute I with chronic I.

8.3.2 *Problems in interpretation*

Objective taxonomies such as these have an important role to play in aphasiological research, but it should be remembered that they depend on the quality of the information that is fed in to the analysis. As we have already suggested, the way language test-items are selected and scored is a crucial issue, and decisions here will have a large effect on the sorts of taxonomies that emerge, and on the way these taxonomies are to be interpreted. Many interpretative problems remain, therefore, and we shall start our discussion of a representative group of these within the WAB framework, and then go on to consider some other outstanding issues (section 8.4).

The status of written language abilities

If we take the seventeen subtests of the WAB, we can ask how they compare with each other in overall difficulty level across a range of aphasic syndromes. Are certain aspects of performance, as elicited and measured on the WAB, consistently more easy or more difficult than others? If we refer back to table 8.5, showing the scoring categories on the WAB, and make use of Kertesz' (1979) normalised scale of performance on all these categories, from 100 (severe loss) to 900 (normal abilities), we can identify three broad difficulty-bands, across sixty-four acute aphasics with infarcts. In the best performance range, between 500–650, there are three language measures: *yes/no* comprehension; fluency and auditory word-recognition; and the non-language measure, praxis. In the midrange, between 325–450, there are six language measures: comprehension of sequential commands; repetition; reading; object naming; responsive speech and sentence completion; and the non-language measure, drawing. In the worst performance band, between 250–325, there are writing, and word fluency.

Now, word fluency is rather a difficult task, involving the exhaustive listing of all members of a given word category (e.g. 'Name all the fruits you can think of'), within a given space of time. Normal adults generally start off fluently on this task, then stop, start repeating items, and grind to a halt. Arguably, it is a rather unusual demand to place on the retrieval dynamics of one's mental lexicon. More interestingly, writing is also in this worst-performance band. We need to consider in more detail why writing should be difficult, both in relation to reading, and in relation to the spoken-language items on the WAB.

It appears that writing is a language skill (rather, complex group of skills) that is highly vulnerable to disturbance. This relatively exposed status of writing abilities is underlined by a further consideration. Where language disorders arise in association with left-hemisphere damage, spoken- and written-language abilities are frequently impaired together, though to different degrees; patients are found whose impairment is more or less equivalent in each modality, at whatever level of severity, and others are found whose written-language abilities are selectively impaired in the presence of relatively

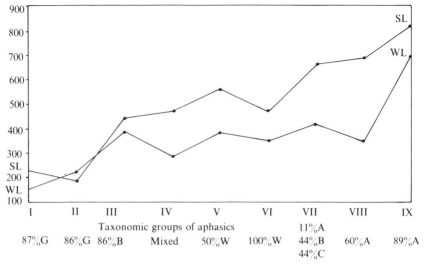

SL = SPOKEN LANGUAGE COMPONENTS
—Information content
—Fluency
—Yes/no comprehension
—Auditory word recognition
—Sequential commands

WL = WRITTEN LANGUAGE COMPONENTS
—Reading total
—Writing total

I = 2 Wernicke's, 9 Global
II = 1 Isolation, 6 Global
III = 1 Conduction, 6 Broca's
IV = TM/TS/Isolation (5 in all)
V = 1 TS, 2 Conduction, 3 Wernicke's
VI = 5 Wernicke's
VII = 1 Anomic, 4 Broca's, 4 Conduction ('Efferent' Conduction)
VIII = 1 TS, 1 Wernicke's, 3 Anomic
IX = 1 Conduction, 8 Anomic

Figure 8.9 Spoken and written language abilities, on a normalised scale of
100 (severe impairment) – 900 (normal performance), as measured on the
WAB, for a population of sixty-four acute aphasics with infarcts. (Based on
Kertesz 1979: table 7.5, p. 110.)

normal spoken-language abilities. But vanishingly few cases have been reported of the reverse situation, where written language is relatively spared in
the presence of largely impaired spoken language. This suggests a *unidirec-
tional dissociation* between these two types of language abilities. See figure 8.9
for the relative performance levels of written- and spoken-language abilities

on the WAB, across nine groups of the acute aphasics with infarcts in Kertesz (1979). This is something of a mystery if our spoken- and written-language abilities simply coexist in the left-cerebral language space, since such a situation would normally result in either a *lack of dissociation* (the two abilities would be impaired, or spared, together), or a *double dissociation* (one, or the other, as well as both together, could be impaired). It may turn out that the reason for this state of affairs lies in the cytoarchitectonics of the left cerebral language area, or in the connections into this area, including right–left hemispheric interactions.

8.4 The interpretation of aphasic syndromes

We now turn to consider some representative problems of interpretation in more detail. In general, we are faced with the following problem: given some particular surface manifestation(s) of linguistic impairment, how far is it possible to hypothesise some causal deficit(s) in the processing system? By and large, we might expect syntactic impairments to derive from syntactic levels of processing, lexical impairments from deficits in the lexicon, and so on. But this is too simple, in two ways: the first is that it may be too imprecise, as it stands, since syntax and lexicon are complex systems, within which different processing deficits might occur; secondly, and more problematically, there is the possibility that the deficit-manifestation link may be fundamentally complex, with one deficit giving rise to manifestation(s) in unexpected parts of the language system. This situation is not surprising, given the relation between underlying and surface phenomena that we considered in 3.1.2.

8.4.1 *Dyslexia*

We start with alexia, or dyslexia as it is usually called in the neuropsychological tradition that we are now going to examine (one of the curious aspects of terminology in this area is that researchers may use one or the other term, depending on their shared assumptions about its interpretation).

Marshall and Newcombe (1973, 1981) have pointed out that, among adult acquired reading-disorders following brain damage, two distinct patterns emerge, which have been named *deep dyslexia* and *surface dyslexia* (see table 8.8). In deep dyslexia, reading for comprehension is available up to a point, particularly where highly concrete and imageable nouns are involved; performance on more abstract words, including grammatical elements such as determiners and auxiliary verbs, is much less good. On repetition, it is found that non-words (i.e. having no lexical entry) cannot be responded to at all, even if they are homophonous with real words (e.g. *seel*), while real words tend to yield what are referred to as *semantic errors* (see Coltheart 1980a,

Table 8.8 *Characteristics of surface and deep dyslexia, after Marshall and Newcombe (1973)*

Surface dyslexia

1. Can read (some) nonsense syllables
2. Errors are typically phonologically similar to the stimulus
3. Errors are very frequently phonologically possible but non-existent lexical forms
4. Semantic reading of the visual stimulus is determined by the (frequently erroneous) phonology of the response (e.g. *listen*→/lɪstən/, → 'it's that boxer, isn't it?': *begin* → /begɪn/ → 'collecting money . . . when you ask someone')

Deep dyslexia

1. Cannot read nonsense syllables
2. Errors are often semantically similar to the stimulus
3. Errors are (almost) never non-existent lexical forms
4. Semantic misreading of the stimulus is sometimes preceded by a (partially) erroneous visual analysis of the stimulus (e.g. *sympathy* → 'orchestra'; *perfect* → 'scent', *allegory* → 'lizard')

From Marshall 1976: 114.

1980b). These may be analysed as either *paradigmatic* (substitutions from the same class, *father* → 'dad') or as *syntagmatic* (sequentially linked, *hot* → 'custard'), although some of these latter may be paradigmatic also, in terms of some larger semantic field (e.g. *Christmas* → 'turkey'). The usual interpretation is that these patients suffer from a blockage of the grapheme–phoneme conversion route (see ch. 5), and therefore rely on what is often referred to as the 'semantic route' (i.e. direct access).

It is rather unclear, however, how a primary symptom of 'semantic error' might arise from a 'phonological blockage'. One possibility is that the term 'semantic error' may be misleading in this context, in suggesting that there actually is a semantic disability in the syndrome. Another, weaker interpretation of the term is 'disorder characterisable in semantic terms', and this may be more appropriate. On the face of it, the input–output relationship evidenced in *father* → 'dad' is hardly to be described as errorful semantic functioning, even though the relationship between the two forms can be described in semantic terms. Even less straightforward cases, such as *Christmas* → 'turkey', generally show a semantic link where no other dimension of similarity exists.

What this suggests, then, is that the semantic level of processing is actually the *strongest* aspect of these dyslexics' performance. It is not inconceivable that these patients are showing to us what actually goes on at the semantic level in normal lexical access, when this is, because of the (non-semantic) disorder, not supported by other crucial aspects of the accessing process. Recall that we are talking about patients' performance on a reading-aloud task: we may imagine the first step to involve semantic activation of the relevant area (network of items) in the lexicon, followed by selection of the particular item which matches the graphological form of the written-word stimulus. Now, if some disorder makes it impossible to carry out a point-by-point analysis of the input, i.e. if it is perceivable only in terms of its global visual properties, then it is possible to understand how appropriate semantic activation, via direct access, might be achieved, with subsequent failure to carry out the matching process. In so far as graphological form is concerned, it is noticeable that deep dyslexic patients do make letter-based errors (e.g. *bead* → 'bread'); and in respect of grapheme–phoneme analysis, it may be significant that impaired short-term auditory memory has been frequently observed in deep dyslexics (though, it must be admitted, many case histories exist where this feature has not been assessed, apparently). From this account, it may be appreciated why some researchers have preferred the term 'phonemic dyslexia' for the same syndrome. But the issue is not yet resolved.

Similarly, *surface dyslexia*, characterised by preservation of the grapheme-to-phoneme route, and yielding phonological errors, may provide a window on the normal operation of grapheme–phoneme conversions. These, by virtue of the degree of mismatch between English sounds and spelling, must be prone to failure (see table 8.8 for some description of these errors). Here again, we are forced to consider the possibility that errors that are describable at one level of linguistic structure may arise through a disorder at some other level(s). Bearing this point in mind, we may now consider another class of interpretative problem.

8.4.2 *Agrammatism*

Agrammatism, as found for instance in Broca's aphasia and transcortical motor aphasia, is the traditional label for a rather well-studied phenomenon which has proved to be controversial in its interpretation. Traditionally, it has been viewed, as the name makes clear, as a loss of grammatical functioning; and the concept 'grammatical' has been interpreted fairly widely (critics might say loosely). Marshall (1977) conveniently summarises the way the tradition has characterised agrammatism: (a) arising frequently with frontal lesions; (b) involving a small active vocabulary, mainly consisting of nouns, verbs and adjectives; (c) showing widespread omission of grammatical formatives (closed-system elements, including affixes); and (d) in extreme cases, 'all expression is reduced to nominal form'. The passage in (1), from a conversation between therapist (T) and patient (P), looking at an advertisement depicting cowboy figures breaking in a horse, may serve to underline what form agrammatism may take (– indicates a pause; ' marks main stress; = indicates a prolonged articulatory onset):

(1) T: what's this
     P: erm –
     T: mm
     P: 'cowboys' and –
     T: mm
     P: 'cowboy 'and 'wrestler –
          'wrestler 'and –
     T: well
          the horse is tied with a rope
          isn't it
     P: a 'rope
          'ah 'yes yes
     T: what are they doing with the rope
     P: –
     T: what are they doing with the rope
     P: = string
     T: mm
     P: yes –
          = string
          = string
     T: mm
          mm
          they're pulling it
     P: 'pu'lling it
          'ah yes
          'pu (whisper)

This patient (see Crystal, Fletcher and Garman 1976; Garman 1982 for further details) shows a selective difficulty with verbs over nouns, and articulatory problems are evident in certain sequences of sounds such as consonant clusters. His most fluent control is over sequences of minor social utterances such as *ah yes yes* and *oh no no*, which occur appropriately often enough to convey the impression that he understands much more than he is able to produce.

Clearly, many of the required linguistic forms are simply not appearing – perhaps being systematically omitted – in such output. The tradition recognises that, in such cases, the determinants of what is omitted may be complex and interactive, with so-called phonological as well as grammatical factors

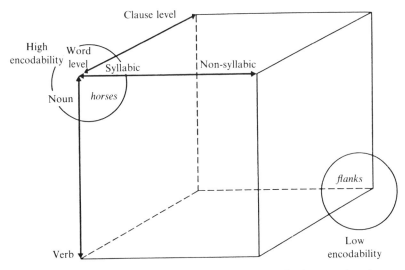

Figure 8.10 Three-dimensional model of interaction between phonology, word class and syntactic level, affecting the encodability of inflectional morphemes in agrammatism. (Based on Garman 1982: fig. 12.2, p. 156.)

being involved, as figure 8.10 illustrates. Thus, for instance, a Broca's aphasic is more likely to have difficulty in articulating the formation of *flanks* (as a third-person singular verb) because it involves an *abstract, low frequency* word stem, which is a *verb* rather than a noun; has a *clause*-level (subject–verb concord) affix rather than a word-level one (such as noun plural -*s*); and has a *non-syllabic* form of the affix, involving a *consonant cluster*. By contrast, and on the same criteria, the form *horses* (noun plural) is much less likely to present difficulty.

Now, against this traditional view of a compromise of various levels in agrammatism, Kean (1978) put forward a radical hypothesis regarding agrammatism in Broca's aphasia, positing a *single, phonological* deficit to account for *all* the characteristics of agrammatism. More specifically, Kean argued that 'the manifested linguistic deficits of Broca's aphasia can be accounted for only in terms of *the interaction between an impaired phonological capacity and otherwise intact linguistic capacities*' (68; emphasis added). Such a comprehensive approach, in terms of a single deficit, is interesting in its own right; but it is all the more important since Kean sees this case as an example of what may be achieved in 'the linguistic interpretation of aphasic syndromes'. In order to see what her proposal rests on, consider the sketch of grammatical and phonological relationships set out in figure 8.11. This shows a range of different grammatical structures converging on essentially

Grammatical level structures:

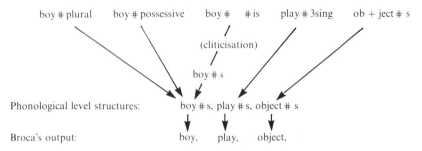

boy # plural   boy # possessive   boy #   # is   play # 3sing   ob + ject # s

(cliticisation)

boy # s

Phonological level structures: boy # s, play # s, object # s

Broca's output: boy,   play,   object,

Figure 8.11 Grammatical and phonological elements in relation to Broca's aphasic speech output. (Based on discussion in Kean 1978: 79–89.)

unitary phonological forms, which may be expressed most generally as: # # word # affix #, i.e. a word (indicated by the word-boundary symbols # ... #) whose internal contents are a word (also marked off by # ... #), plus an affix whose status is not that of a word. The sense of 'word' being referred to here is 'phonological word', being defined, in English, partly in terms of word stress (so '*black* '*bird* is two words, while '*blackbird* is one). The phonological-deficit hypothesis derives from the observation that the linguistically significant generalisation to be made from figure 8.11 is that it is at the level of phonological, rather than grammatical, structure that the # s affixal elements are to be characterised; and it is precisely such elements that show a tendency to be omitted in the speech of Broca's aphasics. The argument receives support from the observation that words formed out of non-word elements such as *ob-* and *-ject*, marked by the + -boundary, do not show omission of these elements in Broca's speech. The situation, then, seems to be that just those elements that are themselves not words, and which are attached to words (i.e. across a # -boundary), will tend to be omitted; these elements Kean refers to as *clitics*.

The force of this interpretation, when brought to bear on the traditional assumptions of agrammatism, will be apparent from a consideration of example (2):

(2)   The boys are playing on the grass

Phonological structure:

the # 'boy # s #   # are # 'play # ing #   # on the # 'grass #
—Word 1—   —Word 2—   —Word 3—
 C   W   C   C   W   C   C C   W

Broca's output:

'boy   'play   'grass

458

This example has just three phonological word-stress domains, marked 'Word 1–3'. Under each element in these domains, the symbols C (clitic) and W (word) have been added, for clarity. Kean points out that the omission of *the* falls into line with its phonological status as clitic, and no appeal need be made to its grammatical status as determiner. And so also for the preposition/clitic *on*.

This clearly suggests, at the very least, a redrawing of the boundary between phonological and grammatical phenomena in the speech of Broca's aphasics: elements that appear to be definable in grammatical terms (e.g. determiners, auxiliary verbs, propositions and so on) may show a tendency to be omitted, not because of some loss of grammatical ability, but by virtue of their phonological status. But there is a complication. Kean points out that certain aspects of linguistic knowledge, such as the relation between forms like '*definite* and *de'finitive* are preserved in Broca's aphasia, and may interact with the phonological-deficit pattern just outlined. Thus, if we find, for instance, that the form '*definite # ness* does not appear, we can say that this observation is consistent with the hypothesis; but what might we conclude regarding the non-appearance of *de'finit + ive*? Kean points out that this runs against the hypothesis, because *-ive* is a + -boundary affix (by virtue of the observation that the stress-altered form that it attaches to, *de'finit-*, is not a word), and hence is supposed to be retained.

Kean proposes that Broca's aphasics perceive that *de'finit + ive* is built on a stem *de'finit-* that is 'lexically construable with' '*definite*; on this basis, we can (a) account for our observation, and (b) lay the basis for a number of other interactive-type observations. These would include some that we have already mentioned, such as the tendency to omit verb affixes rather than noun affixes; non-syllabic affixes rather than syllabic ones; gerundial *-ing* (*the losing of the race*) rather than progressive *-ing* (*he was losing the race*); and other observations such as the tendency for Broca's aphasics to show prosodic disturbance. All these observations, in Kean's approach, are to be regarded as aspects of normal hierarchies of difficulty, preserved in Broca's speech: hence, they are not part of the aphasic syndrome to be accounted for. Clearly, knowing what is *not* part of an aphasic condition is just as important as knowing what is.

Unfortunately, this complication makes the hypothesis difficult to test (see Garman 1982). For instance, it would permit us to account for the lack of complex sentences in Broca's speech by referring to the phonological defect, and pointing to the well-known fact that complex sentences are higher up the hierarchy of difficulty for normal speakers, too. This 'saves' the phonological hypothesis, but raises the problem of what might conceivably falsify it.

There is also a problem (and, incidentally, it is a virtue of Kean's approach that it raises the issue) in characterising what we mean by a *clitic*. This term is used in a number of different senses, but essentially applies to phonologically unstressed elements in English word-structure. However, in many cases determiners, auxiliary verbs and prepositions may be phonologically stressed, where the distinction between stressed and unstressed forms may reflect the roles of these elements in grammatical and message structure. In such cases, we may want to say that it is these roles, rather than their phonological consequences, that determine the appearance or omission of these elements in the speech of Broca's aphasics.

Faced with such difficulties in abolishing the traditional concept of agrammatism altogether, other recent approaches have relied on updating the concept, refining it in the light of current models of grammar and language production. Thus, Berndt and Caramazza (1981) argue that 'the constellation of symptoms present in the production and comprehension of Broca's aphasics can be explained as a central disruption of the syntactic component of the language-processing system, typically co-occurring with an independent disorder of articulation' (p. 171). See also Bradley, Garrett and Zurif (1980). We have already referred briefly to Lapointe's (1985) conception of the syntactic stores that might be envisaged within Garrett's model of production (7.4.2); he proposes these in the context of what we may describe as a 'surface-syntax' account of agrammatism (specifically with reference to verb forms) which is based on a specific inability to access these stores. Byng and Coltheart's (1986) study, in contrast, is set in terms of high-level, or propositional, syntax. Their evidence derives from the effectiveness of therapy that was aimed specifically at improving the ability of their Broca's patient to establish thematic roles (in high-level syntax, close to message-structure requirements) in comprehension of input: the improvement in comprehension that resulted from this therapy programme also generalised to the patient's language production.

Thus, we may say that agrammatism is still a challenging issue. The phonological hypothesis may account for some of the effects that were previously attributed to agrammatism. A basic issue which still remains to be explained is the often-noted cooccurrence of agrammatism and impaired articulatory sequencing.

8.4.3 *Paragrammatism*

Our next problem in interpretation may appear to be rather like the Hunting of the Snark, since the main issue is whether the Snark – paragrammatism – can be said to exist at all. It is mentioned, but not always, in the context of fluent types of aphasia such as Wernicke's. Lesser (1978) quotes Goodglass (1976: 238) describing paragrammatism as involving (in contrast to agrammatism) 'not so much the reduction of grammatical organisation as the juxtaposition of unacceptable sequences: confusions of verb tense, errors in pronoun case and gender and incorrect choice of prepositions – the chief defect is paraphasia or the unwitting substitution of ill-chosen words and phrases in the stream of speech'. (See also Butterworth 1979 and Buckingham 1985.) Now, there are many quite distinct characteristics here, and, as Lesser says, 'the central question ... is the extent to which these syntactic errors can be attributed to a lexical disorder, and the extent to which they reflect syntactic limitations' (p. 147). If we are dealing with a lexical disorder, then it may be that the concept of verbal paraphasia is all that is required to account for whatever syntactic 'knock-on' effects are observed.

Edwards and Garman (1988) looked at this issue among others in the speech of a Wernicke's patient, Mr V. They were concerned to investigate three possible characteristics reported of such cases: (a) so-called press of speech (Albert *et al.* 1981), according to which part of the manifestation of impairment lies in a hyperfluency – i.e. the fluency is actually part of the disorder; (b) paraphasia, in the sense of semantically, grammatically and phonologically based word-substitutions and neologisms; and (c) paragrammatism. They used spontaneous speech as the basis for a comparison between Mr V and a suitably matched normal adult, Mr W. Concerning press of speech, no evidence emerged on such measures as rate of emission, ratio of planning units to expression units, or pausing characteristics; but in turn-taking, Mr V was noticeably more prone to run on until he was interrupted (with difficulty). Next, on a range of surface-syntax measures drawn from the LARSP grammatical assessment procedure (Crystal, Fletcher and Garman 1976), Mr V appeared not to be different from Mr W in the range or incidence of structural patterns deployed, although he did have many more unintelligible (and therefore unanalysable utterances). On a lexical analysis (similar to that illustrated in 3.3.2 above), Mr V appeared to have very similar type and token figures for all word classes except that of nouns, which were less well represented than in the speech sample from Mr W. It was further possible to account for the difference by treating Mr V's neologisms as attempts to produce nouns, rather than other word classes. So, Mr V's lexical deficit consisted in a specific difficulty of accessing nouns appropriately – but it proved possible to narrow this statement down still further. Table 8.9 shows all the noun types in the sample from Mr W (W), and from two recordings of Mr V (V1 and V2). It appears from this display that there is a distinct difference in the use of the entity nouns as between Mr V and Mr W. To some extent, this may reflect a strategy on the part of the normal speaker: Mr W found it difficult to formulate in a spontaneous fashion the requested description of himself and his activities and interests (the

Table 8.9 *The noun types in the samples of speech from a normal adult (W) and two recordings of an aphasic (V1, V2)*

	W	V1	V2
Entity	boat(s)	hand	drink(s)
	keel		(wife)
	frame(s)		
	batten		
	stripes		
	plank		
	gunwale		
	fibreglass		
	woodwork		
Temporal	years	yesterday	Wednesday
	morning	morning	tomorrow
	8 o'clock	day	week
	time	night	night
Spatial	top		way
	place		
Activity	boatbuilding		
	planking		
Other		bit	
		number	

From Edwards and Garman 1989: table 4, p. 174.

same request had been made of Mr V previously), and he appeared to take refuge at one point in a description of how he had used to help make wooden boats. It was in this context that the entity nouns occurred. But we may also suspect that something of Mr V's impairment shows up here: partly because, when faced with a similar situation, he did not resort to such a strategy (perhaps because he could not); and partly because we might suspect entity nouns to occur with reasonable frequency in any sample of spontaneous speech.

However that may be, it seems to leave us with a characterisation of Mr V's sample as one which shows evidence of poor turn-taking ability (deriving from impaired self-monitoring); much unintelligibility, most of which is linked to noun-based neologisms in place of entity nouns; and a deployment of other lexical elements and structural patterns that is not different from the normal adult control. It would appear, then, that paragrammatism is not present in this case: but it leaves open the possibility that it might be found to be present in other cases, or possibly even in this one if more sensitive analyses can be employed. For instance, it is a feature of LARSP that it assesses utterances individually, and concentrates on their structural rather than their lexical content: it may be that paragrammatism in many cases will reveal itself in the form of lexical and structural factors taken together, and possibly in the syntactic organisation of utterances in relation to each other. However this may turn out, it is a worthwhile task to try to arrive at a reasonable analysis of the concept of paragrammatism. And there is an important methodological point here, which is that such analyses must be based on an assessment of aphasic language in comparison to suitable control data, if untoward assumptions about the 'ungrammaticality' of spontaneous-speech samples are not to cloud the issue.

Dyspraxia and dysarthria

Part of the definition of aphasia is that it concerns a *central* language impairment, as opposed to a more peripheral dysfunction affecting the access to, or the execution from, the central language system. Such a distinction is clinically fundamental, since it is imperative to assess whether a patient's problem lies on one side or another of this boundary; and it appears to accord with the division we have recognised, between signal processing (ch. 1) and the abstract language system (ch. 3). However, as our discussion of processing models in chapters 5–7 may have revealed, the boundary between peripheral signal and central language processing can prove hard to draw cleanly. For instance, we have observed that stored forms of words in the lexicon (surely a part of the central system) may be directly involved in perception and production of the signal. In the context of aphasiology, the concepts of dysarthria and dyspraxia point up this issue.

Dysarthria is the easier one to define. The essence of it is that, since it involves a muscular weakness, it is clearly peripheral, and hence its effects are not confined to speech production alone. Thus, difficulties in other functions associated with the speech musculature are noticed, such as sipping, chewing, swallowing and coughing. Pathology may be of various types, including disease affecting the extra-pyramidal system, the brainstem nuclei, the cerebellum, or the lower motor neurons (the cranial motor nerves). It is frequently found in degenerative conditions such as Parkinson's disease. A transient variety might appear in association with cortical damage in the minor hemisphere; this is generally regarded as self-correcting, as the major hemisphere reorganises its controlling functions to take account of the minor hemisphere dysfunction. From these considerations, it may be appreciated that the 'peripheral' muscle weakness may derive from damage to some strikingly central neuromotor nuclei and processes.

Dyspraxia, or apraxia, is a much more difficult concept. To begin with, it is a very general term, covering much more than control of the musculature associated with speech. Secondly, it refers to a motor disability that exists without apparent neuromuscular disorder. For our purposes, we may recognise three broad types: (a) a general motor type, found in a wide range of visuo-motor or ideo-motor impairments, e.g. in constructional tasks where eye–hand coordination is required, or in sequences of activities such as are involved in putting on clothes (so-called 'dressing apraxia'); (b) oral apraxia, in which there is impairment of the ability to perform, and especially to sequence oro-facial movements such as to yawn, whistle, protrude the tongue, etc.; (c) apraxia of speech, or verbal apraxia, which is our concern here. The essence of apraxia is that spontaneous movement is preserved, in involuntary or unconscious actions such as are involved in stereotypic routines and expressions, but that conscious, voluntary movements, especially in imitation or to command, are impaired. This generally arises in association with lesions in the dominant hemisphere, and the usual interpretation is that the minor hemisphere's control of the oro-facial musculature is insufficient for the peculiar demands of speech production, although it may compensate for less demanding non-speech functions to some extent. Thus, there are patients who exhibit apraxia of speech with some variable degree of oral apraxia as well.

We may say that we have here two hypothesised types of *articulatory* impairment, in terms of which the presence or absence of muscular weakness may be discriminating. But how is this to be established? Primarily by asking the patient to perform certain oro-facial movements, to determine how the muscles respond. But within either diagnostic category this sort of behaviour may be impaired, though for different hypothesised causes. So, there seems to be a real problem of interpretation here; are there truly two different types of disorder?

Discussion of apraxia of speech has been further complicated by three further distinctions in the use of the term: first, to refer to a disturbance of the motor control of speech production (this is the main sense which we are concerned with here); second, as a sort of lexical–articulatory disruption that is characteristic of conduction aphasia (see 8.2.5 above); and thirdly, as a sensory-feedback impairment, as is found in Wernicke's aphasia (8.2.4 above). If we concentrate just on the first of these senses, we have to recognise that two other terms have been used for it, namely *cortical dysarthria*, and *anarthria*. Table 8.10 shows the order that Darley (1968) managed to impose on this unruly situation, to highlight the concept that we are trying to elucidate. Just two of his features may be usefully commented on here: the suggestion that dyspraxia gives rise to inconsistent, variable errors in articulation, as opposed to those of dysarthria, which are more systematic; and the requirement that

Table 8.10 *The symptoms of dyspraxia*

1. Absence of significant weakness, paralysis and incoordination of the speech musculature.
2. Speaking performance appears worse than performance in listening, reading or writing.
3. The most prominent feature of the disorder is the existence of phonemic errors.
4. The patient makes effortful groping attempts to produce approximations to the target sounds.
5. Errors are inconsistent.
6. Imitation of heard words is poor.
7. The correctness of the articulation depends on the complexity of the required articulatory positions.
8. Longer words are more difficult than shorter.
9. There is a discrepancy between automatic and volitional performances.
10. The patient is usually aware of his errors.
11. Speech prosody is impaired; the pace is slower, with even spacing of syllables (*syllabic*, or *scanning* speech).
12. Severe difficulty in initiating words produces an effect like stuttering.
13. Some but not all patients also have an associated non-verbal oral apraxia.

From Lesser 1978: 159, based on Darley 1968.

speech production should be the most severely impaired dimension of language ability in a syndrome before dyspraxia can be diagnosed, whereas dysarthria may be present as a minor symptom, or indeed as a deficit standing entirely outside a picture of aphasia as such (i.e. no recognised aphasic syndrome need accompany the diagnosed dysarthria).

The first point here, regarding the systematicity of articulatory errors, attempts to make contact with the linguistic distinction between phonetic (unsystematic) vs phonological (systematic) aspects of speech production. But the equation of 'phonetic' and 'unsystematic' is misleading, and in practice the distinction between a 'phonological' disorder and 'articulatory-phonetic' disorder may be impossible to work with. Changes in normal articulatory control-processes may have effects that are to be simultaneously described along more than one phonetic dimension (e.g. lax vs tense, position of maximum constriction, the presence of coarticulatory phenomena, etc.), of which some, but not all, may have phonological consequences, through the loss of a systemic contrast. In these terms, the 'phonological' aspects of the disorder may be effects rather than central causes, although they may, of course, be the most disruptive aspects of the ability to communicate. Given these remarks, it may come as no great surprise that attempts to establish that 'dyspraxic' patients have essentially '*un*-systematic' errors in articulation have proved inconclusive.

Fluctuating residual control of an impaired system, and interaction effects between different levels of processing, help to obscure the picture. For these reasons, it seems to be more realistic to speak in terms of impairment of articulatory processes (thus covering the phonetics–phonology domain), and to regard consistency of error as just one aspect of the investigation, alongside other parameters of articulatory control, and the degree and the contexts of their impairment.

The second point, the requirement that articulatory production should be the most severely impaired aspect of a wider disorder, appears to be another instance (see 8.2.9 above) of the possible overemphasis on the independent status of a syndrome. Discussion of whether or not dyspraxia is present in a case where it is not felt to be clearly dominant may be complicated by the consideration that dyspraxia, like any other language disorder, may presumably also be envisaged as occurring alongside some other syndrome in a complex pattern of impairment. Here again, one may feel that syndromes are less useful concepts than symptoms for getting to grips with the nature of the presenting disorders, at least in the current state of our knowledge.

Hardcastle, Morgan-Barry and Clark (1985) suggest that an instrumental approach, such as that afforded by electropalatography (EPG: see ch. 1, fig. 1.4 and discussion) may be beneficial in such a controversial area. Looking at voice onset time (VOT: see ch. 4, section 4.2.4) and vowel-duration characteristics in the speech of two diagnosed dysarthrics and one diagnosed verbal dyspraxic, they concluded that

> the two dysarthric speakers in this study can thus be said to manifest inadequate control over muscular tension requirements for the consonant articulations. There is also evidence of temporal reduction in the speech of the dysarthric patients ... Also VOT values were generally lower than for normals.
>
> For the dyspraxic speaker the general patterns indicated a problem in sensorimotor programming of speech with errors characterised primarily as selection, sequencing and temporal integration of target articulations ...
>
> Both dysarthric and dyspraxic speakers showed evidence of spatial and temporal variability in achieving target articulation goals. This was more noticeable for the dyspraxic speaker and is in accordance with the generally accepted view that the problem lies at the programming or regulation stage of speech processing rather than at the more peripheral or neuromuscular stage. (pp. 265–8)

This sort of investigation, and conclusion, appears to offer support for the essential nature of the distinction between dysarthria and (speech) dyspraxia, while revealing at the same time how complex the details may be, how difficult the differential diagnosis may be, and how important it is that we gain further evidence from a range of instrumental approaches to bear on the issue. In processing terms, we may be dealing with a fundamental distinction, between (in dyspraxia) the impaired selection and specification of articulatory targets (Shattuck-Hufnagel's (1979) scan-copier device) and the sensory goals of Perkell's (1980) model of speech production; see ch. 4), and the impaired implementation of motor commands (involving the lower motor-command centre, in Perkell's (1980) model). But the evidence from traditional auditory–impressionistic transcription of speech appears to be empirically inadequate in settling the issue, and, so far, conclusions based on instrumental evidence may be premature. See also Netsell (1984) and Rosenbek, Kent and Lapointe (1984) for further discussion of the issues and approaches.

8.5 Conclusion

This concludes our review of an area of psycholinguistics which has always, for historical reasons as well as because of its subject matter, appeared to be rather separate from the mainstream studies of normal language-processing. There are signs in more recent aphasiological and also normal psycholinguistic research, however, that the two areas are moving closer together. As this happens, certain really fundamental issues in aphasiology are likely to attract new discussion, and possibly even redefinition. These issues are so basic that virtually any brief treatment of the field inevitably presupposes some decision to view them in one way or another. Since this is true of the preceding sections, it is appropriate that something of these decisions should be uncovered here. The first issue concerns whether or not language functions can legitimately be associated with focal localisations in the brain; the second involves the opposition between unitary vs componential views of aphasia; and the third arises from the possible relationship between aphasia and the impairment of intelligence.

8.5.1 *Localisationism versus holism*

It will be appreciated that our discussion has assumed the validity of a broadly localisationist position, especially in sections 8.2.1 and following. We need to ask how appropriate such an approach is.

We have noted that the beginnings of aphasiology may be found in Broca's study of Leborgne, which is also essentially an early exercise in localisation of language symptoms with site of lesion. The challenge to such an approach may be regarded as starting with Marie's explicit critique of Broca's interpretation, provocatively sub-titled 'The third frontal convolution plays no special role in language function' (Marie 1906).

This was not an attack on the specific localisation that Broca had proposed for the observed language impairment; rather, it was a denial that attempts to identify language functions with brain areas could be made at all, on the basis of patterns of language impairment. It is an issue that is still not settled, although we can benefit from a fairly long historical perspective on it now, and it is noticeable that a contemporary consensus viewpoint seems to have emerged, which may best be described as 'modified localisationism'.

Naive localisationism, such as was prevalent among much nineteenth-century research, may be illustrated by the case of *Exner's centre*: this was supposedly the seat of 'writing', and situated in the motor-association cortex of the left hemisphere. It relied on an uncritical acceptance of an unanalysed notion of 'writing', which in terms of any sophisticated localisation theory of today would be regarded as a complex of many component skills, representing the functional involvement of many different areas of the brain. Not surprisingly, therefore, Exner's centre found very little empirical support from contemporary studies of lesion sites, and was quickly and successfully attacked by the early holists.

On the other hand, naive or extreme holism – in so far as it has ever been seriously espoused by anyone – seems equally unsatisfactory. For instance, if the brain functions in a truly non-localised, *en masse* fashion, then the phenomenon of left-cerebral dominance for language (and other functions) is simply unaccountable: this is, as it were, the prime instance of localisation. The expectation, according to such a naive holistic viewpoint, that intercerebral differences would simply be irrelevant to the issue of language impairment in cases of brain damage, is massively refuted by the empirical evidence.

In practice, then, holism has concentrated on *intra*cerebral localisations that have been proposed. Historically, one can discern a tendency for specific localisations to be hypothesised on the basis of preliminary evidence, and then to be tested against further data. In this process, the holist view has represented the null hypothesis, and has, therefore, not required precise definition: in respect of any localisation hypothesis, any case which shows the required symptoms in association with any lesion site other than the one predicted by the localisation hypothesis is consistent with the holist view.

In effect, the current consensus view is as follows: that some syndromes are more easily localised than others; that site of lesion cannot simply be equated with site of (impaired) function; that further refinements are required in the means used to determine the site and nature of lesions; and that refinements are also required in our understanding of what specific language functions involve (and it is here that current normal psycholinguistic research is particularly relevant). It is this modified localisationist view that has been assumed throughout our discussion.

8.5.2 *Is aphasia a unitary phenomenon?*

We have organised our discussion in terms of the independent existence of a number of aphasic syndromes. Within this framework, we have had occasion to comment on the difficult status of some of these, such as anomic aphasia, dyspraxia and agraphia and alexia. Do these difficulties arise because we are trying vainly to impose a categorisation scheme on an essentially unitary phenomenon?

Let us assume for the moment that this is the case. How then can we account for the observed differences between symptoms such as greater or less difficulty in comprehension, word finding, speech production and so on, in individual patients?

Part of the answer is that the dimension of *severity* does not affect the issue of whether or not aphasia is unitary. If we think of aphasia as a single disease, then we can certainly expect to find a range of symptoms that are more or less severe, in individual patients. But we can go further than this: it may also be the case that more or fewer symptoms will be observed, depending on how severe the aphasia is. Within this approach, then, we can recognise the need for differential diagnosis, just as in the syndromic approach. It is also possible to distinguish different involvements of one and the same disease, e.g. whether it primarily affects the speech-output modality, or the visual-input modality, or combinations of modalities. A good example of such an approach is Schuell's (1965) *Minnesota Test for the Differential Diagnosis of Aphasia*; constructed by a clinician, and intended as a practical clinical assessment procedure, it embodies the view that aphasia is unitary, but provides for diagnostic categories that are largely compatible with those that are recognised within largely syndromic approaches.

Given that there is a good deal of overlap between a sophisticated unitary aphasia view such as Schuell's and sophisticated syndromic approaches (involving recognition of syndrome vs symptom issues), there may seem to be very little to argue about, especially given the current state of our knowledge. Therefore, just two points require emphasis here: the first is that no unitary view of language impairment can be accepted which depends on the incorrect assumption that normal language-processing is a unified concept; and the second is that no worthwhile unitary view can be established by the simple device of defining aphasia in terms of some arbitrary subset of symptoms.

It is this latter point that calls for some comment. We have already noted that aphasia is traditionally restricted to cases of *brain* damage, and it may be argued that the distinction that is involved here, however well-motivated from a neuroanatomical viewpoint, may be arbitrary for the purpose of looking at language impairment as a whole. There is a further distinction in most definitions of aphasia, however, between *language* and *speech*: only 'language' is subject to 'aphasia'. Now, this is certainly arbitrary and unhelpful: it is responsible for some of the difficulties we noticed in discussing agraphia, alexia and dyspraxia, to name just a few examples. It appears to rest on the view that speech processing is excludable from central language-processing, a view that may not be tenable for the auditory–oral functions of language, and it unnecessarily obscures certain similarities between (to take just one example) speech and written-language production impairment in Wernicke's aphasia and parieto-temporal agraphia. The arbitrary nature of the speech/language distinction is signalled by the fact that it has never been satisfactorily defined even by those who appeal to it. It has been productive of some of the most radical debates in the field, witness Marie's view that Broca's aphasia was not really aphasia at all, since it primarily affects speech output. It is difficult to avoid the conclusion that the time has come for the research field to be widened from traditional concepts of 'aphasia' to something closer to 'speech and language pathology'. How far a unitary view of such a concept would prove to be sustainable is open to question.

8.5.3 *Aphasia and intelligence*

Debates about the relationship, if any, between aphasia and loss of intelligence have been hampered by the notorious difficulties in defining 'intelligence', and the various, and possibly arbitrary, definitions that have been offered for 'aphasia' (see the preceding section). Where the concept of aphasia has been restricted to something like 'auditory comprehension deficit, with greater or less reading-comprehension involvement', then the question of a relationship with loss of intelligence seems to arise quite naturally. If, on the other hand, aphasia is defined more widely (as we have argued for), then the issue of the relationship becomes exactly parallel with that between normal language-processing and normal intelligence. This is not to say that it immediately becomes any easier to understand, but at least certain answers are ruled out, viz. those that unequivocally deny either the distinction, or any relationship. At the periphery of the psycholinguistic system, among the sensory and motor components that are involved in signal processing, it is relatively easy to draw a distinction between linguistic vs non-linguistic functions. But, nearer the central domain of language processing, it is much harder to draw a distinction between specifically linguistic and non-linguistic capacities, and it may be that what we want to call 'intelligence' is found in both. It is possible, but not necessary, that brain damage may impair general as well as specifically linguistic abilities. Hamsher (1981) recognises two hypotheses for why this might be so:

> One general hypothesis is that some portion of the cerebral cortex in the left hemisphere, which lies near or overlaps with the language zone, subserves the same general mental functions as mediated by the right hemisphere. If lesions resulting in aphasia happen to invade this region as well, then nonverbal intellectual deficits will result. This hypothesis denies the existence of a functional relation between nonverbal intelligence and aphasia. The other general hypothesis suggests the opposite and links disturbances in language with disturbances in thought processes. So far, the evidence brought to bear on this issue is mixed and so if sampled selectively allows one to support or refute either hypothesis. (pp. 354–5)

Not just damage to the brain, but the aging process, too, presents a challenge to our assessment of the relation between language and intelligence (Obler and Albert 1981; Maxim 1985). Obler and Albert point out that 'cognitive decline associated with normal aging or with early dementia ... must be taken into account when asking how age interacts with severity of aphasia and recovery from aphasia' (1981: 387). The discrimination between normal cognitive decline and specific dementias may be possible on the basis of associated language abilities (see also Rochester, Thuston and Rupp 1977). Obler and Albert suggest that 'there are numerous dementing illnesses that will each have a range of characteristic language behaviours associated with it. As neurologists and neuropsychologists detail the diverse forms of dementia, neuro-linguists will document the associated language disorders, and speech pathologists will explore new modes of treatment' (pp. 396–7). We might add that psycholinguists will be interested in the light such studies shed on the relation between language and intelligence in the normal individual.

REFERENCES

Ades, A.E. 1974. Bilateral component in speech perception? *Journal of the Acoustical Society of America* 56: 610–16.

1976. Adapting the property detectors for speech perception. In Wales and Walker (eds.) 1976.

Aitchison, J. 1987. *Words in the mind: an introduction to the mental lexicon.* Oxford: Blackwell.

Albert, M.L., H. Goodglass, N. Helm, A.B. Rubens and M.P. Alexander 1981. *Clinical aspects of dysphasia.* Vienna and New York: Springer.

Albrow, K.H. 1972. *The English writing system: notes towards a definition.* London: Longman.

Allport, D.A. 1985. Distributed memory, modular subsystems and dysphasia. In Newman and Epstein (eds.) 1985.

Allport, D.A. and E. Funnell 1981. The components of the mental lexicon. *Philosophical Transactions of the Royal Society of London* B 295: 397–410.

Ammon, P.R. 1968. The perception of grammatical relations in sentences; a methodological exploration. *Journal of Verbal Learning and Verbal Behaviour* 7: 869–75.

Anderson, J.R. 1984. Spreading activation. In Anderson and Kosslyn (eds.) 1984.

Anderson, J.R. and S.M. Kosslyn (eds.) 1984. *Tutorials in learning and memory: essays in honour of Gordon Bower.* San Francisco: Freeman.

Baddeley, A.D. 1976. *The psychology of memory.* London: Harper and Row.

1979. Working memory and reading. In Kolers, Wrolstad and Bouma (eds.) 1979.

1981. The concept of working memory: a view of its current state and probable future development. *Cognition* 10: 17–23.

Baddeley, A.D. and G.J. Hitch 1974. Working memory. In Bower (ed.) 1974.

Baddeley, A.D., N. Thompson and M. Buchanan 1975. Word length and the structure of short-term memory. *Journal of Verbal Learning and Verbal Behaviour* 14: 575–89.

Baron, J.R. 1973. Phonemic stage not necessary for reading. *Quarterly Journal of Experimental Psychology* 25: 241–6.

Barrington, E.J.W. 1971. Photoreception. In: Chalmers, Crawley and Rose (eds.) 1971. First published in *Invertebrate structure and function*, 1967, London: Nelson.

Barry, W.J. and K.J. Kohler (eds.) 1979. '*Time*' *in the production and the perception of speech.* Arbeitsberichte 12, Institut für Phonetik, University of Kiel.

Bauer, L. 1983. *English word formation.* Cambridge and London: Cambridge University Press.

Beattie, G.W. 1980. The role of language production processes in the organisation of behaviour in face-to-face interaction. In Butterworth (ed.) 1980a.

1983. *Talk: an analysis of speech and nonverbal behaviour in conversation.* Milton Keynes: Open University.

Bellugi, U. 1980. Clues from the similarities between signed and spoken language. In Bellugi and Studdert-Kennedy (eds.) 1980.

Bellugi, U. and M. Studdert-Kennedy (eds.) 1980. *Signed and spoken language: biological constraints on linguistic form.* Dahlem Conference 1980. Weinheim: Chemie.

Bennett, J. 1976. *Linguistic behaviour.* Cambridge: Cambridge University Press.

Benson, D.F. 1979. *Aphasia, alexia and, agraphia.* New York and Edinburgh: Churchill-Livingstone.

Berndt, R.S. and A. Caramazza 1981. Syntactic aspects of aphasia. In Sarno (ed.) *Acquired aphasia.* New York: Academic Press.

Berwick, R. and A. Weinberg 1984. *The grammatical basis of linguistic performance.* Cambridge, Mass.: MIT Press.

1985. Deterministic parsing and linguistic explanation. *Language and Cognitive Processes* 1: 109–34.

Best, C.T., B. Morrongiello and R. Robson 1981. Perceptual equivalence of acoustic cues in speech and nonspeech perception. *Perception and Psychophysics* 29: 191–211.

Bever, T.G. 1970. The cognitive basis for linguistic structures. In Hayes (ed.) 1970.

Bever, T.G., J.M. Carroll and L.A. Miller 1984. *Talking minds: the study of a language in cognitive science.* Cambridge, Mass.: MIT Press.

Bever, T.G., J.R. Lackner and R. Kirk 1969. The underlying structures of sentences are the primary units of immediate speech processing. *Perception and Psychophysics* 5: 225–34.

Biggs, C. 1982. In a word, meaning. In Crystal (ed.) 1982.

Bizzi, E. 1983. Central processes involved in arm movement control. In MacNeilage (ed.) 1983.

Black, N. (ed.) 1981. *Imagery.* Cambridge, Mass.: MIT Press.

Blakemore, C. 1975. Central visual processing. In Gazzaniga and Blakemore (eds.) 1975.

Blankenship, J. and C. Kay 1964. Hesitation phenomena in English speech: a study in distribution. *Word* 20: 360–72.

Bloomfield, L. 1933. *Language.* New York: Holt, Rinehart and Winston.

Blumenthal, A.S. 1970. *Language and psychology: historical aspects of psycholinguistics.* New York: Wiley.

Blumstein, S.E. and K.N. Stevens 1979. Acoustic invariance in speech production:

evidence from measurements of the spectral characteristics of stop consonants. *Journal of the Acoustical Society of America* 66: 1001–17.

1980. Perceptual invariance and onset spectra for stop consonants in different vowel environments. *Journal of the Acoustical Society of America* 67: 648–62.

1981. Phonetic features and acoustic invariance in speech. *Cognition* 10: 25–32.

Bobrow, D. and B. Fraser 1969. An augmented state transition network analysis procedure. In Walker and Norton (eds.) *Proceedings of the International Joint Conference on Artificial Intelligence*. Washington, D.C.

Bock, J.K. 1982. Toward a cognitive psychology of syntax: information processing contributions to sentence formulation. *Psychological Review* 89: 1–47.

Bolinger, D. 1965. The atomization of meaning. *Language* 41: 555–73.

Boomer, D. 1970. Review article, F. Goldman-Eisler, *Psycholinguistics: experiments in spontaneous speech. Lingua* 25: 152–64.

Borden, G.J. and K.S. Harris 1980. *Speech science primer: physiology, acoustics and perception of speech*. Baltimore, Md.: Williams and Wilkins.

Bouma, H. 1978. Visual search and reading: eye movements and functional visual field: a tutorial review. In Requin (ed.) 1978a.

Bouma, H. and D. Bouwhuis (eds.) 1984. *Attention and performance*, Volume X: *Control of language processes*. London and Hillsdale, N.J.: Erlbaum.

Bower, G. (ed.) 1974. *The psychology of learning and motivation, vol.* VIII. New York: Academic Press.

(ed.) 1975. *Psychology of learning and motivation, vol.* IX. New York: Academic Press.

Bradley, D.C., M.F. Garrett and E.B. Zurif 1980. Syntactic deficits in Broca's aphasia. In Caplan (ed.) 1980.

Bradshaw, J.L. 1974. Peripherally presented and unreported words may bias the perceived meaning of centrally fixated homograph. *Journal of Experimental Psychology* 103: 1200–2.

Brady, M. 1981. Towards a computational theory of early visual processing in reading. *Visible Language* 15, 2: 183–214.

Bransford, J.D. and M.K. Johnson 1973. Consideration of some problems of comprehension. In Chase (ed.) 1973.

Bransford, J.D. and N.S. McCarrell 1974. A sketch of a cognitive approach to comprehension: some thoughts about understanding what it means to comprehend. In Weimer and Palermo (eds.) 1974.

Bresnan, J. 1978. A realistic transformational grammar. In Halle, Bresnan and Miller (eds.) 1978.

Briggs, R. and D. Hocevar 1975, A new distinctive feature theory for upper case letters. *Journal of General Psychology* 93: 87–93.

Broadbent, D.E. 1954. The role of auditory localisation in attention and memory span. *Journal of Experimental Psychology* 3: 47.

Brodmann, K. 1909. *Vergleichende Lokalisationslehre der Grosshirnrinde in ihren Prinzipien dargestellt auf Grund des Zellenbaues*. Leipzig: Barth.

Brokx, J.P.L. 1979. Waargenom continuiteit in spraak: het belang van toonhoogte. Doctoral dissertation, Eindhoven University of Technology.

Browman, C.P. 1980. Perceptual processing: evidence from slips of the ear. In Fromkin (ed.) 1980.

Brown, G. 1983. Prosodic structure and the given/new distinction. In Cutler and Ladd (eds.) 1983.

Brown, G. and G. Yule 1983. *Discourse analysis*. Cambridge: Cambridge University Press.

Brown, J.W. 1980. Brain structure and language production: a dynamic view. In Caplan (ed.) 1980.

Brown, R., A. Black and A. Horowitz 1955. Phonetic symbolism in natural languages. *Journal of Abnormal and Social Psychology* 50: 388–93.

Brown, R. and C. Hanlon 1970. Derivational complexity and the order of acquisition in child speech. In Hayes (ed.) 1970.

Brown, R. and D. McNeill 1966. The 'tip of the tongue' phenomenon. *Journal of Verbal Learning and Verbal Behaviour* 5: 325–37.

Buckingham, H.W. 1985. Perseveration in aphasia. In Newman and Epstein (eds.) 1985.

Butcher, A. 1973. *Experimente zur Pausenperzeption*. Arbeitsberichte 1, University of Kiel.

　1981. Aspects of the speech pause: phonetic correlates and communicative functions. Doctoral dissertation, University of Kiel. Published as Arbeitsberichte 15, July, Institut für Phonetik, University of Kiel.

Butterworth, B. 1975. Hesitation and semantic planning in speech. *Journal of Psycholinguistic Research* 4: 75–87.

　1979. Hesitation and the production of verbal paraphasias and neologisms in jargon aphasia. *Brain and Language* 8: 133–61.

　(ed.) 1980a. *Language production*, Volume I: *Speech and talk*. London: Academic Press.

　1980b. Evidence from pauses in speech. In Butterworth (ed.) 1980a.

　(ed.) 1983. *Language production*, Volume II: *Development, writing and other language processes*. London: Academic Press.

Buxton, H. 1983. Temporal predictability in the perception of English speech. In Cutler and Ladd (eds.) 1983.

Byng, S. and M. Coltheart 1986. Aphasia therapy research: methodological requirements and illustrative results. In Hjelmquist and Nillsen (eds.) 1986.

Cairns, H.S. and J. Kamerman 1975. Lexical information processing during sentence comprehension. *Journal of Verbal Learning and Verbal Behaviour* 14: 170–9.

Calvin, W.H. and G.A. Ojemann 1980. *Inside the brain*. New York: The New American Library, and London: The New English Library.

Campbell, R.N. 1979. Cognitive development and child language. In Fletcher and Garman (eds.) 1979.

Campbell, R.N. and R.J. Wales 1970. The study of language acquisition. In Lyons (ed.) 1970.

Caplan, D. (ed.) 1980. *Biological studies of mental processes.* Cambridge, Mass. and London: MIT Press.

1987. *Neurolinguistics and linguistic aphasiology: an introduction.* Cambridge: Cambridge University Press.

Caramazza, A. and E.B. Zurif (eds.) 1978. *Language acquisition and language breakdown.* Baltimore, Md.: Johns Hopkins Press.

Carroll, J.M. and T.G. Bever 1976. Sentence comprehension: a case study in the relation of knowledge and perception. In Carterette and Friedman (eds.) 1976.

Carroll, J.M., M.K. Tanenhaus and T.G. Bever 1978. The perception of relations: the interaction of structural, functional and contextual factors in the segmentation of sentences. In Levelt and Flores D'Arcais (eds.) 1978.

Carterette, E.C. and M.P. Friedman (eds.) 1976. *The handbook of perception,* Volume VII: *Language and speech.* New York: Academic Press.

Castellan, N.J., Jr, D.B. Pisoni and G.R. Potts (eds.) 1977. *Cognitive theory,* II. Hillsdale, N.J.: Erlbaum.

Catford, J.C. 1977. *Fundamental problems in phonetics.* Edinburgh: Edinburgh University Press.

Cattell, J.M. 1886. The time it takes to see and name objects. *Mind* 11: 63–5.

Chalmers, N., R. Crawley and S.P.R. Rose (eds.) 1971. *The biological bases of behaviour.* London: Harper and Row for the Open University Press.

Chamberlain, S.C. 1983. Visual nervous system. In Harré and Lamb (eds.) 1983.

Chambers, S.M. and K.I. Forster 1975. Evidence for lexical access in a simultaneous matching task. *Memory and Cognition* 3: 549–59.

Chapin, P., T. Smith and A. Abrahamson 1972. Two factors in perceptual segmentation of speech. *Journal of Verbal Learning and Verbal Behaviour* 11: 164–73.

Chase, W.G. (ed.) 1973. *Visual information processing.* New York: Academic Press.

Chmiel, N. 1984. Phonological recoding for reading: the effect of concurrent articulation in a Stroop task. *British Journal of Psychology* 75: 213–20.

Chomsky, N. 1957. *Syntactic structures.* The Hague: Mouton.

1964. *Current issues in linguistic theory.* The Hague: Mouton.

1965. *Aspects of the theory of syntax.* Cambridge, Mass.: MIT Press.

1981. *Lectures on government and binding.* Dordrecht: Foris.

1986. *Knowledge of language.* New York: Praeger.

Chomsky, N. and M. Halle 1968. *The sound pattern of English.* New York: Harper and Row.

Clark, H.H. 1978. Inferring what is meant. In Levelt and Flores D'Arcais (eds.) 1978.

1983. Making sense of nonce sense. In Flores D'Arcais and Jarvella (eds.) 1983.

Clark, H.H. and J.S. Begun 1971. The semantics of sentence subjects. *Language and Speech* 14: 34–46.

Clark, H.H. and T.B. Carlson 1982. Speech acts and hearers' beliefs. In Smith (ed.) 1982.

Clark, H.H. and E.V. Clark 1977. *Psychology and language: an introduction to psycholinguistics.* New York: Harcourt Brace Jovanovich.

Clark, H.H. and C.R. Marshall 1981. Definite reference and mutual knowledge. In Joshi, Webber and Sag (eds.) 1981.

Cole, P. and J.L. Morgan (eds.) 1975. *Studies in syntax,* Volume III; *Speech acts.* New York: Academic.

Collins, A.M. and E.F. Loftus 1975. A spreading-activation theory of semantic processing. *Psychological Review* 82: 407–28.

Collins, A.M. and M.R. Quillian 1972. How to make a language user. In Tulving and Donaldson (eds.) 1972.

Coltheart, M. 1980a. Deep dyslexia: a review of the syndrome. In Coltheart, Patterson and Marshall (eds.) 1980.

1980b. The semantic error: types and theories. In Coltheart, Patterson and Marshall (eds.) 1980.

Coltheart, M., K. Patterson and J.C. Marshall (eds.) 1980. *Deep dyslexia.* London: Routledge and Kegan Paul.

Coltheart, M., E. Davelaar, J.T. Jonasson and D. Besner 1976. Access to the internal lexicon. In Dornic (ed.) 1976.

Conrad, R. 1964. Acoustic confusion in immediate memory. *British Journal of Psychology* 55: 75–84.

1972. Speech and reading. In Kavanagh and Mattingly (eds.) 1972.

Conway, N.E. 1963. Design of a separable transition-diagram compiler. *Communications of the Association for Computational Machinery* 6/7: 396–408.

Cooper, F.S. 1983. Some reflections on speech research. In MacNeilage (ed.) 1983.

Cooper, W.E. 1980. Syntactic-to-phonetic coding. In Butterworth (ed.) 1980a.

Cooper, W.E. and J. Paccia-Cooper 1980. *Syntax and speech.* Cambridge, Mass. and London: Harvard University Press.

Cooper, W.E. and E.C.T. Walker (eds.) 1979. *Sentence processing: psycholinguistic studies presented to Merrill Garrett.* Hillsdale, N.J.: Erlbaum.

Cooper, W.E. and E.B. Zurif 1983. Aphasia: information-processing in language production and reception. In Butterworth (ed.) 1983.

Cosky, M.J. 1980. Word length effects in word recognition: evidence from word meaning latency. Unpublished ms., St Olaf College, Maine.

Cowie, R. (1985). Reading errors as clues to the nature of reading. In Ellis (ed.) 1985a.

Craik, K. 1943. *The nature of explanation.* Cambridge: Cambridge University Press.

Crain, S. and M. Steedman 1985. On not being led up the garden path: the use of context by the psychological syntax processor. In Dowty, Kartunnen and Zwicky (eds.) 1985.

Crosson, B., J.C. Parker, A.K. Kim, R.L. Warren, J.J. Kepes and R. Tully 1986. A case of thalamic aphasia with postmortem verification. *Brain and Language* 29: 301–14.

Crowder, R.G. 1971. The sound of vowels and consonants in immediate memory. *Journal of Verbal Learning and Verbal Behaviour* 10: 587–96.

References

Crowder, R.G. and J. Morton 1969. Pre-categorical acoustic storage (PAS). *Perception and Psychophysics*, 5: 365–73.

Crystal, D. 1969. *Prosodic systems and intonation in English*. London: Cambridge University Press.

1980. Neglected grammatical factors in conversational English. In Greenbaum, Leech and Svartvik (eds.) 1980.

(ed.) 1982. *Linguistic controversies*. London: Longman.

Crystal, D. and D. Davy 1975. *Advanced conversational English*. London: Longman.

Crystal, D., P. Fletcher and M. Garman 1976. *The grammatical analysis of language disability*. Revised, 1981. London: Arnold. Second edition with additional material, 1989, London: Cole and Whurr.

Cutler, A. 1976. Beyond parsing and lexical look-up; an enriched description of auditory sentence comprehension. In Wales and Walker (eds.) 1976.

1980. Errors of stress and intonation. In Fromkin (ed.) 1980.

(ed.) 1982. *Slips of the tongue and language production*. Berlin: Mouton. (Also special issue of *Linguistics* 19, 7/8, 245/246.)

1983. Lexical complexity and sentence processing. In Flores D'Arcais and Jarvella (eds.) 1983.

Cutler, A. and S. Isard 1980. The production of prosody. In Butterworth (ed.) 1980a.

Cutler, A. and D.R. Ladd (eds.) 1983. *Prosody: models and measurements*. Berlin and New York: Springer.

Cutting, J.E. 1973. A parallel between encodedness and the ear advantage: evidence from an ear-monitoring task. *Journal of the Acoustical Society of America* 53: 358(A).

1978. There may be nothing peculiar to perceiving in a speech mode. In Requin (ed.) 1978a.

Cutting, J.E. and B.S. Rosner 1974. Categories and boundaries in speech and music. *Perception and Psychophysics* 16: 564–70.

Darley, F.L. 1968. Apraxia of speech: 107 years of terminological confusion. Paper presented to ASHA Convention.

Darwin, C.J. 1987. Speech perception and recognition. In Lyons *et al.* (eds.) 1987.

Darwin, C.J. and A.D. Baddeley 1974. Acoustic memory and the perception of speech. *Cognitive Psychology* 6: 41–60.

Davis, H. 1961. Some principles of sensory receptor action. *Physiological Review* 41: 391–416.

Day, R.S. and J.M. Vigorito 1973. A parallel between encodedness and the ear advantage: evidence from a temporal-order judgement task. *Journal of the Acoustical Society of America* 53: 358(A).

Dechert, H. and M. Raupach (eds.) 1980. *Temporal variables in speech: studies in honour of Frieda Goldman-Eisler*. The Hague: Mouton.

Delattre, P., A.M. Liberman and F.S. Cooper 1955. Acoustic loci and transitional cues for consonants. *Journal of the Acoustical Society of America* 27: 769–73.

478

Dell, G.S. 1986. A spreading-activation theory of retrieval in sentence production. *Psychological Review* 93: 283–321.

Dell, G.S. and P.A. Reich 1981. Stages in sentence production: an analysis of speech-error data. *Journal of Verbal Learning and Verbal Behaviour* 20: 611–29.

Denes, P.B. and E.N. Pinson 1963. *The speech chain.* Baltimore: Bell Telephone Laboratories.

Dick, A.O. 1974. Iconic memory and its relation to perceptual processing and other memory mechanisms. *Perception and Psychophysics* 16: 575–96.

Doctor, E.A. and M. Coltheart 1980. Children's use of phonological encoding when reading for meaning. *Memory and Cognition* 8: 195–209.

Dornic, S. (ed.) 1976. *Attention and performance,* vol. VI. Hillsdale, N.J.: Erlbaum.

Dowty, D., L. Kartunnen and A. Zwicky (eds.) 1985. *Natural language parsing: psychological, theoretical and computational perspectives.* New York: Cambridge University Press.

Draper, I.T. 1980. *Lecture notes on neurology,* 5th edition, Oxford: Blackwell.

Eccles, J.C. 1977. *The understanding of the brain,* 2nd edition. New York: McGraw-Hill.

Edgerton, W.F. 1941. Ideograms in English writing. *Language* 17: 148–50.
1952. On the theory of writing. *Journal of Near Eastern Studies* 11: 287–90.

Edwards, S. and M. Garman 1989. Case study of a fluent aphasic. In Grunwell and James (eds.) 1989.

Eimas, P.D. and J.D. Corbit 1973. Selective adaptation of linguistic feature detectors. *Cognitive Psychology* 4: 99–109.

Eimas, P.D. and J.L. Miller (eds.) 1981. *Perspectives on the study of speech.* Hillsdale, N.J.: Erlbaum.

Elliot, A.J. 1981 *Child language.* Cambridge: Cambridge University Press.

Ellis, A.W. (ed.) 1982. *Normality and pathology in cognitive functions.* London: Academic Press.
(ed.) 1985a. *Progress in the psychology of language,* vol. I. London: Erlbaum.
(ed.) 1985b. *Progress in the psychology of language,* vol. II. London: Erlbaum.

Espir, M.L.E. and F.C. Rose 1983. *The basic neurology of speech and language,* 3rd edition. Oxford: Blackwell.

Faerch, C. and G. Kasper (eds.) 1987. *Introspection in second language research.* Clevedon: Multilingual Matters.

Fay, D. and A. Cutler 1977. Malapropisms and the structure of the mental lexicon. *Linguistic Inquiry* 8: 505–20.

Ferreira, F. and C. Clifton 1986. The independence of syntactic processing. *Journal of Memory and Language* 25: 348–68.

Fillenbaum, S. 1971. Psycholinguistics. *Annual Review of Psychology* 22: 251–308.

Fischler, I. and P. Bloom 1979. Automatic and attentional processes in the effects of sentence contexts on word recognition. *Journal of Verbal Learning and Verbal Behaviour* 18: 1–20.

Fisher, D., R. Monty and S. Glucksberg 1969. Visual confusion matrices: fact or artifact? *Journal of Psychology* 71: 111–25.

Fletcher, P. and M. Garman (eds.) 1979. *Studies in language acquisition*. Cambridge: Cambridge University Press.

Flores D'Arcais, G.B. and W.J.M. Levelt (eds.) 1970. *Advances in psycholinguistics*. Amsterdam: North-Holland.

Flores D'Arcais, G.B. and R.J. Jarvella (eds.) 1983. *The process of language understanding*. Chichester: Wiley.

Fodor, J.A. 1983. *The modularity of mind: an essay on faculty psychology*. Cambridge, Mass.: Bradford.

Fodor, J.A. and T.G. Bever 1965. The psychological reality of linguistic segments. *Journal of Verbal Learning and Verbal Behaviour* 4: 414–20.

Fodor, J.A. and M.F. Garrett 1966. Some reflections on competence and performance. In Lyons and Wales (eds.) 1966.

Fodor, J.A., T.G. Bever, and M.F. Garrett 1974. *The psychology of language: an introduction to psycholinguistics and generative grammar*. New York: McGraw-Hill.

Fodor, J.D. 1977. *Semantics: theories of meaning in generative grammar*. Hassocks: Harvester.

1985. Deterministic parsing and subjacency. *Language and Cognitive Processes* 1: 3–42.

Fodor, J.D. and L. Frazier 1980. Is the human sentence parsing mechanism an ATN? *Cognition* 8: 417–59.

Forster, K.I. 1976. Accessing the mental lexicon. In Wales and Walker (eds.) 1976.

Forster, K.I. and E.S. Bednall 1976. Terminating and exhaustive search in lexical access. *Memory and Cognition* 4: 53–61.

Forster, K.I. and S.M. Chambers 1973. Lexical access and naming time. *Journal of Verbal Learning and Verbal Behaviour* 12: 627–35.

Foss, D.J. and D.T. Hakes 1978. *Psycholinguistics: an introduction to the psychology of language*. Englewood Cliffs, N.J.: Prentice-Hall.

Foss, D.J. and R.H. Lynch 1969. Decision processes during sentence comprehension: effects of surface structure on decision times. *Perception and Psychophysics* 5: 145–8.

Foss, D.J., T.G. Bever and M. Silver 1968. The comprehension and verification of ambiguous sentences. *Perception and Psychophysics* 4: 304–6.

Fowler, C.A., P. Rubin, R.E. Remez and M.T. Turvey 1980. Implications for speech production of a general theory of action. In Butterworth (ed.) 1980a.

Francis, W.N. and H. Kučera 1982. *Frequency analysis of English usage: lexicon and grammar*. Boston: Houghton Mifflin.

Frauenfelder, U.H. and S.M. Marcus 1985. Phonetic decisions and lexical constraints in the real-time process of speech perception. Eindhoven: Institute for Perception Research (IPO), manuscript no. 488.

Frauenfelder, U.H. and L.K. Tyler (eds.) 1987. *Spoken word recognition. Cognition* 25 (special issue).

Frazier, L. and J.D. Fodor 1978. The sausage machine: a new two-stage parsing model. *Cognition* 6: 291–325.

Frederiksen, J.R. and J.F. Kroll 1974. Phonemic recoding and lexical search in the perception of letter arrays. Paper presented at Psychonomic Society, Boston.

Freedle, R.O. (ed.) 1977. *Discourse production and comprehension*, Volume I: Discourse processes: advances in research and theory. Norwood, N.J.: Ablex.

French, J.D. 1957. The reticular formation. *Scientific American* 196: 54–60. Reprinted as chapter 18, The reticular formation, in Chalmers, Crawley and Rose (eds.) 1971.

French, M.A. 1976. Observations on the Chinese script. In Haas (ed.) 1976b.

Frith, U. (ed.) 1980. *Cognitive processes in spelling*. London: Academic Press.

Fromkin, V.A. 1971. The non-anomalous nature of anomalous utterances. *Language* 47: 27–52.

(ed.) 1973. *Speech errors as linguistic evidence*. The Hague: Mouton.

(ed.) 1980. *Errors in linguistic performance: slips of the tongue, ear, pen and hand*. New York: Academic Press.

Fromkin, V.A., S. Krashen, D.R. Curtiss and M. Ritger 1974. The development of language in Genie: a case of language acquisition beyond the critical period. *Brain and Language* 1: 81–108.

Fry, D.B. 1979. *The physics of speech*. Cambridge: Cambridge University Press.

Fudge, E.C. 1967. The nature of phonological primes. *Journal of Linguistics* 3: 1–36. 1969. Syllables. *Journal of Linguistics* 5: 253–86.

Gardner, H., H. Brownell, W. Wapner and D. Michelow 1983. Missing the point: the role of the right hemisphere in the processing of complex linguistic materials. In Perecman (ed.) 1983.

Garman, M. 1982. Is Broca's aphasia a phonological deficit? In Crystal (ed.) 1982. 1989. The role of linguistics in speech therapy: from assessment to interpretation. In Grunwell and James (eds.) 1989.

Garman, M. and A. Hughes 1983. *English cloze exercises*. Kingston upon Thames: Lingual House/Filmscan (first published Oxford: Blackwell).

Garnes, S. and Z.S. Bond 1980. A slip of the ear: a snip of the ear? a slip of the year? In Fromkin (ed.) 1980.

Garnham, A. 1983. What's wrong with story grammars? *Cognition* 15: 145–54.

Garnham, A., R.C. Shillcock, G.D.A. Brown, A.I.D. Mill and A. Cutler 1982. Slips of the tongue in the London–Lund corpus of spontaneous conversation. In Cutler (ed.) 1982.

Garrett, M.F. 1970. Does ambiguity complicate the perception of sentences? In Flores D'Arcais and Levelt (eds.) 1970. 1975. The analysis of sentence production. In Bower (ed.) 1975. 1980a. Levels of processing in sentence production. In Butterworth (ed.) 1980a. 1980b. The limits of accommodation: arguments for independent processing levels in sentence production. In Fromkin (ed.) 1980.

1982. Production of speech: observations from normal and pathological language use. In Ellis (ed.) 1982.

Garrod, S. and A.J. Sanford 1985. On the real-time character of interpretation during reading. *Language and Cognitive Processes* 1: 43–59.

Gazdar, G. 1980. Pragmatic constraints on linguistic production. In Butterworth (ed.) 1980a.

1981. Unbounded dependencies and coordinate structure. *Linguistic Inquiry* 12: 155–84.

Gazzaniga, M.S. 1967. The split brain in man. *Scientific American* 217 (August): 24–9.

1983. Right hemisphere language following brain bisection: a 20-year perspective. *American Psychologist* 38: 525–49.

Gazzaniga, M.S. and C. Blakemore (eds.) 1975. *Handbook of psychobiology.* London: Academic Press.

Gazzaniga, M.S. and S.A. Hillyard 1971. Language and speech capacity of the right hemisphere. *Neuropsychologia* 9: 273–80.

Gee, P. and F. Grosjean 1983. Performance structures: a psycholinguistic and linguistic appraisal. *Cognitive Psychology* 15: 411–58.

Gelb, I. J. 1963. *A study of writing*, 2nd edition. Chicago: University of Chicago Press.

Gimson, A.C. 1970. *An introduction to the pronunciation of English*, 2nd edition. London: Arnold.

Givón, T. 1979. *On understanding grammar.* New York: Academic Press.

Glanzer, M. and S.L. Erhenreich 1979. Structure and search of the internal lexicon. *Journal of Verbal Learning and Verbal Behaviour* 18: 381–98.

Glucksberg, S. and J.H. Danks 1975. *Experimental psycholinguistics: an introduction.* New York: Wiley.

Glushko, R.J. 1979. The organisation and activation of orthographic knowledge in reading aloud. *Journal of Experimental Psychology: Human Perception and Performance* 5: 674–91.

1980. Cognitive and pedagogical implications of orthography. In Kavanagh and Venezky (eds.) 1980.

Goldberg, S. 1979. *Clinical neuroanatomy.* Miami, Fla.: MedMaster.

Goldman-Eisler, F. 1956. The determinants of the rate of speech and their mutual relations. *Journal of Psychosomatic Research* 2: 137–43.

1968. *Psycholinguistics: experiments in spontaneous speech.* London: Academic Press.

1972. Pauses, clauses and sentences. *Language and Speech* 15: 103–13.

Goldsmith, J. 1976. *Autosegmental phonology.* PhD thesis, MIT (published by Garland Press, New York, 1979).

Goldstein, L. 1980. Bias and asymmetry in speech perception, In Fromkin (ed.) 1980.

Goodglass, H. 1976. Agrammatism. In Whitaker and Whitaker (eds.) 1976.

Gough, P.B. 1972. One second of reading. In Kavanagh and Mattingly (eds.) 1972.

Gough, P.B. and M.J. Cosky 1977. One second of reading again. In Castellan, Pisani and Potts (eds.) 1977.

Greenbaum, S., G. Leech and J. Svartvik (eds.) 1980. *Studies in English linguistics: for Randolph Quirk*. London: Longman.

Grice, P. 1975. Logic and conversation. In Cole and Morgan (eds.) 1975.

Griffiths, P. 1986. Constituent structure in text-copying. *York Papers in Linguistics* (University of York, England) 12: 75–116.

Grishman, R. 1986. *Computational linguistics: an introduction*. Cambridge: Cambridge University Press.

Groff, P. 1975. Shapes as cues to word recognition. *Visible Language* 9: 67–71.

Grosjean, F. 1980. Comparative studies of temporal variables in spoken and sign languages: a short review. In Dechert and Raupach (eds.) 1980.

1985. The recognition of words after their acoustic offset: evidence and implications. *Perception and Psychophysics* 38: 299–310.

Grosjean, F. and M. Collins 1979. Breathing, pausing and reading. *Phonetica* 36: 98–114.

Grosjean, F. and A. Deschamps 1975. Analyse contrastive des variables temporelles de l'anglais et du français: vitesse de parole et variables composantes, phénomènes d'hésitation. *Phonetica* 31: 144–84.

Gruber, F.A. and S.J. Segalowitz 1977. Some issues and methods in the neuropsychology of language. In Segalowitz and Gruber (eds.) 1977.

Grunwell, P. and A. James (eds.) 1989. *The functional evaluation of language disorders*. Beckenham: Croom Helm.

Haas, W. (ed.) 1969. *Alphabets for English*. Manchester: Manchester University Press.

1976a. Writing: the basic options. In Haas (ed.) 1976b.

(ed.) 1976b. *Writing without letters*. Manchester: Manchester University Press.

Haggard, M.P. and A.M. Parkinson 1971. Stimulus and task factors as determinants of ear advantages. *Quarterly Journal of Experimental Psychology* 23: 168–77.

Halle, M., J. Bresnan and G.A. Miller (eds.) 1978. *Linguistic theory and psychological reality*. Cambridge, Mass.: MIT Press.

Hamsher, K. 1981. Intelligence and aphasia. In Sarno (ed.) 1981.

Hardcastle, W.J. 1976. *Physiology of speech production: an introduction for speech scientists*. London: Academic Press.

1984. New methods of profiling lingual palatal contact patterns with electropalatography. *Phonetics Laboratory, University of Reading, Work in Progress* 4: 1–40.

Hardcastle, W.J., R.A. Morgan-Barry and C.J. Clark 1985. Articulatory and voicing characteristics of adult dysarthric and verbal dyspraxic speakers: an instrumental study. *British Journal of Disorders of Communication* 20: 249–70.

1987. An instrumental phonetic study of lingual activity in articulation-disordered children. *Journal of Speech and Hearing Research* 30: 171–84.

Harré, R. and R. Lamb (eds.) 1983. *The encyclopaedic dictionary of psychology*. Oxford: Blackwell.

Harris, J.E. and P.E. Morris (eds.) 1984. Everyday memory, actions, and absent-mindedness. London: Academic Press.

References

Havens, L.L. and W.E. Foote 1963. The effect of competition on visual duration threshold and its independence of stimulus frequency. *Journal of Experimental Psychology* 65: 6–11.

Haviland, S.E. and H.H. Clark 1974. What's new? Acquiring new information as a process in comprehension. *Journal of Verbal Learning and Verbal Behaviour* 13: 512–21.

Hayes, J.R. (ed.) 1970. *Cognition and the development of language.* New York: Wiley.

Helmholtz, H.L.F. 1863. *Die Lehre von den Tonenfindungen als physiologische Grundlage für die Theorie der Musik.* English translation of the 3rd edition by A.J. Ellis, *On the sensation of tone.* London: Longmans Green, 1875.

Hemphill, L.A. 1975. A conceptual approach to automated language understanding and belief structures: with disambiguation of the word 'for'. PhD dissertation, Department of Linguistics, Stanford University.

Henderson, L. 1982. *Orthography and word recognition in reading.* London: Academic Press.

(ed.) 1984. *Orthographies and reading: perspectives from cognitive psychology, neuropsychology, and linguistics.* London and Hillsdale, N.J.: Erlbaum.

1985. Towards a psychology of morphemes. In Ellis (ed.) 1985a.

Henderson, L., J. Wallis and D. Knight 1984. Morphemic structure and lexical access. In Bouma and Bouwhuis (eds.) 1984.

Hinton, G.E. 1981. Implementing semantic networks in parallel hardware. In Hinton and Anderson (eds.) 1981.

Hinton, G.E. and J.A. Anderson (eds.) 1981. *Parallel models of human associative memory.* Hillsdale, N.J.: Erlbaum.

Hjelmquist, E. and L.B. Nilssen (eds.) 1986. *Communication and handicap.* Amsterdam: Elsevier.

Hockett, C.F. 1970. *The state of the art.* The Hague: Mouton.

Horowitz, L.M., M.A. White and D.W. Atwood 1968. Word fragments as aids to recall: the organization of a word. *Journal of Experimental Psychology* 76: 219–26.

Hotopf, W.N. 1983. Lexical slips of the pen and tongue: what they tell us about language production. In Butterworth (ed.) 1983.

Howard, D. 1985. Agrammatism. In Newman and Epstein (eds.) 1985.

Howell, P, and N. Harvey 1983. Perceptual equivalence and motor equivalence in speech. In Butterworth (ed.) 1983.

Hubel, D.A. 1963. The visual cortex of the brain. *Scientific American* 209: 54–62. Reprinted as chapter 10, The visual cortex of the brain, in Chalmers, Crawley and Rose (eds.) 1971.

Hurford, J.R. and B. Heasley 1983. *Semantics: a coursebook.* Cambridge: Cambridge University Press.

Hymes, D. 1972. On communicative competence. In Pride and Holmes (eds.) 1972.

Inhelder, B. and J. Piaget 1958. *The growth of logical thinking from childhood to adolescence: an essay in the construction of formal operational structures.* Translated by A. Parsons and S. Milgram. London: Routledge and Kegan Paul.

Jaffe, J., S. Breskin and L.J. Gerstman 1972. Random generation of apparent speech rhythms. *Language and Speech* 15: 68–71.

Jarvella, R.J. and G. Meijers 1983. Recognising morphemes in spoken words: some evidence for a stem-organised mental lexicon. In Flores D'Arcais and Jarvella (eds.) 1983.

Jeffress, L.A. (ed.) 1951. *Cerebral mechanisms in behaviour*. New York: Wiley.

Johnson, N.F. 1975. On the function of letters in word identification: some data and a preliminary model. *Journal of Verbal Learning and Verbal Behaviour* 14: 17–29.

Johnson, R. 1983. Parsing with transition networks. In King (ed.) 1983.

Johnson-Laird, P.N. 1983. *Mental models*. Cambridge: Cambridge University Press.

Joshi, A.K., B. Webber and I. Sag (eds.) 1981. *Elements of discourse understanding*. Cambridge: Cambridge University Press.

Jusczyk, P.W. 1981. Infant speech perception: a critical appraisal. In Eimas and Miller (eds.) 1981.

Kabrisky, M. 1966. *A proposed model for visual information processing in the human brain*. Urbana, Ill.: University of Illinois.

Kahn, D. 1976. *Syllable-based generalisations in English phonology*. PhD thesis, MIT (published by Garland Press, New York, 1980).

Kaplan, R.M. 1972. Augmented transition networks as psychological models of sentence comprehension. *Artificial Intelligence* 3: 77–100.

1973. A general syntactic processor. In Rustin (ed.) 1973.

Katz, J.J. and P. Postal (1964). *An integrated theory of linguistic descriptions*. Cambridge, Mass.: MIT Press.

Kavanagh, J.F. and I.G. Mattingly (eds.) 1972. *Language by ear and by eye*. Cambridge, Mass.: MIT Press.

Kavanagh, J.F. and R. Venezky (eds.) 1980. *Orthography, reading and dyslexia*. Baltimore, Md.: University Park Press.

Kay, M. 1976. Experiments with a powerful parser. *American Journal of Computational Linguistics*, microfiche no. 43.

Kean, M.-L. 1978. The linguistic interpretation of aphasic syndromes. In Walker (ed.) 1978.

Kelso, J.A.S., B. Tuller and K.S. Harris 1983. A 'dynamic pattern' perspective on the control and coordination of movement. In MacNeilage (ed.) 1983.

Kempson, R. 1977. *Semantics*. Cambridge: Cambridge University Press.

Kent, R. 1983. The segmental organisation of speech. In MacNeilage (ed.) 1983.

1984. Brain mechanisms of speech and language with special reference to emotional interactions. In Naremore (ed.) 1984.

Kertesz, A. 1979. *Aphasia and associated disorders*. New York: Grune and Stratton.

Kimball, J. 1973. Seven principles of surface structure parsing in natural language. *Cognition* 2: 15–47.

Kimura, D. 1961. Cerebral dominance and the perception of verbal stimuli. *Canadian Journal of Psychology* 15: 166–71.

1964. Left right differences in the perception of melodies. *Quarterly Journal of Experimental Psychology* 16: 355–9.

1967. Functional asymmetry of the brain in dichotic listening. *Cortex* 3: 163–78.

Kinchla, R. 1977. The role of structural redundancy in the perception of visual targets. *Perception and Psychophysics* 22: 19–30.

King, M. (ed.) 1983. *Parsing natural language*. London: Academic Press.

Kinsbourne, M. and M. Hiscock 1977. Does cerebral dominance develop? In Segalowitz and Gruber (eds.) 1977.

Kintsch, W. 1974. *The representation of meaning in memory*. Hillsdale, N.J.: Erlbaum.

Klatt, D.H. 1979. Speech perception: a model of acoustic-phonetic analysis and lexical access. *Journal of Phonetics* 7: 279–312.

Klein, W. 1986. *Second language acquisition*. Cambridge: Cambridge University Press.

Klima, E.S. 1972. How alphabets might reflect language. In Kavanagh and Mattingly (eds.) 1972.

Knox, C. and D. Kimura 1970. Cerebral processing of nonverbal sounds in boys and girls. *Neuropsychologia* 8: 227–37.

Kolers, P.A., M.E. Wrolstad and H. Bouma (eds.) 1979. *The processing of visible language*, vol. I. New York: Plenum Press.

(eds.) 1980. *The processing of visible language*, vol. II. New York: Plenum Press.

Kornhuber, H.H. 1974. Cerebral cortex, cerebellum and basal ganglia: an introduction to their motor function. In Schmitt and Worden (eds.) 1974.

Kosslyn, S.M. 1980. *Images and mind*. Cambridge, Mass.: Harvard University Press.

Krashen, S. 1972. Language and the left hemisphere. *Working Papers in Phonetics* 24, University of California at Los Angeles.

Kučera, H. and W.N. Francis 1967. *Computational analysis of present-day American English*. Providence, R.I.: Brown University Press.

Kuhl, P.K. 1981. Discrimination of speech by nonhuman animals: basic auditory sensitivities conducive to the perception of speech-sound categories. *Journal of the Acoustical Society of America* 70: 340–9.

Landauer, T.K. 1975. Memory without organization: properties of a model with random storage and undirected retrieval. *Cognitive Psychology* 7: 495–531.

Lapointe, S.G. 1985. A theory of verb form use in the speech of agrammatic aphasics. *Brain and Language* 24: 100–55.

Lashley, K.S. 1951. The problem of serial organisation of behaviour. In Jeffress (ed.) 1951.

Lass, N.J. (ed.) 1976. *Contemporary issues in experimental phonetics*. New York: Academic Press.

Lassen, N.A., D.H. Ingvar, and E. Skinhøj 1978. Brain function and blood flow. *Scientific American* 239: 50–9.

Laver, J.M.H. 1980. *The phonetic description of voice quality*. Cambridge: Cambridge University Press.

Lenneberg, E.H. 1967. *Biological foundations of language*. New York: Wiley.

Lesser, R. 1978. *Linguistic investigations of aphasia*. London: Arnold.

Levelt, W.J.M. 1970. A scaling approach to the study of syntactic relations. In Flores D'Arcais and Levelt (eds.) 1970.

1978. A survey of studies in sentence perception: 1970–1976. In Levelt and Flores D'Arcais (eds.) 1978.

1983. Monitoring and self-repair in speech. *Cognition* 14: 41–104.

Levelt, W.J.M. and G.B. Flores D'Arcais (eds.) 1978. *Studies in the perception of language*. Chichester: Wiley.

Levinson, P. and C. Sloan (eds.) 1980. *Auditory processing and language: clinical and research perspectives*. New York and London: Grune and Stratton.

Levinson, S. 1983. *Pragmatics*. Cambridge: Cambridge University Press.

Levy-Schoen, A. and K. O'Regan 1979. The control of eye movements in reading. In Kolers, Wrolstad and Bouma (eds.) 1979.

Liberman, A.M., F.S. Cooper, D.P. Shankweiler and M. Studdert-Kennedy 1967. Perception of the speech code. *Psychological Review* 74: 431–61.

Liberman, A.M., P.C. Delattre, L.J. Gerstmann and F.S. Cooper 1956. Tempo of frequency change as a cue for distinguishing classes of speech sounds. *Journal of Experimental Psychology* 52: 127–37.

Liberman, A.M., K.S. Harris, H.S. Hoffman and B.C. Griffith 1957. The discrimination of speech sounds within and across phoneme boundaries. *Journal of Experimental Psychology* 54: 358–68.

Liberman, M. and A. Prince 1977. On stress and linguistic rhythm. *Linguistic Inquiry* 8: 249–336.

Liberman, I.Y., D. Shankweiler, A. M. Liberman, C. Fowler and F. W. Fisher 1977. Phonetic segmentation and recoding in the beginning reader. In Reber and Scarborough (eds.) 1977.

Lieberman, P. 1975. *On the origin of language: an introduction to the evolution of human speech*. New York: Macmillan.

Lindblom, B. 1983. Economy of speech gestures, In MacNeilage (ed.) 1983.

Lindsay, P.H. and D.A. Norman 1977. *Human information processing: an introduction to psychology*, 2nd edition. New York: Academic Press.

Lisker, L. 1975. Is it VOT or a first-formant transition detector? *Journal of the Acoustical Society of America* 57: 1547–51.

Locke, S., D. Caplan and L. Kellar 1973. *A study in neurolinguistics*. Springfield, Ill.: Thomas.

Long, G. 1980. Iconic memory: a review and critique of the study of short term visual storage. *Psychological Bulletin* 88: 785–820.

Lotz, J. 1972. How language is conveyed by script. In Kavanagh and Mattingly (eds.) 1972.

Lyons, J. 1968. *An introduction to theoretical linguistics*. London: Cambridge University Press.

(ed.) 1970. *New horizons in linguistics*. Harmondsworth: Penguin.

Lyons, J. and R.J. Wales (eds.) 1966. *Psycholinguistics papers*. Edinburgh: Edinburgh University Press.

References

Lyons, J., R. Coates, M. Deuchar and G. Gazdar (eds.) 1987. *New horizons in linguistics*, vol. II. London: Penguin.

McClelland, J.L. 1976. Preliminary letter identification in the perception of words and nonwords. *Quarterly Journal of Experimental Psychology: Human Perception and Performance* 2: 80–91.

McClelland, J.L. and D.E. Rumelhart 1986. *Parallel distributed processing: explorations in the microstructure of cognition*. Volume II: *Psychological and biological models*. Cambridge, Mass.: MIT Press.

McConkie, G.W. and K. Rayner 1975. The span of the effective stimulus during a fixation in reading. *Perception and Psychophysics* 17: 576–86.

McGurk, H. and J. McDonald 1976. Hearing lips and seeing voices. *Nature* 264: 746–8.

MacKay, D.G. 1966. To end ambiguous sentences. *Perception and Psychophysics* 1: 426–36.

1970a. Mental diplopia: toward a model of speech perception at the semantic level. In Flores D'Arcais and Levelt (eds.) 1970.

1970b. Spoonerisms: the structure of errors in the serial order of speech. *Neuropsychologia* 8: 323–50.

Maclay, H. and C.E. Osgood 1959. Hesitation phenomena in spontaneous English speech. *Word* 15: 19–44.

McNeil, M.R., J.C. Rosenbek and A.E. Aronson (eds.) 1984. *The dysarthrias*. San Diego: College Hill.

MacNeilage, P.F. 1970. Motor control of serial ordering of speech. *Psychological Review* 77: 182–96.

(ed.) 1983. *The production of speech*. New York: Springer.

McNeill, D. 1985. So you think gestures are nonverbal? *Psychological Review* 92: 350–71.

Malt, B.C. 1985. The role of discourse structure in understanding anaphora. *Journal of Memory and Language* 24: 271–89.

Mandler, J.M. and N.S. Johnson 1977. Remembrance of things parsed: story structure and recall. *Cognitive Science* 9: 111–51.

Manelis, L. and D.A. Tharp 1977. The processing of affixed words. *Memory and Cognition* 5: 690–5.

Marcel, A.J. 1978. Explaining selective effects of prior context on perception: the need to distinguish conscious and pre-conscious processes in word-recognition. In Requin (ed.) 1978a.

Marcus, S.M. and U.H. Frauenfelder 1985. Word recognition – uniqueness or deviation? A theoretical note. *Language and Cognitive Processes* 1: 163–9.

Marie, P. 1906. Revision de la question de l'aphasie: la troisième circonvolution frontale gauche ne joue aucun rôle spéciale dans la fonction du·langage. *Semaine Médicale* (Paris) 26: 241–7.

Marks, L.E. 1967. Judgements of grammaticalness of some English sentences and semi-sentences. *American Psychologist* 80: 196–204.

Marr, D. 1982. *Vision*. San Francisco: Freeman.

Marshall, J.C. 1976. Neuropsychological aspects of orthographic representation. In Wales and Walker (eds.) 1976.

1977. Disorders in the expression of language. In Morton and Marshall (eds.) 1977.

Marshall, J.C. and F. Newcombe 1973. Patterns of paralexia: a psycholinguistic approach. *Journal of Psycholinguistic Research* 2: 175–99.

1981. Lexical access: a perspective from pathology. *Cognition* 10: 209–14.

Marslen-Wilson, W.D. 1973a. Linguistic structure and speech shadowing at very short latencies. *Nature* (August) 244: 522–3.

1973b. Speech shadowing and speech perception. PhD dissertation, MIT Psychology Department.

1984. Function and process in spoken word recognition. In Bouma and Bouwhuis (eds.) 1984.

Marslen-Wilson, W.D. and L.K. Tyler 1975. Processing structure of sentence perception. *Nature* (London) 257: 784–6.

1980. The temporal structure of spoken language understanding. *Cognition* 8: 1–71.

Marslen-Wilson, W.D. and A. Welsh 1978. Processing interactions and lexical access during word recognition in continuous speech. *Cognitive Psychology* 10: 29–63.

Marslen-Wilson, W.D., L.K. Tyler and M. Seidenberg 1978. Sentence processing and the clause boundary. In Levelt and Flores D'Arcais (eds.) 1978.

Martin, J.G. 1972. Rhythmic (hierarchical) versus serial structure in speech and other behaviour. *Psychological Review* 79: 487–509.

Martin, S.E. 1972. Non-alphabetic writing systems: some observations. In Kavanagh and Mattingly (eds.) 1972.

Massaro, D.W. and M.M. Cohen 1983. Categorical or continuous speech perception: a new test. *Speech Communication* 2: 15–35.

Matthews, P.H. 1974. *Morphology*. Cambridge and London: Cambridge University Press.

Maturana, H.R., J.Y. Lettvin, W.S. McCulloch and W.H. Pitts 1960. Anatomy and physiology of vision in the frog (*Rana pipiens*). *Journal of Genetic Physiology* 43: 129–76.

Maxim, J. 1985. A grammatical analysis of the language of the senescent. PhD thesis, University of Reading.

Mehler, J. 1963. Some effects of grammatical transformations on the recall of English sentences. *Journal of Verbal Learning and Verbal Behaviour* 2: 250–62.

Mehler, J., M.F. Garrett and E. Walker (eds.) 1982. *Perspectives in mental representation*. Hillsdale, N.J.: Erlbaum.

Meyer, D.E. and R.W. Schvaneveldt 1971. Facilitation in recognising pairs of words: evidence of a dependence between retrieval operations. *Journal of Experimental Psychology* 90: 227–34.

Miller, G.A. 1956. The magical number seven, plus or minus two: some limits on our capacity for processing information. *Psychological Review* 63: 81–97.

1962. Some psychological studies of grammar. *American Psychologist* 17: 748–62.

1979. Images and models, similes and metaphors. In Ortony (ed.) 1979.

1981. Trends and debates in cognitive psychology. *Cognition* 10: 215–25.

Miller, G.A., E. Galanter and K. Pribram 1960. *Plans and the structure of behaviour.* New York: Holt Rinehart and Winston.

Miller, G.A., G. Heise and W. Lichten 1951. The intelligibility of speech as a function of the context of the test materials. *Journal of Experimental Psychology* 41: 329–35.

Miller, J. 1987. A grammatical characterisation of language disorder. In *Proceedings of the first international symposium on specific speech and language disorders in children.* London: Association for All Speech Impaired Children (AFASIC).

Miller, J.D., C.C. Wier, R. Pastore, W.J. Kelly and R.J. Dooling 1976. Discrimination and labelling of noise-buzz sequences with varying noise-lead times: an example of categorical perception. *Journal of the Acoustical Society of America* 60: 410–17.

Minsky, M. 1975. A framework for representing knowledge. In Winston (ed.) 1975b.

Mohr, J. 1976. Broca's area and Broca's aphasia. In Whitaker and Whitaker (eds.) 1976.

Møller, A.R. 1983. *Auditory physiology.* New York: Academic Press.

Morton, J. 1969. Interaction of information in word recognition. *Psychological Review* 76: 165–78.

1970. A functional model of human memory. In Norman (ed.) 1970.

1979. Word recognition. In Morton and Marshall (eds.) 1979.

1980. The logogen model and orthographic structure. In Frith (ed.) 1980.

Morton, J. and J.C. Marshall (eds.) 1977. *Psycholinguistics: developmental and pathological.* London: Elek.

(eds.) 1979. *Psycholinguistics series 2: structures and processes.* London: Elek.

Morton, J. and K. Patterson 1980. A new attempt at an interpretation, or, an attempt at a new interpretation. In Coltheart, Patterson and Marshall (eds.) 1980.

Morton, J. and S. Sasanuma 1984. Lexical access in Japanese. In Henderson (ed.) 1984.

Moskovitch, M. 1977. The development of lateralisation of language functions and its relation to cognitive and linguistic development: a review and some theoretical speculations, In Segalowitz and Gruber (eds.) 1977.

Murrell, G. and J. Morton 1974. Word recognition and morphemic structure. *Journal of Experimental Psychology* 102: 963–8.

Myers, T., J. Laver and J. Anderson (eds.) 1981. *The cognitive representation of speech.* Amsterdam: North-Holland.

Naremore, R. (ed.) 1984. *Language science: recent advances.* San Diego: College-Hill.

Neisser, U. 1954. An experimental distinction between perceptual process and verbal response. *Journal of Experimental Psychology* 47: 399–402.

1967. *Cognitive psychology.* New York: Appleton, Century, Crofts.

Netsell, R. 1984. A neurobiologic view of the dysarthrias. In McNeil, Rosenbek and Aronson (eds.) 1984.

Newkirk, D., E.S. Klima, C. C. Pedersen and U. Bellugi 1980. Linguistic evidence from slips of the hand. In Fromkin (ed.) 1980.

Newman, S. and R. Epstein (eds.) 1985. *Current perspectives in dysphasia*. Edinburgh: Churchill Livingstone.

Nodine, C.F. and J.V. Hardt 1969. A measure of pronounceability of CVC trigrams. *Behavioural Research Methods and Instrumentation* 1: 210–16.

Nooteboom, S.G. 1979. The time course of speech perception. In Barry and Kohler (eds.) 1979.

Nooteboom, S.G., J.P.L. Brokx and J.J. de Rooij 1978. Contributions of prosody to speech perception. In Levelt and Flores D'Arcais (eds.) 1978.

Norman, D.A. (ed.) 1970. *Models of human memory*. New York: Academic Press.

Norman, D.A. and D.E. Rumelhart (eds.) 1975. *Explorations in cognition*. San Francisco: Freeman.

Obler, L.K. and M.L. Albert 1981. Language in the elderly aphasic and in the dementing patient. In Sarno (ed.) 1981.

Obler, L. and L. Menn (eds.) 1982. *Exceptional language and linguistics*. New York: Academic Press.

Ochs, E. 1983. Planned and unplanned discourse. In Ochs and Schieffelin 1983.

Ochs, E. and B. B. Schieffelin 1983. *Acquiring conversational competence*. London: Routledge and Kegan Paul.

O'Connell, D.C. 1977. One of many units: the sentence. In Rosenberg (ed.) 1977.

O'Connor, J.D. and Arnold, G.F. 1961. *Intonation of colloquial English*. London: Longman.

Oden, G.C. 1979. A fuzzy logical model of letter identification. *Journal of Experimental Psychology: Human Perception and Performance* 5: 336–52.

Ohala, J.J. 1983. The origin of sound patterns in vocal tract constraints. In MacNeilage (ed.) 1983.

Ojemann, G.A. Subcortical language mechanisms. In Whitaker and Whitaker (eds.) 1976.

Oldfield, R.C. 1963. Individual vocabulary and semantic currency. *British Journal of Social and Clinical Psychology* 2: 122–30.

1966. Things, words and the brain. *Quarterly Journal of Experimental Psychology* 18: 340–53.

Oller, D.K. and P.F. MacNeilage 1983. Development of speech production: perspectives from natural and perturbed speech. In MacNeilage (ed.) 1983.

Ong Tee Wah 1980. *Fun with Chinese characters*, vol. I. Singapore: Federal Publications/The Straits Times.

Onifer, W. and D.A. Swinney 1981. Accessing lexical ambiguities during sentence comprehension: effects of frequency of meaning and contextual bias. *Memory and Cognition* 9: 225–36.

Ortony, A. (ed.) 1979. *Metaphor and thought*. Cambridge: Cambridge University Press.

Ottevanger, I.B. 1984. The detection of mispronunciations and the influence of context. In van den Broecke and Cohen (eds.) 1984.

References

Paivio, A. 1971. *Imagery and verbal processes*. New York: Holt, Rinehart and Winston.

Palmer, F.R. 1981. *Semantics*, 2nd edition. Cambridge: Cambridge University Press.

Pei, M. 1965. *The story of language*. Philadelphia: Lippincott.

Penfield, W. 1959. The interpretative cortex. *Science* 129: 1719–25.

Penfield, W. and L. Roberts 1959. *Speech and brain mechanisms*. Princeton, N.J.: Princeton University Press.

Perecman, E. (ed.) 1983. *Cognitive processes in the right hemisphere*. New York: Academic Press.

Perera, K. 1984. *Children's writing and reading: analysis of classroom language*. Oxford: Blackwell.

Perkell, J.S. 1980. Phonetic features and the physiology of speech production. In Butterworth (ed.) 1980a.

Perkins, W.H. and R.D. Kent 1986. *Textbook of functional anatomy of speech, language, and hearing*. London and Philadelphia: Taylor and Francis.

Pick, T. Pickering and R. Howden 1901. *Gray's anatomy*, 15th edition revised, with an introduction by John A. Crocco, 1977. New York: Bounty Books.

Pickles, J.O. 1982. *An introduction to the physiology of hearing*. London: Academic Press.

Pinker, S. 1984a. Visual cognition: an introduction. In Pinker (ed.) 1984b.

  (ed.) 1984b. *Visual cognition*. *Cognition* 18 (special issue, S. Pinker, guest editor).

Pisoni, D.B. 1977. Identification and discrimination of the relative onset of two component tones: implications for the perception of voicing in stops. *Journal of the Acoustical Society of America* 61: 1352–61.

  1981. Some current theoretical issues in speech perception. *Cognition* 10: 249–59.

Pisoni, D.B. and J. Nash 1974. Reaction times to comparisons within and across phonetic categories. *Perception and Psychophysics* 15: 285–90.

Plomp, R. 1964. Rate of decay of auditory sensation. *Journal of the Acoustical Society of America* 36: 277–82.

Postal, P.M. 1968. *Aspects of phonological theory*. New York: Harper and Row.

Potter, J.M. 1980. What was the matter with Dr. Spooner? In Fromkin (ed.) 1980.

Power, M. 1983. Are there cognitive rhythms in speech? *Language and Speech* 26: 253–61.

Pride, J.B. and J. Holmes (eds.) 1972. *Sociolinguistics*. Harmondsworth: Penguin.

Pylyshyn, Z.W. 1973. What the mind's eye tells the mind's brain: a critique of mental imagery. *Psychological Bulletin* 80: 1–24.

  1981. The imagery debate: analogue media versus tacit knowledge. In Black (ed.) 1981.

Quantz, J.O. 1897. Problems in the psychology of reading. *Psychological Monograph Supplements* 2, vol. I.

Quirk, R., S. Greenbaum, G. Leech and J. Svartvik 1985. *A comprehensive grammar of the English language*. London: Longman.

Radford, A. 1981. *Transformational syntax: a student's guide to Chomsky's Extended Standard Theory*. Cambridge: Cambridge University Press.

492

Rayner, K. 1979. Eye movements in reading: eye guidance and integration. In Kolers, Wrolstad and Bouma (eds.) 1979.

Rayner, K., G.W. McConkie and S. Erhlich 1978. Eye movements and integrating information across fixations. *Journal of Experimental Psychology: Human Perception and Performance* 4: 529–44.

Reber, A.S. and D. Scarborough (eds.) 1977. *Towards a psychology of reading.* Hillsdale, N.J.: Erlbaum.

Remez, R.E., P.E. Rubin, D.B. Pisoni and T.D. Carrell 1981. Speech perception without traditional speech cues. *Science* 212: 947–50.

Remington, R. 1977. Processing of phonemes in speech: a speed–accuracy study. *Journal of the Acoustical Society of America* 62: 1279–90.

Repp, B.H. 1982. Phonetic trading relations and context effects: new experimental evidence for a speech mode of perception. *Psychological Bulletin* 92: 81–110.

Requin, J. (ed.) 1978a. *Attention and performance*, vol. VII. Hillsdale, N.J.: Erlbaum.
(ed.) 1978b. *Anticipation et comportement.* Paris: Editions du CNRS.

Riesbeck, C. 1975. Conceptual analysis. In Schank (ed.) 1975.

Riesbeck, C. and R.C. Schank 1978. Comprehension by computer: expectation-based analysis of sentences in context. In Levelt and Flores D'Arcais (eds.) 1978.

Roberts, M. and Q. Summerfield 1981. Audio-visual adaptation in speech perception. *Perception and Psychophysics* 30: 309–14.

Robinson, G.M. and D.J. Solomon 1974. Rhythm is processed by the speech hemisphere. *Journal of Experimental Psychology* 102: 508–11.

Rochester, S.R. 1973. The significance of pauses in spontaneous speech. *Journal of Psycholinguistic Research* 2: 51–81.

Rochester, S.R. and J.R. Martin 1977. The act of referring: the speaker's use of noun-phrases to instruct the listener. In Freedle (ed.) 1977.

Rochester, S.R., S. Thuston and J. Rupp 1977. Hesitations as clues to failures in coherence: a study of the thought-disordered speaker. In Rosenberg (ed.) 1977.

Romanes, G.J. 1979. *Cunningham's manual of practical anatomy*, Volume III: *Head and neck and brain*, 14th edition. Oxford: Oxford University Press.

Romer, A.S. 1971a. The origin of the ear. In Chalmers, Crawley and Rose (eds.) 1971. Reprinted from *The vertebrate body*, 4th edition. Philadelphia and London: Saunders.
1971b. The eye. In Chalmers, Crawley and Rose (eds.) 1971. Reprinted from *The vertebrate body*, 4th edition. Philadelphia and London: Saunders.

Rosenbek, J.C., R.D. Kent and L.L. LaPointe 1984. Apraxia of speech: an overview and some perspectives. In Rosenbek, McNeil and Aronson (eds.) 1984.

Rosenbek, J.C., M.R. McNeil and A.E. Aronson (eds.) 1984. *Apraxia of speech.* San Diego: College Hill.

Rosenberg, S. (ed.) 1977. *Sentence production: development in research and theory.* Hillsdale, N.J.: Erlbaum.

Ross, E. and M. Mesulam 1979. Dominant language functions of the right hemisphere? Prosody and emotional gesturing. *Archives of Neurology* 36: 144–8.

References

Rubenstein, H., L. Garfield and J.A. Millikan 1970. Homographic entries in the internal lexicon. *Journal of Verbal Learning and Verbal Behaviour* 9: 487–92.

Rubenstein, H., S.S. Lewis and M. Rubenstein 1971. Evidence for phonemic recoding in visual word recognition. *Journal of Verbal Learning and Verbal Behaviour* 10: 645–57.

Rubin, D.C. 1975. Within-word structure in the TOT phenomenon. *Journal of Verbal Learning and Verbal Behaviour* 14: 392–7.

Rumelhart, D.E. and J.L. McClelland 1986. *Parallel distributed processing: explorations in the microstructure of cognition*, Volume I: *Foundations*. Cambridge, Mass.: MIT Press.

Rumelhart, D.E., P.H. Lindsay and D.A. Norman 1972. A process model for long-term memory. In Tulving and Donaldson (eds.) 1972.

Rumelhart, D.E., P. Smolensky, J.L. McClelland and G.E. Hinton 1986. Schemata and sequential thought processes in PDP models. In McClelland and Rumelhart (eds.) 1986.

Rustin, R. (ed.) 1973. *Natural language processing*. New York: Algorithmics Press.

Rutherford, W. 1886. A new theory of hearing. *Journal of Anatomy and Physiology* 21: 166–8.

Sachs, J. 1967. Recognition memory for syntactic and semantic aspects of connected discourse. *Perception and Psychophysics* 2: 437–42.

Saffran, E.M., M.F. Schwartz and O.S.M. Martin 1980. Evidence from aphasia: isolating the components of a production model. In Butterworth (ed.) 1980a.

Sampson, G. 1985. *Writing systems*. London: Hutchinson.

Sarno, M.T. (ed.) 1981. *Acquired aphasia*. New York: Academic Press.

Schank, R.C. 1972. Conceptual dependency: a theory of natural language understanding. *Cognitive Psychology* 3: 552–631.

1973. Identification of conceptualisations underlying natural language. In Schank and Colby (eds.) 1973.

(ed.) 1975. *Conceptual information processing*. Amsterdam: North-Holland.

Schank, R. and R. Abelson 1977. *Scripts, plans, goals and understanding*. Hillsdale, N.J.: Erlbaum.

Schank, R.C. and K.M. Colby (eds.) 1973. *Computer models of thought and language*. San Francisco: Freeman.

Schiffer, S.R. 1972. *Meaning*. Oxford: Clarendon.

Schmitt, F.O. and F.G. Worden (eds.) 1974. *The neurosciences*, 3rd study program. Cambridge, Mass.: MIT Press.

Schneiderman, C.R. 1984. *Basic anatomy and physiology in speech and hearing*. San Diego, Ca.: College-Hill Press and London: Croom Helm.

Scholes, R.J. 1978. Syntactic and lexical components of sentence comprehension. In Caramazza and Zuriff (eds.) 1978.

Schouten, M.E.H. 1980. The case against a speech mode of perception. *Acta Psychologia* 44: 71–98.

Schvaneveldt, R.W., D.E. Meyer and C.A. Becker 1976. Lexical ambiguity, semantic context and visual word recognition. *Journal of Experimental Psychology: Human Perception and Performance* 2: 243–56.

Scott-Kelso, J.A., B. Tuller and K.S. Harris 1983. A 'dynamic pattern' perspective on the control and coordination of movement. In MacNeilage (ed.) 1983.

Segalowitz, S.J. and F.A. Gruber (eds.) 1977. *Language development and neurological theory*. New York: Academic Press.

Selfridge, O.G. 1959. Pandemonium: a paradigm for learning. In *Symposium on the mechanisation of thought processes*. London: HMSO.

Selnes, O.A. and H.A. Whitaker 1977. Neurological substrates of language and speech production. In Rosenberg (ed.) 1977.

Seymour, P.H.K. and C.D. Porpodas 1980. Lexical and non-lexical processing of spelling in developmental dyslexia. In Frith (ed.) 1980.

Sharpe, L.T. 1983. Visual perception. In Harré and Lamb (eds.) 1983.

Shattuck-Hufnagel, S. 1975. Speech errors and sentence processing. PhD thesis, MIT.
1979. Speech errors as evidence for a serial-ordering mechanism in sentence production. In Cooper and Walker (eds.) 1979.
1983. Sublexical units and suprasegmental structure in speech production planning. In MacNeilage (ed.) 1983.

Shattuck-Hufnagel, S. and D. Klatt 1980. How single phoneme error data rule out two models of error generation. In Fromkin (ed.) 1980.

Slis, I.H. and P.J. Van Nierop 1970. On the forward masking threshold of vowels in VC-combinations. *Institute for Perception Research Annual Progress Report* 5: 68–72.

Slobin, D.I. 1966. Grammatical transformations and sentence comprehension in childhood and adulthood. *Journal of Verbal Learning and Verbal Behaviour* 5: 219–27.
1971. *Psycholinguistics*. Glenview, Ill.: Scott Foresman.

Smith, N.V. (ed.) 1982. *Mutual knowledge*. London: Academic Press.

Smith, P.T., T. Meredith, H.M. Pattison and C. Sterling 1984. The representation of internal word structure in English. In Henderson (ed.) 1984.

Solso, R.L. (ed.) 1973. *Contemporary issues in cognitive psychology: the Loyola symposium*. Washington, D.C.: Winston.

Spellacy, F. and S. Blumstein 1970. The influence of language set on ear preferences in phoneme recognition. *Cortex* 6: 430–9.

Sperber, D. and D. Wilson 1982. Mutual knowledge and relevance in theories of comprehension. In Smith (ed.) 1982.

Sperling, G. 1960. The information available in brief visual presentations. *Psychological Monographs* 74, no. 11.

Sperry, R.W. 1964. The great cerebral commisure. *Scientific American* 210: 42–52. Reprinted as chapter 21, The great cerebral commisure, in Chalmers, Crawley and Rose (eds.) 1971.

Stanners, R.F., J.J. Neiser, W.P. Hernon and R. Hall 1979. Memory representation for morphologically related words. *Journal of Verbal Learning and Verbal Behaviour* 18: 399–412.

References

Stanovich, K.E. and D.W. Bauer 1978. Experimentation on the spelling-to-sound regularity effect in word recognition. *Memory and Cognition* 6: 410–15.

Stein, J.F. and M.S. Fowler 1982. Diagnosis of dyslexia by means of a new indicator of eye dominance. *British Journal of Ophthalmology* 66: 332–6.

Stelmach, G.E. 1978. *Information processing in motor control and learning*. New York: Academic Press.

Stemberger, J.P. 1985. An interactive activation model of language production. In Ellis (ed.) 1985a.

Stevens, A.L. and D.E. Rumelhart 1975. Errors in reading: analysis using an augmented transition network model of grammar. In Norman and Rumelhart (eds.) 1975.

Stevens, K.N. 1981. Constraints imposed by the auditory system on the properties of speech sounds: data from phonology, acoustics and psychoacoustics. In Myers, Laver and Anderson (eds.) 1981.

Stevens, K.N. and S.E. Blumstein 1978. Invariant cues for place of articulation in stop consonants. *Journal of the Acoustical Society of America* 64: 1358–68.

Stillman, R. 1980. Auditory brain mechanisms. In Levinson and Sloane (eds.) 1980.

Stolz, W.S. 1967. A study of the ability to decode grammatically novel sentences. *Journal of Verbal Learning and Verbal Behaviour* 6: 867–73.

Streeter, L.A. and G.N. Nigro 1979. The role of medial consonant transitions in word perception. *Journal of the Acoustical Society of America* 65: 1533–41.

Stroop, J.R. 1935. Studies of interference in serial verbal reactions. *Journal of Experimental Psychology* 18: 643–62.

Stubbs, M. 1983. *Discourse analysis: the sociolinguistic analysis of natural language*. Oxford: Blackwell.

Studdert-Kennedy, M. 1976. Speech perception. In Lass (ed.) 1976.

  1981. The emergence of phonetic structure. *Cognition* 10: 301–6.

  1982. A note on the biology of speech perception. In Mehler, Garrett and Walker (eds.) 1982.

Summerfield, Q. 1979. Timing in phonetic perception: extrinsic or intrinsic? In Barry and Kohler (eds.) 1979.

Sutherland, N.S. 1966. Comments on the Fodor and Garrett paper. In Lyons and Wales (eds.) 1966.

Taft, M. 1979. Recognition of affixed words and the word frequency effect. *Memory and Cognition* 7: 263–72.

  1981. Prefix stripping revisited. *Journal of Verbal Learning and Verbal Behaviour* 20: 289–97.

Taft, M. and K.I. Forster 1975. Lexical storage and retrieval of prefixed words. *Journal of Verbal Learning and Verbal Behaviour* 14: 638–47.

Taylor, I. 1980. The Korean writing system. In Kolers, Wrolstad and Bouma (eds.) 1980.

  1981. Writing systems and reading. In Waller and McKinnon (eds.) 1981.

Theios, J. and J.G. Muise 1977. The word identification process in reading. In Castellan, Pisoni and Potts (eds.) 1977.

Thompson, R. 1967. *Foundations of physiological psychology*. New York and London: Harper and Row.

Thorne, J.P., P. Bratley and H. Dewar 1968. The syntactic analysis of English by machine. In D. Michie (ed.), *Machine intelligence 3*. Edinburgh: Edinburgh University Press.

Trehub, A. 1977. Neuronal models for cognitive processes: networks for learning, perception and imagination. *Journal of Theoretical Biology* 65: 141–69.

Tuller, B. and C.A. Fowler 1980. Some articulatory correlates of perceptual isochrony. *Perception and Psychophysics* 27: 277–83.

Tulving, E. and W. Donaldson (eds.) 1972. *Organization of memory*. New York: Academic Press.

Tyler, L.K. and W.D. Marslen-Wilson 1977. The on-line effects of semantic context on syntactic processing. *Journal of Verbal Learning and Verbal Behaviour* 16: 683–92.

Tyler, L.K. and J. Wessels 1983. Quantifying contextual contributions to word recognition processes. *Perception and Psychophysics* 34: 409–20.

Underwood, G. 1985. Eye movements during the comprehension of written language. In Ellis (ed.) 1985b.

van den Broecke, M.P.R. and A. Cohen (eds.) 1984. *Proceedings of the tenth international congress of phonetic sciences*, vol. IIb. Dordrecht: Foris.

Van Lancker, D. and V.A. Fromkin 1973. Hemispheric specialisation for pitch and 'tone': evidence from Thai. *Journal of Phonetics* 1: 101–9.

Varile, N. 1983. Charts: a data structure for parsing. In King (ed.) 1983.

Venezky, R.L. 1970. *The structure of English orthography*. The Hague: Mouton.

Viviani, P. and C. Terzuolo 1983. The organisation of movement in handwriting and typing. In Butterworth (ed.) 1983.

von Békésy, G. 1957. The ear. *Scientific American* 197 (August): 66–78. Reprinted as chapter 7, The ear, in Chalmers, Crawley and Rose (eds.) 1971.

Wada, J. 1949. A new method for the determination of the side of cerebral speech dominance. *Medical Biology* 14: 221–2.

Wales, R.J. and E. Walker (eds.) 1976. *New approaches to language mechanisms*. Amsterdam: North-Holland.

Walker, E. (ed.) 1978. *Explorations in the biology of language*. Hassocks: Harvester.

Waller, T.G. and G.E. McKinnon (eds.) 1981. *Reading research: advances in theory and practice*. New York: Academic Press.

Wallesch, C.-W. and M. Wyke 1985. Language and the subcortical nuclei. In Newman and Epstein (eds.) 1985.

Walsh, K.W. 1978. *Neuropsychology: a clinical approach*. Edinburgh: Churchill Livingstone.

Wanner, E. 1980. The ATN and the sausage machine: which one is baloney? *Cognition* 8: 209–25.

References

Wanner, E. and M. Maratsos 1978. An ATN approach to comprehension. In Halle, Bresnan and Miller (eds.) 1978.

Ward, J. 1920. *Psychological principles*, 2nd edition. Cambridge: Cambridge University Press.

Warren, R.M. and G.R. Sherman 1974. Phonetic restorations based on subsequent context. *Perception and Psychophysics* 16: 150–6.

Wason, P.C. 1959. The processing of positive and negative information. *Quarterly Journal of Experimental Psychology* 11: 92–107.

 1961. Response to affirmative and negative binary statements. *British Journal of Psychology* 52: 133–42.

Watt, W.C. 1970. On two hypotheses concerning psycholinguistics. In Hayes (ed.) 1970.

Weimer, W.B. and D.S. Palermo (eds.) 1974. *Cognition and the symbolic processes*. Hillsdale, N.J.: Erlbaum.

Weisstein, N. 1973. Beyond the yellow-volkswagen detector and the grandmother cell: a general strategy for the exploration of operations in human pattern recognition. In Solso (ed.) 1973.

Wever, E.G. 1949. *Theory of hearing*. New York: Wiley.

Whalen, D.H. 1983. The influence of subcategorical mismatches on lexical access. In *Status Report on Speech Research SR-73*. Connecticut: Haskins Laboratories.

Whitaker, H. and H.A. Whitaker (eds.) 1976. *Studies in neurolinguistics*, vol. I. New York: Academic Press.

Whitfield, I.C. 1967. Coding in the auditory nervous system. *Nature* 213 (February): 756–60.

Whitten, W.B., W.N. Suter and M.L. Frank 1979. Bidirectional synonym ratings of 464 noun pairs. *Journal of Verbal Learning and Verbal Behaviour* 18: 109–27.

Wickelgren, W.A. 1969. Context-sensitive coding, associative memory, and serial order in (speech) behaviour. *Psychological Review* 4: 118–28.

 1976. Phonetic coding and serial order. In Carterette and Friedman (eds.) 1976.

Wing, A.M. and A.D. Baddeley 1980. Spelling errors in handwriting: a corpus and distributional analysis. In Frith (ed.) 1980.

Winnick, W.A. and S.A. Daniel 1970. Two kinds of response priming in tachistoscopic recognition. *Journal of Experimental Psychology* 84: 74–81.

Winston, P.H. 1975a. Learning structural descriptions from examples. In Winston (ed.) 1975b.

 (ed.) 1975b. *The psychology of computer vision*. New York: McGraw-Hill.

Witelson, S.F. 1977. Early hemisphere specialisation and interhemispheric plasticity: an empirical and theoretical review. In Segalowitz and Gruber (eds.) 1977.

Woll, B. and J. Kyle (eds.) 1983. *Language in sign*. Beckenham: Croom Helm.

Wood, C.C. 1975. Auditory and phonetic levels of processing in speech perception: neurophysiological and information-processing analyses. *Journal of Experimental Psychology: Human Perception and Performance* 104: 3–20.

Woods, W.A. 1970. Transition network grammars for natural language analysis.

Communications of the Association for Computational Machinery 13, 10 (October): 591–606.

1973. An experimental parsing system for transition network grammars. In Rustin (ed.) 1973.

Woodworth, R.S. 1931. *Contemporary schools of psychology*. London: Methuen.

Yamadori, A. 1975. Ideogram reading in alexia. *Brain* 98: 231–8.

Zaidel, E. 1978. Auditory language comprehension in the right hemisphere following cerebral commisurotomy and hemispherectomy: a comparison with child language and aphasia. In Caramazza and Zuriff (eds.) 1978.

Zwicky, A.M. 1982. Classical malapropisms and the creation of a mental lexicon. In Obler and Menn (eds.) 1982.

INDEX OF NAMES

SUBJECT INDEX